Harold Wilson

HAROLD
WILSON

Austen Morgan

PLUTO PRESS

First published 1992 by
Pluto Press, 345 Archway Road, London N6 5AA

A catalogue record of this book is available from the British Library

ISBN 0 7453 0635 7

Library of Congress Cataloging in Publication Data
Morgan, Austen, 1949–
  Harold Wilson : a life / Austen Morgan.
  p. cm.
  Includes bibliographical references and index.
  ISBN 0-7453-0635-7
  1. Wilson, Harold, Sir, 1916– . 2. Prime ministers–Great
Britain–Biography. 3. Great Britain–Politics and
government–1945–1964. I. Title.
DA591.W5M67 1992
941.085'6'092–dc20   92-2730
                                                      CIP

Typeset from author's discs and paginated
by Stanford DTP Services, Milton Keynes
Printed and bound in Great Britain
by Billings Bookplan Ltd, Worcs.

Contents

Preface

This is the story of Harold Wilson's life. It is a full-scale political biography, based on all available sources. Harold Wilson 'destroyed most of his papers as he went along',[1] until Marcia Williams took responsibility for his office in 1956. Surviving papers remain private to Wilson, and some doubt must be expressed about when, whether, and to what extent, his archive will be made publicly available for scholarly research.

I have drawn on the wide range of sources available to active scholars in Britain. First, primary sources: private papers held by individuals or in public archives, state papers in the public record office at Kew, covering Harold Wilson's time in the wartime civil service and Attlee's two governments (available since 1982), published official documents, and published and unpublished labour party material. (The papers of Wilson's premierships will become available in the public record office between 1995 and 2007, and it will then be possible to write monographs on those administrations. It is not expected that this biography will have to be recast dramatically, partly because personal and political information is not rife in administrative archives.) Second, local and national newspapers, and periodicals. Third, Wilson's own writings, principally two books on his periods in office, and a volume of memoirs on the making of the prime minister. Fourth, secondary sources: these include accounts by Marcia Williams, later Lady Falkender, the published diaries of Richard Crossman, Barbara Castle and Tony Benn, other cabinet ministers' memoirs, biographies of Wilson and others, and books and articles on contemporary British history. Fifth, a source still overlooked by academics, radio and television programmes and transcripts. Sixth, recorded interviews with Wilson's friends and associates at all periods in his life, telephone conversations and correspondence. There is a great deal of material – unprecedented for a leading British politician – available on Harold Wilson.

He remains ill-served by biographies. Four of the seven books on Harold Wilson appeared in 1964, the year he became prime minister, and two more during his first premiership; only one has been published since his retirement in 1976, an aborted multi-volume work.[2]

There are a number of reasons for this lacuna in contemporary British history, to do with the man and the party. One is Lord Wilson's prerogative to hold on to his private papers, in so far as they exist, though he abandoned the writing of his memoirs long ago. It is not known what provision is being made for a literary executor. He has appointed a 'semi-official'[3] biographer, but it is not clear whether this individual will be allowed to work unhindered by Lady Falkender. A second reason is, what might be called, the old-boy convention, whereby some key associates decline to talk about their relationship with Wilson without his permission. This is a case of ageing politicians, who practised their craft in the public domain, manipulating the writing of political history. When academics argue that such statesmen should be allowed to bow out gracefully, having made appropriate arrangements for their private papers, this is to collude in a pernicious form of patronage. A third reason is the thirty-year rule governing the release of official records. More important is the lord chancellor's power to keep files closed, the civil service's weeding of its own documents, and the ability of politicians to extract so-called political papers from the official records (Harold Wilson seems to have done this when he left the board of trade in 1951, and only he has access to his prime ministerial papers in the cabinet office). The fourth reason has to do with the divisive state of the labour party in the years after Wilson's leadership: many non-tory intellectuals rallied to the social democratic party in 1981, and the life of a former labour prime minister was considered of little conceivable interest; the socialist intelligentsia followed Tony Benn for a time in the 1980s, having cut its political teeth in 1968 on the heels of Harold Wilson the failed socialist hero.

Apologia and hagiography are as inappropriate for the living as the dead. I did not seek, and would not have accepted, a commission to be Harold Wilson's official biographer. Such a role would not, on balance, be productive, unless one wished to be an advocate for his historical reputation. This biography is, and will remain, an independent work. I agreed in 1986 to undertake this life of Harold Wilson for two related reasons. First, the dust was settling on the post-war political consensus, from 1945 to perhaps 1976, in which Harold Wilson was a leading player, as the politics of the market widened the distance from that era of welfare capitalism. Secondly, the labour opposition was again offering itself as an alternative government, with a new generation of leaders bent upon dissociating itself from the administrations of the 1960s and 1970s. A minority has been implicated in Wilsonism, and the Callaghan tail-end of 1976–9, but most, including Neil Kinnock, were genuine socialist critics of varying degrees.

This volume allows the former young turks of the labour party to be measured against the template of Harold Wilson's career. *Harold Wilson* is not a fundamentalist critique of ambition in politics, nor a dogmatic assertion of true socialism. It is one thing to be personally ambitious, quite another to want to advance a good cause. The wish to build a better society used to be considered one of the best. Harold Wilson, I argue, was a careerist in the main, his opportunism being apparent in his failed attempt to modernize Britain through the archaic institutions of its state. I have written an objective, and, I believe, fair account of his rise to the labour leadership, and two periods in government, though it is not neutral, and certainly not uncritical. It is in the nature of biography to tell the story of a life with the subject centre stage, to present his or her version of events, insofar as one is allowed, even if all about are content to accept conventional negative wisdoms. The objective of all good biography is to capture the subject's personality, something which is not always easy with political actors. It requires a continuing interrogation of motives, and an appreciation of social and political context. Harold Wilson has laid a few false trails in his time, but politics became his life, and there were nearly always others around.

The genre of biography is best practised with little respect for the intellectual division of labour, resultant from the professional interests of communities of communicators. In an age of the specialist, with his or her colleagues, it is still possible, and highly desirable, to attempt a life, as humble writer to great subject, which will be accessible to a diverse range of readers. An understanding of an historical character must be sought using a range of tools, and such polarities as analytical versus factual, academic or popular, public versus private, science or art, denied. Facts are the material on which one draws, but they are human or natural products, usable only in an interpretative framework. The contradictions of life should riddle all narratives. Over-intellectualizing has become an occupational hazard of middle-aged scholars with deep armchairs and little experience of life. The distinction between academic and popular is, in contemporary radical patois, elitist, scholarship for the thoughtful person being still a more humane ambition. Harold Wilson was a private figure on the public stage, who projected images of his personal and family life for political ends. Respect for his privacy in his declining years should not imply the censorship of biographical material, especially when the person in history can only be understood as a social being. Science implies rational construction of an intellectual product, but, whether biography is, or is not, a literary endeavour, there is most definitely a human artistry required in the use of the writings and sayings of even political actors. Harold Wilson, and some of his colleagues, have tried to discredit Richard Crossman's brilliant diaries, which a cynic might interpret as confirmation of accuracy. They are indispensable when used critically, like all other – usually duller – sources, giving unique access to the pedestrian, but sometimes dramatic, world of Harold Wilson the labour politician.

Acknowledgements

This work was commissioned originally by J.M. Dent & Sons, and I am grateful to Bill Neill-Hall, my editor, for suggesting the idea of a biography of Harold Wilson. I was finishing a book on Ramsay MacDonald in early 1986 for Manchester University Press, and there was not a great deal of interest in labour's third prime minister ten years after his resignation. I saw the idea as a challenge, and writing about Wilson was to prove surprisingly enjoyable, partly due to the man himself, but mainly because of where my researches would take me. I informed Lord Wilson of Rievaulx in the late summer of 1986 that I was embarking upon this project, and received a – characteristically – kind but evasive reply. Ginny Iliff took charge at Dent's of tracking down photographs of Wilson, on the basis of my suggestions, and continued to take an interest in the book. I am indebted to the socialist weekly, *Tribune*, which I happened upon just as a member of staff was about to consign the paper's collection of Wilson photographs to the dustbin of history; these I rescued for posterity, and they adorned my study as an inspiration when I was writing. This was interrupted by the final disappearance of Dent's, my editor and his assistant, about early 1988, and I found myself subsequently in the Clapham fastness of Weidenfeld & Nicolson, attached to what remained of my original publishers. This was not an enriching experience, though I delivered a manuscript in early 1989 before fleeing to India. Neither I, nor the noble Lord Weidenfeld, who had published Harold Wilson time after time, sought this relationship, and it was eventually brought to an end without consummation, the high politics of the publishing world being left to my agent Bill Hamilton, of A.M. Heath. Commercial and cultural considerations continued to interact, much as a juggernaut does with a brick wall, with academic greybeards mumbling on the side, and I returned to the quiet pastures of Irish history. I was writing a book on Belfast, in 1989, for the new Pluto Press, which was located up the hill in Highgate. This relationship proved fruitful, and I was delighted to offer them my completed Wilson manuscript. Pluto accepted. I now find myself thanking Roger van Zwanenberg and Anne Beech once again, and acknowledging Anne's editorial prowess.

The most interesting part of the project was interviewing, conversations of up to ninety minutes on average being recorded on audio cassette tape, at locations which ranged from suburban sitting rooms to the House of Lords. I am extremely grateful to the following (in – as they say in the movies – alphabetical order): the late Sir Richard Acland, Harold Ainley, John Branagan, Bill Callaghan, Lord Bottomley, Lord Bruce of Donington, Sir Alec Cairncross, David Candler, Gordon Carr, Lord Cledwyn of Penhros, the late Lord Cromer, Emeritus Prof. Stanley Dennison, Michael Foot MP, Martin Gilbert, Geoffrey Goodman, Emeritus Prof. Albert Goodwin, Andrew Graham, Paul Greengrass, Joe Haines, Denis Healey MP, Stuart Holland (then MP), the late Sean Hughes MP, the late Edward Jackson, Lord [Douglas] Jay, Lord Jenkins of Putney, Lord Kagan, David Lea, Joan Lestor MP, Lord Longford, Lord Mason, Peter Meyer, Ian Mikardo (former MP), Jane Mills (formerly Cousins), Lord [Lionel] Murray, Muriel Nissel (née Jenkins), Dr John O'Connell, Doreen Pitts (née Richmond), Jo Richardson MP, Douglas Richmond, Andrew Roth, the Rev. Eric Sharpe, Lord Shawcross, Peter Shore MP, Emeritus Prof. Robert Steel, and Sir Oliver Wright. A number of other individuals, in public and private life, spoke to me off the record, and, where I quote from a transcript, I refer to 'Private Information'. Pressure of time meant I could not interview further Wilson associates, and some, of course, chose not to talk to me. I visited Wilson's old schools in Huddersfield, and spoke to a number of individuals on the Wirral, including Dorothy Fuller. Colin Pickthall introduced me to Wilson's old Ormskirk constituency, and I spoke to the following labour activists: Walter Brown, Miss Durle, Hugh Edden, Councillor Hodge (now a Conservative), Ronald Matheison, and Louisa Norris. Sean Hughes helped me in Wilson's Huyton constituency, and I spoke to Jim Keight, John King, Peter Longworth, Phil McCarthy, and Larry Nowlan. Others I spoke to included members of the Government Car Service, the late Eric Heffer MP, Gerald Kaufman MP, Lord Houghton, and Richard Norton-Taylor.

I corresponded with, and/or spoke on the phone to: Harold Ainley (again), the Alzheimer's Disease Society, Nora Beloff-Makins, R.F. Bretherton, Sir Harry Campion, Edward Cass, Joan Catermold (née Mitchell), John Coates, John Cole, Lord [Gerry] Fitt, the Rev. Keith Forecast (through Prof. Robert Steel), Lady Fulton, Michael G. Heenan, John Jewkes, the late Jennie Lee, Prof. David Marquand, James Meade, Kenneth O. Morgan, John Mortimer, Chris Mullin MP, Sir Donald MacDougall, Margaret McCallum, M.J. Peagram, managing director of Holliday Dyes and Chemicals Ltd. (who provided me with much useful information on Herbert Wilson), Barrie Penrose, Emeritus Prof. Sir Henry Phelps Brown, Sir Frank Roberts, Emeritus Prof. Sir Austin Robinson, David Rose, Sir David Serpell, Sir Richard Stone, Lady Stone of Hendon, S. Thompson of the National Union of Mineworkers, Viscount Tenby, Barbara Twigg, Mrs M. Venning, Sir Anthony Wagner of the College of Arms, Alexander Walker, the Hon. Mr Justice Walton, Mrs W.A. Whitwam, the Very Rev. John Wild, Marjorie Wilson, and David Worswick. I am grateful to Sir Goronwy Daniel, who sent me an account of his relationship with Wilson. A number of other individuals did not wish to be identified. Keith Fielding, an old boy of Royds Hall in Huddersfield, supplied me with the names and addresses of Wilson contemporaries; Winifred Bishop, Betty Clark, E.H. Diggle (son of H.F. Diggle), Kathleen Goyne, Winifred Gurney, Muriel F. Heaton, and Irene M. Smith provided information. Other Wilson biographers – Paul Foot, Ernest Kay, Gerard Noel – were helpful. I wrote in 1986 to the editors of some sixty-two local and regional newspapers, and my letter appealing for information on Harold Wilson was published by many. Among those who responded, I would like to thank: Mrs Edna Cox, Mrs A.J. Hatherill, I.S. Jones, Gwyneth Jones, Miss J.A. Rimmer, Councillor Tom Sherratt, Jack Tipping, Bob Wooler, and Kathleen Wright. I'm also grateful to the Royal Statistical Society for publishing a request in *News and Notes*, and the Institute of Statisticians for the same in *Professional Statistician*.

I made use principally of the British Library in Bloomsbury, plus the Newspaper Library at Colindale, and the British Library of Political and Economic Science at the London School of Economics, but received help from many other librarians and archivists. I examined a great number of files, minutes, and papers at the Public Record Office at Kew, covering Harold Wilson's time in the civil service, and membership of the Attlee governments, and also further material in the Public Record Office of Northern Ireland. I was given access to private papers in public archives: the Attlee Papers, the Lord George-Brown Papers, courtesy of Frieda Warman-Brown, and the Richard Stokes Papers, courtesy of John Hull, at the Bodleian Library, Oxford; the Chuter Ede Papers at the British Library; the Lord Beveridge Papers, the Anthony Crosland Papers, the Hugh Dalton Papers, the James Meade Papers, and the British Oral Archive of Political and Administrative History in the British Library of Political and Economic Science; the Tom Driberg Papers at Christ Church College, Oxford; the Attlee Papers, the Dingle Foot Papers, the Lord Francis-Williams Papers, the Patrick Gordon Walker Papers, and the Philip Noel-Baker Papers in the Churchill Archives Centre at Churchill College, Cambridge; a collection on Harold Wilson at Huyton Central Library; files, photographs, and very many newscuttings on Harold Wilson in the Labour Party Library at Walworth Road; the GDH Cole Papers, the Fabian

Society Papers, the Herbert Morrison Papers, and the transcript of an interview with Kenneth Younger, at Nuffield College, Oxford; the Ramsay MacDonald Papers at the Public Record Office; the James & Lucy Middleton Papers, and those of Oxford City Labour Party, at Ruskin College, Oxford. I am grateful to Helen Langley at the Bodleian Library, Oxford; Angela Raspin at the British Library of Political and Economic Science; D.A. Rees, the archivist at Jesus College, Oxford; Caroline Dalton, the assistant archivist at New College, Oxford; Alexander Murray, the archivist at University College, Oxford; Margaret Medcalf, in the Battye Library of the State Library Service of Western Australia (for information on Harold Seddon); and Huddersfield Central Library. I received private papers, including photographs, from Harold Ainley, Muriel Nissel, Doreen Pitts, Douglas Richmond, and Martin Roiser (concerning Tony Benn). Bob Purdie furnished me with materials, and sections of his unpublished doctoral thesis on the civil rights movement in Northern Ireland.

As befits the first electronic prime minister, I listened to many radio programmes about Harold Wilson and his political friends, watched a great deal of television, and read transcripts of programmes as well as material used in the making of television documentaries. Fran Acheson helped me in a singular way; Bernice Black at Palladium Media Enterprises allowed me into their screening room, to watch all thirteen parts of *A Prime Minister on Prime Ministers*; Barry Cockcroft talked to me about Harold Wilson, and Cathy Rooney at Yorkshire Television showed me his film on Lord Kagan; Sally Doganis talked to me about *Television and Number 10*; Tim Slessor helped; Nancy Lineton of Forum TV in Bristol leant me a video, directed by David Parker, on the third volume of Tony Benn's diaries; Ken Loach talked to me about his film, *Hidden Agenda*, before being rescued by an aide; Alan Plater talked to me about *A Very British Coup*; John Ware talked to me about his Panorama programme on Peter Wright; I am grateful to Phillip Whitehead of Brook Productions, and Angela Raspin, for letting me read the seventy-six interviews used in the making of *The Writing on the Wall* (working title: The Seventies).

Living as a writer, I forgot the distinction between work and play, friends and contacts becoming people out there on whom I was dependent for intellectual and emotional oxygen: Robert and Basia Andrews have continued to make me welcome in their Bristol home; Paul Bew and Greta Jones provided information on Patrick Blackett, and sympathized over an abuse of scholarship; Celia Bishop and Andy Fairclough provided material assistance, and emotional support; David Brindle expressed a continuing interest; Shelley Charlesworth is always there; Marion Doyen put me up in Manchester one foggy night, and Jake and Jenny Jackson in Nottingham; David Farnham of Portsmouth Polytechnic furnished me with information on John Wilson; Marion Gow, and Ben Jones, looked on from above; Cathy

Gunn told me about some spiked Wilson pieces; John Hampson speculated with me frequently on the nature of publishing; Stephen Hayward told me an interesting story about Harold Wilson joining the labour party; Stephen Howe shared observations, and provided encouragement; David Howell, an eminent student of labour history, was supportive; Emma Judd (née Laybourne) must have heard more about Harold Wilson than any friend deserves; Aidan Lunn helped keep me confident; John Mattausch of Royal Holloway and Bedford New College showed me some of his work on CND, and shared observations on 1980s' radicalism in a Hampstead hostelry; Miriam Margolyes told me about her father; Roisin McAuley told me about Stephen Rea discomfiting the former prime minister; Manuela Narjes was there at a low moment; Henry Patterson kept asking me if I was finished yet; Clive Ponting offered to offload newspaper cuttings from Andrew Roth; David Poyser was an early enthusiast for the project, and provided material assistance in Yorkshire; Bob Purdie provided me with a base in Oxford; Edward Stein told me about a Wilson visit to Moscow; Ralph Stephenson recalled a photographic encounter; Paul Thompson helped with introductions; Prof. John Vincent of the University of Bristol was kind; David Walker gave me an early look at an article on Wilson. All these, and others, helped; I alone am responsible for the finished product.

Crouch End, June 1991

To Evangelie

CHAPTER 1

Introduction

Tuesday, 1 October was the second day of the 1963 labour conference at Scarborough. This was the twelfth such seaside gathering since the party, under Clement Attlee, had lost power in 1951. Harold Wilson was about to address delegates – wearing makeup for television – for the first time since his election as leader of the opposition.

Wilson had chosen to introduce a national executive document on science policy, a topic considered safe for a labour party conference. This was the speech in which he proclaimed the need for a white-hot techno-logical revolution; as is often the case with historic quotations, he never used this exact phrase. After his uncharacteristic venture into socialist ideology at Scarborough, Harold Wilson received a standing ovation from the trade-union and constituency delegates. The memory of his predecessor, Hugh Gaitskell's, fight and fight and fight again speech, against unilater-alism, in the same hall three years earlier, was purged. The labour party had been reunited, and British socialism seemingly made relevant to the 1960s, with the forty-seven-year-old Harold Wilson's version of the managerial revolution. Man and measures were considered inseparable, though few realized that dull morning that Wilson's speech was largely a manoeuvre. Harold Wilson, the northern grammar-school boy of the interwar years, appealed to sections of the middle class, as well as much of the working class. He was coming to symbolize the common, or ordinary, man in an age when mass television was breaking down barriers. Harold Wilson's Scarborough speech signalled that labour intended to modernize Britain, against the background of the political consensus which had survived the war, with a professional onslaught on upper-class incompetence. When the fourteenth earl of Home unexpectedly became conservative prime minister seventeen days later, the stage was set for labour to leave behind the years of parliamentary opposition and internal party division.

Born near Huddersfield during the first world war, Harold Wilson was extremely fortunate to get into Oxford in the 1930s. Graduating towards the end of the decade, he got on to the lower rungs of the academic ladder, courtesy of Sir William Beveridge, an errant but able member of the governing class, who secured Wilson a place in Whitehall as a temporary civil servant at the start of the second world war. Associates were surprised in 1944, when Harold Wilson decided to go into politics, and even more amazed that he chose the labour party. The rhetoric of socialism and democracy was recently acquired. From a petty-bourgeois nonconformist background, Wilson had been an undistinguished liberal at Oxford. He came neither from the working class, which provided labour's mass support, nor the professional upper middle class, from where it drew Attlee and then Gaitskell. Harold Wilson's wartime administrative experience lay behind his entry into government in 1945, having been elected one of nearly 400 labour MPs, though luck, as well as limited success, helped him into the cabinet two years later. He was the youngest cabinet minister of the century, when Attlee made him president of the board of trade. Wilson's father was delighted, being a keen follower of his only son's career. Harold Wilson was considered a right-wing, but above all technocratic, trade minister. His unexpected resignation from the cabinet in 1951 was an attempt to flee a failing government, at a time of British rearmament, and before an expected general election – though Wilson's association with Aneurin Bevan was to be the making of his political reputation within the party in the 1950s. His left-wing roots were shallow, and his loyalty to Bevan weak, but this did not prevent him being considered the champion of the left in 1963.

Gaitskell had made Wilson shadow chancellor in 1956, and opposition spokesman on foreign affairs in 1961. But it was the leader's sudden death in January 1963 which gave Harold Wilson the chance to compete for the job. He defeated the deputy leader, George Brown, due to the intervention of a third candidate, James Callaghan. He had been climbing the greasy pole for less than twenty years.

Wilson saw himself as a meritocrat from the people up against aristocratic amateurs (and this contradiction was to characterize Wilsonism in later years). He possessed considerable energy and not a little enthusiasm, but limited talent meant the pursuit of his career was not quite as effortless as he liked to pretend. He was a driven personality in the world of British politics. Harold Wilson might have opted for another profession, but eventually chose an area dominated by party political competition, in front of an electorate which became more sophisticated and cynical about politicians. Wilson induced little warmth and some mistrust in others, and devious was to be the word most used to describe him. This was matched only by notions he held about himself, Harold Wilson being described as a Walter Mitty figure from early in his political career. The wit of private life was deployed later to considerable political effect, but he persisted in being insecure about himself.

Political parties often get the leaders they deserve, and this was especially the case with Harold Wilson in 1963. Party unity had long been Wilson's major aim, and he sought to remodel labour as, once again, a potential party of government. He was a political healer, after the divisive 1950s, though many Gaitskellites and Bevanites were to argue that he inherited a new political equilibrium. Wilson's answer to the conundrum of a socialist party in a capitalist society was to return to labour's tradition of ambiguity. He was the man to fudge, dressing up an administrative tactic as a political strategy, while he shadow boxed with his conservative opponents, and tried to respond to civil service briefs on a growing complexity of problems. The labour left, especially those who had shifted from Bevan to Wilson, genuinely believed he was a coming man in British politics, though their attempt to make labour a socialist party had been constrained, from the first, by their commitment to a broad church (Bevan, the ultimate rebel, had, after all, made his peace on Gaitskell's terms). The labour right may have taken comfort in the fact that Wilson was a civil servant manqué, but the snobbery of the Hampstead set, which saw him excluded from Gaitskell's leadership, militated against his active membership of the governing class in the 1950s. Harold Wilson was to perfect the practice of ruling by fooling, not the establishment as it was being called increasingly in the 1960s, but the labour party he had been elected to lead.

Harold Wilson succeeded in leading labour back to office in 1964, albeit with a tiny parliamentary majority. He found himself – as he would put it – on top of the elephant. The labour party secured a healthy mandate in 1966, and it looked as if Wilson's government might go from strength to strength. He had more administrative experience than any of his colleagues, but it was precisely in the area of public policy, both domestic and foreign, that he failed so disastrously. There were considerable setbacks in foreign and domestic affairs – Vietnam, Rhodesia and, especially, devaluation in 1967 – though the loss of office in 1970 was unexpected. If Harold Wilson had won that election, he would probably have stepped down before the end of the parliament. He made it back to Downing Street in less than four years, and, despite a second election in 1974, labour had a weak overall majority. Where Ted Heath had failed with the economy, blaming the inflation resultant upon oil-price rises on the unions, Harold Wilson followed. The economic crisis of the first summer of his second premiership continued into 1975, when Wilson, having accepted the idea of a referendum, finally secured Britain's continuing involvement in Europe. Harold Wilson turned belatedly to cutting public expenditure, only to announce suddenly in March 1976 – shortly after his sixtieth birthday –

that he was resigning as prime minister, and retiring to the backbenches. Many people smelt a rat, and few believed Wilson's own explanation that he had had enough. Though Harold Wilson had presided over a loss in working-class members in the labour party, and then the entry of a new petty bourgeoisie into constituency parties, many of its MPs would have preferred him to stay. After all the criticism he had attracted from his own side, Harold Wilson may have missed this irony. He left Downing Street with little to show by way of historical contribution, his own nomination, the open university, while an eminent institution, hardly amounting to a transformation of Britain.

Lord Wilson, whose political career stretched from the second world war to the 1980s, is remembered mainly for two things. One, his secretary, Marcia Williams, whom he made Lady Falkender in 1974, when he was in difficulty with the press. Two, as having come under suspicion within MI5. The death of Gaitskell, at the age of fifty-six, saw two members of the security service seek to prove he had been poisoned by the Soviet Union. It is also alleged there was an attempt to destabilize the labour government in the 1970s, this being associated with Peter Wright, and, more recently, Colin Wallace. Both stories – which belong to the *Private Eye* school of political understanding – continue to fuel speculation about Wilson's surprise resignation.

The real intellectual problem, for scholars and anyone concerned about the state of Britain, is how, and why, the political promise of 1963, as exemplified by Wilson's Scarborough speech, was squandered. Such a historical question requires an appreciation of three things: one, Harold Wilson the person; two, the politics of labour in government; and, three, the structural problems of the British state in the 1960s and 1970s. This is not a book on the limits of labourism, or the decline of Britain, but both topics impinge on the politics of Harold Wilson as labour leader. It will be argued that he lacked ruling passion, in a state where executive power had to be aggregated, and showed insufficient reforming zeal, being at heart an administrator lacking imagination. He was a good civil servants' prime minister, who knew he had to perform politically for parliament and the electorate, but his socialist project was so hollow that he quickly lost credibility.

Harold Wilson was the only person under fifty to have become prime minister in the twentieth century, until John Major seized this record in 1990. Wilson's record of nearly eight years as a peacetime premier was snatched by Margaret Thatcher in 1987, but he remains the longest-serving of the four labour prime ministers there have been since the 1920s. Wilson's name, with that of Callaghan, dominates the political history of the 1960s and 1970s, the second half of the post-war consensus, fuelled by the long economic boom of 1950–74. British social democracy, as the term was then understood, showed its true political colours. Harold Wilson failed to manage capitalism within the terms he set himself, being the one British politician to be associated with two devaluations of the pound. He did a little better with the labour party, despite its continuing loss of individual members. Harold Wilson kept the labour party united for thirteen years, only to see it divide again in the 1980s with Mrs Thatcher in power. The Jenkinsites, the inheritors of the mantle of Gaitskell, did not break away until 1981, when they formed the social democratic party. This was the year Tony Benn nearly won the deputy leadership, at the head of a huge left-wing upsurge in the labour paty, which then drained towards the centre throughout the rest of the decade.

Harold Wilson has passed largely into contemporary British history; the 1960s is already part of the national school curriculum. His years at the top, I would hazard, will be assessed, in the 1990s and beyond, in terms of what happens in British politics. The longer labour remains in opposition, the more the governments of the 1960s and 1970s will be revisited sympathetically. Getting the party into office, simply to remove Mrs Thatcher, was accepted increasingly as a desirable socialist goal – until the tories pinched labour's best cards by burying Thatcherism themselves. Harold Wilson's reputation can only rise from its low point, in spite of whatever historical responsibility is ascribed to him, and his party colleagues, for the subsequent years of tory rule. He may even find some willing to sing his praises. The performance of any future labour administration will, quite simply, determine how we think about Harold Wilson's thirteen years as labour leader. The prospects for his historical reputation are not inevitably all bad.

CHAPTER 2

Young Harold, 1916–27

James Harold Wilson was born to Herbert and Ethel Wilson on 11 March 1916 in Milnsbridge, a village in the Colne Valley of Yorkshire, about a mile west of the town of Huddersfield. No historical event marks the day, though forty-five British sailors were lost when two naval vessels struck mines off the east coast. The country was embroiled in the European war, and Herbert Asquith, the liberal leader, was still prime minister. Lloyd George, the minister of munitions, had yet to make his bid to become political supremo, thereby splitting the party. Labour, which was part of the wartime coalition government, was still a minority force in British politics.

Harold Wilson's genealogy has supposedly been traced, on his father's side of the family, to the late fifteenth century. It is said that a paternal ancestor worked on the lands of Rievaulx Abbey, an early Cistercian settlement, in the Rye Valley by the north York moors. When Sir Alec Douglas-Home emerged as prime minister, in October 1963, Wilson referred scathingly to the fourteenth earl, only to be described, in a television riposte, as the fourteenth Mr Wilson. This excited the national press, and the hunt began for Harold Wilson's roots, Rievaulx being bandied about in 1965. Genealogical scholars who have investigated have found themselves swamped in Wilsons – from Will's son – in that part of Yorkshire. Caution is urged about the period before around 1800. 'The reliable descent' of Harold Wilson's family, according to a local expert, 'was lost about four generations back because of the profusions of Wilsons in parish registers etc.'[1] All that can be said with real certainty is that there were Wilsons farming near Helmsley, a market town beneath the southern rim of the moors, for a very considerable time, and that some were yeomen while others also worked as artisans.

Harold Wilson's first reliable paternal ancestor is his great grandfather, John Wilson, who was baptized in Helmsley in 1817. He farmed, probably on the Duncombe Park estate, and worked as a cobbler in the village.

6

Following his marriage in 1841, to a farmer's daughter who had been born in Old Byland, he took charge of the local workhouse at Pottergate, Helmsley. He moved south to become master of the Monk Bar, York workhouse sometime before 1851, the year of his death. Harold Wilson remembers that, as a boy, he met John Wilson's daughter, his great aunt, who must have been of an advanced age, and that she was matron of the workhouse in York.

His grandfather, James, who is thought to have been born at Rievaulx in 1843, did not farm. He became apprenticed to a linen draper in York, and, when he was about seventeen, crossed the Pennines into Lancashire, where he worked as a warehouse salesman. Later he prospered in Manchester as a draper. This may have had something to do with his marriage in Huddersfield in 1872, in a baptist chapel, to Eliza Jane Thewlis, the daughter of a local cotton-warp manufacturer and self-made mill-owner. The Thewlis family came from Huddersfield weavers and spinners, but rose socially with industrialization; Titus Thewlis employed 104 workers, at one stage, including sweated child labour. Eliza's brother, Herbert Thewlis, who was to manufacture umbrellas in Stockport, Lancashire, became, in time, a leading liberal in Manchester politics. James and Eliza Wilson were, if not bourgeois, then petty bourgeois with important family connections across the north of England.

They had six children. James Herbert (Harold's father) – known as Herbert after his uncle – was born in Chorlton upon Medlock, Lancashire in 1882. He was brought up in a deeply religious atmosphere in Openshaw, where the family was prominent in the Lees Street congregational community. Herbert Wilson displayed considerable intellectual agility at St Matthew's higher grade school in Manchester, having an excellent memory and arithmetical ability.

His older brother, John, known as Jack, became a teacher in technical education, seemingly at Battersea Polytechnic, set up at the turn of the century by the London county council. Fear of foreign competition had led the state to invest in the training of skilled workers, mainly in evening classes. The London polytechnics even provided degree courses. In 1904, when the new local education authorities were concentrating upon the secondary level, Wilson convened a meeting at Birkbeck College, out of which emerged the association of teachers in technical institutions (ATTI). Most of the London members, who dominated the leadership of the organization, were from Lancashire or Yorkshire. Wilson was the first honorary secretary of the ATTI, more a professional body than a trade union, and president from 1909 to 1911, when national membership approached 1,000 – about one in every three technical teachers. Writing in the association's journal, in 1909, on the non-representation of technical teachers on public educational bodies, he contrasted the English way of 'muddling through' with German bureaucratic control: 'Foreign observers in commenting upon English methods of conducting public affairs frequently draw attention to the curious subordination of the expert and the over-whelming importance of the amateur in all branches of national and municipal collective effort ... There must be a more ready attention on the part of the elected authority to those who are experts in the specialised questions which the public representative is called upon to solve.'[2] One need look no further for later inspiration! In his presidential address, to the third annual conference, at Liverpool, Jack Wilson said that, while employers and managers were increasingly receiving scientific and technical education, '[their] main obstacle still [lay] in the opposition of the foremen and the Trades Unions, and the apathy of the workers themselves during the critical period from fourteen to twenty-one years of age'.[3] Jack Wilson left the profession about 1917, to become the first inspector of technical colleges for the board of education, then under the liberal, H.A.L. Fisher.

Herbert Wilson, in contrast, left school in 1898, when he was sixteen. He went to work in Levinstein's, a Manchester dye factory, where he learned his trade as an industrial chemist, studying part time in the city's technical college. He was subject to periods of unemployment, due to competition from abroad, and it was during such times he engaged in political work on behalf of the liberal party, then in opposition.

His uncle, Alderman Herbert Thewlis, chaired the liberal election committee in Manchester in 1906, when the new liberal government, led by Campbell-Bannerman, was confirmed in office. Winston Churchill, having been elected conservative MP for Oldham, before crossing the house in 1904, was one of the successful liberal candidates in Manchester, being returned as a free trader for the important northwestern division of the city. Churchill returned to London as the junior minister in the colonial office. In the 1906 general election, Herbert Wilson worked in Gorton in east Manchester, then a Lancashire seat, for the return of John Hodge, of the steel smelters union. Hodge, a founder of the labour representation committee in 1900, was one of the twenty-nine labour candidates to be elected across the country. This did not mean that Herbert was breaking from lib-labism, the political position of working-class supporters of the liberal party. The labour party owed its arrival in parliament in 1906, when there was a liberal landslide, to a secret national agreement with the liberals. Keir Hardie and Ramsay MacDonald had been granted a free run in a minority of seats for their nascent party, in order to minimize contests between anti-tory candidates. It was feared conservatives might be returned on minority votes. John Hodge was acceptable as a trade-union leader to Manchester liberals. He had served on the city council as a member of the party until 1901, though he joined the independent labour party in 1900. Gorton was a conservative seat, where the member of parliament, a free trader, had been replaced by a candidate advocating protection. Herbert Wilson worked there as a supporter of the Campbell-Bannerman government, and, most likely, a member of the liberal party. His support for John Hodge was not indicative of sympathy for the independent labour party. Almost certainly, Herbert Wilson voted labour in the two following elections, in 1910. Hodge, as the member for Gorton, was to join Lloyd George's coalition government during the war; his conservative parliamentary secretary, in the ministry of pensions, later described him as 'really a rampaging and most patriotic Tory working-man, who would have delighted the heart of Disraeli'.[4]

Harold Wilson's father was undoubtedly a radical, but certainly no socialist. In 1908, Churchill ran in a by-election in northwest Manchester, having been appointed to the cabinet by the new prime minister, Asquith, as president of the board of trade. Herbert Thewlis was now constituency president, and the deputy election agent was Herbert Wilson, again apparently out of work.

Many years later, in 1928, while on holiday in Scotland with his family, Herbert Wilson was to seek out a statue of Sir Henry Campbell-Bannerman which had been erected in Stirling, the constituency for which he had been a member of parliament. Campbell-Bannerman had been the first national politician Herbert went to hear speak in Manchester, at a meeting in the Free Trade Hall during the Boer war. Though the liberal prime minister had been dead twenty years, Wilson *père*, then middle-aged, was still full of admiration. Young Harold, at twelve years of age, was profoundly impressed. Much later, he would date his interest in politics from the oration at Campbell-Bannerman's statue, during that overnight stop in Stirling. In front of it, his father expounded on the meaning of the 1906 election victory, when conservatism had been overthrown. It was clearly a key moment in Herbert's political experience. Though time had moved on, and the conservatives had come back into power in 1922, Herbert Wilson was, emotionally, still a liberal.

Shortly after that historic election, on 14 March 1906, Herbert Wilson married Ethel Seddon in Lees Street congregational chapel, in Openshaw, Manchester. She was twenty-four. Relatively little is known of Ethel Seddon's family background. She was born a few months before her husband, in 1882, seemingly in the same part of Manchester. Her paternal grandfather – who came from Wigan – had been a coalman on the Manchester, Sheffield and Lincolnshire railway. Her father, William Seddon, was a ticket clerk on the same line, and became deacon and treasurer of the Lees Street chapel. Ethel in turn taught Sunday school in Openshaw, as did her future husband. Her father was considered to have an 'equally sharp memory', and has been described as a 'very brilliant astronomer'.[5]

The Seddons of Manchester were working class, albeit upwardly mobile. Three generations had worked on the railways, for the same company. In later years, Harold Wilson was to boast repeatedly of his familial connection with railway trade unionism. On other occasions, Harold Wilson would talk about 'innumerable aunts and uncles' having become teachers.[6] This was indeed the case in Ethel's family. She became a pupil teacher, probably at elementary level, in the late 1890s. A second brother may have been a teacher of technical education.

Herbert and Ethel Wilson, who were in their mid-twenties, made their marital home in Manchester. Ethel continued to teach for a time. In 1909, their first child – a girl called Marjorie – was born. Herbert, insufficiently qualified to research or teach as a chemist, still found it difficult to maintain continuous employment, but, as an industrial chemist, and the son of a draper, he was certainly middle class.

In 1912, Herbert and family quit Lancashire for Yorkshire. He had secured a post with John W. Leitch & Co. in the Colne Valley. The factory was in Milnsbridge, one of the many mill villages on which the Yorkshire woollen industry was based. Wilson was paid £2-10s-0d (£2.50) monthly by cheque, an indication of his increased status. In Leitch's, Herbert Wilson was to take charge of a department, becoming a member of management. He did not settle in Milnsbridge itself, but found a house further up the hill in Cowlersley, as it was known locally. The Wilsons rented 4 Warneford Road for twelve shillings (60p) a week. It was a three-up and three-down terraced house, plus bathroom and garden back and front, set against open ground. In the eyes of the mill folk clustered round the Colne river, from which the valley took its name, these 'comers-in' from across the Pennines were well up in the ranks of respectability.

The Wilsons were just about thirty, and Marjorie three years of age. Herbert Wilson was tall, approaching six feet. He is remembered as a 'well-made bloke', though, until middle age, he was probably quite slim; he was to thicken out considerably in later years. He dressed conservatively and would have given the appearance of a professional man, with stiff collar, waistcoat and watch chain, or perhaps a black-coated worker. He wore a modest moustache, though this was to go in later years. Certainly by the 1920s, he was a heavy smoker of cigarettes, a habit with which he persisted. Herbert, not surprisingly, had a pronounced northern, but not Yorkshire, accent. He has been described as 'inclined to be jolly', and did not use corporal punishment. 'He certainly wasn't a stern person.' Ethel Wilson is remembered as a 'charming ... and friendly person',[7] and reputed to have had a sense of humour. Ethel too would have spoken as a Lancastrian, with an edge of refinement as a teacher. From her late twenties, she worked as a housewife, but she got outside the home in her own right, through community activity. She dressed respectably, and would have stood out from women millworkers in Milnsbridge. Physically, she was a large woman, and probably taller than average.

Religion shaped the life of the Wilson family. Nonconformism was then still a popular social force, implying a set of anti-aristocratic values, and democratic practices. There was no congregational chapel in Milnsbridge, but Herbert and Ethel felt able to join the local baptist community, whose chapel was hidden behind the main street of the village, close to the river. There was also a separate Sunday school building, where Herbert and Ethel taught each week. The baptists were only one nonconformist sect in Milnsbridge, but they seem to have been the most active. The chapel and school became the centre for a wide range of activities, and the Wilsons played a leading role. There was a cub pack and boy scout troop – Herbert Wilson would become a rover leader and, later, district commissioner. He also became secretary of the chapel's amateur operatic society. Ethel looked after the girl guides, and became a captain. She also founded the women's guild.

Family life was underpinned by continuous industrial employment. The demand for the TNT manufactured by Leitch's soared with the outbreak of war, and Herbert Wilson did his duty by manufacturing munitions. Production ran on through Sunday. In early 1916, the factory was substantially reorganized, and he had to give up Sunday school teaching. Herbert Wilson became eligible for conscription about this time, but was exempted on grounds of his work. Wartime inflation saw his salary rise to £260 a year plus a bonus of £100. With Ethel Wilson managing the household economy carefully, a comfortable standard of living was enjoyed at 4 Warneford Road.

At this point, James Harold arrived in the world, seven years after his sister. He was called James after his father and paternal grandfather, and Harold after his uncle in Australia and a cousin of Ethel's, who had been killed at Gallipoli the year before. He would be known as Harold at home and among friends in Milnsbridge, but he was to be formally called J. Harold Wilson, and would use the initials 'JHW' all the way through his education, and beyond. Ethel's second child was to be her last.

Harold Wilson was born in Yorkshire, like three of his four grandparents, but Herbert and Ethel were Mancunians, and his sister had been born in Lancashire. In the spring of 1916, the new baby was taken back to Manchester, to Lees Street congregational chapel, to be baptized. This was surely an indication of where the Wilsons felt they belonged, though they were never to live in the city again. As their son grew up near Huddersfield, his identity was formed in terms of local places. But he was to leave Yorkshire, for good, in his mid-teens. Whatever influences operated upon Harold Wilson in his early years, his later stressing of these Yorkshire roots may reveal something slightly forced in his personality. Very many years later, Aneurin Bevan was to meet Herbert Wilson at a labour party conference. The latter began to talk of old political times in Manchester, and Bevan, perplexed, asked Harold where he had been born. 'With a York-shireman's natural pride', Wilson tells the story, 'I said, thinking of Sheffield's steel, "Yorkshiremen are not born; they are forged."' He then recounts Bevan's riposte, apparently oblivous of a telling observation. '"Forged were you?" said Nye in that musical Welsh lilt of his, "I always thought there was something counterfeit about you!"'[8]

When he was about one year old, the family moved a short distance in Cowlersley, to what is now 40 Western Road. The house had been built in 1914, and Herbert Wilson paid £440 for it, half from his savings, a mortgage covering the rest. Western Road was another step up in the world, signified by the bay window with leaded panes. The house – then called 'Lea Royd' – was terraced, but passageways through to the back in that part of Western Road gave it a semi-detached appearance. It had a cellar, where Ethel did the laundry, and an attic, which became, in due course, Harold's bedroom-cum-playroom. Marjorie slept on the first floor, in a room next to her parents.

Sometime towards the end of the war, Herbert left Leitch's. In 1917, a Major Lionel Brook Holliday, with government assistance, established a new factory north east of Huddersfield, to manufacture picric acid 'for the war effort'.[9] Herbert Wilson was taken on by Holliday's at a salary of £425, and was to remain there for many years. With the end of the war, picric acid reverted to its peacetime use in dyeing. Herbert Wilson is recalled by a worker as 'a really nice man'.[10] He was a manager, in charge of azo dye production, with three process chemists under him, plus processmen. Herbert – according to his son – got away with sacking employees, only 'where drink or carelessness caused danger to fellow workers'.[11] 'He still regarded himself as lower middle-class,' according to Leslie Smith, Harold Wilson's first biographer, 'but always defiantly described himself as "working-class" to Tory friends.'[12]

Harold Wilson was relatively fortunate in the domestic circumstances of his birth. His sister Marjorie was old enough not to be jealous of the new arrival, and in his early years she was strongly protective. A relationship of dependence developed, on his part, with his older sibling. Marjorie became, and remained, an important influence on Harold, and, since she was never to marry, would take a close interest in his well-being.

For Ethel, Harold was 'the blue-eyed boy'.[13] He physically resembled his mother, being pudgy as a child, and having a face with some similar characteristics. He inherited her low blood pressure and very slow pulse rate, and to this has been attributed a certain equanimity in his personality. She was shy, and he took after his mother in this respect – though he learned to compensate. His sense of humour is attributed to her, though he developed from imp to wit, and continued to deploy it in adult life as a weapon. His relationship with his mother was close, and he is thought to have very occasionally sought her advice.

Herbert Wilson was delighted to have a son. As head of a – small – nuclear family, he was determined to do the best for his children. He aspired to their self-advancement, through educational opportunity, and must have expressed such expectations, in carrying out his role of father. Whether or not his father was stern or harsh, Harold Wilson was to show considerable drive. Ambition, often a desire to please a parent, substantially defines Harold Wilson. He was continually to seek reassurance, asking for it by proclaiming his achievements; presumably failing to get adequate response, he persisted all the more in trying to satisfy his father's wishes. Harold Wilson inherited something of his father's prodigious memory, a resource the latter used in work and play. Herbert was ebullient and gregarious, but his son took some time to acquire social skills.

The Wilsons did not believe in a puritanical Christianity, but a religious seriousness pervaded their lives. They believed in doing the right thing, and they brought their children up with this social doctrine. In the Colne valley, the protestant ethic had been coterminous with industrialization. Hard work was an end in itself, but also a means to social advancement. Within such an ideological universe, Herbert Wilson believed not only in religious instruction, but also in the importance of secular education. 'I've taken my own religious views for granted', Harold Wilson would say. 'I'd never had any emotional or intellectual crisis which made me think them out.'[14]

There was a purpose to much in Wilson's family life. He was given toys – at a time when only a minority of boys and girls were so fortunate. At an early age he received a Meccano set, becoming an aficionado of mechanical construction. When he was seven, he was given a Hornby train set for Christmas – the king of toys – which was set up in his attic bedroom at Western Road. With such an asset he would make his first real friend through a common interest.

Herbert bought a second-hand motorcycle with sidecar for £50 in 1918, which he used to cross Huddersfield to Hollidays. It also allowed for visits back to Manchester, to see relations, and regular family holidays. Each Whitsun and August, with Marjorie on the back and Ethel in the sidecar with Harold, Herbert would journey to the north York moors. There in Old Byland village, the family lodged with cousins of Herbert's, who owned the pub on the village green. One of Harold's first memories is of a band in Old Byland, celebrating the Versailles peace treaty in the summer of 1919, when he was three. These holidays were to come to an end after several years, though Herbert had quickly graduated to a new motorcycle and sidecar. In 1925, he bought an Austin 7 motorcar for £149, one of only a handful in Western Road. Herbert later acquired a Jowett, a larger and altogether more impressive model.

Marjorie, who was at elementary school, won a county minor scholarship in 1920, the only pupil in her class to do so. This allowed her to attend Greenhead high school in Huddersfield. It was also that autumn, when he was four and a half, that Harold started his formal learning, walking to the local Milnsbridge council school, known locally as New Street. It was an imposing school, built of Yorkshire stone by the West Riding education committee at the turn of the century, and catered for all the children of the area. As a child of less than five, Harold entered a class of some forty pupils – boys and girls together – who were predominantly mill people. A school photograph from 1925 shows him – a little less pudgy – sitting on the ground in the front row, and among the best dressed in his class, wearing a shirt, tie and blazer.

An older pupil at New Street remembers that 'academically [the teachers] weren't very brilliant',[15] and attributes this to the post-war rush to get teachers. Harold Wilson had a 'miserable year' in the infants' class, in 1920–1, being terrified of a Miss Oddy, who introduced him, for the first time, to corporal punishment. He recalls her as 'an incompetent teacher or a sadist, probably both'.[16] Harold suffered in silence, keeping his fear to himself. But he came out top, and went on to the elementary school proper, jumping two grades. It is from this point – when he was less than six – that his reputation for brilliance apparently stems. Edgar Whitwam, who was to teach him later at New Street, recalled: 'To Harold it was effortless. There was never anyone to touch him ... He was the sort of boy a teacher comes across only once or twice in a lifetime. He was more or less top in everything'.[17] Sometime in the mid-1920s, a new headmaster called Greenwood took over. He quickly knocked the school into shape, and even introduced the 'pretty revolutionary'[18] idea of a uniform, but this was towards the end of Harold's time at New Street. By the age of eleven, he was sharing a desk with a fourteen-year-old boy.

In 1927, Harold was one of eight, out of forty or so boys and girls, in his class to pass the county minor examination, being awarded a scholarship. He had to answer papers in arithmetic and English. Asked to write an essay about a photograph – of Millet's painting, *The Angelus* – Harold imagined that the man had been lured on a drinking spree, and was now telling his wife he had no money to feed their children. At least one temperance propagandist had done a good job on a ten-year-old!

Whether Harold Wilson was the most brilliant pupil at New Street or not, it took parental encouragement to stimulate his intelligence, and personal drive to achieve a high academic performance. Two large bookcases in the Wilson household indicated the existence of cultural life. Harold, like all schoolboys, read comics such as *Bubbles* and *Chips*. At the age of seven, he was interested in Buffalo Bill. His early reading tended to be more serious. Thus, the household took *Meccano* magazine and, after he got his train set, *Hornby* magazine. He was also to read the *Scout*. Herbert bought the *Children's Newspaper* for his family, and had presented Harold with a book, *Engineering for Boys*. He was able to turn to Marjorie's set of Arthur Mee's *Children's Encyclopaedia* in 1924, taking an especial interest in history. Harold Wilson claims that he was an early reader of the *Manchester Guardian*, a paper that espoused his parents' view of the world. He was also allowed to select books off the shelves with a certain amount of guidance.

The Wilson family was one of the few in Milnsbridge to possess a radio. The broadcasting of news, talks and music, all of which might be described as middle of the road, was undoubtedly to have an impact, and Herbert Wilson controlled his son's cultural development. Harold Wilson learned early the habit of radio listening, and, as prime minister, would have BBC Radio 2, and even Radio 1, playing in the background in his study. Herbert Wilson had no time for the gramophone; he had no apparent interest in classical music, and popular music may have been considered as verging on the sinful or flippant. When, at secondary school, Harold Wilson found himself writing an essay in the role of a future chancellor of the exchequer, he singled out gramophone records for particularly harsh treatment: 'To me [they] were a mark of the idle rich, not to say the sybaritic, and my proposed tax of one shilling was undoubtedly intended as a deterrent.'[19]

Harold's early life was not totally serious. When he was about seven, young Wilson became friends with Harold Ainley, the son of an architect, who lived nearby. Harold Ainley was a year ahead at New Street. Their common interests initially were Meccano and Hornby trains; they would play in the attic at Western Road after school and on Saturday mornings. Harold Ainley felt, at least in retrospect, that he was not considered the ideal friend by the Wilsons, mainly because Ainley senior had little time for non-conformist values. The young Wilson may have been attracted to his namesake because he was 'a bit rough and ready'. 'I think possibly ... he looked up to me', recalls Harold Ainley, because 'I could look after myself on a football field.' There is no recollection of this future prime minister behaving in anything other than a proper manner: 'I think he'd have liked to have been adventurous but I don't think he ever was.' When Harold Wilson visited the Ainley household, he always took his cap off before entering.

Sport was Harold Ainley's 'number one subject'. A sort of cricket was played in New Street, a wicket being chalked on the school wall. Cowersley boys also had a bit of a football field nearby at the bottom of a hill. Harold Wilson engaged in these games, 'though he wasn't a brilliant sportsman'. He did make up for a lack of physical acumen by relying on his mental

powers. He would know all the positions on a cricket field, while his friends
were more interested in prowess. When it came to football he was 'a trier',
and was invariably made the goalkeeper. The local football team, Huddersfield Town, was particularly prominent in the 1920s. Harold Wilson
followed Huddersfield's fortunes, and, in 1964, he was still carrying a
photograph of the 1926 team. There is some doubt as to how often he saw
his football heroes play. He has written recently that he attended home
matches, taking the tram into town with a shilling given by his mother.
According to Harold Ainley, it was 'a bit adventurous going to the other
end of town'; he claims that Harold Wilson never accompanied him and
his friends. His father took him first at the age of seven, and Harold
remembers being hit by a ball in the 1925–6 season.

Harold Wilson cannot have been that gregarious. Among his peers, he
failed to excel in ways that probably mattered to them. When he tried to
compensate, it only further distanced him. 'He was as popular as it is
[possible] for the brightest boy in the school to be popular', recalls Harold
Ainley. 'A lot of people looked upon him as a swot but I think it was
jealousy.' He may not have learned how to trust – or even like – people
outside his family. But he appears to have been kind, willing to give of
himself later by helping others with their homework. Being studious may
have become a means of relating to others.

He suffered two major illnesses as a boy, and nearly died from the
second one. In 1923, at the age of seven, he went down with appendici-
tis. He was admitted to a private nursing home, now that his father had a
salary of £500 a year; the bill would come to £60. In early December –
the day of the general election called by Stanley Baldwin – he had an
operation. He was allowed home on Christmas eve. His recuperation
took until Easter, and he missed a whole term at elementary school. It was
during this period, when the first labour government, led by Ramsay
MacDonald, was showing how it could administer the affairs of state
responsibly, that he began to read the *Children's Encyclopaedia*.

Harold Wilson is supposed to have expressed his first serious political
opinion on 6 December 1923, when his parents visited him as he was
recovering from a general anaesthetic. Just over a year earlier, Philip
Snowden had won Colne Valley for labour. He was a member of the independent labour party, and had lost his Blackburn seat in 1918 for opposing
the war. In his new constituency, Snowden was known as a man who had
been hostile to Victor Grayson's brand of socialism. According to Harold
Wilson, he insisted that his parents should hasten back to Milnsbridge to
vote before the polls closed. Too much can be inferred from such an
utterance, especially from a seven-year-old boy who could not return to
school for several months. But something along those lines seems to have
been said, because Herbert and Ethel, who were delayed by fog and failed

to vote, chose to keep this failing from their son for some years. 'It would be easy to exaggerate the significance of this episode ... In reality he understood very little about the issues involved in the election, and regarded the contest in the same kind of light as he regarded a match played by Huddersfield Town.'[20]

Philip Snowden was elected, and became chancellor of the exchequer in the first labour government in 1924. Ramsay MacDonald's administration fell within the year, labour losing the election in October. It should occasion no surprise that the labour voters in Colne Valley felt proud that their member of parliament – a physically handicapped political preacher from the West Riding – had occupied 11 Downing Street for a time. Nor is it strange that an eleven-year-old Harold Wilson, when asked to write an essay on himself in twenty-five years time, should have chosen the role of chancellor of the exchequer. It was an advanced position in the world of Yorkshire nonconformity, and Harold Wilson's 'hero worship'[21] of Philip Snowden, in his first year at secondary school, hardly implies a socialist political consciousness.

Travel had already done something to broaden Harold's mind. Herbert took Harold to the British Empire exhibition at Wembley in the summer of 1924. It was his first visit to London. They stayed in Russell Square, in Bloomsbury, and did the usual tourist things – Westminster, Buckingham Palace, Hyde Park, St Paul's, the Tower of London. Father and son walked along Downing Street, and Herbert photographed Harold standing in front of Number 10, in short trousers and cap. There was no sign of Ramsay MacDonald, though Harold touched the knocker for luck. This photograph was to find its way into the national press thirty-nine years later (though Harold had lost the print in 1950 when he had his wallet stolen). Herbert sold the negative to the *Express* for £50 when his son was elected leader of the labour party, and it would be used to suggest a lifelong desire on the part of Harold Wilson to be prime minister. There is no evidence of any such ambition at this time, and the photograph is easily understood as the work of a provincial tourist with a camera for taking family snapshots. Harold had acquired a smattering of national – English – history during his recuperation earlier that year, and, as they motorcycled home via Runnymede, Oxford, Rugby and Stratford-upon-Avon, he corrected tour guides at the monuments of tradition in the manner of a slightly earnest eight-year-old.

In 1926, Harold's maternal grandfather, William Seddon, reportedly fell seriously ill in Australia. Ethel, believing the worst, wished to visit her father, then in his early seventies. Herbert offered to meet the cost of the sea passage for her and Harold. Herbert was to remain at home, with Marjorie – now seventeen – looking after him. Harold was taken out of New Street school, and, in May, the month of the general strike, Herbert drove them to

London, where they embarked upon the *Esperance Bay* for the long voyage
to the antipodes. It was a thrilling experience for a ten-year-old, not least
the stops in Egypt and Ceylon, en route to Perth. In Western Australia they
found members of the Seddon family living on a small farm, and his
grandfather in much better health. Young Harold helped with the fruit
picking, his first – and only – experience of manual labour, and appears to
have thoroughly enjoyed himself in the outback. Harold and his mother
were also driven to Kalgoorlie, to stay with Harold Seddon and his wife.
The climax of his time in Australia was a visit to the legislative council in
Perth, to see his uncle Harold, now a politician, in action. (Harold Seddon
had quit the Labour Party as a supporter of the war and, as Liberal President
of the Council, would be knighted by King George VI.) The young
Harold Wilson cannot but have been impressed by what was his first time
in 'any of His Majesty's Parliaments'.[22]

Back in Milnsbridge, Harold Wilson was a boy with stories to tell. He
prepared a talk, and duly lectured to each class at New Street – apparently
impressing the teachers with his erudition. He also wrote an article about
his visit to a Kalgoorlie gold mine, arranged no doubt by his uncle. This
was rejected by *Meccano* magazine and the *Scout*, but later appeared in a
magazine produced in secondary school, and is his first known publication.
'A Visit to an Australian Gold Mine' is a short, well-structured, and clearly
written piece. After stating that few of his readers will have had such an
opportunity, he recounts visiting the engine room 'where are the massive
engines that work the Pit Head Gear', before proceeding to explain the
process of gold extraction from ore; 'powder is scattered about everywhere,
and I got some on my boots and clothes, making me look very dirty
indeed.'[23]

CHAPTER 3

Grammar School Boy, 1927–34

In the summer of 1928 the Wilson family had their motoring holiday in Scotland, during which Harold recalls that he 'asked for elucidation'[1] on the meaning of 1906, at Campbell-Bannerman's statue in Stirling. Leslie Smith has Herbert extemporizing on the rise of labour, and even speaking uncritically of the socialist Tom Mann, who had fought an uphill struggle in Colne Valley in 1895. All this sounds like an attempt to establish a personal political biography in 1964 for a new leader of the labour party. Harold Wilson may have been infused with a missionary zeal as an intelligent twelve-year-old, but the objective is not at all clear. Years later, he articulated a liberal view of British political history: '[Campbell-Bannerman] was the Prime Minister who presided over the initiation of the long-overdue social revolution of the early years of the century, of which Asquith in a minor and Lloyd George in a major degree were the instruments.'[2]

Harold's major non-academic preoccupation at this time was the boy scouts. He had been introduced to scouting when his mother had to take him to the guides on Tuesday evenings. He became impatient to belong to the wolf cubs on his eighth birthday, and joined – minus his appendix – a week early. He introduced Harold Ainley, and was to help him with knots and tests. The two Harolds became members of the 3rd Colne Valley Milnsbridge Baptist scouts. It was the largest group in Yorkshire, numbering some 150 boys; membership required attendance at the afternoon Sunday school. The baptist minister, William Henry Potter, was an impressive figure in Milnsbridge, and, through the scouts, of which he was master, many boys in the village – from all backgrounds – had access to a range of activities. They called this large man, who had seven children of his own, 'Pa' Potter, invariably out of respect.

While there was no ostensible talk of politics at scout meetings, Potter instilled an awareness of social conditions; he was even to hold discussions on sex and morals at the request of his boys, and the programme of training included debates. Harold Ainley might have joined the scouts as

19

a means to various ends, but, like Harold Wilson, he was strongly influenced by the organization's conception of social conduct: 'In the scouts you were taught to do a good turn each day. That's part of the scout philosophy. Do a good deed. Well, I think Harold would.'

The main attraction of scouting was going away to camp, which was made possible by fund-raising activity and the generosity of Milnsbridge trades-people. Weekend camps were held in a salubrious part of Huddersfield, Honley, during the summer months. It was at one of these that Harold Wilson contracted typhoid fever in 1930. He was fourteen years old, and it was his second major illness. He was infected by drinking milk, as were some dozen of the local farmer's customers. They were rushed to an isolation hospital in Meltham, where six were to die. The treatment, such as it was, consisted largely of – boiled – milk and water. Given Harold's age and the fact that he was otherwise healthy, the prognosis was probably good – and, indeed, he made slow progress during October. His parents could only visit once a week, but Herbert telephoned each morning and evening from a call-box for a medical report. Then, suddenly, Harold relapsed, and it looked as if he would be the seventh victim. He was critical for nearly six weeks, but began to recover again. He himself was unaware of how serious his illness had been, though he was apparently the marginal survivor. He used his medical incarceration to continue his reading, and seems to have found an interest in fiction. He was released at the beginning of 1931, having been in hospital for thirteen weeks. He weighed a little over four-and-a-half stone, and was given a bed in front of the gasfire in his parents' room. He had to convalesce again until Easter.

Possibly in 1929, he and Harold Ainley had been part of a joint Milns-bridge and Meltham scout trip to Holland, apparently arranged through the chapel. The Yorkshire boys were guests of some Dutch scouts at Beek, near Nijmegen, close to the German border. Though 'Pa' Potter arranged for reduced fares, the cost of something under £4 may have restricted it to those from better-off homes. For most of them, it was their first trip abroad; for Harold Wilson, the North Sea hardly compared with the journey to Australia, though he succumbed to seasickness. The two Harolds wandered over into Germany unchallenged, at a time when the great war was still remembered. Harold Wilson did not join those scouts, including Harold Ainley, who had their first taste of beer there: 'I was a bit of a lad and Harold was a bit timid.'[3]

Despite – or perhaps because of – this, Wilson became a patrol leader. When Harold Wilson was elected in 1945, he joined the parliamentary branch of the guild of old scouts – a nostalgic act with masonic overtones. As chief guest at a scout dinner in London, following his election to the leadership of the labour party in 1963, he stated there was still a role for the movement 'given the … danger of a loss of individual, and above all of moral purpose, especially among the young'.[4] Harold Wilson has written recently: 'I happily acknowledge my membership as one of the main elements in my formative years.'[5]

While he may have learned to relate to other boys as a patrol leader in the scouts, it was on the stage that he showed an early talent for communicating with people in general.

At the age of eleven, when he had to sing a solo in the baptist choir during a Sunday evening service, Harold Wilson – as he recalled two decades later – was petrified. He was quickly to learn to overcome his fear, with the help of his father. Herbert introduced him to amateur dramatics as part of the activity of the chapel. Harold first began as a call boy behind the scenes in the operatic society, which was well known in the Colne Valley for its D'Oyly Carte productions. When he was about twelve, he played Midshipmite in a production of *HMS Pinafore*. A photograph of him in his costume shows a lively, confident boy. He was to be less appreciated in his school choir, possibly because his voice was changing, though he appears to have enjoyed singing.

Gilbert and Sullivan – maybe not surprisingly – represents the limit of Harold Wilson's aesthetic development. This is in spite, or perhaps because, of his experience of Shakespeare and other dramatists at secondary school. He was to play Shylock in a form production of *The Merchant of Venice*, and be praised for his handling of this role in his first play. In a school production of Goldsmith's *She Stoops to Conquer* in January 1932, he received a good notice from a local schoolgirl, Mary Thorpe, of Elland secondary school, for his comic performance as Tony Lumpkin: '[H. Wilson] is worthy of first mention since he is the soul of the play. He took his part with gusto, in fact over-acting in places, for he diverted the attention of the audience from the other proceedings.'[6] Harold Wilson had discovered by his midteens, that he could win the approval of peers and adults.

He was one of the few in his class to go on to secondary education at eleven. In the early autumn of 1927, Harold Wilson made his way to Royds Hall school, up the hill from Milnsbridge. He was dressed, like the other pupils, in a brown blazer with pale blue piping. Royds Hall was originally a rather beautiful mill-owner's home, which became a military hospital during the great war. In 1921 the West Riding education committee opened it as a secondary school, building a new block close to the house. It was 1930 before the playing fields were properly laid out. Royds Hall was to serve the valley, many of the pupils coming down by train to Longwood station. It was coeducational, as the authority was unable to run two separate schools. Some of the pupils were fee-paying, but many were scholarship boys and girls. In 1930–1, the rolls topped 500, 243 boys and 261 girls. Royds Hall set out to provide an academic education, and its range of subjects stretched as far as biology. There was also physical education (including sport), and a strong emphasis on extra-curricular activity through school societies. These were reported in the school magazine, the *Roydsian*, which appeared at the end of every term; 700 copies of the December 1930 number were to be printed. Under its first headmaster, E. F. Chaney, a considerable school spirit was built up. In January 1930, 140 former pupils were to attend the fourth annual dinner of the Roydsian Fellowship. There was an old boys' football club, smaller rambling and cycling clubs, and a drama society.

Royds Hall was not New Street, and Harold Wilson found himself surrounded by other bright boys and girls from all over the valley. He was placed in form Ic, first-year pupils being divided into four groups on the basis of age. A fellow pupil recalls him as 'a grinning schoolboy [somewhat smaller in stature than his male classmates] a bit giggly, and always willing to please, so presented no problems with the staff, who viewed him as an angelic cherub'.[7] He seems to have taken some time to find his feet, and was criticized in reports for not trying hard enough. The following year, 1928–9, he was in form IIc. He improved in time. In 1929–30, he was in IIIb, reaching the 'a' stream in autumn 1930, when he entered the fourth form. He had been in trouble for not working hard enough. Irene Smith, who was in the same year, remembers that 'he certainly got the best end of term reports among the boys in our form, though there were 2 girls who always outshone him!'[8] One of them was Jessie Hadfield, from New Street, who was also in IVa in 1930–1. This was the year he missed two terms, but he came third in the class at the end of the academic year. A teacher, in his last full year (1931–2), remembers Harold had 'an impish sense of humour'.[9] Others recall him as 'one of [my] very ablest pupils' and a 'high-flyer', and his English mistress in the fifth form has described him as 'very bright': 'It was always a relief to get to his essay when marking 35 more mediocre efforts.'[10] In Royds Hall, as the 1920s became the 1930s, 'most of the staff considered him to have no more special promise than many another hard-working pupil with first-class brains.'[11]

He impressed at least three teachers – H. F. Diggle (French), F. S. Wilmut (mathematics) and Miss Caruth (biology). Another female member of staff, Betty Forshaw, as she then was, who came to Royds Hall in 1931, feels that they influenced Harold Wilson. 'Politically the three teachers were Socialist, very concerned about the Depression of that time and looking upon Socialism, as did many of its early adherents, as almost a mission.'[12] It is certainly the case that these three, who were very much a minority on the staff, might have been particularly motivated to help scholarship pupils. It is also likely that Harold Wilson admired them in turn. It cannot be inferred that, because they were left wing, their socialism passed, by osmosis or indoctrination, into the mind of a favoured pupil.

Given Harold Wilson's numeracy, it is perhaps not surprising that F.S. Wilmut, teacher of mathematics, should have taken an especial interest in such a pupil. But it was literature – or rather, writing – which brought them together. Wilmut edited the school magazine, and included Wilson's article on an Australian gold mine in the July 1928 issue, believing it to be a work of imagination! Harold's subsequent pieces, written in a puckish vein, may well have been encouraged by Wilmut. One such was 'Diary of a Choir-Boy', in April 1930, which irreverently noted events in the school choir, from the annual picnic at Hope Bank pleasure grounds, Honley, the previous July, through the winter of practice in preparation for speech day at the town hall in Huddersfield. Wilmut included a note in the December number, reporting Wilson's typhoid fever; 'He wishes to thank his many friends at the School who have written to him during his isolation.'[13]

In 1945, Wilmut would profess himself unsurprised at Harold Wilson's 'achievements'[14] in the preceding thirteen years, but it cannot be inferred from this kind comment that the maths teacher had been nurturing a labour politician in the summer of 1931. As a fifth former, Wilson discussed politics in school at the time of the general election in October, though there is no evidence that he supported labour. Harold Wilson's first real interest in politics – in October 1932, when he was sixteen – came about because of a government plan to introduce school fees. It is not surprising that a scholarship boy should have become incensed, especially given his father was in straitened circumstances at the time. The first political meeting Harold Wilson is recorded as having attended was one organized by the liberals, whose guest speaker was Dingle Foot, a Samuelite MP for Dundee. Harold went with some pupils from Royds Hall, and when questions were invited at the end of the speeches, they sent up a note about the proposed school fees.

Harold Wilson was not brilliant at sport at school. He played as goalkeeper in his form's football team, and, on one occasion, when he let six goals through, he was chased off the field by a team mate. He faired better in school societies, but was by no means the most active.

The most prominent, if not entertaining, ought to have been the debating society, but it seems to have been poorly supported in Harold Wilson's early years. In one of his first attempts at public speaking, in his second year, he 'delivered a brilliant opening sentence that unfortunately got no further'.[15] Having one point to make, he did so briskly. In time, he was to learn the art of exposition, and became one of the better speakers in the school. He first spoke on a motion at the beginning of his third year, seconding the proposition that educating boys and girls together was lunacy; it was lost by an overwhelming majority. Shortly before his sixteenth birthday, on the occasion of the opening of the international disarmament conference at Geneva, the society debated the citizen's duty to fight in wartime. This was a full year before the famous Oxford union vote for pacifism. 'After a protracted and heated discussion', the pupils of Royds Hall came out against war, 'by a large majority'.[16] This is unlikely to have had much significance, even in Huddersfield. Harold Wilson was a principal speaker, and, though the *Roydsian* report is brief, it seems that he took a patriotic stand. At the beginning of the following academic year, he became a committee member of the debating society.

Harold Wilson was a member of the scientific society, but he did not play a leading part. He was more interested in the historical society. After it had been dormant for two years, he became a committee member in late 1931. At the first meeting on 30 November, he gave the second talk, 'From Ark to Aquitania'.[17] He remained on the committee, for what would be his first year in the sixth form, and spoke on 'The Romance of Modern Transport'[18] at the first meeting, on 17 October.

Harold Wilson had to leave Royds Hall because his father had to move to find employment. Herbert had been made redundant in December 1930, at the age of forty-eight, shortly before Harold returned from the isolation hospital. He was given a month's salary and joined the ranks of the unemployed, then rising towards three million, although it may not have had the same impact on Harold as other fifteen-year-olds in the area. The family had a middle-class concern for its reputation, and the fact was concealed from neighbours and friends. Herbert had savings, and he did not have to give up his motor car. He also got some consultancy work, and invigilated in elementary school examinations. Food became more basic, but Harold always received enough, though clothing had to last a little longer. Whatever of Herbert's reaction to his plight, there is no contemporary evidence of it affecting Harold. He worked hard to catch up at the end of the fourth year, and through the following academic year. His success on the school stage as Tony Lumpkin came after a year of relative economic deprivation. There was talk of Harold possibly taking a job in the family business in Manchester, but his father, most likely, was too committed to getting him an education. It was a few more months before Herbert found a job. When he did, the Wilsons, including Marjorie, who was now a teacher, had to leave Yorkshire, their home for the past twenty years. Herbert held on to the house, and was to rent it out for many years.

In November 1932, the family moved to the Wirral in Cheshire. A tunnel was then being constructed under the Mersey, linking Birkenhead with Liverpool, and the Wirral would become a middle-class commuter area on Merseyside. Herbert had secured employment at Brotherton's, a chemical works in Bromborough, about four miles from Birkenhead on the road to Chester. He was employed in a managerial capacity, as chief chemist, and worked here through the 1930s. His new employer supplied the family with a flat nearby in Bromborough. This was part of the ground floor of a large, mid-nineteenth-century house, called 'Woodslee', on Spital Road. It belonged to Brotherton's, the grounds having become playing fields for the firm. Four other families had flats there, including two process workers on the second floor. Other workers lived in cottages at the back. A daughter of Ernest Harrison, a mechanic at Brotherton's, remembers the Wilsons, but does not think Harold had much to do with the other children. Harold Wilson lived in the Wirral for less than two years, but they were crucial for his formal education.

University was considered within his grasp, but some of his teachers in Huddersfield felt he would have to work harder. He himself may have begun to aspire to Oxford. Herbert seems to have been particularly concerned for his son in the autumn of 1932. He consulted his brother Jack, about whether Harold should be sent possibly to a public school in Liverpool on his scholarship. The latter apparently recommended a local grammar, Wirral County School in Bebington, a couple of miles away, which had recently opened.

A brand new red brick building, with white fascia, in Cross Lane, Wirral County was a boys' school, and Harold no longer had to compete with girls. They had their own county school in an adjacent building, with the entrance in Heath Road. The boys' school had started with about 100 first-formers in 1931, and a handful who had come from other schools. He was the first, and only, pupil in the sixth form in 1932–3, and in the following academic year. The teachers were young and enthusiastic, and, with the exception of the woodwork master, had degrees. The headmaster, J.M. Moir, who had come from Wigan grammar school, was a master of science. He is remembered as 'an awful snob',[19] a man who would have preferred the name Wirral School.

The school drew boys from the Wirral, except Birkenhead, some coming by train and others cycling. Most were scholarship boys, and the school was to. have a good examinations record in time. Uniforms were not compulsory, but boys had to raise their caps to masters in the street. They were assigned to one of four houses, Leverhulme, Barber, Dodds and Hodgson, named after leading school governors; Lord Leverhulme ran Lever Brothers at nearby Port Sunlight, and Hodgson was a local baker. Harold Wilson became head of Leverhulme House, being the most senior boy at Wirral County, and he was the school captain in 1933–4. In his first year in the sixth form, he had to continue with Latin, and, apparently, mathematics. He had less of an aptitude for the latter. In the second year, he studied English, French and – mainly – history for the higher school certificate. Lessons were held in the school library, and took the form of tutorials from senior masters. Harold Wilson was fortunate in having such educational opportunity, and he blossomed as a seventeen-year-old. Wirral

County may have been initially reluctant to take him, but he was to be their first star pupil.

There were no other boys of his own age. As a sixteen-year-old, he became friends with Douglas Richmond, who joined the second form in late 1932. Douglas lived closer to Ellesmere Port, and, each morning, Harold waited for him near Woodslee, so that they might cycle together to Bebington. Richmond *père* was an accountant, who had just moved his family back to Merseyside after a year in Hull. Harold Wilson apparently focused on Doug, as he was called, as someone from Yorkshire. The Richmond family was established church, and also conservative, but neither Harold, nor his parents, seem to have found this unacceptable in the Wirral. Harold and Doug cycled back from school each day, and occasionally knocked about with a bat or ball in Brotherton's grounds. Douglas Richmond remembers Harold as a supporter of Huddersfield Town, though there was at least one visit to Goodison Park, to see Stoke play Everton, the two queueing for players' autographs, including the young Stanley Matthews's. As time went on, the age difference saw them drift apart.

The senior classics master at Wirral County, Frank Allen, was 'a big influence on Harold Wilson'.[20] He was in his twenties, 'a socialist and probably a pacifist'.[21] The teaching of Latin was seemingly interrupted when Allen 'deployed his classical knowledge and deep religious faith to widen [Wilson's] appreciation of current political events'.[22] Allen also taught music and cricket. He took Harold to hear Gilbert and Sullivan in Liverpool, and he may also have done a great deal to encourage an interest in sport.

Harold's main subject was history, which was taught by P.L. Norrish, a senior teacher at the school. He had studied the nineteenth century at Royds Hall, and, at Wirral County, his new master introduced him to the seventeenth century. This was the subject he envisaged reading at university. Norrish was himself studying for an external master's from London, and he shared some of the books with his pupil.

Harold Wilson was very much the senior boy. As the school captain in 1933, he took his responsibility seriously. He suggested to the head master that there should be football at lunch time to prevent sexual mischief among older boys. He strongly believed in the grammar school ethos, and praised the house system – borrowed from the public school tradition. He was not 'terribly good at [sport] though he used to think he was'.[23] He was reluctantly recruited to the rugby team, Wirral County being that sort of school, for a game against Birkenhead Park high school. They lost seventy-four to nil, and took some time to live it down.

Harold Wilson was particularly lithe at this time, and concentrated on running. Having joined the Wirral Athletics Club, he won their three-mile junior cross country championship by a whisker. He captained the junior team in the Merseyside championships, and led it to third place overall.

Back at Wirral County, Harold Wilson continued with his old interests. He founded a debating society, and acted in some plays. Herbert Wilson was still interested in scouting, and ran a rover crew for a time at Woodslee. The physics master at Wirral County, Oscar Wilson, attended, and, with the help of Harold, formed the 28th Birkenhead troop at Wirral County; Harold Wilson became patrol leader. He attended school scout camps at Aberystwyth, in 1933, and, the following year, the Isle of Arran. Speaking as school captain at the annual prizegiving the previous December, a local journalist reported him as saying: "'The activities of the school", he said, "were so rich and varied that no boy could fail to find a subject in which to interest himself.'"[24]

He was due to sit his higher school certificate, in English, French and history, in the summer of 1934. The headmaster wanted him to try for an open scholarship at Oxford, but Mr Norrish felt he was not yet ready. That March, Harold took the train to the city of dreaming spires. He had applied to the Merton group of colleges, placing Jesus at the bottom of the list. This was the only college to take an interest in him, after his papers had been examined. Though he had come from a rather obscure secondary school in the Wirral, the senior tutor and the modern history fellow interviewed him. The senior tutor was interested in his Yorkshire background, and the interview went well. Jesus decided it would accept him, but not offer one of the eleven open scholarships, worth £100 a year. The senior tutor, who had a reputation for spotting good candidates, thought Harold Wilson was a risk worth taking. He was very lucky to gain admittance to the university in 1934, but was only awarded an open exhibition, worth £60 a year. An exhibition also suggested he was not amongst the most brilliant of applicants. He later sat the higher school certificate, passing in English and history, and getting a distinction in French. Norrish thought he ought to do a third year in the sixth form, and resit the Oxford entrance, but the headmaster successfully pressured the education authorities to give him a grant of £190. Herbert offered to bring the total sum up to £300 a year, out of a £2 a week increase in his salary from Brotherton's.

At New Street council school, and afterwards in Milnsbridge, Harold Wilson had shown no obvious interest in girls. Harold Ainley remembers: 'I think he preferred his academic efforts to having flirtations.' He did become attracted to a girl in the same year, Olga Gledhill, who acted in *She Stoops to Conquer* in 1932. He was to talk to others about his feelings for her. While he was able to share some common pursuits with her, he could only muster the courage to walk home with her best friend. She, whether from lack of interest or from strict adherence to protocol, was unable to break through his shyness. While nothing came of this youthful infatuation, she was included among 'some of Mr. Wilson's old school and Scouting friends',[25] who were invited to the town hall, when, as prime minister in 1968, he was made a freeman of Huddersfield.

Once he moved to the Wirral, he took an interest in Douglas Richmond's older sister, Doreen. She was younger than Harold, had had a boyfriend in Hull, and went to the girls' county school in Bebington. The relationship began during the Easter holidays, on 10 April 1933; he was seventeen, she not yet fifteen. The venue was a local aerodrome. Doreen, through two friends, had met an acrobatic pilot, and, on the fateful day, he was to take up Doug, and his friend Harold. 'Doug's face was absolutely green' when they came down, but Harold 'loved it'. Having no fear of flying, he and Doreen started going out together. They went to the pictures, maybe once every three weeks, usually on a Saturday evening. Harold had already seen *Congress Dances* (1931), a German film also shot in English, which was an historical romance about the congress of Berlin in 1878. Doreen remembers Harold being particularly impressed: 'It intrigued him, I think ... He thought [the foreign service] would be quite a good career.' Doreen does not remember Harold expressing any interest in politics, admittedly at a dull time between the 1931 and 1935 elections. He was 'very interested in history'. Wilson came quite often to the Richmond home, on one occasion accompanying his girlfriend to the annual dance of an old comrades association, of which her father was a member: 'He was sort of doing his best, but neither of us [were] dancers at all.' There was not much time together, since Harold was to be revising for the Oxford scholarship, and Doreen had matriculation.

Some letters from him to her survive. They are written in a forced jokey style, though are sharp and succinct. He was probably not unduly gauche for a schoolboy of the times, though he was exceedingly self-conscious about a photograph he sent Doreen. Harold Wilson was principally concerned about school, and was certainly not the young man he later pretended he had been. He was keen on Doreen, a feeling she reciprocated, but he was – in the technical sense – slightly paranoid: '[Harold] had a sort of fixation that some of the other boys were trying to break it up ... They'd never met me, but he liked to make a sort of intrigue of it.'[26] 'Above all don't believe anything they tell you', he had written in late 1933, 'it will be as far off the truth as the tripe they tell me.'[27] On his eighteenth birthday, he wrote thanking her for a novel about motoring, *High Speed*; the gesture he variously interpreted as a hint about learning to drive at Easter, a comment on his poor cross-country performance, and an allusion to his 'fastness' in their relationship; the postscript read: '$y = 14x$. Also many more paper ones, which will have to suffice for the present.'[28] He then went off to Oxford, hoping to 'let off steam' by taking her to the pictures on the Saturday. The relationship ceased soon after, Doreen fearing that Doug might not have passed on a message. She thought later she might have failed to express sufficient pleasure at his open exhibition.

One evening in June, Harold decided to accompany his father to the tennis club at Brotherton's, where Herbert was to give a display of his agility at mental arithmetic, as part of a bet. Many years later, he was still able to square, and square root, telephone numbers. After his father triumphed, Harold stopped to watch some tennis. He was, as he tells it now, to fall for one of the players immediately. This was Gladys Mary Baldwin. She was also eighteen, but working away from home, and was certainly attractive. Gladys Baldwin had been born at Diss in Norfolk, her father being a congregational minister. The family moved to Cambridgeshire and, later, Nottinghamshire. Gladys was sent to boarding school in Sussex. She and her brother were brought up strictly, and were not able to form many friendships. When Gladys left school in 1932, at sixteen, she did a secretarial course in the lake district. The school was able to find her a post at Lever Brothers in Port Sunlight. There she joined the central typing pool, and lived in lodgings in Bebington, most of her earnings of £1.4.0 (£1.25) going to her landlady. One of the benefits of employment in Lord Leverhulme's model industrial concern was access to the sporting facilities at Brotherton's.

The following Saturday, Harold Wilson joined the tennis club. He was either a more confident individual, or had simply thrown caution to the wind at the end of his exams. As a tennis player he was not much good, and Gladys, for her part, had simply noticed a rather untidy schoolboy staring at her a few days earlier. He quickly approached her, and later walked her back to her lodgings. They went to the same service at the Highfield Congregational chapel, Rock Ferry, the next morning, and walked back to Bromborough. Harold found himself falling in love with her, though he may not have thought of it in quite those terms. He concluded quickly that he wanted to marry her, though recognized that that was something which had to come later. Gladys was flattered, but it took a little longer for her to be impressed by his character. By the following weekend, they were 'walking out'. On, probably, 18 July 1934, he informed her of his desire to marry.

Their relationship was kept secret, though Gladys was introduced to the Wilsons. Harold said nothing, but they, as parents, were delighted that he might be making a commitment before going off to university. Gladys's Bebington landlady took her *in loco parentis* responsibility seriously, and wrote to the Rev. and Mrs Baldwin about their daughter having a young man. The Baldwins travelled down from Penrith, on the occasion of a local preaching engagement. They were introduced to Harold, and relieved to find Gladys had chosen well. The Baldwins and Wilsons were socially and politically compatible.

Harold Wilson recalls that, on 18 July, he also told Gladys he was going to become a member of parliament, and even prime minister. There is no reference, in any version of this story, to the political party he intended to lead. The Wilsons had voted labour in the 1920s, but Harold – and Gladys – were firmly rooted in a liberal nonconformist tradition. After 1931, the labour party, now led by the socialist and pacifist George Lansbury, declined to its pre-war status as a minority pressure group. A political career in the labour party was an uncertain aspiration in 1934. The evidence, such as it is, suggests that Harold Wilson was really looking to become a professional married man. He himself writes of that important day with Gladys: 'Had she believed one word of all this [about becoming prime minister], it would have been the end of a promising romance.'[29] It wasn't, and Oxford was where his future lay.

In his nineteenth year, about to leave home, Harold Wilson stood five foot nine inches tall. His adult height looked less, since he stooped, with shoulders rounded; his head seemed to come out of his chest, rather than sit on his shoulders. As he left school, he was uncharacteristically slim, weighing a modest nine and a half stone. His face, at its most oval, was interesting and alert. His mouth was too wide, but he often smiled, a little uneasily. His eyes were his most attractive feature, but his eyeballs rode up when he tensed, the basis of his later hooded look. His light brown hair, parted on the left, was, at this stage, short and neat. Already dressing as an adult, he was otherwise lacking in sartorial elegance, though this was to change, for a time. He showed little sign of physical acumen, and his legs looked thin for his body.

Harold Wilson was a cerebral youth. He had an alert mind, though one that was probably too quick for reflection or profundity. History was his favourite subject, French his best, and English the one in which he was least proficient. Science may not have been possible at school, though mathematics seems to have captured his imagination. He clearly worked hard, and was extremely fortunate in the personal tuition he received at Wirral County, to say nothing of the ambitions a new head master had for him. But, Harold Wilson only just made it to Oxford in 1934.

CHAPTER 4

Oxford Undergraduate, 1934–7

Harold Wilson went up to Jesus College, Oxford in October 1934, to read for a degree in modern history. Situated on Turl Street, and known less reverentially as 'Jaggers', Jesus is relatively modern by English standards, dating only from the sixteenth century. It was one of twenty-seven sexually-segregated colleges in the university of Oxford, teaching over 4,000 undergraduates. The university was still formally Anglican, and an important institution of the British establishment; morning and evening services were still held in college chapels.

Jesus was one of the smallest Oxford colleges, with only a dozen or so fellows covering 'all the traditional disciplines'. The principal, Dr A.E.W. Hazel, a Wesleyan and 'a very severe nonconformist', had been liberal MP for West Bromwich from 1906 to 1910, as well as a prospective Asquithian peer in the struggle against the lords. Jesus was traditionally a Welsh college, with closed scholarships, but, after the great war, it increasingly accepted students from other areas; a service was still held on St David's day, but no longer in Welsh. Its undergraduates tended to come from major industrial areas, including Wales, and the college has been described as 'very largely nonconformist'. Jesus was more meritocratic than other colleges, admitting its share of, largely middle-class, grammar-school boys with local authority scholarships. College scholarships went to about a third of the three dozen or so freshmen in 1934. There were also exhibitioners, including Harold Wilson, and commoners, who received nothing from the college. The senior tutor, Goronwy Edwards, is considered 'really the creator of Jesus College in its modern phase'.[1] He had been in a Welsh regiment during the war, and, coming to admire Yorkshire miners fighting alongside, looked favourably upon applicants from the county.

For those not inculcated from birth in the strange rites of the ruling class, an Oxford education could be an intimidating experience. The eighteen-year-old Harold Wilson from Wirral County School, who came up in the Michaelmas (autumn) term, was looking to join a modern history honours

31

school of 840 persons (including 141 women). It was a larger world than he had experienced in Yorkshire or Cheshire, and very different socially. He was confronted, for the first time, by public-school men (and women), invariably from wealthy backgrounds, and with the self-confidence which money, if not breeding, instilled. Tom Driberg, who would later be associated with Wilson, was at Christ Church in the 1920s, and remembers it was 'peopled largely by wealthy Etonians who devoted much of their time to hunting, rowing and drinking'; he heard a fellow undergraduate tell a tutor: 'I thought I'd just let you know that I shan't be coming to any tutorials or lectures this term, because I've managed to get four days' hunting a week.'[2] The foxes of Oxfordshire had less to fear from the men of Jesus, but the impact of Oxford on Harold Wilson must have been considerable.

A friend he made in college recalls of other undergraduates that 'their way of life was very different from ours'. There was 'plenty of drinking and parties and that sort of thing ... in college ... a lot of high living going on.' 'I know that Harold was very disgusted at a lot of the behaviour ... Perhaps it came as an eye-opener in some ways.'[3] He had worked hard to get to Oxford, and defined himself against those who were wasting the educational opportunity which had come easily to them. He was to allude to a geographical distinction between north and south, when addressing a college society in his third year. In a paper entitled 'The Two Nations', he contrasted 'the old England and that on which nineteenth century industrialism had left its indelible mark'.[4] This was less the division between rich and poor, of which Disraeli had written in 1845, and more the contradiction between the idle and productive classes.

University was Harold Wilson's first time away from home, and he missed family life. His first letters show his now characteristic concern with detail, to the virtual exclusion of all other reactions. Each week he sent washing home to save expense, while his mother posted him a regular food parcel. His battels bill should have been about £2.5.0 (£2.25) a week, but Harold set out to get it under two pounds, even with compulsory dinner five nights a week; he did not partake of cigarettes or beer. He was not hesitant about asking for money, though it is clear that he had imbibed his mother's husbandry. Gladys wrote twice a week, and she was to motor down with his parents on a Saturday, once a term, the three staying over in Oxford until the Sunday afternoon. He had no other girlfriends in Oxford. A fellow student remembers meeting his parents one bank holiday: 'they weren't outstanding monuments, just quite ordinary people'.[5] Harold was to return to Cheshire at the end of term, the vacations at Oxford accounting for just over half the calendar year.

In his first year, he was given rooms in the second quadrangle, which he shared with A.H.J. Thomas, the son of a plumber from Tenby, in southwest Wales. Thomas had been awarded a Welsh foundation scholarship to read modern history, and was described as having a 'subtle, knavish smile'.[6] 'He is an exceptionally nice fellow', Harold told his parents, 'and we get on well.'[7] In his letters home, details were given of Thomas's progress. When he fainted in a lecture on one occasion, Harold 'jolly well took charge of the affair ... while everybody else was clucking and fussing about'; 'Lucky I took that ambulance course last year', he wrote, 'or I wouldn't have known the difference in treatment between a "white faint" and a "red" one.'[8]

He also made friends with Eric Sharpe, a freshman living out of college in 1934–5, who was to read greats (classics). They met some mornings at roll call, at 7.45, or, alternatively, matins, which began at 8.00 in the chapel. Eric Sharpe had a similar background to Harold Wilson. He came from Liverpool, and his father was a salesman in Lewis's. The family was lower-middle class, nonconformist and liberal. Eric had been a scholarship boy at Liverpool Collegiate School. In their second year (1935–6), both young men lived on staircase five, in the front quadrangle, Eric on the ground floor, and Harold above on the first, in rooms that had been occupied, before the war, by T.E. Lawrence – Lawrence of Arabia. Eric Sharpe remembers that Wilson was very proud of this historical association, less because of anything Lawrence was, or did, and more because he became a famous British figure.

The scout (servant) on Sharpe and Wilson's staircase was Tony West. He cleaned their rooms, made coal fires, brought them hot water in the morning, and, if requested, fetched breakfast and lunch from the college kitchens. Dinner was served in hall. Robert Steel, a geography exhibitioner, who also came up in 1934, sat at the same table each night, and became another friend of Wilson's. His father was a congregational minister from near Cambridge, the Steel family then occupying the manse at Fulbourn where Gladys Baldwin had lived in the 1920s (Mary Wilson was later to write a poem about the house). Robert Steel's relationship with Wilson was to develop in time, both having academic ambitions.

In his third year, Harold moved into digs at 58 Fairacres Road, across Magdalen Bridge on the Iffley Road. He tended to use Eric Sharpe's room in college during the day, and eat cheaply in Miss Brown's, a cafe at 14a Broad Street, opposite Balliol. That was the year Harold Wilson was working for his finals, disturbed only by the RAF planes which had taken to flying over Oxford.

Religion was still important in Harold's life. Eric Sharpe came from a baptist background, was a committed Christian, and would later become a minister. He recalls Harold was religious, but not extravagantly so. Within days of arriving at Oxford, he went to see Dr Nathaniel Micklem, principal of Mansfield College, a congregational theological college, and one of the institutions then on the periphery of the university. Micklem, who was the professor of dogmatic theology at Oxford, was a liberal, and would become a leading international figure in the movement. He offered to put Wilson in touch with the student congregational society.

Harold Wilson went to the chapel at Mansfield each Sunday morning, Eric Sharpe sometimes accompanying him to hear the visiting preachers. Robert Steel also attended, and remembers the preaching of 'an out and out pacifist'[9] from Birmingham. Wilson and Sharpe also attended Anglican evensong in Jesus on Sundays. Harold very often attended matins during the week, it being a – slightly later – alternative to the daily roll call. He would be married in the chapel at Mansfield College – on new year's day in 1940 – by Dr Micklem and the Rev. Baldwin.

Work was Harold Wilson's main preoccupation at Oxford. Eric Sharpe remembers him as quiet, and as seeing university as a place to study. Wilson immediately got down to it. He had to sit his first public examinations, pass moderations, at the end of the Michaelmas term. Only then could he proceed to work for the final honours school. Aside from modern history, he had to study Latin, French and, significantly, a little economics. 'None of these was studied in any great depth',[10] but the idea was to learn to think and write. Harold Wilson was diligent in attending university lectures, and the classes organized for small groups of students in their first term. At this stage, there was only one tutorial a week, where he was set an essay on which he would be questioned.

In December 1934, Harold Wilson flew through his exams, coming top in economics and joint top in French and Latin. This performance, after less than eight weeks, was to prove decisive for his intellectual formation. Though he had an open exhibition in modern history, he decided he did not want to work for the final honours school. This had nothing to do with his feelings about history. Nor did it have to do with Jesus College, though the authorities may not have been amused. Harold Wilson had become attracted to economics in his first term. He had clearly taken to the new subject, no doubt because of his mathematical mind. There is a story that he phoned his father, who consulted the teachers at Wirral County. It is also said that he decided upon economics, given his intention of embarking upon a political career. The decision was probably a calculated educational move. Robert Steel remembers that the newer discipline had a 'slightly more vocational' reputation than history.

To study economics, Harold Wilson had to read for a modern greats degree, which also included philosophy and politics. The honours school of philosophy, politics and economics (PPE) had been established as recently as 1922, on the basis of courses taught earlier. Permission was sought from Hazel to transfer, though Harold Wilson found he had to pass in two European languages. He already had French, and the college agreed he should study German during the Christmas vacation. He performed poorly in a test in early 1935, but was allowed to proceed. He was examined in Italian for his finals. Albert Goodwin, who had been taken on to develop the college connection with PPE, on the strength of a special subject in finance he had studied as an undergraduate, remained his tutor. He had to send Harold Wilson to other colleges for tutorials. Within Jesus, Wilson also became involved with another tutor.

At the beginning of the Hilary (spring) term of his first year, Wilson now found himself in a much smaller academic world. There were only 468 undergraduates in the PPE honours school in 1934–5, 143 of whom would sit their finals in 1937. Jesus College had only two other PPE candidates, but Harold Wilson was not afraid of academic competition. He had impressed the college with his first term's work, and they expected him to do well. He was diligent, and could handle the material. No particular originality was noted, but this was not expected at this age. Jesus College felt the risk taken in offering the open exhibition had quickly paid off.

Harold Wilson persisted in working hard. In May 1935, he wrote to his parents that he had averaged seven hours work a day in the previous week. The following academic year, on staircase five, he and Eric Sharpe paced each other. Each had a large Boots diary, which he kept in his room, and in which was recorded details of work done, including attendance at lectures and tutorials. Harold Wilson's idea was that they should compete. He was the proud possessor of a pencil, blue at one end and red at the other. Each morning, they compared the previous day's performances. If it was over eight hours, a red circle was entered in the diary for that day; a blue circle round the date meant more than ten hours. The winner was allowed to keep the pencil. Eric Sharpe remembers that, while he had it for a few days that year, it remained mainly with Harold.

The practice was not continued when Wilson went into digs, but he continued to work hard in his final year. He wrote to Doreen Richmond on 1 November 1936: 'I'm certainly enjoying life at Oxford, and also having to behave myself – there's no time not to. This last week I had to work morning, afternoon and evening every day with only Wednesday afternoon off – and then I played squash with my tutor.' These were the words of a single-minded young man.

The philosophy tutor at Jesus College was the thirty-four-year-old Malcolm Knox. He had been born in Birkenhead, the son of a congregational minister. Knox's father was then working for Lever Brothers at Port Sunlight, in charge of staff training. Knox junior had only recently become a fellow, having come to the college in 1931, after selling soap for Lord Leverhulme in west Africa for six years, and was also teaching Greek philosophy at Queen's College. Harold Wilson believed he was indebted to Knox for his place at Oxford, given the Wirral connection. Whatever of this, the latter did a great deal to help the young man from Cheshire.

Wilson found tutorials with Knox 'very fine', and told his parents: '[Knox] thinks I have a penetrating mind which should be useful in philosophy.'[11] Harold Wilson was certainly an impressive pupil, though he was not to show any great conceptual ability. If, early in his second year, he was coming to terms with Kant, it can only have been because of hard work in the summer vacation.

Harold Wilson preferred the academic study of politics. The emphasis was very much on institutions, and the subject allowed him to use his historical knowledge. In the Hilary term of 1935, he was attending lectures by Lord Elton, a leading supporter of Ramsay MacDonald, Prof. Zimmerman, the Montague Burton professor of international relations, and other commentators on the world of political action. International relations, not surprisingly in the 1930s, was the most popular further subject in the final honours school. In his second and third years, Wilson was taught political institutions by Dr R.B. McCallum, fellow of Pembroke College, who recalled that, in his tutorials with Harold Wilson, he emphasized the superiority of Campbell-Bannerman as a liberal leader, and the need for 'specialist committees' in the house of commons.[12] McCallum remembered his pupil as a 'very bright boy',[13] and was not surprised at his later successes.

The third – and main – subject in the new school of PPE was economics, and this was the area in which Harold Wilson specialized. Albert Goodwin did the tutoring at Jesus, and his knowledge of Gladstonian public finance was to be particularly useful to Harold Wilson. Harold Wilson also attended G.D.H. Cole's lectures on economic and social history. Cole's 'seminars for second year students', Harold Wilson would recall, 'meant work ... based on statistics and original records – no help could be found in textbooks for the kind of subjects he set'.[14] He seems not to have taken Cole's special subject, labour movements since 1815, the course which was the focus of undergraduate socialist culture in the 1930s.

For the rest of his economics, Harold Wilson had to go outside Jesus College for tutoring. He read with Lindley Fraser at Queen's, Maurice Allen, an economic theorist at Balliol, and R.F. Bretherton of Wadham College, who taught economic organization. Harold Wilson impressed his tutors, but his weakness was economic theory. In his last term, one of his tutors, possibly Fraser, wrote:

> There can be no doubt about his ability. On the economic history and institutions side ... his work is extremely good: his economic theory is not so outstanding ... He has shown many signs of being able to deal originally with material; plenty of common sense: he knows his own mind on a question; and his industry can only compel admiration. I have never felt more prepared to write for a man.[15]

The mark of Harold Wilson's academic determination was his willingness to enter for prizes. In his first year, he submitted an essay on the armaments industry for the Cecil peace prize, named after Lord Robert Cecil, the conservative champion of the league of nations. Wilson was unsuccessful, and attributed this to the rhetorical tone he had adopted. Abandoning political advocacy for scholarly research, Wilson was to be more fortunate. In his second year, he began work on a set essay entitled 'The State and the Railways in Great Britain, 1823–1863', to be submitted for the Gladstone memorial prize. Britain's railway network was a monument to capitalist overproduction, which the state had done little to control, and it was clearly a subject dear to the heart of Harold Wilson. He worked each afternoon in the Bodleian library, and, during the Christmas vacation of his second year, he did some research at Hawarden, Gladstone's country house in Cheshire, as well as in Liverpool's Picton library. He had written 18,000 words by March 1936. Wilson apparently submitted his entry believing he could not win, but this did not prevent him reading a paper on 'The Transport Revolution of the Nineteenth Century' to the college historical society, 'adding a quite unheralded glamour to the economic problems of that day'.[16] He did Jesus proud by winning the prize for 1936, to the value of £100. Albert Goodwin thought it worth publishing, having paid Blackwell's to issue his own essay. As part of the encaenia, the annual commemoration in June of the university's benefactors, Harold Wilson was one of seven prizemen to read a sample page from their compositions, in front of a gathering in the Sheldonian Theatre, which included the new foreign secretary, Sir Anthony Eden.

He plunged into working for the George Webb Medley junior scholarship that summer, sitting the examination in October with other economics undergraduates. He was again successful, and the £100 scholarship, on top of the £60 from his college, allowed him to become financially free of his father. He was also elected an honorary scholar of Jesus, and allowed to wear the longer gown, a symbol that he was one of those undergraduates who was statutorily part of the establishment of college. G.D.H. Cole was one of the examiners, and he told Maurice Allen that Wilson had won because of his answers on economic organization. He had done well in economic history, but poorly in the theory section of the paper. His photograph featured prominently in the June 1937 number of the *Jesus College Magazine*, along with that of the 1937 winner of the Gladstone prize.

All this extra academic work ate into his time for sport. In his first term, he had put his name down for running, one of five in Jesus to do so. He failed to secure a place in the freshmen's half mile. In the inter-collegiate relays, he was part of a long-distance medley team which came second. He gave up going to the Iffley Road track in his second year, while working for the Gladstone prize. In the Trinity (summer) term of 1936 he resumed training, telling his parents: 'I am not wasting time going to see people and messing about in their rooms, for this is more interesting.'[17] Harold Wilson was evidently not gregarious, though Eric Sharpe, who was probably closest to him, considered he had a friendly manner. He was picked to run in a second university team – the Centipedes – against Reading athletic club, and managed to finish seventh out of a field of sixteen in the cross-country event. He never aspired to a blue, and gave up athletics altogether in his third year.

He was somewhat more successful in Jesus College societies, though he took some time to shine as a personality. In his third term, he was noted for contributing to the discussions of the Sankey society, which celebrated George V's silver jubilee on 3 May 1935. This was the college debating forum, named after Lord Sankey, the college's most eminent old boy, who, having served on the bench, became lord chancellor in the second labour government, and followed Ramsay MacDonald out of the party two years later. Harold Wilson attended most meetings of the society from the beginning, and began to work his way up the hierarchy of offices. He was secretary in the Hilary term of 1936, when it was arranged to invite Lord Sankey to the society's first dinner, at which Sankey addressed the members on 'ordinary incidents' during his time as head of the judiciary.[18] At the dinner, Wilson, by now the society's treasurer, had a chance to talk to this former senior member of three MacDonald governments. Wilson became president in the Michaelmas term of his third year, when two debates were held with other colleges. Despite the increasing tension in Europe in late 1936, not least the outbreak of the civil war in Spain, 'it [was] regretted that the attendances ... [had] been so small.'[19]

Wilson's involvement in other societies was secondary. The invitation to read his paper on railway history to the college historical society in May 1936 led him to serve as secretary in the Hilary term of his third year. He was to return, as a graduate, in the Michaelmas term of 1937 to speak on 'The End of Laissez-faire'. Also in the spring of that year, he was secretary of the Meyriche society, a sort of philosophical gathering. He had also addressed the Henry Vaughan society in the Michaelmas term of his last year, on 'The Last Depression and the Next'; it was reported that 'his paper gained the approval of the whole Society, including even the ex-President, who, for some odd reason, resented Mr. Wilson's remarks about "mugs" on the Stock Exchange.'[20]

In the wider world of the university, he was not particularly noticeable during his three years as a PPE student. An exact contemporary was Teddy Jackson, reading modern greats at Magdalen College. He had already obtained a degree from Birmingham, and won the George Webb Medley junior scholarship in 1935, the year before Harold. Jackson, a socialist and, later, a communist, was active in the undergraduate politics and economics society. It had no funds, but was able to invite academics to address young men and women, on leading intellectual and political questions of the day. Jackson was, for a time, secretary, a position he had been invited to fill. At some point, Jackson noticed, what he described as, a little fellow hunched over, attending the meetings. No one seemed to know who he was, but he was in the habit of going up to talk to the speaker after the meeting. This seems to have been typical of Harold Wilson. Jackson cannot have thought too badly of him, since he invited Wilson to take over the active leadership of the society for a term. No doubt he got on with the job, but he showed no interest in intellectual iconoclasm.

The central institution in undergraduate life was the Oxford Union. It was not a representative body for students, but a debating society and club with library attached; a sort of junior combination of Westminster and Pall Mall. Here young gentlemen – women had only just been admitted as guests to the dining room – displayed their rhetorical skills in the company of invited public figures. Edward Heath, a scholar at Balliol, who was a few months younger than Wilson, would begin his climb to the premiership from the presidency of the Oxford Union. The real world was rarely allowed to spoil the fun, not even in the 1930s, though Heath was probably more sincere than most. Eric Sharpe joined the union when he came up to Oxford, taking out life membership. He thinks Harold also did, and others tend to agree. It would only have confirmed his prejudice against public-school boys. Sharpe was to speak only once in four years, from the floor, and against taking part in war. He remembers going with Harold to debates, and that he was interested. It is significant that Harold Wilson felt intimidated by the frivolous culture of the Oxford Union, to the point of resolving never to speak. He feared he might be the object of fun with a northern accent, and his argument would be ridiculed, coming from an obvious grammar-school man. He was to intervene once, in an end-of-term debate, which had the virtue of being unreported in *Isis*.

Nor was Wilson prominent in Oxford undergraduate politics in 1934–7, and certainly not as a socialist. Clement Attlee became leader of the labour party in 1935, early in Wilson's second year at Oxford. Whatever of his later respect for Attlee, Harold Wilson was then an undergraduate liberal.

Undergraduate liberals were worried about Europe, though the party of Gladstone and Asquith, which Lloyd George had taken over in 1926, split before, and again after, the formation of the national government in 1931. Sir Herbert Samuel led twenty – divided – liberal MPs in the 1935 parliament, this poor showing having been reflected at Oxford where the liberal club nearly collapsed in 1934. 'Apart from Jimmy Brown (Balliol) ... there was nobody of the slightest weight in the Club. There then arrived a whole new intake of greater weight, who pushed the Club along to much better times.'[21] Frank Byers, a freshman at Christ Church, was a leading enthusiast, and the Oxford liberals, under the honorary presidency of Lloyd George, were able to bring out the weekly *Oxford Guardian* during term time from October 1936. The club grew from 110 to 305 members in this academic year. Lloyd George had embraced deficit financing in 1929 with *We Can Conquer Unemployment*, and unveiled his own 'new deal' in 1935, but Oxford liberal undergraduates were more concerned with disarmament in Europe. The *Oxford Guardian* even editorialized in April 1937 in favour of conciliating Hitler, on the grounds that the Versailles treaty had been an injustice done the German people.

Oxford socialists were grouped in the university labour club, founded after the war, and with 484 men and women members in late 1932. (It was separate from labour in extramural Oxford, though its officers had to be members of the city party.) Some labour club members had blacklegged during the 1926 general strike, but most rallied to the university strike committee at the Coles' house in Holywell Street, shortly after he took up his fellowship at University College. Cole became president of the club in 1931, in succession to Ramsay MacDonald (who retained a few active undergraduate supporters), a privately circulated history of 'Red Oxford' in the early 1930s noting that 'senior members [of the university] who profess Labour opinions, if still looked upon as eccentrics, are at least no longer believed to be definitely immoral'.[22] The labour club 'always found room for a healthy element of heresy and scepticism'[23] to left and right. The communist-orientated October club, which was 300 strong in late 1932, was absorbed into the labour club in December 1935. In reaction, the democratic socialist group, whose members wore a red silk tie with silver arrows pointing to the right, was formed at a meeting in Christ Church in which Christopher Mayhew played a leading role. Oxford socialists, under communist influence if not leadership, were especially concerned about Europe, where the threat of fascism, it was believed, could only be countered by a united front.

There was a certain convergence in Oxford between the labour and liberal clubs. The communist party had been arguing for the strategy of a united front of all socialists from 1933, and the labour left promoted this as a tactic of left unity, especially after the outbreak of the Spanish civil war. The labour party believed it could defeat the national government on its own, with socialist policies, and the 1937 conference rejected the united front, many leaders being strongly anti-communist. G.D.H. Cole, who was also chairman of the university labour party in Oxford, had been risking expulsion for what he called a people's front, an electoral compact between the liberal and labour parties. He backed Salter's parliamentary candidacy from as early as October 1936, and when Cole and Richard Crossman, a fellow of New College, addressed the labour club, there was 'great applause';[24] the Oxford socialists later voted, by 69 to 21, for a popular front.

Cole outlined a five-point programme in the *Oxford Guardian* of 9 November 1936, the editor, A.W. Wood noting: 'The vital difference in politics today is not between Socialism and non-Socialism, but between the National Government and a sane government.'[25] He observed the following term that 'recently [Cole] has become so Liberal in his outlook that we believe he is in danger of being expelled by the Labour Party for being too progresssive'.[26]

When he became prime minister, Harold Wilson stated that 'most of [his] passionate feelings at [that] time were in terms of unemployment and home affairs, rather than foreign affairs'.[27] His early biographers all insisted that he had been a socialist while an undergraduate at Oxford. It took Paul Foot, who had been a leading liberal undergraduate there in the 1950s, to expose this myth in *The Politics of Harold Wilson*, in 1968. Wilson, Foot revealed, had been an active liberal. Lord Wilson still maintains that he only flirted with the liberal party while a student, because of Marxist domination of the university labour club. This is untrue. His membership of the university liberal club was continuous through his undergraduate years, though his interest in politics was overshadowed by his academic work. He was not a socialist of any sort. In so far as he had passionate feelings, they were about international relations, a religiously inspired pacifism being the main characteristic of his politics in the 1930s.

As an eighteen-year-old in 1934, Harold Wilson was opposed, like very many British people, to war. Labour and the Samuelite liberals were urging international disarmament on the national government. While Ramsay MacDonald had been a founder of the union of democratic control, twenty years before, in the 1930s he was being pulled by the Simonite liberals and conservatives in the cabinet in the direction of British rearmament, at the behest of the service chiefs, rather than the progressive forces in Europe. The disarmament conference in Geneva had collapsed in April. In the Michaelmas term at Oxford, concerned students were rallying for an international anti-war congress in December. Within days of arriving at Jesus, Harold Wilson attended a college meeting of the 'Anti-war Movement'. As he wrote to Marjorie early in October: 'I tried to counteract the Labour element with the Christian lines of argument so to speak, advocating close co-operation with the churches etc.'[28] It is his first – documented – political statement. Harold Wilson was concerned that organized religion should champion the pacifist message, and there can be no doubt of his opposition to 'labour', in the form of student socialists in Jesus College. Possibly he disliked their anti-capitalist rhetoric, but, since he was to oppose private arms manufacturers along with Sir Norman Angell, it is probable that he was still thinking of the split of 1931 on the domestic financial crisis. If Harold Wilson was not a Samuelite liberal from then, he may have become a free-trade opponent of the conservative-dominated national government in September 1932. Or he could have become a sympathiser, sometime after November 1933, when the three dozen or so liberals joined the opposition in parliament, because of increasing tension in Europe. Hitler might have come to power in early 1933, and pulled Germany out of the league of nations later that year, but, in his first term at Oxford, Harold Wilson's main preoccupation was passing his exams.

The leading socialist student at Jesus College, John Morris, was to stand, as a postgraduate, for labour in the general election in November 1935 in Honiton, Devon. He may have encouraged Wilson, as a freshman, to attend a meeting of the labour club in October 1934. There is no evidence that he did, but, in the most recent version of his apologia, Wilson states that 'one meeting ... was enough for me'. 'What I felt I could not stomach', he argues, 'was all those Marxist public school products rambling on about the exploited workers and the need for a socialist revolution ... I have never read Marx – and still have not.'[29] Wilson has often claimed that the long footnote on the second page of *Capital* prevented him reading further, but, since it does not exist, he cannot have tried too hard. There was little need for a modern greats student in Oxford to tackle Marx; reading the *Communist Manifesto* was largely a political imperative. Harold Wilson was required to read a great deal of theory, and he persisted with Kant to please Knox. He was never a revolutionary socialist, being a committed parliamentarian, and, if he later became what is now called a democratic socialist, he was no sort of socialist at Oxford. The October club had not merged with the labour club in 1934, and, when it did the following year, this takeover generated an antithetical social democratic faction.

On his own admission, Wilson joined the university liberal club in early 1935, just after he had changed to PPE. He may have become college secretary in the Hilary term, responsible for all members in Jesus. He was not joining a political crowd at Oxford, thus his motive, as he has insisted repeatedly, cannot have been to convert liberals to socialism. It has been claimed that there were only 'two active members'[30] in early 1935, but Frank Byers must have already begun to revive undergraduate liberalism 'on sherry'.[31] This culminated in a club dinner on 1 March for 150, addressed by Sir Herbert Samuel. Harold Wilson presumably attended, since he was to be elected to the committee of the liberal club in Trinity term. On 26 March, he and another undergraduate joined four Oxford liberals as members of the eighty club, an inner-party caucus of British liberalism. Founded in 1880, as a meeting point for leading liberals in the country, it had largely become, by the 1930s, an organization trying to revitalize liberalism through a new generation of university students. Five of the six admitted by the club's committee in London went on to become leading liberals in later life; Harold Wilson was to be the exception. Some on the committee complained that 'any Tom Dick or Harry [could] get into the Eighty Club nowadays',[32] but the majority view was that all these undergraduates had been impressive in their interviews, held presumably in Oxford. Harold Wilson was to remain a member of the eighty club for over three years; it would not be until February 1938, eight or so months after graduation, that he resigned.

As a member of the club, he attended annual conferences of the union of university liberal societies, open to all liberal undergraduates. During the Easter vacation, he represented Oxford, with others, at the fourteenth annual conference in 1935, held in Liverpool between 9 and 11 April. 'I cannot now recall what part he took in it', a fellow delegate comments, 'but he certainly did participate, and ... nothing he said or urged appeared in the slightest to be out of line with mainstream Liberal policies.'[33]

Two photographs of the delegates survive, showing Harold Wilson, at the age of nineteen, as an active liberal, albeit of a few months standing. Harold Wilson also attended the next conference, in January 1936, in Manchester, where he spoke in favour of an Oxford motion condemning the private manufacture of arms. Another speech of his was reported in the *Manchester Guardian* for 11 January. He argued that the league of nations should not be criticized too strongly, in spite of recent revelations that the British and French governments were colluding with Mussolini to end the war in Abyssinia, and hoped to get the league to force Haile Selassie to give up territory to appease the Italians. It was his first published political statement.

J.H. Wilson, as he was known, at a time when the use of initials was still the convention, was dubbed 'Jimmy Wilson' by his fellow liberals at Oxford. He remained college secretary until the Hilary term of 1937, just before he sat his finals. At the beginning of his second year, Harold Wilson became an officer of the club, being elected treasurer. This post was held for three whole terms, in the 1935–6 academic year, possibly because he was efficient, as he himself still claims, but probably because no one else wanted it. Harold Wilson handed over as treasurer to J.H. Curtis of Keble College. He himself became secretary of the club for the term, with Frank Byers as president, and A.L. Lamaison of Exeter College as librarian. Robert Steel remembers him rushing to the post office in Oxford before midnight, with reports of club meetings for the *Manchester Guardian*; 'he was always rather fussy about it.'[34] Harold Wilson was in a position to stand for president, though this may have gone to Raymond Walton, of Balliol, in early 1937. Mr Justice Walton, as he now is, recalls: 'The reason he gave for not seeking higher office – which he would undoubtedly have attained – was that he wished to work for a good degree ... he *did* [however] remain on the committee.'[35]

The Michaelmas term of 1936 was probably the most important for the university liberal club that decade. In the autumn of 1936 Cole, inspired by Leon Blum's *front populaire* in France and alarmed by the rising against the republican government in Spain, began to call for his people's front. E.L. Mallalieu, who had been the Samuelite MP for Colne Valley from 1931 until 1935, wrote to the *Oxford Guardian* in mid-November 1936 from his chambers in the Temple in London, supporting a popular front for Britain; by then Colne Valley was once again a labour seat. (E.L. Mallalieu would become a labour MP in 1948, and his brother the labour member for Huddersfield in 1945.) In Harold Wilson's last year as a PPE student, while he must have supported the popular front, as advocated by the self-styled 'progressive'[36] university liberal club, there is absolutely no evidence of him making any particular political contribution.

This is in accord with Raymond Walton's recollection: 'There [is] absolutely no truth in the rumour which he has since assiduously cultivated that he joined the Club to try to swing it to the left; he was then simply a good mainstream Liberal, no further to the left than Frank Byers, myself, or really any other of the Club members. As he was studying PPE, he may have been a better economist than those of us who were studying other disciplines, but none of the ideas he put forward were other than mainstream Liberal policy.'[37] Honor Balfour recalled in early 1964:

> When I was President of the Liberal Club [Harold Wilson] was college secretary for Jesus. I remember him trotting along in his Exhibitioner's gown with an armful of books and that smooth cherrystone face. He never took any initiative or decisions, but if you wanted him to whistle up some members or subscriptions it was always done perfectly. Oxford in the 1930s was alive with political protest ... but you never heard Harold's voice. He preferred to burrow behind the scenes.[38]

Wilson himself remembers that, as treasurer, '[his] financial efforts took a little time and were surprisingly successful': 'College secretaries of the club sent their collective subscriptions to me in cash, which I kept in an old suitcase under my bed in College ... As Treasurer I paid off the whole accumulated debt, between £60 and £70, yet my total receipts, ignoring expenditure, were less than £50.'[39] No doubt this pleased R.B. McCallum, who had been forced, as the club's senior treasurer, to organize a whip round in late 1934 among senior members to pay off undergraduate debts. Many years later, he '[could] not recall anything but the highest efficiency with the Club accounts during this period'.[40] McCallum, who tutored Harold Wilson in politics in 1935–7, could not remember him being politically conscious: 'I think I could have told that he was not a Tory. That is all.'[41] And Frank Byers, who was to be elected a liberal MP in 1945 and later become a peer, remembers: 'He was very efficient [as treasurer], but I cannot remember his taking any strong political line at any time ... Certainly I remember being very friendly with Harold ... and there was nothing political which separated us as far as I know.'[42] 'He was a pleasant companion', writes another office holder, 'not over-talkative, and probably more devoted to working than most of us. Certainly I have no recollection whatsoever of any drunken orgy or anything even remotely approaching that, or indeed any other outlandish behaviour. He was a somewhat – but not overtly – dour northerner.'[43]

Harold Wilson may have felt intellectually insecure among fellow liberals at Oxford. Some, no doubt, were public-school products, but it is interesting that the president in the Hilary term of 1937 should attack Oxford as 'still ... one of the spiritual homes of the English aristocracy and ... plutocracy'.[44]

In so far as he was observed by others, Wilson was considered a swot; in Oxford parlance, a 'gnome'. The college magazine, which regularly carried quotes, 'Sayings of Schoolmen', from leading undergraduates, attributed to him in his last term the phrase, 'I dreamt of Leibniz last night.'[45] It was the only one attributed to him. Raymond Walton believed he was concerned mainly with getting a first-class degree: 'He was clearly on the make but he hadn't yet decided where he wanted to go.'[46] There were nine papers in the final honours school of PPE, and he worried about the one in economic theory. The moment of truth came in May 1937. He found he could barely comprehend a question on his third paper, on economic theory. He became stuck on a geometric diagram, 'which [he] hope[d] would prove something or other',[47] but resisted walking out of the examination. The remaining papers went more smoothly. At the end of term Harold Wilson returned to Cheshire, to await his oral examination. He was so concerned that he repaired to the Liverpool public library to read up on a political history question he had answered poorly. Back in Oxford for the viva, his examiners, meeting in High Street, began by congratulating him on his papers. He became speechless with relief, and had difficulty responding when he was asked about his weak spot in political history. Later that day, he heard indirectly from Knox that he had got a first-class degree. This was duly confirmed. With two examiners per paper, he is reputed to have got seventeen alphas and one beta. On economic theory, he apparently got an alpha plus. The beta, seemingly, was in politics.

Harold Wilson did extremely well in his finals in 1937. According to one of his examiners, he got the best first in PPE in 1937, that is, he came top out of some 143 candidates. Harold Wilson cites Knox, indirectly, as having told him this at the time. But his performance, remarkable though it be, has been exaggerated. A little over a year later, his name was given to the *Sunday Times*'s literary editor, as having 'obtained one of the best "Firsts" in Economics on record'.[48] Wilson himself has claimed that his mark in economic theory was the best since the establishment of the school. He quotes Frank Pakenham, now Lord Longford, as confirming this, but the latter states that he was originally told this by Wilson. Longford believes that he himself got the best first in PPE in 1927, but admits that such claims are based upon academic hearsay. In the university world, it is very difficult to rank candidates who are awarded the same class of degree, and it is virtually impossible to compare performance over the years. Harold Wilson's undoubted achievement has been boosted to, either, the best first in PPE since 1922, or, the best degree in the whole university 'for a long time'.[49] There is no evidence for any such claims. All that can be asserted, is that Harold Wilson got the best first in 1937, in the sixteenth year of PPE. The college magazine in 1937 put the Jesus results interestingly in a political context: 'Our politicians disagree on whether the fact that the Liberal Party claims the greatest number of Jesus "Firsts" this year indicates the soundness of Liberal principles or a future departure from Liberal fallacies.'[50]

CHAPTER 5

Working for Beveridge, 1937–40

Harold Wilson had talked little of his intentions after sitting the final honours school. There was Gladys Baldwin, to whom he had promised marriage in 1934, and the expectations of his family. At some point, he began to aspire to an academic career. The goal of becoming an Oxford don constituted a serious challenge for Harold Wilson, though Robert Steel, who also got a first and became an academic, remembers that colleges were on the look out for men. Wilson may have felt Jesus College would offer him something, there being no economics fellow. 'Even Harold Wilson', the college magazine noted in June 1937, 'may leave to continue his brilliant academic career elsewhere.'[1] Behind this, possibly, was a rumour in the college that he had been applying for academic jobs, even before he completed his finals. This was hardly the correct way to go about things. There is some evidence that he sought references from tutors before graduating, copies of which he forwarded to his parents. Leslie Smith quotes two such testimonials. One seems to be from Albert Goodwin, though the latter only remembers giving him an open testimonial after graduation. It is known that Harold Wilson applied for two posts, probably in economics. One was a lectureship at St Andrew's University, where Knox had been given a chair in 1936. Wilson may have thought this would help in some way. The other was in Oxford itself, a lectureship at Christ Church. Frank Pakenham had taught politics there since 1932, but he knew nothing of this application. Goodwin recalls writing a testimonial for Christ Church. Wilson heard shortly after finishing his exams that he had been unsuccessful at both places.

Still unsure of what his degree would be, he sought out McCallum at Pembroke. Harold Wilson wanted advice, presumably about careers outside academia. The latter suggested he should write to the editor of the *Manchester Guardian*, W.P. Crozier; Harold Wilson had been sending reports on the university liberal club to the paper. He was offered a temporary post by Crozier, as a leader writer, the job to start after his viva, and he would be on probation during the summer. Harold Wilson had gained little journalistic experience while at Oxford, and the circumstances of his appointment suggest that he was being tried as a bright young liberal, who might be some intellectual use to the cause.

His urgency to find employment at this point may have had something to do with a change in the family's fortune. Herbert Wilson had lost his job at Brotherton's, at the age of fifty-four, for reasons unknown. Harold heard the news in a letter from Marjorie, shortly before he left Oxford to return to Cheshire. While Marjorie had her salary as a teacher, there was an implication that he would have to start contributing to the family income. Herbert's misfortune had not stood in the way of Harold's education in the past, and it is unlikely that he was prepared to abandon all in 1937. The firm allowed the Wilsons to remain in their flat at Woodslee in the interim, though they were to be living nearby, at 'Fieldside' in Croft Avenue, the following year.

For an aspiring academic, a period of intellectual apprenticeship was considered normal. Harold Wilson had won a junior scholarship in the Michaelmas term of 1936, and, under the terms of the George Webb Medley award, it could be augmented to a senior scholarship. This would allow him to remain at Oxford as a research student, working for a higher degree. He was aware of two other winners of the junior scholarship, one at Magdalen, Teddy Jackson, and the other at University College. He claims he thought that he was unlikely to get the senior scholarship, but it is probably more the case that he wanted a job with status and money. Perhaps even before he returned to Oxford for his viva, it was announced that he was the winner of the George Webb Medley senior scholarship. It was worth £300 a year, for two years. Harold Wilson had no burning passion to investigate a topic of personal or political interest, and £300 was what he had lived on as an undergraduate when he spent over half the year in Cheshire. He would have to be in Oxford during the vacations, and marriage to Gladys would be out of the question. Nothing further seems to have turned up during the summer of 1937, so, that autumn, Harold Wilson moved back to Oxford, to become a postgraduate student, still formally attached to Jesus College. He got digs at 32 Divinity Road, again in south Oxford, off Cowley Road, where he was to live for over two years. In the Michaelmas term, he was given a desk in the institute of statistics, a new academic animal in the Oxford zoo, founded as recently as 1935, and funded by the Rockefeller Foundation in New York, in the recently opened Bodleian extension on Parks Road. Harold Wilson had enrolled for a D.Phil. thesis on 'Aspects of the Demand for Labour: a factual study of employment and unemployment',[2] to be submitted in 1940. The thesis was never begun, and Harold Wilson quickly forgot that he had ever been a research student in the institute of statistics. The institute's chairman – significantly for the career of Harold Wilson – was Sir William Beveridge.

Wilson was allocated room number three in the institute with Goronwy Daniel, then twenty-three years old. Daniel was a new postgraduate student at Jesus, working for a doctorate on labour migration to Oxford. He recalls Harold Wilson's 'personal kindnesses' to him, such as nominating him for membership of the union. 'There was perhaps an affinity between us', writes Daniel, 'deriving from our both being ambitious young men from humble homes who had got to Oxford from state schools with the help of scholarships and from his having arrived there also as something of an outsider.' Harold Wilson was 'outstanding in his dedication to work and his confidence in his own abilities'; 'the self-confidence was apparent in conversations with him which involved mainly listening to what he had to say.' Sir Goronwy, as he is today, remembers his room mate, ultimately, as ambitious, 'the dedication required to achieve it rul[ing] out friendships of the normal kind with him'.[3]

Also that October, Sir William Beveridge, after nearly thirty years away from Oxford, became master of University College. On 11 November, less than halfway through his first term, he disclosed his intentions to the Rockefeller Foundation: 'I have come to think that what I can personally do best for the social sciences is to do some work on them myself (with a few like-minded people) in place of spending all my time organising opportunities for others.' He continued his letter: 'I am beginning to find a little leisure for serious study, and have actually got one first-class research student doing just what I am going about saying all research students should do: i.e., working under my supervision on a problem that I want solved and on which I am working myself, in place of writing a thesis to please himself.'[4] The research student was Harold Wilson, but it is not clear how he had found his way to Beveridge in 1937. As Wilson tells the story, Beveridge, on the look out for a research assistant in Oxford, wrote to John Fulton, a fellow at Balliol. They had known each other in London. Fulton consulted Maurice Allen, who suggested Harold Wilson. The master-designate of University College then wrote to the Jesus graduate, offering him a position on the basis that he could finance himself. However the contact was made, Wilson and Beveridge were to have a relationship of considerable mutual convenience. It was, of course, more convenient to Sir William, but Harold Wilson was to profit greatly from the experience. Beveridge was meant to be Harold Wilson's supervisor, responsible to the university for the progress of his work. It is clear the latter became another in the series of unpaid research assistants, for which this academic mandarin was notorious. Harold Wilson had no desire to spend three years writing a thesis, and he saw Beveridge as a patron. The relationship, unusually for Beveridge, was to be enduring. The credit for this must go largely to Harold

Wilson. He was only twenty-one, while Beveridge was fifty-eight and at the height of his career.

The new master was a man of obsessive – if not eccentric – intellectual views. At the end of the summer term of 1937, he bade farewell to the London School of Economics (LSE), where he had been director, on oration day, 24 June, with an address on 'The Place of the Social Sciences in Human Knowledge', later published in *Politica*. He advanced two themes, as he was to recall in his autobiography, 'neither of a kind to be welcomed by most of my academic audience'. The first was his view that the social sciences were inductive, 'based on observation, rather than deduction from concepts'.[5] Beveridge 'went on to attack the leading economist of [their] time for his most famous work';[6] 'The subject of Mr Keynes' theory is unemployment and its causes; his chief conclusion is that a main cause of unemployment is found in rigidity of the rate of interest demanded by capital.' Beveridge argued 'Keynes had not started from any fact but from a definition of a concept. He had announced his conclusions as certainties without verification of any kind. And Keynes's procedure had been accepted as adequate by practically all professional economists.' 'I know that in speaking thus', he observed, 'I make enemies.'[7]

Beveridge's second theme in his farewell address was 'a demand for detachment from political association of the teachers of any social science', a view he proclaimed with Harold Laski, the professor of political science and a leading labour intellectual, sitting beside him. Laski, in turn, had been critical of Lionel Robbins, the professor of economics, considering him a propagandist for laissez-faire. Beveridge, for his part, had insisted upon his right to stand for parliament, when he came to the LSE, and was associated with the liberal summer school for a time, but after eighteen years running the LSE, he was a reformed character. He had to concede that it was the Webbs's socialism which inspired their scholarship and the school, 'but if the Webbs could have had their interest in society without their socialism, can anyone doubt that their purely scientific achievement would be even greater than it is and that the position of the Social Sciences would be more secure?'[8] The departing director believed that the social sciences were in their infancy, that observation and detachment were 'the two keys that [could] unlock the gateway to [the] promised land',[9] and that, as in the natural sciences, the division of labour between the disciplines would remain for some time. 'There were unpleasant incidents during [Beveridge's] farewell address', Beatrice Webb later noted, '[and] a marked coldness in the audience'.[10]

None of these strong views on intellectual responsibility meant that Beveridge was antipathetic to state power. He was, above all, an administrator, who believed in the right and duty of a trained elite to manage public affairs. He had been summoned to Whitehall by the liberals before the war, and stayed to fight for his country in the ministries of munitions and food. In the 1920s and 1930s, he continued to work for the government. When the war against Hitler eventually came, Beveridge was to act as a rogue planner in the civil service. By this time, he was beginning to see himself as the saviour of the country, having become an expert in social reform. In the autumn of 1944, he would be elected liberal MP for Berwick on Tweed. He would remain a philosophical positivist, attached to an exaggerated form of English empiricism in which the facts alone counted. This was his attitude to contemporary intellectual and practical problems. In order to escape what he considered political bias, economic history had long been his forte.

Beveridge was to publish *Prices and Wages in England from the Twelfth to the Nineteenth Century* in 1939. This was a near eight-hundred page volume of price tables from the mercantile era, part of an international project on price history, which had originated at the LSE in the early 1920s. Beveridge had been working on this since 1933 and in his preface, dated December 1938, he saw virtue in publishing 'a volume of details and materials, rather than one of broad results and interesting conclusions': 'I can have no bias towards interpreting the prices and wages to fit any preconceived view of the surroundings, to support or to refute any theory of economic development for I have no theories; I have not learned from other explorers what I ought to discover ... .The figures must tell their story, for I have no story to tell.'[11]

The same attitude dominated his approach to unemployment. Beveridge had been among the first seriously to study the phenomenon, when it became a political issue in Britain in the Edwardian era. In his book of 1909, *Unemployment: A Problem of Industry*, he concentrated on the frictional unemployment brought about by the failure to fit workers and jobs together, in accord with economic assumptions about capitalist equilibrium. The work was republished in 1930. Towards the end of his time at the LSE, Britain was recovering from the slump, though 1937 was to be an uncharacteristically good year. Writing to Keynes the previous summer, Beveridge outlined his alternative approach to that of the *General Theory (1936)*: 'I am now hoping to be able to do a little work at any rate on the statistics of unemployment with a view to seeing how far the volume of unemployment can be explained as frictional or connected with personal disabilities of any kind. I am hoping to set on foot some kind of direct study of the actual demand for labour as recorded at the Labour Exchanges and elsewhere.'[12] His *Analysis of Unemployment* of 1937 was to be a breakdown of the monthly unemployment statistics. Beveridge addressed the British Association in September 1936, at Blackpool, the first meeting since the publication of Keynes's book. He acknowledged the existence of post-war structural unemployment, due to declining international competitiveness. But he also attributed it to personal infirmities, and acknowledged that it was long term. Beveridge then went on to state that 'frictional, seasonal and cyclical unemployment form the natural field for unemployment insurance – a spreading of wages over good times and bad.'[13] Here was proof of Beveridge's administrative view of the world. His facts were those amenable to state manipulation, within a given economic and political context. Beveridge concluded his analysis of current figures by pointing, first, to the likelihood of increasing frictional unemployment, that is the delay in workers moving between jobs, and, secondly, the continuation of cyclical depressions on a pre-war basis.

Sir William was a difficult man to be near. He insisted immediately that the master's lodgings, in, appropriately, Logic Lane, should be modernized to his strict requirements. All open fires were abolished, and a deck tennis court was installed to 'provide against growing fat'. Unlike Harold Wilson, he was what was then considered to be a physical fitness fanatic. Beveridge secured the services of his relative, Elspeth Mair, as 'lady of the house,'[14] until she married. Her mother Janet (Jessie) Mair visited constantly, and, when war was imminent, she moved into the master's lodgings, 'thereby reputedly outraging the "lady censors of the University world"'.[15] She had transferred her affections from her husband, Beveridge's cousin, many years before. The new master also rationalized the college, changing the kitchens over from coal to electricity. The traditional collegiate system at Oxford, which, even in the case of University, a wealthy college, allowed little room for the sort of empire-building he had attempted at the LSE, rendered him more of a figurehead. 'With his senior colleagues[,] Beveridge[,] though he could be charming[,] was prickly and authoritarian.'[16] As for students, he took a great deal of interest in some. He welcomed the time Oxford provided for research.

Harold Wilson worked alongside others, in the shadow of Sir William. Green Street, a house on the downs in Wiltshire, above Avebury, now owned by Mrs Mair, was an extension of his Oxford life. The day began at 6.00 a.m., with Beveridge swimming in the unheated outdoor pool. He worked for two hours before breakfast. This continued until 12.30 p.m., when there was a game of deck tennis, and another swim. After lunch, less demanding physical work proceeded in the garden or house, until tea time. Beveridge then resumed academic work until dinner. After the fourth meal of the day, guests were encouraged to join Mrs Mair for bridge.

When Harold Wilson became associated with him in the Michaelmas term of 1937, it was to continue working on unemployment figures. There was a 'group on unfulfilled demand for labour'[17] in the institute of statistics, which seems to have been Wilson and nobody else. Beveridge envisaged looking at Oxford initially, in order to find out why frictional unemployment continued in prosperous parts of the country. He was, despite all his protestations about scientific research, essentially a classical economist. He believed in the idea of equilibrium in the economy, in a natural harmony between capital's demand for labour and its supply by workers; this was ordinarily achieved by the rise and fall of wages. Beveridge seems to have felt that unemployment insurance, on which he advised the government, slowed down the operation of the labour market, a process labour exchanges had been instituted to speed up. He also had his share of class prejudices, such as there was no justification for being unemployed when there was plenty of work available. This proposition could be empirically tested, but it required a different political economy to accept that unemployment was natural under capitalism.

On 1 November 1937 Harold Wilson went to the local labour exchange, to analyse why workers had not taken jobs to which they had been sent. Beveridge, as the architect of the labour exchange system, could only see it as a public institution which, in an efficient manner, mediated the supply and demand of labour in a free market. Harold Wilson simply looked at each cancelled vacancy, finding invariably that the job had already gone, either because the employer had exaggerated his requirement, or had found workers by other means. The Oxford manager reported the conclusions to London, and suggested to Wilson he should conduct the same exercise in Reading, Banbury, Swindon, Luton, Slough, Northampton and Coventry. These were all areas of low unemployment, with, presumably, jobs going wanting, some of them near to Oxford. Beveridge was perturbed as to why workers were not moving from areas of high unemployment. He and Wilson arranged to report on their findings, on 12 February 1938, to the institute's research seminar in economic statistics. Wilson then proceeded to repeat the Oxford exercise, substituting Bedford for Slough. He was assisted by a ministry of labour statistician, A. Reeder. The month of November 1937 was selected for the test. Analysing all the unfilled vacancies, Wilson concluded that, on the basis of his sample, the unsatisfied demand for labour in the United Kingdom was, at most, 2,210 jobs, when there were one and a half million workers unemployed in the month of November. The implication was that the free market was not perfect. At a time of relative prosperity, there were still unemployed workers; an equilibrium could be found, but at a level significantly lower than the working population. Beveridge was faced with accepting the idea of unemployment as a result of a deficiency of demand for labour. He had difficulty believing that employers would not emerge to create new jobs, given that wage levels were not prohibitive. Many years later, in an address as president to the royal statistical society, Wilson was to recall his legwork round the exchanges in terms of the reliability of vacancy figures: 'My conclusions ... were that as a total the figures were meaningless, as were variations, behaving in an exaggerated way when the labour situation was locally tight: nevertheless trends in them were – and are – significant over a few months.'[18]

More recently, Wilson claims he demonstrated the existence of an under-demand for labour even in the prosperous areas, and that Beveridge had to abandon his ideas about unemployment. It is more likely that Wilson simply demonstrated the unreliability of labour exchange vacancy figures, and did not force Beveridge to rethink his conception of unemployment as being largely frictional. It was hardly a revelation that exchanges had failed fully to occupy the market for labour, and the admission that the labour market was less than efficient did not imply a devastating critique of classical economics. The pair moved on to other work that summer, and Beveridge, uncharacteristically, made no attempt to publish Wilson's work.

Other evidence suggests that the master remained unreconstructed. He visited Beatrice and Sidney Webb in August, at their home, Passfield Corner. There was no reference to new discoveries, only to his chairmanship of the unemployment insurance statutory committee. 'We had two three-mile walks together', Beatrice noted in her diary, 'discussing mainly unemployment and its remedies': 'His conclusion is that the major, if not the only remedy for chronic unemployment is lower wages, according to the old argument that if this does not happen the capitalist will take his money and his brains to other countries where labour is cheap ... He, however, expressed the desire to see family allowances introduced which would allow wages to be lowered without endangering the birth-rate or the health of the rising generation.'[19] Beveridge was still concerned about the level of wages, looking to ways to make it attractive for employers to take on workers. There was an element of catastrophism in his view: '[Beveridge] admitted almost defiantly that he was not personally concerned with the condition of the common people ... . If men were fools in not accepting sound economics – and the common people represented by the Labour party might be fools – there would be universal poverty and war.'[20]

It was to be another six years before he would pontificate differently on the question of unemployment, throwing sound economics out the window. In his historic 1942 report on social insurance, he affirmed the goal of full employment after the war, allowing for a margin of 3 per cent unemployed. He thereupon set up a personal inquiry, and turned to the question of unemployment with the zeal of a social reformer. *Full Employment in a Free Society* was published in November 1944. There he generously acknowledged Wilson's assistance on the question of a deficiency in demand, explaining the work on the November 1937 unemployment figures in the south of England. Beveridge went on to argue in his report that, before the first world war, there had been 'cyclical fluctuation' and 'disorganization of the labour market'. Between the wars, unemployment was largely due to a 'general and persistent weakness of demand for labour'.[21] This was an historical, but not a theoretical, revision. Whatever honour he bestowed on 'J.H. Wilson', by acknowledging his work, there is no evidence that the young research assistant seriously challenged his master's view of unemployment in 1938. Harold Wilson admits that 'it was not until more persuasive economists than [he] were able to get at [Beveridge] some years after 1937 that he accepted that there was still under-demand for labour, even in times of cyclical boom, and under-demand going far beyond the figures of the frictional theories.'[22]

Wilson was determined to pursue an academic career, and in the summer of 1938 he and Gladys became engaged. He was clearly getting on with Beveridge. It was also about this time that he bought his first motor car, a 1931 Austin 7, for which he paid an Oxford dealer £11. He took Robert Steel to Avebury a number of times in 1939, and even let his geographer friend take his driving test in the car. That summer, Wilson was to sell the Austin, in part exchange for a seven-year-old Wolsey Hornet, which cost £25.

Beveridge's work on a contemporary social problem was rapidly superseded by a return to economic history, where he felt more comfortable. He was interested in the trade cycle, the Victorian observation that, with industrialization, the economy went through an upturn and downturn roughly every decade. Harold Wilson showed no signs of being disinclined to follow Beveridge into the past.

He had, on his own initiative, found some teaching work for the first two terms of 1938. At some point after receiving his degree, he was approached by Henry Phelps Brown, the economics tutor at New College, a 'stronghold of Liberalism'.[23] Wilson met H.A.L. Fisher, the warden, at an early point, and told him he was working under Beveridge's supervision. Fisher wrote to Beveridge on 24 November, asking what was 'the likelihood of [Wilson] being able to turn into a good coach'. The master of University replied to the warden of New the following day: 'I can say that he has a good head, is extremely methodical, and is prepared to work really hard.' He thought he would be good at coaching, but left Fisher to interview him along with others; Beveridge hoped he would not lose Wilson:

> One of the difficulties of economics in the past has been that anybody who did really well in the Schools (as Wilson did) has been liable at once to start teaching, and pass on just what he has been taught of necessarily theoretical work in his undergraduate course. Wilson now with me is applying his economic training to the study of concrete problems, and I am anxious that he should be able to make a success of them, as I believe he will so that he might be a still better teacher and economist two years hence.[24]

On 1 December, the college's tuition committee agreed that the warden should appoint Wilson to a lecturership in economics from January 1938. He would receive £125 per annum, teaching six hours a week for two terms; the post was 'to be remunerable for two subsequent terms'.[25]

Harold Wilson became an Oxford don in 1938, when he was nearly twenty-two. His lecturership was only temporary, part-time teaching, and very far from a fellowship. He was barely on the bottom rung of the academic ladder. In the Michaelmas term of 1938, Teddy Jackson would take over from Wilson, the latter being acknowledged in the college record for having 'help[ed] last year in the teaching of Economics'.[26]

Harold Wilson was assigned to teach a third-year class on 'economic organisation', and he also had to tutor PPE students in pairs. David Worswick, who had just graduated in mathematics, but stayed on at New College to do a diploma in economics and political science, remembers being tutored in economic history in the Hilary term. Harold Wilson recalls the superior attitude of the public-school undergraduates he taught, 'a characteristic about which I had been warned many years earlier by my father'.[27] It seems that Harold's lack of social confidence was not overcome by his new academic status. He was only a few months older than Worswick, and having to cross the divide between student and teacher.

His time in Fisher's fiefdom was short-lived, coming to an end in June 1938. Beveridge, presumably in order to keep a hold of his research assistant, had, as master of University College, secured a junior research fellowship for Wilson there, which began in the Michaelmas term of 1938. He was formally elected to this post, though G.D.H. Cole was probably the only fellow who knew Wilson. He had 'thought very well of a paper which Wilson read in a seminar conducted by him'.[28] Wilson was not invited to live in college, though he was given a study, next to John Maud's rooms. Wilson had to forego the second year of his senior scholarship, at £300, but he got £400, plus dining rights, from University College. He was given 'some teaching duties'.[29] These cannot have been taken too seriously. Cole, though university reader in economics, taught widely, as a fellow at University College, across the spectrum of subjects covered by the faculty of social studies. He was thus quite keen to drop economic theory, and Harold Wilson, despite his apparent aversion, took on this responsibility. This responsibility explains why, when Beveridge's secretary wrote to the *Sunday Times*'s literary editor in October 1938, mentioning Wilson as a possible reviewer, she described him as 'chiefly interested in Unemployment, and Economic Theory'.[30] The master is unlikely to have allowed Wilson to slip his leash, and he showed no sign of independent intellectual development at University College. Beveridge invariably subordinated his teaching duties, in the form of university lectures, to his current research interests. He lectured alone in 1938 on 'The New Face of Unemployment', at University College. In 1939, probably the Hilary term, Wilson assisted with a series of lectures on the trade cycle. In his second year as a junior research fellow, 1939–40, Beveridge and Wilson were scheduled to lecture on 'The Trade Cycle in Fact and

Theory', on Fridays at eleven in the Hilary term. Wilson was also listed in this term as conducting a seminar on current (economic) problems, with Beveridge and Cole, on Friday at 5.00 to 6.30 p.m.[31]

G.D.H. Cole was not a major influence on Harold Wilson, in spite of the fact that, after Cole had returned to Oxford in 1925, he, and his wife, Margaret, nurtured many who were subsequently active in the labour party. Margaret Cole recalled in her autobiography that, in the 1920s, a 'study group of the keenest ... socialist undergraduates' met at their house on Monday evenings over coffee to read and discuss papers: 'This fact has contributed largely to the comparatively greater influence of Oxford men among the younger intellectuals of the Labour Party.'[32] Writing in the late 1940s, Margaret Cole recalled the names of Colin Clark, E.A. Radice, James Meade, J. Betjeman, John Parker, Eugene Forcey, W.H. Auden, Evan Durbin, Hugh Gaitskell, Lord Listowel, Michael Stewart and John Dugdale: 'Most of these followed up their efforts in discussion by more practical training, in the 1926 General Strike, in adult education, lecturing, and in the work of the New Fabian Research Bureau and the Fabian Society; and there is no doubt that the Oxford group contributed a great deal to the organisation and policy of the Labour movement of the 'forties. It was certainly worth the time spent on it.'[33]

The Coles moved their residence back to London in 1929–30, Douglas Cole spending part of the week, during term, in Oxford, at his rooms in University College. In addition to his lectures and tutorials, he held a meeting of undergraduates, mainly PPE and history, drawn from across the university, where papers were read, under Cole's chairmanship. David Worswick recalls: 'it was thought of by many of its members as far the most exciting and educative experience of their Oxford life.'[34] Also in the early 1930s, he had helped found a 'Pink Dons' Lunch Club',[35] which met on Thursdays. Cole was also chairman of this gathering of socialists and fellow thinkers, though it was not necessary to be a member of the labour party. Douglas and Margaret Cole had also been instrumental in founding the New Fabian Research Bureau (NFRB) in 1931, and, when it fused with the much older Fabian Society in 1939, he became chairman of the new organization under the old name. Any socialist at Oxford in the 1930s would have had contact with G.D.H. Cole, and those with intellectual gifts would have been intimately involved in his circle. As a liberal, Harold Wilson did not attend Cole's undergraduate group between 1934 and 1937. He was to claim he did, when he wrote Cole's obituary in 1959 for *The Times*; this was unsolicited, and its publication disappointed at least one admirer of Cole's. Nor did Wilson attend the pink lunches on Thursdays after he became a don in 1938, as he would have been identified as 'belong[ing] to the school of Beveridge'.[36] Among those who did participate in the lunches was Frank Pakenham. He had become a socialist in June 1936, a labour councillor for

Cowley and Iffley in late 1937, sometime secretary of the city labour
party, and, by early 1939, the candidate for the Oxford parliamentary
seat. He recalls that, 'when war broke out I didn't know of [Harold
Wilson's] existence and I was very active in the labour party.'[37]

Wilson certainly came into contact with Cole at University College, from
the Michaelmas term of 1938, but it was well into 1939, and even the
1939–40 academic year, before there was an intellectual association. Wilson
may have helped him with some articles for the *New Statesman and Nation*,
perhaps after the outbreak of war. Cole, in turn, seems to have suggested,
sometime in 1939, that he should contribute an article on railways to a Fabian
Society book on public regulation. This would have been about the time
Harold Wilson was thinking of publishing his Gladstone prize essay.
Sometime that year (between March and May), he made a journey to
London to attend a meeting at the Fabian Society office, chaired by
Michael Stewart. The latter, one of the Oxford socialists of the 1920s, and
now a labour candidate and school teacher, was involved in workers'
education. While Wilson wrote the article, the book never appeared,
seemingly because of the outbreak of war. Wilson's chapter on 'Government
Control of Railways', in which he hinted at a transport corporation, only
to state it was beyond his scope, was acknowledged in June. It remains in
the society's archives, having been criticized by a reader as too historical.
None of this suggests anything more than a junior research fellow working
for a leading Oxford academic in the same college. But Margaret Cole,
writing in 1949 about Oxford socialist undergraduates, added a footnote
to her autobiography: 'The outstanding example is Harold Wilson.' She
was discussing the 'rather smaller crop in the years just before the last war[,]
many of them in Parliament now',[38] and comparing that cohort with
those of the late 1920s. It is clear from the context of her account of the
1920s' socialists that she simply inferred that Harold Wilson, then a member
of the Attlee cabinet, must have been a socialist at Oxford, like Gaitskell
and others of his generation. In 1967, she told Paul Foot that her husband,
who had then been dead eight years, '[had] had a high opinion of [Wilson]
as a worker and an economist'.[39] This rings more true, as the view of a fellow
at University College, who taught Wilson, and then saw him as a junior
don. There is no evidence that Cole believed Wilson to be a budding
socialist intellectual, much less a promising labour politician.

There remains the problem of his politics. After Harold Wilson graduated,
Derek Tasker, who had edited the *Oxford Guardian*, wrote to Frank Byers
suggesting a book on liberalism, with chapters by university liberals. Tasker
suggested that Wilson should be asked to write on unemployment in the
depressed areas, though nothing seems to have come of the idea. Just after
this Wilson resigned from the eighty club, probably because he wished to
put his undergraduate politics behind him. Sometime in the 1938–9

academic year, Robert Shackleton, a liberal undergraduate in his third year, attended a study group on federal union organized by Beveridge at University College. Shackleton remembers that the group met in Wilson's study, and that he was secretary. 'I certainly regarded him as a socialist then (probably a right-wing socialist), and knew nothing of his Liberal past.'[40]

These were stirring times, particularly in Europe, but Harold Wilson, despite, or perhaps because of, his erstwhile pacifism, showed no signs of being moved in any political way. The death of the sitting tory MP for Oxford City occasioned a by-election on 27 October 1938. This was after Germany had annexed the Sudetenland, and Neville Chamberlain, the new prime minister, returned from talks in Munich with Hitler to proclaim peace in our time. Patrick Gordon Walker, a don at Christ Church, was forced to stand down as labour candidate on 13 October, due to the strength of the left in the city party. Crossman and Pakenham helped, much to the annoyance of Transport House. The master of Balliol, and university vice-chancellor, Sandy Lindsay, a socialist, stood on an independent, or popular front, programme. Lindsay had labour and liberal support, and his candidacy was welcomed generally throughout the university. Edward Heath, who was to be president of the union in 1939, supported his master, though a member of the conservative party. Lindsay picked up some conservative votes, but Quintin Hogg of All Souls, son of Viscount Hailsham, a senior member of the cabinet, took the seat. It was one of the most famous by-elections of the decade, a fight, according to Christopher Hill, of 'good against evil, democracy against fascism, Balliol against All Souls'.[41] There is no evidence that Harold Wilson became caught up in this struggle, or joined the labour party in Oxford in 1938. No one remembers him rallying to Lindsay over Czechoslovakia, and, while he would not have supported Hogg, there is no evidence of Harold Wilson seeing the need to resist Hitler.

Beveridge had moved on to the trade cycle, 'the mysterious alteration between boom and depression which dominated economic life'.[42] He and Wilson turned to British unemployment statistics, from 1927 to 1938, in particular the depression of 1931–2 and the downturn of 1938, and it was not long before Beveridge made a new discovery. He came up with two findings, or facts as he quaintly put it: first, that the export industries led Britain in and out of cyclical depressions; secondly, that these occurred at the times of northern and southern harvests, and must therefore be related to world agricultural prices. This work was described at the 1938 British Association meeting in Cambridge in late August. The paper was subsequently submitted to the *Economic Journal*, and, after a row with Keynes, the editor, who wanted to put it in the economic history supplement, it was published, with the title 'Unemployment in the Trade Cycle' in March 1939. Beveridge concluded that the two 'facts' might be related: 'On the hypothesis here suggested the secret of the trade cycle is to be found, not in bankers' parlours or business bond-rooms, but on the prairies and the rice-fields; the preventive of recurrent devastations of prosperity is to be sought, not in the management of money or the control of investment or the regulation of wages, but in the international planning of agricultural output.'[43] In positing a statistical relationship between industry and agriculture, internally or externally, Beveridge was drawing, probably unconsciously, on the Victorian economist, J. S. Jevons, who had attributed the trade cycle to sun spots, which cause weather cycles, and thus harvest cycles. Beveridge may, or may not, have been interested in sun spots, but he was to have a continuing fascination in the pattern of weather across the world.

Perhaps to help Beveridge prepare his paper for Cambridge, Harold Wilson spent ten days at Green Street in August 1938. On 18 August, he wrote from Bromborough, saying he had 'enjoyed every minute of it, both work and play', and was sending some photographs he had taken to Mrs Mair. He was also clearly working on statistics, probably trade–union unemployment figures, for 1872 to 1913. On 8 September 1938, he was 'very interested in the press reception of [Beveridge's] paper [reported in *The Times* on 23 August]. Did you see the Low cartoon of yourself and the trade cycle [in the *Evening Standard*] this week?' he asked. Beveridge replied two days later, explaining that he had now set aside trade cycle work, in order to do the proofs of his price history, and also because of his work on weather. Wilson thanked him for this information, on 14 September 1938, supplying further statistics. More figures followed on 20 September, confirming the northern and southern hemispheres hypothesis. 'Your forecast of the nature of the elephant upholding the world thus appears to be vindicated', Wilson wrote. 'The next step will be the tortoise on whom the elephant stands – in other words the cause of the fall in "agricultural purchasing power".'[44]

After a brief spell of illness at the end of 1938, Beveridge was back in harness by February 1939, arranging to send Wilson to the board of trade to obtain data from the census of production. In the Hilary term, Beveridge, with Wilson, gave the course of lectures on the trade cycle, subsequently described as an 'outline of facts of trade cycle (old and new) and comments on theories in relation to these facts'.[45]

About this time, Beveridge declined to do another edition of his 1909 book on unemployment. He envisaged instead two new volumes, one on unemployment statistics, with D.G. Champernowne of Cambridge, and a second on the trade cycle, with Wilson: 'I think that in fact everything new and important that I have to say about unemployment will be contained [therein].'[46] He proposed to spend the second half of July and the whole of August at Green Street with Wilson, working on the trade cycle book: 'We contemplate that this should be a simple book of the sort that could and should be read by all undergraduates taking an economics course, and might even be intelligible to senior school-boys though it will at the same time contain the results of new research.'[47]

In June 1939, Beveridge, who had his fingers in many different academic pies, drew up a 'Programme of Research' for the 'projected or near future'.[48] For publication, he mentioned the books with Champernowne and Wilson, work with A.M. Mackintosh on cyclical fluctuation between 1770 and 1850, plus the next two volumes of the price history. As for future research, he envisaged continued work with Wilson on the trade cycle, hopefully as part of the Oxford economists' research group. Wilson would also be involved in work on the labour market, to do with labour exchanges. He mentioned, in addition, questions of unemployment insurance, and weather periodicity.

That summer, he and Wilson repaired to Green Street, to work on their joint book. An outline for *The Trade Cycle: A New Approach* suggests an elaboration of Beveridge's March 1939 article, and it seems that 'a good many' of the chapters were written. The first, entitled 'The Problem Posed', comprised nothing more than a quotation from Conan Doyle, in which the ever-quizzical Dr Watson asks the meaning of a 'mystery', and Sherlock Holmes replies: 'It is a capital mistake to theorise before one has data.' The two authors then plunged into 'a sea of data' on the general employment rate in Britain.[49] As they worked through August, they were rapidly overtaken by events. The book was not finished that summer, and Mrs Mair later claimed only 'half of [it] was ... written'.[50] The war then intervened. 'It stopped not us alone', Beveridge was to write in his auto-biography, 'but appears for the present to have brought the Trade Cycle to an end.'[51] He saw it as a priority in February 1940 to complete the volume, now called *Trade Cycle in Fact and in Theory*. He had already discovered similarities and differences between countries, and there would be a chapter on international comparisons. Beveridge was now looking for a researcher to embark upon such a comparative study. In *Oxford Economic Papers*, No. 3, he examined over thirty series of statistics on production or trade for the period 1785 to 1850, and showed that there had been a rhythmical fluctuation in British industrial activity over those years. Harold Wilson did a great deal of this work, and Beveridge used his statistical series for railways, 'in spite of its somewhat unusual character',[52] now that Wilson's Gladstone essay was not being published. Beveridge's research assistant was even to venture back beyond 1785. Writing to the master, literally on the eve of his wedding, on 31 December 1939, Wilson stated he had worked on the eighteenth-century index and corollations all through the vacation, except on Christmas Day. He was now handing the material over to Beveridge, though would add a few words 'merely as a postscript to yours'.[53] Wilson had concluded that the trade cycle did not exist before the early nineteenth century. This he argued in an article, 'Industrial Activity in the Eighteenth Century', in *Economica* in May 1940. It was his first, and last, academic publication.

Beveridge and Wilson had been preparing at Green Street for the British Association meeting in Dundee, due to begin on the evening of Wednesday, 30 August 1939. Beveridge reached Dundee, but news of developments in Europe led him to decide to return south, on 30 August, via Newcastle, and he was back in Oxford on the Thursday, keen to receive a summons to Whitehall in the eventuality of war. The British Association suddenly became largely irrelevant. On the afternoon of Friday, 1 September, when news of Germany's invasion of Poland reached those attending, it was decided to abandon the meeting. A discussion in section F on the economics of socialism was brought to an abrupt halt. Harold Wilson had been left in Dundee to present Beveridge's latest paper on 'Exports and imports in the trade cycle', his abstract being published in the April 1940 report, though the paper seems not to have been delivered. It was Wilson's first, and last, academic conference, though Dundee was the occasion when several economists, who would later be important in Whitehall, first met him. He left that afternoon, offered Robert Steel a lift, and the two shared a bed that night at a stopover in the Scottish lowlands. Saturday night was spent near Fleetwood, Wilson missing the college meeting on 2 September. Wilson was to recall being in a small Lancashire village, and hearing an agricultural labourer say, 'Well that job is on.'[54] Robert Steel heard the announcement at his bed and breakfast, and thinks Harold might have been in chapel with the Baldwin family. They returned to Oxford on the Monday. Robert Steel was appalled at the idea of war, but does not remember Harold's reaction: 'I probably listened to a long exposition by him on what he thought would happen.'[55]

Harold Wilson was free to volunteer for military service. This was certainly the case in the first few months of war, and he could probably have joined the army, navy or air force at any point until 1945. Without evidence to the contrary, it must be concluded that he chose not to enlist. He sought to stay at Oxford as a don, and then enter Whitehall as a wartime civil servant. This was to be the basis of his later political career, although, when he was trying to get into parliament in 1945, he let it be suggested that he had volunteered for the forces, only to be directed into the civil service. He was twenty-three in September 1939, and unmarried.

Harold Wilson may have gone to the joint recruiting board, and possibly told to stay at University College. As an academic he would not have been exempt from conscription on age grounds until March 1941, by which time the limit had been raised to thirty years. He was due to register with the 1916 cohort on 17 February 1940 under the national service act, but had ensured he was placed in category D sometime in the summer or autumn of 1939.

It was assumed at Oxford that dons would go into the civil service, though Lindsay urged in September that 'our University and College teachers should not besiege the doors of Ministries'. Some senior academics had already taken up government work, but 'for the rest there [was] still plenty to do in Oxford'.[56] The ministry of labour also had responsibility for the wartime civil service, and, in the wake of Munich, very many non-scientific academics across the country had written offering their services in the eventuality of war. A central register was set up in January 1939, of qualified professional and technical people willing to be considered for government jobs, though it was June before a second set of cards was sent out to all academics. Whitehall departments had to draw temporary staff from the register in the first instance. University teachers were asked that summer to make a commitment to accept suitable government service if so offered, though it was appreciated that skeleton staffs had to be maintained in institutions. 'For straight-forward administrative jobs at the higher level, the Civil Service favoured the recruitment of university dons, whom they regarded as more or less their professional equals.'[57] Given the educational background of Whitehall mandarins, it is likely that Oxbridge men and women were particularly favoured. Circumstantial evidence suggests that, at this point, Harold Wilson gave his name to the central register, thereby volunteering to become a civil servant if needed. There was no compulsion involved.

When he left Dundee on 1 September 1939 with Robert Steel, Harold Wilson was no doubt thinking about his future. They may have discussed marriage on the drive down, and Wilson's travelling companion and his fiancée were to take out the banns a week later. Gladys Baldwin had just given up her job at Port Sunlight, seemingly to learn housewifery skills from her mother. The imminence of war led them to bring forward their marriage plans. When Harold called at Preesall, it was to suggest that Gladys should return with him to Oxford. This was, apparently, against her parents' wishes, though she seems to have followed him. Gladys found digs over a cafe in Oxford, and got a secretarial job with the potato marketing board (probably with Harold's help). Harold Wilson, though still a junior research fellow, also took a job with this embryonic organization in September. Pending a formal appointment, he was registered as a temporary clerk, at a little over £3 per week, less than half his academic salary, presumably in order to qualify as a civil servant. On 2 October, Beveridge noted in a diary he kept briefly at the time: 'Harold Wilson has some experience in Potatoes: will be free to teach economics.'[58]

Beveridge returned to the gentle pace of Oxford academic life. Some evacuation from London had taken place, but University College was less disturbed than other colleges. He set about trying to get war work for himself and others. He succeeded in many cases, but was unable to get himself a commanding position in Whitehall. Beveridge attended a meeting of the Oxford economists' research group, on 22 September, in the Christ Church rooms of Roy Harrod, to find 'they [were] all set to do war work'.[59] It seems that Harold Wilson spent the Michaelmas term of 1939 continuing his research, helping Beveridge and Cole with lectures and seminars in the following term. He and Gladys finally decided, in late 1939, to marry. It was a quiet affair at Mansfield College on new year's day, with about fifty guests at the reception, mainly family but also some Oxford colleagues. The married couple left for a few days in a hotel in Oxfordshire. Harold and Gladys Wilson moved into a flat on the main site of University College in time for the Hilary term of 1940. This period at Oxford – a town of young people and old buildings – Gladys was to recall as the happiest in her married life. It was to be short-lived.

CHAPTER 6

Wartime Civil Servant, 1940–1

When Sir William Beveridge left Dundee on 30 August 1939, he was hoping to be summoned back to Whitehall. He had the interests of former students, colleagues and relatives to look after and he was also keen to get his research assistant into the wartime civil service. He wrote on 18 October to J.S. Nicholson, at the ministry of labour, 'about J.H. Wilson and [the] Potato Board'.[1] Since Nicholson was involved in the national service side of the ministry, this may have been an attempt to keep Wilson out of the forces. Beveridge also saw Nicholson, at some point, and was to write of this period in his autobiography: 'I was successful in introducing younger colleagues and friends to departments'.[2] This took some time, and Harold Wilson did some research on the unemployment figures for the first few weeks of the war, leaving a note on 'War and Unemployment' for Beveridge on 31 December. According to Wilson, it was not the case that the war was having little effect on unemployment: three quarters of a million workers had been released, in twenty-nine industries, but, in seventy-three others, a slightly higher number had come from labour exchanges; unemployment had fallen by about 90,000, but there was considerable dislocation due to mobilization. 'If the unemployment position gives little ground for acute mental discomfort', Harold Wilson concluded, 'it gives none for complacency.'[3] (This is the first recorded statement of Harold Wilson trying to have it both ways, a profoundly psychic response which would later characterize his handling of labour politics.)

Wilson sent a copy to the *Economist*, with a view to publication. Shortly after the article was published, anonymously, on 3 February 1940, Wilson was interviewed for a position as statistical officer in the ministry of supply. His name probably came from the central register, since the ministry of labour was now allowing category D men into the civil service. On 12 February, Harold Wilson wrote accepting the post, at £400 per annum. He asked to be allowed to finish his teaching duties at University College, by returning on Fridays and Saturdays for the last two weeks of the Hilary term.

On Monday, 19 February, Harold Wilson reported to room 319 at The Adelphi, as a temporary civil servant in the central statistics department. Geoffrey Cass also reported that Monday, and the two were given a room together. 'I remember him as a bright and friendly person',[4] writes Cass. Hugh Weeks, the director of the department, wanted to recruit Teddy Jackson, who was also on the central register, but he was not to join the civil service until 1941. Douglas Jay, city editor of the *Daily Herald*, also joined the ministry of supply in 1941, as an assistant secretary.

When Harold Wilson joined central statistics, 'things were fairly chaotic'.[5] The ministry's statisticians were involved in compiling figures from the production departments, which went into the printed monthly report to the war cabinet. Harold Wilson worked on labour supply and demand, but seems not to have had enough to do. 'Before we had settled down to a steady job of work', recalls Cass, 'Wilson ... found himself work elsewhere.'[6] One of the people he tried was John Maud, of University College, now in the ministry of food. Wilson has claimed Maud tried to recruit him, offering work on a more interesting area than he was getting from Weeks. Wilson apparently agreed to go, but the transfer did not come through.

Another opportunity was in the process of being created by Stanley Dennison. Though only in his late twenties, Dennison had recently been appointed professor of economics at University College, Swansea, after four years at Manchester University. By February 1940, Dennison was also a temporary civil servant, acting as economic assistant to Jean Monnet, the chairman of the Anglo-French coordinating committee, which had been set up in late 1939 in the offices of the war cabinet. The committee, a small group of British and French officials, coordinated the work of the five permanent executive committees, linking ministries in London and Paris, which were responsible for wartime supplies from abroad. Britain was interested in the defence of its ally, France, and Monnet, an American-based businessman who had been involved in the league of nations, drove his small organization as an allied official, working closely with a joint purchasing board in the United States. Monnet found it difficult to create a common defence programme between two national bureaucracies, and recalled in his memoirs: 'It is astonishing how little the word "alliance", which people find so reassuring, really means in practice if all it implies is the traditional machinery of co-operation.'[7] In January 1940, he had asked for an economist to prepare figures and statements for the coordinating committee. When Dennison took up his post, he set to work on the export of coal from south Wales to France. He requested a statistical assistant, and another member for the central computing staff, in the war cabinet offices. The latter was granted from on high. Though £350 was considered sufficient 'to obtain an adequately trained worker',[8] the cabinet secretary, Sir Edward Bridges, asked, on 13 February, that the appointment of a statistical assistant should be deferred. It was 20 April before the coordinating committee's secretary, Gorell Barnes, again raised the question with Bridges. Sometime in the following two weeks, Dennison, who had been at the British Association meeting in Dundee the previous August, came up with the name of J.H. Wilson. Dennison thinks the latter may have got in touch with him, and remembers Wilson as being 'rather fed up'.[9] The question of the post was discussed with Bridges on 3 May, the cabinet secretary finally agreeing that Harold Wilson could be employed.

The British failure in Norway was being blamed on Neville Chamberlain personally, and Churchill became prime minister at the head of an all-party coalition government on 10 May. Hitler had just invaded neutral Holland and Belgium, and the German army broke through into France at Sedan four days later. On 27 May, there began the week-long evacuation of the British expeditionary force, and some French troops, from Dunkirk. France had fallen, and it looked like Britain might not be far behind, though bureaucratic life proceeded as normal in Whitehall.

Harold Wilson started work for the Anglo-French committee on Monday, 27 May, joining the war cabinet offices, as a statistical assistant. Economic events were being rapidly overtaken by military disaster. By the time Wilson started working for the committee, it had begun to collapse, and was dissolved on 4 July.

The establishments branch of the war cabinet offices reassigned Dennison, and therefore Wilson, to the central economic information service in July 1940. The service was a group of academic economists and statisticians, which had been set up in the autumn of 1939. It represented the first serious involvement of professional economists in the British administrative system, though these temporary civil servants were far from happy.

A year earlier, the Chamberlain government, as part of its belated preparations for war, had requested Lord Stamp, assisted by Sir Hubert Henderson and Sir Henry Clay, to provide economic intelligence within the cabinet office. Francis Hemming, who had been secretary of the economic advisory council since 1930, became the administrative head in the autumn of 1939. He was entrusted with recruiting a central economic information service, to assist Stamp and his colleagues in their survey of wartime economic problems. The first members were John Jewkes, who owed the job to Clay, an earlier professor of economics at Manchester University, and Austin Robinson, from Cambridge. Jewkes was to help on manpower problems, and Robinson on industry. They were soon joined by Harry Campion, a statistician, also from Manchester. There followed, in 1940, Lionel Robbins, Alec Cairncross, D.N. Chester, Ely Devons, James Meade, and, later, Richard Stone. On 4 June, in the house of commons, Attlee, the new lord privy seal, envisioned that the expanding group of economists would 'provide digests of statistics bearing on the development of the war effort, and reports on the progress achieved by departments in giving effect to decisions on economic questions reached by the ministerial committees'.[10] This was to reckon without Churchill. In the 1930s, his wilderness years, he had, as scientific adviser, Prof. Lindemann, the Oxford physicist. When he took over the admiralty in September 1939, Churchill set up a statistical branch under Lindemann, who was assisted by Roy Harrod and Donald MacDougall. Lindemann's branch became part of the prime minister's office the following May. Though Bridges was reluctant, shortage of space at number 10 meant it had to be accommodated in the cabinet offices. Churchill used Lindemann to extract information from Whitehall, particularly the service and supply ministries. These facts and figures were then deployed by the prime minister to secure the action he wanted, to the annoyance of ministers and officials alike. It was Lindemann's branch which had the ear of the prime minister in the summer of 1940.

Lionel Robbins, from the London School of Economics, found Hemming's group, 'although not actually disbanded, had fallen into complete oblivion, and the economists and statisticians assumed a more or less independent existence preparing material for the new network of committees'.[11] By October, Bridges was trying to encircle Lindemann's branch, using liaison officers from the departments to track information supplied to the branch. Churchill insisted that the facts passed directly to him had to be accepted as the basis of decision-making. The cabinet secretary acquiesced in the existence of two statistical sections, but he secured Churchill's agreement to a committee on information gathering throughout the civil service. The prime minister's statistical branch survived the review, but, in early 1941, the central statistical office was founded. This was under Hemming, and then Campion, and was to collect information from the departments for general use. The cabinet office economists became the economic section under Jewkes, and then Robbins, working to the lord president's committee. This was now being directed by Sir John Anderson. The central statistical office and the economic section were gradually to become part of the Whitehall machine.

Harold Wilson had been given a room with Stanley Dennison in July 1940, both being classed as economic assistants, on a salary scale of £600 to £800. Dennison was close to Jewkes, both being Manchester liberals, and neither Dennison, nor Jewkes later, had cause to believe Harold Wilson was any different. He seemed to know a great deal of history, and was always quoting Gladstone. Dennison now remembers Harold Wilson as a person who had been 'devilling' for Beveridge, and believes he 'admired [Beveridge] enormously': 'I don't think Harold had any intellectual interests whatsoever; ... I don't think he believed in anything.' He was 'very, very bright' and 'very amusing – which he always was.' Wilson was 'fundamentally a statistician ... [;] he merely took stuff and manipulated it'.[12]

Dennison, who became the administrator of the economic section, quickly lost Harold Wilson to John Jewkes, as general director. Prof. Sir Austin Robinson, as he now is, recalls that he was in touch with Beveridge, and that the latter 'very strongly recommended to me the young Harold Wilson'.[13]

When Harold and Gladys had moved to London in February, they took rooms in Earl's Court, and then Pimlico. The young couple then rented a small flat, at the top of a block, in suburban Twickenham in Middlesex. Gladys became a full-time housewife, and Harold returned home each evening on the train. Though he had been in Oxford since 1934, and Mary had gone to school at Crawley in Sussex, they shared a northern suspicion of life in London. When London was subjected to heavy bombing every night from 7 September to 2 November, civil servants in the Richmond Terrace cabinet offices repaired to the basement under the adjacent New Police Building. Harold Wilson remembers spending nights there during the week, in the company of Lionel Robbins. Some nights he returned to Gladys and Twickenham, where they, and the block's other inhabitants, dragged mattresses down to the ground floor, while German bombers passed overhead. The young couple also seem to have spent some weekends in Oxford, where the cabinet offices had access to accommodation in one of the colleges. Gladys Wilson found the bombing too much, and went to stay with Harold's parents at Liskeard in Cornwall, lodging later in Oxford in the house of a fellow of Jesus College.

While Wilson recalled the nights of the blitz, spent under what was then Scotland Yard, he does not mention the economic debates which took place. Since the central economic information service comprised academics, the habits of peacetime were carried into the wartime civil service. But intellectual debates now had a practical significance. The idea of reconstruction was already being floated. Sir Alec Cairncross, as he now is, remembers Harold Wilson as 'rather shy': 'he never declared an interest in politics to me at that time'. At some point, Wilson asked Cairncross if he believed all the stuff Robbins was spouting, the LSE professor accepting the necessity of intervention in wartime. 'Harold [of course] must have been the baby of the show.'[14] According to Roy Harrod, the most impressive statistician was Richard Stone, from the ministry of economic warfare. James Meade had returned from the league of nations in Geneva, and between June and August, Meade wrote a paper, 'Financial Aspects of War Economy'. He and Stone then conducted a statistical analysis of national income and expenditure, for the years 1938 and 1940. This was inspired by Keynes's *How to Pay for the War* (1940), and their work was to revolutionize national accounting by the treasury. It was published as a white paper at the time of the 1941 budget.

Keynes, who had suffered a major heart attack in 1937, was, by the start of the war, 'the most distinguished British economist of his generation, both in the eyes of the "profession" and among the wider public'.[15] He had theoretically demolished the idea that inflation was caused by the supply of money, and, in the context of excessive wartime demand, he came out, in his 1940 pamphlet, with the idea of deferred pay. This was a form of deficit financing, in which the national debt would come to be held mainly by wage earners. He was to be more successful in urging that interest rates should be kept low, thereby minimizing the charge on the national debt after the war. There had been opposition to Keynes's macro-economic approach: first, at the LSE, where Robbins flew the standard of non-interventionism; secondly, at Oxford, where the economists' research group and the institute of statistics showed the strength of empiricism. Keynes was also a leading 'political' economist, who exerted influence on state functionaries, and, from late 1939, attempted to sell the idea of compulsory saving to the labour movement. In the summer of 1940 he moved into the treasury as an adviser. While he was to work mainly on the problem of external finance for the war, he was responsible, through Meade and Stone, for ensuring that the 1941 budget was the first to be shaped by his broader fiscal view. It was an historic turning point, between the pre- and post-war worlds. In the first weeks of war, Keynes had hosted, at his London house in Gordon Square, Bloomsbury, a series of meetings of 'old dogs',[16] such as Sir Arthur Salter, Sir Walter Layton and Sir William Beveridge. The old dogs had all been in government service during the first world war, and then returned to academic life. They were now critical of the state's mobilization for war. While Beveridge looked back to what he remembered as the successes of 1914–18, Keynes, with very different memories of the peace in 1919, was the most intellectually creative. Salter got a government job in November from Chamberlain, but Layton, like Keynes, had to wait until after Churchill came to power, to be recruited by Whitehall. Beveridge was to be the least favoured, and this rejection had a profound impact. He was to become a popular champion of social reform. During the phoney war, this small group of well-known experts attempted to influence ruling-class opinion through letters to the press, newspaper articles and pamphlets. A typical broadside was Keynes's contribution to *The Times* of 14 and 15 November 1939, when he first advanced his views on internal finance for the war.

Beveridge had used the same august organ, on 3 October, to advocate again a war cabinet of ministers without departmental responsibilities, assisted by an 'economic general staff'. This was so that Britain might fight a 'war without waste'. Though he wished to be placed in charge of manpower, or even economic planning, Beveridge found his offers rejected repeatedly by Whitehall. He was therefore forced, in the first months of the war, to act mainly as an advocate of federal union, world government for Europe and the English-speaking countries. Thus, he accompanied Lionel Robbins and Barbara Wootton to a conference in Paris, in April 1940, to discuss international peace. Beveridge became a complete statist, especially after the fall of France. Keynes, in contrast, remained a minor interventionist. While Beveridge had welcomed his Cambridge colleague's ideas on internal finance, he opposed Keynes's macro-economic approach, especially as it pertained to the question of wartime unemployment. He believed that frictional unemployment, as he still saw it, could only be tackled by administrative controls, to make the wrong people suitable for the right jobs. On the day before Churchill came to power, Beveridge wrote: 'one of the weaknesses of our present economic organisation for war is the incompleteness of its socialism.'[17] He reassured the middle classes, in a BBC broadcast in early June: 'The term "socialist planning" as I have used it has nothing whatever to do with taking away people's property and savings. It means simply that production is directed to serve State purposes at State risk instead of being directed by private enterprise at private risk. One can just as well speak of it as State planning.'[18] Socialism was statism. He came to advocate what was being called 'total war', on the military front but also at home; Beveridge would write, again in *The Times*, that, 'when we beat ploughshares into swords, we should exchange also three other P's for S's: profit for service, party for State, procrastination for speed'.[19] He was never in any doubt that he, and selected members of the governing class, could save Britain in the role of public officials with absolute powers; as he told the Royal Economic Society on 7 June: the provision of man-power 'involve[d] the knitting into a single organisation at the top and at all stages, of the Ministry of Labour and of all the supply departments, [but also] the effective decentralisation of execution'.[20]

Ernest Bevin, the transport workers' leader, whom Churchill had made minister of labour and national service, offered Beveridge, in June 1940, a position in charge of a new welfare department in the ministry of labour, to include the factory inspectorate. Beveridge tried to bargain about his return to the civil service, and lost the only wartime post as an administrator he was to be especially offered. But he was not to be excluded totally from the war effort in Whitehall. Bevin appointed him an adviser, and Beveridge had to work his way back, during the summer, before getting close to the centre of power. As late as 11 August, when he saw the Webbs at Passfield Corner, he was demoralized. 'Poor Beveridge was in a state of collapse', Beatrice noted. 'I have never seen him so despondent about public affairs, so depressed about his own part in bettering them.' The fall of France, against the background of appeasement, left him despondent about the war. 'What is even more personally depressing is that he has been ignored; his services as an administrator have not been requisitioned – all that has happened is that Bevin ... has appointed him as adviser ... He agrees that there must be a revolution in the economic structure of society; but it must be guided by persons with knowledge and training – i.e. by himself and those he chooses as his colleagues.'[21] One of these was to be Harold Wilson, who was not having a good war. Though he would continue to work with Jewkes on labour issues, Harold Wilson returned to serve Beveridge, in the war cabinet offices, during the battle of Britain. Alec Cairncross remembers Wilson continuing to work for Beveridge on manpower issues, even while employed in the economic section, and recalls that John Jewkes, with Wilson, saw themselves as trying to keep Beveridge from rampaging like an untamed elephant.

Bevin had announced Beveridge's appointment as commissioner for manpower survey on 28 June 1940. Manpower, a term Bevin preferred to labour, despite the presence of women in the workforce, was to be the most critical factor in wartime production. It is significant that the ministry of labour was also made responsible for national service, but it was one thing to combine the responsibilities, and another for civil servants in London to control the allocation of men and women to essential services. The manpower needs of the munitions industries, which supplied the armed forces, had been examined by the Wolfe committee in late 1939, but its statistical projections were inadequate. Bevin was committed, as a member of the new government, to harnessing the working class, through trade unions, to the war effort. While military conscription had been in operation from the beginning, he was not an advocate of industrial compulsion. Beveridge was. He had learned from Layton, at a meeting of the old dogs, on 20 September, that the ministry of labour entered the war with no manpower plans. Now in the summer of 1940, the new minister of labour wanted to know how the working class could be better used on the home front. Beveridge, at least in retrospect, was to consider the exercise relatively unimportant, but he set about this social scientific task with characteristic enthusiasm.

The manpower survey was given, as secretary, A. Reeder, now deputy director of statistics in London. Beveridge had control of a 'considerable staff'[22] across the country, and secured treasury permission to employ two senior and five junior investigators, plus two Oxford men – Golay, an American, and Ghiselin, a Canadian, both from University College. Most of the remaining staff were volunteers. Beveridge planned to use academic economists in the long vacation, paying only expenses, and secured the collaboration of G.D.H. Cole, who organized local surveys, and Mrs Mair, to deal with women's organizations. Cole's survey was designed to find out if there were reserves of unused manpower, what the reasons for this unmet demand might be, and the steps that could possibly be taken to put workers in appropriate jobs. Investigators were asked to scour their areas, in search of local ministry officials, educationalists, leading trade-union officials and labour managers, and to talk to them about reputed failings in the operation of the labour market. 'With little more than a letter of introduction these investigators interviewed employers, employment exchange managers, and others, dug out statistics, and surveyed like anything.'[23] All this material was relayed to London, for Beveridge and his assistants to analyse.

It was finished in a remarkably short time, Beveridge sending his 68-page report, comprising mainly memoranda, to Bevin on 4 October. The manpower survey was not, as might have been expected, a statistical study. 'The Report,' as he told Bevin, 'deal[t] less with quantities and more with the problems of organisation.'[24] London was being bombed nightly, and Beveridge was greatly struck by the change in 'spirit' he observed in the capital. He concluded that, in time of peace, private enterprise worked, but the price mechanism could not govern production in wartime: 'State planning becomes inevitable and proves effective in proportion to its completeness.'[25] This was a highly philosophical end to a discussion of the mechanisms of the labour market in mid-1940. Beveridge's secret report was printed for circulation to departmental heads, but Hitler's Luftwaffe destroyed the print works before further copies could be produced. 'Whether any of its select recipients used it in any way', he wrote later, 'I do not know.'[26] Beveridge expressed the wish to submit a supplementary report, using recently available data which could be subjected to statistical study. He also indicated that his mind had moved on to another aspect of the problem. He still had his eye on a senior position in the ministry of labour, and, before he had sent his report to the minister, the loss of some temporary offices in the blitz necessitated his removal to the New Police Building in Richmond Terrace. Other work was waiting here, since his services were already being used in the offices of the war cabinet.

Churchill had set up a production council in May 1940, chaired by Arthur Greenwood, to coordinate industrial production for the fighting services. The other members were to be Sir Andrew Duncan, the new minister of supply, Bevin, Herbert Morrison, the new home secretary, and the parliamentary secretaries from the admiralty, aircraft production, labour and supply. Greenwood proved to be ineffective, and both his committees were to be abolished at the end of the year. The production council set up a subcommittee, the manpower requirements committee, to study the labour needs of the munitions industries. Beveridge had sent out a memorandum from Oxford in June, in which he raised the problem of whether the service departments' programmes could be fulfilled. Probably because he was already working on the manpower survey, Bevin suggested, seemingly in

August, that he should chair this inter-departmental meeting of officials. The manpower requirements committee was asked, by ministers, statistically to compare the departmental programmes with the manpower resources of the country. It was another investigation, but, being located in the offices of the war cabinet, there was a better chance of Beveridge influencing policy. The committee met regularly in room 314 of the New Police Building in the autumn of 1940, and set about extracting secrets from the service and supply departments. It included G.D.H. Cole, then a temporary official in the ministry of labour, and John Jewkes. Roy Harrod, who was an observer on the committee from Churchill's statistical section, would tell Beveridge many years later: 'I was deeply impressed by the manful way in which you grappled with [the] mass of statistics and persuaded the departments to provide the necessary information.'[27]

Beveridge was allowed to have, as joint secretary of the manpower requirements committee, his '"first-rate research assistant" from Oxford'.[28] (The other secretary was G.J. Nash, of the ministry of labour). Wilson seems to have been mainly involved in servicing Beveridge's manpower requirements committee, and he was also given some statistical work to do by the chairman. Douglas Jay was to attend one of the committee's last meetings: 'There they both were across the table in a large Whitehall committee room, rather like an owl and sparrow: Beveridge, august, white-haired, venerable and dogmatic; and Wilson diminutive, chubby and chirpy.'[29]

Harold Wilson was sent to Northern Ireland in December, on behalf of the committee, to investigate why the province was not making a greater contribution to wartime production. Military conscription did not apply there, and unemployment was rising. It was a major assignment for a twenty-four-year-old temporary civil servant, though Ulster, from the point of view of Whitehall, was something of a backwater. The RAF flew Wilson to Aldergrove, near Belfast, where he was met by the minister of commerce, Sir Basil Brooke's, private secretary. That afternoon and the following morning (11/12 or 12/13 December), he talked to a number of civil servants about Northern Ireland's unemployment problem. Bad weather over England forced him to spend a second night in Belfast, during which the city experienced some bombing. Harold Wilson documented the spare capacity, in a 'long report'[30] for the manpower committee, dated 17 December, describing Northern Ireland as 'a depressed area'. Since the beginning of the war, there had not been one new factory, while the orders with existing firms were 'exceedingly meagre'. The unionist administration in Belfast had clearly found a sympathetic listener. He concluded that 'so far as can be seen there is little or no economic co-ordination between Great Britain and Northern Ireland'.[31] Harold Wilson recommended the area's integration into the machinery of wartime government, through the home office, and also envisaged a production council for Ulster. 'I hope we shall see him here again', the vice chancellor of Queen's University was to write to Brooke. 'I am sure he would like to come, for he obviously enjoyed his visit tremendously and liked being here and meeting so many of our people.'[32] Wilson's draft was sent to Belfast for comments, and the report – a copy of which he kept – was circulated on 2 January 1941. But the production council was on its last legs. Andrews, the prime minister of Northern Ireland, suggested to Morrison that a member of the British government might look after the interests of the province, but the cabinet secretary vetoed the idea. Churchill saw Wilson's report, but Bevin dismissed it as an out of date document by a junior civil servant.

Beveridge had worked briskly on the manpower requirements committee, producing an interim report in early November, and a second one by 11 December. The committee estimated that nearly ten million people would be needed for the war effort by late 1941, and that well over half were required for the munitions industries. Over two million men had to be found, and nearly a million women. Beveridge predicted a labour shortage, with the forces taking men out of industry, and urged that skilled jobs should be filled by women. He asserted that the problem could be overcome, given sufficient state control, though there would be a commensurate need for welfare provisions. After the interim report, the committee set about preparing a master table, which showed to what extent all the non-essential industries would have to release men for munitions work and the armed forces, and where women would have to engage in war production. The second report, like the interim one, went to a joint meeting of the production council and economic policy committee on 19 December 1940. The regular ministerial members were joined, on this occasion, 'by a large disorderly concourse of representatives from departments'.[33] Years later, the official historian of Britain's manpower budgeting was to write: 'The great service which Sir William Beveridge rendered was that for the first time the manpower picture had been looked at as a whole.'[34] But 'the statistics were still far too unreliable and questions of timing still too uncertain to make the report[s] more than a very general guide to action.'[35] The council resolved to submit a summary memorandum to the war cabinet, 'inviting it to authorise the methods proposed for obtaining the necessary manpower'.[36] This was a characteristic response, given the machinery of government inherited from peacetime. Since Beveridge did not have his report recommended directly to the war cabinet, he tended to take the view, at least in retrospect, that he was once again a prophet ignored in his own land. But this was to underestimate the impetus he gave to the state machine on the question of manpower planning, even though it was the last meeting of the production council.

Arthur Greenwood told his war cabinet colleagues that the army council should be asked to reconsider its recruitment plans, and Churchill decided to reorganize the committees on the civil side of government. As minister without portfolio, labour's deputy leader was shunted on to the question of reconstruction, his two committees being dissolved at the end of 1940. Bevin had been brought into the war cabinet in October, during a reshuffle, and, in January 1941, he became chairman of a new production executive, which was to coordinate supplies for the armed services. It met, in Lord Beaverbrook's room, on 3 January. The manpower requirements committee was inherited by the production executive, which soon moved to the new cabinet offices in Great George Street. Following his second report, Beveridge had continued to work on problems for the committee. On 31 December, he mentioned colonial manpower, Northern Ireland, production departments, regional labour requirements, industrial compulsion, and manpower and materials, as areas on which the committee would work. An inactive ministerial manpower committee absorbed the Beveridge committee on 16 January 1941, becoming the production executive's new manpower committee. It was chaired by Ralph Assheton, Bevin's par-liamentary secretary, and Beveridge became vice-chairman, the ministry of labour assuming responsibility for it. Beveridge and Harold Wilson had taken up new posts in Bevin's ministry, though the manpower committee, comprising junior ministers and officials, was to meet in the new cabinet offices. Beveridge 'continued through it to pour out memoranda about man-power problems'.[37]

Harold Wilson sank with Beveridge's committee of officials, but, by 28 January, he was joint secretary, with S.G. Holloway, of the new manpower committee, working with ministers for the first time. He was still a small cog in the administrative machine, though, since late August 1940, he had been riding, once again, on Beveridge's coat-tails. It is relatively easy to reconstruct Beveridge from the bureaucratic flows of paper which have survived. Harold Wilson is more difficult to place in the labyrinth of Whitehall. There is one extant sheet in his handwriting, which may be revealing. Beveridge favoured industrial compulsion, and had written in a memorandum in December: 'The case ... rests on the strategic necessity of speed, on the psychological necessity of fair play, and on the impossi-bility of convincing the public of urgency so long as the Government refrains from using powers which it is known to possess.'[38] He advocated the position again, on 5 January 1941, in a paper for the manpower require-ments committee. A copy was shown to Wilson, and the latter returned it, with thanks, appending a note with two queries. The first was a numerical miscalculation he detected, and the second, on the problem of restricting employment in consumer services, was to repeat a 'prohibition'[39] he had urged the previous day. Jewkes put in a paper for the committee later, endorsing industrial compulsion, but arguing that 'the issue is not one of principle but of expediency'.[40] Harold Wilson seemed uncritical of Beveridge's position, but he was still working harmoniously with Jewkes in the cabinet offices. Whatever the academic economists might advise, for Bevin it was a practical political problem. He began to develop a policy for manpower in wartime in 1941, and, probably as a result of Beveridge's reports, the war cabinet agreed, on 20 January, to the principle that military call-up should be dependent upon the supply of armaments. The following day, Bevin told parliament that the government would be taking certain measures, under the emergency powers act of May 1940, to control the supply of labour to munitions industries. But it was the lord president's committee, under Sir John Anderson, where the first manpower budget was attempted that year. The national service act was extended, to include women by the end of 1941. A number of orders, especially one on essential work in March, saw labour exchanges increasingly involved in regulating manpower. All this was too little and too late for Beveridge. After the war, Layton was to tell him that 'the first Manpower Budget' was produced in the ministry of supply in 1942 'as a rough guide to enable Great Britain to discuss both the Munitions and Services allocation of manpower with the Americans ... for the year 1943'.[41]

Beveridge had been given another go at manpower planning, when, in December 1940, the second undersecretary in the ministry of labour, in Montagu House, Sir James Price, fell ill. With the manpower survey completed, and two reports with the production council, Beveridge agreed to fill the position on a temporary basis. He was finally a wartime civil servant. He had considered the question of reservation from military conscription in his second report, and thought the schedule might be used to encourage men into essential civilian work. He recalls being placed in charge of the 'military service department',[42] though this undersecretary then had responsibility for the military recruitment department and the national service department. The latter's 'function ... was to ensure that the available manpower was properly distributed between the Armed Forces, Civil Defence and industry'.[43] It is clear that Beveridge was engaged mainly on revising the schedule of reserved occupations. Under the schedule, men were reserved from military service if they were above a certain age, fixed by the government for their occupation. Beveridge raised most of the ages, but he also introduced an important new principle; a 'register of protected establishments' was to be drawn up, whereby men engaged on war work would be reserved at a lower age. The armed forces would get more men, civilians would be encouraged to move to essential work, and those in protected establishments would not be so readily conscripted. This 150-page document was quickly completed, approved by Bevin, and published on 10 April 1941. Beveridge was not acknowledged as the author, but he had a copy bound in a volume of his miscellaneous publications.

As a senior official in the ministry, Beveridge was also a member of the labour supply board, and 'took any chance open to [him] to put forward memoranda and proposals over a wide field'.[44] Bevin had set up the labour supply board, in order to discuss the implementation of government policy with his senior officials. On 26 November 1940, Beveridge wrote to the board about visits made by Jewkes and Wilson, on behalf of the manpower requirements committee, to the north western and north midlands regions; there was a heavy imbalance in the dispersal of factories to these regions. This may have been the first time Harold Wilson was mentioned to Bevin, but there is no evidence that this leading member of the coalition government was particularly impressed by his junior official. Beveridge, as an undersecretary, joined the board, and, as early as 21 December, he was submitting the 'outline of a man-power plan'. He was particularly concerned about workers leaving munitions factories, and, after Bevin sugared Beveridge's pill, an essential work order was issued in March 1941. This gave the ministry a role in hiring and firing. Beveridge, with his eye on the need for industrial dilution, also began to press for conscription into the women's services, but it was to be December 1941 before Bevin resorted to this. Beveridge dated his demise in the ministry from a memorandum, dated 21 May, in which he argued for the conscription of women. By then, the labour supply board had become the labour coordinating committee, with a somewhat different function. Much remained to be done.

The ministry of labour and national service had been reorganized in June 1941. One deputy secretary took control, essentially, of the peacetime departments, while another, to be known as the director-general of manpower, was assigned the wartime responsibilities. This was to have been Beveridge's job with a new description, and increased responsibilities, but so bad were his relations with Bevin and other senior officials, that it went to G.H. Ince. Beveridge's time in the civil service had lasted less than six months. Harold Wilson was transferred to the ministry of labour and national service in early 1941, as, once again, a statistician, earning £550 by the summer. It seems likely that Beveridge arranged for him to join the manpower statistics and intelligence branch in Ebury Bridge House, some distance from Whitehall. This branch, which had been set up by Bevin, was to be part of Ince's responsibility. It is best seen as a small statistical unit, directly serving senior officials at headquarters, and Beveridge may have encouraged its formation, separate from the ministry's regular statistics department, which had been dispersed to Southport. There is no doubt that the manpower statistics branch supplied Beveridge with his information when he was an undersecretary. Harold Wilson may have been its head, but it comprised only a handful of officials. Given Wilson's attempt to avoid military service, it is interesting that he helped Beveridge on the revision of the schedule of reserved occupations. There is a brief statistical estimate in the Beveridge papers, dated 30 January, dealing with the changes and initialled 'J.H.W.'. While Harold Wilson only reached the age of reservation on 11 March, his twenty-fifth birthday, Beveridge soon increased it to thirty years for dons. As a wartime civil servant, Wilson's eligibility under the national service acts was to be 'subject to special conditions'.[45]

There is no doubt that Wilson worked on the general area of national service, because, on 8 April, Beveridge circulated three memoranda from him on manpower demand and supply. In the first, Wilson discussed how more men might be made available for the forces. He considered it might be difficult, in the second memorandum, to force skilled men into general military service. In the third document, he listed likely abuses of the system of reservation. Wilson stated that 'the figures' of men becoming de-reserved were 'being watched and plotted regionally'[46] to prevent jobs being redefined as skilled. This undoubtedly pleased Beveridge. Wilson's statement that 'the political and trade-union difficulties of sending skilled men to the forces as foot-sloggers [were] practically insuperable'[47] may, paradoxically, have appealed to the advocate of increased munitions production. Wilson certainly helped Beveridge on general issues for the labour supply board. He also helped him on the question of demobilization, Beveridge serving on a war cabinet committee appointed to report on the likely extent of unemployment after the war.

Harold Wilson remained in the ministry of labour after 9 June 1941, the day Beveridge was once again appointed an adviser to Bevin, to explore the use of skilled men in the forces. The following day, Greenwood announced that Beveridge was to chair an inter-departmental committee on post-war social insurance. Bevin – and Beveridge – considered this a dead-end job, since it took him away from manpower planning. As the latter was to put it in his autobiography: 'The critic on the hearth was driven into the winter of post-war reconstruction with a small fire of temporary war work on Skilled Men in the Services to keep him warm. I did not like this bowing out.'[48]

It is ironic that Beveridge's work on social insurance, following the publication of his report in December 1942, would make him a national, indeed international, hero. He was hailed as a leading social reformer. In his report, he described want as one of five giants on the road of reconstruction, the others being disease, ignorance, squalor and idleness. He proposed to tackle want with a system of full social security, from cradle to grave, in a state insurance scheme based on contributions. Beveridge stated it rested on three assumptions: children's allowances; health and rehabilitation facilities for all; and the maintenance of employment. These were all areas he succeeded in introducing into wartime political debate, without reporting

directly upon them. 'The historian of social administration', it is commonly
argued, 'finds in the Beveridge Report the blueprint of the post-war
welfare state in Britain.'[49] The greater irony, in the case of the career of
Harold Wilson, is that he was offered the position of secretary of the
inter-departmental committee on social insurance. This he declined. In the
summer of 1941, thinking probably that the master had nowhere to go
within the civil service, Harold Wilson set out to pursue his career alone.

He was involved in Beveridge's other report for J.S. Nicholson, being
appointed secretary of the committee on skilled men in the services in June.
With Beveridge as chairman, the committee comprised George Bailey, an
industrialist, J.C. Little of the engineers' union, and R.G. Simpson, an
Edinburgh accountant. The master of University College had, as personal
assistants, Frank Pakenham, who joined him as a volunteer from Christ
Church, and, once again, Jack Golay. The committee was asked to advise
on whether the services were using skilled men economically, training them
to the required standards, and whether more needed to be called up. The
chairman told his colleagues on 11 June, that, since the services were
demanding more skilled men, the committee would attempt to 'prove that
the men in these numbers were needed'.[50] Beveridge and his staff looked
first at the army and air force, it being the first to offer facilities. The army
was the most important service, and Frank Pakenham was to do many of
the station interviews in September and October. Bevin asked on 22 July
for an interim report, as he was due to meet engineering employers
concerned about the shortage of skilled manpower. Beveridge submitted
it eight days later, and the report, which no doubt pleased the engineering employers, was published as a command paper in August. Harold
Wilson was identified as the secretary of the committee.

The interim report gave rise to much public discussion about the likely
call-up of skilled workers. The committee seems to have been preparing
a negative case, namely that they should be kept in industry. Beveridge then
tackled the navy. On 5 September, he visited Fairmile and Brighton, and
was to remember seeing at Rodean, the select girls' school, that each of the
cubicles was now occupied by two naval personnel. Rodean had in fact
become HMS *Vernon*, most of the torpedo instructional department being
transferred there from Portsmouth because of bombing. Harold Wilson has
also recalled the Rodean visit, but it is unlikely that he accompanied
Beveridge throughout his investigations in the summer and autumn of 1941.
The visit of the chairman and two other members of the committee to
Brighton was used as an occasion for a seventh meeting. Thus, Harold
Wilson, as committee secretary, had a reason for being at HMS *Vernon* that
day. He seems to have been very much an administrator for the committee,
which was now being pulled, by industry, in a direction opposite to that
originally envisaged by the service departments. It was probably about this

time that Beveridge broadcast, asking skilled men in the services, who thought they were not being fully used, to get in touch with him. Employers and trade unions forwarded the names of men, who were allegedly being wasted in the forces. Beveridge, with 'the faithful Frank Pakenham',[51] conducted interviews with 169 servicemen at Egginton House later in September. The committee submitted a second report on 31 October. On the question of the economic use of skilled men, Beveridge answered 'yes' for the navy, 'not yet' for the army, and 'not yet wholly' for the air force.[52] The secretary for war, Captain Margesson, had tried to explain the army's difficulties to Beveridge and his colleagues, but, as he told Bevin, 'we have not succeeded in persuading them to modify very materially the attitude which [the] Committee take up in regard to the War Office.'[53] Sir John Anderson thought the report should go direct to the war cabinet. There Churchill, as minister of defence, encouraged the war office to concoct a reply. Bevin had been impressed by its findings, but urged in vain for a government decision. The committee became alarmed, but Beveridge dissuaded his colleagues from going public. Publication was delayed until 18 February 1942, when it was presented to parliament, accompanied by a war office memorandum. The army tried to suggest that a committee of civilians could not appreciate military organization, in order to play down Beveridge's suggestions that there should be general enlistment initially, and a new corps of electrical and mechanical engineers. These ideas were accepted by the new secretary for war, Sir James Grigg, following his appointment on 22 February.

CHAPTER 7

Coal Statistician, 1941–4

Harold Wilson slipped away from Beveridge in the summer of 1941, becoming a statistical officer in the mines department, in Dean Stanley Street, Millbank. The mines department was then an autonomous division of the board of trade, and, at the end of June, Sir Andrew Duncan, a non-party conservative, had been reappointed president. David Grenfell, a former trade-union official, continued as secretary for mines. The department was to become the ministry of fuel and power in June 1942, under Gwilym Lloyd George, a liberal MP and son of the former prime minister. The new ministry's responsibility was coal, petroleum, gas and electricity, but coal was the principal energy source for industrial production, the lifeblood of the war effort.

The mines department had been looking for a new head of its statistics branch, and, when Duncan, as the minister with ultimate responsibility, began to take a strong interest in coal, the undersecretary for mines, Sir Alfred Hurst, pressed for an appointment. The branch, which comprised about sixty people, produced regular series of statistics on the consumption and production of coal. It also secured returns from major users in wartime, as well as data on the movement of coal.

Harold Wilson came into the picture suddenly in July. Alec Cairncross had been working on coal, in the economic section of the war cabinet offices, and he recalls mentioning Wilson's name to the mines department. It is unlikely that Wilson was considered for the post at the level of a principal, but what is certain is that there was something irregular in the way the mines department secured his transfer. Wilson was to tell Wright, the establishments officer, and W.G. Nott-Bower, the deputy under-secretary, that he was 'redundant' in the ministry of labour, being engaged on 'administrative work' in Ebury Bridge House. He stated he was 'dis-satisfied', as 'his position there has never been clearly defined'.[1] The mines department had been aware of the position before any formal interview was held, and it was also under the impression that labour would release him, though the ministry did not disclose this to the treasury, which was responsible for civil service appointments. On 30 July, Wright, in a 'personal' letter to his opposite number in labour, was to refer to 'circumstances which were perhaps as distasteful to you as they were difficult for me, resulting from very strong pressure applied by the Head of my Department [Grenfell] and by the President of the Board of Trade [Duncan].'[2] Two days later, in another 'personal' letter, this time to the treasury, he told L.L.H. Thompson that he would have acted differently, if he had been given more time.

Wright and Nott-Bower interviewed Wilson sometime before 17 July, and reported: 'Personality decidedly good; extremely alert mentally and not afraid of tackling anything in the statistical line.'[3] While Wright wanted to hear from the admiralty about Loraine, another possible statistician, Nott-Bower told Hurst that supply was after Wilson: 'I was very impressed with him, and I think we should do well to decide on him at once.' He was exempt from call-up and, though only twenty-five, 'he certainly [gave] the impression of much greater maturity'.[4] On 18 July, the undersecretary agreed that Wilson should be offered a post at £700 per annum. There were discussions with the treasury on 21 and 22 July. The ministry of labour was then formally asked to release Wilson, Wright stating that he was to be paid £550. This was granted on 28 July, and he was asked to report on 5 August. Harold Wilson heard the news in Cornwall, where he and Gladys were staying with his parents. He had secured an increase of at least £100 a year, by agreeing to move from labour to the mines department, without there having been consultation.

Harold Wilson had broken away from Beveridge after four long years, and relations between them were to be affected by the rise of the younger man. After eighteen months as a wartime civil servant, Wilson was now on his way.

When Harold Wilson moved to Dean Stanley Street, he found a paper on expected coal consumption in 1942, in which the figures had been extrapolated from the percentage increase, between the summer of 1940 and the following winter, without seasonal adjustment. 'These statistical eccentricities rapidly passed into desuetude.'[5] A coal shortage was feared, given the increase in consumption in 1940 and 1941, which was to continue into the following year. In the second half of 1941, Harold Wilson set about overhauling the statistics collected by the mines department. This involved, in the first instance, redesigning the questionnaires, which colliery managers had to answer each week. The data then had to be analysed. This was to become a routine procedure, conducted by the clerical staff of the statistics branch, in Lytham St Annes. A weekly report had to be prepared for Grenfell, and there was also a weekly survey of production. 'Within two years', according to Wilson, 'during which period the Department became operational, with a management role, we were able to account for nearly every ton of coal consumed, by type of consumer, for stocks, identifying the winter weeks' consumption of every significant consumer, coal, gas, electricity, railways, industrial, house coal depot, and soon afterwards to trace the movement of every ton of coal from every coalfield – and where necesary every pit – by rail, road, sea and canal, to every consuming point, in terms of each grade of coal, singles, doubles, peas, grains, the lot.'[6]

Harold Wilson also provided the figures for the regular meetings of the coal production council, which had been set up to increase production. Though the council called upon the districts to set up pit production committees, the disruption of the export trade delayed this until May 1941. The council was at the apex of a structure of supposed industrial coop-eration, through which the state hoped to encourage increased output. When Harold Wilson attended his first meeting on 13 August, as a representative of the mines department, Duncan was in the chair. The secretary of the coal production council was John Fulton, the Oxford don who had come out in support of Lindsay in 1938. It was in August 1941 that Harold Wilson first came into contact with trade-union leaders, the miners' federation being represented on the council by Will Lawther, James Bowman and Ebby Edwards. As the department's statistician, Wilson provided some of the information for both sides of the industry. He was witness to class opponents blaming each other for insufficient production. On 1 October, he had to explain a discrepancy between his manpower figures and those of the ministry of labour. As time went on, he became more prominent in its delib-erations. On 3 December, its members finally considered a memorandum of Wilson's, on absenteeism and productivity. Absenteeism was the employers' explanation for unsatisfactory output. Productivity, that is output per shift, was a relatively new concept. Wilson's paper pointed to the falling number of shifts being worked at the coalface, due to miners being called up and going to work in munitions factories. The implication was the need to get more men, and boys, into the pits.

Headquarters had been reorganized a number of times since the beginning of the war. When Harold Wilson joined the statistics branch, it was part of the general division, under R.N. Quirk, an acting assistant secretary, who reported to Nott-Bower as deputy undersecretary. In October 1941, the mines department was reorganized into eight divisions, under the immediate control of Nott-Bower and Lord Hyndley, the government's honorary commercial adviser. Harold Wilson was a junior official, in charge of 'statistics and reports', one of the four sections in division I. Fulton, promoted assistant secretary, headed division V, where he continued to look after the coal production council. Duncan gave up the presidency of the board of trade in early February 1942, and was succeeded, after a brief inter-regnum, by Hugh Dalton, a leading labour figure. He brought with him, as principal private secretary, the thirty-five-year-old Hugh Gaitskell, who had become a temporary civil servant in 1939. In a memorandum for the president, in February 1942, Gaitskell wrote that Harold Wilson was 'extraordinarily able'; 'he is only twenty-six, or thereabouts, and is one of the most brilliant younger people about ... He has revolutionised the coal statistics ... The great thing about him is that he understands what statistics are administratively important and interesting. We must on no account surrender him either to the Army or to any other Department.'[7] Duncan, who had returned to the ministry of supply, offered Dalton advice on the mines department over lunch on 3 March. Fulton should be made number two, and he would 'also promote Harold Wilson to be Director of Programmes'.[8] Dalton was to recall Harold Wilson as a 'junior official[s] ... who ... show[ed] a gift for forecasting, with quite uncanny accuracy, our monthly coal output'.[9]

Fears about a coal shortage increased in early 1942, and Dalton decided in favour of fuel rationing. He asked Beveridge, on 12 March, to prepare a scheme, this being reported to parliament. Though Wilson's branch in the mines department was to help Beveridge, it was the Canadian, R.S. Ghiselin, who actually worked on the project. Beveridge's scheme was accepted by the new president of the board of trade, and, on 31 March, Dalton noted in his diary: 'I hear tonight that it is being said in the Mines Department, at least by Wilson and his friends, that my paper on coal is "the best ever".'[10] Beveridge's scheme secured government approval, but, when this was announced in the house of commons on 21 April, conservative backbenchers revolted. A government white paper had to be promised. As Churchill backtracked on the question of rationing, Dalton considered reorganizing the mines to increase production. The miners, their union, and Grenfell, a former miner, favoured nationalization during the war. The owners, and most tory MPs, opposed any further government interference. Dalton advocated state control for the duration, and this was enshrined in a white paper on 3 June, called simply *Coal*. A national coal board was to be set up, with responsibility for production, mechanization, manpower and productivity, supply of materials, and health and safety. Regional controllers were to be given a range of powers. Rationing was to be postponed, though there were further restrictions on consumption. Wartime control was vested in a minister, and Gwilym Lloyd George was promoted within the government. He was given two joint parliamentary secretaries, one, Tom Smith, a Yorkshire miners' MP, looking after coal. The ministry of fuel and power, based on the mines department, came into being on 11 June.

Lloyd George's new ministry was divided into three divisions, for coal, petroleum, and gas and electricity, with Sir Frank Tribe as permanent secretary. Lord Hyndley became the administrative head of the coal division as controller general, with overall charge of the directorates of production, labour, services and finance. Nott–Bower, as deputy secretary, assumed responsibility for the common services of the ministry, including 'statistics and planning' under Harold Wilson. The latter was only to handle coal statistics in the immediate future. Petroleum, having been another autonomous part of the board of trade, remained effectively a separate department, under the second parliamentary secretary. Gas and electricity, in contrast, was under Nott–Bower. Wilson became a principal statistical officer in the summer of 1942.

The statistics branch had been ninety-two strong at the beginning of 1942, and the Lytham St Annes's contingent returned to London in the spring. Robinson was assigned to house coal statistics, while departmental statistical offices were being set up in each of the twelve (civil defence) divisions. When the government's white paper appeared, two-thirds of the branch's complement of 117 worked outside headquarters. Harold Wilson had been involved in making new appointments, but he failed to secure the transfer of two civil servants from other departments; one, an ex-miner and former student of his, T.W. Twells, from the ministry of labour, and another, with experience of business statistics, from the admiralty. A year after he had joined the mines department, he was 'spend[ing] a large amount of [his] time on the research and planning side'[11] of the work of the statistics department. Much of the general statistical work was the responsibility of J.E. Brookbank, an officer who had worked his way up in the civil service from 1917. Harold Wilson wanted him made deputy director, with the position of statistical officer, and his advocacy of this case was to become pronounced in the following months.

Muriel Nissel, then called Jenkins, became a temporary assistant principal in the statistics and planning branch about June. She was recently down from Oxford, having read PPE, and was interviewed by Wilson, Fulton and J. Innes, director general of services. Harold Wilson, in assigning her work on her first day, drew two organization charts. The first was of the ministry of fuel and power as a whole, while the second showed the statistics and planning branch in greater detail. At the top was 'J.H.W.', with his private secretary Mrs Murphy. Much of the branch was devoted to statistics, under Brookbank. Wilson emphasised planning and research, distinguishing Ghiselin's work on consumption, from that of P.M.D. Roberts on production. Muriel Jenkins was to work with Roberts, who had been at Jesus College. Wilson included the administrative civil servants' college backgrounds on the chart, putting himself down as 'Jesus, New College, & Univ.', Ghiselin as University, a Miss Joan Mitchell as St Hilda's, and concluded 'Cambridge is not represented'.

He assigned his new appointee a number of tasks: 'all questions of research into output, manpower, absenteeism etc. ... a very large assignment'; the four-weekly surveys of production; preparation of research for cabinet documents; progressing of individual pits and districts; calculation of new targets and progressing against targets. 'You will of course', he wrote, 'have research assistance, clerical off[icer] & the use of the calculating pool'.[12] Only members of the executive class of the civil service had direct dealings with coal mines. Muriel Jenkins was soon joined by Pauline Woodhouse, later Silver, who was 'very much a rebel'. She was in fact a member of the communist party. Jenkins remembers Harold 'came in very excitedly one day and said: "I've found the person I want".' There was little sex in the air. 'I don't think he attracted me in that way', recalls Muriel Nissel. 'He was good fun, lively, nice to work with, but one didn't warm to him. I don't think I ever felt a warmth.' She remembers him coming back from a meeting with Lord Hyndley, 'giggling all over his face'. His personal drive was almost singular, in her experience as a civil servant. It was 'obviously frustration of one kind or another': 'I think he wanted to be able to control things and push people around'.[13]

The production of coal had been a problem from the beginning of the war, and the responsibility of the private owners for the poor state of their industry was recognized. The required output was seen as coming about through the employment of more men, but, from 1944, the emphasis would be on increasing output per shift, by means of technical changes – improved productivity.

The industry had employed 766,000 men in 1939, but a shortage of shipping affected distribution during the winter, and the lord president established a coal committee in the autumn of 1940. Munitions work had drawn many miners away from the pits, and an order in June was intended to arrest the drift. The fall of France led to the loss of much of the export trade, and considerable unemployment ensued. The size of the workforce fell from 749,000 – a wartime peak which was never regained. The problem became one of securing the return of miners from other industries and the armed forces, though the latter were untouchable in the opinion of Churchill and the service ministries. A mixture of incentive and coercion was applied to civilian ex-miners. An increase in consumption in 1941–2, combined with a continuing fall in production, produced the alarm which coincided with Dalton's move to the board of trade in February. Some 58,000 miners were involved in strikes in May, and their union put in a demand for an increase of four shillings (20p) a shift, with a national minimum wage of £4.5.0 (£4.25). In Dalton's white paper of early June, it was announced that mining was to become a priority industry for the purposes of national service. Incentives would be offered to juveniles, and absentees could be prosecuted by national service officers. The national coal board was not to have responsibility for wages, and, at the insistence of Bevin in particular, the government agreed that a national wages body should be established for the industry.

Even before the house of commons approved the white paper on 11 June 1942, Bevin and Dalton had set up a board of investigation to enquire into the miners' wage claim, and the permanent machinery for dealing with wages and conditions. It was a panic measure, the government having been alerted to the possibility of 'social upheaval'[14] in the coalfields. The chairman was Lord Greene, the master of the rolls, and it was to meet in private at the royal courts of justice in the Strand. The other members were Sir John Forster, of the national arbitration tribunal, Dr Arnold Duncan MacNair, vice-chancellor of Liverpool University, Col. Ernest Briggs, who was associated with Port Sunlight, and George Chester, general secretary, in Northampton, of the boot and shoe operatives. The joint secretaries were D.T. Jack, of the ministry of labour, and, from the proposed ministry of fuel and power, Harold Wilson. The board met on Tuesday, 9 June to consider the immediate wages issue, and also took evidence on the Friday, and the following Monday. The miners, in the form of their secretary, Ebby Edwards, insisted upon the principle of a national minimum wage. The war wage agreement of March 1940 had suspended local bargaining for the duration. Harold Wilson took Muriel Jenkins along to one of the sittings, and this is when he scribbled on the back of one of his organization charts, 'Lay preacher, I should say. Most of them are.'[15] It is his first recorded comment on an unidentified trade-union leader. The owners, through their leader Sir Evan Williams, argued for new district agreements, in which increases would be related to improved output. When the board had finished listening to both sides, Lord Greene, according to Harold Wilson's recollections, discussed the problem with him over lunch. The chairman thought of awarding two shillings (10p) per shift, and Wilson suggested two shillings and sixpence (12^1/2p) to appease the militants. He also endorsed the idea of a national minimum, and suggested figures to Greene. The board reported to the government on 18 June, unanimously recommending two shillings and sixpence (12^1/2p), and a national minimum weekly wage of £4.3.0. (£4.15), with less for some grades; an output bonus was to be fixed for each pit.

Bevin and Lloyd George accepted this. The two ministers considered that the increased costs of £23 million would be passed on in price rises, the state meeting them through the coal charges account – a financial device whereby the more productive coalfields, through a levy, helped the less profitable. Both sides of the industry accepted what came to be called the 'Greene award', and the immediate problem was solved. Harold Wilson, while observing the discretion expected of a former joint secretary, was to refer later to 'the extremely business-like, thorough and urgent way in which this Board did its work ... [to] the leadership shown by its Chairman, and the co-operation shown by members.'[16] Ten weeks later, on 28 August, the board, after two further meetings with the industry, issued a supplemental report on an output bonus scheme. The lord president's committee had endorsed the idea of a pit bonus, and, after talks between the government and the industry, Greene was asked to draw up a district-based scheme. The owners feared that different bonuses would cause labour to move between pits, and the unions were interested in protecting their lowest-paid members. The supplemental report was implemented from 6 September, but it failed to produce a long-term increase in output. When the bonus scheme was reviewed after a year, the board, in its fourth and final report in September 1943, pronounced it a failure. It accepted the miners' idea of a pit scheme.

The board had moved on to the question of collective bargaining machinery for the industry by the autumn of 1942, a more complicated exercise. Greene only met the industry on 1 December, and the board became something of an independent force in this industrial relations quagmire. The problem was the negotiation of future wages and conditions for the miners, the owners wanting to draw up their own conciliation scheme. After the master of the rolls showed a redrafted report to both sides on 17 December, the miners came out in favour at a special conference on 22 January 1943. Greene had decided upon a national board, in which conciliation was backed up by arbitration. The two sides of the industry were to have a twenty-two-strong negotiating committee, but there would be a three-man independent national tribunal which had the final say on all questions. On 9 February, sending the latest draft to Lloyd George, Wilson wrote: 'To protect the Board from criticism by the Industry when any Government pressure has been put to the Board, these papers have not been officially seen in the Department until this week, though at every stage the Joint Secretaries have been able to put such points as they consider desirable to the Board.'[17] The support of both sides was secured in the following two weeks. Though copies of Greene's third report were sent to Bevin and Lloyd George before publication, the government welcomed it as an independent agreement when it appeared on 15 March. Harold Wilson signed this report, like the previous two, as joint secretary.

The tribunal, appointed later by Greene, comprised Lord Porter, a law lord, J.F. Rees, a university college principal, and Prof. T.M. Knox. The ministry of fuel and power had arranged for the master of the rolls to speak on the BBC on 2 April. He announced a new dawn for the coal industry from 1 May, but this was not to be.

There were immediate problems with the board's solution. Northumberland (and Cumberland) miners declined to sign, having discovered that their employers were strictly adhering to the 1940 war wage agreement, and refusing to pay increased overtime. This action of local employers had been upheld by the national arbitration tribunal. It threatened to stifle the principle of compulsion in the mining industry, before the Porter tribunal was even born. The miners' federation insisted that the employers should assent to amend the 1940 agreement, but Wilson reported to his minister that the men's leaders were divided on tactics: 'Lawther is pressing for an immediate settlement, and invoking the Minister in order to get it, while Ebby [Edwards] takes a view that we should carry on and hope for the best.'[18] The national board nevertheless came into being on the appointed day, and Greene managed to achieve a solution in private, making an award on 11 May, whereby all district agreements were absorbed by the new national conciliation scheme. Harold Wilson reported to the minister on 21 May (though the memorandum was not sent until 16 June): 'Without ever feeling confident about anything in connection with this subject ... I feel that the Northumberland troubles have, in fact, had the effect of improving the machinery.'[19]

Wilson had been actively involved in the work of the Greene board for over a year, implementing government policy by helping to improve industrial relations in the mining industry. Under the dual control instituted in June 1942, it had been envisaged that the ministry would not be involved in questions of wages. By the time of the fourth report in September 1943, Harold Wilson had resigned as joint secretary, handing over to Brookbank in July.

While Wilson had been working for the Greene board, he remained responsible for coal division statistics in the ministry. His staff more than doubled to 273 by March 1944, though there were only some sixty employed at headquarters. His position had been designated as that of a temporary assistant secretary in October 1943, which carried a salary of £1,000–1,200. The directorate of economics and statistics may have been instituted about then, putting Wilson on a par with more senior officials responsible for wartime control of the industry.

Harold Wilson was formally accountable for three areas of work. The first was the twelve regional statistical offices, which collected weekly returns from 1,600 pits, 2,500 industrial consumers, 2,000 non-industrial consumers, 1,100 gas works, 200 electricity works, and 100 water works. There were also four-weekly returns of other consumption, and a quarterly audit of production. The second was the statistics section at headquarters, where his three staff officers, under Brookbank, were diverted from supervising routine work, with queries from within and without the ministry, to say nothing of parliamentary questions. The section was divided into three areas – production and manpower fluctuations (the latter Wilson handled personally until early 1944), finance and wages, and statutory returns. His third responsibility was the economics section, and he himself worked full-time on planning and policy, assisted by Miss Mitchell and Mike Roberts. Wilson considered them both 'on the young side', though realized that 'perhaps [he] should be the last person to say this'![20]

Like many other officials, he had begun to think about post-war questions towards the end of 1943, but he failed to become involved in planning within the ministry. Wilson thought that fuel and power should have a voice, alongside the treasury and board of trade, in Washington talks about foreign exchange. As he told the permanent secretary on 22 December: 'we have not been able to initiate representations on it, apart from certain oral discussions which I have had with Robbins, Meade and Keynes. I have not been able to give the study to the subject which I should have liked.'[21] This comment, in a departmental memorandum, is the only evidence that Harold Wilson ever came in contact with Keynes.

The national coal board set up in 1942 proved a poor arena for policy debate, not least because it was intended as an advisory body. It was only after the white paper had been presented, that the miners and owners were given seats at a national level. The first meeting was not held until 18 December, due to the need to set up the regional coal boards. The vice-chairmen of these, from both sides of the industry, were on the national board, and there were also representatives from the distributive trade and consumers' organizations. Lloyd George took the chair, and the controller general was the vice-chairman. They were accompanied by the joint parliamentary secretary (Tom Smith MP), the permanent secretary, the four directors, plus Fulton and Wilson. Two years later the latter was to write: 'Perhaps the best commentary on it was a typing error by one of my staff in the Ministry who referred to it as the "Notional Coal Board".'[22] Ministry officials thought so little of the board that papers for the first meeting were sent out late. It was nominally responsible for all aspects of wartime control, but was only to meet quarterly. More manageable sub-committees were appointed, but these were chaired by officials. Harold Wilson was not involved, though he attended the only meeting of the output bonus sub-committee on 23 December, because of his involvement with Greene. He liaised with Edwards and Lee, of the mining association, on the loading of figures, and promised an agreed procedure for the second meeting of the board. Wilson was more interested in having the board take over a statistics committee, chaired by Nott-Bower, from the redundant production council. This did not happen on 17 February 1943, and it seems that the ministry declined to discuss the rationalization of returns with the industry. He attended the third meeting, with other officials, on 21 May, but missed the next two. Harold Wilson appeared as director of economics and statistics on 29 March 1944, but the board was not to be convened again for seven months due to the invasion of Europe.

Harold and Gladys had found a new flat about the beginning of 1941 in a block across the Thames, 19 Fitzwilliam House, on The Green, in Richmond. Harold was sometimes duty officer in the ministry of fuel and power, or fire watcher on the roof, and felt he fulfilled his obligation in Whitehall. No doubt he was pleased when Gladys became pregnant in 1943. A son, Robin, was to be born in December. Gladys took the baby to her parents, now at Duxford in Cambridgeshire. They stayed seven weeks, Harold commuting part of the time by train. 'Can you imagine me a father?'[23], Harold wrote to an old Oxford friend in March 1944.

Having resigned as joint secretary of the Greene board in July 1943, Wilson was free to work on the question of coal supply and requirement, in the run up to the invasion of Europe. Churchill and Roosevelt had met in Washington the previous summer, to discuss further the war against Germany, Anglo-American cooperation having already been cemented in the combined chiefs of staff committee. This was extended to the civilian field in mid-1942, and a combined production and resources board (CPRB) was among those set up in the United States. The liberation of Europe required the active participation of the Americans, and Britain needed their help in assuming responsibility for decimated countries. Coal was emerging as an important issue in Anglo-American discussions by the middle of 1943. In August, CPRB and CRMB (combined raw materials board) established a combined coal committee in Washington, to work with a recently formed London committee, on problems of production in both countries. Hyndley chaired the London coal committee, and Harold Wilson soon took over as joint secretary. His opposite number was Lieut. S.D. Berger, of the joint American secretariat, in the offices of the war cabinet. There was a third secretary from the ministry of production, which accommodated the committee in Great George Street, though British and American officials held their joint meetings in Dean Stanley Street.

The London committee of the CPRB was informed on 24 September that a British mission was shortly to leave for Washington, to agree the figures in a world coal budget for 1944–5. British estimates were promised for the following week. Harold Wilson, S.D. Berger and A. Notman, another American official in London, left at the end of the month by seaplane, stopping overnight in Eire, flying to New York, and travelling on the next day to Washington. Harold Wilson was to spend from 2 to 17 October in the American capital, his two colleagues remaining a further three weeks to deal with other matters. It was his first visit to the United States, and he was to come away with decided views on its governance. Harold Wilson had to make contact with all those dealing with coal, and, in fifteen days, he had meetings at CPRB, the war production board, the office of economic warfare, the solid fuels administration, the bureau of mines, and with those responsible for various stockpiling and rationing schemes.

He also saw British representatives, in CPRB, and, at the embassy, those dealing with economic and relief questions.

Wilson was in Washington to handle the technical matter of how both sides estimated coal supply and requirement, in the first year of the European invasion. Once he – and his two colleagues – had worked their way through the labyrinthine bureaucracy, agreement was quickly reached with the staff of the combined coal committee. Wilson also attended a joint meeting of CPRB and CRMB on 15 October, as a staff member of the coal committee. He had sat in on a meeting of the Washington committee, and sub-committees on mechanization and supply and requirements. The American offer of secondhand equipment for surface extraction, and the arrival of the mission from London speeded up the question of underground machinery. As for the second sub-committee, while he had no authority to discuss the question of supply, he was able to report that a Dr Elliot of the war production board, who was 'a Balliol man', wanted South Africa's coal reserves fully exploited. 'On this subject', Wilson reported to Lord Hyndley, 'in accordance with the line we had previously agreed in London, I played the part of an idiot boy, a part which I found quite congenial.'[24]

He seems to have made a good impression on his American hosts, being shown, 'very unofficially', a memorandum from the head of CPRB to the head of the British supply mission. The American, as Harold told Gladys in a letter, praised him: '[He said] that the British really ought to send far more like me and less old school tie wallahs. He said my Yorks accent was a great asset and also my direct manner, both much more understood by the Americans. He said my handling of them was superlative and some of them were very difficult.'[25] If he had pleased his new American masters, he was still keen to ingratiate himself further with the mandarins of Whitehall. In his written report to the controller general, Harold Wilson also gave some impressions he had formed of the United States. He found that the forthcoming presidential election was dominating everything, and there was very little Anglo-American economic cooperation. There was little attempt to restrict domestic consumption, and he thought a word from the US military authorities in Britain might encourage Washington to limit the army's use of coal in the United States. He found the administrative machine to be in 'complete chaos'. The combined coal committee was badly conducted, and isolated in a confused decision-making process. Harold Wilson was, above all, critical of his professional colleagues: 'On the statistical side, similarly, in spite of an army of economists and statisticians, no statistics exist which are any use under wartime conditions. The inferiority complex which I had always felt about U.S. coal statistics – and in this I was perhaps influenced by Mr. Quirk's statements on the American peace-time statistics – I have now left behind in

Washington.'[26] He returned from Washington 'more in favour of British methods than before'.[27]

Wilson had handed over the secretaryship of the London Coal Committee at the end of July, probably because of an internal battle in fuel and power. Shortly after his return from the United States, he asked for more staff in his recently created directorate. In a lengthy memorandum to the permanent secretary on 14 January 1944, he once again asked that his immediate subordinates should be promoted. To emphasize their responsibilities, he stated that, 'at the present time[, he was] a less busy person than at any time since [he] came to the Ministry'.[28] Lloyd George had already expressed the view that promotion was not justified, and Nott-Bower later told Wright that Wilson's 'unreasoning prejudice had outstepped the bounds both of caution and common decency': 'the thought must have been far from deep ... and inspired by Mr. Wilson's usual overwheening desire to boost individual members of his staff and his Directorate generally, without regard to their position, either in relation to the work actually performed or other staff and sections within the Ministry.'[29] This outburst from the deputy secretary was surely uncivil, even by Whitehall standards. It marked a trough in a saga which had begun in early 1942, and was to drag on to the autumn of 1944, though it is difficult to determine what really lay behind it. Nott-Bower is remembered as a 'stuffy old character',[30] and, as a representative of the permanent civil service, he would have looked upon temporaries as, at best, a nuisance. Harold Wilson was young to be a director at twenty-seven, 'a position not normally held by anyone under 40',[31] as he told Beveridge. This was not quite true. He lacked experience of life, but no more than many with whom he was associated. But he was evidently conceited. He had sent Wright a copy of his Washington report to Lord Hyndley, stating that he had 'returned as a fervent apostle of such things, when applied within reason, as Treasury control, Establishments control, the restriction of staff, and the restriction of the (University) output of economists and statisticians.' He ended: 'I should add, of course, that this note does not mean that I have no more territorial demands in Europe.'[32] Such jokey comments were not unusual in his memos and letters, and he had to apologize on at least one occasion for 'hyperbolic oratory'.[33] Harold Wilson was undoubtedly having a good war in fuel and power, though he may have remained socially insecure. Other officials, not all of whom had an interest in being negative, maintained that the director of economics and statistics' demands for staff were unreasonable.

His requests to establishments went unanswered in the early months of 1944, due largely to Nott-Bower's peppery dismissals of his claims. On 17 March, Wilson told Tribe that, 'faced as I am with a complete breakdown of our headquarters' statistical service, I must press that *either* the necessary staff be made available or that I be relieved of a responsibility which I cannot carry out.'[34] He was being chased to produce a statistical white paper, and this digest of figures from 1938, comprising thirty-eight tables, was to be presented to parliament finally in early July. There was a last minute rush, due to the printing works being bombed. Wilson had informed the members of the national coal board on 9 March that he could not supply them with figures for their next meeting. He told the permanent secretary that both the ministry of reconstruction and the war office were keen to have him. Some attempt was made to alleviate the problem, but it was referred to Tom Smith, the secretary for coal, in late June. The issue dragged on, and the treasury sent in an official to study the work of the directorate. Harold Wilson protested that this was not to be comparative. He refused to agree in advance to any such arbitration on 27 September, and referred – for the first time – to his leaving the ministry. It had been agreed that morning on the phone, Wilson wrote to establishments, that '[he was] going on the basis that [he was] regarded as being in full charge in this and other senses until 31st October after which [his] successor [would] take over'.[35] Harold Wilson allowed himself to be driven out of the wartime civil service, but the absence of documentation suggests he may have been allowed to go with an unblemished record. He was in other words sacked. A career civil servant succeeded as director of economic and statistic services on 1 November. The issue was not statistics, as Harold Wilson would have it, but the role of a statistician. The civil service saw this as a particular professsional skill, ancillary to the amateur culture of the administrative class. There is no doubt that Harold Wilson was successful in the ministry of fuel and power, but it is also the case that overwheening ambition brought to an end his days as a wartime civil servant.

CHAPTER 8

Into Politics, 1944–5

Harold Wilson had not joined the labour party in Oxford, and there is no sign of him becoming a member in London. It is of course the case that a political truce prevailed from 1939, and party activity was overshadowed by the war. As a temporary official, he was bound by a 1927 order in council which prevented civil servants being involved in politics. Some temporary civil servants, such as Gaitskell and Durbin, had already fought parliamentary seats, and Muriel Jenkins, a regular civil servant, joined the Westminster labour party while at fuel and power; she became secretary in 1944, and was to stand as a councillor in Soho. Harold Wilson was never a member of the Westminster party. The staff side of the civil service national Whitley council had asked for a relaxation of the political ban in May 1943, and the government ruled that temporary civil servants would be treated exceptionally as regards the first post-war election. 'They were allowed to appear before a selection committee, and if necessary to address an adoption meeting, without resigning. It was only after the easing of the political ban that Harold Wilson became involved with the labour party.

Beveridge's official report on social insurance was published eventually in late 1942. He celebrated by marrying Mrs Mair on 15 December. Upon reading the announcement, Harold Wilson wrote to his master, sending his and Gladys's best wishes. They received an invitation to the reception in the Dorchester Hotel. He asked Beveridge if he would autograph his copy of the report some day: 'the way in which it has hit the public, & especially the Press, is really marvellous. I have not yet, of course, read all the report, though I am gradually getting familiar with it.'[1] Harold Wilson was moving politically after Beveridge, who went on to study unemployment.

Beveridge formally joined the liberal party in September 1944, in order to fight Berwick. On 20 October, Wilson wrote to Beveridge, apologizing for having been unable to watch him take his seat in the commons. This may simply have been courtesy, tinged with a degree of discretion, given that Beveridge was still master of University College. But it suggests that Harold Wilson saw no great difference between the labour and liberal parties, in a parliament elected in 1935. While labour was more important than the liberal party, it was by no means clear in 1944 that Attlee could lead a post-war government. Beveridge was now actively committed to advancing the interests of the liberal party. When Frank Pakenham, who was the labour candidate in Oxford in 1945, intimated that he would prefer Beveridge not to speak for the liberals in the campaign, the latter replied, on 30 May, saying he would make 'friendly references to [Pakenham] as a really good man unfortunately gone into the wrong Party'.[2]

Harold Wilson had come into brief contact with the Fabian Society just before the war, only to lose touch (though the research committee decided, in November 1941, to write to Wilson, Durbin, Austen Albu, and Barbara Wootton, with a view to forming a sub-committee on socialization.) In the summer of 1943, the executive agreed to coopt Wilson, though he did not begin attending until 8 November. Insignificant though this cooption is in the history of Fabianism, it may indicate when Harold Wilson the politician began to first emerge. Membership of the executive was hardly a public position, and he kept his involvement with the Fabians quiet. He was coopted again in July 1944.

Wilson was to state in his memoirs, in a rare moment of philosophical reflection: 'It has never been any part of my political attitude to tear up society by the roots ... The best style of government is like rowing – the ideal solution is to get the boat along as quickly as possible without turning it over.'[3] John Parker, who had become a labour MP as early as 1935, was general secretary of the Fabian Society. He recalls that, about 1944 (in fact, August), the society published a pamphlet, *The Dutch State Coal Mines*. The author, Llewellyn Morgan, was, in fact, a number of anonymous civil servants, one of whom was Harold Wilson.

John Parker, though he was too modest to admit it, is one of Harold Wilson's political parents. He it was who brought him into association with the labour party, through the Fabian Society. King's Buildings in Dean Stanley Street, where Harold Wilson worked, looked on to Smith Square. There, almost adjacent, was Transport House, the head office of Bevin's union, which also housed labour party headquarters. Harold Wilson was in the ministry of fuel and power for nearly three years, before he made that short journey. His guide, and other political parent, was the senior leadership of the miners' union. When he had first dealt with trade unionists, such as George Chester on the Greene board, Harold Wilson was the proper civil servant. Writing to the general secretary of the boot and shoe operatives, in August 1942, he greeted him as 'Dear Chester', and addressed the letter to 'George Chester'.[4] This may have been considered socially patronizing, because, on 15 September, Wilson apologized for leaving off 'Mr', attributing this to 'a typing error'.[5] It was no such thing. The use of forenames was more common in the labour movement, than in many other areas of society, and Harold Wilson was to learn to address miners' leaders in this manner, and to so refer to them behind their backs. He became well known to Ebby Edwards in 1942–3, and the other two officers of the miners' federation, Will Lawther and James Bowman. His job was to get the miners to cooperate with the state during wartime, in order to produce more coal. It is not surprising that their leaders considered they were making substantial gains by cooperating with civil servants and ministers. Will Lawther was to claim later that 'Harold used to meet with us and talk. He got his socialist outlook then.'[6] There is little evidence of socialism in Harold Wilson's politics at the time, and another union official, Sidney Ford, recalled: 'He always looked at the facts, and made his judgements accordingly. He didn't have that immediate bias towards the miners which you found in most socialists at the time. If you'd asked me at the time, honestly, I'd have said he was a Liberal.'[7]

Wilson's name was mentioned to Tom Smith, the parliamentary secretary in fuel and power, who seems to have spent a great deal of time with fellow mining MPs. John Parker and Tom Smith suggested Wilson's name to Transport House, at some point in the winter of 1943–4. The party executive was preparing for the return of post-war political competition, and there was a search on for parliamentary candidates. The party in the country had been run down during the war, and Transport House was even more central in organizing the return to the electoral process than it had been before the war. The invasion of Europe had yet to take place, and a number of future labour MPs were officers in the forces. There was a shortage of political talent, and party figures uninvolved in the government were the key patrons. Sometime in early 1944, Harold Wilson allowed his name to be added to the list circulated to constituency labour parties.

Wilson received a letter from Eric Sharpe in the early spring of 1944. His former Jesus College friend was a conscientious objector, and working on the land in Wales. He announced he had a vocation to become a baptist preacher. Harold Wilson replied on 26 March, in a long letter, expressing pleasure at Eric Sharpe's decision: 'I hope I can feel that in my way too we shall be doing the same kind of work and perhaps when opportunity offers meeting.' He stated that the labour party had asked him to become a candidate. 'I have at last come close to beginning on the work I have always wanted to do since I was a kid', he continued. 'I have often told you about it – politics. I've seen it at very close quarters and sometimes seen it at its worst in the past three years, but an opportunity has presented itself ... We shall need all the ideals and statesmanship we can get in national politics.'

Eric Sharpe, now retired, suggests that Harold Wilson was inaccurately recalling their conversations at Oxford only a few years earlier:

I think he is wrong there. Thinking back, I don't think we did discuss his desire to enter politics ... The honest answer I have got to give is 'no, never', and I don't think any of his friends who knew him in those undergraduate days would have thought that, because he didn't wear his political opinions on his sleeve, any more than he wore his religious opinions, or anything else. He was not an extrovert type, so he wouldn't have done, even in deep conversation with us in these matters. He certainly never gave me the impression that he had any ambition to become a politician let alone the prime minister ... My own feeling is that it was very largely chance and the succession of political events which brought him into the political field.[8]

Several constituencies invited Harold Wilson to apply to become their prospective parliamentary candidate, presumably on the basis of information circulated. He attended a selection conference in Peterborough, then a conservative seat, just before D Day, but was unsuccessful. Wilson travelled back on the train with Kenneth Younger, who had also been summoned to the conference. Younger believed he came second, and Wilson third, out of the short list of three. Wilson was also on short lists for Elland, Sowerby Bridge, Darlington and Grimsby, again all held by tories. He received an approach from Ormskirk in Lancashire in the summer. This was a conservative seat (except for 1918–22), which had gone labour in 1929. Its MP followed MacDonald in 1931, and, when he resigned in late 1939, he was replaced, without a contest, by W.S.R. King-Hall. Commander Stephen King-Hall, as he was known, was a retired naval officer, and well-known broadcaster, who was appointed director of publicity in the ministry of fuel and power in August 1942. King-Hall was a colleague, and apparently a friend, of Harold Wilson's.

Ormskirk was a geographically extensive constituency in Lancashire, on the other side of Liverpool from Cheshire. It was bounded by Southport, Preston, Wigan and Liverpool. Much of it was agricultural, potatoes being the principal crop. It included the towns of Croxteth (population 30,000), Ormskirk (13,000), Maghull (6,500), Formby (5,800) and the villages of Skelmersdale, Aughton, Rainford, Tarleton and Aintree. Liverpool had moved many of its municipal tenants outside the old city boundary, to new towns like Croxteth, but the constituency contained a wide range of social groups.

Harold Wilson's first reported political act was to attend the Ormskirk selection conference on Saturday, 9 September 1944. He was one of four to address the divisional executive committee, in Ormskirk's congregational school, the other three being C. Keynon, a farmer from Rossendale, but also the nominee of the Ormskirk trades council, Harold Dickson, a trade-union organizer from Great Crosby, and a Wigan railway ticket collector, Frank Roberts. Harold Wilson of Richmond, Surrey was selected that night, and his photograph appeared in the following Thursday's *Ormskirk Advertiser*. The new candidate, still with a moustache, looked dour. His association with Beveridge was reported, it was claimed he had volunteered in 1939, and his work in the ministries of supply and labour was reported. No mention was made of fuel and power.

When Wilson referred, on 27 September, to leaving the civil service, there was no reference to him becoming a parliamentary candidate. The rules also allowed temporary civil servants to address adoption meetings, and this he did three days later, on Saturday, 30 September, at the same venue. His exeunt from the civil service preceded his adoption as a parliamentary candidate, and there is little evidence, other than Harold Wilson's own subsequent mutterings, that he was politically persecuted by Whitehall. In his first reported political speech, he showed how recent was his socialism: 'He urged that Socialists should get rid of the inferiority complex, for much that had been advocated by the Labour Party for the last 40 years had been introduced into war time Legislation. The Labour Party was not an opposition Government but an alternative Government. The Labour Ministers in the present Government had been given the muckiest jobs, and they had done them in a way which was credible to themselves and the party.'[9] He went on to describe Beveridge's 1942 report as socialist, as would be the forthcoming one on unemployment. Wilson was back in Ormskirk within a fortnight, speaking at the same venue. 'During the war', he argued, 'there had been a great industrial and technical revolution. Great changes had taken place in science, radio, electricity and in other directions. Immense discoveries had been made and there had been a revolution in production which had been greatly increased and would go on increasing if they did the right thing after the war.... .If they only took advantage of this great revolution they could make the conditions of the people far happier and very much different than they were previously.'[10]

Wilson expected an election within months, and was clearly prepared to work hard for the seat. Just about all his colleagues were taken by surprise that autumn when they heard he was going into politics. Teddy Jackson, working in the central statistical office, encountered Harold on a Whitehall bus. When the latter said he was standing for parliament, Jackson had to ask 'which side'?[11] He told John Jewkes, then in the ministry of aircraft production, that he was standing in Ormskirk. 'I don't think in that area a Liberal has got very much chance,'[12] Jewkes is reputed to have said. Sir Alec Cairncross, who was to succeed Jewkes, recalls that 1944 was the first time he was aware of Harold Wilson's interest in politics. The latter attended his first labour party conference, in London, that December, as a prospective parliamentary candidate, but made no contribution. Robert Steel ran into him in Oxford's High Street in early 1945, and was also told about his parliamentary ambitions. 'You can hardly believe this, and I said: "which party". And he said the labour party.'[13] Philip Mair, hearing he was abandoning the civil service for a political career asked, 'Isn't that a rum sort of thing for you to do?'

'It depends', Harold replied, 'what you think you can make of it'.[14]

He had been making efforts to secure his return to Oxford as early as December 1943, the month Robin was born. Wilson's junior research fellowship had been suspended in 1940, shortly after he went to Whitehall, allowing him to keep his salary as a temporary civil servant. Towards the end of his fourth year in the civil service, Wilson lunched with the master at the Reform Club. According to a letter Harold Wilson wrote after the lunch, on 11 January 1944, he was intent upon resuming his academic career after the armistice. His 'preference' was for a return to Oxford, and, because of Beveridge and Cole, University College.

Harold Wilson was probably earning £1,150 per annum and only twenty-seven. He claimed that the treasury had just offered him a 'short-period engagement' after the war, and there had also been 'an offer from a preferable source [possibly Sir Andrew Duncan on behalf of the iron and steel federation] at a considerably higher rate (nearer treble than double my present salary) and for more interesting and useful work.' Referring to other people who wanted him was becoming a habit! Wilson was prepared to take a slight cut to return to Oxford, but was insistent that he should have a full tutorial fellowship. He could have applied for this in 1941 if he had stayed at Oxford. 'My signing on at this stage, if I were invited to', Wilson told Beveridge, 'would ... be partly for personal reasons and partly for the feeling of economic attachment to the college.'[15] Beveridge may not have been in a position to accede to his request, especially as Harold Wilson wanted to see the war out in Whitehall. It seems that the fellows of University were keen to fill the vacancies in their college. Candidates were being considered, and they were unable, in early 1944, to throw the former junior research fellow any sort of economic line. The estates bursar even seems to have wanted to settle his superannuation.

The 1944–5 academic year was approaching. Wilson commenced part-time teaching in Oxford at the beginning of the Michaelmas term, probably at University College, since G.D.H. Cole moved on at this point. Wilson was still at the ministry of fuel and power, but working out a month's notice. He then found himself, on 1 November 1944, without a full-time job, but with a wife and son to support in Richmond. This was the first time he was faced with economic insecurity, and it was by no means certain that he would be elected a MP. Harold Wilson, and very many others, had limited aspirations for the labour party, even as the war was drawing to a close.

He had begun writing a Fabian pamphlet, and turned to this as soon as he left Whitehall. As chief statistician in fuel and power, he had had access to much information, but was still bound by the official secrets act. The publication of the *Statistical Digest* the previous July released much important data on his industry. Coal statistics fed no mouths, and it cannot have been easy for the Wilsons that winter. Harold is reputed to have spent five weeks on his work on coal, and it quickly burst the bounds of a Fabian pamphlet, he would claim, to become a book. This was to be published, under the title, *New Deal for Coal*, in June 1945, by a young Jewish refugee from Vienna, George Weidenfeld.

Harold Wilson acted as consultant to the railway clerks' association at some point, producing a report on the likely nationalization of their industry. He also did some lecturing on current affairs that winter, for the admiralty at Blackheath. As the war in Europe neared its end, he waited for the general election, and also for news from Oxford.

He was finally given a position at University College in 1945, praelector in economics, though possibly not until well into the Hilary term. Beveridge was on his way out, retiring as master at the age of sixty-six, and in the process of handing over to the pro-master, the Rev. John Wild. The latter remembers Wilson from the pre-war years as 'a most congenial colleague in the Senior Common Room',[16] and it was probably during Wild's mastership that he returned to University College. At the age of twenty-nine, he had become a regular Oxford don. His family did not move back to Oxford until Easter, when a college flat was made available on staircase 11 in the back quad. Harold taught in the Trinity term.

He was remarkably unreconstructed as an economist, in spite of more than four years' experience of wartime government, to say nothing of his identification with the labour party. Beveridge even believed he was going to resume their pre-war research. Wilson had been made domestic bursar, and much of his time was probably taken up with college administration.

He had nursed Ormskirk through the last winter of the war, agriculture being an important issue. On 16 November 1944, Wilson, accompanied by his constituency president, F.J. Sayer, met the local national farmers' union. He advocated later that agricultural workers should be paid the same as skilled workers. Farmers would also be guaranteed prices. The industry could be expanded to everyone's benefit, improved wages in the city coping with increased prices. 'Unemployment', Wilson had argued a few days before, 'could only be prevented by a radical policy which would imply national capital control and the planning of the country's economic resources as in war-time, and the taking over by the State of a number of key basic industries.' This was said at a special meeting on social security, where Wilson expounded on Beveridge's 'historical document'.[17] He thought it should be legislated for now, as a post-war government, presumably tory, would not do so.

Wilson's OBE, awarded in the 1945 new year's honours, helped greatly in Ormskirk. The local paper was to cite the award, during the election campaign, as proof of his wartime contribution. Without a conservative candidate in place, Wilson opened up against King-Hall, now calling himself 'national independent'. 'This independent hocus pocus', he wrote, 'is merely a red herring drawn across the path of those who are seeking a new Britain.'[18] Manny Shinwell was the first prominent labour figure to speak for Wilson in the division on 12 April. There was now a conservative candidate, A.C. Greg, a farmer from Cheshire. On May Day, Wilson issued a party message: 'May Day is traditionally the day on which we in the Labour movement renew our faith in our Socialist principles, and dedicate ourselves afresh to our fight to a new order in Britain and the world.'[19] 'Renew' may have been a bit strong in his own case.

Harold Wilson revealed himself, on the eve of the 1945 general election, in *New Deal for Coal*. The book was dull and overwritten, concise but repetitive. It was very much the work of an economist, being full of tables and statistics. It was also the product of a civil service mind, the paragraphs being numbered like an official report. The book probably expressed a consensual view in the ministry of fuel and power, at least among temporary civil servants. Harold Wilson maintained that he was only using publicly available data, but it was an insider's view which avoided breaching the official secrets act. There were emotive references to the hardship of mining, dotted through the flow of facts and assertions. The book was dedicated 'to [his] many friends employed in and about the industry'. He had incorporated the suggestions of Will Lawther and Sam Watson, chairman of the labour party's coal and power committee. It advocated nationalization of the industry, and, in the post-war general election, this was the major issue between the parties. Coal had been under partial state control since 1942, and, in October the following year, Gwilym Lloyd George came out in favour of full socialization for the duration. Public ownership, for anyone responsible for handling the problems of the industry, was considered, by 1945, to be the only viable solution.

In *New Deal*, Harold Wilson proffered a realistic plan for coal. The labour party, and the miners' union, had long been committed to public ownership, but it was the Reid report on technical reform, published earlier in 1945, which had stimulated policy development.

Manny Shinwell had come close to replacing Gwilym Lloyd George in April 1944, and, when labour won the post-war general election, Attlee made him minister of fuel and power. Shinwell may have asked Harold

Wilson to become his parliamentary private secretary, given his administrative experience in the ministry. The new prime minister told Shinwell to bring the mines into public ownership, and coal nationalization, along with that of the bank of England, was to be included in the king's speech of 16 August, only a matter of weeks after Harold Wilson's book was published. Shinwell may have grown to dislike Wilson, but, in *Conflict without Malice*, published in 1955, he was to make no reference to *New Deal* in 1945:

> I immediately took up the task of preparing the legislation for nationalizing of the mines ... I had believed, as other ministers had, that in the Party archives a blue-print was ready. Now, as Minister of Fuel and Power, I found that nothing practical and tangible existed. There were some pamphlets, some memos produced for private circulation, and nothing else. I had to start on a clear desk.[20]

The Churchill coalition had come to an end on 23 May, following the defeat of Germany, the prime minister forming a caretaker government made up largely of conservative ministers. He called a general election. Nominations were to close on 25 June, and polling would be on Thursday, 5 July. It was Churchill, responding to party colleagues, who precipitated this rapid return to peacetime politics. Both parties were manoeuvring for electoral advantage, and it was known that labour was determined to fight as an independent party. Attlee, the deputy prime minister, was attending the labour party conference, arranged for Blackpool between 21 and 25 May, when he heard of the election. Harold Wilson was the delegate from Ormskirk, representing 283 men and 152 women, a small constituency party. He and another party candidate hurriedly left Blackpool on 23 May, in the company of Hugh Dalton, who was returning to London to resign as president of the board of trade. Wilson was back in Lancashire on 29 May, to address an Ormskirk meeting. Shortly after the break-up of the coalition government, he spoke warmly of Churchill as a war leader, but he repeated Bevin's attack of early April, when the then minister of labour had said that it was not 'a one-man government'.[21] 'The people of this country', Wilson was reported, 'had the unique opportunity to settle their futures on lines which would ensure the planning of the country's resources in their interests and not for the profits of a few. He believed that the mood of the country ... after seeing the nation's resources fully mobilised for war, was for no compromise or trifling in mobilising them for peace and abundance.'[22]

Harold Wilson was to be adopted on Saturday, 16 June, the day after parliament was dissolved. He had Lord Faringdon, a member of the Fabian executive, address a meeting in Formby on 13 June. At Wilson's adoption meeting, in Ormskirk grammar school, attended by both his and Gladys's parents, he was described as 'fellow, University College'. F.J. Sayer said

Wilson 'came from the working class people, and believed in the working class'.[23]

Wilson was an assiduous parliamentary candidate, though he admits he gave 'long and turgid speeches': 'Looking back, my orations were painfully dull, factual and overweighted with statistics.'[24] But he was no slouch when it came to the tools of the political trade, and he followed King-Hall in using loud-speaker equipment.

He toured many of the 152 polling stations in the constituency on 5 July, clocking up the miles. The ballot boxes were then held by the police, for the service votes to be received from the various theatres of war and occupation. There were 8,747 such electors in Ormskirk, nearly one in ten in the constituency, so Wilson's non-existent military service was not unimportant.

The count was held three weeks later, in the Drill Hall, Ormskirk, on Thursday, 26 July. Harold Wilson was present, with his father, to hear he had obtained 30,126 votes, out of a poll of 65,078. This represented a turnout of almost 70 per cent. The opposition vote was split between Greg, the conservative (23,104) and King-Hall, as a national independent (11,848). Harold Wilson was duly elected member of parliament for Ormskirk on a minority vote. Wilson, the *Ormskirk Advertiser* noted, 'comes north with a high reputation. He is not a stranger for he is a native of Yorkshire and spent many of his earlier years on Merseyside. A scholar of high standing and a recognised authority on economics, Mr. Wilson, who is far from being an extremist, is fully conscious of the grave responsibilities that lie ahead, both for him and the party he represents; but he will not shirk from them and will do his utmost to merit the confidence which a vast body of the electorate in the Division [has] reposed in him.'[25]

Interviewed after the result was declared, Wilson had said that 'it was not a personal victory, but showed that the electors of the Ormskirk division wanted to see the country organised after the war in the interests of the people as it had been organised in war time in the interests of victory.' 'Whether he would be going to London', he concluded, 'as a member of a victorious Labour government or as a member of the backbench opposition he did not know, but in either event he pledged himself to the service of his constituents.'[26]

CHAPTER 9

Junior Minister, 1945–7

Peterborough in the *Daily Telegraph* had referred to Harold Wilson the previous October as 'a coming President of the Board of Trade or Chancellor of the Exchequer'.[1] This must have represented the limits of his most secret ambitions as he was about to go into politics, or it may also have been a hope Hugh Dalton expressed off the record to a friendly journalist. Wilson's candidacy was greatly overshadowed by Sir William Beveridge's during the general election, and *The Times* simply noted the new member for Ormskirk as a 'Fellow and Lecturer in Economics' who had 'assisted' Beveridge.[2] The *News Chronicle*'s Ian Mackay saw him as a man of the future: 'Outstanding among the really "new" men on the Labour benches I would put the brilliant young civil servant, Harold Wilson ... [He] is regarded by the Whitehall high-ups as one of the discoveries of the war. Wilson it was who supplied the Minister of Fuel and Power with his facts and figures, and his statistical digest of the coal industry ... was such a model of clear and concise statement that even the industrial correspondents could not find any fault with it.'[3] The defeated MP, Harold Nicolson, regretted that he would not 'see how the brilliant Harold Wilson really does. He is only 22 [sic].'[4] Wilson was in fact twenty-nine.

If Harold Wilson was not surprised at his own result, he shared in the country's amazement at a labour victory. Many labour figures had privately expected to lose, not least because Attlee cut a poor figure as leader. There was a swing to the left in 1945, and the party fought hard with *Let Us Face the Future*. When the results were counted on 26 July, it was found that labour had secured nearly twelve million votes (48 per cent). 'British history', *The Times* opined the next day, 'affords no such example of the reversal in national leadership on the morrow of a crowning victory.' The conservatives dropped to ten million votes (40 per cent), while the liberals increased to two-and-a-quarter million (9 per cent). Labour won 393 seats to the conservatives' 213 and the liberals' 12 (there being 22 other, mainly independent, MPs). For the first time, labour had secured an overall majority – of 146 seats – due to the party having broken through in England. 110 labour MPs were returned in the county seats to 112 conservatives, Harold Wilson being one of these.

Churchill and Attlee had flown home from Potsdam for the declaration of the results on 26 July. The prime minister resigned before they were all declared, and Attlee was immediately summoned to the palace. The political class was momentarily shocked at the victory of socialism, but *The Times* quickly articulated a moderate interpretation: 'it is a vote, decisive in its effect, for specific courses of action, most of them common ground in the late Coalition, in the belief that, on the balance of the arguments put forward at the election, the Labour Party have established the right to be trusted with them. Their mandate now is national not sectional.'[5]

Herbert Morrison, at the behest of Harold Laski, chairman of the party executive, was arguing for the election of a new labour leader, but Bevin hastily arranged for a meeting of the parliamentary labour party on 28 July, at Beaver Hall in the city. Trade unionists only constituted some 19 per cent of the new party, labour MPs being described as mainly 'black-coated workers'.[6]

Bevin quickly secured the endorsement of Attlee's leadership, the new prime minister having already appointed his senior ministers on 27 July. Morrison as lord president was effectively Attlee's deputy. The new prime minister had first thought of giving Bevin the treasury and Dalton the foreign office, but switched them around to please the king. The other leading members were Greenwood (lord privy seal), Jowitt (lord chancellor), and Cripps (board of trade). All significantly had been members of the coalition government. While the parliamentary party meeting continued, Attlee and Bevin left for Berlin, to resume the talks with Truman and Stalin.

Two days after the Beaver Hall meeting, Harold Wilson attended 'a Young Victors Party', at St Ermin's Hotel in Westminster, hosted by Hugh Dalton for newly elected MPs. The other guests that evening, aside from John Wilmot, Dalton's former parliamentary private secretary, were Raymond Blackburn, George Brown, George Chetwynd, Dick Crossman, Evan Durbin, John Freeman, Hugh Gaitskell, Christopher Mayhew, William Wells, Woodrow Wyatt and Kenneth Younger (Aidan Crawley and David Hardman were unable to attend). Eight of the twelve present were to become ministers within six years, and Christopher Mayhew thought there must be 'one or two Prime Ministers among this lot'. Mayhew felt inadequate in the company of the former civil servants, and mentioned in a letter home 'a pleasant young man called Harold Wilson': 'I watched his bulging cranium with anxiety as he talked, expecting the teeming, boiling brain within to burst out at any moment.'[7]

The new session of parliament began on Wednesday, 1 August with the election of the speaker. Harold Wilson took the oath the following day, sitting on a government backbench between Sidney Silverman and Benn Levy, two leftwingers. The meeting of the American, British and Russian leaders concluded on 2 August, and Attlee announced further appointments after his return to London: prominent members of the cabinet were Chuter Ede (home secretary), A.V. Alexander (admiralty), Ellen Wilkinson (education), Emanuel Shinwell (fuel and power), and Aneurin Bevan (health). Among the non-cabinet ministers appointed on Saturday, 4 August was George Tomlinson, at the ministry of works, who had been one of Bevin's parliamentary secretaries during the war. Only one senior minister – Aneurin Bevan – was under fifty, though Attlee was to appoint younger MPs to junior positions. Harold Wilson returned a telephone call to University College from 10 Downing Street, to find he was being offered the parliamentary secretaryship at the ministry of works. He became a junior minister at twenty-nine, with a salary of £1,500, in addition to his remuneration of £600 as an MP. Attlee recalled later that, knowing of Wilson, '[he] therefore put him into the Government at once'.[8] The new prime minister believed in balancing intellectuals and trade unionists in office, and, since 'no one could contend that organisation was one of George Tomlinson's strongest points',[9] it was clear he needed someone with Wilson's administrative background to assist him. The other new MPs given jobs were George Lindgren, who became parliamentary secretary in national insurance, and Prof. Hilary Marquand, who was made secretary for overseas trade. 'I am not sure that this was really good for any of them', Dalton wrote later, '[b]ut there were a lot of posts to fill and not a great array of possibles among the old brigade.'[10] Harold Wilson was the youngest member of the government, indeed of any administration since 1900.

The ministry of works, whose headquarters were across the river in Lambeth Bridge House on the Albert Embankment, was ultimately responsible for public buildings and lands, owned or leased by central government. This responsibility had increased greatly during the war, but, with the end of hostilities, a great many units had to be derequisitioned and even dismantled, in particular military camps. The ministry of works had also become the sponsoring department for the building and civil engineering industries, state control, such as it was, operating mainly through consultation with representatives of the employers and employees. Tomlinson saw this as his department's *raison d'être* during reconstruction, his biographer recording that 'his great success lay in human contacts'.[11] The new minister inherited wartime regulations of building materials and components, and, with the excessive post-war demand for labour in construction, this control, as Tomlinson informed the cabinet in October, would have to be retained in peacetime. Once the ministry of labour determined the supply available, the ministry of works prepared a draft national building programme showing each department's labour entitlement.

The ministry was also responsible for the technical aspects of building policy, which had an important bearing on post-war reconstruction. Housing had been one of the most important issues in the general election, labour promising a ministry of housing and planning in *Let Us Face the Future*, though Churchill had rejected this on the grounds of legislative difficulty. Of the country's stock of some twelve million houses, nearly a third had been damaged in the war, while the remainder went without repair. Unemployment had reduced demand before the war, but, with the loss of nearly three-quarters of a million houses, it was going to be difficult to offer homes to the many new families in post-war Britain.

Attlee confirmed Bevan as housing overlord (in England and Wales) on 16 August, thereby setting aside an election promise. Attlee also established a cabinet housing committee, insisting that 'the utmost drive and vigour must be put into the campaign for houses'.[12] This was to be waged on the ground by the local authorities, who would build and manage most of the badly needed units, and Attlee took personal charge of a revamped housing committee in December. The coalition government had set a target in March 1945 of 750,000, in order to house every family. Plans were made for 300,000 permanent houses in the first two years after the war, plus something less than 200,000 (prefabricated) temporary units. The labour government decided not to publish any objective, but Bevan accepted his conservative predecessor's programme, making a modification for 100,000 prefabricated permanent houses.

Harold Wilson reported as parliamentary secretary on, presumably, 6 August, and it was not long before he resumed his battle with the civil service. The secretary of the ministry of works, Sir Percival Robinson, who had started as a clerk in 1911, was of the old school. Harold Wilson, 'a young man full of ideas and enthusiasm', was appointed to assist Tomlinson. Parliamentary secretaries had originally represented senior ministers in the house of commons, when the latter belonged to the house of lords, but the junior post was now seen as a training ground for higher office. The minister of works, a former cotton weaver, 'was never one to dampen enthusiasm[,] and the Parliamentary Secretary was given his head'.[13] Junior ministers had no authority in departments, being unable to instruct permanent secretaries, who, in turn, only had to obey parliamentary secretaries to the extent that they were acting on behalf of the minister. Wilson's ministerial salary was £200 less than that of a principal assistant secretary, of which there were a number in Lambeth Bridge House.

Robinson began by stressing that the junior minister's duties were largely in parliament, an injunction the latter ignored by immediately consulting civil servants, seemingly when Robinson went on leave. The permanent secretary appears to have been complacent about his department's failings, particularly in the programme of prefabrication, though a directorate of temporary housing had been established under T.P. Bennett as controller. When Robinson heard that Wilson had been talking to civil servants, he 'eyed him sternly. "Look – I must speak frankly to you. After all, I'm twice your age, you know ... I really must explain", he continued, "that this sort of thing simply isn't done."' Robinson was apparently aghast that Wilson had talked to anybody that mattered, oblivious of civil service decorum. According to Leslie Smith, 'Wilson's retort came sharply. "Look here", he said, "you'd better get this clear. I've served in more Government departments than you. And this was how the war was won."'[14]

The return to peace saw considerable reorganization in the ministry, including the appointment of a director general of building materials. Tomlinson, as he told Attlee on 12 December, had a high-powered executive in mind to replace the departing encumbent. The minister generally deferred to his officials on such questions, and he 'held out for a long time'[15] when he came under political pressure to replace one in particular. Towards the end of the year, according to Wilson, Attlee summoned him to Downing Street to report on his ministry's poor performance in temporary housing, the parliamentary secretary laying the blame at the permanent secretary's door. Robinson was promoted out of the ministry in the spring of 1946, a sinecure being found for him on the board of the Anglo-Iranian oil company. Wilson told the commons on 23 January: 'I do not want to go into the question of the personnel of the Ministry of Works, except to say that it is a very different place now from what it was in August.'[16]

The minister of works in the coalition government, Lord Portal, had begun the temporary housing programme in 1944. Portal was keen to use mainly pressed steel, but the revelation that there would be no steel available saw the prototype Portal house dropped in December by his successor, the conservative MP Duncan Sandys. The government shifted its policy towards permanent housing in February 1945, though the unpopular temporary structures were necessary to meet immediate demand. Allocations had already been made to local authorities, but the search for alternative materials and designs delayed that year's prefabs, the target for 1945 being revised downwards. There can be no doubt of Churchill's desire to see returning troops housed, because, on 5 July, election day, he reconstituted what he called the 'housing squad' of ministers 'to drive forward the housing programme as a military operation'.[17] The end of lendlease saw a reduction in the planned number of units from the United States, and the costs began to rise after the war. Labour inherited a chaotic policy for temporary housing.

When Harold Wilson examined the programme, he found it 'was simply not working'.[18] He attended an informal meeting on 8 August in the room of the lord privy seal, Arthur Greenwood, in Gwydyr House, where the question of housing was first discussed. As the junior minister in works, Wilson was not to be included on the cabinet housing committee, but, at the first meeting of the new committee in December, Attlee stated that 'it was essential that housing should be regarded as having the same sort of urgency as military operations in the war years'.[19] A draft white paper on temporary housing reported an inflated cost of £185 million, which went to the cabinet on 15 October. Tomlinson and other ministers attended especially for this first discussion, occasioned by an opposition motion due for debate two days later. The government decided to accept the March 1945 target of 165,000 temporary houses, within two years of the end of the war in Europe. There were six different designs (plus a more expensive aluminium house, being produced in aircraft factories). Bevan would report to the cabinet housing committee, in January 1947, that most of the 96,000 planned for England and Wales by the end of 1946 had been completed. A junior Scottish minister admitted a shortfall from their target of 16,000 units. The minister of health was to consider this 'a very satisfactory result',[20] and the progress was noted with approval.

Harold Wilson had given up day-to-day responsibility for emergency housing, though more were constructed in 1947 than previous years. Tomlinson was succeeded in February by Charles Key, who had been Bevan's parliamentary secretary. It was well into 1948 before 154,000 houses were completed, at a final projected cost of £216 million. This was a long way from the half million temporary houses Churchill had envisaged in March 1944, when he promised post-war homes for those engaged in the national effort.

The palace of Westminster had been bombed in 1941, and the Attlee government inherited the responsibility for rebuilding the house of commons. A select committee had been set up in late 1943, parliament approving in January 1945 the plans of Sir Gyles Gilbert Scott to rebuild in the Gothic style. Demolition work began in June, but completion was not expected until late 1949. The extremely traditional view of the parliament elected in 1935 was unacceptable to many new labour MPs elected in 1945, but, with work in progress, they were unable to influence the government. Attlee, replying to a parliamentary question on 9 October, stated that the new plans provided 'all possible facilities for Members having regard to the limitations imposed by the site and to the accepted procedure of [the] House'.[21] The rebuilding of the house of commons should have been an important practical and symbolic issue in the new Britain, and Will Griffiths, who was to serve as Bevan's parliamentary private secretary, criticized Scott's house of commons for not being circular and

able to seat all its members. 'The Houses of Parliament', he wrote in the
Daily Worker, were built for MPs who were landowners, financiers and
business men, elected by a tiny, well-to-do section of the population.'[22]
Griffiths condemned the plans for not providing MPs and their secretaries
with rooms, and also advocated greater public access, suggesting, perhaps
a little unrealistically, that the abolition of the lords – where the commons
was then meeting – would provide more space immediately.

Harold Wilson had no radical opinions on the British constitution, and
he was required to deal with MPs' office and living accommodation in
London in his maiden speech on 9 October. This he did almost apolo-
getically, mentioning that Tomlinson had now found somewhere to live
in the capital, and defending the under-used ministerial rooms in parliament.
He later handled requests for a gymnasium in the palace of Westminster,
and agreed to the temporary use of the reporters' dining room.

It was Wilson's job to answer MPs' questions not dealt with by
Tomlinson, both at the despatch box and in writing. He also spent a great
deal of time in the commons, listening to members' complaints about house
building, and answering for the government in the adjournment debates
which closed each day's sitting. These were all too often on the supply of
building materials. While it was Tomlinson and his responsibility to
maintain partial state control of the building and civil engineering industries
during reconstruction, the forces of production did not come easily under
the government's writ. Harold Wilson quickly learned to blame the
previous government, and just as readily boasted of his superior knowledge
as a civil servant. On 23 January 1946, he said: 'Having had some experience
of war-time controls of the distribution of materials, I was appalled at the
absence of control in building materials up to the time this Government
assumed responsibility.'[23] He said in another debate two months later: 'I
am sorry to have to say, as one who saw a great deal of munitions planning
during the war, that the planning of the temporary housing programme was
inadequate and amateurish in the extreme.'[24] Wilson was invariably given
a hearing, and it was February 1947 before a conservative MP gave him a
rough time: 'The honorable Gentleman has a great reputation in planning
circles; we look forward to the day when that reputation will be matched
by his reputation in construction circles for ability in providing homes for
the people.'[25]

Wilson made his major contribution to housing the people by seeking
the cooperation of the construction industry. The ministry had established advisory machinery from 1940, when a labour MP, George Hicks,
became parliamentary secretary, and a building and civil engineering joint
committee was announced in October 1945. It comprised representatives
of the employers and employees, and was to 'advise on problems arising
in connection with the execution of the building and civil engineering

programme',[26] other than wages and conditions. Harold Wilson chaired this national joint committee from late 1945, and it met seven times in the first three months. The employers were politically unsympathetic to the Attlee government, but, as Harold Wilson recalls, 'their cooperation could not be faulted, although many of them, in public and private, expressed considerable criticism of Aneurin Bevan, and particularly of his decision to concentrate all available resources on building houses for local authorities'.[27]

The ministry of works only established a decentralized organization, based on the civil defence network, after the war. As part of this, there were regional joint consultative committees, which advised local directors of the ministry. In the first few months, Tomlinson, accompanied by his principal private secretary, and usually Wilson, visited each of the ministry's regional offices. The parliamentary secretary announced in early 1946 that he was to tour the regions in the company of national representatives from both sides. This three-week tour took place in February. Wilson also accompanied Tomlinson and George Isaacs, the minister of labour, in March to York, where they answered questions, at the request of Attlee, from the general council of the building trade unions. On another of his excursions from London, in the late summer, to Yorkshire, he met up with his boyhood friend, Harold Ainley, who was having difficulty finding a house. Labour chaired the housing committee in Huddersfield, but it did not control the council. Harold Wilson, who considered the city's building programme to be 'damnable', pressed Bevan, as he told Harold Ainley in a letter, 'to step in and take control out of the hands of those particular thugs who are running it today'.[28] He was developing a facility for rough language in private.

The principal problem remained the supply of building materials. In areas such as brick making, Tomlinson attributed this to the shortage of labour. Attlee had designated works and supply as the production authorities to expedite production, but the ministry of works, through an inter-departmental building materials coordinating committee, was largely responsible for the national building programme. In February 1946, perhaps in response to the row between health and works, Bevan, Tomlinson, the Scottish housing minister, and John Wilmot, the minister of supply, suggested a housing production executive to Attlee. Modelled on the radio production executive, which had controlled the manufacture of military and even civilian utility radios during the war, it was designed to manage all the forces of building production. Bevan was to chair a meeting of ministers, who would supervise a chief executive and his staff having 'the responsibility of surveying the whole field of housing materials and components production'.[29] This involved works, supply, and other departments devolving particular functions to a body which was to be serviced by the ministry of health. It was April before Attlee gave his permission, agreeing that the new body should not be publicly announced. The executive was set up at 1 Richmond Terrace, and staffed by civil servants drawn from the departments concerned. Ministers seem to have cooperated, and Harold Wilson recalls that this is when he first worked with Aneurin Bevan.

Works also had responsibility for some of the very many military camps which had been established during the war. In the summer of 1946, the homeless began to squat in empty huts. 'In Whitehall empty camps were a largely invisible problem. To the homeless they were all too visible – a hope, and eventually an outrage. In the end they responded by helping themselves.'[30] It began in July, in Scunthorpe, spreading across the country spontaneously, as cinema newsreels carried the story. The *Daily Mail* opportunistically welcomed people making difficulties for a labour government, though local communists played a role in organization in parts of the country. Some camps were still required by the services, but others, declared redundant, were with the ministry of works, pending other uses. Officials processed the problem in a spirit of bureaucratic rationality, oblivious of how ordinary people were coping with the return to peacetime. When the squatting was brought to Attlee's attention, he instructed the war office, in consultation with works, to ensure that camps declared redundant were not left empty. These instructions seem not to have been formally passed on to the departments.

The issue came to the cabinet on 14 August, when many senior ministers were on holiday. Their juniors from the war office, health and works were summoned for the item on squatting. This was Harold Wilson's first cabinet. He was minuted as favouring eviction from the four camps under his department, where the camp was destined for use as 'a Government training centre or some similar purpose',[31] but not if required for German prisoners of war. Such ambiguous advice was to be characteristic of his conduct of government policy. The Germans, pending repatriation, were being used as labour, though Polish troops, who had been on the side of the allies, were also being accommodated in camps in Britain. There was popular indignation at such priorities, the nationalism of the British people always at risk of slipping into chauvinism. The ministry of health announced, under popular pressure, that redundant camps would be considered for housing purposes, though there were practical difficulties, especially given the deployment of resources on the temporary and permanent housing programmes. The cabinet agreed on 14 August to set up a committee on the question of squatting, but this was not before Attlee demanded written reports from the war office and ministry of works, as to why his instructions had not been implemented. Harold Wilson rushed back to Lambeth Bridge House, and, in the reply he drafted for the prime minister, he surmised that Tomlinson, whom he was unable to consult, had probably not passed on the instructions. The ministry had been pressing the war office on the question of camps, and he blamed the army for giving insufficient notice of vacation. Attlee's curt reply could have been the end of the matter, but Wilson, with Tomlinson's approval, further reported that the camps in question had been handed over to the ministry of works before the prime minister spoke to the two ministers. Attlee decided it was not necessary to circulate the junior ministers' reports to the cabinet.

Chuter Ede summoned an ad hoc meeting of relevant ministers for 20 August in the cabinet office, the home secretary being joined by the lord chancellor and five junior ministers, including Wilson. Civil servants reported that 2 admiralty camps, 235 war office, 21 air ministry, and 31 camps under the ministry of works were now being squatted. One of the admiralty camps was at Barscough in Wilson's constituency. His only minuted intervention was a report that some of the camps in works' hands were squatted while awaiting transfer to other departments. Police reports were available, showing that 'the majority of squatters were ex-servicemen or the wives of serving men', seeking to 'escape intolerable conditions of overcrowding': 'all are described of good character, and where they are in large camps are co-operating to run the camps efficiently.'[32] With widespread public support for the squatters, the committee called upon the services to lease camps for housing, and also give notice of when they were to become redundant. A committee of officials was established to watch the issue, and they were instructed to refer to ministers before taking any legal action. This benign course of action was approved by the prime minister. Harold Wilson does not appear to have been involved subsequently, in spite of the fact that it was discussed at the next four cabinet meetings. Senior ministers, with Tomlinson attending, accepted the cabinet committee's report on 4 September.

Four days later, 1,500 squatters, organized by the London district committee of the communist party, seized several blocks of flats in fashionable parts of west London. Included was Duchess of Bedford House in Kensington, then still with the ministry of works; a block in Weymouth Street in Marylebone was also occupied. The strategic objective of promoting class struggle was clear, but the shift from empty military camps to urban residential property, some of which had been requisitioned by local authorities for allocation, after repair, to working-class people on the housing list, altered the nature of the conflict. The communist party was unable to control the tide of housing need it ignited. The authorities came to feel that the communist party was waiting to see the government's reaction, before organizing squatting in provincial cities.

The cabinet accepted that force might have to be used, but felt there would be less public sympathy for those occupying residential accommodation in the capital. John Peck of the foreign office, who considered himself an expert in communist affairs, took exception to the fact that the squatters set up committees. He described one block as 'a minature police state', and observed drily: 'the first type of furniture to be installed in the building is the iron curtain'.[33] Number 10 replied to the foreign office that Francis Williams, a left-wing journalist then working for Attlee, would stress the line of communist manipulation to some press friends. A state counter-offensive was in the making.

Five of the London squatters' leaders, one of whom was known to be living 'in the most deplorable housing conditions',[34] were charged with conspiracy on 14 September. The ministry of works later secured an injunction to regain possession in Weymouth Street, which made the government unpopular with its supporters. The occupation of hutted camps continued, and, by September, there were over 40,000 people in more than 1,000 camps. 'The Government, however sympathetic to the plight of individuals', Bevan told the commons on 10 October, 'is bound to condemn the action of squatters.'[35] But ministers also stressed the allocation of scarce housing had to be on the basis of need. The practice of queueing was in keeping with the democratic ethos of wartime.

The communist party had stimulated local authorities to speed up reha-bilitation of properties, but it backed off when faced by a defiant central government. This saw the government's authority restored during the winter of 1946–7. The weather, and the gradual transfer of camps from the services to local authorities for temporary accommodation, undoubtedly also helped. The labour government, having been paternalistic in its concept of the government's relations with the people, showed itself pragmatic in practice. The issue was diffused in the distinction drawn between military camps and privately owned residential property. 'Whether the people were pawns or partners of the planners', a historian of the squatters' movement has written, 'would, in the end, determine whether the planners were masters or servants of the vested interests.'[36]

Wilson stopped working on the housing programme in October 1946, when Attlee appointed him, at the age of thirty, to head the United Kingdom delegation to a preparatory commission in Washington of the food and agriculture organization (FAO). The FAO was shortly to become one of the agencies of the new united nations' organization (UNO). Douglas Jay, who had been elected a labour MP in the summer, was the first choice of John Strachey, the minister of food. It was decided he should deputize for Wilson at Lambeth Bridge House, and, though not a member of the government, he agreed to do the job part-time for three months without salary, while also writing for the *Daily Herald*. The cabinet secretary concurred, as long as the arrangement was kept secret.

Harold Wilson briefed Jay on the train from Oxford. He had a number of 'grand ideas',[37] including a government architect to revolutionize the practice of the profession. The prime minister must have had good reports, the squatting issue aside, on Wilson's time at the ministry of works, to ask him to lead a British delegation. But the radical world food proposals of the FAO's director general, Britain's Sir John Boyd Orr, a leading nutritionist and now an independent MP for the Scottish universities, were far from being a foreign policy priority. Dr Edith Summerskill, the parliamentary secretary at the ministry of food, had reported to the cabinet food supplies committee, on return from an earlier Washington conference, that Orr, with 'his prophetic wisdom and imagination … grasped the possibilities of the [FAO], but his administrative experience [was] not sufficient to enable him to create the machine for achieving his ideals.'[38]

While the ministry of food had produced two white papers on the world food shortage, and John Strachey, a former Marxist, became minister in May, Whitehall did not want the FAO to become a strong international force. The ministry of food and the board of trade argued in a joint cabinet paper that the United Kingdom's financial position was the most important issue. Gorell Barnes, who was now working in number 10, advised Attlee that, while there was an international consensus in favour of price stability, 'there [was] inevitably some conflict of interest [between] the importing and exporting countries'.[39] Britain was a leading importer, and had long pursued a cheap food policy.

The preparatory commission does not appear to have been a subject of cabinet deliberations, and Harold Wilson's political brief was only to allow minor reform in international economic relations. For this he was given a large team of official advisers, with the commission due to begin work on 28 October.

Harold Wilson had been to Washington once before, but he had little experience of the problem this time. Britain had continued to import food during the war to feed the allied armies, but there was now a looming problem of foreign exchange, as well as increased demand throughout the empire. The Attlee government was determined to 'maintain the basic standard of feeding in [the] country and endeavour to relieve some of its monotony'.[40] With a world shortage of wheat, Strachey was forced to introduce bread rationing for the first time in July 1946. Starvation and famine were already occurring in the backward areas of the world, and the FAO's international emergency food council, set up at a conference in May on urgent food problems, was proving unable to mobilize adequate resources.

The organization was also just as concerned about the problem of food surpluses at this time, the minds of planners being very much on the economic reconstruction which had taken place after the first world war. Agricultural overproduction, in the context of low consumption across the globe, had led to the slump of 1929. Planners were concerned to avert such an outcome again. The FAO was established at a conference in Quebec in late 1945, when Sir John Orr, attending as an unofficial member of the British delegation, was elected to lead the inter-governmental effort to coordinate food supply and demand between the nations. His contract was for two years. By the following July, the new director general was actively espousing his idea of a world food board to promote the production and distribution of basic foodstuffs, with executive powers to purchase, hold and sell stocks. It implied a radical development in the role of the FAO.

The idea of an international buffer stocks authority had originated with Keynes in 1938, and been developed in a 1941 memorandum, but it was rejected by the Americans in wartime talks on international currency management. Though Orr was slow to realize it, the state department in Washington, where the FAO was being established, considered a world food board to be 'impracticable and inimical to [the United States's] international trade policy'.[41] Other representatives of the American government were more supportive in public. Orr might not have been surprised, if he had known that Britain was content to see the Americans scupper the idea.

Despite transatlantic machinations, forty-seven nations, including the United States and Britain, accepted the 'general objectives' Orr enunciated at the second session of the FAO conference in Copenhagen in September. A preparatory commission was established, under Lord Bruce, former prime minister of Australia, 'to carry the proposals further'.[42]

The terms of reference, possibly thanks to the British, cleverly permitted the examination of alternatives to Orr's world food board idea. The Soviet Union, as a major producer, was invited to attend, but the overture was ominously declined. When the sixteen members of the commission, backed up by their delegations, met in late October, they each made opening statements. The United States came out in favour of a free market. With Canada undecided, it was confronted by thirteen nations backing the idea of international management. China and India especially saw Orr's board as the source of relief food and agricultural supplies. The director general recalled that, at the opening, 'the delegations were so stunned by th[e] reversal of policy by the United States that no other ... wanted to speak and the meeting broke up in confusion'. Bruce decided to continue 'in the hope of salvaging something from the wreckage'.[43] The United Kingdom took what Harold Wilson considered a 'middle view', which allowed it to '[hold] the initiative throughout the Commission and ... [make] most of the running'.

The members had divided into two committees, one on development and food programmes, and the other on commodity stabilization; each spawned a number of working parties. The British delegation's instructions were to argue that, on food production and nutritional questions, 'everything which is possible and desirable [could] be done under the existing Charter and Constitution of the F.A.O.'. Whitehall officials were to ensure that the international trade organization (ITO), of the united nations' economic and social council, whose preparatory committee was then meeting in London, would secure the responsibility for commodity management. This was something on which the Americans were particularly keen. A British delegate, possibly R.R. Enfield of the ministry of agriculture and fisheries, did much to sabotage 'the wild and woolly F.A.O. schemes for establishing new international financial agencies'. Wilson's team stressed the need for a technical revolution in backward agriculture and industrial development, to allow poor countries to buy food at world prices. The British endorsed the American idea of an annual exchange of information, and were all for turning the FAO conference into one on world nutrition. On the second committee, Wilson tried to slow down its work, until the ITO conference ended. The state department accepted the idea of rules of international commodity management, but the American 'theologians' in London were more nationally minded. The British favoured agreements on some individual commodities, and rejected the 'Keynesite' concept, preferring national stocks of particular commodities. Britain came under 'continuous running fire from the Indian delegation',[44] the latter complicating the British proposals for 'a positive commodity policy'[45] with the idea of regional prices.

On 18 December Wilson returned to London, presumably for consultations with the interdepartmental working party based in the ministry of food. He also brought a letter from Bruce for Attlee. After praising Wilson for being an 'admirable leader', the Australian appealed to Britain 'to come in behind us in what we are trying to do'.[46]

Back in his own ministry, Wilson wrote an interim report on the work of the delegation, which was sent to Bevin on 31 December. 'By [our] proposals', he wrote, 'we are making possible what we all want to do, namely to link possible overproduction with the great potential, but so far economically ineffective demand of the backward countries, and to do so in such a way that Britain is not called on to bear the financial cost.'[47] A new American idea to sell surplus food at concessionary prices, with safeguards, to undernourished countries had been taken up by Bruce, and officials in London began to fear that the commission would 'degenerate into a dogfight in which [Britain would] be in a hopeless minority'.[48] London thought that the Americans would make up for this by increasing the price of commercial exports. Broadley, the second secretary in the ministry of food, had been expressing 'a great deal of disappointment' on 31 December, ruminating on the lack of American enthusiasm, the militant demands of India, and the low calibre of the delegations. 'Only the U.K. delegation', he mused, 'seems to have gone out adequately equipped and briefed. Harold Wilson was an excellent choice, but he has had to bat on a very sticky wicket.'[49] Broadley recommended the suspension of the commission for a year, in response largely to a depressing cable from J.E. Wall of the ministry of food, who was acting leader. 'Everyone is having second thoughts and writing a vast amount of worthless paper', Wall reported to London. 'Wilson will need to take control of the Commission on his return and we are preparing the various debating points for him today.'[50] Wilson was due to leave for Washington, and Strachey asked him to report on the position as he found it, in time for the interdepartmental meeting on 6 January. He failed to make it by 2 January, trapped in Gander by bad weather. Even Strachey speculated about an adjournment of twelve months, and the commission reconvening in Geneva.

The British were clearly worried that the Americans would antagonize other nations, but the commission was gradually put back on the rails. Wilson cabled Strachey on 6 January: 'position here improved greatly and my present assessment is we shall have no difficulty in killing any concessionary price scheme costing us a cent.'[51] A draft report emerged, chapter by chapter, the British delegation redrafting each one, as it came from the secretariat. It was then submitted the following day to the other members of the commission. A final report was adopted on 24 January, running to ninety-five pages in the version presented by Strachey to parliament. Harold Wilson had hoped that 'the United States rather than the United Kingdom [would] carry the odium for having killed the World Food Board',[52] but the British ambassador was to report that, in the United States, left-wing periodicals attributed the 'murder'[53] of Orr's idea to the state department and foreign office.

Attlee had finally replied to Bruce on 11 January, hoping for an early and successful end to the commission, mentioning that he needed 'Harold Wilson back in England as soon as he can be spared'.[54] Attlee agreed that Wilson could return to the ministry of works, though the prime minister may have been petitioned by Jay, who felt three months as 'a crypto-junior Minister'[55] was enough.

Harold Wilson was back in London by 24 January. There he presented the conclusions of the commission, at a press conference in the ministry of food.

Wilson opened an adjournment debate on the report on 6 February. Attlee stayed on the front bench, to hear his youngest junior minister make his first major speech. The parliamentary secretary to the ministry of works praised Orr. He explained the commission's conclusions in terms of the ITO's proposed commodity authority, and the unwillingness or inability of several leading nations to provide the initial capital for international buffer stocks. He predicted a new wheat agreement in the near future, though the foreign office was sceptical. Harold Wilson clearly failed to convince labour backbenchers that the commission had strengthened Orr's proposals.

Wilson still retained the connection with Oxford, having agreed in August 1945, when appointed a junior minister, to do some teaching at University College on Saturdays and Sundays. Former students were returning from the forces, to say nothing of new cohorts coming up. The number reading PPE was 'very large',[56] and economics dons were in short supply. But Wilson was not able to carry on beyond the Michaelmas term.

Oxford remained the Wilsons' home, though they still retained the flat in Richmond. Gladys and Robin had continued to live at University College, moving out at some point to a college flat on Banbury Road. Harold returned to Oxford each weekend, though he was often away on ministerial or constituency business.

The Wilson family were to remain in Oxford until the beginning of 1948. Harold was open to the idea of buying a house in Hampstead Garden Surburb in north London as early as November 1945, but took no action. There was also still the question of his parents. They had left their home in Liskeard, and moved into the Richmond flat. The reason was Herbert's temporary employment, though near retiring age, with the ministry of supply in London. Harold was undoubtedly instrumental in bringing this about, though Herbert recalled that he gave his son considerable advice in 1945–8. During the week, the junior minister returned late each evening to his mother, something which may have had an impact on his wife.

Gladys Wilson had never believed he would become an MP, much less a member of the government. His return to Oxford after Whitehall proved short lived, and her father died after a short illness in October 1945. She can have seen little of Harold in the first session of parliament, even during his Oxford weekends. Robin, as a two-year-old toddler, was entirely her responsibility. '[Harold] was not very perceptive about female needs and emotions; his articulate, level-headed and undemonstrative parents had done little to prepare him for the temperament and desires of a hypersensitive wife confused by her own changing moods. From the beginning he did not appear to involve [Gladys] in his political life.'[57] The crunch came towards the end of 1946, over his absence in the United States. They had been married almost seven years, and both were thirty. It is said that 'the Wilsons' marriage tottered'.[58] When he came back at Christmas, he found Gladys 'had been rather disturbed at being left alone in Oxford with ... Robin for so long'.[59]

Whatever of the difficulty in their relationship, Harold took Gladys back to Washington, when he returned in January 1947. Robin went to stay with her widowed mother. A new stablility was achieved in the marriage, allowing Harold to continue his political career.

At this stage in his career, Harold Wilson was more a civil servant manqué, and less a politician. Arthur Ewing, who had been at Oxford with him, was, in 1945, a senior official at the ministry of works. He was also active in the Finchley labour party, living at Southway in Hampstead Garden Suburb. On the occasion of municipal elections that November, Ewing brought Wilson along to speak at a meeting. Ernest Kay, a journalist, and one of the labour candidates, was also on the platform. He later recalled what may have been one of Harold Wilson's first political speeches outside his own constituency:

> He spoke without notes for little over half an hour. I was disappointed as I listened to him and I knew that some of my colleagues were sharing my feelings. By the time he was halfway through his speech the audience had grown to perhaps thirty: it was easy to hear the shuffling of feet and to watch the suppression of yawns. He was not a good speaker. He was dull. There was no fire in him. I thought he spoke as though he were delivering a lecture at Oxford ... He ended his speech to little more than a murmur of applause – and most of this came from the platform. Soon afterwards the meeting ended – well in advance of the scheduled time.

The small labour cadre repaired to Ewing's home for a drink. 'Harold Wilson was charming', recalls Kay. 'He scintillated with wit. He was amusing. He cracked jokes. He was relaxed. Why, I found myself thinking, doesn't he put over some of this wit in his speeches?'[60]

There was no sign of this either in Ormskirk. He quickly established a good reputation, if the *Ormskirk Advertiser* can be taken as a measure of local opinion. The paper seems to have been fed material regularly by Harold Wilson, and his private office. He travelled frequently to Merseyside, often staying with the local secretary, Leslie Last, in Maghull. Wilson boasted in October 1946, just before he went to America, that he had visited his constituency twenty-six times since the general election. This was roughly every fortnight. He had also answered some 3,000 letters, half of which he was able to pass on to other government departments. He initiated what he called 'at homes', a forerunner of the MP's surgery or clinic, held at various points in his large constituency. He also had twenty sessions with electors, presumably public meetings, in his first year. Harold Wilson was to be praised as an efficient and effective member of parliament, and the consensus seemed to be that he was 'put[ting] Ormskirk on the map'.[61] His election in 1945 was a fillip to the local party, and it quickly secured the services of a full-time agent. There were to be over 1,000 men, and 500 women, in membership by 1947. This was a local example of a national political phenomenon, the labour party's individual membership rising from under half a million in 1945, to over a million – an all-time record – in the early 1950s.

Wilson was to speak at labour meetings throughout his constituency, though there were complaints that local party members did not see enough of him. It was on such occasions that he talked politics, mostly about the tasks and achievements of the labour government. He stated in September 1945 that the government 'would deal with industry after industry and problem after problem. He asked them to be patient, and put their eyes to three years ahead, as the re-building of Britain would be a long job.'[62] Just as in war, he said the following January, 'the resources of the country ... should be fully mobilised for the purpose of winning the peace and raising the standard of living, and improving the lot of the ordinary people.'[63] This was a recurring theme, even the basis of Wilson's politics. At the May Day celebrations in 1946, he proclaimed that the party was engaged in 'a fight for this new Britain'.[64]

Scientists were to play an important role. Thinking about the peaceful uses of 'atomic power', he had claimed that, 'before the war[,] scientists were far too often left to decay, or were used merely for somebody's rapid profit. Now the scientists were to be used to improve the standard of the people.'[65] Unemployment was an important issue, particularly in the area of Skelmersdale, and he let it be known that he was seeking to direct industry there. Wilson told a meeting in October 1946, in Church House, Ormskirk: 'He often felt that in the day to day struggle with so many problems that they were further than ever from the Socialist Commonwealth on which their eyes were fixed a year ago.'[66]

CHAPTER 10

Board of Trade, 1947–50

Douglas Jay left a written report for Harold Wilson at Lambeth Bridge House in late January 1947, but 'was rather surprised to find he displayed extraordinary little interest'[1] upon his return from the United States. The death of Ellen Wilkinson created a vacancy in the cabinet, promising promotion prospects. It had been mooted in May 1946 that Wilson might be offered the parliamentary secretaryship at fuel and power, but the job went instead to Hugh Gaitskell (beginning his ministerial career). Harold Wilson was disappointed on a second occasion, it being rumoured in September that he would be made minister of transport. Attlee appointed Tomlinson to the cabinet as minister of education in February 1947, and Charles Key took over at Lambeth Bridge House. Harold Wilson was left in place, and disappointed a third time. But he only worked with Key for three weeks, becoming secretary for overseas trade on 5 March. This was another outpost of the board of trade, under Sir Stafford Cripps, the number two economics minister to Dalton at the treasury. Wilson was still a junior minister on £1500, but a cut above the others.

Wilson's promotion may have been connected with timber, then in great demand given the housing programme. While in the United States, he had encouraged the board of trade to buy American timber, which necessitated Britain using its precious dollars. The overseas trade department was looking actively to secure supplies from Russia, and Stalin was thought also to have wheat available, which might allow the government to ease bread rationing. But 1947 was not a propitious year for a junior British minister to attempt an opening to the east.

Cripps had advised Wilson's predecessor, Hilary Marquand, to go to Moscow at the end of January 1947, but Russian stalling tactics saw the visit postponed a number of times. Bevin travelled there by train in March for another council of foreign ministers, which was to last seven weeks. At a meeting with Stalin on 24 March, he expressed surprise at the failure of Mikoyan, the minister for foreign trade, to reply to British overtures.

Bevin stressed Britain's need for timber, and Stalin mentioned the possibility of grain from the 1947 harvest; he expressed himself in favour of Anglo-Soviet trade. When the British foreign secretary offered capital goods, Stalin stated Russia had a need for light rails and rolling stock for a network of 30,000 to 40,000 kilometres. The go-ahead for talks had been given at last.

Cripps told the commons on 15 April that Wilson was to head a trade delegation, comprising officials from the board of trade, the ministries of supply and food, and the commercial counsellor in Moscow. The public position of the government was that no formal trade agreement was expected, merely the reaching of an understanding, but timber and foodstuffs experts were to be on standby in London, ready to fly to Moscow if summoned by Wilson. Marquand had chaired the cabinet committee on external policy and overseas trade, comprising undersecretaries, but this was replaced by the overseas economic policy committee, under Attlee, from early 1947. Harold Wilson was not a member, and senior ministers gave little thought to his mission, before it left for Moscow by air, via Berlin, on 18 April.

Wilson discussed the negotiations with Bevin as soon as he arrived, agreeing that Britain should go for as much timber as it could get. Cripps believed he was carrying out a divine mission, and was worried about an agreed timber allocation arrangement for Europe. He wanted to take the Bevin/Wilson idea to cabinet, as it could be bad for Britain's foreign relations. Hector McNeill, a junior foreign office minister, telegraphed Bevin on 25 April, as the latter was about to leave for Berlin: 'Such a departure from our previous adherence to equitable sharing in Western Europe', he stated with all the authority of the foreign office, 'could not come at a worst time ... The argument that we should use our superior bargaining power (in this case steel) is a bad one politically ... Moreover, we may not always be in the superior bargaining position, e.g. Poland and coal.'[2]

Wilson's team met the Russians on 22 April, coming face to face with Anastas Ivanovich Mikoyan, an Armenian, reputedly from a long line of carpet salesmen. The British presented a revised shopping list, and Mikoyan quickly offered to supply some of the required items. He repeated an argument of Stalin's, namely that they needed transport and plant to mechanize their timber industry. Mikoyan then mentioned a preference for dealing through private channels, while Harold Wilson expressed a desire to keep control of foreign trade. He seems to have missed the irony in this exchange between the communist and capitalist worlds. The Russians then raised the question of credit, asking for improved terms under the 1941 civil supplies agreement, as they were still paying in gold for non-military goods sent from Britain during the war. Wilson replied that he had no authority to renegotiate that agreement, and Bevin, and London, confirmed that trade had to be discussed before credit.

At a second plenary on 24 April, to consider the respective lists, Wilson talked about Britain's balance of payments problem. The talks became deadlocked, but Mikoyan then agreed, in a private meeting, following a letter from Wilson of 30 April, to raise the question of credit through diplomatic channels. It was taken out of the talks about talks. Wilson then dropped a bombshell, namely that there would be a delay on the supply of rails. He also asked for some elasticity on specifications and contract terms. This was also to become a British habit in the post-war world! Lack of success in the talks did not prevent the Russians holding a reception for the trade delegation, during the three-day May Day holiday.

The British and Russians both stuck to their quantities in two further meetings, though the parallel expert discussions on individual commodities proved more useful. The Russians then introduced the question of delivery dates for jet aircraft and engines they had been promised. These had been offered in less troubled times, and were not a matter simply for the board of trade. A deal had been agreed in principle, and contracts for fifty-five gas turbine engines signed between August 1946 and March 1947. But all of the 1947 production of aircraft was earmarked for the RAF (less twelve planes for Argentina). Wilson let it be understood that the Russians would have to be more forthcoming on foodstuffs. The talks came to an end on 8 May without agreement, and Wilson and his officials prepared to fly back to Britain.

Molotov, the Soviet foreign minister, formally requested a revision of the 1941 agreement two days later, which was sent to the British ambassador in Moscow, Sir Maurice Peterson, for transmission to the foreign office. Wilson, still in Russia, drafted a parliamentary statement for Cripps. Officials in London considered this 'too optimistic', and the president of the board of trade accepted a less sanguine view of possible future trade. After returning to Britain, Wilson wrote a report on his exploratory visit, which was sent by Cripps to the overseas economic policy committee on 16 May. The secretary for overseas trade wrote that the Russians had shown 'a certain keenness' for an agreement. 'I am convinced', he reported, 'and was given assurances on this[,] that figures considerably higher than those quoted ... would be available.'[3] The Russians were concerned about wartime credit. In return for supplying timber, they wanted some machinery for the industry. Wilson favoured a concession on credit, and advanced seven reasons, the last being the political one that it would do something to maintain Anglo-Soviet relations. Leaving the credit question to be decided, he suggested a working party to draw up the minimum conditions on which negotiations should be resumed. Dalton and Cripps saw the Russian ambassador, Zaroubin, in London on 3 June, and insisted there would have to be a trade agreement before credit was reconsidered. The chancellor favoured Wilson returning, if the Russians accepted this, and told Bevin he would send a treasury official to keep an eye on finance. Wilson, who was leading another delegation to the preparatory committee of the world trade conference in Geneva, immediately began to plan his return to Moscow. The foreign secretary was less enthusiastic: 'I am particularly anxious that we should not go into this negotiation in too much of a hurry, letting the Russians see that we are hard pressed to know where to get food or timber.'[4] Wilson was invited to the overseas economic policy committee on 12 June, and endorsed the official working party's minimum demands on timber and wheat. Hector McNeil and Dalton were cautious, but Cripps favoured leaving it to Wilson's discretion. The committee decided the negotiations should resume as soon as possible, a view confirmed by the cabinet on 19 June.

Wilson's delegation left the following day. The negotiations were to be 'prolonged and arduous',[5] he and his officials remaining in Moscow until 25 July. 'Apart from finance[, the British] ... had few cards to play.'[6] They were unable to guarantee deliveries or prices. The first phase of the talks, as Wilson subsequently recalled, involved getting Mikoyan to admit that there had been a good harvest, and make an offer. From 25 June to 5 July, the British tried to increase the supply of wheat being offered. Cripps told the overseas economic policy committee on 10 July that the cereals offer was good. The figure for timber did not justify a concession on supplies or finance. Mikoyan had raised the question of finance on 7 July, and Wilson, who was instructed by London to make no concession, did not regain the initiative until 14 July. Then he sent the Russians a letter reaffirming the British position. According to a cable he sent to London that night, Mikoyan had summoned him two days after the meeting of the cabinet committee, to offer a compromise on finance. 'We then', Wilson wrote, 'had an extremely tough but for me a very enjoyable two-hours clouting one another all over the room in the course of which he was told a number of things designed to improve his educational development.'

The junior minister's arrogance may have been matched only by his self-delusion. Mikoyan was an old bolshevik with a proven capacity for survival. He hinted at repudiating the 1941 agreement. According to Wilson, '[Mikoyan] got such a thick ear ... he did not come back on this point.'[7] Wilson himself was in a difficulty over light rails: Whitehall had no idea how much surplus stock was dumped at home and overseas. One official in the board of trade cabled him: 'In a fairly varied administrative experience I cannot recall a worse story of muddled misleading figures than the performance of the War Office (and to a much less degree) the Ministry of Supply.'[8]

The detailed discussion of a trade agreement began on 15 July. With the Canadian government threatening the renegotiation of its wheat agreement with Britain, Attlee, summing up in cabinet committee on 17 July, instructed that Wilson should shortly go to the limit considered unavoidable on wheat in order to avoid a breakdown. Between 21 and 24 July a breakdown on cereal prices threatened. Wilson's mission was aborted, though Mikoyan asked him to postpone his departure by one day, at a final courtesy call on 23 July.

Final agreement came in sight on 24 July, when Mikoyan dropped his prices and accepted the British ones, but his offer was scuppered by the 1941 credit terms. He came down to having half the sum extended, but the British only went up to a quarter. There was a final meeting late at night. Wilson was prepared to return home empty handed rather than make a concession on finance. He had come up earlier with an idea which involved a bit of give and take on both sides, but neither Mikoyan nor London liked it. The talks broke down at 1.00 a.m. on 25 July, and the British delegation flew out of Moscow at 2.00 p.m.

Wilson drafted another report for senior ministers, which Cripps sent to the overseas economic policy committee on 11 August. Wilson made it clear that a trade agreement had collapsed at the last moment on the question of credit. It had not been as easy to extract timber and wheat from the Russians as he had claimed. He regaled senior ministers with some general observations on the character of the negotiations, which, he wrote, took on 'the nature almost of a military manoeuvre'. 'Every step', Wilson reported, 'has to be carefully planned, and timed, against the general strategy of the talks, every small action must be consonant with the tactics of the day (or made deliberately inconsonant to cause confusion); every use must be made of propaganda, communiqués and all the methods which go to make up a war of nerves.' Secondly, Mikoyan personally exuded 'a hint of the Eastern bazaar'. Wilson had walked out of his 'shop' four times, only to be called back, but not on the fifth occasion. His third point was that the negotiations had been buffeted by international politics, though he was not able to say whether for good or ill. The main British weakness was his inability to supply the Russians with what they wanted: 'the position on light rails, which might have been our strongest card, was confused and unsatisfactory from the beginning, and I found it necessary to play for time … in the hope that further quantities would become available.'[9]

Wilson had to convince the cabinet committee that he had done the right thing, but he had difficulty interpreting Mikoyan's motives at the end. He admitted that the Russians had a good case on finance. Sir Frank Roberts, the acting minister in the Moscow embassy, wrote privately on 25 July to Robin Hankey, of the northern department in the foreign office, expressing disappointment at the breakdown. 'Wilson', he wrote, 'conducted the talks with great skill and firmness and proved himself fully a match for that redoubtable and much more experienced negotiator, Mikoyan. He got out of him more than I should have thought possible on cereals and on the trade questions and he really deserved to return home with a success. His team were also first-rate and worked admirably together.'[10]

Cripps reported to parliament on the failure of the trade delegation on 28 July. Wilson had already spoken to Bevin and other ministers, and the Russian version was released the following day in Moscow and London. A squall then ensued in Anglo-Soviet relations, when the *Moscow Bolshevik* paper carried an attack on the British delegation on 1 August. It alleged that a drunken official, W. Strath, had broken a glass panel in a door, as the delegates made their way from the restaurant to Wilson's room in the National Hotel. Further, on a Sunday outing to a lake near Moscow, male and female members of the delegation humiliated some peasant children by offering them food and then taking photographs. Peterson reported that the first charge was 'substantially true', but the second a 'complete travesty',[11] and recommended that the report should be ignored. Wilson had already been quoted in the *Daily Express*, denying any improprieties; 'we were probably the only sober people in the hotel that night'.[12] It is his first documented lie in government.

The overseas economic policy committee was now virtually dead, and Harold Wilson attended an ad hoc meeting with Attlee, Dalton, Bevin and Cripps on 5 August, when it was decided to defer the question of reopening the negotiations. Wilson accompanied Cripps to the cabinet meeting on 7 August, when the latter reported that the Russians had repaid some of the credit due on 1 August. If a financial agreement was signed before 1 November, the British would make it retrospective. Vyshinsky, the Soviet deputy foreign minister, was keen to have the negotiations reopened, but the British government decided that there had to be a full repayment of the 1 August sum. It left Cripps, Dalton, Bevin, who was all for temporizing, and Strachey to draw up the terms for resuming talks. Wilson, on Cripps's instructions, saw Zaroubin the following day in London. The Russian ambassador stated that Mikoyan was unlikely to accept the British position, at which the secretary for overseas trade threatened serious repercussions 'throughout foreign relations'.[13] The Russian ambassador replied that, following Molotov's original letter of 10 May, the British had agreed in principle to amend the 1941 agreement. An interdepartmental meeting of officials was held a few days later, at which a treasury man, who had been on the delegation, came up with two ideas on the question of finance. The first involved a concession against increased supplies, and the second, in order simply to finish off the earlier negotiations, entailed a writing down of the credit terms. Bevin, Dalton and Attlee discussed the resumption issue on 18 August, but decided to keep the Russians waiting for a week. The chancellor was forced to suspend the convertibility of sterling two days later, one of the conditions of the American loan negotiated in the months after the war. It was a major turning point in the government's management of the economy. As for trade with the Soviet Union, Bevin and Dalton agreed that there could be no further drain on the dollar reserves. The prime minister virtually closed the issue down. Wilson had been keen on a further financial concession, though Bevin had told him on 19 August that he should try and get wheat from Australia. He then wrote to Attlee, as if it had been his idea to cold shoulder the Russians. There were exchanges and contacts between the two governments through September, but the Russians continued to insist that they were being discriminated against.

It was to be the end of 1947 before progress was achieved. Bevin waived his objections on 27 October, Anglo-Soviet trade having no implications for international relations in general. At what was to be the last council of foreign ministers, held in London that autumn, Bevin told the United States secretary of state, General Marshall, on 24 November, that Britain would not supply any more jet engines or aircraft to the Soviet Union. Forty aircraft and six engines were outstanding. The British foreign secretary may not have been fully authorized to make this promise, but 'Mr. Marshall said he noted this situation with satisfaction.'[14] A week later, the cabinet, which now included Harold Wilson as president of the board of trade, agreed that the ministry of food should expedite supplies from Canada and Australia, and also reopen talks with the Russians later in the month. The latter did not require to be paid in dollars, and Britain had become concerned about the question of currency since the last round of talks. It was now prepared to make a further concession to obtain Russian cereals. Wheat had been obtained from Australia, and there was the prospect of more from Canada. Wilson decided to go to Russia for a few days.

He flew out on 3 December with only seven colleagues, Bevin having personally informed Marshall of the resumption of talks. Bad weather delayed the party in Berlin, and Wilson did not reach Moscow until 5 December. He had intended a courtesy call the first evening, followed by a plenary meeting. Wilson wanted to negotiate formally during the day, and have personal meetings in the evening with Mikoyan, but the Russians had got into the habit of doing business late at night. Wilson was prepared to go further on the question of credit, before fixing a price for grains in a second part of the talks. Mikoyan secured all he wanted on the 1941 agreement, Britain even waiving most of the claims it had on wartime military supplies to the Soviet Union. The Russians offered 750,000 tons of coarse grains in 1948, for £20 million, there being a shortage of wheat. They secured British government backing for their orders for capital goods, though the Soviet Union did less well on Indian rails, getting only 25,000 tons for £460,000.

Wilson stayed only a few days, agreement in principle being reached at 6.00 a.m. on 10 December after eleven hours. Peterson led in the drafting talks, which became bogged down in detail. The president of the board of trade flew out of Moscow the same morning, a relatively junior team being left behind. After attending a meeting of the economic policy committee the following day, Wilson reported to the commons. He announced that Mikoyan and the ambassador were shortly to sign a trade agreement, though this did not take place until after Christmas. It was a great deal less than the resumption of pre-war Anglo-Soviet trade, though there was provision for further talks by May 1948. Sir Maurice Peterson believed the agreement was 'the thin end of the wedge',[15] Wilson expressing the view that Russia would have an increasing need for British goods.

His three visits to the Soviet Union in 1947 quickly overshadowed his first mission to Washington. There was nothing perverse in Wilson looking east, while Bevin was forming a substantial relationship with the United States. The Moscow connection had started with the search for timber to build houses. It became a chance for Harold Wilson to use his wits against a formidable commercial negotiator, and an opportunity to prove himself to his colleagues in London. He sought to build on his achievement of 1947, by virtually monopolizing the issue of Anglo-Soviet trade.

He had other responsibilities abroad in 1947, leading the British delegation to the ITO conference in Geneva in April. This was another preparatory committee, though one that was to be even less fruitful than the FAO. He returned to Switzerland between his first and second visits to Moscow, and assisted in the drawing up of a draft charter on world trade. This American-inspired attempt at regulation was having difficulty getting off the ground. The secretary for overseas trade was not the president's understudy in the commons, but Wilson was a regular attender at Cripps's 'morning meetings' with senior officials in the board of trade.

1947 was the year of crises for the labour government. It began with an exceptionally bad winter, and consequent widespread disruption. Snow lay across the country from the end of January to the middle of March, and Shinwell, at fuel and power, was forced to ration electricity supplies, contributing to general inactivity. Many were thrown out of work. Without coal to export, Britain could not import raw materials, making it difficult to export sufficient goods to keep up the external balance. There was a risk of national bankruptcy, from the dollar credits running out. A balance of payments crisis threatened. This had its roots in the export markets lost to Britain during the war, but Dalton, whose expertise lay in the realm of internal finance, remained relatively optimistic. The treasury simply advocated cuts in imports. The pound became convertible against the dollar on 15 July, leading to a high capital outflow. The government panicked, appealing to the United States to allow it to suspend convertibility. Washington reluctantly allowed Dalton to do this on 20 August.

The labour government was dominated by the big five – Attlee, Morrison, Bevin, Dalton and Cripps – with Bevan an emerging figure. 1947 was the year Attlee's leadership was called into question, the prime minister being blamed for the drift in government policy. The key issue was the economy, and planning was seen as the solution. The other four all had views, as well as personal political ambitions, but Attlee was safe, as long as they were divided. Sir Stafford Cripps emerged early as Attlee's principal critic; he had decided views on the economy, and his own political destination. The president of the board of trade was to bring about an important change in the government's direction, which had implications for Harold Wilson. Following the suspension of convertibility in August, there was to be a reassignment of ministers and responsibilities. Harold Wilson had returned from the United States to the coal crisis, and the housing programme was badly affected. But he was moved to overseas trade before the snow cleared, and his preoccupation with the Soviet Union in 1947 kept him out of domestic politics. Wilson was seen to be a technocratic minister, working in an administrative manner, who had little recourse to parliament, and less to the party. Attlee was his political patron, and, though Wilson was also close to Cripps at the board of trade, he was not a fellow political conspirator. This did not stop him having notions later about being a key player that year.

The story begins with Dalton in the treasury, nursing an ambition to become foreign secretary. Political space seemed to be opening up early in 1947, given Morrison and Bevin were both ill. Cripps suggested to Dalton in April that Bevin should be put in charge of planning on the home front. Dalton quickly put this to Attlee, who remarked simply that Morrison and Bevin had to be kept apart. The – new – national planning board, under Sir Edward Plowden, was given to Morrison in July, but there was to be no ministry of planning.

Politicking increased. Dalton's parliamentary private secretary, George Brown, allied with Morrison's, Patrick Gordon Walker, to get rid of Attlee by stirring up the parliamentary party. Dalton was informed of what has been called 'the July plot',[16] and tried to offer Bevin a political dagger. The foreign secretary was not one for treachery against the prime minister, and he was preoccupied with the idea of American economic aid to Europe. Bevin was concerned to get the continent into shape, and later summoned George Brown, who had been an official in his union, for a dressing down, by which time the plot had fizzled out. The attempt to usurp Attlee's position was resumed the following month, when Morrison, who had been standing in for Attlee as deputy prime minister, went on holiday on 8 September. Cripps had suggested to Dalton that they should recruit Morrison, the aim still being to make Bevin prime minister. Cripps and Dalton would then have become chancellor (or lord president) and foreign secretary respectively. This was to underestimate Morrison's hostility to Bevin, and Cripps was now preoccupied with getting planning away from the lord president. He hoped Bevin as prime minister would see off Morrison. Cripps saw himself running production, a role he had originally evisaged being performed by Bevin from number 10, and was prepared to let Attlee have the treasury as a consolation. A suspicious Morrison thought he should be prime minister.

Cripps thereupon decided to confront Attlee single-handedly, and their meeting on 9 September was to be decisive. The prime minister had been aware that something was afoot throughout the summer, the *Daily Mail* predicting on 20 August that he was to be unseated. Attlee responded to Cripps by stating that he could not go to the treasury as he had no head for finance. Bevin did not want to leave the foreign office, and he was unacceptable to the party as leader. Bevin and Morrison still had to be kept at arms' length. The implication was that Attlee had to occupy the top job, to keep the other four working in the government. Morrison's absence in Jersey delayed the government's reorientation.

Harold Wilson was not intimately involved in the August convertibility crisis, though he subsequently reported to Dalton that there had been speculation against the pound abroad. It is the first such observation, in a series that was to become obsessive much later. He chaired the first meetings of the committee on exports, part of the machinery, staffed by a phalanx of senior officials, set up in the late summer to deal with the balance of payments. The government, through the foreign office, was being gradually attached to the United States, Bevin, a strong anti-communist, believing implicitly in Atlanticism. When this also took on an element of economic rescue, he saw the solution to British domestic problems in terms of good Anglo-American relations. Questions of socialism and capitalism went out the political window, and Bevin chaired a conference on European economic cooperation in Paris. Britain was to be the second pillar in the emerging western bloc. This was still an economic project, but, as planning continued, a military aspect emerged. Harold Wilson had a responsibility for imports and exports, but there is no sign of him expressing anxiety about the implications of what was to be known as Marshall aid.

Cripps's meeting with the prime minister had a surprising outcome. Attlee responded to the bearer of critical tidings, by offering the president of the board of trade directly much of what he had been trying to achieve through intrigue. He could take charge of production, said Attlee, and be the overall planner in a new ministry of economic affairs. There would also be an inner cabinet running the economy, the big five plus Lord Addison.

Cripps subsequently accepted this, Dalton expressing his willingness to work with the new minister. Attlee, in correspondence with the lord president over the following couple of weeks, effectively stripped Morrison of his economic powers.

The prime minister was considering how to reallocate portfolios by the middle of September. Greenwood was to be dropped, Shinwell pushed out of the cabinet, and Bevan was due for promotion to the ministry of supply. Gaitskell could become minister of fuel and power, and Harold Wilson take Cripps's place. Both would become new members of the cabinet. Cripps also recommended Wilson's promotion. Gaitskell was to note in his diary on 14 October: 'Harold Wilson was obviously Cripps' nominee – and a very good one too.'[17] But Attlee was to offer Bevan either supply or the board of trade. The minister of health, perhaps smelling a rat, chose to stay where he was. Attlee followed Morrison's advice, and gave the minister of supply to George Strauss. Morrison accepted Wilson and Gaitskell's promotion, but failed to keep Shinwell in the cabinet. Greenwood went on 29 September, the day Cripps was made minister of economic affairs. Harold Wilson's appointment was also announced. Morrison had to be conciliated further; Shinwell was sent to the war office, and Gaitskell kept out of the cabinet. The final changes were announced on 7 October, with Morrison back in harness as deputy prime minister. Philip Noel-Baker, at commonwealth relations, was the other new cabinet member. Harold Wilson's elevation coincided with advancement to junior positions for George Brown, Alf Robens, James Callaghan, Kenneth Younger and Michael Stewart. The cast for a later labour government was assembling. Arthur Bottomley, already in the government, became secretary for overseas trade. John Freeman was also moved. Douglas Jay had to be content with becoming Dalton's parliamentary private secretary, but he entered the government in December as economic secretary to the treasury. Here was the shape of things to come.

Harold had taken Gladys and Robin for a belated week's holiday to Mullion Cove, not far from the Lizard in Cornwall, where they had use of a friend's cottage. He was summoned by telephone, probably during the week beginning 21 September, to lunch at Chequers the following Sunday, the official on the other end hinting that promotion might be imminent. Wilson expected to be offered one of several ministries – fuel and power, supply, food. Attlee showed him round the prime minister's country retreat on 28 September, and after lunch offered him the board of trade. 'His amazement was rapidly replaced', Leslie Smith was to write, 'by a feeling he had never before experienced. For the first time in his life, he felt inadequate. It was not that he doubted at all his ability to administer the department ... Nor did he doubt for a moment his ability to direct all the negotiating side ... It was in the realm of higher political initiative and leadership that he felt inexperienced and immature. Visions of Cripps in action kept shooting through his mind ... No matter what the problem, Cripps knew exactly what to do – and invariably introduced a touch of diplomatic panache which Wilson knew he had yet to achieve ... He had not yet been a ruler himself, and this was exactly what he now had to become.'[18] In 1947, Wilson was the youngest person appointed to a British cabinet since 1900, and was also the only member born in the twentieth century. 'In the country at large', wrote a young Cecil King in his diary, 'Wilson is quite unknown and his is a purely Whitehall reputation. But if he can add to his reputation as an administrator the ability to do a spot of political spell-binding, he is then quite a long way on the road to No 10.'[19]

Harold Wilson owed his position to Cripps and Dalton, but ultimately to Attlee. The board of trade lost some powers to the new ministry of economic affairs, Cripps having authority over his old department, plus the ministries of labour, supply, fuel and power, and works. He also took control of the economic section in the cabinet office, and the new planning staff. Hugh Gaitskell noted on 14 October that 'Cripps wants to run things with H[arold] W[ilson], R[ussell] [sic] Strauss and myself as his lieutenants. He made this quite plain to us. We are to have sort of inner discussions on the economic front.'[20]

Dalton backed the new planning department, though senior treasury officials were less enthusiastic. Harold Wilson was now able to participate formally in the development of economic policy, in spite of his lack of political authority. Attlee did not make him a member of the new economic policy committee – initially Attlee, Morrison, Addison, Dalton, Cripps and Bevin – but he was to be a regular attender from early November.

Cripps took command of the economy, urging austerity, and Dalton introduced an emergency budget on 12 November, his fourth – and last. Personal spending was reduced significantly, by increased indirect taxation. Deflation was not to Dalton's liking. The chancellor had accidently leaked some details to a journalist on his way to the chamber, and he resigned the following day. Attlee gave Cripps the treasury, while allowing him to remain minister of economic affairs. He was now economic overlord, and was to be – perhaps – the most powerful chancellor in the twentieth century. The new president of the board of trade recalls writing 'a ... sad ... letter of condolence'[21] to Dalton, Wilson having, in an earlier letter, thanked Dalton for advising him on a series of problems. Harold Wilson was even closer to the new chancellor, and a cabinet colleague, but the labour government was now firmly committed to retrenchment. When Cripps created the new post of economic secretary, to allow Jay to join the government towards the end of 1947, Hugh Gaitskell noted: 'We must now try and bring Evan [Durbin] into the inner Cripps circle. If we can do this I shall really begin to feel quite happy about the Government.'[22]

Evan Durbin, who had succeeded Wilson at the ministry of works, came from a west country nonconformist background. In this, he resembled the new president of the board of trade. Both made it to Oxford, where Durbin, ten years Wilson's senior, met Gaitskell. Economic policy in the labour government was now predominantly in the hands of Wykehamists. Cripps had been to Winchester (but not Oxford), as, of course, had Gaitskell. Douglas Jay was two years behind Gaitskell, though he was not actually to speak to him at Winchester or New College. George Strauss had been to Rugby, and John Strachey – like Dalton – at Eton. Harold Wilson, like some of the others, had been an economics don. But he was the odd person out, by virtue of social origins, age, recent political success, and an absence of a socialist intellectual culture – or even a decided view about economics.

Gaitskell had a power base, if the term may be used, in the XYZ Club. This had been established after the 1931 débâcle for the labour party, which saw the national government forced to devalue the pound. Two secret labour supporters, Vaughan Berry and Nicholas Davenport, who believed still in private enterprise, held a first meeting at a restaurant in the city in early 1932. They sought to influence the party's economic and financial policies. Davenport, a financial journalist, proposed a national investment board, and an industrial finance corporation. Berry was an early advocate of the nationalization of the Bank of England.

The XYZ Club was to be secret, but also informal. Its founders hoped to educate what was then the party of George Lansbury in the ways of the city. Hugh Dalton used the club to shape party policy in the 1930s. He recruited, at various times, Hugh Gaitskell, then an academic, Francis Williams, at the time city editor of the *Daily Herald*, his successor Douglas Jay, and Evan Durbin, then also an academic in London. These intellectuals , all with political ambitions, regularly met progressive financiers, such as George Strauss and John Wilmot, in Soho restaurants or each other's flats. It was hardly a political conspiracy, more a freemasonry of socialist economists. The XYZ Club sought to anticipate the shape of an imminent war economy from 1936. It formally ceased to advise the labour party in 1939, but, by then, the job had been done.

Many of its members became temporary civil servants during the war, lunching together regularly at a pub in Villiers Street, near the ministry of supply. Right-wing labourism, under the coalition government, was becoming a practical proposition. During the succeeding years of the Attlee government, the club dined, once a fortnight, on Wednesdays, in a private room at the house of commons. It was then a talking shop for trained economists. Factionalism in the labour party had yet to develop, but XYZ was a would-be social democratic grouping. Douglas Jay lists Harold Wilson as one of those recruited in the 1940s and 1950s (the others included Jack Diamond, Frank Pakenham, Jim Callaghan, Douglas Houghton, Bill Rodgers, Nicholas Kaldor, James Meade, Patrick Gordon Walker, Anthony Crosland, Roy Jenkins, Len Murray and Robert Neild). Francis Williams was to summarize the impact of XYZ: 'It has ... some claim to have exercised in a quiet sort of way more influence on future government policy than any other group of the time and to have done so in the most private manner without attracting publicity to itself.'[23]

Cripps had not been involved in XYZ in the 1930s, beyond the occasional visit as a guest. He was then very much on the left, being expelled from the labour party in early 1939, along with Aneurin Bevan and George Strauss, on the question of the popular front. The war allowed him to become a national leader, in the fight against Nazism, as a member of the war cabinet and, later, minister of aircraft production. He rejoined the labour party in 1945, having long abandoned any Marxian ideas. George Orwell had been surprised to find him indifferent to the question of capitalism or socialism: 'I saw that I was up against the official mind, which sees everything as a problem in administration and does not grasp that at a certain point, i.e. when certain economic interests are threatened, public spirit ceases to function.'[24] Cripps was an extremely dynamic minister at the board of trade, and the ideal chancellor to impose austerity on the British people. His moralism was not self-seeking. Having accumulated power, the new chancellor chose to direct the economy through a collegiality of ministers. It took the institutional form of fortnightly dinners, again at the house of commons, on Thursdays, in the weeks XYZ did not meet. Cripps looked after the bill, having amassed a fortune when at the bar. He was joined by Bevan (from April 1948) and Wilson, fellow cabinet ministers, and Douglas Jay from the treasury. Senior ministers included Marquand (who was to be moved to pensions in 1948), Gaitskell, Strauss and Strachey. The debates at the group dinners, Douglas Jay recalls, 'varied between general economic disquisitions from Strachey and factual reports on the world cereal, timber or metal markets from Harold Wilson.'[25] Gaitskell shared Jay's view of the minister of food as 'too inclined to abstract theory'.[26] He was not yet critical of Wilson. After a dinner on 22 April 1948, he wrote in his diary: 'I could not help feeling that Stafford was surveying his future Cabinet.'

The economists of XYZ felt they were well placed, even with the change of chancellor. Cripps listened to them, but he remained his own man. Bevan had been a major political ally. Harold Wilson, having slipped the leash of Beveridge, was dependent on labour's new economic visionary. Sir Stafford became Harold Wilson's new model: 'He had always much admired Cripps, and thought him a great man. But now he suddenly seemed even greater. Cripps, the man he was to succeed, was an elder statesman. Wilson, in comparison, felt he was still a glorified civil servant.' He later repeated the first words of his new permanent secretary, Sir John Woods: 'I'm sure I'm speaking for all of us when I say nobody can replace Stafford. But I'm sure they've chosen you as the person who'll come nearest to it. We've all a great respect for you – but nobody will ever be another Stafford.'[27]

Harold Wilson can have seen little of Gladys and Robin in 1947, as he was in Oxford for only one weekend that summer. Herbert Wilson – still in London – reached retiring age in December 1947. He and Ethel sold the house in Huddersfield, and seem to have retired to the west country, to St Austell. The way was now clear for the Wilsons to move back to Richmond. But Gladys had become pregnant in the late summer, and it was a question of finding a family house. The new president of the board of trade experienced a jump in his ministerial salary from £1,500 to £5,000. Herbert also had capital available. It was reported in the press that the young cabinet minister was on the lookout for somewhere to live in London. A local vicar, knowing that a conservative MP was moving out of Hampstead Garden Suburb, passed this information to Patrick Gordon Walker, now a junior minister, who lived in South Square. Wilson came to purchase 10 Southway for £5,100. His father gave him a loan of £800, more than enough to cover the deposit, and the rest was raised on a mortgage. It was a substantial three-bedroomed, detached house with garden, asymmetrical and partly tile-hung. Dating from the Edwardian years, but part of the planned garden suburb movement, Southway had been built for artisans. By the late 1940s it was most definitely middle class. The Wilson family moved in around the turn of the year. They joined the local free church, though religion meant little to Harold. Robin was sent to the mixed nursery at the nearby school, and, in May 1948, Gladys gave birth to another boy. Thanking the prime minister for a telegram of congratulations, Wilson wrote to 'My dear Clem': The baby 'for his part, although about the size and general appearance of a trout, would, if he were capable of it, wish to be associated with me in writing to thank you for your message.'[28] He was named Giles after an Oxford friend, Giles Allington, a brother-in-law of the future conservative prime minister, Sir Alec Douglas-Home. The Attlees became his godparents

Hampstead Garden Suburb was attractive to a provincial professional man, and 10 Southway remained private to the Wilson family, and the few friends Gladys made locally. Harold did not bring party colleagues there, largely because he eschewed political entertaining, and Gladys had little desire to be a politician's wife. The garden suburb was not too far up the Finchley Road from Hampstead, where Hugh Gaitskell had bought a house, in Frognal Gardens, in 1946. The Wilsons were to attend the Gaitskells' new year's eve party in 1950. After drinking in the new year, Eva Robens, wife of Alf, then parliamentary secretary at fuel and power, 'looked hard at Harold Wilson and said, "You come from North of the Trent, don't you? Surely, you know how to behave!" And then proceeded to fling her arms around him and kiss him passionately, to his very great embarrassment. As he had previously been giving a lecture on why the ladies could not obtain nylons – which was full of statistics but all very sober – the incident gave great pleasure.'[29]

Frank Pakenham, now ennobled and a member of the government, and one of Gaitskell's strongest admirers, lived near to the Wilsons between 1947 and 1950. They had the same doctor, and their children were to attend each others' parties. The Wilsons were not incorporated into the local socialist intelligentsia, but this was not because Harold was left wing. Wilson was ten years younger than Gaitskell, and had also made it to the cabinet in a little over two years. 'He was very much our junior, yet could not be treated as such.' 'His views on social intercourse [were] so unusual among the professional classes', preferring work to dinner parties and other social occasions. This 'inhibit[ed] the development of friendships and the warmer kind of relationships with other politicians'.[30] He was not clubbable.

Wilson and Gaitskell were then heavy cigarette smokers. Nicotine addiction was understood as conducive to sociability, and smoking was even permitted in cabinet meetings. Shortly after Wilson took over at the board of trade, the import of United States's tobacco was suspended by the prime minister, in order to save dollars. Attlee banned smoking in cabinet. Duty had been increased by 50 per cent in the spring, but the cabinet decided against any further rise in Dalton's autumn budget. Gaitskell gave up smoking when the price of cigarettes rose, and Harold Wilson recalls that it was in Moscow, in December 1947, that he began to smoke a pipe, in order to temporize in negotiations. It was to be an important prop in his political stagecraft.

The *Ormskirk Advertiser* described Wilson's promotion to the cabinet in 1947 as giving 'the utmost satisfaction to all sections of his constituents',[31] at the point at which he was considering abandoning the seat. The boundary commission had moved quickly to equalize votes across the country after the war, the proposed redistribution of Lancashire and Liverpool seats being known by June 1947. It was clear for some months that Croxteth was to be returned to Liverpool, and that Ormskirk would revert to being a predominantly rural seat. It was considerably reduced in size. Harold Wilson might be a successful senior minister, but he was facing political defeat – it was thought – in 1949. The issue was to be resolved at a four-hour meeting of the divisional labour party on Saturday, 27 November 1948. Wilson declined the local party's invitation to be its candidate in the next general election, claiming that ministerial duties

prevented him attending to such a large constituency. It was known he had
been invited to stand for a new Lancashire seat. At a meeting in Progress
Hall in Page Moss the following day, he formally became the candidate for
Huyton. It included a part of the old Ormskirk, but there was no significant continuity, it being more the existing Widnes seat.

Harold Wilson concentrated for much of 1948 on the board of trade,
the bureaucratic leviathan in Millbank which accounted for 10 per cent of
the administrative class of the civil service. He had a general responsibility for trade and industry, including production, exports and imports, and
prices. There was also a miscellany of unrelated items, such as industrial
location, films, clothes rationing, and company law. The president of the
board of trade took departmental issues to cabinet committees. He spoke
on trade and industry, rather than the full range of economic and political
affairs. He was required to make announcements in the house, but was not
responsible for any major legislation.

Stafford Cripps's parliamentary private secretaries at the board of trade
had been John Evans and Barbara Castle. Castle was an administrative officer
in the ministry of food during the war, and entered parliament in 1945.
When Cripps was made minister of economic affairs, he declined to take
her to the treasury, on the grounds that it would be too boring for her.
'Look, I don't go with the furniture', she told him, but Harold Wilson was
willing to keep her on when he became president of the board of trade.
This political relationship, so casually begun, was to be enduring. She
remembers Wilson was 'dreadfully dull as a parliamentary speaker', his
speeches being mainly exhortations to increase exports. Wilson was made
aware of the problem, and was willing to accept criticism. Later he would
be considered almost masochistic, in the way he allowed some members
of his staff to berate him when prime minister. 'He obviously made a
conscious decision that he was going to become a parliamentary speaker.
We worked on it', recalls Castle, 'and he quickly developed a much better
debating style ... a quite remarkable transformation.'[32] Castle recalls him
as 'a very conventional man in some ways', though 'instinctively egalitar-
ian'. He was proud of his background, his achievements, and had 'a good
healthy self confidence'. This may have been the appearance.

'His main concern was to ensure that Board of Trade affairs ran smoothly
under him',[33] by becoming involved in much detailed work. Harold
Wilson strongly identified with civil servants. 'There was no "side" to him
[as president,] and he easily established friendly relations with all ranks.'[34]
He was extremely cautious about taking decisions, and was compared
unfavourably with Cripps in this respect. But his method was seen to be
more soundly based on the facts of the matter. Wilson would later deny
having been self confident in the board of trade, claiming that he was only
51 per cent certain of decisions on which he had spent hours. If senior civil

servants were irritated, they were also able to avert other decisions by swamping the president in paper. He was also – ominously – keen to please manufacturers and other businessmen, and accepted invitations to many lunches and dinners given by trade associations. This increased his workload, since he usually had to give a speech. It also brought a labour minister into contact with importers and exporters, all of whom were keen to make money out of the peace.

Harold Wilson became an expert on international trade, in particular Britain's position in the world economy. The country's exports before the war, mainly of manufactured goods, plus so-called invisible earnings, had paid for its imports, comprising largely food and raw materials. Trade had been in balance. The invisible earnings, especially foreign investments and shipping, were lost during the war, and the continuing military commitment overseas was adding to external liabilities, the empire becoming less a source of supply. The United States's policy of lend-lease during the war saw Britain continue to import from across the Atlantic. General world shortages increased prices, while the pre-war pattern of exporting to British dominions and colonies continued. There had been a loss of markets to the United States and other competitors, while productivity abroad was also higher. Harold Wilson saw the retention of British prestige in terms of a new balance in international trade, though he was unable to admit that the United States was now dominant. As the possessor of the hard-currency dollar, the US was in a position to help Europe, by importing from Britain and other former leading economies. But it was not clear why the American government, and especially congress, should seek to balance its trade with Europe. Harold Wilson's job was simply to do something. An export target was fixed for 1948, of 60 per cent over the 1938 figure. The 1946 exports had been slightly below, and those of 1947 just above the pre-war figure. Government policy was justifed by optimism about the future: 'when the present sellers' market comes to an end we may, as the world's greatest buyer have less to fear than most.'[35] The emphasis was on exports to the United States, to earn the dollars to pay for essential imports.

Wilson was concerned mainly with the rules governing the international market and the expansion of trade, the British government being committed to enshrining the idea of a 'one world multilateral trading system'[36] in the charter of the ITO. It also attempted to reduce protectionism in the form of tariffs, quotas and preferences, where and whenever it could. The first months of Wilson's presidency had coincided with the united nations conference on trade and employment in Cuba, involving 62 countries. Arthur Bottomley, his successor in overseas trade, led the British delegation to the Havana conference. Lord Bottomley, as he now is, recalls that Wilson 'was quite content to leave me to handle things. He had confidence in me ... And I formed a friendship with him, got to know his parents and his sister.'[37] Wilson presented a white paper to parliament in April 1948, containing the final act and the Havana charter for an international trade organization, but it was to be May 1949 before he advised Attlee that the charter should be ratified. Multilateral tariff negotiations had also taken place at the Geneva preparatory committee in 1947, resulting in the general agreement on tariffs and trade, to be known as GATT. Britain applied this provisionally, since, with the export drive, it was in its immediate interest to bring down trade barriers. As for the ITO, 'in the long run', Wilson wrote, 'we are more likely to gain than to lose from promoting multilateral international co-operation in the trade sphere.'[38] The refusal of the American congress to ratify the charter undermined the ITO, and this meant that Britain did not have to ratify GATT. Economic nationalism was again frustrating global free trade. The United States then committed itself to the GATT process, but, in the unlikely setting of Torquay, in early 1951, bilateral tariff negotiations between the United States and Britain were to break down. The latter refused to abandon preferences for empire goods. One member of the economic policy committee, possibly Bevan, made the point that 'our refusal to agree to the United States proposals afforded evidence, which might be useful, that we did not on all occasions follow the United States line.'[39]

Harold Wilson came to public attention over the removal of wartime controls. The labour left cherished their continuation, but as Ian Mikardo, a backbench MP, admits, it was 'not easy to work out opposition against something which [was] popular'.[40] Cripps, anxious to encourage private industry in the export drive, favoured a gradual return to economic freedom. Physical controls had only worked when there was scarcity. Rationing was now irrelevant, but the key was timing. Decontrol became government policy, but it was handled in a piecemeal way. On 4 November 1948, Wilson announced a 'bonfire of [production] controls'. This was a veritable battery of measures by which the state had manipulated industry since 1940. Cripps had continued the rationing of food and other domestic items into 1948, restrictions on bread being lifted in July after two years. The principle met with least opposition among the working class, it being seen as the fairest way of distributing resources. But Harold Wilson believed that rationing only protected the inefficient and penalized the enterprising. As a liberalizer, he came under pressure from manufacturers, who were happy to work within rationing constraints, since they were at least guaranteed a share of the market. Clothes rationing came to an end in March 1949, Wilson's officials having been pressing for this. The president of the board of trade again exploited the event, tearing up a ration book in front of photographers. Gladys Wilson was even roped in, for what may have been her first appearance in the national press as the wife of an up-and-coming political figure. A second 'bonfire of controls' followed a few days later. Much of this, plus the relaxation of food rationing, was encouraged by Morrison. He had an eye to the middle-class vote in the general election, the housewives' league being an important pressure group. It was felt that rationing and controls were the main contribution to the government's unpopularity. The *New Statesman*, however, remained especially critical of the president of the board of trade, and he was to be accused as late as March 1951 of 'bland capitulation to rationing by price'.[41]

Harold Wilson's most notable achievement in this period was in the help he gave the British film industry. It was an area in which Cripps took an interest. The United States set out to regain its commercial, and therefore cultural, preeminence after the war, and Cripps imposed a levy on imported product. The American government was displeased, and Hollywood retaliated with a trade embargo. No new American films came to Britain. There was an opportunity for the British film industry, though leading producers looked to the government for investment.

Wilson inherited the problem of the American embargo in September 1947, the new president of the board of trade being partly concerned about Marshall aid. This required an improvement in Anglo-American commercial relations. Old American films were being run time and time again, and a million dollars a week remitted to the United States. Under pressure from domestic distributors and exhibitors, Wilson opened negotiations in London with Hollywood executives. An agreement was announced in February 1948. The British levy was abolished, but American production companies would only be allowed to take £17 million out each year for a period. This was on the assumption that British films did not earn in the United States. Capital acquisition was not to be permitted, and excess income had to be devoted to the arts and sciences in Britain. Hollywood was to donate two million dollars to the project for a national theatre. Wilson won himself some friends in Britain in the film industry, and also helped remove an obstacle in the way of the European recovery programme. But a subsequent increase in the quota for British films was considered, by the Americans, to be sharp practice.

The president of the board of trade, with Cripps in the treasury, came to accept the idea of state subsidy, and the government legislated for a levy on cinema tickets, to be known after a senior treasury official, Sir Wilfrid Eady. This money was to be disbursed to producers by a national film finance corporation (NFFC) set up in 1949. Harold Wilson made Nigel Davenport, the radical financier and journalist, a member of the NFFC, but the latter was to resign from the corporation. 'If [Harold Wilson] had been a real socialist', Davenport wrote years later, 'he would, of course, have nationalised or municipalised the two great cinema circuits.'[42]

Cripps may be considered the first real Keynesian chancellor, given his use of demand management. He sought to increase production and productivity, the machinery of the state, through the government's economic policy and production committees, being geared to an export drive. The former committee was usually chaired by Attlee, the latter, which took over the economic work of the lord president's committee, was run by Cripps. Harold Wilson was a full member of the production committee, the board of trade having a general responsibility for industry. It was also Wilson's job regularly to announce the trade figures, which gradually became better. Britain's share of Marshall aid – $1,263 million in 1948–9 – helped to boost economic growth. So did a boom in north America. 1948 was one of the best years for the British economy in a long time, the balance of payments going into the black. Cripps maintained something approximating to full employment, keeping inflation down by controlling consumption. There was considerable planning, not for socialism, but economic self-sufficiency, rebuilding the national economy by paying for imports with exports. Cripps sought to improve the conditions in which employers produced goods and services for export, this determining the policy on controls. The government's attempt to control wages, with an indefinite freeze announced in early 1948, was not to the liking of the trade unions. His budgets of 1948 and 1949 were designed to restrict personal consumption further, though a high level of social spending was maintained. Harold Wilson gradually came to play a role in economic management, but was remarkably attentive to US interests. Cripps was prepared to accept American dollars, but he did not believe in becoming dependent. Following the convertibility crisis of 1947, the government decided to cut the investment programme by £200 million. The president of the board of trade took a departmental line in the production committee, trying to defend the engineering industry at the forefront of the export drive. The major struggle was waged by Bevan and Key, who resisted bringing the housing programme into balance before mid-1949. There is no evidence of Harold Wilson supporting the government's leading socialist at this stage. The United States was keen on a customs union for western Europe, but he espoused 'the achievement of a closer economic integration ... by more practical and immediate means'.[43] This meant in effect slowing down the work of the international study group set up in Brussels at the behest of the Americans.

Harold Wilson was less prominent in the deliberations about European economic cooperation, possibly because it was a matter principally for the foreign office. He was more forthcoming about the ITO, being committed to international free trade. Though the economic policy committee took a tactical anti-American line at the end of 1947, when the conference in Havana to consider the draft charter looked like breaking up, Wilson succeeded in pulling it back when the crisis passed. He was unsympathetic to the desire of underdeveloped countries to impose quotas, while insistent that Britain, given its balance of payments difficulty, should have the right to resort to protection. He was equally nationalistic in 1948, when the question of Soviet trade came up again, and was prepared to exploit the Russians' shortage of sterling. On the industrial regeneration of the American and British zones in Germany – Bizonia – he warned about the damage which could be done to British exports. When there was talk of an international tin agreement in early 1949, he, again unsuccessfully, argued for discussions with Belgium and the Netherlands as producers 'related solely to purchases of tin for the United States stockpile'.[44] He was able to help Ormskirk and Huyton, being responsible for the 1945 act under which development areas were designated. A white paper was published in October 1948 on the working of the act. In the three and a half years he was to be at Millbank, Wilson designated two areas – one was part of the highlands and islands of Scotland, the other Merseyside. This was announced in early 1949, the year in which he expected a general election. 'It wasn't for love of Wilson', recalls Peter Longworth who had proposed his adoption for Huyton, 'but we wanted to be included in the development area.'[45]

A whiff of scandal, the only one to affect the Attlee government, had touched the board of trade in the autumn of 1948. Harold Wilson was not personally implicated, but he was to be attacked by Churchill over the involvement of his parliamentary secretary, John Belcher, who had been appointed in Cripps's time.

The scandal concerned one Sydney Stanley, originally Solomon Kohsyzcky, a Polish-born Jewish businessman. Stanley conned money by pretending to have powerful friends. It was to be alleged that Stanley, and other Jewish businessmen, had bribed ministers and public servants for licences and contracts. Belcher had been a worry to both Cripps and Wilson. In May 1948, when Belcher failed to take an adjournment debate, Wilson spoke to Attlee about the parliamentary secretary's drinking. Wilson was to maintain that nothing was known about Belcher's friendship with Stanley, in spite of the fact that the latter frequently visited Belcher's private office, much to the consternation of civil servants.

The unease of officials in the board of trade was brought formally to the president's notice on 30 August. The permanent secretary, Sir John Woods, told Wilson of rumours that Belcher was being influenced to withdraw a prosecution against a football pools firm for breaching the paper control. Wilson seems to have called in the police. He also reported directly to Attlee, and the lord chancellor became involved. The police investigation proceeded, and Belcher appeared to incriminate himself by mentioning his friendship with Stanley. It was Friday, 15 October before the parliamentary secretary, after a meeting with Wilson, asked to go on leave for the duration of the inquiry. The president suggested to Attlee it would be wise to avoid the Sunday press, so he was allowing Belcher to open the Dorset industries exhibition on the following day. The cabinet approved the membership of a tribunal, on 28 October, to be chaired by Mr Justice Lynskey, to inquire into allegations reflecting on the official conduct of ministers of the crown and other public servants. It sat for twenty-five days in November and December, during which fifty-eight people gave oral evidence (and there were two affidavits), nineteen of the witnesses being represented by lawyers. Those called before the tribunal were examined by the attorney general, Sir Hartley Shawcross.

Attlee told the cabinet on 6 December that Stanley was due to give his evidence. It was feared a number of ministers were to be named. The lord chancellor suggested that members of the government should make themselves available, but leave it to the tribunal to summon them if necessary. Not appearing would not be construed as guilt. This suggests Lynskey and his two legal colleagues were helping the government as a whole. Among those named, aside from Belcher, was Hugh Dalton, now back in the government as chancellor of the duchy of Lancaster, Charles Key, and George Gibson, a trade unionist who had been made a director of the bank of England. An unprecedented amount of information about ministers' dealings with businessmen was made public. All allegations were examined. Belcher had sought to remove the controls in the cosmetics industry, and Harold Wilson had overruled him.

The Stanley affair was one of the most serious issues to face the Attlee government. Proof of corruption, from a tribunal of inquiry, was enough to blow an administration out of office, and the future of labour leaders depended, to some extent, on Harold Wilson, the weak link in the cabinet. Though he was to try to rope Cripps into the question of responsibility for Belcher, he had to admit privately to Attlee that most of the alleged incidents had occurred under his presidency. It cannot have been a pleasant time for him during the winter of 1948-9, and he succumbed to 'a comparatively mild attack of jaundice'.[46]

It was 21 January 1949 before Lynskey and his colleagues released their findings, initially to the government. They found that Belcher had been friendly with Stanley, but only that he had dropped the prosecution against Sherman, the head of the football pools firm. Belcher had resigned from the government during the inquiry, but he was not replaced, by J. Edwards, until 1 February.

Harold Wilson was to say later 'that he himself thought privately that if the Tribunal could have been more familiar with the complexities and pressures of a vast department ... where each day scores of quick decisions might have to be reached on such vital matters as controls or dispensations or special allocations, the findings on Belcher might have been less critical.'[47]

Gibson also stood down. Dalton survived as a member of the cabinet. Key, with some effort, managed to remain minister of works. Lynskey stressed that there was nothing against the permanent secretary of the board of trade, but James Cross, Belcher's private secretary, was found to have accepted gifts. The tribunal attributed most of the rumours to Stanley. For his own financial gain, he had put it about that he could secure favours from, in particular, the board of trade. 'Mr Stanley', read the report, 'is a man who will make any statement, whether true or untrue, if he thinks that it is to his own advantage to so do. He was, however, able to give colour to his statements because Mr. Belcher, Mr. Gibson and Mr. Key received him on apparently friendly terms and it is not therefore surprising that rumours arose and that these baseless allegations of payments of large sums of money were made.'[48]

The report was debated in parliament on 3 February, when Belcher made a resignation speech. Harold Wilson spoke briefly, stating that James Cross had not been criticized. Churchill and Sir John Anderson criticized the government in general, and Wilson in particular, on the grounds of ministerial responsibility. Wilson was clearly rattled, and the issue must have simmered. He wrote a 'Personal and Secret' letter to the prime minister on 15 February, seeking, and receiving, permission to send copies to Morrison and Cripps. On Churchill and Anderson's criticism, Wilson wrote that 'it was easy enough to make these comments after the event, but apart from the general question of drink and Belcher's intemperate habits, neither Stafford nor [he] had, or could have had, any idea of the seriousness of what was going on.' Neither of them could have known about Stanley, 'unless [they] had started from the hypothesis that [Belcher] was not to be trusted and had, in fact, had him spied on'. Belcher's two private secretaries had, separately, reported to Wilson's private secretary on the question of drink, but were unaware of meetings outside the ministry. Wilson admitted that the civil servants in question had set aside their loyalty to their minister.[49] Attlee let the issue rest.

In the spring of 1949, a recession in the United States led to a downturn in British exports, threatening another balance of payments crisis. This was to lead to a change in the exchange rate of the pound from $4.03 to $2.80, the chancellor announcing this devaluation of 30 per cent on Sunday, 18 September. The illness of Cripps in the summer saw Harold Wilson intimately involved in the crisis, but the key role came to be played by Hugh Gaitskell.

Wilson flew to Canada on 10 May on a trade mission. Barbara Castle was in the party. Wilson was to have flown 15,000 miles by 1 June, as he told his cabinet colleagues on return, visiting all but two provinces. He gave nine formal, and fourteen informal, speeches, nine broadcasts (including one in French on Quebec radio), held thirty-six meetings with various organizations, and had forty interviews with business representatives. All this was reported in a characteristically lengthy paper, packed with detail and illustrative annexes.

The president of the board of trade came up with nineteen specific recommendations, urging an emphasis on exports to Canada in order to earn dollars. He admitted that the recession would make it difficult to maintain even present levels of trade. Wilson claimed that, '[during his] visit the main line of comment on United Kingdom economic policy switched from attacks on the limited scale of our purchases to criticism of our inadequate export efforts.' He noted of a meeting with his Canadian and United States oppposite numbers in Toronto, that 'the Trade Ministers of the three greatest trading countries ... met together for the first time in history'.[50] This was a typically boastful assessment. When the report was circulated on 23 June to members of the economic policy committee, it accompanied a simple memorandum on exports to Canada.

The government was taking the 'economic situation' seriously by June, the gold and dollar reserves draining month after month as a result of speculation. Some British officials were convinced of the need for a change in the exchange rate, but ministers, by and large, were wary of precipitate action. Alec Cairncross had argued in the board of trade at the end of 1948 for devaluation, and reiterated his view in a paper to Wilson the following March, though Cairncross knew from Max Brown, the president's principal private secretary, that their master did not fight in cabinet. Cripps, Dalton, Alexander and Addison discussed the dollar position at the economic policy committee on 15 June. Wilson was also present throughout, but Gaitskell only attended for two other items. At a group dinner in late June, with Cripps absent, the economic ministers all came out against devaluation and deflation; 'we would have to move in the direction', Gaitskell noted, 'of a more closely controlled trade system with discrimination against the dollar, but try to build up multilateralism in non-dollar areas.'[51]

The economic policy committee considered the balance of payments problem into July; the reserves of $1,564 million seemed on the tenth like running out in forty weeks. National bankruptcy stared Britain in the face. Cripps had already made a statement on 6 July, when Bridges, now the permanent secretary at the treasury, urged 'disinflation'.[52] The commons debated the issue between 14 and 18 July. Devaluation had been discussed on 1 July in the economic policy committee, but Cripps rejected it on 9 July when suggested by Snyder, the United States's treasury secretary. The British did not like the American hints about devaluation, but the chancellor promised to keep the Americans informed. Cripps was to be concerned, above all, with this promise to the treasury secretary. He also felt bound by all his previous denials of devaluation. It is thought that Attlee and Morrison were in favour at an early point, but Dalton opposed to devaluation. 'Harold Wilson', according to a Gaitskell note of 3 August, 'now says he also favoured it then, but if so he certainly did not say so.'

Cripps fell ill. He was to leave for a sanitorium in Zürich on 19 July, and Attlee took formal responsibility for the treasury. He left day-to-day financial policy to the three Oxford economists, Wilson, Gaitskell and Jay, plus the financial secretary to the treasury. Wilson was the most senior, and only cabinet minister, but Jay, in the treasury, was close to Gaitskell. Gaitskell 'fanc[ied] that [he] was brought in largely because [he] happened to be one of the few Ministers in London in the first three weeks of August.'[53] Commonwealth finance ministers had been meeting in London, and Wilson was to report on the conference to the cabinet on 25 July. This conference was crucial to Jay, who was included on the British team. The United States had cut purchases throughout the sterling area, and Britain's exports were now priced too highly. Wilson, who had responsibility for circulating treasury papers, told his senior colleagues that an agreed package of dollar import cuts might be reported confidentially to members of the United States administration. Cripps had instituted regular reporting on the dollar reserves, and it fell to Wilson to sign the chits to sell gold from the reserves.

Douglas Jay had come down on the side of devaluation on 17 July. The same conclusion was reached, independently, by Hugh Gaitskell. The two men discussed this policy on 20 July, and, at a group dinner the following night, won over Bevan, Strachey and Strauss. Harold Wilson was absent, but Gaitskell and Jay had seen him earlier that day: 'He ... made it plain that he agreed in the main, though he was not so sure on the timing. He favoured devaluation *fairly* soon but not before the Washington talks.'[54] Trade talks were to be held with the United States and Canadian governments, between 7 and 12 September, before an international monetary fund meeting the following day. Douglas Jay was to recall that the three economists reached agreement on 21 July, and the treasury knights were told on 22 July, by Sir Edward Bridges, to prepare for devaluation. The economic ministers still wished to keep their options open, and were reluctant to fix a date. Wilson, Gaitskell and Jay, in a meeting with Bridges and two of his colleagues on Monday, 25 July, agreed that devaluation was necessary before the end of September. This view they put to Attlee, Morrison and Dalton, that evening. It was apparently at this meeting that Wilson, in the opinion of Gaitskell and Jay, shifted position, being much less keen on devaluation. He thought there might be an early general election. The cabinet, at three meetings that week, declined to take the decision. Though Harold Wilson had argued the treasury line on 25 July, that Britain should devalue during the planned talks in Washington, he was less forceful. Two days later, probably with reference to Jay, he complained '"there was too much talking"'.[55] The three economists met with Attlee and Morrison on 28 July, and it was agreed to recommend devaluation, after Cripps returned but before the Washington talks. This position had been advocated by Attlee and Gaitskell, against Morrison and Jay, who were for immediate devaluation, and Harold Wilson, who still wanted to wait until Washington.

Douglas Jay was to recall a second shift of opinion on the part of the president of the board of trade at this meeting. Walking across Palace Yard after the meeting, Morrison, according to Jay, 'used some unsympathetic expressions about Wilson'.[56] His Janian response, a product of dependence on, partly, the treasury but, mainly, Cripps, led Gaitskell and Jay to distrust him. 'He trims and wavers', Dalton was to note in his diary, 'and is thinking more of what senior Ministers – and even senior officials – are thinking of him than of what is right.'[57] It was decided that Wilson, who was planning to drive to Annecy, close to the Swiss border, should seek the opinion of Cripps in his Zürich clinic. He was also to sound out Bevin. Only a member of the cabinet could do this, but Attlee asked Gaitskell and Jay to draft the letter. At a final cabinet on 29 July, he ruled that there were to be no emergency meetings of the government in August. He would take any necessary decision after consulting available ministers. The treasury sought to reaffirm its preferred date, in its version of the draft letter to Cripps, causing Gaitskell to fight for Jay's original version. It is possibly at this point, that Wilson was eclipsed – in the opinion of Attlee – by Gaitskell.

Gaitskell and Jay negotiated with the treasury on the text of the letter, which they took down to Attlee at Chequers on 5 August. The prime minister signed the compromise draft, representing devaluation as now the consensual view of economic ministers and officials. Attlee wanted a government decision on the timing, before the Washington talks. Max Brown actually brought the prime minister's letter to Zürich, handing it to Wilson, who gave it to Cripps on 8 August. Attlee took the view that there was no hope of American aid. He ruled out Sunday, 11 September as devaluation day, since finance ministers would then be travelling to the meeting of the international monetary fund. 18 September was the last possible Sunday. The chancellor seems to have concurred, but urged the need for a general election. Wilson helped him write a letter. Douglas Jay certainly believes the chancellor assented, though he was not privy to the conversation of the two ministers. Only Attlee heard Cripps's opinions directly, via the letter Wilson brought back. The latter reported to his ministerial colleagues the following week, on his discussions with Cripps and Bevin. Cripps was described as 'by no means convinced of the need for devaluation, and in any case did not at all like the idea of doing it before the Washington Conference'.[58] The foreign secretary felt the same about

Washington, though he was to accept the idea of devaluation in due course.

When Cripps returned for a meeting of ministers at Chequers on 19 August, he had to be persuaded all over again in the course of three hours. The treasury, having belatedly accepted devaluation, now saw little virtue in postponing it. Wilson and Gaitskell (plus Bridges) joined Attlee, Bevin and Cripps in finally deciding upon devaluation. Gaitskell argued in favour, but Harold Wilson was against an early date. Bevin came round to the idea, and, though Cripps was still sceptical, it seemed to be accepted. The chancellor was against an early date, and Attlee did not force him. The treasury knights were informed the following morning. Gaitskell was to accept later that Cripps's illness prevented an early devaluation. The cabinet concurred on 29 August, though the decision was not unanimous. Cripps and Bevin were due to sail to Washington, and it was now accepted that the United States government had to be forewarned.

Gaitskell was clearly now in the ascendant. He, with Jay, had directed the interdepartmental group of officials who prepared the brief for Washington. Attlee stated he would watch the progress of the talks with his economic triumvirate. Sunday, 18 September had long been the most likely day. At 6.45 p.m. on 17 September, following the return of Cripps and Bevin from Washington, ministers assembled in 10 Downing Street to approve the chancellor's broadcast talk. Wilson, Gaitskell and Jay entered through the front door of Number 11, as if to see Cripps. Other members of the cabinet scurried in by other entrances. The chancellor broadcast on the radio that night. Monday was declared a bank holiday. By the following day, the British half crown (2/6 or 12$\frac{1}{2}$p) was no longer equivalent to half an American dollar. Parliament was recalled. Bevan opened for the government on 29 September, the third day of the debate. This was the occasion when Harold Wilson, according to Michael Foot, 'gave the first hint the Commons had seen that he might wish to abandon his civil service brief and engage in the wider political argument'.[59]

In November – according to the memoirs of Douglas Jay – Wilson leaked his version of the devaluation saga to two national papers. According to this, he had been in favour, and secured the backing of Cripps in Zürich, while Gaitskell was opposed to devaluation. If he did leak, and there is circumstantial evidence to show that Wilson was already concerned about press coverage, this suggests he was out to do down Gaitskell. Given Cripps's ill health, Gaitskell was a candidate for the chancellorship. It is likely that Wilson saw this as a future prize for himself. Wilson had to move fast, claiming he was the architect of an apparently successful devaluation. Bridges's opinion about a new chancellor would, it seems, carry some weight with Attlee, but those of Cripps and Morrison were also thought to count. Jay attributes Wilson's actual dilatoriness in July to the latter's belief that

Bridges was then still opposed, but Wilson may have been deferring to Cripps. Wilson, despite all his energy, froze creatively when faced with a decision as gigantic as devaluation.

There followed a further round of public expenditure cuts, which had been considered during the dollar crisis, the government accepting that deflation was a necessary consequence of a devaluation. The issue had to be fought out in October. At two meetings of the economic policy committee on 14 October, ministers, including Wilson and Gaitskell, discussed Cripps's papers on the international financial position and combating inflation. Gaitskell was supportive of the chancellor, but Wilson did not take a strong line either way. Bevan again put up a fight, trying to defend his housing programme and the national health service. The cabinet reluctantly accepted on 21 October the treasury view that there should be prescription charges of a shilling (5p). Old age pensioners were excluded. Perhaps more importantly, it cut 25,000 houses from the planned 200,000 programme. The minister of health subsequently told Attlee this was 'ill-balanced', since he had expected a real cut in the defence budget. 'Even at this late hour', Bevan wrote, 'I suggest that we modify our plans accordingly.'[60] Bevan had been threatening to resign. Having supported devaluation, and therefore the government's economic strategy, it was now difficult to come out in defence of socialist principles. The government went on to prune national and local administration, in order not to destroy the social services. The prescription charge was quietly enacted on 9 December, but Bevan announced that implementation would depend on a fair and workable scheme being devised.

Wilson had crossed the Atlantic for a second time that year in November, leading the United Kingdom delegation to another FAO conference in Washington. He also worked on the dollar export drive and Anglo-American film problems while in the federal capital. He visited Chicago, New Orleans and New York in his second week, three of the four centres where superintending trade counsels were in post. As had been agreed beforehand, he made no public speeches, but there were informal addresses, press conferences, and two broadcasts, plus a television interview in Chicago. He met mainly American importers, and the agents of British exporters, and, at a social occasion in Washington, organized by the motion picture association, he had what he claimed was a lengthy discussion with President Truman and members of his cabinet. Wilson attended a lunch in New York given by the chairman of the same organization:

In the party were some of the leading and toughest New York businessmen ... In my capacity as Daniel in this den of lions I was able to deal with a wide range of questions on our national and international economic policies and I think, to get rid of a good deal of their misconceptions. While it would be very far from the truth to suggest that these tycoons were converted to Socialism during the lunch, they appeared to be going away with a much better understanding of what our economic problems were and how our Government was dealing with them ... Perhaps my most useful achievement at this and similar gatherings, was the proof I was able to give them that Social Democracy in Britain, so far from being a halfway house to Communism, was the most live and practical alternative to it.

It was a good argument for social democracy, but Wilson is unlikely to have altered the perceptions of these robber barons to the extent he suggests. His mission had been to increase British exports to the United States.

Wilson again reported to colleagues on his return, in a printed cabinet paper of thirty-five pages, including eight annexes. He came up with a list of sixteen recommendations, plus the conclusion that the poor state of trade was due to 'the inability and/or unwillingness (principally the latter) of United Kingdom exporters to seize the opportunities facing them'.[61]

CHAPTER 11

Out of Office, 1950–1

Some weeks after devaluation, Hugh Gaitskell was to write in his diary:

> It is a pity that Harold Wilson, whom I regard as extremely able and for
> that reason alone most valuable to the Government, should offend so
> many people by being so swollen headed. It may, of course, be that I
> am regarded as a rival of his and therefore my friends are always talking
> to me in deprecating terms about him. But I do not think this is
> altogether the case. What is depressing really is not so much that he is
> swollen headed but that his is such a very impersonal person. You don't
> feel that really you could ever be close friends with him, or in fact that
> he would ever have close friends. The dangers of friendship in politics
> are so great that when one starts with drawbacks of this kind the
> prospects are not too good.[1]

An impersonal person is a good description of Harold Wilson, though
Gaitskell's – very different – personality was to be a liability in his leadership
of the labour party.

A general election was expected through much of 1949, Herbert
Morrison having called for 'a victory of consolidation'.[2] His draft programme,
Labour Believes in Britain, which contained further nationalization measures,
was accepted by the party conference that year. The government was keen
to end controls and rationing, the bugbear of the most vocal sections of the
community, but the economy was affected, above all, by devaluation in
September. Cripps and Bevan continued to favour an early general election.
For the chancellor, it was a case of needing a new mandate from the people,
while Bevan was keen on a political resolution of the government's difficulties. Harold Wilson was in this camp, though he also gave the impression
of supporting the prime minister. The cabinet agreed, by a majority on 13
October, not to rush to the country before the end of 1949. Gaitskell was
dismayed to hear of this postponement, having advised Attlee to go to the
country before December, or not until after March 1950. Cripps and

Bevan were to divide, the next day, on the question of public expenditure cuts. There ensued a battle, with the chancellor hinting at retirement, and the minister of health threatening political resignation; Douglas Jay considered 'S[tafford] C[ripps] very messianic and A[neurin] B[evan] very ideological about what are practical administrative questions not really lending themselves to either form of high emotion.'[3] Hugh Dalton supported Bevan, and believed treasury officials had got at Gaitskell. A split was avoided on the question of cuts, and the timing of the election left to the prime minister.

In early December, he discussed possibilities with some senior ministers, plus the chief whip. Cripps argued that it would be difficult to hold sterling beyond the first few weeks of 1950, and a date for the election was selected, Attlee being influenced mainly by the knowledge that Cripps's 1950 budget would have to be a tough one. The chancellor was not prepared to electioneer from the treasury. Five sitting labour MPs were elevated to the peerage, Attlee telling the cabinet of his decision on 10 January. Number 10 announced late that night that polling would be on Thursday, 23 February.

The Gallup poll had shown a conservative lead of 10 per cent over labour in November 1949. The tories now accepted the goal of full employment, and even basic nationalization, but sought to capitalize, not only on Churchill's leadership, but on grumbles about labour rule. They also articulated fears about a socialist future, *Let Us Win Through Together*, the labour manifesto, containing a 'shopping list' of industries to be taken into public ownership. The party stressed economic recovery, with jobs and welfare for all, with most of the cabinet expecting a slightly reduced labour majority. Gaitskell predicted a majority of only thirty, but Bevan feared a weak tory government might get in for a while. Even before parliament was dissolved on 3 February, labour had a slight lead in the polls, and Harold Wilson announced the previous month's trade figures on 10 February 'from a campaigning platform'.[4] Attlee toured Britain in the family's car, offering reassurances about the return of a labour government. This was the first campaign in which radio election broadcasts played a role, labour and the conservatives using their leading figures, plus personalities like the wartime populists, J. B. Priestley and Charles Hill. On the eve of poll, labour was in the lead by 1.5 per cent.

Turn-out was a remarkable 84 per cent, February being a mild month. This represented nearly twenty-nine million voters. Labour secured over 13 million votes (46.1 per cent) to the conservatives' 12.5 million (43.5 per cent), but government supporters declined from 393 seats in 1945 to 315. The loss of MPs was due substantially to a major redistribution in 1948–9, boundary changes alone accounting for thirty labour losses. The house of commons was also reduced in size by fifteen seats. The conservatives increased from 213 seats to 298, and the liberals, at less than 10 per cent of the vote, secured 9 seats. The slight swing against labour had taken place in the suburbs, especially in London, as well as in some leading provincial cities. A working majority was then considered to be about forty. The government had an overall majority of only five, Hugh Dalton describing it as the 'worst possible result ... We have office without authority or power, and it is difficult to see how we can improve our position.'[5]

Wilson concentrated on the new seat of Huyton after his selection. The local tories, and the *Prescot and District Reporter*, were determined to prevent him winning. His opponent, Sydney Smart, was a forty-nine-year-old catering contractor, who had unseated a trade unionist in Croxteth to become a member of Liverpool city council. Some of the political characteristics of the city were being laid down in the new constituency, the Huyton labour party expelling a local councillor in early 1949 for unsocialist behaviour over the allocation of houses. The aggrieved member attacked an element in the local party for being anti-Semitic, anti-Irish and pro-fascist.

Wilson was adopted on 2 February 1950, his agent being R. Foulkes. There ensued a lively three-week contest. Referring to Wilson having proclaimed a new development area, Alderman Sheenan, leader of the Liverpool conservatives, said: 'The Walter Mitty of the Socialist party is Mr. Harold Wilson ... Talk about castles in the air! He can build factories in the air on Merseyside.'[6] The name was to stick.

Wilson opened his election address with a commitment to economic recovery, and ended on a note of anti-communism. He regaled the voters of Huyton with a lengthy account of the dollar problem, an explanation of the social reforms achieved by the government, and an outline of future economic policy, contrasting 1950 with the years after the first world war. The reference to communism was a response, not only to the cold war, but to the communist party, which put up 100 candidates in 1950, and was now in outright opposition to the labour government. Leo McGree, a Liverpool official of the woodworkers' union, was put up against Wilson in Huyton, while D.N. Pritt, a crypto-communist MP in Hammersmith, was to characterize the 1947 trade talks as a British rejection of Russian economic help on the grounds of 'long-standing hostility to the U.S.S.R.'.[7] Anti-communism appealed to Irish catholics, who made up 52 per cent of the electorate. Wilson was vulnerable on the question of sectarian education, not least because of his own nonconformist background. The 1944 education act greatly expanded the state sector, but religious schools in England and Wales were less favourably treated. The question of state support for Catholic schools was a dominant issue of the 1950 election, in Liverpool and parts of Lancashire. The communist, and a liberal, secured only 2,292 votes, in a constituency with 52,363 electors.

There was a turn-out of 85 per cent, which was to be a record for Huyton. Harold Wilson secured 21,536 votes, to the conservative's 20,702. With a majority of only 834, he had a relatively close shave.

He attributed this privately 'to the fact that at the last minute several thousands of votes swung over on the question of Catholic Schools, on which my opponent made some very rosy promises, contrary to the policy of his Party'.[8] Harold Wilson thought he had lost the seat. He was later quoted as telling Huyton Catholics: 'don't rock the boat.'[9] The cabinet had decided on 4 May not to amend the 1944 education act, but to get legal advice on administering it more liberally. Harold Wilson was trying to help three Catholic schools behind the scenes, but only wanted to proceed openly on the basis of political consensus. This did not prevent him attacking the conservative local authority in Prescot, which had refused financial aid. He stated his support for George Tomlinson, as minister of education, but this was enough for John Murnaghan, secretary of the Huyton labour party: 'As a Catholic, I can assure you that no person has done more for Catholic schools than Harold Wilson ... For God sake, let us all pull together and work with a good man on this issue.'[10] Wilson was to get Frank, then Lord, Pakenham to speak for him in Huyton in later elections. The latter found the local MP 'on close and friendly terms with the clergy'. 'Harold Wilson', he was to write, 'is naturally at home in a Catholic presbytery with a Catholic priest whose social origin is the same as his own. He is naturally, and without effort, in sympathy with the struggles and sacrifices of a simple Catholic working-class community in pursuit of a reasonable education. Much more at home, in fact, in such surroundings than in upper-class society.'[11]

There was little optimism left in the labour party in 1950, in spite of the growth in exports after devaluation. Its leading members were in their eleventh year of office. The party had attracted more votes than ever before, and individual membership, at 908,000, represented a significant increase on the less than half a million in 1945. Attlee stated at the cabinet on 25 February 1950 that there was no question of proceeding with the controversial legislation in the manifesto. But Hugh Gaitskell had detected little waning of enthusiasm during the campaign: 'Perhaps one might say that on the one side they had acquired a sort of additional confidence in the capacity of Labour to govern, and on the other side had accumulated inevitably a collection of grievances against us for the way some aspects of government had affected them.'[12] The king's speech of 7 March was that of an administration treading water. Attlee's second government experienced its first parliamentary defeat on 29 March, on a motion to adjourn. The cabinet had even considered another appeal to the country before the end of the year, and it was evident in Whitehall and Westminster that the labour government had lost its reforming edge. Harold Wilson's view, expressed privately on 28 February, was that he had 'made it [back to parliament], for as long as it lasts'.[13]

Harold Wilson retained the presidency of the board of trade, though he was to have a new parliamentary secretary, H. Rhodes, from 2 March. The second labour government was not substantially different from the one which had been in power for nearly five years. Alexander, now ennobled, became chancellor of the duchy, while Dalton took over town and country planning. Shinwell was brought back into the cabinet, as minister of defence. Hector McNeil, Patrick Gordon Walker and James Griffiths were the only new members, in charge, respectively, of the Scottish, commonwealth relations and colonial offices. There were to be two further changes in the autumn and winter, both of which were to have implications for Harold Wilson, and the future of the second labour government. Sir Stafford Cripps, still ailing, retained the treasury, and the role of economic overlord, but Attlee had been persuaded to ease his burden. Hugh Gaitskell became minister of state for economic affairs on 28 February, becoming responsible for the more traditional functions of the treasury. Douglas Jay was promoted to the financial secretaryship on 2 March, though it was to be October before the economic secretaryship was filled, by John Edwards.

Hugh Dalton had a hand in all this. He had discussed with Attlee on 27 January the government's management of the economy after the general election. 'Going below Stafford', Dalton said, as Gaitskell later noted, 'there was nobody until you came to the younger Ministers, that is really Harold Wilson, Douglas and myself.'[14] This was also Cripps's view, given a deterioration in his relationship with Bevan. Dalton was keen to keep Morrison out, and he also did not rate Bevan highly for the treasury.

Gaitskell had contributed to a discussion on economic planning and trade liberalization at the economic policy committee eight days earlier. He argued for caution about the abolition of physical controls: 'He did not believe that it was practicable to maintain full employment without a slight excess of money incomes and this required the retention of physical controls in order to prevent inflation.' Gaitskell recognized that US pressure for liberalization stemmed from the interests of American industry, 'but this should not be allowed to prejudice the planned economy of the country'.[15] This was a policy for a future chancellor of the exchequer. Gaitskell was still outside the cabinet, probably due to the need to accommodate Shinwell, and Harold Wilson may not have felt too threatened. Attlee then appointed both men to the economic policy committee in March, narrowing the gap between the minister of state at the treasury and the president of the board of trade.

Following the loss of nearly eighty labour seats in 1950, the national executive and cabinet repaired to Beatrice Webb House near Dorking for a conference on the weekend of 20–21 May. Herbert Morrison urged the dropping of all public ownership. He also wanted a new definition of socialism, as 'the assertion of social responsibility for matters which are properly of social concern'.[16] Morrison was known for his tautologies. He is reputed to have said that socialism was what labour governments did. Meaningless in terms of a theory of politics, this was an adequate cultural dressing for the political practice of the first Attlee administration.

Bevan, with the support of Morgan Phillips, the general secretary of the party, plus a leading trade unionist, prevented Morrison's attempt at doctrinal revision. Cripps, and Harold Wilson after him, generally favoured the idea of government planning as the essence of socialist action. Planning, *pace* Herbert Morrison, was what public administration was about. There was no split in the labour leadership at Dorking, but the electoral setback was the dominant preoccupation. There emerged a consensus that the party would have to present its policies to appeal to the public. Attlee sat silent for much of the weekend, having little inclination for ideological struggle. Dorking was the first – muted – confrontation in, what was to be an intra-party war. On the one side, there were to be socialist ideologues; on the other, practical reformers. The struggle was to last for over a decade.

Harold Wilson was be a leading unifier in the party, but, in 1950, he set out to mark his own political card. He had mentioned to Attlee on 4 May that he had just finished a memorandum, entitled 'The State and Private Industry', based on his experience at the board of trade over three years. It was written in the immediate wake of the 1950 election, and remains Harold Wilson's major contribution to British socialist thinking. He sent it to number 10 the following day, for consideration by ministerial colleagues.

The labour president of the board of trade seemed reluctant to admit to the structural separation between administration and politics; he acknowledged the memorandum was a political document, but confined party points to a covering note. It was more the work of a government minister than a would-be socialist strategist. He mentioned it could only go to legislation after another general election, but Harold Wilson clearly wanted it sent to a cabinet committee. He also had his eye on the party organization in Transport House. If the president of the board of trade was really intent upon the objectives he espoused, it would have taken more than the normal processes of Whitehall and Westminster to manage capitalism in the way he advocated. 'The State and Private Industry' was a bid for political recognition. For a technocratic minister who may have been considered on the right of the labour party, Harold Wilson gave the impression of socialist fundamentalism. 'The State and Private Industry' was a call for something like wartime control, which Wilson, under Cripps, had helped undermine. He recognized that peacetime required a different form of control, but it is not credible that he could have believed that the labour party was committed to full socialization, although he predicted socialism in Britain by 1975. Nor can he have expected that the British state was prepared to interfere extensively in private companies, even though he used the civil service language of consultation and consideration in his document. Herbert Morrison would later succeed in removing the 'shopping list' of industries to be nationalized from the party manifesto. Wilson must have realized that extensive public ownership was no longer part of labour's strategy. Much the same applied to the idea of control.

Attlee replied on 7 May, suggesting that the memorandum should be considered by the party at forthcoming weekend conferences. It could be discussed initially by a group of senior ministers, and also by a junior group chaired by Wilson. 'In the nature of things', Attlee wrote, 'the men of my generation will before long be passing out, and the responsibility will be passing to the younger generation.'[17] This must have pleased Wilson, though it was to take a few years. The prime minister recommended, for the meeting of junior ministers, Gaitskell, Jay, James Callaghan (a junior minister since late 1947), Hervey Rhodes, John Edwards and Christopher Mayhew. (The two latter had lost their seats in February.) Wilson agreed, and suggested Gaitskell should also come to the senior meeting, on 17 May, several days before Dorking. Wilson and Attlee were joined by Morrison, Cripps, Dalton, Bevan, Maurice Webb, the new minister of food, George Strauss and Richard Stokes, the new minister of works. The meeting came out against government directors, Wilson's idea for peacetime control. It also reaffirmed the mixed economy, which had been implied by *Labour Believes in Britain*. 'It is clear', Wilson summarized, 'that very many voters were being lost through fear of ultimate nationalisation of industries ...'.[18] Gaitskell and Jay drove further nails in the coffin of socialism two days later, at the meeting of junior ministers. Callaghan did not attend, but those suggested by Attlee were joined by Tom Cook, Wilson's former parliamentary private secretary, Fred Lee, Lord Lucas, John Freeman (Strauss's parliamentary secretary), and Fred Willey. Mayhew argued that labour, hitherto the party of producers, had to see the electorate as consumers. Jay came out in favour of 'competitive socialism'. Gaitskell was minuted as having the last word: 'he did not believe in controls on the private sector for the sake of controls. In general, his view was that we should get rid of monopoly practices and let competition work.'[19]

Wilson's memorandum was not totally dead. Morrison sent it, in confidence, to the research department at Transport House. It was also discussed at Dorking, at a Fabian weekend conference in Oxford (30 June–2 July), and with the trade and industry group of MPs. Wilson privately gave Cole a revised copy in late June, arguing for the mixed economy on grounds of electoral necessity. Cole described it as a most excellent piece of work, and expressed himself as in pretty close agreement. On the basis of all this, Wilson produced a second version. He dropped the idea of government directors, described the mixed economy concept as 'most important',[20] and endorsed Mayhews's point about seeing voters as consumers. The document continued to argue for the nationalization of the chemical industry, as part of a state strategy for controlling capitalist industry. The revision was sent to Attlee on 14 July, the prime minister agreeing to forward it to Morgan Phillips, for use in framing party policy. It was, in other words, kicked into touch. This had been Harold Wilson's first excursion in the politics of labour. It may be that he had been stimulated by the planned conference, but he was hamstrung by being a member of the cabinet, without any significant standing in the party. Attention had to be paid to his memorandum within the government, but Attlee allowed it to be neutered by discussion before Dorking.

A major concern of the government had been the budget for 1950–1. While it was being prepared, Cripps presented supplementary estimates on 14 March. He wanted a 'ceiling' on national health service expenditure in the forthcoming financial year. Gaitskell shared the chancellor's view that Bevan was responsible for the financial mess in his department. Health had been underfunded when set up in 1948, unpredictable demand being met by supplementary estimates. The idea of a ceiling forced unpleasant choices on Bevan. The chancellor was attentive to the need for rearmament, under the North Atlantic Treaty Organization (NATO) set up a year earlier. In presenting estimates of health expenditure to the cabinet on 3 April, Cripps suggested charges for dentures, spectacles (and other free items). Bevan had successfully resisted the implementation of prescription charges after devaluation, and insisted that 'the Government's abandonment of the principle of a free and comprehensive health service would be a shock to their supporters in the country and a grave disappointment to Socialist opinion throughout the world.'[21] The cabinet agreed to a ceiling of £392 million after further meetings on 4 and 6 April, leaving the question of charges to be decided.

Gaitskell, had been a not-uncritical admirer of Bevan in 1948. 'Personality is a funny thing', Gaitskell noted in his diary, after a group dinner. 'Bevan, of course, has it very decidedly. He is powerful, though maddening as well.'[22] He became more dismissive. 'It would be much better', he wrote in August, 'if Aneurin Bevan simply said that he was Welsh, he spoke as he felt, and sometimes he felt very strongly, instead of trying to make a philosophy out of the use of invective. Perhaps this is really a clash between romanticism and classicism.'[23] Gaitskell had put his finger on it. However, as minister of fuel and power in the summer of 1949, he showed himself to be, quite simply, anti-Welsh, attributing the 'bad atmosphere' at the annual dinner of colliery managers, partly to the fact that it was being held in Cardiff, and 'there were a large number of Welshmen present'.[24] These personal and cultural differences did not assume a political form until the autumn of 1949. Devaluation increased Gaitskell's standing, but it did not bring him into the treasury immediately. Bevan showed himself resistant to public expenditure cuts, but he had allowed the enactment of prescription charges. There was no split in the run up to the 1950 general election, though the atmosphere at the Cripps's dinners had deteriorated. At some point Bevan had called Gaitskell an 'arid intellectual' to his face. When Strachey later sought to defend Gaitskell, Bevan dismissed him as a man of no political consequence. Discussing religion at a group dinner, Gaitskell, who had written Bevan off as 'a hopeless nineteenth century mystic',[25] was pleasantly surprised to find they shared eighteenth-century rationalist views. But he had been privately dismayed at Attlee's failure to move Bevan out of a spending department. Gaitskell thought he would make a good minister of labour, but Bevan was left in charge of health in Attlee's second government.

A national health service committee was set up in April 1950, under Attlee, to monitor expenditure on a monthly basis, to keep within the budgeted limit for 1950–1. The committee's other members were Morrison, Addison, Bevan, Isaacs, McNeil, Summerskill, Marquand and Gaitskell. It was running Bevan's department, over the head of the minister. Hector McNeil, who had a responsibility for health in Scotland, was Bevan's most prominent supporter in the cabinet. Harold Wilson was still in the shadow of Cripps, but beginning to assert himself politically. One weekend at Buscot Park, the Berkshire home of Lord Faringdon, Wilson had heard Bevan threatening to resign. Wilson thereupon begged Cripps not to impose health charges, and asked Bevan to go easy on the ailing chancellor. Whether this mediation took place or not, it shows Wilson's inclination to defuse what was becoming an important issue. When Cripps introduced his budget on 18 April, there was a ceiling on health expenditure, but no charges. The earlier cut in the housing programme was restored. Being forced to justify himself to Gaitskell throughout 1950 focused Bevan's propensity to resign on the question of health charges. There was an early warning on 29 June, when he informed Cripps that he would no longer attend the group dinners. Gaitskell was to describe his role on the national health service committee as that of treasury prosecutor against Bevan and McNeil: 'The meetings are not exactly easy or comfortable, and on one occasion the Minister of Health, provoked by something I had said, slammed his papers down and started to walk out of the room. The P.M., however, summoned him back and smoothed him down ... It is a very wearing affair – always having to nag one's colleagues, and especially when they are as slippery and difficult as the Minister of Health.'[26]

Cripps's health deteriorated again in the summer of 1950, and he was persuaded to go away for three months. Gaitskell took temporary charge of the treasury, though still not a member of the cabinet. He even moved into Cripps's room for the summer. The chancellor did not recover, and resigned from the government, and even parliament. Gaitskell was appointed chancellor of the exchequer on 19 October, and heard the news in New York on his first visit to north America. He had worked well with the Americans in the establishment of a European payments union as minister of state: 'It is rather odd that after acquiring a reputation within the UK Government for objecting to so much of what the Americans were trying to do in Europe I should yet have been able to get on well with them ... They were and are economic new-dealer types, and anxious to get the same kind of payments system going as we were ourselves.'[27] Gaitskell was only forty-four. He was the second youngest chancellor of the twentieth century, and with the least parliamentary experience of any since the beginning of the nineteenth. He had little standing in the labour party. Morrison did not perceive Gaitskell as a political threat, and Bevin seems to have considered him qualified as principal economics minister. Bevan had political respect for Cripps, and considered Gaitskell little more than a glorified civil servant. Attlee told Gaitskell he was trying to move Bevan out of health, no doubt to prevent a recurrence of the rows about spending. Douglas Jay did not expect 'the violent explosion which hit [him] from Nye Bevan',[28] though he was prepared for Harold Wilson's resentment. The latter had been denied the job he wanted by Cripps's resignation. But he must have seen it coming, in February, and then again in the summer. Gaitskell noted in his diary on 3 November: 'I suspect that Nye is not so much jealous but humiliated at my being put over him. But Harold Wilson, and others confirm, is inordinately jealous, though in view of his age there is really no reason for it. But then one does not look for reasons for jealousy.'[29] The chancellor was to record early in the new year: 'Harold Wilson is probably still exceedingly jealous, but I must say I have had no great difficulty with him. But all this is rather premature because the real struggle will come when we try and settle expenditure policy and get nearer to the Budget.'[30]

Other changes soon followed. Bevan was finally moved to the ministry of labour on 17 January 1951. Hilary Marquand, still outside the cabinet, took over health. Housing, renamed local government and planning, was assigned to Dalton. Bevan was made lord privy seal less than two months later, and was to die in office on 14 April. Bevan was not considered for the foreign office. Herbert Morrison, who had suffered a thrombosis in 1947, had to be moved there, to face the nationalization of the Anglo-Iranian oil company by the Mossadeq government. At Easter, Attlee's duodenal ulcer, from which he had suffered for a number of years, forced him into hospital for several weeks. The stress and strain of high office, compounded by the narrow parliamentary majority in the 1950 parliament, did much to undermine the labour cabinet in the spring of 1951. But it was international politics which led to a major government crisis.

North Korea had invaded the south on 25 June 1950. The united nations – at the behest of the Americans – resolved to repel this communist offensive, General MacArthur taking command of a multinational force on 7 July. The British government had responded with naval support, committing ground troops on 25 July, though Bevan voiced doubts in cabinet on 1 August. The party conference, at Margate in October, was to endorse Britain's involvement. MacArthur, having landed in the north, would come under attack from Chinese 'volunteers', the united nations' forces retreating below the 38th parallel. The British government had agreed – under American pressure – greatly to increase defence spending in the three following years, though national expenditure was to inflate rapidly by January 1951. President Truman seemingly threatened on 30 November 1950 to use the atomic bomb on communist China, a horrendous prospect which led Attlee to fly to Washington. He returned on 11 December having apparently talked the Americans down, but the United States military was now thinking in terms of a £6,000 million programme for Britain. The cabinet was forced to agree to the principle of German rearmament on 14 December, in the name of European defence. The British government came under further pressure in the new year to brand communist China as an aggressor, Gaitskell, in the absence of Bevin, forcing this through the cabinet. The programme for German rearmament was not to be ready until September 1951. By then the united nations, following the recall of MacArthur by his own government, and a military stalemate, was engaged in truce talks with the North Koreans.

The Korean war was the labour government's Rubicon. British ministers and officials were alarmed at Soviet expansionism, fearing a repetition of the 1930s, when pacifism had led to war against Germany. Military deterrence was once again considered necessary, only a few short years after the second world war. Attlee was to tell the cabinet on 25 January 1951 that 'the Chiefs of Staff had paid regard to the fact that war was possible in 1951, and, in 1952, Russia would be powerful enough to go to war if she so desired.'[31] Britain still saw itself as the leading power in Europe, but it was now dependent, through NATO, on the United States. The labour government, fearing a return to isolationism in America, was almost keen to accede to any requests from Washington. As the strongest country in Europe, Britain had to give an example to lesser western powers. It was not possible to limit the British response to a realistic programme such as was at first contemplated or to avoid a disproportionate burden on the United Kingdom. Not for the first time, falling in with American wishes exposed the British economy to stresses that precipitated a crisis – a crisis greatly intensified by coincident pressures on the world economy and, as a consequence, on Britain's terms of trade and balance of payments.[32]

The Americans had asked their NATO partners on 26 July 1950 by how much they could increase military spending in the three following years. Gaitskell as acting chancellor came up with a figure of £3,400 million (plus an additional £200 million for service pay) on 4 August. This represented an increase of £1,100 million on planned military expenditure, of which it was hoped the Americans might pay £550 million. Attlee had been led to believe, by the United States ambassador, that Washington would '"pick up the cheque"'.[33] The national economy could just about produce this level of armaments, disregarding the effect of the Korean war on the price of raw materials. But the cost of British imports, as of every nation's, rose, there having been stockpiling in the United States from early 1950. Harold Wilson, as trade minister, was particularly conscious of the world shortages in commodities. Gaitskell flew to Washington in October, but got little joy on import prices and financial assistance. Once he entered the cabinet as chancellor, he had to face the extra problem of Shinwell as minister of defence. He ended Marshall aid six weeks before 1 January 1951. Believing that Britain now had a strong economy, he moved towards the American military's demand of £6,000 million, which may have been accepted by Shinwell. Attlee told parliament on 29 January that Britain would spend £4,700 million on defence over three years. This involved an additional £500 million in 1951–2, which had to be found in the budget in April. Having represented 8 per cent of Britain's gross national product, defence was to take a planned 14 per cent. It was known there would be no real American help.

The increased military programme dominated the preparation of the 1951 budget. Bevan had opposed the £3,400 million figure of August 1950, associating it with cuts in the social services. He protested to Attlee in October, on the grounds that the new chancellor 'would [not] commend himself to the main elements and currents of opinion in the Party'.[34] Attlee was clearly tiring of Bevan, and finally moved him sideways in the new year.

Bevan also had a role to play in the defence programme, and was still able to defend his cherished national health service. The government accepted the defence estimate of £4,700 million on 25 January, Gaitskell politically advocating this huge increase, while predicting considerable economic difficulties. Bevan, and others, objected to surrendering so completely to the United States, especially when it would do so much damage to the British economy. Harold Wilson recalls that 'this squandering of our resources is what brought me out fighting at Bevan's side.' He claims he backed Bevan in having 'cautionary words'[35] inserted into the statement Attlee made to parliament. These were to the effect that the economy might not be able to sustain such an armaments programme, due to a shortage of raw materials, components and, especially, machine tools.

Wilson was hardly yet in alliance with the new minister of labour. His worry was the rearmament programme, which Gaitskell had pushed through. The chancellor had already tangled with Bevan on the question of health service charges, and the new minister of labour seems not to have been to the fore in resisting the £4,700 million figure. Gaitskell, judging by his diary entry of 2 February, was sanguine:

> We have got the rearmament programme through however rather more easily than might have been expected ... It was expected that Bevan would put up a lot more resistance. I never thought so myself ... Both the President of the Board of Trade and Minister of Supply [Strauss] made some effort to resist it, partly just as an alibi in case the programme could not be fulfilled or exports dropped catastrophically.[36]

Strauss was to recall that he and Wilson led the opposition on 25 January. Wilson was to claim he considered resigning in February, on the raw materials shortage, and recalls Bevan talked him out of it. Woodrow Wyatt would remember Wilson fearing he might become a scapegoat for losses in the overseas trading account. Britain had secured a surplus of £244 million in 1950. Rearmament implied increased imports, at inflated prices, plus a loss of crucial exports. This would reflect badly on the president of the board of trade. Wilson later recalled his experience of wartime production, with reference to 1951. 'He knew', Leslie Smith would write, 'from his war-time administrative experience of programming and progressing that the country was poorly equipped for an effort of such magnitude.'[37]

The chancellor saw it all in terms of political careerism: 'One cannot ignore the fact that in all this there are personal ambitions and rivalries at work. Harold Wilson is clearly ganging up with the Minister of Labour, not that he cuts much ice because one feels that he has no fundamental views on his own, but it is another voice. The others on Bevan's side are more genuine.'[38] He was thinking then of Jim Griffiths, the new colonial secretary, Chuter Ede, the home secretary, and Dalton himself.

Gaitskell attempted to hold the ceiling of the national health service at £393 million for 1951–2, Marquand being denied the extra £30 million he needed. The chancellor reintroduced the idea of charges for dentures and spectacles in cabinet on 22 March, whereby mainly older people would have to pay 50 per cent of the actual cost of the former, and £1 towards the latter. There was also to be a shilling (5p) on prescriptions, as had been legislated for in 1949.

Gaitskell saw various members of the government before the cabinet meeting, but not Harold Wilson: 'I knew quite well that he was almost certain to side with Bevan since he had been ganging up with him for a long time.'[39] Though the cabinet, chaired by Morrison, opposed prescription charges, Bevan – and Wilson – were the only defenders of the principle of a free health service. Each minister, unusually, was minuted; Wilson spoke very late: 'he would ... have preferred to see a cut in defence expenditure rather than a scheme of charges under the National Health Service'.[40] Chuter Ede and Jim Griffiths 'were a little doubtful',[41] but they did not oppose the chancellor. Gaitskell had allowed the ceiling to rise to £400 million, a figure suggested by Bevin. The charges were to apply from 12 April. Bevan attacked the rearmament programme, and clashed with Shinwell. The chancellor proceeded to prepare his budget.

Attlee was in hospital through April, and Morrison made no effort to call a meeting of ministers on this domestic issue, concerned as he was with foreign affairs. Bevan threatened in public on 3 April to resign, at a meeting in Bermondsey where he was heckled about the recent prosecution of seven dockers. Gaitskell told Dalton two days later that it would do the party good in the country to stand firm. When informed by Hugh Dalton that this would mean the resignation, not only of Bevan, but also of Wilson and John Strachey, now at the war office, the chancellor replied: 'we will be well rid of the three of them'.[42] 'I thought', Dalton recorded in his diary, 'that H[ugh] G[aitskell] thought too little of the Party and too much of the general mood of the electorate.'[43] It was an apposite observation. Bevan repeated his threat in cabinet on 9 April, on the eve of Gaitskell's budget, arguing, with Wilson, that a £23 million saving was a paltry figure, compared with a defence programme which could not be implemented. Ede did not like Bevan's threats, but Tomlinson now emerged as a supporter. The chancellor had an audience with the king late that afternoon, and told him of Bevan's threat: '[The king] said, "He must be mad to resign over a thing like that. I really don't see why people should have false teeth free any more than they have shoes free", waving his foot at me as he said it. He is, of course, a fairly reactionary person.'[44]

Attlee counselled against disagreement from his bed in St Mary's Hospital, Paddington. He called for support for the chancellor, which Morrison and Whiteley reported to the cabinet when it reassembled in the evening at the house of commons.

Gaitskell rejected all compromises. He stated he would quietly resign if the 22 March decision was overturned. Bevan and Wilson also promised to resign, if charges were imposed. The minister of labour was minuted: 'latterly, he had come to feel that he could bring more influence to bear on Government policy from outside the Cabinet than he could ever hope to exercise within it; and, when a Minister reached that position, it was time for him to go.' The cabinet secretary, as always, was working for the prime minister. Bevan stated that, if he went, it would be on more than dentures and spectacles: 'While he supported the policy of rebuilding the armed strength of the western democracies, he was concerned about the pace and volume of their rearmament programme. He believed that, by trying to do too much too quickly in response to United States pressure, the western democracies were in grave danger of undermining their economic strength.'[45] Tomlinson joined the cabinet radicals in voting against the chancellor, but Morrison liked Bevan's idea of a ceiling and no charges, and put this later to Attlee. The prime minister saw Bevan and Wilson at St Mary's, probably that night. They seemed prepared to accept the compromise, and even the possibility of charges if costs ran over £400 million. Wilson believed Attlee was going to have a word with the chancellor.

The next morning, Gaitskell refused to compromise just before the budget, offered his resignation, and finally obtained the support of Attlee. It was believed Bevan was determined to resign in any case. Gaitskell went on to introduce his budget that afternoon, deciding at the last minute to leave out a sentence whereby the charges would be imposed from 12 April. He conceded a point on retrospective legislation, though it would involve the loss of some money. The charges on dentures and spectacles would bring in £13 million in 1951–2, and £23 million in a full year.

Bevan and Wilson again visited Attlee, and were advised to attend the parliamentary party meeting the next morning, and urge postponement of the charges. John Freeman, the parliamentary secretary at supply, privately begged Bevan not to resign on the budget. He should wait a few weeks and go on 'the drive towards war, the absence of any coherent foreign policy, the inflationary and anti-working class character of our rearmament economies'.[46]

Bevan and Wilson again opposed charges for dentures and spectacles in cabinet, two days after the budget, on 12 April. The former insisted that the bill should be held back, until after a general election. This was considered possible in June. Wilson argued that the cabinet should continue to discuss the difference, after the prime minister was out of hospital. The bill should be postponed: 'There was a good deal of feeling about this in the Party, and he thought it would be wiser on that account not to rush the introduction of the legislation.'[47] It was decided to introduce the bill on 17 April, and have the second reading in the week beginning 23 April. Wilson tried again to play the role of conciliator at some point. He privately lectured Gaitskell on the need for consensus in cabinet, and urged Bevan to give up his obsession with a free health service. Wilson had told Dalton on 11 April, that he was 'trying to persuade Nye not to resign'.[48]

Gaitskell shifted very slightly in the following days. Bevan and Wilson saw Bevin, who was acting as mediator at Attlee's request. Wilson attributed the whole thing to Morrison, and claims Bevin was sympathetic to his and Bevan's position. Bevin died on 14 April. Attlee, in a letter to Bevan on 18 April, expressed the wish that the differences could be forgotten. It is Harold Wilson's view that, 'had [Bevin] lived, the whole course of Labour Party history and certainly the outcome of the Bevan–Gaitskell dispute might have been very different'.[49] He has also expressed the opinion that, 'if Attlee had not been in hospital – with Morrison in charge – [the resignations] would not have taken place.'[50] Attlee was to concur years later: 'I was ill at the time when Aneurin Bevan raised difficulties over the Budget and was rather surprised when Wilson took the same stand. I considered that his action was due to the influence of his older colleague and his relative lack of experience.'[51]

The cabinet decided on 19 April to introduce the bill allowing for health charges. Bevan threatened to resign on the third reading. When Shinwell suggested the charges might only be temporary, Gaitskell agreed they might not be permanent. 'We've got them on the run',[52] Bevan scribbled in a note to Wilson. The home secretary was to discuss a form of words, for the second reading debate on 24 April, with Gaitskell, Bevan, Marquand and McNeil. Few seemed to have paid much attention to Harold Wilson. 'He appeared ... to be following his usual diligent routine in his usual unruffled manner.'[53] Bevan found Gaitskell's verbal concession inadequate after the meeting. The left-wing *Tribune* criticized the budget as 'dangerous' on Friday, 20 April, comparing Gaitskell to Philip Snowden. Sympathy for Bevan was waning, but it was this number of *Tribune*, in particular Michael Foot's article, which brought things to a head. Attlee, after holding discussions at St Mary's, sent Bevan an ultimatum, asking for a guarantee that he would behave properly as a member of the government. Bevan telephoned Wilson to say that the government was proceeding with the bill. He finally wrote his letter of resignation on Saturday, 21 April, having invited Donald Bruce, his former parliamentary private secretary, round to his home for lunch. 'I was present in the room in Cliveden Place', Lord Bruce, as he now is, recalls, 'when Nye made the telephone call to Harold to ask him where he stood, and the reply was instantaneous – instantaneous, there was no question of doubt in it.'[54] The health service charges were the occasion, but Bevan went on in his letter of resignation to criticize the rearmament programme. Attlee noted in his reply that Bevan had 'extended the area of disagreement a long way beyond the specific matter'.[55] Bevan had wanted this to be a single gesture, in order not to damage the party, and urged Wilson and Freeman to stay in the government.

It seems Freeman was more willing to accept this advice, but both went to see Bevan on the Sunday.

Wilson was determined to be associated with this major political resignation, and John Freeman, 'noting the unbending resolve ... wondered whether he was witnessing a future party leader in action'.[56] 'Most Ministers who resign from governments', Bevan's biographer was to write, 'find particularly awkward the task of defining when agreed policies become intolerable, and they are always told they should have gone sooner or stayed longer.'[57] Harold Wilson resigned on 23 April. He was absent from the cabinet when it met at 10.00 a.m., it being agreed that Marquand and McNeil should open and close the following day's debate. Wilson, it seems, was with Attlee at St Mary's, and 'the interview was typically short and sharp'.[58] Hugh Dalton was to recall in his autobiography eleven years later: 'I made no effort to dissuade Harold Wilson from resigning ... I had counted him as very promising some years before and there was no doubt that he was very clever, "but a bit of a cold fish", people said. In contrast with the other two, he did not seem to have much warmth or strength of character.'[59] Dalton had referred to 'Nye and the dog' during the row, the sobriquet 'Nye's little dog' sticking to Wilson.[60] In his resignation speech in the commons on Monday, 23 April, Bevan attacked Gaitskell's 'arithmetic of Bedlam'.[61] Wilson's exchange of letters with the prime minister was not published, and he was to claim that 'there was nothing in that correspondence that was not covered in [his] statement in the House of Commons, and both the Prime Minister and [he] felt it unnecessary to publish it.'[62]

Press reaction the following morning was muted. In his resignation speech, after Bevin's memorial service on 24 April, Wilson stated he would be 'brief and ... uncontroversial'. He did not believe the rearmament programme was possible, admitted £13 million was 'a minor cut', but 'the principle of a free health service ha[d] been breached ... [possibly to] be widened in future years'.[63] He promised to support the government and party. 'Mr. Bevan', wrote one reporter, 'had ended with his boats ablaze. Mr. Wilson's boats carried fire-fighting equipment.'[64]

John Freeman, who seems to have promised to support Bevan at the time of the budget, resigned on 24 April, and was also to express concern about the economic effects of rearmament. Freeman was the only one to come under extensive pressure to stay, including a promise of the financial secretaryship at the treasury, and even Wilson's old job. The national health service bill had its second reading the same day, five labour MPs eventually voting against, with twenty abstaining. Marquand and McNeil told the cabinet two days later a special effort was required to secure the passage of the bill before the Whitsun recess. Dentures and spectacles, apparently, were being snapped up at a great rate, and there would be little saving to the treasury.

The 1951 resignations, after Gaitskell's first – and last – budget, were historic. They are on a par with those of the free traders, including Snowden, who quit MacDonald's national government in 1932. Harold Wilson's surprise exeunt was to be remembered erroneously as taking a stand in defence of the health service. 'At least his public statements on matters at all relevant to the dispute were quite consistent and concerned with the rearmament programme', Joan Mitchell has written in a study of the 1951 financial crisis. 'But even now [1963] it is not at all easy to see at what stage the Government could have taken any different political decision on a matter of principle, nor what they could have done on the key question of easing supplies of raw materials – except on the assumption that Britain's bargaining power with the U.S. Administration was much stronger than it could in fact have been.'[65] Gaitskell had said in a discussion with Dalton that 'it [was] really a fight for the soul of the Labour Party'.[66] Writing in his diary on 30 April, he was to suggest that the affair 'may indeed be regarded as of considerable significance in the history of the Labour Party and even therefore in politics in general in Britain.'[67] He had not been so sure of victory: 'Although I embarked on this with the knowledge that it would be a hard struggle I did not think it would be quite so tough. I suppose that if I had realised that there were so many things which could have meant defeat, I might never have begun; or at least I would have surrendered early on. If Ernie [Bevin] had not suggested the compromise; if some of the Cabinet had been more frightened; if Bevan had played his cards better; if the Budget speech had not been a success; if the Broadcast had been a flop; if I had not won the battle decisively in the Party meeting. If any of these things had not happened it might have meant failure.'[68]

Sir Hartley Shawcross, who had no sympathy for Wilson, was made president of the board of trade on 24 April. 'There was no wailing and nashing of teeth that I can recall',[69] says Lord Shawcross of the civil servants he inherited at Millbank. Resignation freed Wilson from the ministerial duties which had dominated his life for nearly six years. He had been in the world of Whitehall since 1940, yet he was still only thirty-five. Harold Wilson was now a parliamentary associate of Aneurin Bevan, the man who had resigned on a question of socialist principle. The 1951 resignations were to do the ex-president of the board of trade's political career a great deal of good. If Wilson had been a victim of the proverbial Whitehall bus before 23 April 1951, he would be remembered as an energetic, but rather colourless, member of Attlee's cabinet. A man of promise, not necessarily of substance. If Harold Wilson had been made chancellor in succession to Cripps, he would, on the occasion of his first budget, have been on the side opposite to Bevan. Wilson would not have prevented the latter's resignation, nor labour's loss of office later in the year. He claims that political calculation played no part in the decision he made at home on 22–23 April. 'At the time[,] it looked far more like an act of political suicide.'[70] Perish the thought! Harold Wilson showed himself most reluctant to resign. His journey towards this point had begun the previous October, when the equally ambitious Gaitskell was given the treasury. Without the guidance of his patron, Cripps, it is likely that Harold Wilson had little commitment to the new chancellor's policies. He may even have considered him a rival. Wilson had seemingly been pro-American, and anti-Russian, but opposition to militarism was a deeply rooted political sentiment. Thus he came out against Gaitskell's second increase to £4,700 million in January 1951. It is not surprising that Wilson considered it disastrous for the British economy, at worse, and, at best, totally unrealistic. But he had accepted the £3,400 million figure. His resignation shows him to be both calculating and indecisive, rather than fired with the sense of a great political injustice being done.

CHAPTER 12

Bevanism, 1951–5

Several weeks after resigning, Wilson wrote to a friend that he had 'no regrets at all either politically or personally. Politically we felt we had to make a stand somewhere ... Personally, after six years in office – and at the finish working sixteen hours a day, including Sundays – I was getting pretty near the end of my tether ... Most people who know me say I now look ten years younger.'[1] Hugh Gaitskell was to visit the dying Cripps at his home in Gloucestershire later in 1951. 'We talked about Aneurin Bevan', Gaitskell wrote in his diary. 'I told [Cripps] that I had heard that [Bevan] was very bitter and I said that I thought that both he and Harold Wilson had been jealous when I became Chancellor.' Cripps thought there was no reason for Bevan to be surprised, as he had made it clear that the latter would not be succeeding him. 'As to Harold Wilson, Stafford said, "Why on earth did he do this?"'[2]

No real answer was forthcoming from the emergency meeting of the parliamentary party on 24 April. Many labour MPs were thinking of the previous week's *Tribune*, but two members of the cabinet had now resigned. Wilson and John Freeman made personal statements to fellow labour MPs, and they were followed by Gaitskell, whose defence of the budget was well received. Bevan then rose. Having attacked the chancellor the previous day in his resignation speech, he continued in similar vein. His 'shocking outburst of bad temper ... was evidently a revelation to many people in the Party. He almost screamed at the platform. At one point he said, "I won't have it. I won't have it." And, this of course was greeted with derision. "*You* won't have it?" called other Members of the Party.'[3] Dalton whispered loudly to Morrison, 'this is [Oswald] Mosley speaking'. Roy Jenkins thought it 'sub-human'.[4] Perhaps having overheard Dalton, Chuter Ede, as leader of the house, returned to *Tribune's* comparison with 1931, inferring that Bevan might be another Mosley. Michael Foot was to write that 'it must have been that ... meeting ... which gave the Grand Committee Room its villainous reputation ... a gloomy Gothic penitentiary, where by some gruesome accident [labour MPs] were always condemned to assemble when "hanging" matters were on the agenda.'[5]

Labour's national executive committee, elected each year at the party conference, was marshalled, the following morning, by Morgan Phillips, in support of the government. This was unusual, especially when a section of the party was opposed to government policy. Bevan, and three supporters on the executive, wrote a letter of protest to Morgan Phillips on 26 April, stating he had behaved unconstitutionally. It was the first concerted action of what was now to be call the Bevanites.

Labour MPs, who had customarily congregated in the tea room at the house of commons in the inter-war years, spilled over into the smoking room in 1945, a tory preserve where alcohol was served. Bevan appropriated the corner with a big round table, gathering younger MPs around him. He appointed Donald Bruce his parliamentary private secretary. 'The conversation' at the Bevan corner, according to Michael Foot, 'was much more a general political debate in which, while he was a member of the Government, Bevan might offer a subtle and elaborate defence of some of the administration's most indefensible actions. In protecting the Cabinet and its secrets, he was ultra-loyal and ultra-secretive; no Privy Councillor ever respected his oath more faithfully, and it was largely for this reason that, while he was in the Government, no interchange occurred between him and any Left-wing groups in Parliament.'[6] Donald Bruce liaised with the left, as part of his parliamentary duties, protecting Bevan from breaches of collective responsibility. Lord Bruce, who was then a backbench rebel, now admits that Bevan tried to keep him in line. After one revolt, 'he said: "Donald, my boy, you will not do that again, otherwise you're out!"'[7] Bevan was something of a loner within the government, with a network of friends outside politics, but his battle with Gaitskell was to flush out backbench supporters. By the time Harold Wilson came on the political scene, perhaps towards the end of 1950, there were Bevanites in the wings. He was to tell Leslie Smith of 'a meeting of the informal Parliamentary "Bevanite" group',[8] Wilson dating its existence from the beginning of 1951. He was to be less discreet later: 'Several of us used to meet from time to time rather than being seen about the House. I would pick up two or three of them in my car and go for a stand-up supper at one residence or the other, including the Bevan establishment in Cliveden Place.'[9]

In fact, a small number of left-wing MPs had begun to meet regularly from as early as November 1946, the month in which fifty-five backbenchers signed an amendment to the address calling for 'a democratic and constructive Socialist alternative to an otherwise inevitable conflict between American capitalism and Soviet Communism.'[10] Richard Crossman, whose burgeoning Zionism distanced him from Bevin, was the instigator, and their Keep Left group was formally launched in April 1947. Richard Crossman,

Michael Foot and Ian Mikardo wrote the policy document published by the *New Statesman*; the former had long been associated with the weekly, and the two latter were members of the editorial board of *Tribune*. It was published the following month as the pamphlet *Keep Left*. A number of members met weekly, with Mikardo as secretary, the group having the regular support of *Tribune*. But the paper began to carry party material paid for by Transport House in January 1949, Michael Foot having been elected to the executive the previous May. A new pamphlet, *Keeping Left*, was published at the beginning of 1950. Foot was to be replaced by Mikardo on the executive that October, and though *Tribune* broke away from the party organization in September, neither was openly associated with the pamphlet. Mikardo also gave up the secretaryship of the group. The new signatories included Barbara Castle, Tom Horabin and Richard Acland. *Keeping Left* was situated firmly within the politics of the western camp, though it called for cooperation with the east. Keep Left had yet to find its political way in a complicated international world by the time of the ministerial resignations in April 1951. It was an inauspicious foundation for Bevan, Wilson and Freeman to launch a left-wing parliamentary crusade, drawing on socialist activists in the constituencies and industrial militants in the unions.

The three former ministers met privately on 26 April with twelve fellow MPs, eight of whom had been identified with Keep Left. Crossman, Davies, Foot, Hale, MacKay and Mikardo were present, along with Richard Acland and Barbara Castle. Hugh Delargy, Tom Driberg, Will Griffiths and Jennie Lee turned up with Bevan, Wilson and Freeman. Ian Mikardo was elected to the chair, and his secretary, Jo Richardson, continued as secretary to the group. These fourteen men and one woman founded the Bevanites within the parliamentary party, though the name Keep Left was retained so as not to alarm the party leadership. Nine further MPs joined the group, and members of Keep Left discussed which other parliamentary colleagues were to be approached. It had thirty-two members in 1951, and forty-seven (plus two peers) the following year. Keep Left was small, but it had established a presence on the national executive. Bevan had first been elected in 1944, to one of the seven constituency seats, topping the poll each year. He was joined by Michael Foot in 1948, Tom Driberg in 1949, and, in 1950, Ian Mikardo and Barbara Castle. Keep Left had attempted to reach party activists through a series of 'brains trusts' up and down the country from the summer of 1950, an idea taken from a radio programme of the same name.

There was definite contact with Bevan certainly from July 1950, but it was the following March before Harold Wilson was associated with the parliamentary left. He was reported in the *Sunday Times* to be sympathetic to the thinking of Thomas Balogh, an Oxford economist, and an adviser to the labour party since 1943.

Bevan, Wilson and Freeman put their names to a *Tribune* pamphlet, *One Way Only*, in July, a statement on behalf of twenty-five Bevanites. The original authors of *Keep Left* took responsibility for the foreign affairs section, and Bevan wrote the introduction. *One Way Only* was to sell 100,000 copies. It criticized the government's rearmament programme, arguing that this could not be sustained by the British economy without American aid. *Going our Way*, a second Bevanite pamphlet, written by Mikardo, which included an attack on right-wing trade-union leaders, appeared in time for the party conference. Harold Wilson claims he did not see an advance copy, 'its publication [being] a great embarrassment to him'.[11] Priority was given to mutual aid that summer, a general election being considered imminent. The group was concerned about the most marginal seats held by Bevanites, who planned speaking tours and brains trusts, and even individual schedules for the duration of the election campaign. Harold Wilson booked an early brains trust for Huyton, and Bevan spoke for him on 22 July. His seat was the third most vulnerable held by a Bevanite, and he must have feared defeat.

Mikardo recalls being 'a bit surprised' at Wilson's resignation: 'I always did think his resignation was not on the same footing as that of Bevan and Freeman ... Nye resigned out of anger, John Freeman resigned out of real conviction, and Harold resigned as a step in his career strategy. It was a piece on his curriculum vitae ... The decisive piece.'[12] Acland remembers returning by car from a brains trust weekend in Yorkshire, and hearing Harold Wilson tell his new political friends: 'Do you know what I'm going to do, what I'm going to concentrate my attention on now that I'm relieved of departmental responsibility. I'm going to read Erskine May from cover to cover.'[13]

The resignations gave Harold Wilson a left-wing reputation on Merseyside, but he still lacked a political presence in the party nationally. Thus he decided to put himself forward that autumn as a candidate for the executive, along with Bevan, Driberg, Mikardo and Castle. At Scarborough in October, Castle came second to Bevan, who obtained 858,000 votes. Driberg and Mikardo were also reelected. Shinwell was unseated, and Wilson was second runner up with 396,000 votes. Transport House may have tried to do him down using 'J.H. Wilson' on the ballot paper, but it is more likely he was simply a relative political newcomer.

Attlee had decided during the summer of 1951 that the government could not endure a third session of parliament, given that the tories were, in the words of Robert Boothby, 'harrying the life out of [labour MPs]'[14] with late-night sittings and so on. The cabinet, with Morrison, Gaitskell and Shinwell in Canada, agreed to a general election being called for 25 October. The precipitating event appears to have been a planned overseas tour by the king. Attlee wanted the election out of the way in case George VI was later inconvenienced by having to hurry back to Britain. The Scarborough conference – labour's fiftieth – was shortened to allow MPs to return for the dissolution on 5 October, and the election campaign was relatively quiet. The *Daily Mirror* posed the question 'Whose Finger on the Trigger?' in the run up to polling day, but the conservatives, still under Churchill, played it low key, in order to get the liberal vote. With a turn out of 82.5 per cent, labour secured almost 14 million votes (48.8 per cent), the largest ever secured by a British party. The conservatives were only 231,067 votes behind (with 48.0 per cent), but the liberal vote swung significantly to Churchill. There were 321 tory to 295 labour MPs (with 6 liberals and 3 others), giving an overall majority of 17. The conservatives took 21 seats from labour, over half of them in London and the south east, the electoral system, and tactical voting, depriving Attlee of a third successive election victory. 'No one will ever know', Michael Foot was to argue, 'whether Bevan lost more votes for Labour by the onslaughts on his colleagues, so heavily personalized in the newspapers, than he gained by the general invigoration of politics.'[15] Labour would deal with this structural dilemma by striving for party unity after the left was to spend the 1950s trying to radicalize electoral politics.

Harold Wilson appears to have begun electioneering in the early summer of 1951, as local conservatives were giving no quarter. Their candidate, F. L. Neep, claimed Wilson had jumped because he was about to be pushed. The *Prescot and Huyton Reporter* described the sitting MP as wearing his now-famous 'monkey-nut suit',[16] a reference presumably to the ground nuts fiasco in east Africa. Wilson had been accompanied by the likes of Bessie Braddock, a strong anti-communist Liverpool MP, when he was in the government, but, after his resignation, it was people such as Hugh Delargy, a left-winger, who spoke for him at labour meetings in the constituency. He was identified now as a Bevanite, but took a stand, as he had always done, on the government's record: 'At mention of the word revolution one immediately thinks of blood, etc., but in this country since 1945 you have carried out a peaceful revolution.'[17] Wilson had to defend a majority of 834. There was no communist this time, but also no liberal, though he was helped by the continuing shift of population from Liverpool on to new council estates. Wilson secured 23,582 votes to the conservative's 22,389, a majority of 1,193, a good result for one of the leading left-wingers in the parliamentary labour party.

On 30 October, twenty-four out of thirty-two Bevanites met at Crossman's Westminster home to consider their post-election strategy. Bevan announced that he was not prepared to stand for the parliamentary committee, the elected shadow cabinet of twelve (plus six ex officio members). Some newer Bevanites pressed for the group to become less exclusive, and it was later agreed to hold a series of meetings open to all labour MPs to be addressed by outside speakers. Crossman mused privately on the new Keep Left on 4 December: 'The fact is that Bevanism and the Bevanites seem much more important, well-organized and machiavellian to the rest of the Labour Party, and indeed to the U.S.A., than they do to us who are in the Group and who know that we are not organized, that Aneurin can never be persuaded to have any consistent or coherent strategy and that we have not even got to the beginning of a coherent, constructive policy. What we have, and it is very important, is a group of M.P.s who meet regularly, who know and like each other and who have come to represent "real Socialism" to a large number of constituency members.'[18] Thus began a process of political self-flagellation, with the intellectual Crossman honestly, if not recklessly, submitting the left's strategy to liquidating inquiry. Harold Wilson was invited to take the chair from Mikardo. The latter remembers him as 'a bloody good chairman': he was 'a talented young man, [with] ministerial experience, a formidable customer, who was an accretion of strength, and, I must say, he put his back into the Bevanites.'[19] Jo Richardson continued as secretary, meeting Wilson before group meetings to arrange the agenda; she recalls no particular warmth: 'He struck me as being totally sure of himself ... bordering on the arrogant.'[20] Crossman wrote later of this rising political star: 'Harold Wilson was as neat and competent as ever, and whenever an idea is put forward, remembers without fail an occasion on which he did it or set up a committee on it at the Board of Trade. His complacency must be unique, but he has a good mind, is an excellent member of the group and is likeable into the bargain.'[21] Crossman was referring to a weekend conference at Buscot Park in mid-December, at which Wilson delivered a lengthy paper on the immediate financial position. Because of Britain's balance of payments problem, he argued for increased east–west trade, but mainly for more imports of raw materials from the commonwealth. The gathering decided that Bevan, Wilson, Crossman and Mikardo should produce a third, updated, pamphlet on behalf of the group, but, when they met on 21 January 1952 at Bevan's home in Belgravia, Harold Wilson mooted the idea of returning to the front bench. Bevanism was beginning to fracture after less than a year.

This was partly because Bevan was preoccupied with his forthcoming book, *In Place of Fear*, which had been assembled from drafts while in Yugoslavia with Jennie Lee the previous summer. James Callaghan had an MP's locker adjacent to Bevan: 'Nye's locker overflowed with papers of all descriptions, and he had a ··· struggle to shut it.'[22] *In Place of Fear* was published in April, selling 37,000 copies. Bevan, if the truth be known, did not satisfy this socialist following with his long-awaited book, which many wanted to be a classic.

In a debate on the defence estimates on 5 March, fifty-seven labour MPs – including Harold Wilson – had voted against the conservative government, the '57 varieties'[23] comprising Bevanites and others in revolt against the official opposition's decision to abstain. The Bevanites had decided not to move their own amendment, cognizant of the advice of trade-union members that this would be seen as going against the parliamentary party. Bevan subsequently expected to be expelled, and Barbara Castle and Harold Wilson urged caution. The parliamentary party voted to restore standing orders on 19 March, after nearly seven years in abeyance, Charles Pannell, a trade unionist, accusing the Bevanites of being a group in the party, 'organized, secret, with their own whips on'.[24] Persistent disobedience by the Bevanites could lead to suspension.

With the constituencies by and large enthusiastic for the rebel MPs, the left–right struggle shifted to the trade unions, where a group of right-wing leaders constituted what was considered a bureaucracy, which sought to guide party policy through the block vote at party conferences. The Bevanite group decided on 22 April to hold open meetings each Tuesday at 1.30 p.m., while also meeting privately on Mondays. In the run up to the party conference at Morecambe, the *News Chronicle*, quoting Richard Stokes, accused the Bevanites of being 'a party within a party'.[25] The paper described Bevan, Crossman and Freeman as its leaders, and Bing, Mikardo and Barbara Castle's husband, Ted, as the organizers. No mention was made of the chairman Harold Wilson. Bevan replied in *Tribune*, confirming the substance of the charge, but denying there was any 'party within a party'. The Bevanites secured a noted success in the elections to the executive at the end of September, winning six of the seven constituency seats. Bevan came top of the poll, and Castle, Driberg and Mikardo were all reelected. Harold Wilson, on his second attempt, secured fifth place, and Richard Crossman, who had been a dissident since 1946, took the seventh seat. They knocked off Dalton and Morrison, the last of the 'big five' leaders, excepting of course Attlee. Dalton minded less being defeated in company with Morrison, but Harold Wilson is reported to have told a friend: 'Nye's little dog has turned round and bitten Dalton where it hurts!'[26] He had achieved this preeminent position on the strength of his resignation, making his first speech to a party conference on 2 October in favour of a cut in the rearmament programme. Gaitskell, who had been unsuccessful in the executive elections, asked in his speech why the three ministers had not resigned in January 1951 if they had been concerned about rearmament.

The rise of an organized left was followed rapidly by a reaction from the right. Arthur Deakin, general secretary of the transport and general workers' union, speaking as fraternal delegate from the TUC, attacked 'the Tribune Organisation' on 1 October: 'Let them cease the vicious attacks they have launched upon those with whom they disagree, abandon their vituperation and their carping criticism which appears regularly in *Tribune*.'[27] Gaitskell delivered a speech at Stalybridge near Manchester on 5 October, warning of communists in the constituency parties. He said of the Bevanites: 'It is time to end the attempt at mob rule by a group of frustrated journalists and restore the authority and leadership of the solid sound sensible majority of the Movement.'[28] The party's right wing was mobilizing. When labour had still been in office in mid-1951, Gaitskell attended a private meeting in Aidan Crawley's flat, with John Edwards, Douglas Jay, Patrick Gordon Walker, Frank Pakenham and Woodrow Wyatt, to 'organise a few people to write to the press, and ... do some more speaking in the country'.[29] Wyatt was clearly moving rightwards. Gaitskell, Hartley Shawcross, Hector McNeil, Gordon Walker and Morrison met twice at Dick Stokes's immediately after the election; while 'there was ... some general discussion about Bevan ... no very clear line [was] laid down'.[30] There was yet another meeting the following March, at Wyatt's flat, involving Christopher Mayhew, Anthony Crosland, who had entered parliament in 1950, Roy Jenkins, Arthur Allen, Alf Robens and Gaitskell, in order to oppose Bevanism in the parliamentary party. The Gaitskellites were forming.

The press pushed the theme of a party within the party in the wake of Stalybridge, and Attlee came out against sectionalism on 11 October. Bevan considered disbanding the group. At a private gathering with Foot, Wilson, Mikardo and Crossman, it was agreed that group meetings would be open, Bevan and Wilson pushing this through a group meeting. Crossman noted in his diary: 'I had a distinctly uncomfortable feeling about diddling forty colleagues in this way and I said so to Harold Wilson on the way out. He was baffled, which shows what good politicians he and Nye are.'[31] His cynicism had begun to show.

The parliamentary party voted on 23 October, by 188 to 51, for the 'immediate abandonment of all group organisation'.[32] Fifty-three labour MPs did not vote. The group formally decided the following week – with Wilson in the chair – to disband, it being understood that Bevan and his supporters would continue to meet clandestinely. Attention now shifted back to the parliamentary party. There was an election for the deputy leadership in November, in which Bevan obtained 82 votes to 194 for Morrison. The leader of the left did secure the twelfth seat on the otherwise right-wing and centrist parliamentary committee for 1952–3, Harold Wilson and Geoffrey Bing being unsuccessful.

At a private dinner in the house on 25 November, the six Bevanites on the executive decided to constitute themselves as a steering committee, joined by Jennie Lee, Michael Foot and J.P.W. Mallalieu from *Tribune* (and later John Freeman from the *New Statesman*). The committee would meet for lunch once a week at Crossman's house when parliament was sitting.

It is not clear whether Harold Wilson remained chairman, now that the Bevanites had become a secret organization, and it is possible Mikardo resumed the position. There were to be six 'scoutmasters',[33] each responsible for a number of supporters, the full group meeting only at private social functions. The Tuesday lunches at Vincent Square began in early 1953. Bevan was to be an irregular attender, having decided to go upon a tour of India.

A shadowy 'second eleven'[34] came into being centred on Mikardo as chief organizer. He 'like[d] to translate talk into action', even though 'an organization man [in the labour party was] considered to be a covert capitalist'.[35] The second eleven was responsible for political work in the constituencies and trade unions, and Mikardo built on the success of the brains trusts. They provided a rare opportunity for political discussion within the electoral organization run by the national party. There was an unsuccessful attempt on the national executive in early 1953 to have the brains trusts banned, after *Tribune* took over the organization. Harold Wilson participated from June, but his contributions are not recalled. Nor does he seem to have been actively involved in the secret work of the Bevanites, unlike Foot, Castle, Freeman, Bing, Stephen Swingler and Davies. Other activists included Hugh Jenkins, Ben Parkin, Ted Castle and Ralph Miliband. From the time of the 1953 conference at Margate the 'informal group' was to be more organized especially in the selection of parliamentary candidates. Ted Castle remembered: 'there were no formal channels of communication between us and the first eleven although of course Jo Richardson was "secretary" to both the first and the second eleven.'[36] Peggy Duff, *Tribune*'s circulation manager, recalls: 'From 1954 on certainly it met regularly once a month, kept minutes of its proceedings, established sub-committees and occasional social gatherings, usually at Lord Faringdon's house at Buscot[t] Park'.[37] Meetings of the second eleven were held, on Sunday afternoons, either in the Castles' flat on Highgate Hill, or in Jo Richardson's home in Hornsey. 'Always Aneurin', according to Ted Castle, 'had a real fear of causing a split in the Party ... None of us could ever forget the effect of the split of 1931 and the terrible consequences for the Party.'[38]

Harold Wilson took an especial interest in nationalization as a member of the executive, the Morecambe conference having agreed to a review of labour's policy. When the first eleven met on 25 November 1952, he, Bevan and, apparently, Thomas Balogh argued that chemicals, heavy engineering, rented land and aircraft production should be taken into public ownership by the next labour government. This, according to Richard Crossman, was acceptable to Douglas Jay. By early 1953 the Bevanites were thinking they might have to resign on the question of policy, standing again at the party conference, but Bevan and Wilson agreed as members of the policy committee to close down two important sub-committees. Crossman asked Wilson, "'Have we got a policy for remedying the appalling situation in the nationalized industries and the private sector?'" He got a negative reply: '[Wilson] admitted he hadn't the faintest idea what we should do about them. The fact is that Nye and Harold are not interested in rethinking policy at all.'[39] At a later lunch, Bevan was indignant that only water had been designated for nationalization, but Wilson tried to suggest that controlling interests in the other industries could be interpreted as full public ownership. Such fancy theoretical footwork would be increasingly deployed to get Wilson out of a problem.

At a weekend meeting of the executive in April, with the majority against land nationalization, Wilson failed in his proposed compromise, and Bevan later suggested it might be an issue on which the minority could break. The new policy document, *Challenge to Britain*, emerged in June, in time for the Margate conference. Bevan welcomed it as a victory for the left, much to the consternation of his own supporters.

Harold Wilson had lost his ministerial salary of £5,000 in 1951, and needed to find work to supplement his £1,000 remuneration as an MP. Journalism was an acceptable profession for a labour politician, and it was announced on 29 April that he was to do a series of articles for *Reynolds News*, 'which [had] the great advantage of being read by most people in the Labour movement'.[40] Upon leaving the board of trade, Wilson was offered, so he claimed, positions in industry to the value of £22,000; one was an executive job in the film industry starting at £13,000. They were all turned down, but he changed his mind when labour lost the election, becoming an 'economic adviser' to Montague L. Meyer in Buckingham Street off the Strand, a family firm of timber importers, with a paid-up capital of a million pounds. Wilson was to remain with Meyers for eight years.

Montague Meyer and his brother had travelled to the Soviet Union after the revolution, becoming the first Britons to resume trading relations. The firm was the largest importer of softwood by the beginning of the second world war, with yards in the leading ports of the country. Montague Meyer became friendly with Ernest Bevin, and it was through the foreign secretary that Harold Wilson met the family. Wilson was able to put one of his officials in touch with Montague's son, Tom, upon his return from Washington in 1946, and he also took John Meyer, another son, with him to the Soviet Union as his timber expert. It was the latter who made the approaches in 1951.

Wilson infers he was asked to help the company with the Russians during the cold war. He claims his salary was less than suggested at the time, but admits it greatly eased his circumstances. Though Montague L. Meyer had no association with labour, or any other party, Harold Wilson was given an office, and possibly a company car. He brought his own secretary, Mrs Elise Cannon, from the house of commons, working at Meyers in the morning, before travelling to Westminster. He was hardly hired to 'prepare special studies for the directors on the trends in overseas markets',[41] but he did predict tory budgets, presumably after he became shadow chancellor. Wilson recalls being 'their political and economic consultant', but also 'diplomatic adviser'.[42] He was paid to do privately what he had done as a minister, represent the company abroad and also give advice to its senior executives. John Meyer's cousin, Peter, considers he was, above all, 'a sounding board'.[43] Wilson left for Moscow on 10 May 1953 with his secretary, probably on behalf of the company. Stalin had died in early March, and sections of western opinion had begun to look for some alleviation in the cold war, trade being a possible harbinger of improved diplomatic relations. Harold Wilson was met at the airport by the heads of the soviet timber export corporation.

He was interested in discussing world politics, and assessing the new leadership in the Kremlin. (He was to stop off in Budapest on his way home, for talks with Hungarian ministers.) Wilson had a meeting with Mikoyan in Moscow, the two discussing Anglo-Soviet trade, in particular timber exports. Wilson claimed this was the first meeting between a Russian and an Englishman since their talks in 1947. He even had an hour with Molotov, once again foreign minister, describing him as 'an original Bolshevik not a parvenu technocrat'. Wilson also met Andrei Gromyko, who had recently been ambassador in London, at a lunch given by the British ambassador.

Harold Wilson spent nine days in the Russian capital, much of his time being occupied meeting members of the diplomatic community and foreign journalists (but not the *Daily Worker*'s correspondent). While taking a photograph in Red Square, he had been arrested by a policeman. Wilson recalls 'it was one of the few times in my life that I have lost my cool ... I raised my voice and used abusive language; when this did not reduce his interest in my camera, I succeeded in conveying to him that I was seeing Mikoyan the following day.'[44] He also visited shops, to inspect the goods on sale, and was permitted, unusually, to visit workers' homes. After his return to Britain, he wrote an uncharacteristically brief report, of seven pages with three appendices. A copy of this was sent to Richard Crossman, and it was eventually circulated to members of the party executive. Harold Wilson boasted that his views on all questions were 'well known' in Moscow, and advanced an authoritative interpretation of the post-Stalinist regime: 'Peaceful co-existence, then, looks like being the theme, and the world will have to get used to a divided Germany, possibly to the quadripartite frustrations in Austria. It is a great deal less desirable than peace, [but] ... it is greatly to be preferred, not only to the horrors of World War III, but to the cold war that has limited our national and international horizons for so long.'[45] Fifty labour MPs turned up to a special meeting of the parliamentary party on 25 June to hear Wilson report in person. 'He did a magnificent job', according to Crossman, 'of blowing out his information so that he could tell us everything that was happening in Russia. The technique [was] to start by saying, "Of course, I only have 2 per cent of the information necessary to form a judgment but most of the pundits in Washington have only 1 per cent", and then go on to give judgments on everything ... Harold did it with the very greatest skill.'[46]

Meyers provided Harold Wilson with direct experience of business. In a book published in 1964, Frank Pakenham, then Lord Longford, was to 'associate Hugh Gaitskell with public service before all else[,] and Harold Wilson with an instinct for business'.[47] For an old Etonian, this was an orthodox, and accurate, view of a Wykehamist. Longford also envisaged Gaitskell as a magnificent chairman of a bank, and predicted that Harold Wilson would be a fine socialist prime minister. Someone closer to Wilson has written of his time in the timber business:

> I have a theory that when he left the Board of Trade and joined the Meyer organization, he became a liberated person. He escaped the restrictions of ministerial life and also the confines of life at the top of a political party. He was less inhibited and was able to let himself go. He expanded and grew tremendously during this period ... He came to understand a great deal about how industry works and about how business firms work ... But now, looking back, I wonder whether this apparent advantage might not have been a disadvantage in the long run, for his specialized knowledge of the difficulties that business firms can encounter, and his sympathy with their problems, might well have made him less tough with some of them than he should have been when he became Prime Minister.[48]

Meyers was not to be Harold Wilson's only involvement in the world of business. Before the war, an Austrian emigré, Frank Schon, had started a detergent firm in Cumberland – Marchon Products. Wilson became involved with the company as president of the board of trade; Schon was providing work, and Wilson was concerned with developing hitherto depressed areas. Marchon received help from the industrial and commercial finance corporation, set up in 1945 with labour government support. When Arthur Creech Jones, the colonial secretary, lost his seat in 1950, the corporation made him its representative on the board of Marchon's. With the Korean war, supplies of American sulphur, used in detergent manufacturing, became difficult to obtain. Wilson, who was to show a distinct recollection of sulphur shortages, set up a committee in the board of trade, to consider indigenous methods of manufacturing sulphuric acid. Considerable government help was forthcoming to Schon, to allow him to build a new plant near to deposits of anhydrite (calcium sulphate) in Cumberland.

Harold Wilson was to be involved with Marchon Products in opposition, and he apparently helped Schon sell a detergent plant to the Russians in 1958. Though a leading member of the opposition front bench, he was put on a retainer of about £1,000 per year, plus all expenses, until 1963. 'This discreet deal ... enabled Wilson to make a great show in 1959 of giving up his publicly-known consultancy with Montague L. Meyer.'[49]

The Bevanites were concerned that they might not retain their six seats on the executive at the 1953 Margate conference. Herbert Morrison was nominated for the treasurership, but the conference decided to make the deputy leader an ex officio member, and the treasurership remained with the ailing Arthur Greenwood. The same members were returned for the constituencies, with Bevan and Castle leading for the Bevanites. Wilson rose to third place, and Crossman also increased his vote. Driberg dropped relatively, and Mikardo, in particular, had been at risk. *Challenge to Britain* was ratified by the delegates, the leading Bevanites being constrained to speak for the executive. In the general debate on financial policies and controls, in which Gaitskell counterposed death duties to nationalization, Harold Wilson, replying to the movers of motions and speakers, defended public ownership. He voiced what was to become a personal theme: 'the first task of any socialist Chancellor of the Exchequer is to nationalise, not the joint stock banks but the Treasury.'[50] Bevan lost the deputy leadership contest by 76 votes to 181 for Morrison when parliament resumed, but he retained his seat on the parliamentary committee. Harold Wilson failed to get elected by one vote. If he had got on, he would have been spared considerable agonizing several months later. There was some discussion about reconstituting the Bevanite group, and it was decided to set up 'unofficial groups on special subjects',[51] in an attempt to permeate the parliamentary party's policy committees. Harold Wilson was a member of the finance group, which was chaired by Gaitskell, its other members, besides Jay, being Jenkins, Crosland, John Diamond, Douglas Houghton and Dick Mitchinson. The parliamentary committee then selected speakers for debates each week, former ministers tending to shadow their successors. Harold Wilson had a right to sit on the front bench as a former minister, but he followed other former ministers on to backbenches, choosing a seat on the second row. The executive set up a finance and economic policy sub-committee in January 1953, its members including Balogh, Gaitskell, Crosland and Wilson, though the latter was not prominent. It was only in 1953 that he began to speak for the opposition, being invited on to the front bench by Gaitskell.

German rearmament once again became an issue in Britain in early 1954, following the failure of the Berlin four-power conference. The parliamentary labour party came out for what was known as the European defence community, within NATO, on 23 February. Labour MPs only supported the shadow cabinet by 113 votes to 104, the Bevanite position being put by Harold Wilson, with 'a quiet, inoffensive speech'.[52] It was his first major political statement, one for which he was to be remembered. His amendment secured 109 votes, losing by only 2 in the party meeting. Bevan and Attlee clashed at the executive on 24 March.

The story broke the following day that the United States had recently exploded a hydrogen bomb in the Pacific. By 5 April, Attlee had forced Churchill to request disarmament talks with the United States and Soviet Union. With the French under considerable pressure in Indo-China, the foreign secretary, Anthony Eden, began to talk on 13 April about collective defence in southeast Asia. Attlee rose in the house to endorse an anti-communist initiative, but Bevan stated Eden's statement would be 'deeply resented by most people in Britain'.[53] This was seen as a public challenge to the leader of the labour party, from a member of the parliamentary committee. The following day, almost three years after an earlier resignation, Bevan quit the shadow cabinet. 'In view of the unpleasant incidents'[54] the previous afternoon, he was minuted, he would sit on the backbenches after Easter.

He immediately bumped into Crossman and Wilson, in the library corridor of the house of commons. Bevan was placing Wilson in a dilemma, since the secretary of the committee immediately notified Wilson of the vacancy. 'If he automatically said no to Nye's place', Crossman observed, 'he would just look like Nye's poodle. If he accepted, he would look as if he were breaking up the Bevanite Group.'[55] These were options Harold Wilson would have characteristically fudged, if it had been simply a case of words. Now it was a question of action, in which he had something to gain by automatically allowing the procedure of the parliamentary committee to work. Crossman and George Wigg agreed on 15 April that he should leave things open during the Easter recess. Wilson was angry at having his fate determined in such a way, but the idea of standing, if there were a new ballot, appealed to him. Bevan 'rebuked [Crossman] for giving [Harold Wilson] wrong advice' after Easter, on 20 April, but Crossman stated that 'Harold had a perfect right to regard himself as freed from all responsibility to Nye.' His next reply is of considerable significance, being the earliest documented statement of its kind: 'I ... said that, in my view, it was now far more likely that Harold Wilson would succeed to the premiership than that Nye would. He was just the type of man who would succeed Attlee. To which Nye replied: "If he's that kind of man, I don't want anything to do with him."'[56]

Crossman 'predict[ed] that Harold [would] play an extremely sophisticated and nicely calculated game'. He wrote to Wilson on 22 April that

Bevan 'looked as though he had the death-wish on him!'[57] It seems that Mikardo was supporting Bevan, and that Crossman, while he liked the idea of a new ballot, wanted Wilson to confer with the Bevanites and decide not to run for the vacant seat. By 26 April it was clear there would be no ballot. Crossman and Wilson then agreed that he should be coopted, but issue a statement saying he supported Bevan, and that the latter agreed to him serving in the interests of party unity. Wilson was unwilling to put this to Bevan on his own, and the latter, in any case, insisted, in 'a friendly but rather uneasy conversation'[58] with the two of them, that it would be seen as a split in the Bevanites.

At the regular Tuesday lunch the next day, Wilson, with Crossman, found himself in opposition to Bevan, Jennie Lee, Bing, Freeman, Balogh, Mikardo and Driberg. Bevan 'made it clear that ... the present parliamentary leadership was hopeless and that an electoral success would be disastrous until [it] had been completely changed as the result of a mass movement in the constituencies, which we were to lead from the backbenches, while staying on the [executive]'.[59] Wilson produced a draft letter later in the afternoon, which he intended to send to the secretary of the parliamentary party, only to meet with Bevan hinting about MacDonaldite betrayal. He decided to go on the committee the following morning, with the support only of Richard Crossman and George Wigg. Wilson then went to see Attlee, Crossman recording: 'Harold says he delivered ... a strong lecture on the need for a proper balance in the Party and re-emphasized his determination to remain loyal to Nye.' He predicted a rough time for Wilson, but hoped that, if the latter 'remain[ed] 100 per cent Bevanite', the leader of the group would 'restrain the two or three members ... who would already like to denounce Harold for MacDonaldism'.[60] Wilson expressed in his letter what was to become the essence of Wilsonism: 'what matters in the last resort is the unity and strength of the Party.'[61]

Shawcross, who was not a member of the parliamentary committee, seems to have continued to shadow the board of trade, when not busy at the bar. This may have been why Wilson, at the parliamentary committee on 26 May 1954, provoked a long discussion on a recent Shawcross speech which was a thinly disguised attack upon Bevan. The speech, Wilson argued, threatened party unity. Gaitskell continued to shadow the treasury, criticizing the conservative chancellor, Rab Butler.

When the tories cut food subsidies in the 1952 budget, Gaitskell opposed the chancellor. In a parliamentary party meeting at the time, Harold Wilson had, apparently, wanted to strengthen labour's response. He recalls of 1952 that 'Hugh and [he] led the fight [against the finance bill], passing the ball to one another for all the world as if we were a pair of well-trained American footballers',[62] but Gaitskell's diary, in which he privately compared Bevan to Hitler, reveals no significant political cooperation with Wilson during the 1951 parliament.

Wilson had also taken an interest in international development. This was hardly a pressing topic with the left of the labour party, and it saw Wilson associate with the sort of reformers who might have been former liberals. He had been involved with the FAO, but took no further interest at the board of trade. Global development, however, was becoming a more familiar issue, the progress of backward – or developing – areas being seen as dependent upon aid and advice from the leading capitalist countries, particularly the United States, and international agencies. Harold Wilson was involved in Britain in the foundation of the organization War on Want, which had its origins in a letter from Victor Gollancz, the left-wing publisher, to the *Manchester Guardian* in early 1951, asking readers to affirm support for east-west negotiations and a north–south programme. Just after the resignation of the three ministers, the association for world peace set up a committee on world development, and Harold Wilson was approached to preside over its work. It comprised eleven men and women, including Ritchie Calder and E.F. Schumacher, its leading members being Richard Acland and Leslie Hale, two Bevanite MPs. Wilson, Acland, Hale and Mary Rosser drafted the ninety-six page report, *War on Want: a Plan for World Development*, which was published by the association in June 1952. Harold Wilson probably drafted much of the document, and Acland recalls 'he was always spot on punctual. [He] always knew what the next thing to be done was. He always listened patiently to any point that I put up.'[63] Acland now describes *War on Want* as 'a very feeble document'.[64] With Gollancz less than fully committed, Acland, with Hale's assistance, took on the task of promoting War on Want. It was launched at the Free Trade Hall in Manchester, Harold Wilson being one of the speakers. About £200,000 was raised for development projects, before the organization was handed on in 1954.

Wilson identified himself with the issue of world development for the next year or so. He addressed a meeting of the Swiss peace council, in the town hall in Berne in October 1952, his speech being published the following year in London as *Today They Die: The Case for World Cooperation*. This pamphlet was published by the national peace council, which published another of Wilson's pamphlets in 1953, *Two out of Three: The Problem of World Poverty*, which was the economic conclusion of a disarmament commission report. Wilson admitted that, while the underdeveloped world would solve the west's problems, 'in the short period, development ... on the required scale [would] involve a drain on the scarce materials of the Western world'.[65] These pamphlets were based on *The War on World Poverty: an Appeal to the Conscience of Mankind*, a book Wilson published with Gollancz in 1953. Running to some 200 pages, it grew out of work he had done for the association of world peace committee. Wilson wrote the epilogue a year after the publication of *War on Want*, and the book rehearsed the case for development, known to the experts but probably not to a wider public. He argued for agricultural and industrial development, but also for capital works programmes, and a concern for social development. Harold Wilson estimated that ten times the existing external finance was needed by developing countries. He was appreciative of Britain's record of colonial development, despite the ground nuts scheme. On the basis of the Colombo plan, he endorsed the idea that the united nations should establish a world development authority, which was currently being resisted by the United States, Britain and the Soviet Union.

When Harold Wilson accepted cooption to the parliamentary committee, he incurred the disapproval of Bevan and most of the group. Though few are prepared to admit it even now, Bevan never forgave him. Ian Mikardo recalls Bevan had seen 'Wilson as a man on the make but didn't allow that to interfer with his relationships with him, until that fatal Tuesday'. He was subsequently 'hostile privately, [and] publicly distant'.[66] At one of the first meetings, he was in a minority of four who opposed a savage attack by Morrison on Bevan in *Socialist Commentary*. Wilson continued to meet with the Bevanites, but Mikardo remembers that Bevan's resignation 'ended the Bevanites as a coherent cohesive group. It certainly ended Harold's association.'[67]

When Arthur Greenwood died, Bevan decided to stand for the treasurership at the 1954 conference in Scarborough, a post the trade-union leaders wanted to give Gaitskell. Bevan was prepared to give up his seat on the executive to stand, to show that Deakin and Williamson, of the two general unions, 'prefer[ed] an intellectual like Gaitskell to a miner like [him]'.[68] Gaitskell was viewed as a coming leader, while Bevan, with his left-wing politics and artistic friends, had long been contemptuous of trade-union leaders and MPs. Gaitskell was elected treasurer by 4,338,000 votes to 2,032,000 for Bevan at the end of September, and was to soon come joint top in the parliamentary committee poll. Bevan, in contrast, had resigned from the shadow cabinet, and given up the executive. Having lost the election, his standing was purely moral as an MP and a socialist speaker in the country.

Harold Wilson supplanted Barbara Castle at the top of the constituencies section, with 1,043,000 votes, an endorsement for having taken Bevan's seat. His four Bevanite colleagues were also returned, and Anthony Greenwood, son of Arthur, who was not yet fully identified as a Bevanite, came on to the executive in third place. Bevan spoke at the *Tribune* rally the following day, and made what was assumed to be a personal attack, when he referred to 'a desiccated calculating machine'[69] leading the labour party. This was taken to be a reference to Gaitskell, although Bevan was to claim it was a 'synthetic figure'.[70] Many considered he had begun his decline as a great socialist leader, and Richard Crossman found Harold Wilson to be 'buoyant' the next morning, noting: 'I can't help suspecting that [this] ... was due to a partly conscious recognition that this speech had given him the leadership.'[71]

The conflict between Bevan and Gaitskell had broken out in 1950–1, and was to be resolved finally with the death of the two men. It would reach its nadir, shortly, in 1955. Bevan was to narrow the distance, once Gaitskell became party leader, and the latter was to be conciliatory, until after the 1959 election. The reforms which Gaitskell was to begin then, in the wake of the party's third defeat, Bevan's demise would allow him to complete in 1961. The triumphant right-wing leader would be struck down less than two years later. The rivalry between Bevan and Gaitskell is of epic proportions, requiring artistry in analysis. It is an historical tragedy, the intimates of both men maintaining, to this day, that their hero would have made a great British prime minister. Bevan's close associates can only be described as in love with the greatest socialist leader Britain never had, while surviving Gaitskellites would probably prefer to think of their hero as the best man for the job. The struggle between Bevan and Gaitskell in the 1950s has a dramatic quality worthy of a modern opera.

The former was born in 1897 the son of a Welsh miner, the latter to an Indian civil servant nine years later. While Hugh Gaitskell progressed from public school to Oxford, Aneurin Bevan was a working-class autodidact. He became a labour MP in 1929, about the time the former embarked on an academic career. While Gaitskell was in the civil service during the war, Bevan was editing *Tribune*. The difference between the two men was one of class. Bevan revealed this when he reproached Sam Watson, of the Durham miners, for backing Gaitskell as treasurer: 'How can you support a public schoolboy from Winchester against a man born in the back streets of Tredegar?'[72] The point is well made, however, that Bevan, as a backbench MP, held many working-class, mainly trade-union members, in contempt in the 1930s. He had been loyal to the likes of Cripps, and would have public schoolboys as leading Bevanites. Bevan, in conversation with Crossman, was to describe himself as an aristocrat, in comparison with the bourgeois Gaitskell. Bevan was a socialist in a way that Gaitskell was not. The latter believed he had a right to rule, and a duty to prove labour could be a responsible government. He stressed Whitehall and Westminster, and, rhetorically, the electorate, since the latter gave legitimacy to the mandarins manqués of the Hampstead set. Bevan's 'primitive Marxism'[73] accepted the institutions of British democracy, and the reality of government power, but he looked to an independent working class, albeit through constituency labour parties, and had a vision of socialism continually enriched by struggles at home and abroad. This was the structural contradiction in the rivalry between Bevan and Gaitskell. It had been manifest in previous decades, within the personalities and politics of labour leaders, and was to be evident later. Gaitskell said in 1960 that 'it was a battle between us for power – [Bevan] knew it and so did I.'[74] But this power struggle, while shaped by the personalities of the two men, was driven by a structural contradiction between two positions on the left of British politics.

The battle was about the character of the labour party, as the Attlee years drew to a close. Bevan feared it was losing a sense of political mission, while Gaitskell believed politics were only a means to administration. The electoral defeat of 1951 had been a total negation for Gaitskell, but for Bevan it was a sign that the party had to renew itself politically. He looked to the activists in the constituencies, and, later, in the unions, while the ex-chancellor preferred parliamentary and trade-union leaders. The conflict was lived at a personal level. This was certainly true of Bevan, who responded emotionally, but Gaitskell was also deeply emotional, despite 'the appalling weight of convention in [his] youth'.[75] Bevan wanted to be leader, but only of a socialist party which represented a mobilized people. This is why he was a great tribune. Gaitskell also wanted to be leader, but of a practical party which would not upset the establishment. This is why he was to prevail in the 1950s. The series of clashes between these two men was a personification of the dilemma of a socialist party in a capitalist society.

Bevanism began to break up after the 1954 conference. Crossman, musing on 12 October about prospects for the left, envisaged Bevan skulking on his farm in the Chilterns: 'Jennie [Lee]'s political influence on him will prevail and make him more and more the spokesman of a lunatic fringe. That is one danger. The other danger, of course, is that people like Harold, myself and Barbara [Castle] will be killed with kindness by the Right.'[76] This was not to be. Harold Wilson, referring several weeks later to a *Tribune* attack on Arthur Deakin, 'made his favourite crack that Bevanism is impossible without Bevan but would be far better without the *Tribune*'.[77] He sat silent on the executive while the meeting, at the behest of the TUC, condemned Jennie Lee, Michael Foot and 'Curly' Mallalieu, but privately backed a pamphlet reply penned by Foot. He also told Attlee, on 10 November, that the expulsion of the editorial board would lead to the resignation of all the paper's supporters from the executive. It was becoming clear that Harold Wilson wanted to lead the left, but from a safe position at the centre of the party.

The party conference had voted narrowly to back the executive on the all-important question of German rearmament. When it came to labour MPs supporting the nine-power agreement, whereby Germany was to be admitted to NATO, it was decided that the parliamentary party would abstain on the vote on 18 November. This seemingly ended a divisive issue for the party; the left secured a moral victory, and the right a practical one. With the state of international relations still uncertain, Bevan sought, towards the end of the year, to reengage the question. He tabled a parliamentary resolution on 15 February 1955, which was supported by over 100 labour MPs, calling for four-power talks on Germany. The parliamentary party rebuked him by 132 votes to 72 nine days later. It had been decided to censure the government in a defence debate, though not oppose the commitment to build the hydrogen – or H – bomb, which had been announced on 17 February in a white paper. Bevan was not opposed to a thermonuclear military strategy, and Crossman agreed with the government, since the H bomb dispensed with the need for German rearmament. When Bevan started to waiver on supporting the party amendment, it looked like the Bevanites would tilt towards a pacifist position. On 2 March during the defence debate, Bevan challenged Attlee on the terms of nuclear first use, making three separate attacks. Some sixty-two labour MPs then abstained on their party's censure. At least eight Bevanites, including Crossman, Wilson and Freeman, followed Attlee through the lobby. It was the beginning of the end. 'The only man who was any good ... was Nye Bevan', wrote Crossman the following day, 'and he took a palpably dishonest decision, whereas the rest of the leadership were nigglers, knaves or cowards.'[78]

The withdrawal of the whip by the shadow cabinet, and even the expulsion of Bevan from the labour party by the national executive, was on the cards for his *lèse majesté*. The parliamentary committee decided, at a special meeting on Monday, 7 March, by nine votes to four, that the whip should be withdrawn. Ede and Callaghan moved the motion, and its opponents included Wilson, who leaked the information to Crossman. Hugh Gaitskell had favoured a strong censure, since withdrawal of the whip would not prevent Bevan from standing for party office, but he voted with the majority. He believed that expulsion from the party could not be got through the national executive and conference. Harold Wilson was to claim 'he wondered whether to resign [from the shadow cabinet], but decided not to.'[79] At the Bevanite lunch the following day, Crossman and Wilson declined to threaten en bloc to resign from the executive, if it should expel Bevan from the party. The alternative tactic of a round robin of 130 MPs, opposing withdrawal of the whip, failed for lack of support. Bevan was ill with flu, and the shadow cabinet, with Wilson absent, decided to wait a week before asking the parliamentary party to support withdrawal of the whip. Harold Wilson thought Bevan was doomed, and arranged to be in Paris when the parliamentary party met on 16 March. Dalton recorded in his diary that 'Wilson ... [was] diplomatically absent.' He was to claim he had asserted his right to abstain in the parliamentary party meeting, but Gaitskell recorded that 'even Harold Wilson indicated that he would of course stand by the Committee'.[80] An amendment that Wednesday to censure Bevan fell by 138 votes to 124, but Attlee's motion for expulsion from the parliamentary party was carried by 141 to 112, hardly an outright victory for the parliamentary leadership. The secretary of the parliamentary party was instructed to write to Morgan Phillips, informing him of the withdrawal of the whip. The issue was to be taken to the national executive on Wednesday, 23 March. Gaitskell finally became committed to this, but Crossman, at a secret meeting with Gaitskell on Tuesday, 22 March, said the left might dump Bevan. He also suggested that Wilson would probably run for the treasurership in October, if Bevan was thrown out of the party by the executive. Attlee made a conciliatory proposal to the executive, namely that a sub-committee should seek assurances from Bevan about his future behaviour, this being accepted by a majority of only one. Bevan owed his reprieve to Mikardo, who had hurried back from his daughter's wedding in Israel, as it is certain that Edith Summerskill would have cast her vote against him. Bevan apologized to Attlee at the sub-committee of eight on Tuesday, 29 March, but declined to refrain from criticizing others. Attlee and Griffiths wanted to accept Bevan's assurances about the future at the executive on 30 March. A tougher amendment was carried by fifteen to ten, with the leader and Griffiths against, and these two abstained, when the substantive motion was carried by sixteen votes to seven. Bevan was saved from expulsion, but warned about his future behaviour. Harold Wilson had tried to amend the motion, losing by twenty votes to six, with Attlee against him. Bevan remained excluded from the labour ranks in parliament, but there was now no need to appeal – as he would have done – to the party conference against expulsion from the party.

Churchill had at last decided to quit as prime minister, resigning on 5 April in the middle of a national newspaper strike, which also obscured the Bevan affair. The shadow cabinet offered to consider restoring the whip to Bevan, and he gave the usual undertaking to accept standing orders when readopted as a labour candidate. He was finally encouraged to give assurances about his future behaviour to the chief whip, the shadow cabinet recommending restoration of the whip to the parliamentary party meeting on 28 April.

The conservative party had not lost a by-election in the whole parliament, and good county council election results encouraged Sir Anthony Eden to go to the country on 26 May. With the promise of a new patrician premier, and opinion polls, from January 1955, showing labour in second place, the omens were good for the conservatives. Butler introduced tax cuts in his budget on 19 April, a blatant electoral bribe. *Forward with Labour*, though drafted by Crossman and Driberg, offered little new in domestic affairs, while promising continuity in foreign policy. It was now the labour opposition which was seen to have an ageing leader; Attlee was perceived as having failed to rid the party of Bevanism. The general election on 26 May saw a significant drop in turnout, with an electorate which had grown little. Labour lost one and a half million votes, its 277 seats being 18 down on the previous result. The conservatives lost half a million votes, but secured 49.7 per cent of the poll. With 344 seats they increased their overall majority to 58.

Harold Wilson was to attribute the conservative victory 'mainly to the apathy created in Labour's rank and file by the public dissensions'.[81] The turn-out at Huyton reflected the national pattern, though the electorate had grown by nearly 6,000. Much attention was paid to Southdene Estate in Kirby. Harold Wilson had the support of Anthony Greenwood at his adoption meeting on Sunday, 8 May, and advertised speakers included Driberg and Pakenham. Attlee spoke for Wilson at Hambleton Hall in Huyton on Wednesday, 18 May. Aneurin Bevan did not visit the constituency.

Asked about the division in the party throughout the parliament, Wilson stated he accepted the 1954 conference position on German rearmament. When a local baptist minister criticized him for holding a meeting on Sunday, 15 May, Wilson replied that, while his 'religious principles' found expression in the labour party, he accepted that 'very many sincere Christians ... equally feel that to them Christianity is fulfilled in the teachings and practice of the Conservative party.'[82] He had done a great deal to look after the interests of his constituents, and his campaign slogan was 'Your friend indeed'.[83] He claimed in his election address that he had honoured his pledge to voluntary schools. The count was held at Rupert Road Modern School on 26 May, a recount being necessary because some ballot papers were overlooked. Harold Wilson received 24,858 votes to his conservative opponent's 22,300, his majority of 2,558 meaning Merseyside had another safe labour seat.

Attlee had been thinking of going for some time, and a new generation of leaders emerged in the early 1950s. He was mainly concerned to stop Morrison, a man who had tried to capture the leadership in 1935 and again 1945. Many assumed Morrison would step into Attlee's shoes, having been reelected deputy leader each session, though he was only five years younger. Bevan had once been a possible party leader, until the rows in the party. Hugh Dalton publicly suggested that those over sixty-five should not stand for the parliamentary committee, this being a way of advancing Gaitskell's bid for the leadership. Dalton exempted Attlee to keep out Morrison, but his 'operation avalanche' applied to eight of the fifteen members of the shadow cabinet from the commons. Harold Wilson, at thirty-nine, was the youngest member of the parliamentary leadership. Lunching with Crossman on 6 June, Wilson conceded the leadership to

Gaitskell in due course. He hinted that he then wanted the deputy leadership, in spite of having been elected last to the shadow cabinet the previous autumn. Bevan, in his opinion, would be the left-wing candidate that year, but not for much longer. Wilson's opportunity was to come, presumably, in the new parliament. 'Gaitskell realized that if ever he made a mess of things Harold was there to step into his shoes as a *tertium gaudens*.'[84]

Attlee informed his parliamentary colleagues he would go at the end of the session, which was to run through the summer and into 1956. In the elections for the shadow cabinet in June 1955, Bevan, George Brown, Anthony Greenwood, Richard Stokes and Dick Mitchinson came on. Gaitskell was second with 184 votes, and Harold Wilson fifth with 147. He considered Bevan, who came seventh, should now consolidate his position in the parliamentary party, an arena he had eschewed as a rebel. Attlee accepted a suggestion from Gaitskell, which had originated with Crossman and Wilson, that designated members of the front bench should shadow government ministers for the session. Wilson was assigned the board of trade in July, and given Arthur Bottomley as his number two. Bevan was asked to look after labour, and Alf Robens was given the foreign office to shadow.

The 1955 election defeat was to provoke a major debate about party policy and even socialism. Harold Wilson, with the support of Crossman and Gaitskell, suggested to the executive on 22 June that there should be a report on party organization. He got himself appointed chairman of a sub-committee, whose other members were Jack Cooper, a leading trade unionist, and Margaret (Peggy) Herbison and Arthur Skeffington, both MPs. Between 5 July and 24 September, the Wilson committee took evidence at forty-nine meetings with MPs and national and regional officials. This was the first serious study of how the labour party functioned in the country, Wilson conducting the inquiry in a manner reminiscent of Beveridge. Evidence, written or oral, was taken from 550 agents, 140 MPs, and 164 candidates, and he managed to keep the other three members of the committee on board. Wilson prepared the statistical tables, and wrote the interim report himself, the printed version presented to the conference running to over forty pages, including eight appendices. Though it had a few good phrases, the report was an extremely detailed piece of organizational analysis, rather than an intellectual contribution to political sociology. Wilson denied it was an 'inquest' into electoral defeat. This was something he was not powerful enough to conduct, and he would have got little thanks within the party. He advanced some of his own ideas about the labour party in his report. 'Obviously full employment, overtime and the widespread employment of married women affected not only political attitudes but also the numbers of voluntary workers willing and able to carry on election activities. Apathy, disputes in the Party, national and local, the absence of sufficient clearly defined differences between the parties, disillusionment with nationalisation in the way it has been presented to the public, the rationing scare; all these have played their part.' He was concerned mainly with the decline in the number of volunteers who had been mobilized by the party. 'Many of those who did work for a Labour victory were older men and women: with many it was habit rather than enthusiasm which provided the motive force.'[85]

'Organisation', Harold Wilson concluded, '[had] become the Cinderella of the Party at all levels.'[86] 'Compared with our opponents, we are still at the penny-farthing stage in a jet-propelled era, and our machine, at that, is getting rusty and deteriorating with age.'[87] He advanced the theory that general elections were won, not by persuading 'floating'[88] voters that the party had the best programme, but by getting out the traditional labour vote. He even calculated that labour could have won an additional sixty-six seats, and therefore the election, with better organization. He and his colleagues had obviously been impressed by the conservatives' professionalism, but he had to acknowledge that such talk was 'offensive alike to our traditions and our principles'.[89] The report focused on how the national party could stimulate voluntary activity at local level. Among the list of forty-one recommendations, the most important dealt with political agents, whom Wilson thought should be given cars, etc. Wilson highlighted the position in large urban areas, where municipal politics had stimulated the development of city parties, invariably at the expense of constituency organizations, an observation which undoubtedly antagonized local labour councillors. He also attacked the labour party for being too centralized as a bureaucracy, there being 'a wrong relationship between Head Office and the Regions ... [of the sort] we should expect to find in a minor department of the War Office, rather than in a great national Party.'[90] His prescription was modernization, the target being a marked register of labour supporters in every constituency in the country, to be completed in two years. Harold Wilson remembers that the report 'pleased the right wing of the Party, not up to that point my natural allies'.[91] He may also have felt that it would appeal to party activists. The report was debated in the private session of the party conference at Margate in October, having already been leaked – by Wilson it was believed – to the *Daily Mirror*, and was 'received'[92] by the delegates. The debate was opened by a trade unionist, who attacked Wilson's integrity. He argued that organization was being used to cover up political dissension as the cause of electoral defeat. Bevan spoke later as an ordinary constituency delegate, 'brush[ing] aside the topic under discussion and [bringing] the Party back to the question of whether it wanted to be a fighting Socialist Party or not'.[93] The interim report was accepted as final by the new executive, and, when it came to appointing sub-committees, Wilson succeeded in having himself and his colleagues entrusted, with others, to implement the recommended changes.

He had successfully imposed his conception of labour's problem on the national executive committee, a solution which might have been expected from a former civil servant. But it did not prevent the right launching a major ideological critique, which was to dominate the second half of the 1950s. Harold Wilson broke formally in 1955 with the socialist fundamentalism of the Bevanite movement, this giving way to the Crossman–Wilson 'Left Centre'.[94] Crossman saw 'a new Centre of the Party ... forming, which [was] trying to create a policy and leadership neither subservient to the unions on the one side nor appeasing Bevan on the other'.[95] Wilson wanted 'a changing personnel'[96] invited to the Tuesday lunches at Crossman's to build a new power base in the parliamentary party.

Bevan had been elected to the parliamentary committee with 118 votes. He did not oppose Morrison for the deputy leadership, but challenged Gaitskell for the treasurership. The latter was reelected with 5,475,000 votes to Bevan's 1,225,000, due partly to the railwaymen and shopworkers switching sides. A 'considerable number of constituency parties had [also] transferred their votes to Gaitskell'.[97] Bevan was again unable to run for the executive, and Wilson topped the poll in the constituencies section for the second time, being joined by the same six members. Castle, Greenwood and Crossman were – by fits and starts – becoming followers of Wilson. Jim Griffiths was the fading compromise candidate between right and left to replace Attlee. Driberg and Mikardo still remained loyal to Bevan. Gaitskell had hitherto only addressed the conference as a member of parliament, but he spoke from the platform as treasurer in the debate on nationalized industries at the Margate conference in 1955, giving, in Michael Foot's words, 'a superbly delivered peroration'.[98] His success was followed by a parliamentary triumph, when, as shadow chancellor, he confronted Butler. Having introduced a giveaway budget in time for the election, the conservative chancellor presented an emergency one on 26 October, increasing taxation and cutting public spending. Gaitskell had prepared a characteristically professional speech, but, at the suggestion of a member of the parliamentary party, he added personal attacks on Butler. 'No doubt', noted Crossman, 'he saw at last the opportunity to destroy once and for all the figure of "Mr Butskell" – a demolition essential if he is to become the Leader of the Labour Party.'[99] Butler was to be replaced on 20 December by Harold Macmillan, and Gaitskell's speech led Attlee to announce on 7 December that he was resigning.

CHAPTER 13

Shadow Chancellor of the Exchequer, 1955–9

Attlee decided to go, in his seventy-third year, when he felt Morrison had irrevocably damaged his chances. The deputy leader's political destruction was arranged, indirectly, by Harold Wilson. It was he who urged that Morrison should open for the opposition in a censure debate on 31 October, when the latter made what was widely considered to be a disastrous speech. Wilson collaborated closely with Gaitskell during the passage of the finance bill in November, creating 'a succession of field-days and field-nights'.[1] He even succeeded in having the bill declared non-existent, but did not oppose its restoration to the order paper. With these 'bright young men taking over the [party] machine',[2] Attlee may have felt he was leaving labour in safe hands. But this alliance of middle-class intellectuals across the left–right ideological divide, saw something of a working-class rapprochement between Bevan and the trade-union MPs.

Gaitskell had not been in the running to succeed Attlee, thinking merely he would stand for the deputy leadership. It was Morrison's parliamentary failure which alerted him to the possibility that he would have to stand as the right-wing candidate, though the idea seems to have been at the back of his mind. Wilson and Gaitskell had made a post-conference broadcast together on 14 October, and, sitting in Gaitskell's car later, in a side street in Soho, Wilson pledged his support. In his own words some years afterwards, he said: 'I don't think you're ideal, Hugh, but I'll back you for [the leadership] wholeheartedly – so long as you stop trying to force every issue, by always trying to get a majority decision on everything that crops up. If you'll really try to work with the whole party, take a unifying not a divisive view of your responsibilities, you can count on my complete support when Attlee goes – and on my continuing loyalty.'[3] The implication may have been that Wilson would become deputy leader, if and when Morrison finally stepped down. Bevan was also after the position, and offered on 3 November to back Morrison for the leadership in the second ballot, in return for support, and office later as foreign secretary. Even Morrison was preferable to Gaitskell in the opinion of the Bevanites, and Bevan may have believed he would take over the leadership in four or so years. The two former adversaries met again on the evening of Attlee's announcement. The following day, 8 December, Bevan offered not to run for the leadership, at the request of ten elderly MPs, if Gaitskell would withdraw in favour of Morrison. This ploy backfired badly, and must have pushed many into the Gaitskell camp. Harold Wilson subsequently claimed that he 'was shocked and affronted by what he considered immoral tactics',[4] which is impossible to believe. When nominations closed, Bevan, Morrison and Gaitskell were all in the ring to succeed Attlee. Balloting ended on 14 December, and, when the votes were counted, it was found that Morrison had secured only a derisory forty. Bevan had the support of seventy MPs. Gaitskell was outright winner, on the first ballot, with 157 votes, including those of Wilson, Crossman and the emerging left centre. Wilson did not state that he voted for Gaitskell in 1955, but it is known he wrote a letter of congratulations on 16 December to the new leader, warning of some hostility from Morrison's supporters.

The labour party was now under a new, right-wing, middle-class leader. Gaitskell owed his position, in part to the decline of an ageing Morrison, partly to his own ability, effort and recent conciliatoriness, and also to the defection of socialist intellectuals from the Bevanite movement. Many may have been tired of the infighting in the party, but Gaitskell was not the leader to create long-term unity; 'Hugh', a more serene Denis Healey now says, 'was not the right sort of man to be leader of the party, or even prime minister. He was too intolerant ... His problem was he really thought people who disagreed with him were either knaves or fools.'[5] Attlee had not considered him a suitable leader of the labour party.

Morrison resigned the deputy leadership in a fit of pique, thereby giving up his membership of the parliamentary committee and national executive. Bevan offered to support the new leader, and announced he was standing for the deputy leadership. The right wing was more keen on the popular Jim Griffiths. 'I was asked to stand for election', he recalled, 'by those who thought that it would be advantageous to choose a deputy who could bring a wider experience to the service of the new leader and who would co-operate loyally with him.'[6] Bevan persisted with his candidacy. Griffiths was elected on 2 February 1956 with 141 votes. Bevan did well in securing the support of 111 MPs, and took the result as a good omen. If Gaitskell had wanted him, the party would have begun to reunite in the 1955 parliament, but, at a *Tribune* mass meeting in Manchester two days after the result, Bevan reopened the battle for the soul of the party: 'If the Labour Party is not going to be a Socialist Party, I don't want to lead it. I don't believe you can measure the progress of society by individual careers ... When you join a team in the expectation that you are going to play rugger, you can't be expected to be enthusiastic if you are asked to play tiddlywinks.'[7]

Gaitskell had to fill the two vacated posts in the shadow cabinet in early 1956. He gave Griffiths's colonies portfolio to Bevan after the Manchester speech, though the latter wanted foreign affairs. This remained with Robens. The new leader had noted in his diary on 9 January of his own portfolio: 'although I have to be cautious on this, it is clear that Harold Wilson will have to have the Treasury.' George Brown had argued against this, but Gaitskell was forced to take account of Wilson's standing: 'he had in fact worked very well ... with me, and although he was a cold fish I thought he knew the need for loyalty ... He was not really dangerous because he would not have much support if he made trouble.'[8] Gaitskell made Wilson number one at the treasury. He appointed Jay and Bottomley joint number ones at the board of trade, and Patrick Gordon Walker was also roped into the trade and finance team. Douglas Jay does 'not remember ever having a serious dispute with Harold Wilson about the sharing of duties.'[9] He holds to the view that Wilson 'was best as a lieutenant to Hugh Gaitskell because, on sort of high policy, you'd never know which way he would turn'.[10] It seems that the shadow chancellorship satisfied Wilson's ambitions: 'for the next twenty years [that is, until 1976, he told Crossman] I shall be dealing with the Treasury either as Chancellor or Shadow Chancellor, so I've been making a special study of financial problems and I can assure you that my first Budget will be the most controversial since Lloyd George's in [1909].'[11]

On 25 February 1956 – though it took some time for the news to filter out of Moscow – Khrushchev denounced Stalin and the 'cult of personality' at the communist party's twentieth congress. Eden had invited the Russians to visit Britain, and, on 18 April, Khrushchev and Marshal Bulganin, the new premier, arrived for a nine-day visit. The prime minister invited Gaitskell, Robens and Griffiths down to Chequers to meet the Russians in private.

The Russian leaders were guests of the labour party national executive on 23 April, at a dinner in the house of commons, members of the shadow cabinet also being invited. Khrushchev was to write in his memoirs that 'one of the leaders of the Labour Party at that time was Wilson, who was considered our friend. Even though he was fairly conservative, he claimed that if he were in power his policy toward us would be friendlier than that of the Eden government.'[12] Labour leaders had prepared after-dinner questions, but Khrushchev, when called upon to speak, delivered a pugnacious address spontaneously. When he was interrupted by George Brown, a right-wing trade unionist and shadow defence minister, who had visited Poland in 1954, 'absolute pandemonium broke out'. 'He and I', recalled Brown, 'went on having an altercation, whenever one could break in, about releasing prisoners and other things.'[13] Sam Watson, a former miner, and Nye Bevan also became involved in exchanges with Khrushchev. The gathering quickly broke up, and Khrushchev refused Brown's hand the following day at a parliamentary lunch. Gaitskell did not want to apologize to the Russians, but the executive was surprisingly united in condemning Brown's behaviour. Harold Wilson almost succeeded in having him rebuked. Bevan defended Brown at the shadow cabinet, the latter making a mild apology to his colleagues. At a final meeting with the Russians at Claridges on 26 April, Gaitskell was invited to visit the Soviet Union. Griffiths attempted an apology: 'George Brown's boisterous humour was but a tough docker talking to a tough miner.'[14] (Brown in fact had been a salesman in the fur department of John Lewis's in Oxford Street.) Khrushchev was to bear a grudge against the labour party until he fell from power in 1964.

Major developments were in train in Egypt, where President Nasser announced the nationalization of the Suez canal in July, in retaliation for the United States withdrawing from the planned high dam at Aswan. British and French investors were the main losers from its seizure, but London was concerned about the loss of British power in Africa and Asia, and Paris about Nasser's support for Algerian nationalists. Nasser had also been conducting unofficial raids into Israel, to the annoyance of the Zionist lobby in the United States. Eden told the commons on 30 July 1956 that force would not be ruled out.

Gaitskell and Bevan differed from the prime minister only in wanting the sanction of the united nations, the labour front bench seeking to oppose military action while refusing to condone Nasser. George Brown was considered pro-Arab, and would remain so, but the labour party as a whole was strongly Zionist. Harold Wilson was to recall that 'Hugh Gaitskell was a committed friend of Israel, as were others of us in the Shadow Cabinet.'[15] Jewish migration to Palestine in the late 1940s had fuelled Zionism, but Bevin, in handling the British mandate, showed himself strongly anti-semitic. The withdrawal of troops in 1948 led to the establishment of the state of Israel, Britain expecting neighbouring arabs to crush the Jewish settlers. The new society being built by mainly Europeans was attractive to western socialists, but Washington had become implicated in the region as an imperial power. Richard Crossman had been one of the first non-Jewish supporters of Israel in the labour party, first visiting the country when it was still under British control. He argued in the early 1950s for a withdrawal from the canal zone. Bevan was also opposed to imperialism, and he, and Jennie Lee, paid their first visit to the middle east in 1953. They formed a close relationship with Yigal Allon, who had fought in 1948–9, was then on a kibbutz, and would later be deputy prime minister.

It is not surprising that Harold Wilson should have become a Zionist, seemingly in the early 1950s; he was to described Allon, much later, as his 'closest friend among all the Israelis',[16] and it is possible they met during a year Allon spent at St Antony's College, Oxford.

Wilson had not been concerned with Palestine when a member of Attlee's government. Ian Mikardo recalls: 'Harold had no principles at all. I don't think Harold has ever had an altruistic, dispassionate thought, any doctrinal beliefs at all. Except one, which I find absolutely incomprehensible, which is his devotion to the cause of Israel.'[17] This loyalty is problematic. Any commitment is excess political baggage for an ambitious politician, but Harold Wilson was to find his Zionism compatible with labour party Realpolitik.

Three months of international diplomacy followed the seizure of the canal. Harold Macmillan took the most aggressive line in cabinet, and Eden began to prepare the military and ideological ground for a classical imperialist intervention. Britain, France and the United States summoned an international conference on 2 August, but, with Eisenhower seeking reelection in November, John Foster Dulles declared in favour of moral force only. The shadow cabinet in Britain began to agitate for the recall of parliament, the labour opposition not being consulted by the government. The international conference met on 16 August, and eighteen of the twenty-two nations attending agreed to recommend to Nasser Dulles's idea of a canal board associated with the united nations. This was rejected early the following month. Eden then announced on 12 September that Britain, with the support of France and the United States, was establishing a canal users' association, which all nations would be invited to join. The opposition moved a vote of censure, calling for the dispute to be referred to the security council. A second international conference opened in London on 19 September, but there was now a division between Dulles and Eden. The association was established on 1 October, with the Americans less keen on supporting their European allies. Britain, with the reluctant support of France, had been forced to the security council, and, in debates on 5 and 13 October, it accepted six principles for a settlement.

On Sunday, 14 October General Challe outlined a French plan to a sympathetic Eden at Chequers, involving Israel invading Egypt, with Britain and France then seizing the canal in the guise of peace-keepers. Eden and his foreign secretary Selwyn Lloyd met Mollet and Pineau in Paris two days later, the plan being agreed in the secret treaty of Sèvres by 26 October. Israel invaded Egypt on 29 October, concerning itself with military targets in the Sinai. The French leaders flew to London the following day, and Eden announced that the two powers were intervening. The combatants were asked to withdraw ten miles either side of the canal, even though the Israelis had not reached it, and the Egyptians were defending the Sinai. British and

French troops were going to occupy the canal towns. The labour opposition could only press for another security council resolution or parliamentary debate. The American government moved that Israel should withdraw, Britain and France vetoing this resolution in the united nations. Planes from Cyprus began to bomb Egyptian airfields on 31 October. Labour moved a vote of censure on 1 November, arguing that intervention was a violation of the united nations' charter. The general assembly voted for an immediate ceasefire early the following day. Eden offered on 3 November to defer to a united nations' peacekeeping force, revealing a central concern with the canal. Gaitskell called for the prime minister's resignation. British and French paratroopers dropped on Port Said at dawn on 5 November, but Eden and Mollet accepted a united nations' ceasefire from midnight on 6 November. This was the day of the American elections, and Britain was brought to heel by a run on the pound, a greatly changed Macmillan applying for a dollar loan from the international monetary fund. A united nations' emergency force was admitted on to Egyptian territory, and Israel withdrew from the Sinai under international pressure. The last British and French troops were out by Christmas.

The Suez affair did much at the time to obscure events in Hungary, where the Russians had encouraged partial deStalinization. In a sixteen-point programme for 'a new Hungary', students in Budapest demanded on 22 October a provisional government under Imre Nagy, liberalization, and greater national freedom. Nagy was reappointed president, but his deputy summoned Soviet tanks to restore order in the capital. Fighting broke out there on 25 October, and quickly spread throughout the country. János Kádár had taken over as first secretary of the communist party, and Nagy formed a coalition government on 1 November. Hungary then declared itself a neutral state. The Soviet Union was quietly stationing troops throughout the country, and Nagy appealed to the united nations. With world attention focused elsewhere, Moscow sought to regain control by force on 4 November. Britain and France were in no moral position to condemn Soviet imperialism, and Kádár assumed power at the head of an all-communist government. There was widespread popular resistance, gradually put down by the Soviet troops, and Nagy was abducted by the authorities on 22 November.

The British labour party was no friend of Russia's, and the year 1956, through the twin foci of Suez and Hungary, demonstrated the reality of imperialism, east and west. Britain lost its role as a world power, challenged within the commonwealth and censured by the united nations, though NATO, and Atlanticism generally, continued to receive a democratic legitimacy from the labour opposition. If nothing else 1956 stimulated opposition to superpower politics in Britain and other advanced countries. Harold Wilson would not be in touch with this seachange, and hostile when it later affected the labour party. The absence of a cathartic political response in 1956 on his part indicated his formation in the war and rootedness in the immediate post-war years. He now had a personal vested interest in the British state, as a leading member of the shadow cabinet. This was also evident in Gaitskell's preoccupation with the political figleaf of the united nations, when the reactionary response of Eden to Nasser required a more thorough challenge from the opposition. Most labour politicians continued to believe that, when British troops were engaged abroad, the only viable political position was to avoid accusations of national treachery. It had nothing to do with the justice of the cause.

As soon as he had been appointed shadow chancellor at the beginning of 1956, Harold Wilson looked forward to being included in 'a small, informal group'[18] around Gaitskell. This was not to be, seemingly because the new labour leader remained loyal to his right-wing friends. But Wilson quickly earned the praise of Gaitskell, who noted of a two-day economic debate in February, that 'both Harold and Douglas made outstanding speeches'.[19] Bevan continued his political agitation, sometimes attending the parliamentary committee. Following one particular attack on the TUC, Wilson 'remarked to [Gaitskell] afterwards, it seemed to be more hatred of the T.U.C. than any hatred of resale price maintenance which motivated him'.[20] Wilson briefed his shadow cabinet colleagues on the eve of the 1956 budget, and made suggestions as to how the party should respond. This 'obviously nettled Nye Bevan, who proceeded to make the usual kind of rather silly speech, saying that we mustn't have a technical attack, that it must be a very broad one in which we should bring in ... defence policy and goodness knows what else.'[21] Wilson also had to address the question of the European Economic Community (EEC), then being negotiated by six states. He told the shadow cabinet in October that he proposed to be 'non committal'[22] on the Eden government's alternative of a free trade area in Europe. If Britain could become a high-investment economy, he argued, it would have nothing to fear from European competition. Entry to the EEC was possible. But 'let us be clear', he wrote in a paper for his colleagues, the common market 'is not a Socialist proposal; it owes more to Cobden than to any Socialist thinker.'[23] A list of nine safeguards was included. This balancing act was to continue for twenty years, and Europe would become perhaps the major issue of Harold Wilson's political career.

He was shadowing Harold Macmillan, a pre-war tory radical, who affected an Edwardian patrician air, but was to epitomize the professsional politician in post-war Britain. As chancellor, Macmillan continued to deflate the economy in his first budget, in 1956, but he also raised profit tax to appease the increasingly powerful unions. Macmillan had described the shadow chancellor as making 'a brilliant debating speech' on 20

February: 'He scored good party points ... But he did not say anything to stir up the trade unions.'[24] Harold Wilson replied to the chancellor's budget broadcast on 19 April, in what must have been his first major appearance on radio and television. He was to have extremely fond memories of one of the conservatives' greatest assets. 'There must have been a chemistry at work', Wilson has written, 'which brought out the best in both of us, and the debates on his first budget and Finance Bill became popular occasions. I suddenly developed an aptitude for dealing with serious economic and financial problems in a humorous and personal way, to which Macmillan responded.'[25] After these contests on the floor of the house, the two repaired to the smoking room for a friendly drink. 'To observers, the mutual admiration society between the two Harolds was always an odd one, but it was largely based on professional esteem. When Wilson made a speech attacking him, Macmillan would as often as not rate it in his diaries as "very amusing", or else treat it with the cautious respect it deserved.'[26] It is significant that Wilson recalls fondly his parliamentary jousts with Macmillan, when he emerged as a parliamentary performer, during what was to be a turning point in post-war British history.

Harold Wilson had been appointed chairman of the party executive's financial and economic policy committee after the 1955 conference, at the beginning of the three-year post-election policy review. Wilson also became a member of the committee on 'equality'. He presented *Towards Equality: Labour's Policy for Social Justice* to the 1956 party conference in Blackpool at the beginning of October, this being his first impressive speech to party delegates. It began with an attempt to have it both ways. 'Equality' was a concept beloved of the social democratic right, but Wilson, in language coded for the left, stated 'there [could] not be socialism in this country ... unless we control the levers of economic power'.[27] Six pages of the national executive's report were devoted to the work of Wilson's sixteen-strong organization sub-committee, a 'regional and field' sub-committee having been established plus another for 'youth'. He had failed to endear himself to the party agents in the country, which was reflected in the votes for the executive, when Barbara Castle supplanted him as the most popular constituency representative. She complained to Richard Crossman the day after that Wilson had not congratulated her on topping the poll; 'I replied', wrote Crossman, 'by asking whether she had condoled with him on sinking to Number Three!'

Crossman later felt that 'by openly breaking with Nye[,] Harold Wilson and [he] had done [them]selves no good as chairman and vice chairman',[28] but erstwhile Bevanites were now about to gain controlling positions on the national executive, on the basis of seniority. Tom Driberg became vice-chairman for 1956–7, and Bevan himself also returned to the executive after two years' absence. He secured the treasurership on his third attempt, after a close fight with George Brown, 3,029,000 votes to 2,755,000 (two minority candidates secured 686,000 votes), and this contest suggests Gaitskell was unwilling to share the leadership with Bevan. The new labour leader was to cast a cold eye over his colleagues after the conference: 'When one looks round at the Executive it is hard to see anybody apart from Jim Griffiths who has both ... courage and intelligence. Harold Wilson has plenty of intelligence and a little courage, but when one gets beyond him, frankly most of the rest are either just incapable of making good speeches ... or just entirely lacking in courage, with only one idea, namely to get as many cheers from the Left Wing as possible.'[29] Bevan moved rapidly towards Gaitskell during the Suez crisis, and privately intimated that the offer of the shadow foreign affairs position would end his rebellion. He was given the job after the shadow cabinet elections, when Harold Wilson came top of the poll of MPs for the first time.

Harold Wilson changed secretaries on the eve of the new session, Mrs Cannon leaving to have a baby. She was replaced by Marcia Williams, formerly Field. Marcia Field had been born in Northamptonshire, into the working class, on 10 March 1932. She had a very good relationship with her father, Harry, who later became a small builder, but did not get on well with her mother, Dorothea, a 'very religious and quite a strait-laced lady'.[30] Marcia had a sister Peggy and brother Tony. She was vaguely conscious of Harold Wilson as a minister associated with rationing when at school in the late 1940s, and it was her idea to go to London University to study history, 'motivated by [a] desire to prove that I could also have a special place in [my parents'] eyes as the other two had: one for being beautiful, the other for being male.'[31] Marcia Field became secretary of the labour society at Queen Mary College in London in the early 1950s, and remembers getting James Callaghan over to speak to students. She graduated in 1955 and married George – Ed – Williams, a fellow student who had been active in the conservative society. At some point the Field family was to move to London. Marcia Williams quickly regretted her marriage: 'we were young, maybe the sex wasn't as good as it should have been, and the two should have come together to make it worthwhile. I still envy people who have a happy marriage.'[32] The union lasted two years, until George Williams went off to work in the United States, and they were divorced in Washington State in 1961.

Marcia Williams had gone to work in Transport House after the 1955 election, becoming a shorthand typist in the office of Morgan Phillips. She was hardly committed to being a secretary: 'I think I'd rather have been a man, because I would have liked to have got things done in my own right rather than have been mainly the staff officer who helped to get things right, or get them wrong. I think it's been a man's world.'[33]

Marcia Williams describes herself as being 'left-wing' at the time, and 'a great admirer of Nye Bevan'.[34] But the Bevanite rebellion was near its end. She was to be offered a job in Hugh Gaitskell's office at Westminster, but turned it down. Her arrival in Smith Square coincided with the Wilson committee on party organization, and she began to see that summer – so she later claimed – that Harold Wilson 'possessed the necessary streak of practicality needed to make ... [left-wing] ideals a reality.'[35] 'He was obviously a coming man', she was to write, 'and I thought it would be more interesting to work for someone younger, who was outside the Party Establishment.'[36] He may have been an outsider in Transport House, but Wilson was shadow chancellor of the exchequer at Westminster. Marcia Williams helped distribute papers at executive meetings, and serve the coffee. After the 1955 conference, she learned of efforts by Phillips to deny Harold Wilson the organisation sub-committee, thereupon sending Wilson anonymous notes about the machinations of the right. 'Harold', recalled Marcia, 'afterwards joked that he had wondered who it was and how this person came to be so well informed.'[37] She remained unknown to Wilson, until the house of commons dinner for Bulganin and Kruschev in April 1956, when, with a senior colleague, she was present to make a shorthand note of the speeches. 'Harold Wilson', she recalled, 'who sat at the end of the top table a short distance away from my seat, sensed my nervousness and was extremely sympathetic.'[38] Sometime afterwards, Harold, recognizing Marcia at a bus stop, gave her a lift into Westminster in his car. Shortly before the 1956 party conference, a member of the executive told her Harold Wilson was looking for a secretary. She was successful in securing the post, starting work at Meyer's about October. Wilson was able to pay her £15 a week, considerably more than she had been earning at Transport House.

Marcia Williams, then twenty-four, was an able and committed woman, but she was unhappy and insecure. She remembers that when she 'first began to work for him [she] was often terrified – she used to draft and redraft [her] letters and advice notes until they were so perfect they could have been framed.'[39] Tall and fair, with blue eyes, she had a long face with prominent teeth. While charming, she could also be tempestuous. Marcia had offered herself as secretary to Harold Wilson, and was to be politically devoted to him. He was the source of her power, and authority, and she served him to excess, becoming intolerant of others' weaknesses and inefficiency. She was also able to exercise an influence over her boss. As early as March 1957, Crossman noted that Wilson had been late for a meeting, because Marcia – as Crossman put it – was having 'a nervous breakdown'. 'He had spent twenty minutes', noted Crossman, 'on the phone with her husband. All this was really endearing, since afterwards he said, "Take my mind off her, for God's sake, by discussing pensions."'[40]

There seems to have been a strong element of maternalism in Marcia Williams: 'In a small way, she probably replaced the influence of Harold's mother, becoming the encouraging figure at his shoulder, as well as the woman who warned him if he was going too far, and spotted dirty marks on his clothes or shabby shoes.'[41] But she was also an intelligent woman, with a sense of politics. She met for a great many years a deep craving within him: for someone else to whom politics were meat and drink and the very air that was breathed; someone who, at her best, had a political mind capable of testing and matching his; someone who, again at her best, possessed a deadly ability to slash her way through the woolliness and verbiage of political argument to get to the heart of an issue. Someone who was prepared to devote all her time to Harold Wilson's service; and someone who, at the very worst moments, was always there.[42]

The relationship became a political marriage, and, like all such unions, could bring out the worst in one or both partners. In the case of Marcia, she lost control under stress, and would come to berate him as prime minister in semi-public. She would eventually admit, in a television interview in 1977, that she was given to outbursts, and Wilson heard her say, on the Jimmy Young Programme, on BBC Radio 2, that she had a temper. As for her employer, Harold simply froze with embarrassment on such occasions, betraying an inability to handle the relationship. He would claim that he was not in the slightest afraid of her. Many years later, she would describe him, with affection, as 'unemotional on the surface, reluctant to show feeling or sentiment of any kind, yet underneath gentle and, if I may use the word, soft.'[43] He was a pushover.

Joseph Kagan, a Jewish businessman from Yorkshire, entered Wilson's life shortly after Marcia Williams. Wilson's relationship with this individual was to prove politically embarrassing. It began with a raincoat.

Joseph Kagan was born on 6 June 1915 in Lithuania, the son of a textile manufacturer. The Kagan family lived in a Jewish ghetto, in Kaunas, and young Joseph attended high school. He came to England in 1933, possibly with his mother, to study textiles at Leeds University, but Joseph and his mother returned to Lithuania, only to be caught there by the second world war. When the country was annexed by Stalin in 1940, his father fled to England, and Joseph took over the family's woollen mill. When the Germans invaded in 1941, Kagan escaped execution, becoming a labourer in a foundry. He married Margaret Shtromas, hiding his new wife's family behind a partition at the foundry. He was already 'good at finding ways of doing things that [could not] be done ... The means were somewhat insensitive, but the ends were sure to work.'[44] After the Russians returned, Kagan, his wife and, possibly, his mother fled to Bucharest, where a government official was entrapped to issue the latter with a visa to Palestine.

Kagan and his wife eventually reached Yorkshire in 1946. They were to have two sons and one daughter.

Joe Kagan worked first in a garage, but, by 1951, he was manufacturing rough blankets in a tin shed near Huddersfield. Kagan Textiles Ltd – 'Gannex' – quickly profited from the unprecedented prosperity of the 1950s, when, with the help of the ministry of defence, he started to manufacture a lightweight coat, made of wool and nylon. His first big order came from the Bradford police. The Gannex raincoat, or mac, was to have a high cultural profile in 1960s' Britain, due to Kagan's marketing ploys.

Kagan first became involved with the shadow chancellor in 1956, though he has recalled various dates, and Wilson says they did not meet until the early 1960s. Kagan has recalled a Wilson business trip to Russia in 1956, and one to China two years later. The relationship between the Yorkshire Jewish manufacturer, whose private and business habits were hardly respectable, and the labour politician, who was considered careful in his dealings with others, was to be mutual, though probably more mutual on Kagan's part – and mediated by Marcia Williams. Joseph Kagan would enjoy, and profit considerably, from the rise of his Huddersfield-born friend. Wilson was to present Khruschev with a Gannex at the Kremlin in 1963, when he was leader of the labour party, and this raincoat became an integral part of the image of Harold Wilson as prime minister during the rest of the decade.

The Suez crisis of 1956 undermined Eden's premiership. His ill health was publicized on 19 November, and Harold Macmillan emerged on 10 January 1957 as the new prime minister, the labour opposition protesting that the tories had 'involve[d] the Crown in party politics'.[45] The reelected American president had wanted Eden out, and announced that Washington would militarily assist any state in the middle east subject to armed aggression by a pro-communist nation. American forces were preparing to resist a Nasserite revolt in Jordan by April, though British paratroopers would again be in action. Macmillan quickly patched up things with the Americans, meeting Eisenhower at Bermuda in late March 1957, and it was on 4 April that Duncan Sandys, in a defence white paper, committed Britain to an independent nuclear deterrent. This would perpetuate the illusion of superpower status, without excessive expenditure on men and arms, the British deterrent comprising Vulcan bombers, carrying the new H bomb, and Blue Streak missiles. By the time Macmillan reported to the commons on the Bermuda talks on 1 April, the shadow defence secretary, George Brown, had already supported British hydrogen bomb tests at Christmas Island in the Pacific. It was known that many labour MPs wanted a postponement, but Gaitskell had been in favour of nuclear weapons, and many in the party welcomed the white paper's promise to phase out conscription by 1960.

The opposition front bench proposed, in a debate on the white paper in mid-April, that British tests should be temporarily suspended, in order to appeal to the United States and the Soviet Union. It was a compromise which had originated with Christopher Mayhew, back in parliament and the deputy spokesman on foreign affairs. Such a position did not entail opposition to nuclear weapons as such, but it embodied an element of unilateral action – tapping the idea of Britain as a moral guardian for the rest of the world. Despite his youthful pacifism, Harold Wilson did not play a prominent role in the tortuous attempt, by the shadow cabinet and national executive, to formulate a policy on nuclear weapons in 1957. Bevan learned from Khrushchev in September, when they met in the Crimea, that the Russians would respond to a British suspension of tests. The Americans would be forced to follow suit. A British decision to cease manufacturing – so Bevan gathered – would not affect the two superpowers, so there was little mileage in unilateralism. Bevan had been prepared to call for an end to H bomb manufacturing, but he changed his position on the eve of the party conference at Brighton. By Sunday, 29 September, he was concerned about the implications of renunciation for the state's defence and foreign policy, particularly under a labour government. This volte face had been achieved by Sam Watson, secretary of the Durham miners. Watson was the most powerful trade unionist on the national executive, and his hostility to British communists informed his view of the world. He had been very close to Attlee, and, though not a member of parliament, was considered a possible successor to Bevin in 1951. In the course of the previous two evenings, Watson – with a bottle of whisky – 'gradually got Nye round to the mood of the next Foreign Secretary and the representative of the world's mineworkers'.[46]

Some 120 constituency parties had come out for the renunciation of nuclear weapons, but the executive was prepared only to commit a labour government to suspend British tests unilaterally. This was seen as a prelude to multilateral suspension, and talks about disarmament. Bevan replied to the debate on nuclear weapons, on the Thursday, as the representative of the executive. He came out against unilateralism, speaking of sending a labour foreign secretary 'naked into the conference chamber ... to preach sermons'. 'All you can do is pass a resolution [and create] a diplomatic shambles ... And you call that statesmanship? I call it an emotional spasm ... The consequence of passing this resolution would be to drive Great Britain into diplomatic purdah.'[47]

With Bevan allied to Gaitskell, and the executive supporting the shadow cabinet, the 1957 labour party conference came out against renouncing nuclear weapons by 5,836,000 votes to 781,000. The transport workers narrowly backed the leadership, but three-quarters of the constituency parties found themselves opposed by the shadow foreign secretary. 'When Bevan sat down', wrote an elderly right-wing MP, 'I had to get up and go away ... I felt as if I had been present at a murder – the murder of the enthusiasm which had built the Labour movement.'[48]

The day after Bevan's speech, the Russians launched the first earth satellite, Sputnik 1, to be followed by Sputnik 2 on 3 November. They plunged the United States, and its allies, into gloom about the strategic implications of this technological breakthrough.

The other major issue at the Brighton conference had been the question of nationalization, and here Harold Wilson played an important part in policy development. Public ownership had been a problem for the labour party from 1950, and, with Gaitskell as leader, it came under attack in 1956. This was the year Anthony Crosland, an Oxford economist and labour MP, until he lost his seat, published *The Future of Socialism*. It was the most important book in the history of British socialism. Crosland wanted the party to adopt the idea of equality as an alternative totem to public ownership, equality of opportunity, rather than levelling, being achieved by tax and other reforms, and economic management. A policy committee on public ownership was established after the 1956 conference, chaired by Griffiths, and with Harold Wilson a member. The executive unanimously endorsed *Industry and Society: Labour's Policy on Future Public Ownership*, a document which promised 'to extend public ownership in any industry or part of industry which, after thorough enquiry, is found to be seriously failing the nation.'[49] There was a commitment only to renationalize steel and long-distance road haulage.

As one critic wrote, *Industry and Society* gave the party 'a mandate to do about public ownership whatever it may happen to like when it returned to office.'[50] Barbara Castle and Ian Mikardo, as members of the executive, had second thoughts, but Bevan told Gaitskell he did not want a 'shopping list'. Opposition to the document came from elements of the trade-union right, still committed to collectivism; Morrison and Shinwell, now ageing backbenchers, spoke against it at Brighton with a sense of nostalgia. Harold Wilson, who came second to Anthony Greenwood in the executive elections, had been selected to introduce this new policy statement, which he described as 'a new analysis of contemporary capitalism'. Wilson admitted there had been some 'misunderstanding' about it, and that the members of the committee, drafting the section on public ownership, had 'found that though the faith was a common one, [they] varied in the emphasis [they] put on particular reasons for it'. He insisted that the document still allowed for 'traditional nationalisation'. With the proposal to acquire equity shares in firms and exercise public control over large companies, they were 'simply going further along the road on which [they] started in 1945–50'.[51]

His attempt to disguise ideological revision was undermined in a long debate, in which Gaitskell summed up for the executive. The platform carried the day, with 5,309,000 votes to 1,276,000 against. The railwaymen were the only union to make a stand, with half the constituency parties, for the traditional party view of complete socialization.

The labour party published a pamphlet by Wilson that autumn, *Remedies for Inflation*, comprising a series of articles which had appeared in the *Manchester Guardian*. Gaitskell described him as 'a distinguished economist and statistician'[52] in the foreword, while noting it was not an official party statement. This was less than a fulsome compliment, Gaitskell being known to consider Wilson only 'a good economist of the second grade'.[53]

The shadow chancellor outlined labour's alternative policy in the third section of his pamphlet. Demand inflation could be tackled with physical controls, such as building licences, and, as for cost-push inflation, this required 'a Crippsian approach to the whole issue of wage restraint'. A labour government needed to have an 'understanding' with the unions. Wilson concluded that labour would have to be tougher in fighting inflation: 'Labour ideologies will not stand in the way of the full use of the monetary weapon, as Conservative ideology has prevented the present Government from using physical controls.'[54] This was tough talk, but nothing very radical. Harold Wilson, in 1957, admitted he would adopt tory fiscal measures as part of his policy, and prefigured the central question of a labour government's relations with the unions in a time of full employment. But Wilson was looking back to the late 1940s, when things had gone relatively well for Attlee's government, rather than forward to the 1960s.

Harold Wilson again came first in the shadow cabinet elections at the beginning of the 1957 session; Bevan was third, followed closely by Callaghan, Robens, Greenwood, and then George Brown. Richard Crossman had noted of his closest political friend: 'Harold Wilson grows fatter, more complacent and more evasive each time you meet him.'[55]

The shadow chancellor was then involved in a political exercise, which was to backfire badly on him, concerning Macmillan's chancellor, Peter Thorneycroft, a pronounced monetarist. Thorneycroft had raised bank rate from 5 to 7 per cent on 19 September – the highest since 1921 – in an effort to stem a run on the pound, and secure a loan from the international monetary fund. Harold Wilson did not want to further weaken the pound, but he had been told by Sigmund Warburg, a banker, that a crisis of 1931 proportions was inevitable. Wilson wrote to Enoch Powell, the financial secretary, on 24 September 1957, alleging that the increase had leaked before publication. He requested an investigation, and moved an emergency resolution on the failing pound at the party conference: 'Time and time again we warned them that their reckless scrapping of controls, their free for all, would leave us vulnerable and defenceless to the first blast of economic crisis.'[56] Wilson maintained he had prima facie evidence of a leak, but the lord chancellor was to conclude this was not the case. Macmillan believed nothing irregular had happened, but learned that Thorneycroft had spoken to newspaper editors 'about the general policy'.[57] Wilson and Griffiths saw Macmillan and the lord chancellor on 7 October: 'They seemed rather nervous [Macmillan recorded], but produced a story about a Mr. X (who was under my "patronage") and a conversation with a Mr. Y (who was under my control).'[58] The prime minister told Gaitskell on 24 October that there would be no inquiry, but Sir Leslie Plummer, prompted by Harold Wilson, mentioned in parliament on 12 November the name of Oliver Poole, deputy chairman of the conservative party. Macmillan, now under pressure from Poole and Thorneycroft, thereupon conceded a tribunal of inquiry under Lord Justice Parker, to investigate what he would call in his memoirs 'The Strange Case of the Bank Rate "Leak"'.[59]

The tribunal began to hear witnesses on 2 December, and, on 19 December, Harold Wilson appeared. He denied he had ever alleged a leak, merely wanting an inquiry to allay stories in the press. The shadow chancellor was forced to admit that his prima facie evidence turned out to be based, in part, on groundless rumours. But Macmillan sacked Thorneycroft after Christmas, for being a deflationist, Powell and the other junior treasury minister resigning in solidarity. The tribunal's report, which was published on 21 January 1958, found that there had been no leak; where there had been prior disclosure of accompanying financial measures, these had not been used for private gain. Gaitskell initially considered it a whitewash, but the shadow cabinet agreed the report had to be accepted. 'Harold Wilson should be shown up', Macmillan ordered from Australia, ' ... Gaitskell should never have yielded to him.'[60] The opposition front bench argued that the rumours justified the inquiry, and labour pressed for a debate. Rab Butler, as lord privy seal, introduced the motion welcoming the report on 3 February. 'It was a task to which he brought an unfamiliar tone of acerbity, mounting a particularly scornful denunciation of the Opposition's resort to "the political weapon of the smear".'[61] Harold Wilson moved the opposition amendment, regretting the chancellor's briefing for journalists and party officials the day before his announcement. 'He flogged his way through', noted Crossman, 'in what was a brilliant but parliamentary forensic performance. What adroitness he showed in flipping over the weak points and putting in laughs just at the right times, and what sheer guts he showed in battling his way through the entrenched hatred he had engendered among the Tories!'[62] The opposition lost the day. Members of the shadow cabinet seem to have continued to believe there had been a whitewash, and Wilson, though he had been caught out, found nothing for which to apologize. The prime minister was not amused.

Harold Wilson was now in love with the Scilly Isles, off Land's End and 40 miles by boat from Penzance. The Wilsons had taken regular holidays in Cornwall in the 1940s, and his parents first made the crossing to the Scillies in 1951. Under friendly pressure from his Hampstead Garden Suburb neighbour, Ernest Kay, Harold and Gladys visited the largest island, St Mary's, the following summer. They were to spend every family holiday there subsequently, usually before the party conference, and also at Easter and Christmas. Harold Wilson approached the duchy of Cornwall for a plot of land, but it was 1958 before the building of a three-bedroom bungalow began outside Hugo Town, the house looking 300 yards across fields to the sea. (The Wilsons had moved next door in Hampstead Garden Suburb in 1953, to 12 Southway, and rented out their old home next door.) 'Lowenva', Cornish for 'house of happiness', and a name suggested by Marjorie Wilson, was ready for occupation in 1959.

The campaign for nuclear disarmament (CND) was formed at the beginning of 1958, on the initiative of Canon John Collins of St Paul's Cathedral, to achieve an end to nuclear weapons. While CND was non-party-political, an early objective was the winning of the labour party, Barbara Castle, Ian Mikardo and especially Anthony Greenwood being prominent unilateralists. The labour party and the TUC jointly agreed in March to a campaign against testing, and also opposed United States nuclear weapons in Britain. Harold Wilson kept a low profile on the executive and shadow cabinet, though he may not have been unsympathetic to CND; shortly after the budget, he '"in private ... assured [Crossman] that, when [they] come to power and something has to go, that something [would] be defence"'.[63] The Wilsons dined with the Crossmans a few weeks later, and, according to his host, Wilson said that, whereas their wives were pacifists really, '"You and I, Dick, are both economic opponents of nuclear weapons."'[64] (He would admit, on television, in 1982, that there were unilateralists in the family, his wife's pacifism having rarely been noted.) Wilson's was altogether a more cautious approach, possibly because he was thinking of a leadership bid after the general election.

A leading supporter of 'ban the bomb' was to be Frank Cousins, who had become general secretary of the transport union in 1956. The TGWU had come out for the suspension of tests, in line with party and TUC policy. While Cousins privately attended the Trafalgar Square rally at Easter 1959, at the end of the second CND march from Aldermaston, it was only at the union's delegate conference in July that Britain's largest union came out against nuclear weapons. But it did not favour the destruction of stockpiles, a position falling short of the the full CND demand. The general and municipal workers had voted for unilateralism the previous month, and

Gaitskell, under pressure from Bevan, advanced to the idea of a non-nuclear club, whereby a labour government would give up its weapons, if all other countries, excepting the two superpowers, agreed not to go nuclear. A minority of five on the national executive, Greenwood, Castle, Mikardo, Driberg and Edwin Gooch of the farmworkers, supported Cousins, but 'Harold Wilson', noted Crossman, 'ha[d] been discreet.'[65] The new policy was contained in *Disarmament and Nuclear War*, published jointly by the labour party and TUC, and, following the TGWU vote, the labour leader asserted, in Workington on 11 July, that a party conference could not instruct a future government under his leadership. When the general and municipal workers, after considerable arm-twisting, cynically reversed its conference decision on 21 August, it looked like the TUC and labour party conference would support the idea of a non-nuclear club, a position conceived in terms of multilateral development on the world stage, rather than the little England approach of CND.

A general election was expected in the autumn. Towards the end of a pleasant summer, Harold Macmillan announced polling day would be 8 October.

The budget in April had been an expansionary one, with cuts in direct and indirect taxation, and the restoration of investment allowances. The economy was going the tories' way, and their manifesto, *The Next Five Years*, was to promise increasing prosperity. It was felt that the labour party was being undermined by the weakening of working-class consciousness, and Gaitskell admitted privately in the summer that labour might lose: 'If the Tories increase their majority, it would only prove that we were even more out of touch with the electorate than [we] now think we are and that our renovation of the Party hasn't gone fast or far enough.'[66]

The conservative party, and private business interests, had been propagandizing against socialism. Eisenhower visited London at Macmillan's invitation on 27 August. A British prime minister who could use an American president to electioneer surely deserved the political sobriquet 'Super-Mac'. The prime minister invited the cameras into number 10, like grateful family retainers, to witness his pre-dinner conversation with Eisenhower.

Labour was now united but bland and unconvincing, with only the bomb as an important issue, and the Gallup poll in the *News Chronicle* indicated no strong reason for the conservatives being replaced by a not-very different labour party. The conservatives had even been showing a slight lead over labour for much of the past year. The reemergence of the liberals, who took Torrington in March 1958 from the conservatives, heralded a possible threat to the two-party system.

Gaitskell was leading a party delegation, which included Bevan, in the Soviet Union, when the 1959 election was called. The TUC had just begun its conference at Blackpool, voting down Cousins's policy on nuclear weapons on 9 September. Gaitskell immediately returned to London, and hastened to Blackpool in a private plane, to open the opposition's campaign – unusually – at the trade unionists' annual gathering. Richard Crossman was appointed chairman of the campaign committee at Transport House, redrafting the manifesto. The campaign committee met daily at party headquarters, at 10.30 a.m., and Morgan Phillips took charge of each press conference in Smith Square. Transport House was responsible for party propaganda, but also for supplying speakers for radio and television programmes. Harold Wilson, along with Greenwood, Gaitskell, Bevan, Griffiths and Crossman, launched the party's election programmes. These were run by Anthony Wedgwood Benn, who had been briefly a producer at the BBC before being elected to parliament in 1950 at the age of 25. Wilson recalls that he was 'more or less kept off the screen by those running the Party's appeal to the electorate',[67] but Woodrow Wyatt interviewed him in his broadcast on how labour intended to finance its programme: 'I made Wilson sound sincere and reliable though it went against my inclination.'[68] A professional campaign was mounted, and Gaitskell's leadership stature improved. It began to look like labour might win, until he promised at Newcastle on 28 September that a labour government would not increase income tax. This was an attempt to preempt a tory smear, and Gaitskell had agreed it with Wilson. It was considered a grievous mistake, because, the next day, Macmillan reminded the public that Gaitskell, in his one and only budget, had increased income tax and imposed health charges. The labour leader made himself look intellectually dishonest.

Wilson had been adopted labour candidate for Huyton, at a meeting at Cherryfield School, in Southdene, Kirby, on 22 September. County councillor James Willie, who was also vice-chairman of the local council, stated that Wilson would be 'a very early future Prime Minister',[69] a prediction picked up by the *Prescot and Huyton Reporter*. Wilson promised a labour government would legislate to allow pensioners bus passes, and a rise in the weekly rate. He also stated it was not policy to abolish grammar schools, merely selection at eleven. He had been working hard on the question of voluntary schools, having confidential discussions with Griffiths and Michael Stewart at the ministry of education.

Wilson also spoke at a meeting in Liverpool, chaired by a local socialist, Eric Heffer. With Frank Cousins on the platform, the shadow chancellor of the exchequer told his audience he held neither stocks nor shares. He promised he would use the budget to maximize productive investment in export industries, make the underprivileged a social priority, and bring about equity in taxation.

The Huyton campaign was considered the liveliest since 1950, but, though there was a greatly increased electorate, the turnout was slightly down. Harold Wilson was safely returned, with 33,111 votes to his conservative opponent's 27,184 – a majority of nearly 6,000.

There were many such safe labour seats in the country, but the party did less well in marginals. Labour never recovered from Gaitskell's gaff over taxation. It secured 12,216,000 votes (43.8 per cent) to the conservatives' 13,750,000 (49.4 per cent). The labour party did particularly badly among young voters. The government improved its position with the electorate, but it was the liberals who greatly increased their vote, to nearly 6 per cent – though they still only had six seats. The conservatives won 365 seats (an increase of 24), and labour 258 (a decrease of 23), giving the government an overall majority of 100 seats.

The 1959 election was an unpleasant landmark in the history of the labour party. It had dropped from nearly 400 seats over four elections, and lost three in succession. Though Gaitskell had made a major tactical mistake, the defeat was not blamed on his leadership. Barbara Castle, who may have been relieved at being returned, was to testify to the party's 'good programme, better organisation than we have ever had and brilliant leadership by Hugh Gaitskell'.[70] The labour leader announced, in words written by Richard Crossman: 'we shall fight and fight and fight again until we win'.[71]

CHAPTER 14

To the Labour Leadership, 1959–63

Hugh Gaitskell was referring to political competition between the two main parties, but he came to fight an intra-party struggle to modernize labour. The positions had already been rehearsed before the general election. Geoffrey Goodman, then a journalist on the *News Chronicle*, remembers attending a private lunch at St Ermin's Hotel as early as June 1958. Gaitskell and Jay talked about turning labour into a 'left of centre radical party'. Harold Wilson was also present, and dissociated himself, 'partly by silence and partly by an open difference of opinion'.[1] Gaitskell's initiative reflected that of the German social democrats, who abandoned Marxism at their 1959 congress at Bad Godesberg. But labour had never been a revolutionary party, even in theory, and the ideology of labourism was rooted in a notion of working-class tradition in Britain, which appealed to both left-wing socialists and right-wing trade unionists.

With a third successive election defeat, right-wing intellectuals immediately tried to remove public ownership from the party's programme. For the Sunday after the election (11 October), Gaitskell had arranged a farewell party at Frognal Gardens for Hugh Dalton, who had just given up his seat in the commons. Douglas Jay, who was a member neither of the executive nor of the shadow cabinet, proposed at this social occasion that nationalization should be dropped, the party should break from the unions, and there should be a change of name, to 'labour and radical' or 'labour and reform', to symbolize the party's willingness to cooperate with the liberals. Jay's was an extreme statement of the need for change. Gaitskell accepted that there had to be a revision of the 1918 constitution. He wanted to strengthen the parliamentarians within the party, and thereby modify the commitment to socialization in clause four of the constitution, which proclaimed the party's aim as 'the common ownership of the means of production, distribution and exchange, and the best obtainable system of popular administration and control of each industry and service.'[2]

Roy Jenkins came out forcefully against nationalization the next day, on the BBC television programme, *Panorama*, and Jay went public on his ideas for a transformed party in the pro–Gaitskell periodical, *Forward*, on 16 October. There was no concerted initiative on Gaitskell's behalf, but, to the party, it looked like a leadership attempt at revision. Douglas Jay was to regret changing his mind, and publishing the article over his own name, and Roy Jenkins would admit that Gaitskell 'and those of us who were close to him, made serious tactical mistakes during the ensuing weeks'. Jenkins continued to believe a battle had to be fought over whether labour was 'a party of power' or 'a party of protest',[3] even though the would-be British social democrats, supposedly the masters of political realism, failed strategically to change the labour party.

Harold Wilson was more concerned about his position on the front bench in the wake of the 1959 election. Gaitskell was 'very anti-Harold',[4] and told Crossman he wanted to move him from the shadow chancellor's post. This was because Wilson was 'too unpopular in the City, was not a good enough economist, and "wouldn't take the tough decisions"'.[5] Crossman relayed this to Wilson, while Douglas Jay considered that the former's 'motive ... was not so much malice, as reckless loquacity'.[6] Wilson was furious that Roy Jenkins might take his place, as the latter was not even in the shadow cabinet. Gaitskell was thinking of offering Wilson the shadow foreign secretaryship, held by Bevan, but Wilson did not want to lose the opportunity of becoming chancellor, and believed Gaitskell expected him to perform badly as shadow foreign secretary. It seems Gaitskell may have envisaged Wilson as leader of the house, if labour had won the general election, and it was suggested he should accept this job on the opposition front bench. Crossman found him 'stand[ing] pat, with the only expression of anger and passion I've ever heard him use'.

Whether Wilson had really overcome his jealousy of Gaitskell or not, the division between the two men now began to widen. Wilson, according to Crossman, 'wasn't prepared for any kind of reforms, for the obvious reason that he wasn't going to be in charge of them'.[7] In the shadow cabinet elections in early November Wilson returned to first position, with 167 votes, showing he was least unpopular with most sections of the parliamentary party. Bevan stepped into the deputy leadership when Griffiths stood down, and retained the party treasurership. Gaitskell also allowed him to continue shadowing the foreign secretary. The labour leader also had to leave the shadow chancellor in place, but failed to reassure Wilson about the future. The latter 'was afraid that his succession to the deputy leadership – and so to the leadership "say fifteen years hence" [in 1974] – was in jeopardy'.[8]

Harold Wilson was appointed chairman in 1959 of the committee on public accounts, an important position in the British system of government.

The public accounts committee was charged with reviewing the handling of public expenditure, and had the power to send for persons, papers and records. Wilson recalls that he asked Gaitskell for the nomination as chairman, and, while it customarily went to a member of the opposition, a former financial secretary to the treasury was more likely to get the position. Wilson had been in opposition for eight years, and felt he 'needed to refresh [his] recollection of the conduct of affairs'.[9] He may have seen it as politically strengthening his position within the opposition leadership, securing his entry to the treasury in a labour government. Marcia Williams, who now moved into the chairman's office in the house of commons, states it was 'one of the crucial phases in the making of the Prime Minister of the future'.[10] Harold Wilson and his secretary left Meyers, the relationship with the firm being brought to an end in case of any perceived conflict of interest. 'The earlier combination of businessman and politician', writes Marcia Williams, 'gave way to the duality of semi-civil servant and politician'.[11]

Harold Wilson worked closely with the comptroller and auditor general, Sir Edmund Compton. A fellow labour member, now Lord Cledwyn of Penhros, thinks Wilson was the best chairman of the public accounts committee: 'Harold had a capacious mind and a remarkable memory. I've never seen anyone with such a memory.'[12] The committee reported two or three times a year to the house of commons, the – expurgated – minutes of evidence being published annually. Much of the work went unnoticed, even among members of parliament, but when, as in the Ferranti case, it was discovered that a private firm grossly overcharged the government, it captured public attention. Harold Wilson was to be renominated to the chairmanship, at the beginning of each session of the 1959 parliament, until discharged in February 1963.

Gaitskell had been privately invoking the spirit of Stalybridge, but it was as party leader that he prepared for the short labour conference in Blackpool on 28/29 November 1959, which had been arranged to elect a new executive. Despite the best efforts of Transport House, this weekend gathering became the occasion for an inquest on the election defeat. Barbara Castle was ending her year as party chairman (sic), and she opened the proceedings with a spirited socialist attack on tory prosperity. Gaitskell, in complete contrast, argued the revisionist thesis about 'a significant change in the economic and social background of politics'. Affluence, it was believed, was leading the working class to desert the party: 'the changing character of labour, full employment, new housing and the new way of living based on the telly, the frig., the car and the glossy magazines – all these have had their effect on our political strength.' The climax of Gaitskell's speech was a call to scrap clause four of labour's constitution. Since the party was committed to a mixed economy, Gaitskell argued, nationalization was, at best, only one of a number of means. The goal of socialism was defined in terms such as equality. His alternative was an anticipation of 1960s' youth culture:

> we should put more stress on the issues which specially appeal to younger people. I believe these include the cause of Colonial freedom, the protection of the individual against ham-headed and arrogant bureaucracy; resistance to the squalid commercialism which threatens to despoil our countryside and disfigure our cities; a dislike of bumbledom of all forms; a greater concern for sport and the arts.[13]

The labour leader had prevented the executive from presenting an agreed statement, but his bid for ideological hegemony, as a preliminary to internal changes, was to fail. This attack upon party tradition, indeed sentiment, was not to the liking of the unions, and left and right vied in the inconclusive debate. Bevan was ambiguous when he wound up for the platform, opposing complete socialization, but also advocating a planned economy. He was not prepared to join Gaitskell's revisionist enterprise, but was almost spent as a heroic dissident.

Harold Wilson did not speak in the debate. He believed agreement could be achieved on specific proposals for nationalization, but not on a discussion of the principle. He claims he spent all day Sunday working on Bevan, to prevent him kicking over the traces of party unity at an evening rally. Wilson had risen to second place in the executive elections, overtaking Greenwood. Anthony Wedgwood Benn, still more of a radical than a socialist, knocked off Mikardo. The latter had been due to become chairman of the executive for 1959–60, and a trade unionist, George Brinham, had to move up from the vice-chairmanship. Wilson and Crossman had both been on the executive seven years, and due to take this position in 1960, but Wilson let Crossman become vice-chairman after the Blackpool conference.

The *Daily Mail* announced in early December that Wilson was to lead the left against Gaitskell. Bevan was fading from the political scene, but Harold Wilson denied that he would lead any challenge. According to Crossman, Wilson believed that Gaitskell, being no Attlee, was on his way out, and hoped the party leader could be got rid of within twelve months. There was little precedent for successful palace revolutions in the labour party. Gaitskell had brought John Harris into the leader of the opposition's office, and this former editor of *Forward*, though formally press officer of the parliamentary party, set about selling political revision to the lobby, an idea most Westminster correspondents were keen to promote. Labour had lost three elections, so the formula – it was argued – had to be changed. Bevan had refused to move against Gaitskell, though it became clear that he was opposed to dropping clause four. His speech at Blackpool on 29 November 1959 was to be the last he made to a party conference. Bevan had been unwell for a year, and his last words in the house of commons were uttered at the beginning of December. He was operated upon for malignant cancer, and his death imminently expected in January 1960. With Bevan clinging to life, Harold Wilson told Crossman and Castle he would stand for the treasurership and as deputy leader, his acolytes being surprised at his determination to step into Bevan's shoes. The latter rallied in late March, but died on 6 July at his farm, aged 62. He was cremated near his birthplace in Wales, and there were memorial services in Tredegar and Westminster Abbey. Gaitskell and Wilson sat with the privy councillors, and not their executive colleagues, in the Abbey.

Bevan's illness had postponed the struggle over clause four. Gaitskell proposed on 27 January that the executive should delay consideration of constitutional reform for a month, but Jennie Lee, who held one of the five women's seats, replied that they should first discuss the party's policy on public ownership. This view was publicly expressed by Harold Wilson, at a parliamentary press gallery lunch on 11 February. Gaitskell insisted two days later that clause four must be rewritten, and a special executive meeting was arranged for 16 March. At a secret confabulation the preceding evening, attended by Crossman, Driberg, Castle and Greenwood, Wilson suggested incorporating Gaitskell's twelve draft proposals into the existing constitution. Fudging was now a typical Wilsonian response to political division, and he was to be publicly criticized by Roy Jenkins. 'To pretend that compromise', Jenkins wrote in the *Daily Telegraph*, 'is always possible and that policy statements can mean both everything and nothing is a certain recipe for the continued erosion of the Labour vote.'[14]

The executive finally agreed, at the 16 March meeting, after much important redrafting, and with only one against, to add an updated statement of aims to the constitution. Specifically on the question of public ownership, Gaitskell, who had seen 'public and private enterprise hav[ing] a place in the economy',[15] had accepted Bevan's Blackpool phrase about the community having control of 'the commanding heights of the economy'.[16] It is clear that 'common ownership', the new preferred term for socialization, was being played down. The 'further extension of common ownership', the agreed statement read, 'should be decided from time to time in the light of [the party's] objectives and according to circumstances, with due regard for the views of the workers and consumers concerned.'[17] It was now a question of the conference accepting the amended constitution, but Gaitskell reckoned without the unions. Four of the six largest came out in defence of clause four in the spring and summer of 1960, and the leader was forced to downgrade his statement to a valuable expression of party aims. The executive agreed by a vote of eighteen to five to present the expression to the 1960 party conference in Scarborough. It was accepted by 4,304,000 votes to 2,226,000 on 6 October as just that. Frank Cousins spoke against, but a TGWU motion to reject 'the commanding heights' formulation was lost. Gaitskell, replying to the debate, had effectively conceded defeat on clause four: 'It was never an issue of principle; it was an issue of presentation ... we were going to have a major division over defence, and we did not want to add to the divisions in the Party unnecessarily. So we are not discussing amending the constitution.'[18] Such a concession was a delegitimizing of leadership.

Defence had reared its head again that February, when the government announced a missile warning station was to be built at Fylingdales in Yorkshire. At this stage, labour was still committed to the idea of a non-nuclear club. With the cancellation of the full conference in 1959, the TGWU had been unable to propose support for the CND cause. But 43 labour MPs refused to vote for an opposition motion on 1 March 1960, because it only mildly criticized the defence white paper. The government later announced the abandonment of the (British) Blue Streak ground-to-air missile, and the possibility of acquiring the (American) Polaris sea-to-air weapon for its submarines. With Gaitskell absent abroad, George Brown, the shadow defence minister, retorted, in a censure debate on 27 April, that labour might have to give up its support for the independent British nuclear deterrent. Harold Wilson, as the most senior member of the shadow cabinet available, wound up. He suggested that, while 'ageing young Conservatives' had shouted 'groundnuts' at labour candidates in the election, the opposition would now have something to throw at the government. He used scorn and wit with effect:

> When [Macmillan] became Prime Minister ... he set out to keep up with his nuclear neighbours. Like so many other rather pathetic individuals whose sense of social prestige outruns their purse, he is left in the situation at the end of the day of the man who dare not admit that he cannot afford a television set and who knows that he cannot afford it and who just puts up the aerial instead.[19]

Labour talk of not supporting the British bomb had much to do, first with CND's 1960 Easter rally, and secondly with a leading union adopting a unilateralist position, helped by a growing trade-union determination to defend clause four. Gaitskell reaffirmed his opposition to unilateralism, portraying it as a challenge to his leadership. The labour leader seemed unwilling to let the confusion in government policy solve the labour party's problem of being for nuclear weapons now, but against them in the future. Crossman and George Wigg meanwhile developed the idea of a non-nuclear NATO in Europe, and, at a joint labour party/TUC meeting on 31 May, it was agreed to draft a new statement on defence policy. Frank Cousins announced on 3 June that the TGWU remained opposed to all nuclear weapons. The labour party – and TUC – eventually came to accept that an independent nuclear deterrent was no more, but conceded that Britain was to be protected by the United States as a nuclear superpower.

Harold Wilson had privately expressed an interest in the deputy leadership even before Bevan died, and this post had to be filled at the start of the 1960 parliamentary session. Wilson saw himself getting into a position to rival Gaitskell, who was expected to survive the Scarborough conference in October. After a dinner on 31 August, attended by Crossman, Castle, Wilson and their spouses, the two former couples were surprised to be invited – for the first time – to Hampstead Garden Suburb, to continue speculating about Gaitskell. The latter's determination to defy the conference, if not on clause four then on the bomb, was putting pressure on the labour party, and Wilson was being forced to move further and faster than he wanted.

In early September, the TUC, at its conference in the Isle of Man, voted to accept the Cousins's and labour party positions on nuclear weapons. This was due largely to the role of the unilateralist engineering union (the AEU), under the leadership of a Gaitskellite. In order to secure support for the official party policy, the union's president, Bill Cannon, argued that his delegation should back both resolutions! George Brown then advocated that the party executive should recommend support for the TGWU resolution at the conference, on the grounds that Cousins stopped short of a unilateralist position. Brown was a member of Cousins's union, and he had his own ambitions in the labour party, but he later returned to the Gaitskell camp. At the pre-conference executive in Scarborough on 2 October, Anthony Wedgwood Benn argued that Gaitskell should attempt to reach agreement with Cousins. When this was rejected, Benn resigned from the national executive, failing to be reelected at the conference. It was not a fatal gesture.

The defence debate was on 5 October. Delegates had before them the executive statement, and a pro-leadership resolution from the wood-workers. They also had, confusingly, the TGWU motion and a unilateralist AEU one. It was only when Cousins decided to go completely unilateralist, in order to get three large unions, including the AEU, to support his resolution, that the fate of the platform was sealed, by a million or so votes. On Wednesday afternoon, closing the debate, Gaitskell made the most important speech of his career. He attacked 'pacifists, unilateralists and fellow travellers'.[20] Privately expecting to have to resign, he ended with a peroration: 'There are some of us, Mr. Chairman, who will fight and fight and fight again to save the party we love. We will fight and fight and fight again to bring back sanity and honesty and dignity, so that our Party with its great past may retain its glory and its greatness.'[21]

Harold Wilson was sitting four seats along on the platform, diligently attending to his pipe. He remained seated, with others, when Gaitskell was given a partial standing ovation. When the votes were counted, the executive, meaning in this case Gaitskell, had lost by 297,000, out of over six million cast. His authority as leader was weakened, but not destroyed. The party had formally gone unilateralist by 407,000 votes, but only just carried Cousins's motion. It was the trade-union block votes which defeated the party leader, just over half the constituencies rallying to his appeal.

The party leader's challenge to the labour conference had failed, but Gaitskell was cheered by Cousins's small majority. He immediately resolved to overturn the unilateralist position at the next conference, during the year (1960–1) when Crossman would be chairman of the party, and Harold Wilson vice-chairman.

Wilson now found himself facing the sort of dilemma that had troubled the party's great left-wing rebel after 1955: whether to advance his position by working for, or against, the leader. Two posts had been vacated by Bevan's death. The treasurership went to Harry Nicholas, number two in the TGWU, at the 1960 conference. The unions did not want a contest, and settled upon Cousins's deputy rather than a member of parliament. As for the deputy leadership, it was known that Gaitskell was backing George Brown. Wilson thought he might have been offered it, but cannot have believed Gaitskell wanted him. The election for the deputy leadership was due when parliament resumed. As Barbara Castle summoned a Bevanite meeting for Wednesday, 12 October at her home, it looked like Wilson would have difficulty stepping into Bevan's shoes. He would be forced to take on Gaitskell for the leadership, on the question of the bomb, while acting as shadow chancellor and vice chairman of the party. 'Here is an object lesson', Crossman wrote, 'in the master-tactician and the super-opportunist, who is so clever that his tactics are disastrous and he destroys his opportunities.'[22]

Anthony Greenwood announced to his fellow conspirators that he was resigning from the shadow cabinet, in order to stand for the leadership. He wished to defend the conference position on unilateralism, which Gaitskell was threatening to overturn. The pressure on Wilson increased, since Greenwood might come to fill the space left vacant by Bevan. But he refused to be pushed into running on 12 October. After a second indecisive meeting at Crossman's on 19 October, Wilson decided to stand against Gaitskell, and his candidacy was announced the following day. Greenwood deferred to him.

Wilson was to fight as a multilateralist, opposed to Gaitskell's policy of splitting the party. He was not taking a stand overtly in favour of the conference resolutions, preferring a compromise between conference and parliamentary party, and a closer relationship between executive and shadow cabinet. This was in the name of party unity, but at the expense of political principle. Crossman was prepared to back this 'left-centre'[23] challenge, in the belief that the left could not neutralize Gaitskell, but a broader alliance might stop the leader tearing the party apart. George Wigg became Wilson's campaign manager.

Gaitskell was reelected by two to one on 3 November, obtaining 166 votes to Wilson's 81. A third of the parliamentary party had refused to back the leader, but Gaitskell did better than in 1955. In the deputy leadership contest a week later, George Brown won by 146 votes to Fred Lee's 83. The post-Bevanite challengers to an incumbent labour leader were to suffer in the shadow cabinet elections, Wilson plummeting to ninth place, and Lee to twelfth. Wilson later described his 1960 leadership challenge as a mistake.

Gaitskell continued to believe he was fighting an issue of principle, namely collective security against neutralism, and considered he was faced with 'a dangerous, malicious, underground conspiracy'.[24] As early as April 1960, Tony Crosland and Bill Rodgers, general secretary of the Fabian Society, had begun to plan a Gaitskellite organization. A right-wing – revisionist – manifesto was issued on 19 October, after the party conference, with the campaign for democratic socialism (CDS) being launched on 24 November. Though Gaitskell kept his distance in public, the CDS was a right-wing version of Bevanism, intent upon working in the constituencies and unions to defeat the left, by winning over the centre. It had taken the vote in favour of unilateralism at Scarborough to propel the right out of its dining clubs and into the party.

The executive, in the wake of the 1960 conference, decided on 23 November to hold talks with the TUC. A motion to present the unilateralist position was lost, by seventeen votes to nine, in spite of the party's recent decision. Two weeks later, the parliamentary and party leaders held a joint meeting, at which it was agreed that a new defence policy had to be drafted. The conference decisions were being sabotaged.

Five days later, George Brown moved an opposition censure of government defence policy. Sixty-eight labour MPs abstained, and, when parliament resumed after Christmas, the Bevanites resumed their Tuesday lunches at Crossman's.

A joint meeting of the TUC general council, the national executive of the labour party and the shadow cabinet was held at Congress House on 24 January 1961. Wilson and Crossman tried to conciliate Cousins at this gathering, while Gaitskell and Brown sought to defeat him. Harold Wilson even put forward a six-point programme, which provided for a non-nuclear Britain in NATO, and no nuclear bases in the country. The meeting decided there should be a twelve-person drafting committee, four from each of the three bodies. The executive elected Crossman, the party chairman, Sam Watson of the Durham miners and Driberg. Harold Wilson, the vice-chairman, lost – by an undetected miscount – to Walter

Padley of the shopworkers. Despite the votes at Douglas and Scarborough the previous autumn, Frank Cousins was joined on the drafting committee by only one other unilateralist. Cousins initially stated he was not opposed to NATO, nor to the alliance retaining nuclear weapons in opposition to the Soviet Union, and this led Crossman to attempt another compromise in the four meetings of the committee. His draft only secured the support of Cousins, Driberg and Padley. A majority of eight supported a draft by Denis Healey, inspired by a Gaitskell determined upon victory. Cousins then reasserted his independence, and submitted a third draft on 15 February. At the executive a week later, this was defeated by sixteen votes to seven. Gaitskell won by sixteen votes to ten, the Crossman/Padley document being only just defeated by fifteen votes to thirteen.

The party leader, with only the initial support of a shadow cabinet majority, was well on his way to reversing the Scarborough conference decision. The parliamentary party rejected Crossman's compromise by 133 to 69 votes the following day. Gaitskell had vanquished Cousins.

With a lead being given by Gaitskell, trade-union conferences now began to swing away from unilateralism. Padley's shopworkers agreed to the Crossman compromise, if all other unions were prepared to back it. The AEU also came out in favour of the compromise, as the Gaitskell position was now being interpreted. The TGWU conference voted to support Cousins in July, making it the only major union to stand out against Gaitskell. When the TGWU was defeated by five and a half million to two million votes at the TUC in September, Gaitskell's victory was inevitable. The party conference at Blackpool rejected Cousins by 4,309,000 votes to 1,891,000, backing the executive by 4,526,000 votes to 1,756,000. Three of the six largest unions had changed sides, accounting for nearly a quarter of the union vote. If the block vote had lain behind unilateralism, labour multilateralism now rested on a similar distortion of democracy. There was still a trace of defiance on the part of delegates, as the conference voted to oppose Polaris submarine bases, but Gaitskell had been vindicated, and compromisers like Crossman and Wilson shown – in the eyes of the establishment – not to be up to the task of leading the labour party.

If unilateralism had been reaffirmed at the 1961 conference, Gaitskell would have been forced to resign, but the labour party found a new unanimity at Blackpool. This was now less about the independent British deterrent, which was thought to be redundant, and more about NATO, which was seen as retaining some sort of nuclear capacity. Labour was learning to live with the bomb, as long as it was American, and the American bases in Britain were non-nuclear.

Gaitskell's victory was not triumphalist, but the leadership initiative had been decisive. He had threatened to split the labour party, only to force responsibility for this upon the unilateralists. While the left was considered the disruptive force in the labour party in the 1950s, it ultimately put political solidarity before any particular position. It was the right which allowed political principle seriously to threaten labour as a mass organization. The question of the bomb slipped off the agenda, and Harold Wilson was not unhappy to see the issue resolved in this way, especially given he would be chairman in 1961–2.

His front-bench responsibility had remained the treasury in the first two sessions of the 1959 parliament, Wilson shadowing Heathcoat Amory, and, from July 1960, Selwyn Lloyd. Harold Wilson moved the opposition amendment welcoming the Radcliffe report on monetary policy on 25 November 1959, this being an historic update of the 1931 'classical analysis of the City'[25] conducted by Lord Macmillan. Wilson wished to play down monetary policy, but found Radcliffe a good stick with which to beat the government. '"There is no gentle hand", argued the report, "on the steering wheel that keeps a well-driven car in its right place on the road."'[26]

In 1960, Wilson published an article in the *Financial Times* on budget day. He took pride in the correctness of some of his predictions, particularly as regards anti-avoidance measures, even though he had been writing as a would-be socialist chancellor. In an economic debate that July, he asserted that production could not be expanded, because the government had thrown away the opportunities of the 1950s, 'the most favourable world economic conditions we had since before 1914'.[27] Harold Wilson first proclaimed the age of the scientific revolution in his speech: 'The potential release of energy ... of productive power, of facilities for material development and for leisure alike, defies the measuring rod of the market place or counting house, or any system dedicated to private profit and speculative gain.'[28] He put forward the idea of a four-year plan for Britain in a debate the following February; economic planning was becoming, once again, a rage in Britain. The idea was developed in an article for the *New Statesman* published on 24 March. Wilson was to argue in 1963 that, if his advice had been taken, tax revenues would have been up £1,000 million. The 1961 budget saw large concessions for those paying the highest rates. Wilson forecast an economic crisis, and deflation followed in July. In a debate on 26 July, he referred to an article in a German periodical, in which Britain was characterized as 'The Sick Man of Europe'. 'Fundamentally', Wilson argued, 'our latent virility, vigour, skill, ingenuity and inventiveness are such that instead of presenting this image of sickness we could present an image to the world of bounding energy and enterprise. All that is lacking is the leadership and inspiration, the call for service and sacrifice which this Administration is unable to give.'

With the defence issue considered settled within the party hierarchy, the national executive committee had begun to consider policy for Blackpool on 10 April. Crossman was complaining a month later: 'the Left on the

Executive has done absolutely nothing and Harold Wilson has left it to Peter Shore [head of the research department], concerning himself, apparently, chiefly with press relations in order to pile up his own position.'[29] Gaitskell and Brown, as the parliamentary leaders, and the party officers, Crossman and Wilson, then set about working on the Transport House draft. This cooperation threatened the resumed Bevanite lunches, and it was clear the left was divided between opponents of Gaitskell, and those who accepted they had to work with him. Crossman and Wilson even found themselves invited to Frognal Gardens for drafting sessions. The policy document was published on 28 June as *Signposts for the Sixties*, and launched in a television broadcast on 12 July by Gaitskell, Brown, Crossman and Wilson.

At Blackpool, Harold Wilson opened, and Hugh Gaitskell closed, the *Signposts for the Sixties* debate, which was accepted by the conference, after three sessions of desultory discussion. Wilson and Crossman came third and fourth in the executive elections, Callaghan – who had come on in 1957 – being the only right-winger elected by the constituencies. Crossman presided at Blackpool, and handed on the chairmanship to Harold Wilson. They had been determined to unite the party, from a left of centre starting point, but, when Crossman closed on the theme that 'the policy and the leadership issue [were] settled', this had the effect of 'infuriat[ing] the Left and … isolat[ing them]selves even more completely'.[30] There was a left-wing challenge to the leadership in the new session of parliament, but Wilson and Crossman were not involved. Greenwood and Castle, neither of whom was a member of the shadow cabinet, respectively secured 59 and 56 votes, against Gaitskell and Brown. The latter strengthened their parliamentary base, obtaining 166 and 169 votes respectively. Wilson recovered his position in the shadow cabinet elections, topping the poll, as he had done on three previous occasions. Crossman was the most successful runner up on the left slate. Gaitskell thereupon made Wilson shadow foreign secretary, formally a promotion to the position which had not been filled since Bevan's death sixteen months earlier. It was also a way of allowing Callaghan to become shadow chancellor. Gaitskell may still have been hoping Harold Wilson would not succeed as shadow foreign secretary, and Crossman confided to his diary at the end of November: 'It was clear … that Hugh had quite deliberately pushed aside any idea of forming a Centre, that he was relying on the Right of the Party, that he was allowing Harold to work with him because he was indispensable on the Front Bench and that I could work on the same terms in Transport House. But, as allies, he didn't want us.'[31]

The shock of Harold Wilson's move from financial to foreign affairs was eased, with the common market emerging as a major issue. The idea of a European common market had been proposed in 1955, but Britain rejected any notion of an external tariff. When Eden came up with his plan for a

European free trade area in October 1956, Harold Wilson took an early interest with the idea of safeguards. The treaty of Rome was signed by France, Germany, Italy and the Benelux countries in early 1957, the European economic community (EEC) coming into being the following year. Britain then negotiated a European free trade area (EFTA) – excluding agricultural products – with the Scandanavian countries, plus Switzerland, Austria and Poland. Macmillan came out in favour of British entry into the EEC in July 1961, largely for strategic reasons, since he hoped to strengthen Europe's link with the United States through NATO. The labour party had not taken a strong line. According to Crossman, 'Hugh Gaitskell and Harold Wilson [were] firmly determined to avoid making the mistake ... which we made on nuclear weapons by trying to work out a detailed ... policy which only splits us.'[32] The right tended to back the government, and the left to oppose entry. Douglas Jay was the principal opponent, believing in the continuing viability of the national economy. There was a basis for unity on the question of Europe in the idea of minimum conditions, and this was the line taken by Harold Wilson, without Gaitskell's approval, in the parliamentary debate on 2/3 August 1961. Opening on the second day, Wilson said: 'Frankly, until we know what terms we can get, anyone who can claim to see this issue in simple black and white terms, in or out, is either a charlatan or a simpleton.'[33] Labour was not opposed to negotiations, and the party would reserve its position until it saw the package. The TUC supported the formal application. No position was taken at the 1961 labour party conference, five days before Edward Heath, the lord privy seal, met European ministers in Paris.

The negotiations were delayed, while the six members of the community worked out a common agricultural policy, and were not resumed until early 1962. The shadow cabinet began working out minimum terms in March, on the basis of a paper by James Meade, the Cambridge economist. Jean Monnet, at Roy Jenkins's invitation, spoke at an XYZ dinner the following month, Gaitskell professing himself unconvinced by the faith in Europeanism. An anti-common market committee, which included Barbara Castle and Douglas Jay, was set up on 30 July, claiming the support of a majority of the parliamentary labour party. Up to 90, mainly younger Gaitskellites, were members of the labour common market committee, led by Roy Jenkins.

It was to be a case of *Gaitskellisme sans Gaitskell*. The commonwealth was extremely apprehensive about its future if Britain became a member of the EEC, and Gaitskell joined labour commonwealth premiers on 9 September in opposing entry on the provisional terms. Gaitskell condemned the government's haste in securing entry at almost any price, in a television broadcast on 21 September, speaking – significantly – of 'the end of a thousand years of [British] history; ... the end of the Commonwealth ...

[to become] just a province of Europe'.[34] Gaitskell forced opposition to the EEC through the shadow cabinet, and, at the national executive, meeting on the eve of the 1962 conference, a mild statement was drawn up, by Gaitskell, Brown, Crossman and Sam Watson. It contained five necessary conditions for entry, but the left abstained, since the statement allowed for further negotiations.

Gaitskell introduced the party's new policy on 3 October. He opposed entry on the existing terms, but warned about 'the end of Britain as an independent nation state'.[35] He sat down to unprecedented applause from a labour party conference. George Brown did his best to wind up for the executive, supporting the statement, but from a pro-European standpoint. He may have realized that, if Macmillan succeeded in taking Britain into the EEC, Gaitskell, if he came to power, was most unlikely to tear up the treaty of Rome. The labour leader was reluctant to demand a general election on the EEC issue, and those arguing for one were defeated by over two to one at the Brighton conference.

There were two further debates on the EEC early in the 1962–3 parliamentary session. Wilson wound up for the opposition on 8 November, describing the two-day debate as 'practical, constructive and detailed ... [without] a striking of general philosophical attitudes for or against the Market'.[36] 'Our position is that if we get the terms, then we go in.'[37] Further developments in the negotiations were debated in the house of commons a month later, Harold Wilson giving what was to be his straightest view of the EEC: 'while the industrial Common Market can be outward-looking and liberal – and I believe it is intended to be – the agricultural Common Market is restrictive, autarkic and Schachtian and is an offence to the trading interests of the free world.'[38] 'Whether in or out of Europe', he argued, 'we should turn our eyes towards an Atlantic trading community, indeed, one covering the whole of the free world rather than a community covering part only of Europe.'[39]

The left, however, was soon to be saved by an unexpected ally. Negotiations resumed in Brussels in January 1963, but, on 14 January, president de Gaulle suggested, at a press conference, that Britain might do better only to associate with the EEC. The French leader was hostile to the Atlantic alliance, dominated by the United States, and thought Britain was not sufficiently enthusiastic for European federation. As for American Polaris missiles, he preferred France to retain its independent nuclear deterrent. The other five powers were not unsympathetic to Britain, and rescheduled the talks, but de Gaulle won over the German leader, Dr Adenauer, and Ted Heath was told on 29 January that the six were unable to proceed with the talks. Hugh Gaitskell died four days after de Gaulle's veto, so it was Harold Wilson who opened the parliamentary debate on 11 February. He argued that the labour conference, at Brighton, had shown a greater sense of national interest than the conservative gathering at Llandudno, and castigated the government for having no alternative policy. 'In any further negotiations in Europe', he said, 'we cannot again allow ourselves to get into the posture of suppliants.'[40] Beggers could be choosers.

Harold Wilson, after a year as chairman, had been elected top of the poll in the executive elections at the Brighton conference. Anthony Wedgwood Benn also returned, knocking off Callaghan. It is perhaps symbolic that the 1962 conference, when labour found a new unity, should have been presided over by Harold Wilson, though opposition to the common market was to be profoundly divisive for the party later.

Harold Wilson must have noticed that George Brown had become somewhat detached from his leader at Brighton. Wilson ran against the incumbent deputy leader in the new session of parliament, securing an impressive 103 votes to Brown's 133 on 8 November. It was his second – unsuccessful – bid for the leadership since 1960. He was clearly marking his card, but may have seriously believed he could unseat Brown to become number two to Gaitskell, and thus heir apparent. Harold Wilson dropped to third place in the shadow cabinet elections, Callaghan coming first, but he continued as shadow spokesman on foreign affairs.

Wilson played a marginal role, with Gaitskell and Brown, in the Cuban missile crisis in the autumn of 1962. The installation of Russian weaponry, following the Cuban revolution led by Fidel Castro, saw the United States, under President Kennedy, escalate the threat to global peace. Washington imposed a military blockade on the island on 22 October. On 23 October, Wilson accompanied Gaitskell and Brown to a meeting with Macmillan. The labour leaders urged the prime minister to fly to Washington, to press Kennedy not to go too far. Macmillan noted 'they hadn't much to say. Brown was more robust than Gaitskell. Wilson looked very shifty. Fortunately, they all distrust each other profoundly.'[41] The party was reluctant to rally to Britain's ally in NATO, and this, apparently, angered the American president. Kennedy had supplied photographic evidence to the British government and MI6, and a member of the central intelligence agency (CIA) in London, Archie Roosevelt, was detailed to inform the labour party: 'The opposition was no problem. The deputy leader of the Labor Party, George Brown, was a friend and I arranged a briefing for him and the party leader, Hugh Gaitskill [sic].'[42] Harold Wilson was evidently not included.

Khruschev agreed on 28 October to withdraw missiles already installed, and the crisis was defused. By early December, Gaitskell was writing a memorandum to Kennedy on his opposition to the common market, the hiccup in relations having been overcome. Both men were to be dead within a year. In the free enterprise culture of the United States, Kennedy's death would be attributed to a range of forces. In the secrecy besotted world of the British state, Gaitskell would become a victim in an absurd communist plot. Harold Wilson was to be the anti-hero.

The leader of the opposition had begun to show signs of physical strain by the summer of 1962, momentarily blacking out on 13 June. Gaitskell was concerned only to have physiotherapy for what he took to be rheumatism in his shoulder. He told friends on 7 December that he had picked up something in Paris, where he had been discussing the common market, but reference was made later to recent trips to India and to Poland in August.

Believing he had influenza, Gaitskell went into the trade-union hospital, Manor House, in Golders Green on 15 December. Doctors were puzzled by his condition, but few visiting labour colleagues suspected anything serious. He was released on 23 December, in order to spend Christmas at home, and expected to be able to leave for Russia on new year's day. This, and other engagements, had to be cancelled, though he had a second remission. Gaitskell entered the Middlesex Hospital on 3 January 1963 with symptoms of pleurisy and pericarditis, these being attributed to some sort of virus. Appropriate specialists were summoned, and a rare and incurable disease, lupus erythematosis, an immunological disorder, was suspected. This – not unusually – was never definitively proved, and Gaitskell was to be described as suffering from an 'unusual fulminating form of lupus erythematosis'.[43] His doctor would say years later: 'It was a condition like Lupus. What he actually had was what we call an immune complex deficiency. His immune system broke down as the cells degenerated.'[44]

Gaitskell became much worse, as the doctors tried various antibiotics. He was put on an artificial kidney on 17 January, and died the next day from pulmonary congestion.

Gaitskell's death was medically complicated, and, in an atmosphere of political speculation about the labour leadership, the British security service (MI5) – or at least a section – began to take an interest. In the twilight world of counter-espionage, reality is often seen in highly conspiratorial terms – what the central intelligence agency calls 'obligatory paranoia'.[45]

Harold Wilson had indeed established a relationship with the Soviet Union. He visited it three times in 1947, being photographed on one occasion in the company of a woman member of his delegation (the photograph would be passed much later to MI6, and thence to MI5). Much is now made of the sale of British jet aircraft to Russia, though it is clear Harold Wilson did not play a decisive role. The hostility of British security organizations to the decision may have led to him being portrayed as soft on the Soviet Union, it being thought that Roger Hollis, head of MI5's C division, and Martin Furnival Jones, head of D division, actively backed the RAF's opposition to sales. Harold Wilson had to answer a parliamen-

tary question on the subject in May 1948, and American opponents of
Marshall aid were to complain of Britain arming the Soviet Union at the
start of the cold war. A version of this story was to be leaked to the press
in 1964 (and again in 1974). Wilson's resignation in 1951 probably saw him
noted as less than keen on the Korean war, and certainly as a left-wing
follower of Bevan's. His visits to the Soviet Union on behalf of Meyers
clearly aroused attention, there being nine in all between 1953 and 1963
– almost one a year. Much was to be made of the fact that Wilson must
have been compromised, his failure to report any Soviet approaches being
the principal cause for suspicion! Fellow travelling was not unknown in the
labour party, but Harold Wilson was not one of those MPs sympathetically
treated in the communist *Daily Worker*. Nor was he included on the list
of more than a dozen supected labour MPs, drawn up by Gaitskell in August
1961 (before the Blackpool conference), with the help of George Brown
and Patrick Gordon Walker. These men, especially the deputy leader, had
elaborate antennae for detecting fellow travellers, and there is no hint of
them suspecting, as opposed to disliking, Harold Wilson.

In December 1961, a Soviet agent, Anatoli Golitsin, who had worked
for the KGB as a major against Britain and the United States, defected to
the west in Helsinki. The reliability of any defector requires analysis of
motives and actions. Soviet agents were privileged citizens in their own
country, but risked retaliation if they fled to the west. The principal
motive for defecting, other than the ideological one, was to avoid
punishment for incompetence. Such individuals were of little use to the
west, and were run as double agents, or defectors in place, gathering as much
information as possible. Golitsin realized that he had to tell the west what
it wanted to hear, in order to become a privileged defector in the United
States, and it is believed he was fed theories, or suggestions, from within
the CIA and MI5, which were then confirmed. Some, but not all, of the
information he passed was correct. It is not impossible that Golitsin was a
fake defector. But it is more likely he was simply a human casualty from
the world of espionage.

Golitsin came to London in March 1963, to be debriefed by MI5, and
stayed until July, in the first months of Harold Wilson's leadership of the
labour party. Golitsin had said nothing to the CIA about Wilson, but he
became keen to blame Gaitskell's death on the KGB. He imparted in
London, for the first time, the story of Harold Wilson being a Soviet agent.
Golitsin claimed, quite simply, that department 13 of the KGB was responsible for Gaitskell's death, because its head, General Rodin, had served in
the London embassy! Back in the United States in the late summer of 1963,
Golitsin for the first time linked the death of Hugh Gaitskell and the rise
of Harold Wilson, to the initial consternation of the CIA.

Golitsin's claim about Gaitskell's death is initially implausible, for a very simple political reason. The most likely successor as labour leader in 1963, so everyone believed, was George Brown. He had won the deputy leadership three years earlier, and retained it in a contest with Harold Wilson in 1962. The Russians knew that George Brown would have been more anti-communist than Gaitskell, as is clear from Khruschev's memoirs, published posthumously in the west in 1971. (According to Ian Mikardo, who acted as the parliamentary bookmaker, some Russians in the London embassy placed bets on Callaghan winning in 1963. 'Shows how bloody well informed they were!'[46]) It was not inevitable that Harold Wilson would be victorious in the leadership contest, his success owing much to the third candidate. This throws the Golitsin theory out of the court of credibility, and there is evidence that this became the official view of the CIA and MI5 in 1963. Following Golitsin's return to the United States, Roger Hollis, as head of the British security service, told the Americans that there was nothing in the Gaitskell/Wilson affair. But the Russian defector had linked the two names that September in front of his American debriefers, and John McCone – head of the CIA – reported to the president personally. 'Kennedy's reaction was brusque: "He said, if you have specific proof, you pursue leads ... In the meantime, as President of the US, I will deal with Wilson if he becomes Prime Minister of the UK. And let's hear nothing more about it until something crops up.""[47]

James Jesus Angleton of the CIA, and Peter Wright of MI5, were nevertheless working overtime to detect communist enemies within the west. Angleton had been educated in England, at Malvern College, before going to Yale. He served in London, during the war, as an intelligence officer, and later became a member of the Soviet division of the new CIA. In 1954, at the age of thirty-seven, he became chief of counter-intelligence, a position he was to hold until 1974. It was Angleton who coined the phrase 'a wilderness of mirrors', to describe the world of counter-intelligence, and who fought for acceptance of Golitsin's views within the CIA.

Peter Wright's father had been an electronic engineer, who lost his job in the 1930s and turned to drink. His son had to leave public school early, and became a scientific civil servant after the war. He was eventually taken on by MI5 in 1955 as a technical officer, in charge of improving methods of eavesdropping. Wright would later boast, in a memorable phrase not his own, of having 'for five years ... bugged and burgled [his] way across London at the State's behest, while pompous bowler-hatted civil servants in Whitehall pretended to look the other way'.[48] He first met Angleton in Washington in 1957, when he went to discuss bugging techniques. Failing to become head of a secret scientific division, Wright had to wait until 1964 before being given a section – D3 (research) – within

MI5. His mentor, Arthur Martin, also a section head in the same department, was soon to be fired, allowing Wright access to Anthony Blunt.

When Arthur Martin came up with the idea in 1963 that Hugh Gaitskell had been assassinated, Golitsin, quickly reinforced it. Martin then contacted the British medical association, only to be told that the labour leader could not have been poisoned. Peter Wright went off to Porton Down, the ministry of defence's chemical and microbiological laboratory. He then asked Angleton to have a search made of Russian scientific literature, this showing that a drug – hydralazine – could produce some of the lupus effects in rats. Wright approached Gaitskell's consultant at the Middlesex, Dr Walter Somerville, only to be disabused of any supicious circumstances. Wright 'clearly did believe there was something in th[e] theory that Gaitskell had been poisoned, and [he was] reluctant to let go of it.'[49] Gaitskell's brother, Arthur, was even approached, and a return visit made to Porton Down. The head of chemical warfare refused to conduct research to test Wright's theory that Gaitskell had been poisoned by a cup of coffee, either in Poland, or in the Soviet embassy, where he had supposedly gone to get a visa for his trip to Russia. The fact that Gaitskell's illness preceded these events counted for little. Though the assassination theory was never proved, it would be leaked to sympathetic journalists. The *News of the World* was to carry the story in 1971, crediting another KGB defector with the information that 'Russian killer squads'[50] had been sorting out their political opponents in the west. *Private Eye* would take up the story about this time, and the theory, according to one prominent London journalist, was 'widely disseminated among journalists in the middle and late 1970s'.[51] After years of hints and rumours, gossip and innuendo, it came to assume the status of a self-evident truth.

The story of Gaitskell's death was revived in 1987, when Peter Wright's book *Spycatcher* was published in the United States. According to Wright, Gaitskell had told him personally of the visit to Russia. After his death, Wright continues, Gaitskell's doctor approached MI5, reporting his suspicions. The rest of the story in *Spycatcher* rings true, though Wright appears keen not to be too strongly connected with the assassination theory. On the point of who approached whom, Wright is wrong. Philip Williams, Gaitskell's official biographer, showed in 1979 that it was MI5 which came belatedly to the doctor and family. Dr Somerville appeared in a special *Panorama* documentary, on BBC television on 13 October 1988, arguing that his patient could not have been killed. The *Panorama* reporter, John Ware, showed that Wright was not a reliable historical witness. Wright admitted the inaccuracy of passages in the book, which had been written by Paul Greengrass. Greengrass denied attempting to 'flam up' the account he took from Wright, but he does admit to writing 'a gossipy, atmospheric account of an interesting life'.[52] Concluding his discussion of

Gaitskell's death, Wright asserts that 'if there was a high-level leak in MI5 to the Russians, they would have been informed of our suspicions and I am sure they would have ensured that no other case came our way.'[53] Assuming conspiracies everywhere, Peter Wright is able to offer explanations for whatever he wants to believe.

Each winter from the late 1950s, Harold Wilson gave a short course of lectures, for a fee, at the University of Chicago. He was there in January 1963 when Gaitskell was in the Middlesex Hospital, but heard the news of his death in New York. Once it had been known Gaitskell's condition was critical, supporters began phoning Wilson. Wilson immediately determined to stand for the leadership, spending £60 on transatlantic calls in two days. He flew back at once to London, where he made a short statement to waiting journalists. Harold Wilson claims he did not campaign, and says very little about the contest in his memoirs, but Marcia Williams has written: 'The leadership election ... was a nasty one, and I for one would rather not recall the way in which the Labour Party conducted itself during that period. It was rough, tough and unpleasant, with no holds barred and many people deeply hurt.'[54] George Brown would write that 'it was not a nice election': 'I discouraged active campaigning on my behalf, but that didn't prevent a bitter campaign from being waged against me.'[55]

The battle for Gaitskell's succession lasted four weeks. George Brown, the favourite candidate, could expect the support of the right wing, and therefore the majority of the parliamentary party. He also knew he could rely on virtually the whole shadow cabinet. Brown lobbied vigorously in the house, threatening members of the front bench, and promising others jobs, as he became more rattled. Wilson was not the candidate of the parliamentary leadership, but he had come top in the shadow cabinet elections four times, and was a popular constituency member on the party executive. He was billed as the left-wing candidate, appearances counting for a great deal in the world of politics. The intervention of James Callaghan as a third candidate was to determine the outcome, and it was fortunate for Wilson that Greenwood did not also stand. Callaghan had been a member of the parliamentary committee since 1951, but had just lost his seat on the executive. He had opposed Gaitskell over clause four, but supported him in overturning unilateralism.

'The Callaghan candidature', according to Richard Crossman, 'was precipitated by the strong-arm methods of the Brownites, combined with the agonized awareness of some of Gaitskell's closest friends that, if Harold Wilson was an odious and impossible man, George Brown was plain impossible.'[56] Brown had not always followed Gaitskell, and the weaknesses in his personality made some right-wing MPs think twice about making the deputy leader a potential prime minister. Callaghan's principal supporters were Tony Crosland and George Thomson, while Wilson's campaign was mounted by George Wigg and Richard Crossman. The latter believed that, 'in view of Harold's reputation for shiftiness and manoeuvring his best campaign was to have no campaign at all and to be seen studiously doing nothing with closed eyes, while leaving the Party to make up its mind.'[57] Wigg had Judith Hart and Stephen Swingler lobby the 70 or so leftists, while John Stonehouse, John Dugdale and Ben Parkin tackled those listed as probables or possibles.

Brown's campaign manager, Charles Pannell, suggested a pact to Crossman on 21 January, whereby each of the two principals would agree in advance to accept the deputy leadership if unsuccessful. Wilson leaked this information to the press, and it led to a row with Brown who publicly disowned the idea. The leadership contest dragged on for nearly three weeks, until the ballot on Thursday, 7 February. Wilson's managers kept him under control. He was nervous in his room before the parliamentary party meeting, but he sat through it showing no sign of worry. He came top with 115 votes, but, since Brown secured 88 and Callaghan 41, he was not the outright winner. Only one member of the shadow cabinet – Fred Lee – voted for Wilson, an indication of what his closest parliamentary colleagues thought of him. Callaghan had to drop out under party rules. Wilson needed only eight of Callaghan's votes to be victorious.

Gladys Wilson and Giles, together with Wilson, had been invited to Crossman's home, where they were joined for supper by Marcia Williams, George Wigg, Leslie Plummer and Tony Greenwood. (Mrs Wilson, as the wife of the leader of the labour party, was to be known from the first as Mary. It is not clear when Gladys was dropped, but Mary was being publicly used from as early as 1954.) Wilson suddenly said: '"There is one toast we must drink, to the man who is not here, the man who should have done it, Nye Bevan."'[58] Anthony Greenwood, for one, was not impressed.

Wilson opened, and Brown closed, for the opposition, in a parliamentary debate on the breakdown of the common market talks, at the beginning of the following week. Crossman thought Brown the better speaker, but Wilson apparently impressed his colleagues as statesmanlike. As the Wilson camp waited for the result of the second ballot on 14 February, concern was expressed that Brown might storm out of the parliamentary party meeting. When the result was declared, it was found that Wilson had won by 144 votes to 103. George Brown stated he wanted to think about his future, but Wilson appealed to him to remain as deputy leader. Ben Parkin praised the new leader at a celebration later at his Pimlico home. 'It was, out of character, almost incredible, but without doubt true': two journalists wrote of Wilson, 'the ice-cold Puritan, who now led the Labour Party had allowed himself the rare luxury of tears.'[59] Crossman discussed the election with John Freeman the following day, resolving to dictate an analysis of Wilson for his diary. He would look at it every twelve months, 'to see how foolish I have been, or how wise'.[60] This he was never to do. Nearing forty-seven, Harold Wilson, the tenth leader of the labour party, was younger than Gaitskell had been in 1955. Though both were known as Oxford economists, the 1963 leadership election represented a change in direction for the labour party.

The two men were very different. Gaitskell was upper middle class, southern, tory and episcopalian in background, Wilson lower middle class, northern, liberal and nonconformist. Winchester made Gaitskell, while Wilson remained the grammar school boy. Both became members of the governing class in the late 1940s. Gaitskell saw his career in terms of duty, but Wilson had to be ambitious – for himself or for a cause – though the weight of the biographical evidence now shows that Harold Wilson had little in the way of political beliefs. The two men certainly had very different conceptions of politics. Gaitskell's reference remained the state, while Wilson learned about the party in the 1950s. The former came out as a right-winger, wishing to lead a modern party. The latter was to aim for the centre, like Attlee, as labour leader. Gaitskell was rhetorically a modernizer of the state and civil society, though party activists remembered above all the split with Bevan in 1951. Wilson was to be popularly perceived as an altogether more democratic political figure. Though his first television address as leader on 27 February was not very professional, Marcia Williams recalls that he subsequently projected 'the image of the extraordinary ordinary man': 'The first in the country people had seen reach the top in politics.'[61] He was to be an inspiration to many upwardly mobile men and women in the 1960s, particularly in the rapidly growing public sector.

The Gaitskellites were not a little bitter. Bill Rodgers, who had become a labour MP in 1962, edited a biographical volume on their dead leader, which was published in 1964. He quoted in his introduction something Gaitskell had written about his political associates of the 1930s:

> While accepting the ultimate emotional basis of moral valuation, they had great faith in the power of reason both to find the answers to social problems and to persuade men to see the light. They were for the pursuit of truth to the bitter end through the patient and unswerving application of logical thought. They wanted no barriers of prejudice to obstruct the free working of the mind or blunt the sharp edge of intellectual integrity.[62]

They were, in other words, sensible socialists. Douglas Jay felt that Gaitskell could have been the best British prime minister of the twentieth century: 'He had strength of character and courage denied to MacDonald or Baldwin; trustworthiness lacking in Lloyd George or Chamberlain; an understanding of the social and economic facts of the modern world denied to Winston Churchill; and an all-round intellectual equipment which Clem Attlee, despite all his other rare gifts, would not aspire to rival.'[63] Roy Jenkins said that, in 1959–61, Gaitskell 'seemed to have secured for himself a long tenure of the leadership on conditions of tolerable authority'. 'What in fact he had done', Jenkins continued, 'was to bequeath this easement to his successor, and to give Harold Wilson the elbow-room which has helped him to look like a Prime Minister.'

Wilson had consorted with the Bevanites through the 1950s, but he told Crossman during the contest that he and Mary would not socialize with individual members of the party. 'No one should be disappointed at not being asked to dinner', he was to tell labour MPs. 'Nobody is being asked to dinner.' This was a case of making political virtue out of personal necessity, as Wilson believed that a man without friends had the makings of a good labour leader. He preferred, in puritanical fashion, to get on with his work. 'I am much more relaxed now', he would tell a journalist. 'With 20 to 50 different problems to deal with every day I never get bored.'[64]

He also told Crossman of his determination to involve scientists and technologists in the party. Wilson had been attending, on Gaitskell's behalf, a series of dinner parties at the reform club, hosted by Patrick Blackett, professor of physics at Imperial College, at which leading scientists exchanged ideas, with a view to formulating public policy. They wanted to 'wave a wand over Whitehall'.[65] Blackett was one of the country's leading scientists, having helped split the atom at Cambridge. He developed operational research during the war, this being an administative way of evaluating the claims of the armed services, and thereby rationalizing the military system – the era of the so-called slide-rule strategy. Blackett was frozen out of Whitehall in 1948, the year he won a Nobel prize, for opposing the military application of atomic energy. He became an opponent of the cold war and imperialism, and an active lobbyist on behalf of the scientific community. In 1953, when Blackett returned to London, Marcus Brumwell convened a group of scientific intellectuals, which included C.P. Snow, Jacob Bronowski and Solly Zuckerman, the idea being to influence the labour party. When Gaitskell became labour leader, he and Callaghan (and later Robens) attended these occasional scientific discussions, although Gaitskell criticized Blackett for technocratism. When Wilson became leader, Crossman, as spokesman on education and science, accompanied him to these meetings, and the relationship improved; Blackett and his colleagues came to feel they might have some influence on a Wilson government. Blackett and Wilson's shared memories of Whitehall in wartime informed much of the discussion, when temporary civil servants mobilized industry for the war effort, in the spirit of national interest, and the state, through the armed forces, was largely the customer.

By the 1960s science had become the spirit of the age, the technology of war being obscured by the optimism of the scientific worldview. Nigel Calder, the editor of *New Scientist*, asked about 100 men and women from all over the world to write on the next twenty years in 1964, these expert predictions being published, in two volumes, by Penguin Books in 1965, under the title *The World in 1984*. The first volume was broadly scientific and technical, the second covering government, domestic life, leisure, etc. Futurology was becoming a discipline. 'There is a growing awareness', Calder wrote in his introduction, 'that rates of change are now so great that medium-range forecasts are a serious requirement if we are not to be caught out by change and if the scientific revolution is to be carried through wisely.'[66] Calder – perhaps unconsciously – was seeking to revise the Orwellian nightmare. Talk of change, especially the complex rather than millennial sort, would have attracted Wilson. Dynamism was to become his means and end in government. He was particularly impressed by political modernization in the United States since 1961, the election of an Irish-American catholic to the presidency being celebrated as a democratic breakthrough. 'What he aims at', Crossman noted of Wilson, ' ... is the British equivalent of Kennedy's New Frontier, with a professional politician at the centre, hard-boiled, ruthless but with a basic inner drive and integrity, and round him a galaxy of talented, able, brilliant men.'[67]

Wilsonism in early 1963 promised the unification of the party, an ideological emphasis upon science and technology, and political professionalism – in short the rise of a meritocracy to political leadership. Its opponent was the British aristocracy, and the cult of amateurism aped by the bourgeoisie. 'At the very time that even the M[arylebone] C[ricket] C[lub] has abolished the distinction between amateurs and professionals', Wilson would argue, 'in science and industry we are content to remain a nation of Gentlemen in a world of Players.'[68] The meritocracy was very much a product of the British grammar school, and Harold Wilson was to be the first grammar school boy to become prime minister

Ironically, the reaction to Harold Wilson would come from elements of the same meritocracy. It was the political children of Harold Wilson who were to turn against him within a few short years, and ensure that 1963, when he fortuitously captured the leadership, was the pinnacle of his political career.

CHAPTER 15

Into Office, 1963–4

Harold Wilson had inherited a Gaitskellite shadow cabinet in February 1963, and told his former Bevanite friends, somewhat preposterously, that they 'must understand [he was] running a Bolshevik Revolution with a Tsarist Shadow Cabinet'.[1] He had few supporters on the opposition front bench, but the change in leadership meant some positions were available for reallocation. The shadow foreign secretaryship he gave to Patrick Gordon Walker. The new labour leader gave George Brown the home office to look after. Denis Healey took over Brown's defence portfolio, and James Callaghan continued to shadow the treasury. Richard Crossman was given the science portfolio, though he had never been elected to the shadow cabinet. Leading labour MPs were otherwise left in the posts Gaitskell had given them, but this did not prevent Crossman heralding a new dawn: 'Compared with what I expected, [Wilson] has gone on making the running and has produced something like a psychological revolution in the Party.'[2]

Harold Macmillan's second government had begun to crumble in the 1959 parliament. The conservative chancellor, Heathcoat Amory, produced another 'stop' on the economy, and Selwyn Lloyd took over in July 1960. In a sterling crisis the following summer, he embarked upon a pay pause. Deflationary policies had no appeal to the unions, but they joined the employers on Macmillan's new national economic development council (NEDC) in 1962, through which the government sought to plan the growth of particular industries. Selwyn Lloyd was replaced in July by Reginald Maudling, who presided over a rise in unemployment to 800,000. With a continuing balance of payments problem, he sought to bring about a boom in 1963, risking the import of raw materials. There were increasing demands on the defence budget. Kennedy agreed that December at Nassau to sell Polaris to Macmillan, the British nuclear submarines becoming part of a multilateral NATO force. This led to de Gaulle's veto on membership of the EEC.

Britain was having difficulty finding a role, while its empire drained away. The process of decolonization continued, but many of the new federations were to prove unstable. Immigration from the new commonwealth came to be defined as a problem in Britain, and the government enacted a racist measure in 1962, whereby quotas were to be imposed on those without jobs or skills. The government's poor showing was reflected in by-elections, with a liberal victory in Orpington in March. That July, Macmillan suddenly sacked one-third of the cabinet, in what was quickly dubbed a 'night of the long knives'. John Vassall, a clerk at the admiralty, was convicted in October of spying for the Russians, having been entrapped as a homosexual. Then, on 1 July, Edward Heath revealed that Kim Philby was the third man. Spy stories were proving a popular form of entertainment, and a good money spinner for the press.

When mixed with sex, they made a scandalous cocktail. Macmillan was confronted with the Profumo affair in 1963, shortly after Harold Wilson became leader of the opposition. John Profumo was the war minister, in charge of the army, and was involved with a 'call girl', Christine Keeler. Stephen Ward, a society osteopath, was, allegedly, her pimp. There was little unusual in this, but Keeler was also selling her services to a Captain Eugene Ivanov, an assistant naval attaché at the Soviet embassy. Rumours of this possible threat to national security, well laced with titillations about the mediating role of Keeler, reached Fleet Street. Little did the salivating newshounds realize that the KGB was seeking revenge, by embarrassing the government. MI5 had sought to use Keeler, through Ward, to entrap Ivanov. George Wigg, who was to play a crucial role, revealed the story at the Castles' dinner party on 10 March, though those present, including Wilson, were disinclined to exploit it.

On Thursday, 21 March, parliament was due to debate the imprisonment of two journalists, who had refused to disclose their sources to the Radcliffe tribunal into the Vassall case. Barbara Castle decided to use parliamentary privilege to bring the Profumo rumours into the open, but Wigg and Crossman preempted her by calling for a select committee. Harold Wilson also spoke in the debate after midnight, defending the freedom of the press. Profumo came back on the Friday morning, attacking the opposition for using privilege. He threatened legal action if the stories were repeated outside parliament. The war minister told the house that he had met Ivanov and Keeler, socially, at Ward's London flat a number of times. He then left, with his wife, to join the queen mother at the races at Sandown Park. This was royal benediction!

Stephen Ward contacted Wigg the following Tuesday, insisting Profumo was lying. A note was made of their conversation at the house, and an appreciation passed to Wilson. The labour leader sent this to Macmillan on 9 April, arguing that the issue was national security, not Profumo's private life. The prime minister replied that he would take no further action, but Ward continued to resist what he saw as an establishment cover up. After a meeting between Wilson and Macmillan on 27 May, the prime minister agreed to an investigation by the lord chancellor.

Profumo agreed to resign from the government and parliament on 4 June, admitting he had misled his colleagues and the house of commons. Ward was charged with living off immoral earnings four days later; his trial was to open at the Old Bailey on 22 June. Three days after being found guilty, he would take a lethal overdose of barbiturates. Profumo's resignation created a crisis within the conservative party, much being made of the sexual angle, but Macmillan survived a censure debate on 17 June, in which Wilson made 'an absolutely magnificent speech'.[3] The prime minister announced four days later that Lord Denning, the master of the rolls, was to hold a judicial inquiry into the question of security. The government now came clean on Philby to avoid further embarrassment, though Macmillan thought Wilson might 'play up'[4] after meeting him and Brown on 15 July (four days earlier, the prime minister had briefed the leader of the opposition on MI5: 'It seemed to me right to do', Macmillan noted, 'and he took it quite well'[5]). The disgraced Profumo was cleared by Lord Denning in September, of having betrayed military secrets to the hapless Miss Keeler. But the master of the rolls prostituted his judicial position in heaping opprobrium on the latter, though he conceded Macmillan had failed to act responsibly when information came his way. Macmillan told Wilson on 19 September of the omissions on security grounds, and the leader of the opposition agreed to support the government. Profumo was a political gift to the labour party, but the labour leader was afraid that the prime minister would resign. He did not want to break Macmillan on the back of his former war minister.

Harold Wilson had already begun to create an international profile as the British leader of the opposition. He had flown to Washington in March, for his first and last visit to the president. Wilson recalls having first met Jack Kennedy in Oxford in 1940, at Beveridge's invitation. The usual photographs were taken, and Wilson had one of him and Kennedy framed.

Wilson addressed the national press club in Washington on 1 April, in the first major presentation of labour's policies for an American audience. He feared 'a major seize-up in free world trade' due to a famine of liquidity. Wilson called for 'an economic summit of the free world', to discuss the increase of credit, using the machinery of the international monetary fund. While reaffirming support for the western position on Berlin, he advocated de facto recognition of East Germany. As for disarmament, Wilson urged nuclear free zones, albeit only latterly in 'central Europe'. He ended by reaffirming labour's commitment to NATO, and thought Britain should increase its contribution to conventional strength. Wilson admitted that the party's desire to '"denegotiate"' the Nassau agreement was well known'.[6]

With Patrick Gordon Walker and David Ennals, the party's international secretary, he then flew to Moscow in June, his twelfth visit since 1947. Meetings had been arranged with Khruschev, Mikoyan, Kosygin and other Soviet leaders, though the test ban treaty was then being negotiated. At the first interview, discussing Berlin, Khrushchev was threatening towards the labour leader. In their second meeting, he 'was all sweetness and light and said he looked forward to seeing [Wilson] again as Prime Minister'.[7] Her majesty's leader of the opposition broadcast on Soviet television on 14 June, addressing the east/west conflict. 'Differences of political institutions or of foreign policy', he said, 'do not mean that we have to settle these problems by recourse to war ... The choice is between co-existence and co-annihilation.' Wilson endorsed the Russian leader's idea of peaceful competition between their two social systems, and looked forward to the 'much greater interchange of scientific knowledge and know-how'.[8] In a foreign affairs debate on 3 July, he suggested that the Russian, British and French premiers should hold a regular summit each October, on the occasion of the united nations' general assembly in New York. In seeking to build on Macmillan's conduct of foreign policy, through increased summitry, the labour leader showed a desire to maintain Britain as an important, if not world, power.

Harold Wilson set out to revamp labour ideology in the summer of 1963, in time for the party conference at Scarborough. He spoke on foreign affairs at a pre-conference rally on Sunday, 29 September, attended by Willy Brandt, the socialist mayor of West Berlin. Roy Jenkins, in that morning's *Observer*, hoped the rapprochement with the SPD was 'a symbol of the Labour Party's rejection of "little Englandism"'. He predicted 'a dull conference'!

Wilson attacked the failures of the tory government in Europe and Africa, but his vision was Gladstonian: 'I believe we are on the eve of a new greatness for Britain, a greatness based not on military oppression or the ability to mount a colonial expedition, not on economic imperialism or colonialism, but on a contribution we have it in our unique power to make to the peace and happiness of mankind.'[9]

Wilson's main speech at conference was to be the opening of the science debate on the Tuesday morning. The idea for this had come from Richard Crossman, following the first significant parliamentary debate on the topic on 15 July. Wilson succeeded in getting a policy statement, drafted by Crossman and Peter Shore, through the executive on 27 September. It was hardly an issue of major concern, and he had not written his speech by the opening of the conference. Patrick Blackett travelled to Scarborough, to hear what Wilson would say. Alan Moorehead wrote of 'a soberly but well-dressed crowd, a middle-aged crowd ... and above all a solid respectable crowd, with the sort of moral principles that made Dr Ward and his *galère* seem like denizens of another planet.'[10] When the conference rose, Wilson left to fulfil a number of social engagements, including the Fabian tea party, where 305 people turned up instead of the expected 70. There he announced – probably inadvertently – that he would create five new departments when he became prime minister, which was to cause him some embarrassment with shadow cabinet colleagues, in particular James Callaghan. He also tried to reassure the civil service that there would be no radical changes. Marcia Williams then made him sit up until 3.30 in the morning, dictating his conference speech.

It was a tired Harold Wilson who rose to introduce *Labour and the Scientific Revolution* to delegates at 10.00 a.m. on 2 October. They sat in 'a conference hall that seemed rather more related to a performance of Lohengrin by the local opera group in Edwardian times than to a launching pad for Labour's new scientific age.'[11] He began his speech with the unprecedented pace of technical change in industry in the 1960s. Asserting that 'there [was] no room for Luddites in the Socialist Party', Wilson insisted that automation, if nothing else, made the case for socialism. Under private enterprise, it would lead only to high unemployment. His theme was the need for more scientists, which meant expanding Britain's educational institutions, particularly at the higher level. Wilson envisaged these scientists being deployed on industrial research, and, with state funding, originating – public – industries to revive the British economy. 'If we were now to use the technique of R[esearch] and D[evelopment] contracts in civil industry I believe we could ... establish new industries which would make us once again one of the foremost industrial nations of the world.' He concluded that labour had to 're-defin[e] and ... re-stat[e] [its] Socialism in terms of the scientific revolution'. Wilson insisted that, 'in the white heat of this revolution', both sides of industry would have to change. Apparently thinking on his feet, he suggested that, for example, apprenticeship schemes should be organized at industry level.[12] Wilson ended his speech with an attack on aristocratic control of industry, and the challenge provided by Soviet education and technology. Finishing towards 10.50 a.m., he received 'a long, standing ovation'.[13] 'The hall rose to him. It almost seemed that he had not expected such enthusiasm for his message. But the party had no doubts that it was going to win.'[14] The conference was euphoric that the memory of Hugh Gaitskell had been purged, and that his successor had revealed a new vision of British society and politics. Richard Crossman, who had done so much to make it possible, was to note: '[Wilson has] provided the revision of Socialism and its application to modern times which Gaitskell and Crosland had tried and completedly failed to do. Harold [has] achieved it.'[15]

This was to be dubbed Wilson's white-hot technological revolution speech, though commentators were to formulate a variety of catchy terms. Blackett had not been involved in the speech, and Wilson, judging by comments months later, thought it perhaps attracted more attention than it deserved. The idea of a scientific revolution was confused with a technological one. By lunchtime, Robert McKenzie, a political scientist and BBC broadcaster, was telling radio listeners that 'Harold Wilson [had] moved the Labour Party forward fifty years'.[16] Print journalists, in the main, were equally complementary. John Cole, the *Guardian*'s labour correspondent, wrote: 'The Labour Party's attempt to marry socialism and science in full view of the electorate was given a superb start today by Mr Harold Wilson, who made the best platform speech of his career. The annual conference has not previously been a happy hunting-ground for Mr Wilson, who prefers the intimacy of the Commons for his subtler shafts of scorn and wit.'[17] *The Times* noted that, 'by common agreement[,] this was the most immediately successful conference speech Mr. Wilson had ever delivered, and the audience showed a fervour that hardly knew any bounds when he sat down.'[18] Even the *Daily Telegraph* could not hide its admiration: 'The Labour Party bought Mr. Wilson, so to speak, wrapped up in brown paper. As he is unpacked, they are delighted to find him in pretty well every way rather better than they had expected.'[19]

The weeklies continued in this vein. In *Tribune*, Michael Foot wrote of the Wilson of 1951. 'He had forgotten nothing and learned much.'[20] The *New Statesman* reported that 'Wilson presented a vision of a new Britain and in doing so redefined socialism.' It was 'the most important speech made by a British politician for many years.'[21] The *Spectator* acknowledged that it had 'become a commonplace during the past week to assert that the Labour Party has changed completely and that the tired old features have been transformed beyond recognition'.[22] The *Economist* was probably the most profound, noting that 'Scarborough might yet mark the second stage in Mr Wilson's clamber upwards into very valuable statesmanship.' Exchanging 'the old cloth cap for a vastly becoming new white coat' captured 'the mood of the grass roots in Britain and throughout the industrial countries of the West'. The editorial speculated 'whether there is hope that ... [a labour] government might fill at least part of what should be its proper role in British history'.

By the Saturday, the *Guardian* was confidently asserting that 'Labour [could] fairly claim that it has not been more united, personally and doctrinally, since 1945.'[23] This was Harold Wilson's finest hour, the climax of his reputation. The *Sunday Times* was more balanced: 'There was probably nothing very much in his speech on the new scientific age that we have not thought of before, but it was a bright notion to pounce upon this safe and interesting theme at the moment, and he put it over with the air of a bold pilot breaking into uncharted seas.'[24] Anthony Sampson, in the *Observer*, who was working on his new *Anatomy of Britain* (1965), was one of the few journalists to contrast Wilson's Tuesday speech with his comments at the Fabian tea. 'He is against putting what he oddly calls "spatchcocking" dons, industrialists or trade unionists into existing Government departments; he thinks they would destroy morale and cause inefficiency.' But the science speech 'gave the impression – which Lord Hailsham has never managed to give – that Labour really *cared* about ideological change. That it *liked* men in white coats and understood cybernetics, whatever they are.' 'It is clear', Sampson concluded, 'that change is not going to be achieved just by substituting one lot of 90 politicians for another. It might be useful if Harold the white-hot revolutionary had a long talk with Harold the sober administrator.'[25]

Harold Wilson's white-hot technological revolution – his 'vision of a socialist future'[26] – was an important moment in British politics. It raised expectations, against which his government was to be judged in the course of the 1960s.

Richard Crossman considered Wilson had 'a rather mythical memory' about his time at the board of trade. The new labour leader was recalling Cripps's national research development council (NRDC) in 1963, which had been set up in 1948 to develop inventions to the production stage. Wilson had appointed Blackett to the NRDC in 1949, and he remained a member until 1964. Crossman considered Wilson was 'set on believing that there are immediate sensational things to be achieved by giving development contracts to private industry'.[27] Wilson's vision was that of the civil servant or technocratic minister, and amounted to a rejigging of the machinery of government. He promised a number of new institutions. There would be a ministry of higher education and another for science, which he had originally envisaged under one minister. They would work jointly with a new minister of planning, while the board of trade became an industry ministry. There were also to be ministries for disarmament and overseas development. Finally, at Scarborough, he repeated the idea of 'a university of the air', which he had first announced the previous month in Glasgow, the idea of educational broadcasting being derived from distance learning in the United States, but mainly Russia. With the exception of the latter, which had originated with Michael Young, now at Cambridge, and was not yet party policy, the idea of new ministries had been kicking around the labour party for some time. It was the Macmillan government, with the establishment of NEDC, and talk of planning, which stimulated the opposition's thinking.

Wilson had found an important way at Scarborough of presenting labour as the party of modernization. Science was not inimical to the right, though some Whitehall–orientated labour figures were not inordinately impressed with the speech. The left, in contrast, heard talk of revolution, though this had more to do with the language of advertising than Marxism. Wilson had a profound hostility to advertising as part of business, but was keen to appropriate the techniques of consumer manipulation when it came to politics.

When Harold Wilson proclaimed the scientific revolution, he was making a democratic appeal to the British people, especially the new educated petty bourgeoisie. The speech was not addressed directly to the establishment. Harold Wilson the politician appeared for once to be speaking from the heart. Control of the state bureaucracy, for him, was the end of politics. Between 1940 and 1945, Crossman was to tell a Fabian audience in November, Britain had probably been the best governed country in the world. Wilson had already told American journalists in Washington: 'We have a reservoir of unused and underused talent, of skill and craftsmanship, of inventiveness, and ingenuity, of administrative ability and scientific creativeness which if mobilised will ... enable us to become – not the workshop of the world; that is no longer our role – but the pilot plant, the toolroom of the world.'[28] This was an appeal for changes in the state and, even, civil society. Wilson wanted economic modernization, and a stronger role played by new social groups. He saw this coming through a labour government. His new ministries would intervene, especially in areas of knowledge and training, while scientists would be absorbed into the system of administration. The white–hot technological revolution, in so far as it meant anything, came down to incorporating scientific decision-makers into the world of Whitehall. This was the Blackett project *par excellence*. Richard Crossman had closed the conference debate on *Labour and the Scientific Revolution* with a warning on precisely this point. 'It would be an absolutely fatal thing', he told delegates, 'if the impression got abroad that, instead of the present Establishment with its "old boy" network, we foresaw the substitution of a scientific meritocracy to exert the same kind of dominance over the worker.' He cited, as a warning, de Gaulle's France, 'a technocratic paradise dominated by an old general'.[29] The part of Plato he always doubted, Crossman said later, was the doctrine of philosophy kings.

While Wilson was basking in the warm glow from Scarborough, labour had an important stroke of political luck. The conservatives were due to meet in conference at Blackpool from 8 to 11 October. Harold Wilson would be a difficult act to follow. Macmillan was scheduled to address a rally on 12 October, just before the test ban treaty, which had now been signed by more than 100 states, came into force. The first evening of conference, the tory ranks heard that the prime minister had been rushed to hospital with prostrate trouble. Shortly before his operation on 10 October, Macmillan summoned the foreign secretary, the fourteenth earl of Home, and asked him to inform the representatives gathered at Blackpool that he would not be leading the party into the next election. The conference immediately became an arena for the three principal candidates for the leadership. Rab Butler, the first secretary of state and deputy premier, a progressive tory, was probably the favourite. Lord Hailsham was popular with the party, until he decided to renounce his peerage in order to achieve the premiership. An outsider, Reginald Maudling, the chancellor, was thought by some to be the young, dynamic candidate.

Tory leaders, even when they were to step straight into the premiership, emerged through an informal process of consultation. This began on 14 October. Macmillan, still in hospital, favoured Hailsham, but he instructed that soundings be taken throughout the party. If one peer was possible, some began to think, then why not another. Lord Home, though he had left the commons in 1951, began to emerge as a compromise candidate. Conspirators around Ian Macleod held a midnight meeting at the home of Enoch Powell to prevent this. The queen visited Macmillan in hospital on 18 October, and was advised to send for Home. The party rallied behind this hereditary Scottish peer, and he was able to form a government, the first appointments being announced on Sunday, 20 October. Home, as prime minister, disclaimed his peerages. Warned that he would have to counter Wilsonian jibes about being the fourteenth earl, he replied: 'Oh well ... I shall refer to him as "the 14th Mr. Wilson".'[30] He did, on television, and the term stuck. As Sir Alec Douglas-Home, the earl won a safe Scottish seat on 8 November.

If Macmillan had only posed as an aristocrat, though married to a Devonshire, Douglas-Home, Eton and Oxford, was the genuine article. He even had political roots in appeasement under Neville Chamberlain. The elevation of Douglas-Home was nothing less than a display of political bankruptcy, in the wake of the moral turpitude associated with Profumo. It was even more likely, with only twelve months of the parliament left, that the conservatives would be defeated at the polls.

Harold Wilson behaved as if he was going to be prime minister, expecting the general election as early as the following March or April. Anthony Wedgwood Benn discussed with him, on 3 December 1963, the idea of a series of meetings the following year, passing on the suggestion of his American wife, Caroline, that there should be a 'New Britain' programme, analogous to the 'New Frontier' of Kennedy in 1960. The Benns believed such an appeal would attract experts and others – 'New Britons' – to the labour cause. To the tories' idea of 'modernisation', he countered that of 'regeneration',[31] though the terms could have been reversed. Party policy did not count for much, since Wilson, on his own later admission, 'was running the Party in a slightly dictatorial way'.[32] Any programme promoted by the party was to be that of a labour government under his leadership. Wilson was sympathetic to Wedgwood Benn's proposal, and, dining with Crossman two weeks later, he announced that Wedgwood Benn was to chair a group, comprising Thomas Balogh, Peter Shore and Richard Crossman, to draft six speeches, to be delivered in the first three months of the new year. He wanted the series to be called 'Purpose in Politics', purposiveness being a Baloghian concept. Wilson was extremely sensitive about using ghost writers, but it was arranged that the texts were to be polished by Ted Willis, James Cameron and Hugh Cudlipp.

Wilson began in Birmingham, on Sunday, 19 January 1964, with a speech on 'The New Britain'. He argued that socialism meant 'applying a sense of purpose to our national life: economic purpose, social purpose, and moral purpose. Purpose means technical skill – be it the skill of a manager, a designer, a craftsman, an engineer, a transport worker, a miner, an architect, a nuclear physicist, a doctor, a nurse, a social worker.'[33] He spoke on economic policy six days later at Swansea, arguing that national production would be expanded, in the short term, by borrowing to avoid a balance of payments crisis, increasing short-term interest rates, and an incomes policy 'based on rising production'. The economy had to be strengthened through structural changes in the long term, involving help for exporters, tax incentives, import substitution, and government research and development contracts, managed by a new ministry of technology. There would also be 'new publicly owned industry based on science'.[34] This idea came from Peter Shore, and had been heralded at Scarborough. The next speech was due to be on foreign affairs, but Wilson '[felt] ... it [was] home issues that really pull[ed] in the support'.[35] He spoke on housing and town planning at Leeds on 8 February, repeating the commitment to take urban building land into public ownership. On a visit to the United States, where he met President Johnson, he spoke on 'Britain and World Peace', in Connecticut on 3 March. Wilson endorsed Kennedy's view of the western alliance as designed to 'enable [them] to make a fuller, more effective contribution to peace and prosperity in the world'.[36] He spoke on full employment in Liverpool five days later, to an audience that included labour activists from Ormskirk and Huyton, invoking the spirit of 1945. He bemoaned Britain's relative decline under the tories in Edinburgh on 21 March: 'If the trends of the last twelve years continue the Japanese will catch up by the middle seventies, and by this time the Germans will be twice as powerful economically as we are.'[37] The final speech of the original series was entitled 'Our National Purpose', and was given at a party rally in the Albert Hall, on Sunday, 5 April, on the eve of the first Greater London Council elections. Wilson promised 'social purpose, economic purpose, and purpose in foreign affairs',[38] and ended by quoting Bevan's last speech to a party conference on the 1959 election defeat.

The new Britain was less a political programme, and more a presentation of Harold Wilson as a dynamic administrator. The speeches themselves were published as a Penguin Special later in 1964. The cover of *New Britain*, with the subtitle, *Labour's Plan Outlined by Harold Wilson*, comprised a black and white photograph of the speaker, with 'Wilson', in large red letters, splashed across his forehead. Weidenfeld and Nicolson published another selection that year, under Wilson's title, *Purpose in Politics*. The volume opened with his 1963 conference contributions, but it mainly comprised speeches he had made from the front bench. Those on monetary and fiscal policy hardly made for entertaining reading, and Wilson's contributions on foreign policy dealt largely with the independent British nuclear deterrent. He hoped it was neither financially, technically nor strategically viable.

Wilson attempted to expound an intellectual view of the world in the late summer of 1963, when he wrote a long article on British socialism for the following year's *Encyclopaedia Britannica*. He was holidaying on the Scillies in the company of press photographers and journalists, and seems to have returned to it after the Scarborough conference. The article was published separately as a book in the United States, and his friend, George Weidenfeld, duly brought out a British edition in 1964, under the title, *The Relevance of British Socialism*. It is defensive about the labour party, given it was written for an American audience, but this creates a certain distance between author and subject, which is filled with argument and thought. *The Relevance of British Socialism* was Wilson's only attempt to advance a theory of socialism for Britain, and it shows his inability to rise above the structures of party and government. Ideas were simply the handmaiden of ideology.

The *New York Times* had published an article on 15 September 1963 entitled 'Wilson Defines British Socialism', which remains the best statement of his political position. He began, for the benefit of Americans, by eschewing revolutionary action and political strikes. Wilson then quoted clause four and the 1960 declaration in favour of the mixed economy, the new testament favouring 'an expansion of common ownership substantial enough to give the community power over the commanding heights of the economy'.[39] This amounted, as Wilson revealed, to the renationalization of steel, the public ownership of water supply, the expansion of existing public industries, and, finally, the development of new industries in the public sector. Wilson stated that a labour government would dynamically strengthen the British economy, promising new, science-based activity. He concluded: '[labour's socialism] is essentially a pragmatic conception, related to the needs of the age and the world in which we live.

And, because we are democratic Socialists, its implementation in terms of legislative and executive action depends entirely on the consent of the British people.'[40] Wilsonism was to be pragmatism.

Wilson himself was becoming known to the British public, quickly adapting to the medium of television. Tom Driberg was an unofficial adviser. Wilson became 'convinced that what he said on television was less important than the impression he gave and what he looked like'.[41] He took delight in presenting himself as the common man, in contrast to the untelegenic Douglas-Home. Wilson's pipe became his characteristic tool of the trade, though he smoked cigars in private. It was even used in television interviews, as a protective device, regardless of studio fire regulations. The pipe was not always lit, particularly when cameras filmed him entering and leaving buildings, and getting in and out of cars. He also wore spectacles, but made sure he was never photographed or filmed with them on. (At some football match or other later, when the camera caught him wearing spectacles and smoking a cigar, Wilson, with only two hands, got rid of both and extracted a pipe from his pocket.) His Gannex raincoat became his second most distinctive accessory. Wilson was later to tell Robert Kennedy that he had studied his late brother's television style. It was less charisma with Wilson, and more communication. Marcia Williams was to remember the 1964 election: 'At last you were able to get into people's homes and to do that you had to be like someone they would know … Fortunately this young man [Wilson], with the sort of background that everyone in those days was aspiring to … Suddenly he was on your screen[,] he was in your home and [you] could identify with him.'[42] (If Marcia Williams thought Wilson was young, the labour prime minister would be 'good old Mr Wilson' to Paul McCartney of the Beatles.)

Wilson was aware that print journalism was biased against the left. Television, he believed, was a way of circumventing this problem, but he relied considerably upon the press for his political image. He became a political character, with photographs and cartoons in newspapers. The *Sunday Times* was to run a feature on Harold Wilson in February 1964 in its new colour magazine, Godfrey Smith having spoken to the Wilsons the previous summer on the Scillies. Mary Wilson was quite unpretentious: 'It would be a complete waste of time doing any fancy cookery for Harold, risottos for instance. Yes, it's true he prefers tinned salmon. Anyway, we couldn't afford smoked salmon. Harold cooks a very nice breakfast. He's good with sausages and things. But I wouldn't trust him with the joint. If Harold has a fault it is that he will drown everything with H.P. sauce.'[43]

Harold Wilson became increasingly prime ministerial in 1964, though, behind the talk of dynamism, lay hesitancy in action. He sought, for example, to retreat from the position of Britain acting alone against South Africa. Barbara Castle and Wedgwood Benn confided on 13 April that they had 'grave reservations about Harold'. 'He just doesn't like a showdown and [is not] ... a political leader ... prepared to fight a stand-up battle with his colleagues for the things in which he believes.'[44] This trait was to become more pronounced, and a cause of frustration to Denis Healey and others. The leader of the opposition was even outvoted in the shadow cabinet in July, the labour front bench supporting the government's terms for Malta's independence. Jim Callaghan had characterized Wilson's leadership as 'a succession of bilateral interviews' with members of the shadow cabinet: this 'might make for admiration while it succeeded[,] but would fail to build personal loyalty on which to rely in bad days'.[45] These words were prophetic.

Wilson believed that his real cabinet would be made in 1966, just as Attlee's had been in 1947 (the year he became president of the board of trade). Tommy Balogh, Peter Shore and Wedgwood Benn constituted an informal group of advisers, but it was 21 July before they could discuss electoral tactics with Wilson. They had wanted less knockabout with Douglas-Home, and more on the new Britain. Wilson did speak about the first 100 days of a labour government on television on 15 July, this being another transatlantic import from the arrival of Kennedy's Camelot in Washington. He had been concerned not to provoke the Americans with an election imminent, and, after the so-called Gulf of Tonkin incident, which gave the United States an excuse to attack North Vietnam, he flew back from the Scillies on 10 August, 'terrified of saying anything that might upset the Americans'.[46]

Labour had been leading the conservatives in the monthly Gallup poll from August 1961. From 15.5 per cent after Wilson's election, this was to drop to 1.5 in September 1964, as the conservatives' pre-election boom worked. Douglas-Home had stated in June that the election would be in the autumn, at the very end of the 1959 parliament. It was called eventually for 15 October 1964, necessitating the postponement of the party conferences.

The prime minister made much of the independent nuclear deterrent, but the tory manifesto, *Prosperity with a Purpose* also promised 400,000 new homes a year. Peter Shore drafted labour's election programme, entitled *The New Britain*, and Wilson launched it on television on 11 September. The party repeated its promise of a ministry of economic affairs, to draw up a national plan, with regional planning boards. There was also to be a ministry of technology, to help modernize industry. The trade gap would be tackled, and there was to be an incomes policy, and tax reform. The labour manifesto contained little on foreign affairs, but a non-nuclear Britain was seen as playing a closer role in a nuclear NATO.

The party held a rally the following day at Wembley. It 'began with an American convention-style entertainment with actors and actresses [including

Vanessa Redgrave] and a pageant'.[47] Douglas-Home was forced on to the road, but found it uncomfortable talking politics to people. He was equally ill at ease on television, and betrayed a scepticism about the medium's tendency to trivialize. Harold Wilson was now a consummate political performer on the small screen, being the first would-be prime minister to talk direct to the British people. The labour party organized a series of rallies up and down the country, where he pressed home the idea of a new Britain. Wilson had a standard speech, with a variable nightly addition. His advisers feared he was 'writing the chapters of a book'[48] in his nightly speeches, rather than hitting Home where he was economically weak. They also criticized Wilson for concentrating too much on the daily press conferences, but he seems to have become convinced by his own image as the man who could defeat the tories. Treasury figures showed a trade gap, and Wilson predicted an annual balance of payments deficit of perhaps £400 million.

He had been adopted labour candidate for Huyton on Monday, 14 September. The local issues were housing and selection at eleven for secondary education. Kirby had gone comprehensive under a labour council, and many parents wanted to transfer to the area. At what was his fifth adoption meeting, Wilson promised he would continue to be a good constituency MP. 'I want you to bring your problems to me', he said, 'irrespective of your politics, creed or colour, and I will deal with them individually. No problem is too big or too small to take up.'[49] The electorate in Huyton was still growing, but there had also been further boundary changes.

Being a potential prime minister undoubtedly helped Wilson's candidacy. There was an independent communist, or Maoist, as third candidate. Wilson was absent from the constituency on his national speaking tour, but his full-time agent, Arthur Smith, a former miner, covered his back. Wilson, to the chagrin of party managers, spent much of the last week in Huyton, and travelled more than 100 miles on 15 October visiting polling stations. As his result was being declared early on Friday, 16 October, Wilson was seen, on television, to be deeply moved. He was safely home with 42,213 votes to 22,940 for a conservative, a majority of 20,000 being worthy of a potential prime minister. The third candidate obtained 899 votes, and was given short shrift by the crowd at the count. '"By voting Labour you are only bolstering capitalism", he started. But his voice was lost in the overpowering din from the angry crowd.'[50]

The campaign had been closely fought for three weeks in the country, the liberals promising a breakthrough. Turn-out was slightly down on 1959 (to 77.1 per cent). The conservatives dropped one-and-three-quarter million votes, to twelve million (49.4 to 43.4 per cent of the poll). These went largely to the liberals, who nearly doubled their vote, to three million. Labour held its support at just over twelve million (rising from 43.8 to 44.1 per cent). The increased liberal vote gave Wilson an overall majority. Labour did well in London as in 1945, suggesting it had made inroads into the professional middle class, but it did not eat into the tory vote in the south-east and midlands. The party also performed well in its heartlands, but the liberals made a showing on the Celtic fringe. Labour secured 317 seats to the conservatives' 303 plus the speaker; the liberals had 9. There were no other minor parties. The labour opposition had come back with an overall majority of five, the smallest since 1847, but Harold Wilson was in a position to form a labour government after thirteen years of tory rule. The promise of a new Britain would now be put to the test.

CHAPTER 16

The First Wilson Government,
1964–6

Harold Wilson had returned to his suite, at the Adelphi Hotel in Liverpool, after the declaration at Huyton. With the outcome still uncertain, he and his party left by train for London on Friday, 16 October at 8.15 a.m. The labour leader was accompanied by his father, Mary Wilson, Marcia Williams and Thomas Balogh, plus John Allen and John Harris from Transport House. The blinds were kept down for much of the journey to allow the Wilsons to doze, but Balogh's transistor radio – though it only worked at stops – meant there was little opportunity for rest.

They were met at Euston by Len Williams, the general secretary, and a media circus. The Wilsons were whisked away to labour headquarters in Smith Square, where the family had begun to gather. It was not until after 2.47 p.m. that Douglas-Home conceded defeat, when labour reached 316 seats. Marcia's brother, Tony Field, who had driven Wilson throughout the campaign, called at Hampstead Garden Suburb and collected a short black jacket (not the morning wear requested by the palace). Two special branch officers arrived, to provide security, and Wilson requested his old board of trade driver, Bill Housden. He then left to meet the queen. With Mary and Robin in a palace Daimler, while the rest of his family, plus Marcia Williams, followed in a second car. To take one's family, and secretary, to Buckingham Palace was unprecedented, but perhaps indicative of a prime minister who would be respected by aides for having absolutely no side. Wilson agreed to form a government, and was surprised to find there was no formal kissing of hands. He then drove to Downing Street, via Transport House, in his prime ministerial car, to be followed by Marcia Williams, and labour's chief whip, Herbert Bowden. After speaking to the press on the steps, Harold Wilson entered number 10 as labour's third prime minister: 'I went along the long corridor from the front door to the Cabinet Room, a little bewildered, more than a little lonely, but above all else conscious of our small majority and the utter unpredictability of even the immediate future.'[1]

The first major task was to form a government. Wilson was the leading political survivor from Attlee's cabinet, though he was younger than many of his front-bench colleagues. James Griffiths and Patrick Gordon Walker had joined the cabinet in 1950, and George Brown and Lord Longford were ministers outside. Arthur Bottomley, Michael Stewart and James Callaghan had been junior ministers. Wilson had 316 colleagues in the commons to choose from, but few supporters in the shadow cabinet. He had been provided with a party list of MPs, but Edward Short, who became chief whip, is not sure he used it.

Wilson filled six senior offices on the first day. George Brown, as deputy leader, had been promised the new department of economic affairs (DEA) in a famous taxi ride from St Ermin's Hotel to the house, and this position was offered to him as first secretary of state. James Callaghan, as expected, went to the treasury. The division of labour, as agreed in a concordat that evening, according to Wilson, was that Callaghan had 'monetary responsibilities', while Brown was in charge of 'industry and everything to do with the mobilisation of real resources for productivity and exports'.[2] Brown claims the concordat was never formally accepted, while Callaghan states it took many weeks to agree what was only a verbal truce. Gordon Walker was made foreign secretary, though he had lost his seat. (In the early hours, Wilson had issued a statement saying he looked forward to his return to the commons, having already telegraphed Gordon Walker to the effect that he would be in the government.) When Gordon Walker also lost a by-election in Leyton in January 1965, he was replaced by Michael Stewart. For lord chancellor, Wilson selected Gerald Gardiner, a respected barrister much committed to law reform, whom he had nominated to the upper house the previous December. Denis Healey became defence secretary, and Herbert Bowden lord president and leader of the house of commons. Frank Cousins, the transport workers' leader, who was not yet a member of parliament, had been earmarked for transport; Wilson gave him the new ministry of technology, supposedly to lead the industrial regeneration of Britain.

The remaining members of the cabinet, selected by 18 October, were: Lord Longford (lord privy seal), Sir Frank Soskice (home office), Fred Peart (agriculture), Anthony Greenwood (colonial office), Arthur Bottomley (commonwealth office), Michael Stewart (education and science), Richard Crossman (housing and local government), Ray Gunter (labour), Douglas Houghton (duchy of Lancaster), Barbara Castle (overseas development), Fred Lee (power), William Ross (Scottish Office), Douglas Jay (board of trade), Tom Fraser (transport), and Jim Griffiths (Welsh Office). When Roy Jenkins declined to become education secretary in January 1965, in succession to Michael Stewart, the job went to Anthony Crosland. Wilson had a cabinet of twenty-three, one less than Douglas-Home's.

The new prime minister sought to create a balance between different party interests. His left-wing colleagues of the 1950s – Crossman, Castle, Greenwood and, to a lesser extent, Cousins – were included, though they were to criticize him for packing his cabinets with Gaitskellites. 'Instead of defeating his enemies intellectually', one would say, 'he tried to buy them off.'[3] Balance was essential to divide and rule. By dividing economic policy between Brown and Callaghan, Wilson strengthened his own control, but he was to be confronted by Douglas Jay, Anthony Crosland and Lord Longford of the old Hampstead set. The labour cabinet, aside from Lord Longford, was predominantly middle class. Nearly half had been to Oxford, and five – Wilson, Longford, Jay, Crossman and Crosland – were dons. Harrow, Eton, Winchester, Merchant Taylor's, St Paul's, and one lesser public school, were all represented. The intellectuals were more right than left wing: 'Most of them [were] "revisionists", bored by old party dogma, rather ill-at-ease in trade union gatherings, and looking towards the kind of classless, half-American society outlined in Anthony Crosland's books.'[4] Only two other universities were represented. Nearly half the cabinet had only been to secondary school, this group including the trade unionists, who, like the deputy leader, were mainly right wing. Being working class by origin, they tended to have deeper roots in the labour party, but only eight members of the cabinet had fathers who were manual workers. Griffiths and Fraser were former miners. Though the minister of technology was something of an exception, this less glamorous wing of the cabinet would be most sensitive to rank and file interests. Although Harold Wilson was not trusted by the intellectuals, as leader of the government, it was to be one or two of the working-class members of the cabinet who would cause him most trouble.

Harold Wilson also appointed thirty-one ministers outside the cabinet, including Wedgwood Benn (postmaster-general), Fred Willey (in the new ministry of land and natural resources), George Wigg (as paymaster-general, to oversee MI5 and MI6, for which he would be known as spymaster general), and Sir Hugh Foot and Alun Gwynne Jones (foreign office ministers, as Lords Caradon and Chalfont, responsible for, respectively, the united nations and disarmament). Wilson had failed to entice Solly Zuckerman, the government's chief scientific adviser, and an old friend of Bevan's, into his 'ministry of all [the] talents',[5] and it was George Wigg who suggested Chalfont, a former professional soldier, as minister for disarmament. There were thirty-nine junior ministers (most noticeably Jennie Lee, to look after the arts). With whips and the royal household, the government numbered just over 100. Of the 317 MPs, 87 were found jobs, in a larger and more democratic administration than the preceding conservative one.

But it was hardly the executive to construct a new frontier. When all the parliamentary private secretaries are taken into account, there were few elements independent of the government on the labour backbenches. The most notable were Michael Foot and Ian Mikardo. Prime ministerial patronage took hold of the parliamentary party. Considerable political and ideological unity had been created under Wilson, but this was directed primarily at getting into power. Party management was now integral to government leadership, but aspects of the factionalism of the 1950s would find expression in individual ambition.

Wilson had spoken reassuringly of his plans for Whitehall, in a radio interview with Norman Hunt of Oxford University in February: 'I do not believe frankly in bringing a lot of top people in and putting them on top of existing civil servants.'[6] 'In the main', he conceded, 'it wo[uld]n't be new departments, it [would] be replacements.'[7] The new ministry of economic planning would be 'in a sense, Neddy [NEDC] writ large and given teeth'.[8] It was necessary not to overload the treasury, but allow it to get on with economizing. Wilson admitted his main reason for having such a planning department: 'when you run into balance of payments difficulties ... the whole Treasury is pervaded with the idea that we must now hold down production.'[9] He was not particularly in favour of the *cabinet* system, and 'rather against the idea of bringing in a series of *eminences grises* or Rasputins or court favourites to advise a Prime Minister'. 'You see', Wilson said, 'perhaps the effect of having been a civil servant is that one is, to some extent in a Whitehall phrase, "house trained", and one wants to see any experts properly dovetailed into the administrative machine – on an organization chart, not floating about in a somewhat irresponsible way.'[10]

He would adopt from President Kennedy the idea of 'project studies', 'with experts – not only ministers – but top civil servants, planners within the department and also, in some cases, people brought in from outside'.[11] 'My conception of the Prime Minister', Wilson argued, 'is that if he's not managing director, he is at any rate and should be very much a full-time executive chairman.'[12] On the question of cabinet versus presidential government, he affirmed commitment to the British practice, and only wanted to build up the cabinet secretariat. 'I am perhaps spoilt in all these things', Wilson concluded, 'by my experience of being a civil servant under Churchill, and a minister under Attlee and that was, I think, the way on which they ran these things – much more than you've had perhaps in the last few years.'[13]

Wilson's conversation of over an hour with Hunt in February was far from radical, and was edited down to thirty minutes for broadcasting. A slightly longer version of the transcript appeared in the *Listener*, and was to be published in a book by the BBC. Lord Bridges later commented in a separate programme, criticizing the separation of economic planning from the treasury. Wilson's reference to Neddy, the former cabinet secretary said, sounded like an attempt to turn it from an advisory to an executive body. As for the treasury holding down production, Bridges could only 'say that this was the one point in Mr Wilson's talk which really puzzled [him], and troubled [him]'. If there were two departments, 'I would have thought that it would make the job of any Chancellor ... extremely difficult and would inevitably result in some tension, if not actual confusion between the two departments.'[14] Douglas Jay knew as much about Cripps's short-lived ministry of economic affairs in 1947: 'Wilson', Jay claims, '... knew the scheme was ill-judged, but for some reason put personal appeasement first.'[15]

The reason was George Brown, who had to be kept out of the foreign office, presumably because he could not be relied upon to be diplomatic. Wilson dined secretly in late July 1964 with Sir Laurence Helsby, then head of the home civil service. He suggests that Helsby was familiar with the unedited version of his broadcast, and raised no objection to either the DEA or the proposed ministry of technology. Helsby would not have been so indiscreet, having been permitted by the prime minister to discuss a possible change of administration with the leader of the opposition. Sir Donald MacDougall of Neddy was earmarked in advance to become director general of DEA, and Sir Eric Roll, the economic minister in Washington, agreed to become permanent under-secretary. George Brown was to regret not asking Sir William Armstrong, the head of the treasury.

Harold Wilson's government was innovative in conception with new ministries – DEA, technology, overseas development, Wales, land and natural resources. The idea of separate ministries for higher education, possibly disarmament, and science had been dropped, and the board of trade was not turned into an industry department. Wilson also brought in outsiders as ministers – Gardiner, Caradon, and Chalfont, but not Patrick Blackett, who refused then to go to the lords. Wilson envisaged number 10 as 'a power house for the the whole nation',[16] but rejected the concept of a prime minister's office. Thomas Balogh thus became economic adviser to the cabinet, and Peter Shore the prime minister's parliamentary private secretary. His secretaries, Marcia Williams and Brenda Dew, whom he had inherited from Gaitskell, plus Susan Lewis, were all brought into number 10, the former as 'personal and political secretary'. Williams was given the waiting room next to the cabinet room, but Wilson was immediately embraced by the private office of the prime minister, on the other side of the cabinet room. He inherited Derek Mitchell as principal private secretary, a man who was to be suspected later by labour ministers as less than completely loyal. Mitchell had wanted to keep Williams out of number 10, but Herbert Bowden was given very short shrift when he suggested this to the new prime minister. The cabinet office was Wilson's main administrative resource, under the cabinet secretary, Sir Burke Trend, and responsible to the prime minister in his role as head of government, in accord with the doctrine of collective responsibility.

The outgoing prime minister and his wife had left for Chequers on 16 October, but the Wilsons did not move immediately into the flat on the second floor of number 10. The new prime minister returned each night to Hampstead Garden Suburb, where a lone police officer was stationed outside the house. Wilson expressed 'schoolboy enthusiasm'[17] the following Monday to Tony Wedgwood Benn, as the last of Maudling's belongings were being removed from no. 11. The Douglas-Homes remained at number 10 for a fortnight, Mary Wilson being invited to tea on one occasion.

Mary Wilson was reluctant to move to Downing Street, and Giles opposed the idea. He was still attending University College School in Hampstead, following in the steps of his brother. His father had been quoted earlier as saying '"He isn't the brightest scholar in the family"',[18] and Giles was then subjected to some public school bullying for being the son of the labour leader. It is no wonder he was to have problems. Mary Wilson eventually accepted the Downing Street flat, without making changes. They decided to move on 12 November at half term. The press photographed the removal, though most of the furniture went into storage. Mary Wilson occupied the main bedroom in the number 10 flat, and Harold slept in the dressing room. Richard Crossman had lunch in the flat several months later: 'Nothing could be more deeply *petit bourgeois* than the way [Harold] lives in those crowded little servants' quarters up there. But the fact that he doesn't … use the state rooms [on the first floor] for sitting in after dinner is only a proof that he is not corrupted by his new station in life. No. 10 doesn't change him, he changes it so that its rooms look exactly like the rooms in his Hampstead home.'[19]

The treasury had presented Wilson with a memorandum on the economy, almost as soon as he entered number 10. When James Callaghan was appointed chancellor he went immediately to number 11, where Sir William Armstrong, his permanent secretary, presented him with 'a foolscap typed volume at least two inches thick of background economic information, with a polite intimation that [he] might wish to read it before the morrow'.[20] A copy of this brief had been spirited earlier to George Brown's flat, and another requested by number 10. The treasury is known to have predicted a deficit of £800 million for 1964, continuing into 1965. Britain had only just gone into the red, between 1962 and 1963, due to the tory chancellor's electioneering budget. A quarterly figure of £290 million had been made public on 30 September 1964. Wilson had referred to a crude trade gap of over £800 million a year in *The Relevance of British Socialism* (1964), but he used the figure of £400 million during the election campaign. This was the normal current deficit. Such figures had been issued in the 1940s, and were again to be presented in the 1970s. According to Douglas Jay, who became president of the board of trade, the treasury overpainted the true position at the start of the labour government, simply by the way it compiled the trade figures.

There was only a hint of this in the short broadcast Wilson made that evening from Downing Street:

> We face immediate difficulties in the economic sphere and those of our colleagues who will be dealing with that sphere will be meeting urgently. When we know what is involved we shall speak frankly to you and say what needs to be done. Over the whole field of Government there will be many changes which we have been given a mandate by you to carry out. We intend to fulfil that mandate. What we are concerned to ensure is that there should be a true partnership between us and the people of Britain. We shall not hesitate to tell you what needs to be done.[21]

Whether Wilson realized it or not, he would have to wrestle with the British economy for the rest of the decade, and was to begin his personal account of the labour administration in 1971: 'This book is the record of a Government all but a year of whose life was dominated by an inherited balance of payments problem which was nearing a crisis at the moment we took office; we lived and governed during a period when that problem made frenetic speculative attack on Britain both easy and profitable.'[22]

This is a political excuse, as Reginald Maudling, the outgoing chancellor, would recognize: 'An incoming Government is liable to depict its inheritance in the gloomiest possible terms, thereby hoping to minimize its own initial mistakes and maximize its subsequent achievements. It is not a habit confined to any one Party.'[23] Wilson should have appreciated the extent of the problem for Britain, as an economist and former minister. When Gaitskell handed over to Butler in 1951, the balance of payments deficit was nearly £700 million, due in part to the Korean War. Higher in real terms, it was corrected within a year. It was the conservatives who changed the method of measuring the balance of payments, and Harold Wilson had to accept the £800 million figure on 16 October. If he had tried to change to the lesser one of £400 million, he might have been accused of playing down the problem. But he proceeded to play politics with the deficit, partly to blame the outgoing conservative government. He would later use the argument about an inherited crisis to justify his own government's tawdry performance. Nothing was sprung on Harold Wilson when he entered Downing Street, but he chose to behave in a dramatic fashion. This only made the crisis worse. The very election of a labour government alarmed the international speculators he was to rail against with exceptional verocity. Much of this could have been foretold.

Wilson, Brown and Callaghan discussed the position informally in the cabinet room on the Friday evening (or Saturday morning). The cover for the meeting was junior appointments, though Armstrong heard from George Brown that the topic was to be devaluation. When the three most senior members of the government met alone, it was in the knowledge that the treasury had outlined three options for dealing with the balance of payments – devaluation, import quotas or import tariffs. The treasury was opposed to devaluation, and Callaghan quietly accepted this. He had promised the treasury secretary in the United States that a labour government would not devalue upon taking office. International bankers invariably considered devaluation a means of defaulting on domestic and foreign holders of a currency. 'The Tory Opposition as well as the press', Callaghan was to recall later, 'would have hammered home day after day that devaluation was always Labour's soft option.'[24] George Brown was also opposed, contrary to the advice of the DEA's director general, Sir Donald MacDougall. Brown 'regarded it as an act against the working class, despite my efforts to explain to him that, though it might reduce real wages somewhat, it would help to maintain employment'.[25] The new first secretary therefore threw away the possibility of making the DEA a growth ministry from day one! MacDougall concluded that 'the first great mistake of the new Government was not to devalue at once'.[26]

Wilson had justified not taking the devaluation course before the election: '"you would water the weeds as well as the flowers."'[27] This was Thomas Balogh's advice, but only because he believed an incomes policy was a precondition. MacDougall states Wilson was opposed 'because he was aware of the economic and political risks that were undoubtedly involved, but also because Balogh had persuaded him it was unnecessary since "socialist" policies could cure the balance of payments problem in quite a short time'.[28] Balogh was to change his mind within three weeks, when Wilson refused to tell the public that the economy was overheated, for fear of a crisis in confidence. But devaluation was the talk of the economists moving close to the centre of power. The press and broadcasting media had no idea that such a drastic initiative might be on the cards, and few in Whitehall or Westminster remembered that the new labour prime minister had been actively involved in the last British devaluation.

The three principals, with Sir William Armstrong of the treasury, Sir Eric Roll of DEA, and Sir Burke Trend, of the cabinet office, formally took the decision in the early evening of Saturday, 17 October. Callaghan had been sitting that morning in the study at number 11, when Maudling put his head round the door, and said: 'Sorry, old cock, to leave it in this shape. I suggested to Alec ... that perhaps we should put up the bank rate but he thought we ought to leave it all to you. Good luck.'[29] The new government's solution was to impose an import surcharge – essentially further tariffs – of 15 per cent, on all items except food, tobacco and basic raw materials. Douglas Jay was informed as soon as he was appointed to the cabinet as trade minister, but he preferred quotas, as more selective, and less offensive to international trade agreements with Britain's partners. Tony Crosland, who was to be made Brown's minister of state, continued to believe in immediate devaluation. This was also the view of Nicholas Kaldor and Robert Neild, two economists who became temporary civil servants at the treasury. The government's economic advisers – Nield, Kaldor, Balogh, Cairncross, John Jukes (deputy director general at DEA), and MacDougall – were to be told at a working supper at number 10 before Christmas not to discuss the exchange rate. Three of the six had taught Callaghan his economics at Nuffield. When they presented a memorandum in 1965, arguing for devaluation, 'Wilson personally ordered its suppression'.[30] At least one copy survives outside the cabinet office.

At the first meeting of the cabinet on Monday, 19 October, the new ministers endorsed a draft statement. Crossman noted in his new – ministerial – diary: 'It really was an absolute farce to have George Brown saying, "Naturally you won't want to be told, for fear of the information leaking, how serious the situation is … [or] what methods we shall take … ".'[31] A white paper was drawn up. With parliament due to met on Tuesday, 27 October, the labour government announced its preparedness to defend the value of sterling, to the extent of cutting public expenditure, including, perhaps, the development of the Concorde aeroplane. Wilson went on television that Monday evening, to announce his determination to tackle the economy through 'an exciting, challenging adventure in partnership … between the Government and the people of Britain'. 'Old-fashioned restrictionist ideas', he argued, 'have no place in our expansionist Britain, whether it is monopoly practices or insistence on overmanning a job, or some costly demarcation argument, or the temptation to indulge in wild-cat strikes.' The alternative had been prefigured rhetorically: 'mobilis[ing] the energies of all our people, in the job of modernising Britain by harnessing to our task the scientific revolution of our time'.[32] Callaghan was to write, many years later, of how neither government nor country 'was then willing to face the degree of change that was necessary to put the situation right … It was not until British industry faced a worldwide recession in the early 1980s … that rigid ideas and practices were shaken loose'.[33] Maudling accepted the government's statement as shadow chancellor, but the import surcharge, as a protectionist policy, was widely considered a breach of GATT and EFTA. Douglas Jay, who had to defend an illegal policy with which he did not agree, argued: 'The right course would have been to restrain less essential imports by an internationally legal method for a fair period; and if after a time this proved plainly ineffective, to let the exchange rate of the currency float freely.'[34]

The premiss of government economic policy became the maintenance of sterling as a reserve currency. It was to be discovered, in 1971, that exchange rates could float, without apparent deleterious economic effects, albeit within a framework of informal international agreement. Wilson had insisted there was a balance of payments problem during the general election, and continued to hold to this view of the British economy in office. He has argued, first, that devaluation, when the problem of the British deficit was not fully appreciated, would have been politically damaging for the labour government. Secondly, it would have encouraged speculation. Thirdly, it might have led to retaliation abroad. And fourthly, it certainly required deflation at home. The advocates of devaluation, on the other hand, contended that it would have pushed the blame on to the conservatives, solved the balance of payments problem, and allowed the government to get on with its other economic policies. According to a study of the government's record, by economists who served it temporarily, 'those who assert that the pound sterling should have been devalued in 1964 know their economics but not their politics.'[35] For Harold Wilson devaluation was simply too big a decision on day one as prime minister. Having accepted that action was necessary, and that other policies had to be prepared, devaluation became the great 'unmentionable'[36] in Whitehall.

President Johnson was facing his electors for the first time, and the United States played an important role. George Brown wrote subsequently: 'It looked as if with American help that we could build up the economy within a reasonably short period of time.'[37] Callaghan would have clutched at treasury caution, particularly when it looked like the government could borrow from the international monetary fund. But Wilson, Brown and Callaghan were principally interested in labour being reelected. Some deflation was necessary, with or without devaluation, and Callaghan was to admit that, with its tiny majority, labour could not afford deflation, because of the need for another election. But their ostensible political concern remained the question of confidence in sterling, 'the strange mixture of the historical mystique and symbolism which equated the strength of sterling with the strength of the economy'.[38] For Harold Wilson, this was an article of faith.

Labour had made electoral promises to its traditional working-class base, and Callaghan introduced an autumn budget on 11 November. Old age pensions were to rise by $62^{1}/2$p (12s 6d) for a single person from March 1965, though Callaghan had only wanted to give 50p (10s). Health prescription charges were to be abolished on 1 February. The chancellor also announced tax increases. The standard rate was to go up by $2^{1}/2$p (6d) in the new tax year, when he would then also introduce a capital gains tax, and a corporation tax.

This was an interim, and slightly deflationary, budget, but holders of sterling were struck by the government's commitment to – albeit modest – social reform. There were immediate sales in Europe and north America, which continued into the following week. Callaghan was to write that he 'never experienced anything more frustrating than sitting at the Chancellor's desk watching [the] currency reserves gurgle down the plug-hole day by day and knowing the drain could not be stopped'.[39] The governor of the Bank of England, Lord Cromer, had held a low opinion of Maudling, but only objected to the conservative chancellor's electioneering dragging on through the summer. The return of a labour government, he recalls, raised no fear of hanging from the lamp posts, though the reaction abroad was more nervous. He welcomed Wilson's television broadcast of 26 October, and was to work well with Callaghan. Cromer quickly urged cuts in public expenditure, invariably on social programmes, while, as governor of the central bank, he had to support the pound in the market. The cabinet decided on Thursday, 19 November not to raise the bank rate, the daily losses of sterling having been kept secret from most members of the government. Callaghan only informed Brown and Wilson. Brown was occupied at DEA, while 'Harold', Callaghan recalls, 'gave me unfailing support and encouragement, helping me through a most trying experience. I was very grateful to him.'[40]

Wilson, Brown and Callaghan were forced, on the evening of Friday, 20 November, to increase bank rate from 5 to 7 per cent, as from the following Monday. Lord Cromer had been urging a 1 per cent increase, but George Brown vigorously resisted this, and the delay necessitated the 2 per cent increase. Some recovery was made on the first day, but, on the Tuesday, 'the speculators had second thoughts'.[41]

Cromer and the deputy governor came to number 11 that evening. The governor of the Bank of England was 'unusually emotional' about the financial crisis, and demanded 'a real credit squeeze, together with legislation to remove trade union restrictive practices, a specific figure for restrictions in government expenditure and the abandonment of steel nationalisation'. 'A fairly rough exchange followed',[42] according to Callaghan. The chancellor felt compelled to take Cromer next door to see Wilson, and they met in the cabinet room late that night, with officials in attendance. George Brown does not seem to have been present, though Sir Donald MacDougall was summoned to Marcia Williams's adjoining room.

The prime minister, according to his 1971 account, asked the governor 'if this meant that it was impossible for any Government, whatever its party label, whatever its manifesto or the policies on which it fought an election, to continue, unless it immediately reverted to full-scale Tory policies.' Wilson goes on to state that Cromer 'had to admit that that was what his argument meant, because of the sheer compulsion of the economic dictation of those who exercised decisive economic power'.[43] Callaghan endorses Wilson's account, and Cromer, who has looked at the former but not the latter, does not dispute the general drift of this historic, if not histrionic, meeting. He claims that he was not seeking to bring down the labour government, and that he was acting constitutionally, in so advising the government of the day.

He admits to being critical of Wilson, for being a politician and not a statesman. The prime minister, in response, threatened to call an election on dictation by overseas financiers. Lord Cromer pointed out that by the time a general election was held we should have no reserves left, to which the Prime Minister replied that in such an event sterling would be allowed to float. In the circumstances of those days this was akin to assailing the Holy Grail, and the Governor fiercely said that a floating pound could precipitate a world financial crisis. Harold Wilson replied that as there was a general interest in preventing such a calamity, the world's central bankers should cooperate against the speculators.[44]

This confrontation is a rare instance of power holders, in discussion, deploying ultimate sanctions in British politics, though the governor had the last word. Wilson accepted that the announcement of such a hypothetical general election would precipitate a world financial crisis, and merely asserted a commonality of interest with Cromer in not bringing this about. MacDougall confirms that Wilson was talking of floating the pound, and he and Neild drafted a paper on this as an alternative to a simple devaluation. George Brown was still adamantly opposed. Wilson implies that he ordered Cromer to arrange an international financial rescue, but the governor claims he suggested this, the following day, to Callaghan at the treasury. He could not be so ordered by a prime minister, his duty to the queen being on a par with that to the pound. Lord Cromer admits he knew more about what was happening to the pound, than did the prime minister or the chancellor. Wilson had argued that President Johnson would back him up, but Cromer was able to find out from a contact, possibly in the White House itself, that this was not the position of the American government. The president was not in active charge of finance in the United States government. Cromer announced, on Wednesday, 25 November, that he had raised a $3,000 million credit overseas, this deal, he claims, being initiated in London, and not New York, as Callaghan came to believe. The Americans were interested in the dollar, and did not want the pound dragging them down. Cromer was probably able to use Wilson's threat to float the pound to good effect in messages to his central bank colleagues. The three billion stopped the speculation, and Wilson's policy of 'strengthen[ing] the basic position of sterling'[45] survived – until the next crisis.

The government had presented its programme for the session in the queen's speech on 3 November. Aside from the concessions to be dealt with in the autumn budget, its major provision was the nationalization of steel – in spite of the wish of the minister of power, Fred Lee, to postpone it. Enoch Powell's rent act of 1957 was to be repealed, and a land commission established by Fred Willey. In the area of housing, there was to be leasehold enfranchisement. There would be a parliamentary commissioner, or ombudsman, and a free vote on capital punishment. Towards the end of his first speech in the house as prime minister, Wilson predicted that the conservative member for Smethwick, who had used the immigration issue against Gordon Walker, would be treated as a 'parliamentary leper'. This produced a furore over what had been an – uncharacteristic – angry outburst. At the party conference later in the year, Wilson was to carry the attack into the labour movement: 'I have condemned and will condemn every so-called Labour Club which operates colour discrimination, every group of misguided workers who try to operate colour prejudice in their working relations. The Labour Party of ours is more than a political organisation: it is a crusade, or it would be better that it did not exist.'[46]

The question of racism, in the form of Rhodesia, had already risen. Northern Rhodesia was about to become independent as Zambia, following the collapse of the Central African Federation, which had included Nyasaland (already Malawi) and Southern Rhodesia. There were over a quarter of a million white settlers in the latter colony, and this self-governing member of the commonwealth operated a political system oppressive to the African majority. Rhodesia took over the federation's air force at the beginning of 1964, and this would-be state, in which 5 per cent of the population ruled over the other 95, wanted its independence. The conservative government had maintained that the racist 1961 constitution was unacceptable, and the new Rhodesia Front government, under Ian Smith, hinted at a possible unilateral declaration of independence (UDI). As soon as he became commonwealth secretary, Arthur Bottomley left for Africa, to continue talks in the Rhodesian capital, Salisbury. The labour cabinet, at only its second meeting on 22 October, acknowledged that it would never use force against white rebels. The policy seems to have been Wilson's own, his main concern being to prevent Douglas-Home taking up a pro-Rhodesia position. The commonwealth office had wanted to retain the possibility of threatening Smith, but, when Wilson failed to get him to London for talks, the British government could only warn, on 27

October, that a rebellious Rhodesia could be economically and diplomatically isolated.

A major issue for Wilson was the labour government's relations with the United States. 'We are a world power and world influence', the prime minister told British financiers at the lord mayor's banquet at the Guildhall on 16 November, 'or we are nothing.'[47] While seeking to reassure the United States about sharing the policing of the non-communist world, Wilson was hardly in a position to deliver. Britain's contribution to NATO was especially important, the moment of truth in Anglo-American relations. Despite the labour party's opposition to nuclear weapons, Wilson, Patrick Gordon Walker and Denis Healey quickly decided, on the grounds of money already spent, to continue building Polaris submarines. Five had been begun by Macmillan, and a cabinet committee decided to carry on with four. Continuity in policy was assured on extremely practical grounds, and labour's idea of a non-nuclear Britain quietly abandoned. Whitehall was reassured by Wilson, who was relying upon the convention whereby cabinet committees, comprising a handful of selected ministers, could take decisions behind the back of the full cabinet. Kennedy had tried to prevent Britain having an independent nuclear deterrent, under the terms of the Nassau agreement, and Wilson would reply to Barbara Castle in cabinet, as late as December 1965, that Britain was going to opt out of the nuclear race. 'He himself', she noted, 'had had to take a decision to conduct a nuclear test, but the only reason was we had to test a new device which would save plutonium and therefore cut defence costs.'[48]

The independent nuclear deterrent was considered at a defence review, held at Chequers over the weekend of 21/22 November 1964. Wilson, and his senior colleagues, hoped to persuade the service chiefs of the need for defence savings, in view of the economic crisis, Britain's huge defence commitment overseas contributing to the balance of payments problem. Wilson hoped to dent the escalating plan to spend £2,400 million in 1969/70, and three aircraft being developed – the P 1154, HS 681 and TSR 2 – were rigorously scrutinized. The possibility of American replacements was mooted. A major battle ensued, with British 'aircraft manufacturers ... knocking on our door'.[49] The government announced the cancellation of the P 1154 and HS 681, in a defence white paper, in February 1965. The TSR 2 led to a three-way split in the cabinet, but Wilson postponed consideration of an American or British replacement; it too became a victim of retrenchment in the April budget. 'I had to keep development going for purely political reasons', Healey recalled, 'at a cost of £4 million a week until April 6th.'[50] Also discussed at Chequers was the American idea of a multilateral nuclear force (MLF) in NATO. Wilson was to adopt an idea of Healey's, which became known as the Atlantic nuclear force (ANF), under which Britain and the United States would, as it were, hand over an equal number of Polaris submarines to NATO control. This was something of a political fiction, but it was put verbally to the cabinet on 26 November. Having conjured away the idea of an independent nuclear deterrent with the ANF, the labour government unwittingly abandoned its opposition to nuclear weapons. It was suggested that the United States might allow Britain to reduce its conventional commitment in Germany, in return for continuing as a nuclear power. The Americans were not keen to renegotiate Nassau, and pressure was exerted on London.

Wilson, Gordon Walker, Healey and Lord Mountbatten, chief of the defence staff, flew to Washington on 6 December, where Wilson was formally greeted the following morning on the White House lawn by President Johnson. The prime minister and president then repaired to the oval office, for private talks on their respective political problems. While Wilson seemed genuinely to be moved by protocol, he was irreverent, in front of his officials and ministers, about the Americans. He might have to kowtow to Johnson, but that did not mean Wilson, or anybody, had any respect for the American president. Johnson, in turn, had little liking for Wilson, a view he revealed to at least one British minister. The two sides met that afternoon in the cabinet room. Wilson stated a preparedness to maintain Britain's position in Africa, while, in Asia, the British commitment in Malaysia, he argued, prevented active support for the United States in Vietnam. But he offered British help with training and counter-insurgency. 'Wilson spoke the language he thought Lyndon Johnson wanted to hear',[51] and, towards the end, he criticized the idea of a multilateral force, on the grounds that it was inimical to the Russians.

At a White House dinner that evening, Wilson redefined 'the special relationship' as 'a *close* relationship', 'governed by the only things that matter, unity of purpose, and unity in our objectives'.[52] Johnson, with his secretary of state, Dean Rusk, and defense secretary, Robert McNamara, considered the British idea of an Atlantic nuclear force on 8 December, and it was agreed this would be studied within NATO. The demise of the multilateral force was considered a success for Wilson, though it was not to be publicly buried. Wilson had been pushing at an open door in Washington, and little was to be heard of the Atlantic nuclear force. But the prime minister's political aides, especially Thomas Balogh, were taking the view that, unlike when in opposition, Wilson was already spending too much time on foreign affairs. After a quick visit to Canada (which seemed obligatory, whenever a British prime minister went to Washington), he arrived back in London, early on Friday, 11 December, and boasted to the cabinet of a new era in Anglo–American relations: '"They want our new constructive ideas after the epoch of sterility. We are now in a position to influence events more than ever before for the last ten years."'[53]

Still 'a trifle disembodied'[54] after his transatlantic flight, Wilson faced a post-election party conference that weekend in Brighton. Delegates pressed for the increase in pensions, which Callaghan had announced, to be brought forward to Christmas. Wilson maintained it was administratively impossible, but George Brown expressed a fear of further speculation. The prime minister had proclaimed his honesty to the party conference, but it was to be shown that he did not tell the truth. 'The reason pensions did not rise until April, 1965, was that extensive economic pressures made it impossible.'[55] The prime minister also referred, on Saturday afternoon, to the country's financial difficulties, stating that 'the spirit of Dunkirk [would] once again carry [them] through to success.'[56] He was to admit in 1971 he got 'carried away ... dictating late at night', but insisted his historical analogy was 'the long period after Dunkirk and through to victory'.[57] Richard Crossman, sitting on the platform, thought it only a good conference speech: 'It didn't seem to me that he struck the right Prime Ministerial note ... he certainly didn't steel our people for the difficulties ahead.'[58]

The department of economic affairs had been taking shape in Great George Street. Sir Donald MacDougall, who had come straight from being economic director at the national economic development office (NEDO), set up a planning department, with the assistance of John Jukes, to work on a national plan. Fred Catherwood, an industrialist, established an industrial advisers' department, to strengthen relations between government and industry. Under the aegis of NEDC, Brown increased the number of 'little Neddies', which looked after particular industries. He also appropriated responsibility for prices and incomes. This – would-be voluntary – policy dominated the early months of labour's attempt at economic planning. Intervening on particular increases, Brown negotiated with the TUC and employers' organizations. Both sides of industry joined the government in signing a 'declaration of intent on productivity, prices and incomes' on 16 December. Tripartism, or corporatism, whereby employers and trade unions became increasingly involved in state policy, was being practised by the labour government. A national board for prices and incomes was announced the following February, to be chaired by Aubrey Jones, a former conservative minister. A norm of 3.5 per cent for incomes was set in April 1965, with the goal of price stability. The DEA also set about establishing regional economic planning boards, to service councils comprising nominees of a wide range of local interests.

Industrial policy was the responsibility of the ministry of technology at Millbank Towers. Frank Cousins, who was to be elected a MP in January 1965, was given, as parliamentary secretary, C.P., later Lord, Snow. While Snow's work on 'the two cultures', and the role of science for government, had prepared some of the ideological way for the labour party, he was not to be a successful minister. (When Zuckerman queried his joining the government, Wilson said "'oh, that's public relations, that's not serious'".[59]) Patrick Blackett became chief adviser at Millbank Towers, but he was not able to control the staffing of the new department. Cousins inherited the technological side of Quinton Hogg's work, the scientific aspect going to education. Wilson planned to prise engineering and shipbuilding away from the board of trade, and wanted to take aircraft production from aviation under Roy Jenkins. It would be mid-1966 before this happened. The new minister of technology was immediately involved in the computer industry, and, by encouraging the formation of International Computers Limited in 1965, helped save the industry for Britain at a time of growing international competition. Wilson, hearing that the treasury was buying an American computer, had ordered it to buy British.

The Wilson government reached the end of its first 100 days on Sunday, 24 January 1965, with its parliamentary majority reduced to three. The prime minister had asked each minister to report on progress. Dynamism had been the theme of the labour government, and Wilson wanted to project an image of continuous action. This American-inspired anniversary was to be an opportunity for a major public relations exercise, but Wilson found himself upstaged by a greater political actor. Early on the morning of 24 January, Winston Churchill finally died. Harold Wilson had been preparing two broadcasts on his first 100 days, but was forced to cancel them when it seemed that Churchill was near his end. He paid tribute to Churchill in a live television broadcast from Downing Street on the Sunday evening: 'We in Britain feel as a family feels, when its eldest, most respected, best-loved member dies, a sense of personal loss, of a gap in our midst that cannot be filled ... The words and deeds of Winston Churchill will form part of the rich heritage of our nation and of our time for as long as history comes to be written and to be read.'

The prime minister spoke, in a parliamentary tribute the following day, of Churchill the house of commons man: 'They misjudge him who could even begin to think of him as a Party operator, or a manipulator, or a trimmer, or a Party hack. He was a warrior, and Party debate was war.'[60] Wilson ended his account of Churchill's contribution to British history with a rare literary flourish: 'For now the noise of the hooves thundering across the *veldt*; the clamour of the hustings in a score of contests; the shots in Sidney Street; the angry guns of Gallipoli, Flanders, Coronel and the Falkland Islands; the sullen feet of marching men in Tonypandy; the urgent warnings of the Nazi threat; the whine of the sirens and the dawn bombardment of the Normandy beaches; all these now are silent. There is a stillness. And in that stillness, echoes and memories.'[61] It was *Boys' Own* stuff, and he probably spoke from the heart. Wilson was privately to describe this peroration on Churchill's life as 'the best speech I ever made'.[62]

Parliament adjourned – exceptionally – for a week, during which 300,000 people filed past the coffin. Wilson, the conservative and liberal leaders, plus the speaker, took a turn standing guard on the Friday evening. The state funeral was held on Saturday, 30 January at St Paul's Cathedral, 'a day', as Richard Crossman put it, 'of orgiastic self-condolence on the end of our imperial destiny.'[63] There were to be more.

The Churchill funeral brought heads of state and government to London, and allowed the prime minister, with the lord chancellor, to meet Ian Smith. The Rhodesian prime minister, though still a constitutional leader, sneaked into number 10 by the garden entrance. According to Wilson, 'he was extremely difficult, extremely sour, and not a little offensive about his obsessional aversions – the Labour Government, the previous Conservative Government, the United Nations ... the Commonwealth ... and ... "the countries to the north of us" – the newly-independent African states.'[64] Smith agreed that Lord Gardiner and Arthur Bottomley might visit Salisbury, for talks with the government and African leaders.

These duly took place in late February, and the two ministers arrived in Rhodesia bearing 'five principles', labour having built on the conservatives' policy. The most important concerned the question of democracy: 'If independence were granted, as proposed, long before majority rule became a reality, no action would be taken subsequently to hold up the progress to majority rule as more Africans qualified for the vote.'[65] As Wilson was later to admit, he had no intention of subjecting 'the Rhodesian people ... [to the] rule[of] an unprepared African majority tomorrow'.[66] Smith appeared to accept a legislature, in which non-Europeans could prevent retrogressive constitutional changes, but nothing came of this, and a Rhodesian government white paper, in April, argued for independence. The Rhodesian Front secured an electoral victory the following month, and, at his first commonwealth conference, held in London from 17 to 25 June, Wilson, under African pressure for a constitutional conference, conceded that Britain might summon one at the appropriate time. With rumours of UDI, contingency plans were drawn up in London. Wilson continued to oppose the use of force, even if British troops went in as part of a united nations force. Smith made a second visit to London, and Wilson reiterated, on 7 and 8 October, that independence would only be granted, if it was clear that progress towards democracy could not be halted. The Rhodesian prime minister attempted to bargain about UDI, before leaving on 12 October, but Wilson, speaking on television that night, offered a commonwealth mission. Though this was rejected, the British prime minister flew to Salisbury, with Arthur Bottomley, the attorney-general Sir Elwyn Jones, and Sir Burke Trend, thirteen days later, in a last-minute attempt to avert UDI. Wilson feared the tories might support the white settlers. He was also worried that Britain's copper supply from Zambia might be cut off, and believed that, if the Russians got involved in a united nations force, they might invade Rhodesia.

From 25 to 30 October, Wilson held talks with the Salisbury government, centrist political groups, and nationalist leaders brought to Government House from detention. Wilson lost his temper at the cruel treatment of African leaders by the authorities, and also toasted newspaper editors for their defence of free speech. At a dinner given by Smith, at which government ministers told prurient stories, he clashed with the Duke of Montrose, the expected regent of a UDI Rhodesia. (Wilson was not always distressed by sexist vulgarity: he had sniggered to colleagues in 1948, waiting in line to receive the then Princess Elizabeth and her husband; 'Harold reminded us', Hugh Gaitskell noted, 'that it was still a capital offence to rape a Royal Princess!'[67])

While it had been demonstrated that the Africans wanted majority rule before independence, Wilson tried to conciliate the whites by offering Smith a royal commission, to test the acceptability of an amended constitution among the people of Rhodesia as a whole. The British prime minister returned to London, via Zambia, Nigeria, Ghana and Gibraltar, to report to parliament on Monday, 1 November. The cabinet agreed to Wilson's idea of a royal commission 'in order to play for time',[68] Barbara Castle and Frank Cousins alone wishing to end negotiations. Further exchanges continued between the two capitals, about whether the commission's report would have to be unanimous. Wilson spoke to Smith on the phone early on 11 November, armistice day, but the Rhodesian government declared itself independent several hours later. The governor dismissed his ministers in the name of the queen, though they had already rejected the authority of the United Kingdom. The prime minister immediately announced the publication of all exchanges that had taken place between London and Salisbury, showing, as a member of the cabinet would put it, that 'he was never happier than when he was drafting a constitution for Rhodesia.'[69]

With Britain now legally responsible for the affairs of its former colony, Harold Wilson sent Michael Stewart to the united nations in New York, where Britain was condemned in the general assembly for not using force. Lord Caradon thought the government had been 'too gentle',[70] but succeeded in preventing a mandatory resolution in the security council without resorting to the veto. Britain imposed economic sanctions by orders in council, while Crossman mused about 'overthrowing the Smith regime by para-military action', involving 'black propaganda or subversive organization'. Military options had been considered, but the ministry of defence discomforted number 10 by asking whether a British landing in Rhodesia would be opposed or unopposed. Kenneth Kaunda of Zambia requested that British troops seize the Kariba Dam, which supplied his country's electricity, and Wilson offered to send troops to the Zambesi. The Royal Air Force was to airlift oil into Lusaka, but Kaunda, seeing there would be no attack on Rhodesia, ordered Britain out. Zambia was exempted from sanctions, since Rhodesian coal and water were needed to extract the copper, and it is more likely that the British government was concerned to be seen to be doing something, rather than economically throttling the rebel regime.

The British prime minister flew to New York on 15 December. The prime minister addressed the general assembly the following day, but there was a walk-out of African delegates. Wilson stated there would be no change of course, but, after meeting President Johnson in Washington, it was announced, on 17 December, that Britain was to ask the security council to impose an international oil sanction on supplies to Rhodesia. The oil embargo saw the conservatives abstain in the house of commons, some supporting the government, while others – effectively – sided with the Rhodesian rebellion. The united nations was to impose general economic sanctions on Rhodesia the following Easter. At the behest of the Nigerians, a commonwealth conference, with 'Britain ... in the dock', was arranged for Lagos on 11/12 January 1966, at which Wilson would come under sustained pressure to use force. He only maintained unity by promising that oil sanctions would prove effective within 'weeks not months',[71] advice which had come from Oliver Wright, his foreign office private secretary at number 10. 'We did think', Sir Oliver now says, 'not that we would bring [Smith] to his knees, but that this might lead him to negotiate.'[72]

Wilson states that, in his first meeting with Johnson, the president did not raise the question of bombing North Vietnam. The prime minister told the cabinet on his return that Britain had offered covert military assistance, undoubtedly portraying himself as a co-fighter against communist subversion. Wilson had 54,000 British troops in Malaysia, resisting the communist government of Dr Sukarno in Indonesia. Australia and New Zealand were to send troops to fight alongside the Americans in Vietnam, as would South Korea, and Wilson's problem was to avoid American pressure to join this western united front, designed largely to share responsibility for what was an American military intervention. Years later, Wilson was to claim Johnson would have been happy with six Scottish highlanders, with kilts and bagpipes. The prime minister argued that, as Britain was co-chairman, with the Soviet Union, of the Geneva conference, under the agreements of 1954 and 1962, the foreign secretary's role might be that of a mediator, even though initial approaches to Andrei Gromyko were unsuccessful. The Americans had started to bomb the north in early February 1965, as a result of which forty-nine labour MPs called upon the government to withdraw support. Wilson telephoned Johnson on 11 February, offering to fly to Washington for talks, only to be rebuffed about being 'willing to share advice but not responsibility'.[73]

Wilson lunched with Johnson on 15 April, on his second visit as prime minister, and claimed subsequently that, while it was clear America would prosecute the war, it had been accepted that Britain could work diplomatically for peace. If this was the British view, it was hardly the American one. Callaghan visited Johnson in the White House that summer, and recalls that the president 'asked me to thank our Prime Minister for his efforts, which he hoped would be continued'.[74] Wilson had already sent Patrick Gordon Walker, as a personal emissary to south-east Asia, but the former foreign secretary was unable to visit Hanoi or Peking. The prime minister found his report engrossing reading. The idea, quite simply, was to distract attention from Britain's continuing support for the United States. An official in number 10 recalled the prime minister's penchant for 'activity', as opposed to real executive 'action'.[75] There was to be activity, not action, on Vietnam.

To avoid disagreement at the commonwealth conference, Wilson, after consulting Johnson, proposed a commonwealth peace mission, to comprise the prime ministers of Britain, Nigeria, Ghana and Trinidad. Tanzania alone opposed this neutral initiative. Richard Crossman believed it was 'another of ... George Wigg['s] ... stunts'.[76]

The four heads of government were instructed to seek a ceasefire in Vietnam, this being a precondition for a conference, which might agree an international peace force under the Geneva agreement. It was thought Wilson would be away for a month, and Washington and Saigon agreed to receive the mission, but Moscow, Peking and Hanoi prevented Wilson's idea getting off the ground. The prime minister secretly sent Harold Davies, the former Bevanite, and then a junior minister, to Hanoi in July, but he was received only by officials.

Fifty labour MPs had signed a private letter in June, warning about the escalation of the war, and Michael Stewart, though not a member of the executive, addressed the party conference in late September. Wilson asked Johnson to suspend the bombing of North Vietnam, on his third visit in December, to see if Hanoi responded. Singapore had meanwhile left the Malaysian Federation in August, and, with Sukarno deposed in Indonesia, this would have allowed Britain to withdraw its troops from Borneo.

Wilson and his wife were invited to the switching on of the Christmas lights outside the White House, at which Johnson, according to Wilson, endorsed the British role of peacemaker. Marcia Williams, who was accompanying Wilson abroad, gives a different interpretation of the speech. 'Far from being complementary to the British', she was to write, it 'was meant critically, hitting out at us in an oblique way maybe but nevertheless an attack upon us for not participating in the Vietnam War.'[77] Williams may not have appreciated just how pro-American the British government was, but she would have been aware that Wilson, and other ministers and officials, found the United States' president 'a little difficult to take'.[78] This Texan did things very differently from other American presidents.

Johnson suspended bombing over Christmas, but Wilson failed again to interest the Soviet Union in a diplomatic gesture. The bombing was resumed on 31 January 1966, a decision supported by the foreign office, though not by Wilson. Ninety labour MPs endorsed Senator Fulbright's criticism of the president, but Wilson blamed Hanoi for intransigence at a meeting of the parliamentary party.

Foreign policy represented something of a distraction from economic management. Wilson had broadcast to the nation on the economic situation on 24 February 1965, with another lecture on the need for improved productivity in Britain. It was necessary for the unions to consider the question of wages in relation to output, he said, ending with Kennedy's exhortation: '[ask] not what our country can do for us, but what each of us can do for our country.'[79] This American sentiment had little impact in Britain.

Callaghan's April budget contained the tax increases announced the previous autumn, and he also restricted business entertaining expenses. The finance bill was given a rough parliamentary ride, the shadow chancellor, Edward Heath, emulating Wilson's performances of the late 1950s. The government suffered three minor defeats in early July 1965. Wilson had debated in Paris the significance of gold for international trade, with de Gaulle's adviser Jacques Rueff, who maintained that its price should be allowed to rise because of scarcity. The French were interested only in acquiring the precious metal, and had no sympathy for Britain's difficulties at the hands of international speculators. Wilson thought this pre-Keynesian economics, believing the dollar, and the pound, should be preserved as the principal world currencies. He addressed the prestigious economic club in New York on 14 April, describing the pound as 'one of the twin great reserve currencies of the world'. Wilson invoked the spirit of Britain in 1940, arguing that this would avert domestic financial collapse. 'I do not believe', he said, that 'the world immediately faces a crisis comparable to that of 1931[,] and even if it did I believe we have the resources both of economic expertise and statesmanship to prevent it.'[80] This was more sanguine than on previous occasions, and showed that his expectations of national unity in the 1960s drew on his experiences of wartime London: 'Our people are capable, once they regard themselves as part of a wider national whole greater than themselves, of efforts of skill and inventiveness, of courage and sacrifice that puts the faint-hearts to shame.'[81]

Steel was to be Wilson's Rubicon. The bill for nationalization was expected in the first session of the 1964 parliament, when the government still had an overall majority. This was to reckon without two labour MPs, Woodrow Wyatt and Desmond Donnelly. Wyatt had long moved away from the left, becoming a Gaitskellite. He distrusted Wilson, but regretted not being offered a job in the government. Donnelly had been a Bevanite, but even then he was reporting to the party leadership on the left's activities. He equally disliked Wilson. While Donnelly was totally opposed to the public ownership of steel, Wyatt favoured government control of the industry. At the end of January, Wyatt had been offered 'an important job or a peerage'[82] to keep him quiet, but refused to budge. The chief whip, Ted Short, offered on 3 February 1965 to arrange for Wyatt to be out of the country at the time of the vote. Wyatt was arguing for only 51 per cent state ownership, which was acceptable to the industry, and sent this idea to Wilson on 12 March. Wilson announced a white paper four days later. Wyatt saw him in his room in the house of commons on Thursday, 18 March. Wilson was 'oozing butter and charm. I was pressed to have whisky or the brandy Wilson was getting fond of in those days.'[83] The prime minister did his best with the recalcitrant backbencher. 'As he walked round and round the big table he kept saying, "I'm a pragmatist"; then, "I don't think there are ten votes in the country in steel one way or another but I'm stuck with it."'[84] There was a second encounter on 12 April, and the white paper appeared at the end of the month, to be debated on 6 May. Wyatt stated his intention of abstaining, and George Brown then privately conceded that the government would listen to the industry's proposals for less than complete nationalization. The first secretary made this public when he wound up the debate. Wyatt asked for clarification, which was forthcoming, though Brown did not keep strictly to the agreed form of words. The two dissident MPs then voted for the white paper, giving the government a majority of four. Steel nationalization was not to be included in the 1965 queen's speech, Michael Foot thereupon venting the objections of the left at an adjourned meeting of the parliamentary party.

Wilson had been forced by EFTA to reduce the import surcharge to 10 per cent from 27 April 1965, and it was to be abolished in November 1966. The trade figures for May 1965 showed an increased deficit. The prime minister's announcement, on 26 June in Glasgow, that there would be no election that year, did not prevent renewed speculation. Failing to get policy concessions from George Brown, the chancellor had to seek support from the international monetary fund and the federal reserve. Callaghan kept the Americans informed, and the United States' opposition to devaluation in Britain was a major constraint on domestic economic policy. No election allowed the tories to ditch Douglas-Home as leader of the opposition. On 28 July, Edward Heath became the first leader elected by the conservative party. Wilson would now be more equally matched with a professional politician. 'Both he and Heath', a conservative historian, and later MP, was to write, 'are serious, lonely men, dedicated to their careers, who have risen through the Westminster maelstrom. But Heath lacks Wilson's imagination and quickness, and Wilson lacks Heath's thoroughness and relentless attention to detail. Wilson's mental agility often tempts him to laziness; Heath, with a much less nimble mind, has to plod doggedly in order to reach conclusions and find solutions. But these, once reached, are adhered to with far greater tenacity.'[85]

The pound was again in trouble, and Callaghan had to introduce a third, emergency, budget on 27 July, providing for a wide range of cuts in public expenditure, including defence. The government also reneged on promises about pensions and prescriptions. Five or six meetings had been held at number 10, between 11 and 18 July, involving Wilson, Brown, Callaghan and Jay, plus officials, this being 'the nearest approach [Jay] knew in the Wilson Government to the smooth and effective method of reaching decisions which prevailed under Attlee and Cripps'.[86]

The government's economic advisers were urging that the pound should be floated, and the bank of England was still fearful of 'the collapse of the world monetary system'.[87] This worried the Americans. Callaghan, according to Barbara Castle, was blaming the multinational corporations. 'We had just got to face it that big business didn't like a Labour Government', she was to write in her diary for 31 August. 'It was almost impossible to curb their operations; if they were denied forward cover here, they merely instructed their agents in another country to get it for them.'[88]

The departure of Wilson, Callaghan and the governor on their planned holidays eased the market, but the United States treasury secretary, whose support was necessary to gain loans from abroad, began to express fears about George Brown's voluntary incomes policy not averting inflation. The cabinet was specially summoned for 1 September, to give the national board for prices and incomes statutory powers. There would have to be an 'early warning' of increases, which Brown could restrain by ministerial order. The TUC responded by agreeing on 6 September to vet wage claims, in order to save the voluntary system. Callaghan maintains this conference vote helped rescue the pound. Seemingly unbeknowst to the chancellor, the federal reserve and the bank of England 'prepared a big offensive operation against the anti-sterling speculators'[89] for 10 September, but Burke Trend had been over to see Mc George Bundy of the White House in late July. An early warning system was to be negotiated in November with both sides of industry. The government had approved the DEA's national plan before the summer recess, covering the five years to 1970. Though George Brown was forced to deal with a threatened revolt by employers, it was welcomed by the NEDC, and eventually published on 16 September.

The speaker had died earlier in the month, leaving Wilson with a possible smaller majority in the second session. With the government's political hopes in tatters, but an economic strategy on paper, and the pound temporarily stabilized, the prime minister faced the party conference at Blackpool, describing the national plan as 'a breakthrough in the whole history of economic Government by consent and consensus'.[90] Delegates voted on 30 September – 3,635,000 to 2,540,000 – to support incomes policy legislation, which reassured international opinion. The pound was to be safe until the late spring of 1966.

The first session of the parliament came to an end on 8 November 1965. Wilson boasted that the sixty-five government bills on the statute book were equivalent to the legislative achievement of any two sessions in the period 1951 to 1963. Labour's overall majority remained three, even with the election of a new speaker, in late October 1965, from the government side of the house. Wilson had managed to find a liberal to become the third non-voting occupant of the chair.

The 1965 queen's speech presented another long list of legislative proposals, including dock modernization, the land commission, a public schools commission, and a British ombudsman. Wilson had tried to reinsert steel nationalization in order to keep Frank Cousins in the government. Roy Jenkins was made home secretary just before Christmas, replacing Sir Frank Soskice, who was made lord privy seal to prevent him bringing about a by-election. Tom Fraser, who had insisted on being given transport in 1964, was replaced by Barbara Castle, Crossman thinking she was being punished for her strong pro-African stand on Rhodesia. Anthony Greenwood went to overseas development, and Lord Longford took over the colonial office, which was to be absorbed shortly by the commonwealth office, and then combined with the foreign office.

Wilson had been against a general election in the autumn of 1965, believing the government had little to show for its year or so in office. The labour MP for Hull North – a marginal seat – died in November, and the party put considerable resources into winning the by-election on 27 January 1966. The return of the labour candidate, Kevin McNamara, averted the need for an imminent general election, in the largest swing to labour in a by-election since 1924. Wilson feared for the failure of his incomes policy, but he was also establishing his reputation in the Rhodesia crisis. Both considerations may have combined to bring him round to the idea of a general election, and, on 28 February, he called one for Thursday, 31 March.

As party leader, Wilson had worked outside the Transport House system, under Len Williams as general secretary. When leading members of the national executive were made ministers, it became necessary to bridge the gap between Westminster and Smith Square. Wilson had set up an informal liaison committee in late January 1965, run by George Wigg. It comprised members of the number 10 political office, representatives of the lord president, Herbert Bowden, and senior Transport House officials, its objective being to encourage ministers, including Wilson, to think about their work politically. Wilson gave Wigg's job to Crossman in September. Crossman saw his role as putting over government policy to the party, and the liaison committee, with Marcia Williams reporting to Wilson, continued to meet through the 1966 general election.

Much more important was the intimate group of Wilson advisers. His few close political friends of the 1950s had come to form an inner group in late 1963, even though Wilson was sensitive to the charge of political cronyism. Once in Downing Street, a battle began to save Wilson from the civil service. The prime minister believed he knew how to work the system, but this only made his friends more anxious. The key role was played by Marcia Williams. Though political secretary, with responsibility for personal, constituency, and party matters, she exercised a considerable influence over her boss. This was unprecedented in the history of number 10. George Wigg was the minister closest to the prime minister, and already ensconced in Downing Street. A third person was Peter Shore, who had moved into the parliamentary private secretaries' room on the second floor, while the political office took over servants' quarters adjacent to the private flat, and also in the attic. Tommy Balogh, though formally a civil servant in the cabinet office, came to occupy an attic room in number 10. He was probably the most important economic – and political – adviser. Richard Crossman was closest to Wilson in cabinet, and, among other ministers, Tony Wedgwood Benn was still an admirer. Wilson had appointed Trevor Lloyd-Hughes of the *Liverpool Daily Post* as press officer in number 10, but the need was felt for a political press officer. Gerald Kaufman left the *New Statesman* in October 1965 and moved into Peter Shore's room.

This group of seven – Williams, Wigg, Shore, Balogh, Crossman, Wedgwood Benn and Kaufman – formed a kitchen cabinet. Crossman first used the term in his diary in late November, but the idea of a 'strategy group'[91] had originated on 13 September when, as chairman of the liaison committee, he met Wedgwood Benn for dinner at the Athenaeum, to discuss a new manifesto. The existence of the kitchen cabinet was to be kept secret from Transport House, but Nora Beloff of the *Observer* was to be 'the first correspondent to latch on to the odd nature of the "Kitchen Cabinet" and the excessive impact of Marcia Williams on the Prime Minister'.[92]

On 1 February 1966, after he had privately decided to go to the country, Wilson met his kitchen cabinet for dinner in the number 10 flat. At a joint meeting of the cabinet and executive at Chequers the following Sunday,

Wilson proposed work on a document for the party conference in October. This was a cover for an election manifesto. Peter Shore presented his own draft to the kitchen cabinet at Chequers, on Sunday, 13 February, this being amended at further meetings on 1 and 6 March. The group does not seem to have met during the election, but when Wilson was to run into political difficulties in June, there was a short-lived regrouping of the prime minister's political friends, now including Judith Hart. Barbara Castle and John Silkin joined much later.

The election campaign began on Tuesday, 1 March, when Callaghan, to avoid the charge of going to the country before the budget, made an economic statement. He promised to subsidize mortgage holders with a new gambling tax. What was most certainly Wilson's manifesto was quickly approved, at a joint meeting of the national executive and cabinet, the following Monday. It was released that evening, after redrafting by Driberg, Crossman and Terry Pitt, under the title, *Time for Decision*. It sought a mandate to continue the work of the government, and emphasized economic and social planning. George Brown and Jack Jones, of the TGWU, had agreed a form of words on prices and incomes policy, within the realm of voluntary action. While steel nationalization was again included, the left secured the withdrawal of a commitment to enter Europe. Parliament was dissolved on 10 March.

As politicians prepared for three weeks on the hustings, an election business committee, comprising Len Williams, as chairman, Ray Gunter, Alice Bacon, Callaghan and Crossman, held its first daily meeting at Transport House. The strategy arranged was that Wilson should remain at number 10, governing the country, and only electioneer in the last week. This was not adhered to, and the prime minister, under the control of his political office, made a speech nearly every night. Wilson was running for reelection in a presidential manner. He refused to debate on television with Edward Heath, a mere party leader. Crossman breakfasted with him each morning in number 10, but the prime minister tended only to have ideas, afterwards, in his bath. Callaghan ran the morning press conferences at Transport House on his own. Mary Wilson had invested in a new wardrobe of clothes, to help point up the contrast between the married prime minister and Ted Heath, who was a bachelor. Marcia Williams feared defeat. She had, through an intermediary, ordered furniture vans for 1 April. A schoolboy in Slough hit the prime minister in the eye with a stink bomb on 23 March, but Wilson declined to exploit the issue. He joked about the miscreant's eligibility for membership of England's cricket team. His morale dropped, with a number of difficult meetings, and it was only in Huyton that his spirits revived.

With the polls predicting a secure majority, Wilson was less anxious about his own seat. Conservatives were running their sixth candidate in Huyton since 1950, and Screaming Lord Sutch managed to get himself nominated as a third candidate. After handing in their papers, he had rushed after Wilson to inquire about the closure of the Cavern Club, associated with the Beatles, in Liverpool. The prime minister, presumably with tongue in cheek, said he would be issuing a statement.

The turn-out in Huyton dropped significantly on 31 March, to 70.1 per cent. Wilson beat the conservative by two to one, with 41,132 votes to 20,182. Sutch obtained 585 votes. The national turn-out was slightly down. Labour increased its vote by nearly a million, to 13,064,951 (47.9 per cent), the conservatives dropping to 11,418,433 votes (41.9 per cent). This was the second highest vote for labour. The government gained 46 seats, with 363 MPs. The conservatives lost 51 seats, with 253 MPs, and the liberals came back with 12 members (there was also 1 minority MP plus the speaker). Wilson had an overall majority of ninety-seven. For the first time in the history of the party, a leader had improved the electoral position of a labour government. While the party was showing signs of losing working-class support, it had made sufficient inroads into the middle class to compensate. This was especially the case with home owners. Many of the seventy plus new labour MPs, as observers quickly noted, were young professionals, with radical political commitments. 'The Labour Party', wrote Wedgwood Benn, 'is in the process of transforming itself into a genuine national party.'[93]

CHAPTER 17

The Year of Opportunity, 1966–7

The members of the government placed their jobs at the disposal of the prime minister on Friday, 1 April, but Wilson made very few changes. 'I have decided to try to get away from the idea of major reshuffles', he said. 'Instead I will move people every year – one or two of them, like the Football League.'[1] There were a number of retirements. Soskice was pushed upstairs, as Lord Stow Hill, but Longford once again became lord privy seal. Griffiths quit politics at an advanced age, and Cledwyn Hughes took over the Welsh Office. Outside the cabinet, Charles Pannell handed over the ministry of works to Reg Prentice, while a minister without portfolio, Sir Eric Fletcher, a solicitor who had been helping the lord chancellor, was made deputy speaker. Two ministers were demoted: Douglas Houghton became minister without portfolio in the cabinet, in order to give the duchy of Lancaster to George Thomson, with special responsibility for European affairs; Fred Lee was moved to the colonial office, and Dick Marsh brought into the cabinet as minister of power. The only notable appointment was Judith Hart's shift from the Scottish to the commonwealth office. Shirley Williams, David Ennals, Merlyn Rees, Dick Taverne, Edmund Dell and Bruce Millan were among those who joined the ranks of junior ministers.

There had been a struggle between the political and private offices at number 10 from 1964. Marcia Williams quickly came to 'hate' Derek Mitchell. When she sought to accompany Wilson on a trip to the United States at public expense, Mitchell suggested it would be possible if she went as Mary Wilson's maid. Williams thought that Wilson would replace him when he tried to 'knife her',[2] but it was not until after the 1966 election that Michael Halls, who had been his private secretary at the board of trade, became the prime minister's principal private secretary.

George Wigg remained as paymaster-general. Unsuccessful in the area of national security, he came to be concerned about Wilson's personal political security, and was to be pushed out, as Lord Wigg, to the horserace betting levy board in November 1967. Peter Shore had become a junior minister at technology, leaving Ernie Fernyhough to continue as parliamentary private secretary. Harold Davies was to step down in early 1967 from being a junior minister, to look after Wilson's political back in the parliamentary labour party. Eric Varley would serve as parliamentary private secretary in 1968–9. Tommy Balogh came into number 10 about this time, and Brenda Dew transferred to the civil service to become his secretary. Gerald Kaufman remained a loyal member of the political office staff, still paid by the labour party to be a press officer in parliament. He brought in David Candler, a Transport House press officer, to take over Stuart Holland's work in the political office. It was Candler's job to answer letters from trade unions and constituency parties, the more important being signed by the prime minister. Candler later helped with political speeches.

Several prominent left-wingers were still left out of the government. Michael Foot had encouraged Frank Cousins, a personal and political friend, to accept Wilson's invitation in 1964, and Cousins, once appointed minister of technology, wanted Foot as his parliamentary secretary. Cousins, it seems, did ask Wilson, and the prime minister certainly knew this was his desire, but Wilson suggested, erroneously, that Foot did not want to join the government, and the minister of technology did not approach Foot. Ernie Fernyhough sought out Michael Foot shortly before the 1966 election, presumably on the prime minister's instructions, and – according to one version – wanted to know if Foot would be prepared to take over technology, presumably after Cousins resigned. Michael Foot considered this close to treachery, and declined Wilson's hypothetical offer. He stated the points on which he was opposed to the government, but expressed an interest in waiting until after the general election, if Wilson wanted to offer him a position in the government. Foot claims Fernyhough came bearing an offer of the home office, to which Roy Jenkins had recently been appointed, and that he replied to Wilson by letter. No approach was made subsequently by the prime minister.

Foot admits to being angry with Wilson, then or later, about the fact that Ian Mikardo was not being used in, or by, the government. Mikardo was to become the first chairman of the select committee on nationalized industries later in 1966, and would hold this position for the rest of the parliament. Foot was to suggest to Wilson that Mikardo would make a good chairman of British Steel, as the industry was being taken into public ownership, but Dick Marsh appointed Lord Melchett in 1967. Mikardo was to be offered more than one public position, which he declines to specify, but turned them all down. None was in the government.

Wilson had assumed formal control of MI5 and MI6 in 1964, with Dick White reporting to the foreign secretary, and Roger Hollis to the home secretary, though the prime minister had to clarify ministerial responsibility. He was to be more concerned with the security service. A labour government was bad news for the denizens of Leconfield House: 'The old school in MI5 didn't like Wilson's politics or his philosophy. There was a feeling which said, "Wilson will screw up" ... [There were] comments like ... "The Empire is going down the drain."'[3] The Profumo scandal had made an impression on Wilson, and he told Hollis that George Wigg was to be informed of any security matters with a bearing on politics. Wedgwood Benn considered the paymaster-general 'a complete madman', and had feared 'a police state run by Colonel Wigg on the security side'.[4] 'I cannot say', Denis Healey would write, that 'my heart always rose when his long ant-eater's proboscis began to quiver, and his mouth began its gobbling splutter.'[5]

Hollis promised to desist from using MPs as agents, and undertook to refrain from tapping the telephones and opening the mail of members of both houses of parliament, but the prime minister's directive was considered unwarranted political interference by many members of the security service.

Hollis had kept Blunt's identity from Wilson, as well as the fact that his subordinates, in the wake of Philby, were engaged in a destructive search for communist moles in MI5. Wilson was also kept in ignorance of the fact that President Johnson ordered a secret review of British security in the summer of 1965, something which was not to be revealed until 1987 by Peter Wright. Angleton was keen that the the CIA should – effectively – take over MI5, and naively believed the American ambassador in London could secure the assent of the British government. Hollis's replacement by Sir Martin Furnival Jones, at the beginning of 1966, probably reassured the Americans about better management of the security service. Wilson, like Attlee before him, had wanted to appoint a chief constable, but Wigg persuaded him to accept the internal candidate. Under Furnival Jones, D branch, or counter-espionage, was greatly strengthened, and the British, for the first time, began to share security information with the Canadians, Americans, New Zealanders and Australians. When he was reelected in 1966, Wilson, it would seem, believed he had MI5 under control. Roy Jenkins had recently taken over the home office, and labour now had a large parliamentary majority. Leconfield House would have to behave itself.

One of Wilson's first acts after he returned to Downing Street was to bring other departments into the handling of prices and incomes. The DEA under George Brown had set up the industrial reorganisation corporation (IRC) shortly before the election, to promote the restructuring, mainly by merger, of likely competitive industries. The IRC had originated in Cousins's department, and was 'very much a Balogh kind of animal'.[6] The IRC was provided for in the queen's speech, on 21 April, when the government also announced its intention of legislating to take steel into public ownership, set up the land commission, and establish a new ministry of social security.

It also promised to begin negotiations to enter the EEC, though Crossman had got this removed from the 1965 queen's speech.

Callaghan's budget on 3 May 1966 was deflationary. He increased corporation tax, and introduced a new selective employment tax (SET), suggested by Nicholas Kaldor, designed to discourage service industries. (Kaldor is reputed to have said to his fellow Hungarian Balogh, shortly after they came into Whitehall: 'Tommy, those bastards in the Treasury tell me I know fuck nothing about economic policy. I tell them they are wrong, I know fuck all!'[7]) Callaghan made a tactical mistake in leaving SET to near the end of his speech, which led the city to believe that he was not attempting to raise revenue. SET was only to be collected from September, and could not make an impact on inflation during the summer.

A major event early in the second Wilson government was a strike by the national union of seamen (NUS), due to begin on Monday, 16 May. Ray Gunter, the minister of labour, urged the union to accept the employers' offer, promising a review of the 1894 merchant shipping act. Having prevented a rail strike in February, by summoning the union executive to Downing Street, Wilson agreed to see the NUS leaders on 13 May, but to no avail. Exports were immediately halted, and the pound had to be supported by the sale of dollars. International bankers saw the seamen as a threat to the British government's – still voluntary – incomes policy. Wilson described it as 'a strike against the State, against the community',[8] but Crossman privately thought that the government was 'paying a very high price for George Brown and his policies'.[9] The navy was put on standby, with a view to helping foreign ships dock.

The strike was being fought by the cabinet emergencies committee, chaired by Roy Jenkins, but Wilson had taken personal control. A state of emergency was declared on 23 May, and Gunter set up a court of inquiry, under Lord Pearson, three days later. It recommended a slight improvement in wages and hours, which was rejected, on 7 June, to the annoyance of the TUC. Wilson intervened again, at the behest of the TUC, meeting both sides of the industry on 15 June, and two days later. Reporting to parliament on 20 June, after five weeks of stoppage, the prime minister accused a 'tightly knit group of politically motivated men', close to members of the NUS executive, of 'endangering the security of the industry and the economic welfare of the nation'.[10] One of these, sitting in the gallery, was John Prescott, an NUS militant and full-time student. The prime minister's source was MI5, in particular Thistlethwaite's F Branch, and George Wigg kept the prime minister informed about Bert Ramelson, the communist party's industrial organizer.

'Wilson's conduct', recalls Wigg, 'reached a high-water mark in his handling of this strike … Single-handed, he smashed a strike which was nearing the point of no return.'[11] The prime minister greatly angered many in the party and the trade unions, and Peter Shore 'thought it was completely bonkers'.[12] In a meeting on privy councillor terms, in the house of commons, Wilson was accompanied by – he hints – senior MI5 officers and 'one of the operators "in the field"'.[13] Wilson tried to defend his charge that the communist party was behind the strike, in a debate eight days later, but had to admit it had no members on the executive of the NUS. He regaled MPs with, what Crossman believed was simply, 'Wiggery-pokery'[14] on 'the Communist party's industrial apparatus'.[15] The prime minister accused the party of being out to destroy the prices and incomes policy, and clearly felt the possible success of his government was being undermined.

Following the first charge, Wilson, Gunter and the TUC had decided that the chairman of the court of inquiry, Lord Pearson, should intervene. Pearson was to encourage a further concession in return for increased productivity. Wilson then lent on the NUS general secretary, and prepared a ploy for the latter to confront the militants, at an executive meeting on 30 June. His second anti-communist speech stimulated the moderates, and the union voted to accept the new offer promoted by the TUC. The seamen went back to work on 1 July, after forty -seven days on strike. The red card had been played, but only at the expense of the labour leader's relations with the trade union movement.

Wilson was faced with the resignation of Frank Cousins two days later, on the eve of the prices and incomes bill being published. The symbolic effect of this, in terms of a possible change in TUC support for the government, cannot be underestimated. The seamen's strike had badly affected exports, and there was still a balance of payments problem despite imports also being held up. Sterling again came under threat, though central banks united in extending a credit to maintain its reserve status. Lord Cromer resigned on 1 July after five years as governor, to be replaced by his deputy, Leslie O'Brien, on the recommendation of Wilson and Callaghan. Britain's reserves were still in danger, the pound dropping to its lowest, against the dollar, in twenty months on 5 July. The government had maintained full employment while tackling the deficit, this being evident in the inflationary effect of wage increases.

By July 1966, in, what he called, 'one of the nastiest and most inexplicable crises sterling had faced',[16] Wilson was convinced of the need for deflation. This meant ending the drive for economic growth. George Brown had finally come round to the alternative, devaluation, on the advice of the government's economists, though Thomas Balogh may have dissented. Brown saw devaluation as an alternative to deflation, but he only had the support of Roy Jenkins and Tony Crosland. Richard Crossman was to bring Barbara Castle and Tony Wedgwood Benn into the camp favouring the floating of the pound, though it was realized this would still require deflation. Once Callaghan had been given the June gold figures by the new governor, he too began to waiver. Callaghan, and especially Brown, had been greatly influenced by talks, in London, with the French prime minister, Georges Pompidou, who recommended devaluation and deflation to get the British economy right for Europe. The chancellor believed that devaluation was becoming increasingly inevitable, but Wilson again vetoed this on 13 July. Bank rate was increased by 1 per cent on the following day, but this compromise between Brown and Callaghan was too little too late. The announcement that further policies would follow had a deleterious effect on the pound. The prime minister left that Saturday (16 July) on a visit abroad, returning, as scheduled, on 19 July. The pro-devaluation lobby was humming in expectation of yet another crucial cabinet meeting.

Callaghan presented a deflationary package of £500 million that evening, which was considered, and agreed, on 20 July. Wilson had been forced to allow a discussion, in principle, of devaluation, but he made it a question of confidence in his leadership. He argued with left-wingers, in private, that devaluation was really connected with EEC membership. It was certainly the case that the Europeans favoured devaluing the pound, but it did not follow that all devaluationists were motivated by the desire to enter the EEC. Six – Brown, Jenkins, Crossman, Crosland, Castle and Wedgwood Benn – were in favour, but the other seventeen, including Wilson and Callaghan, were against. Most of the cabinet followed the prime minister, but he was opposed by a considerable minority straddling left and right.

The 'July measures', as they came to be called, had been secretly prepared by the civil service. They included hire purchase restrictions, cuts in public investment and overseas expenditure (including troops in Germany), and, most significantly, a six-month freeze on wages and prices, followed by six months of severe wage restraint. 'Given the [government's] commitment to full employment and growth the natural – though still unpleasant – policy choice was to devalue. [It] did not. Why not is one of the major political puzzles of the 1960s.'[17]

George Brown resigned that evening, making no mention of devaluation, though he had signalled to a parliamentary colleague in the commons by making a 'D' sign. Having discussed the position with Bowden and Wigg, he announced simply that there had been a disagreement. The first secretary was back in harness the following morning. Callaghan had left for Germany, to secure a larger payment from the Bonn government for British troops stationed there. Johnson feared for NATO. 'Wilson agreed to keep British troops on the Rhine through June 1967',[18] in return for an American promise to purchase $35 million of military equipment in Britain. George Brown presented the – amended – prices and incomes bill to parliament on 4 August, subsequently taking it through committee. The TUC came to accept the wage freeze.

The majority of nearly 100 had freed the second Wilson government from parliamentary uncertainty. The seamen's strike, despite the prime minister's strong stand, combined with the resignation of Frank Cousins, a potential left-wing leader of the labour movement, saw the sterling crises of May and July. Devaluation that summer might have allowed a new departure for the labour government, opening up opportunities for an uncertain Wilsonian project of modernization. A massive deflation, involving, in particular, a statutory incomes policy, was seen to be an attempt at economic management, at the expense of the working class. This is the point at which the trade unions began to slip from supporting the government, and the labour leadership was to find itself in conflict with party members – all as a result of Harold Wilson's refusal to countenance devaluation in July 1966.

The prime minister had given the ministry of technology to Wedgwood Benn, who entered the cabinet on 4 July at the age of forty-one. In mintech – as his department was futuristically known – he gained responsibility for engineering and shipbuilding, and aircraft production, becoming one of the more powerful members of the government. Edward Short was replaced as chief whip by John Silkin, this being thought of as an imaginative appointment since he would stand up to Wilson. It was not until after the July days that the prime minister made further changes in the cabinet. George Brown was relieved of the DEA on 11 August, the prices and incomes bill having received its third reading, and he was promoted as deputy prime minister to the foreign office. Michael Stewart was a deflationist, and he took over the job Brown had made his own, becoming first secretary of state. Callaghan was left in place at the treasury, though he had been reported as wanting the foreign office. He threatened to resign, but maintains this was over the division of functions between the treasury and DEA. With Brown's removal, Callaghan saw his opportunity, demanding the return of economic power to the treasury. Wilson conceded that Stewart would be responsible only for productivity, and his appointment, after the July measures, meant the effective end of the department, and the national plan. It was a boost in the direction of the EEC, Stewart seeing membership as the way forward for Britain. Wilson was to promise a new concordat, but Callaghan and Stewart worked out their own relationship. The prime minister also made Crossman lord president and leader of the house, with an eye to managing the new parliamentary party. Herbert Bowden was demoted to the commonwealth office, but with the major issue of Rhodesia to handle. Bottomley went to overseas development, though still in the cabinet, and Greenwood, considered a poor minister, found himself promoted to housing and local government.

Harold Wilson had visited Moscow shortly before the 1966 election. Arriving, with Frank Cousins, Lord Chalfont, and officials on 21 February, Wilson was greeted by Alexei Kosygin, Khruschev's successor. Mary

Wilson and Brenda Dew, who then worked for the first lady in number 10, accompanied the official British party. Gerald Kaufman was paid for by Transport House, and Marcia Williams was funded 'privately', by, most likely, Joe Kagan.

The talks on trade and technology with Kosygin were productive. Alun Chalfont, like Cousins, was invited back to Moscow, for more detailed talks on the non-proliferation treaty. Vietnam was the major issue: the United States had resumed bombing of the north. Wilson achieved precisely nothing, but Chet Cooper, a former CIA man in London, then in the White House, had hoped the bombing might remain suspended until Wilson's trip. Kosygin refused to budge in formal talks. In a private meeting between Wilson and Leonid Brezhnev, at which Oliver Wright, the foreign office's private secretary in number 10, and Marcia Williams were present, the communist party's secretary repeated traditional Russian concerns about Germany in a forceful manner. The prime minister believed Kosygin was more amenable in private, accepting that the Russian leader was afraid of leaning on North Vietnam, in case China sought to increase its influence. Chalfont had a meeting at the North Vietnamese embassy, but to no avail.

During the seamen's strike, Wilson was informed by an emissary of Johnson's that the United States was to bomb Hanoi and Haiphong, which duly took place on 28/29 June. The prime minister dissociated the British government from the bombing of populated areas, but went on to support American policy, in particular its willingness to enter into negotiations. This did not appease the left of the labour party.

Wilson flew again to Moscow on 16 July, during the sterling crisis, ostensibly to visit the British industrial fair. Wilson may have sought to capitalize on his dissociation from American bombing of civilians. Hanoi had threatened to put captured American pilots on trial for war crimes, and, fearing reprisals on the part of the United States, Wilson sought to get Kosygin to dissuade North Vietnam from further provoking American opinion. No progress was made on the question of negotiations, and he returned to London three days later. The prime minister had repeatedly told his colleagues that Johnson was happy for him to mediate. Now he reported to the cabinet, on 21 July, "'If ever there were another Cuban situation, the[Russians] would want our services.'"[19]

Wilson flew to Washington a week later. At a welcoming lunch on Friday, 29 July, the president, having referred to Churchill, stated England (sic) was 'blessed with a leader whose own enterprise and courage [would] show the way'.[20] Wilson was evidently flattered, but Marcia Williams, generally more astute about people, and American presidents in particular, thought 'somehow it just didn't add up ... not against that awful background of Vietnam'.[21] Wilson maintains there was no criticism of British defence policy, and states Johnson promised to continue supporting the pound. This was not least because the dollar might next come under speculative attack, with mid-term elections due in November.

The prime minister was keen to get back to London. Arriving that Saturday afternoon, he drove straight to Wembley, where he saw Britain win the final of the world cup. For a nation coping with economic and political adversity, success on the soccer field, and the attendant national-ist euphoria, served as a substitute for the solution of problems. Anne Crossman was disbelieving at lunch the following day, when her cabinet minister husband predicted the world cup victory would strengthen sterling by impressing international bankers.

Wilson sent George Brown to Moscow that November. The foreign secretary was carrying a copy of an American ceasefire proposal for the Soviet foreign minister, Andrei Gromyko, but, unknown to the British at the time, the United States was also using a Polish intermediary, and possibly others. This only made Hanoi suspicious, though the intention seems to have been to use two routes to ensure at least one message got through. The Americans were only prepared officially to stop bombing North Vietnam after troops had ceased to cross the demilitarized zone into the south, but Johnson wanted a secret agreement with Ho Chi Minh, whereby the United States would concede by unconditionally stopping the bombing. North Vietnam was to halt its troops, at which point America would stop its own reinforcements. The United States would act alone in the first phase; both sides were to de-escalate in the second. The Americans were to make two concessions, for the price of an end to infiltration by the North Vietnamese. It was envisaged that talks might then follow on the ending of the war.

Despite the confusion over whether London was fully instructed by Washington, Kosygin and Gromyko agreed to pay an official visit to Britain in February 1967. The Russians had concerns other than Vietnam, however. George Brown came to believe that the Russians did not have much influence on North Vietnam, but the United States wanted to use its 1967 bombing pause as a cover for the cessation of action against North Vietnam. Just before the visit, Wilson heard from Chet Cooper, now working for Averell Harriman in the state department, the latter having been appointed ambassador for negotiations with Vietnam. Cooper was sent to London to mend fences. When he left Washington in late January, it was in the belief that the United States was about to talk secretly with the North Vietnamese. Washington was to pass peace proposals, either in Moscow or Warsaw, though Cooper described the secret rendezvous as being 'under a palm-tree'. Wilson believed Washington was asking him to get the Russians to back this initiative, and perhaps even ask them to pass it on to Hanoi. The North Vietnamese foreign minister, in an interview, expressed a willingness to talk on 28 January, though Washington's proposals had been rejected in Moscow the previous day. Cooper returned to London to brief Wilson on 4 February, and was asked to remain for the duration of the Russians' visit. 'Wilson's enthusiasm', Cooper was to write, 'might have been somewhat dampened if he had known that President Johnson, Walt Rostow, and a few people in the State Department took a rather dim view of his eagerness to discuss Vietnam with Kosygin. There was a sense that the British Government was pushing hard, perhaps too hard, to undertake the role of mediator.'[22]

Kosygin and Gromyko arrived in London on 6 February, and Wilson repeated the two-phase proposal at the first plenary the following day. He also suggested a 'Geneva-type conference',[23] seemingly at the behest of the foreign office and George Brown, though Washington was against any such conference. The Russians now wanted Britain to join them in calling for bilateral talks, this being more acceptable to North Vietnam. Wilson stressed on Wednesday, 8 February there would be a delay between the two phases. The United States would act simultaneously with the Vietnamese in the second phase, but fighting would still continue. Kosygin asked for the idea in writing on 10 February, and Wilson later handed over a letter which – he claims – had been checked in Washington. Cooper used the American position as stated two days previously, and sent it to Washington for approval. 'It [had been] apparent', he was to write, 'the British intended to keep me in close touch with the discussions on Vietnam, and expected me in turn to keep in close communication with Washington.'[24] When Cooper did not receive a reply, he considered this a good sign. The White House was then changing its offer, and Wilson believed hawks in the United States administration were out to sabotage a possible breakthrough. He was evidently thinking of Walt Rostow in the state department, and Cooper confirms they 'were in a brand new ballgame'.[25] The infiltration of North Vietnamese troops over the past few days had led the president to reverse the order – the bombing would stop only after the troops were halted. Johnson had put this in a letter to Ho Chi Minh on 8 February, and this was the initiative he was to recall in his memoirs. 'I recognized', Johnson would write, '... that the new proposal altered the ... plan we had discussed earlier with the British and had offered to Hanoi.'[26] Wilson sent the changed offer to Kosygin, as he was about to board a night train for Edinburgh. Brown was to state that the message should have been held back, to allow Britain to ask the United States to rethink yet again. 'After much stewing and floor-pacing', Cooper recalls, 'Wilson called the White House. In the two decades of my diplomatic career I had never seen anyone quite so angry, but Wilson kept himself very much under control as he explained how embarrassing and damaging the Washington message was.'[27] Wilson then tried to sell the original offer to the Americans as well as the Russians. 'Wilson and Brown were operating on the raw edges of exhaustion

... The word "betrayal" was bandied about, and there were some uncomplimentary references to a few high-level American officials. I sensed', writes Cooper, 'Anglo-American relations dissolving before my eyes.'[28] Kosgyin stated, on 12 February, that Moscow was also reverting to its earlier position, and, despite a last minute effort by Johnson to stop infiltration by extending the bombing pause, Hanoi did not respond. The Americans allowed too short a time for a considered reply, and the new year truce came to an end shortly after Kosygin left Britain. 'Washington officials', Cooper was to conclude, 'actually had had little real interest in the London episode; they regarded it privately as a sideshow to the main event they were trying to get under way in Moscow.'[29]

The question of the EEC had once again become prominent during the 1966 election, when de Gaulle announced France was withdrawing fron NATO. Wilson reiterated the party's view on membership, in a speech at Bristol on 18 March. It all depended upon the terms, he argued. Wilson seemed to favour entry, but there was nothing in the speech inconsistent with his past position, though Douglas Jay was to see it as a statement of opposition. There can be no doubt that the foreign office, which was principally responsible for international economic relations, saw Britain's future as lying in Europe. This was not antithetical to Atlanticism: Washington welcomed economic cooperation on the part of its allies. The major internal obstacle was attachment to the commonwealth, but the former white dominions had been eclipsed by the mid-1960s, and Rhodesia, plus its black African opponents, made the commonwealth a less attractive forum. Public opinion in Britain, certainly at this stage, was to be overwhelmingly in favour of joining Europe, and there was an unarticulated assumption that Britain would apply a second time. Where Macmillan had failed, Wilson might succeed. The prime minister thought the party was two to one in favour, but he did not want to come out before the election. George Brown was still at the DEA, and had not yet taken up the European cause. The prime minister seems to have made up his mind at the beginning of the year, helped perhaps by John Freeman, whom he had sent to India as high commissioner.

After the election, Wilson asked George Brown, who was known as a convinced marketeer, to chair a cabinet committee on the social and economic implications of joining. It met first on 9 May. Brown's committee reported to a meeting of ministers and officials at Chequers on Saturday, 22 October. Wilson suggested privately to Brown that the two of them should visit EEC capitals, to discuss terms for entry.

In the morning sessions at Chequers, it became clear that the treasury envisaged entry not before 1968, due to the poor state of the economy. The cabinet met informally in the afternoon, Wilson revealing a concern about devaluation after entry. He also expressed anxiety about Brussels interfering in British economic planning. There was some objection to the common agricultural policy, the left defending 'Little England as the pre-condition for any successful socialist planning whether inside or outside the Common Market'.[30] The majority view seemed to be that Britain needed to join the EEC. Douglas Jay noted the pro-marketeers to be Brown, Jenkins, Crosland, Gardiner, Gunter, Longford, Houghton, Gordon Walker and Cledwyn Hughes. The Wilson/Brown tour was announced in the house on 10 November, after the cabinet, in formal session, had first retreated to the idea of a declaration of intent to apply for membership, and then decided determinately to go for Europe. Wilson now presented Europe as the arena for 'a new technological community'.[31]

The grand tour of the six EEC capitals took place in early 1967. It began – symbolically – with Rome on 15–17 January, where Wilson stated a willingness to accept the treaty governing the economic community. The British envisaged problems with agriculture, the commonwealth, capital movements and regional policy. The following Sunday, 22 January, Wilson flew to Strasbourg, to address the council of Europe, before proceeding to Paris for a confrontation with de Gaulle (24–25 January). The general was critical of the role of sterling as an international currency, and hinted that Britain might not be admitted to the EEC.

The following week – 31 January/1 February – Wilson and Brown were in Brussels. The Belgian government welcomed Britain's application. Following the visit of Kosygin and Gromyko to London, the tour was resumed in Bonn (14–16 February), The Hague (26–27 February), and Luxembourg (7–8 March). The Dutch were the most enthusiastic, now that de Gaulle's doubts had become known to the other five partners. The foreign secretary, and probably the prime minister, believed that the five could win round the French president.

A full record of Wilson and Brown's meetings in the European capitals was circulated to the cabinet for discussion on 21 March. A subsequent series of papers on particular subjects, prepared in a cabinet office special unit under William Neild, was also sent to senior ministers, and discussed at weekly cabinet meetings throughout April. The leading anti-marketeer was Douglas Jay. 'The key to British post-war policy', he was to write, 'should ... have been preservation of the political and economic assets that history had bequeathed us, notably in the Commonwealth and sterling area.'[32] Fred Peart, Denis Healey, Barbara Castle and Richard Crossman were sceptical about the chances of success. There were also three meetings of the parliamentary labour party, at which, Wilson claims, a clear majority in favour of membership emerged.

The cabinet met again over the weekend of 29–30 April. Crossman thought that Wilson and Wedgwood Benn were the only ministers to have been converted since November. He calculated that ten favoured entry. Seven – Jay, Peart, Healey, Castle, Ross, Marsh and Bowden – were opposed. Six, including himself, were in the middle, but they were prepared to support an immediate application. Douglas Jay recorded the vote as being thirteen to eight (including Greenwood) in favour of this. If Crossman, Wedgwood Benn and Callaghan had voted with the antis, as they might have been expected to do, then the cabinet would have come out against applying by eleven to ten.

At a formal cabinet meeting on Tuesday, 2 May, the labour government, with Barbara Castle and Dick Marsh opposing, decided to apply for membership of the EEC. Wilson's draft statement was accepted without any resignations. This historic decision was announced that afternoon, and, after a three-day debate, the house voted 488 to 62 in favour of the white paper. 'It was almost certainly the biggest majority on a major issue since the development of the modern system of party political alignments.'[33] Thirty-five of the dissidents were labour MPs, while another fifty-one had abstained, amounting to nearly a quarter of the parliamentary party.

General de Gaulle effectively vetoed Britain's new application six days later, citing the role of sterling, and the disruptive effects on the common market. The British application was again allowed to lie on the table. Wilson met de Gaulle in Paris in mid-June, and, while they mainly discussed other international issues, the prime minister stressed that Britain's failure to get into the EEC might strengthen Atlanticism throughout Europe. He was clearly trying still to persuade the president, but de Gaulle repeated 'non' at his November press conference. There the issue effectively rested, in spite of the support of the other five members at the council of ministers in December. Another Wilsonian initiative had bitten the dust.

The Smith regime had survived in Rhodesia, and, at the commonwealth conference in London in September 1966, Wilson came under pressure from African and Asian states. He admitted, in his opening address on Tuesday, 6 September, that his Lagos statement about the impact of sanctions had been proved wrong, but denied any sell-out was under discussion. Wilson had formulated a sixth principle, designed to prevent a black majority oppressing the white minority, after the granting of independence.

The majority of delegates, who caucused throughout the conference, wanted direct rule from Britain. They also demanded an immediate declaration of no independence before majority African rule, which became known as NIBMAR. Wilson was subjected to unprecedented verbal attacks for three days, relieved only by the support of Malawi and the former white dominions. Three dinners at Chequers over the weekend saw little diplomatic advance.

A special cabinet meeting was held on the Saturday, the prime minister being authorized to agree to NIBMAR, if it were necessary to prevent the breakup of the commonwealth. Wilson saw this as ending any possibility of negotiations. With Smith able to deal with sanctions, it would take 'bloody revolution [to] create[d] a new situation'.[34] He therefore asked the conference, on Monday, 12 September, for one last chance to talk to Smith. If this was unsuccessful, Britain would seek mandatory UN sanctions against Rhodesia, and come out in favour of NIBMAR. Wilson had threatened to adjourn the conference, and, when it finally met, this proved decisive. The section of the communiqué dealing with Rhodesia was quickly agreed, the commonwealth backing Wilson's attempt to get Salisbury to return to legality.

The prime minister had bought a little time. The new commonwealth secretary, Bert Bowden, flew to Rhodesia, but no progress was made with Smith between 19 and 28 September. The British government then drew up a list of five possible offers, including the integration of Rhodesia into the United Kingdom, which was sent to the governor in Salisbury on 15 October. It was over a month before Smith turned them all down.

Bowden again flew to Rhodesia on 24 November, and got a hint that Smith might abandon UDI. Wilson immediately jumped at the chance of a meeting. After the British cabinet agreed on Tuesday, 29 November, Smith and the governor left Salisbury on the Thursday morning for Gibraltar. Wilson, Bowden, and the attorney general, Sir Elwyn Jones, arrived there that night, 1 December, the British party immediately boarding a launch for HMS *Tiger* in the Mediterranean. Talks on the *Tiger*, a mile offshore, were Wilson's way of pointing up Smith's status as a rebel. The Rhodesian premier came with full powers to settle. Before the formal talks opened the following morning in the wardroom, Wilson explained to him the imminence of mandatory sanctions and NIBMAR. In the formal talks, Wilson's sixth principle seemed to impress Smith, and the Rhodesian leader even discussed a phased development. After returning to legality, a new constitution would be put to all the people. The country might then become independent, the interim government including five new ministers, 'for example, businessmen, and one or two "constitutional" Africans'.[35] But he reserved his position on the timing of a return to legality, and the broad-based government. Smith stated on the Saturday he had to return to Salisbury to consult his colleagues, and then refused to endorse an agreed document which accurately recorded their meetings. The Rhodesian rebel, whatever his limitations, was clearly a match for the wily British prime minister.

Smith and Wilson returned to their respective capitals. An emergency cabinet meeting in London endorsed the draft agreement on 4 December. Barbara Castle was the only member to oppose it. It was rejected in Salisbury the following day, Wilson believing Smith had been outmanoeuvred by right-wingers in his cabinet. Smith's last chance was also Wilson's. The British premier now had to adopt the solution of the com-

monwealth conference. Selective mandatory sanctions on exports to
Rhodesia, which Wilson had resisted out of fear for the British economy,
in particular trade with South Africa, were voted at the united nations in
New York. When he spoke in the parliamentary debate on 8 December,
Wilson was cheered by labour MPs for taking a stand on what he defined
as 'the greatest moral issue Britain ... had to face in the post-war world'.[36]
The *Tiger* offer was withdrawn later in the month, the British government
declaring in favour of NIBMAR. There the issue apparently rested.

Sanctions were still inadequate to the task of bringing Smith down, and,
in the absence of a commonwealth conference in 1967 or 1968, Wilson
was able to maintain contact with Salisbury. Lord Alport, a former conservative commonwealth minister, undertook a fruitless mission the summer
after *Tiger*. The shadow foreign secretary, Douglas-Home, visited Smith
in early 1968. That summer, Wilson secretly sent Sir Max Aitken, of
Beaverbrook Newspapers, and Lord Goodman, a solicitor and adviser in
many areas, to meet Smith. Their mission was to ascertain the possibility
of another meeting, as the Rhodesian leader was now prepared – it was
believed – to accept the six principles. Barbara Castle heard about new talks
from Lord Gardiner; 'I told him miserably that I couldn't justify my
opposition to the talks logically ... Harold had never had his heart in the
moral issue from the start ... But there came a point when one said,
however illogically, "Far enough".'[37]

The two leaders now met on HMS *Fearless*, moored at Gibraltar,
between 9 and 13 October. Wilson was acompanied by George Thomson,
now commonwealth secretary, and Sir Elwyn Jones. Marcia Williams was
again included, as was Gerald Kaufman. There was to be no deadline this
time, and both sides were to refer back to their capitals. The talks covered
the same ground, mainly in plenary sessions in great technical detail,
Wilson being surprised that Smith was a formidable negotiator. Marcia
Williams wrote later: 'I felt that they had rather more in common with each
other than they would probably have liked to admit, particularly in their
approach to politics, and certainly in their expertise and their efficiency in
being able to keep their options open.'[38] The prime minister tabled a
document on Sunday, 13 October, which Smith took back to Salisbury.
Wilson asserted, two days later, in a parliamentary statement that there would
be 'no sell out, no slamming the door by us'.[39] He announced that he was
prepared to send Thomson to Rhodesia if it would help, and the latter, now
as minister without portfolio, was summoned.

In nine meetings with Smith, between 2 and 9 November, and again 13
to 16 November, negotiations continued. To avoid the third anniversary
of UDI on 11 November, Thomson toured neighbouring black states.
Despite British willingness to make concessions, the talks came to an end
with disagreement on eight major points. 'Perhaps one day', Thomson told

parliament, 'the response from the other side of th[e] door will be more constructive than it has so far been.'[40] This was the end.

When the commonwealth prime ministers met eventually, in London between 7 and 15 January 1969, Thomson suggested that Britain was still committed to NIBMAR, though most of the delegates opposed the *Fearless* proposals as still oppressive. Wilson tried to insist that the *Fearless* proposals, or something similar, might be acceptable to all Rhodesians, at which point Britain would grant independence. He would consult the commonwealth on the change of circumstances, and hoped the 1966 principle could then be waived. The Rhodesian government introduced a new republican constitution later in the year, designed to copperfasten white minority rule over the African population.

No attempt was made to repeal the commonwealth immigration act when Wilson assumed office. There had been no reference to the problem in the draft manifesto, until Wedgwood Benn pointed out that labour would have to operate existing controls until it came up with a new policy. Soskice was weakly committed to the free entry of passport holders, but also in thrall to his civil servants, according to Richard Crossman. George Thomas, his parliamentary secretary, remembers him as favouring control: '"If we do not have strict immigration rules"', he quotes Soskice, '"our people will soon all be coffee-coloured."'[41] This is borne out by the permanent secretary, who described Soskice as 'less liberal in his approach than his predecessors'.[42] The prime minister took command in March 1965, announcing a mission to commonwealth countries to examine the machinery of control. Wilson believed the system was being abused, and clearly preferred that immigrants might be halted at embarkation. This had been the approach in the 1950s, and it was his intention to keep the issue of immigration out of British politics. He failed to secure the services of Lord Butler as chairman, but came up eventually with Lord Mountbatten, who was about to retire as chief of the defence staff. Mountbatten toured the commonwealth in three months with little success, and recommended that the number of new immigrants should be reduced to at least 7,000 a year. 'I believe that these drastic restrictions', he wrote, 'will be accepted [in the commonwealth] with understanding so long as they only remain in force during the breathing space needed for assimilation.'[43] Wilson also stated that discrimination would be made illegal, but, according to George Thomas, 'Frank [Soskice] would have none of it. He thought such legislation would add to our problems, and in that I agreed with him.'[44] Wilson designated Maurice Foley, a minister at the DEA, to look after the assimilation of immigrants, but this attempt at a different strategy, being premissed on the idea of control, was to be perceived as racist.

A special cabinet committee had been set up under the lord president, and the cabinet discussed immigration on 8 July, most ministers having shifted from the pre-1962 position of no controls. Wilson wanted to vet accommodation before dependents were admitted, but this was rejected as impractical. The government announced in a white paper, on 2 August 1965, that entry vouchers were to be reduced from 20,800 to 8,500, and available only to those with jobs or skills. Five thousand were to be doctors or other professionals, and the unskilled were to be barred, though there was still a demand for immigrant labour.

The white paper had been prepared in number 10, and Richard Crossman, who was alert to white feeling in the midlands, believed the reason was political. 'I am an old-fashioned Zionist', he wrote, 'who believes that anti-Semitism and racialism are endemic, [and] that one has to deal with them by controlling immigration when it gets beyond a certain level.'[45] The race relations bill had been introduced in April, and was to be enacted in November after being diluted. It had to be extended in 1968.

Soskice failed to establish a royal commission on the subject, and, when Roy Jenkins took over the home office, he was actively to pursue questions of discrimination and integration (Maurice Foley was also moved to the home office). Jenkins was to define integration 'not as a flattening process of assimilation but equal opportunity, accompanied by cultural diversity, in an atmosphere of mutual tolerance',[46] and appointed his publisher, the former liberal MP Mark Bonham Carter, as chairman of the race relations board. The 1965 white paper saw labour through the general election, and, as a result of the administrative change in the controls, the number of immigrants dropped significantly in subsequent years.

The problem of Kenyan Asians, whereby some decided to settle in Britain, having been denied work permits by the Kenyatta government, arose shortly before Roy Jenkins left the home office in late 1967. There were in all 200,000 Asians in Kenya, many being passport holders with rights of entry to Britain. The Kenyan government increased its attack on the Asian minority in February 1968, shortly after James Callaghan took over the home office. Britain had granted Kenya independence in December 1963, and it was Kenyatta who was now being racist; he had offered Asians citizenship, but then sought to punish them for refusing to become Kenyans. 'The truth is that Africans', Barbara Castle noted, 'are no better at racial tolerance than we are here.'[47] 'I had some reason for hoping', Callaghan was to write, 'that if we put up a firm front, [President Kenyatta] would not proceed with mass expulsions.'[48] Callaghan favoured controlling the entry of Kenyan Asians, and Duncan Sandys and Enoch Powell began to stir up the white community. The cabinet delayed Callaghan's bill on 15 February, to allow Wilson to send Malcolm MacDonald to intercede with Kenyatta in Nairobi, but the government decided a week later, with Barbara Castle literally asleep in cabinet, to provide vouchers for 1,500 Asians a year (up to 7,000 including dependants). Callaghan's bill was rushed through parliament by 1 March; thirty-five labour MPs voted against, as did the liberals, and a group of thirteen tories under Ian Macleod. Richard Crossman found himself 'engaged in a furious discussion about immigration. On this issue the whole of the London intelligentsia ... are united in denouncing the Immigration Act as the most shameful and disgraceful Act of any Government.'[49] Researching the issue towards the end of the month, he discovered that 'for two years, between 1965 and 1967, although the problem was known to exist nothing was done about it until suddenly it became acute.' This was 'presumably because the Home Office didn't want to touch the subject'.[50] The home secretary had been Roy Jenkins, and the European commission on human rights was to rule in 1970 that the immigration act was discriminatory. Jenkins had let the draft bill be prepared, but claims he would not have gone ahead with it, and came to regret not putting up a stronger fight in cabinet against the Callaghan policy. Shirley Williams, who was to be moved to the home office in late 1969, was part of a group of junior ministers which tried to get the cabinet to honour British citizenship. The action against the Kenyan Asians was hardly an appropriate context in which to extend the race relations act, the 1968 bill having its second reading on 23 April.

The previous Saturday, Enoch Powell, speaking in Birmingham, had said: 'As I look ahead I am filled with foreboding. Like the Roman, I seem to see the River Tiber foaming with much blood.'[51] Two weeks later, the prime minister replied to Powell, in a speech in Birmingham: 'to maintain the principle of racial equality we must create practical conditions in which these principles are acceptable to all our people, including those who day by day live their lives alongside immigrant communities.'[52] This did little to endear Wilson to the 1969 commonwealth conference, four east African countries, including Kenya, absenting themselves from the working party on citizenship and immigration.

Roy Jenkins had protected his liberal reputation from December 1965 until November 1967, his period at the home office seeing the enactment of a number of reforms which began as private members' bills. Dick Taverne took charge on a day to day basis. Marcia Williams enigmatically records that Harold Wilson 'kept a careful watching brief[53] on the question of personal freedoms. He was not personally in favour of some of the measures, but the support of his government was necessary to secure their enactment. 'Harold Wilson was never particularly obstructive to them', Jenkins would recall, 'and he was never obstructive to me.'[54] Wilson conciliated a minority in the cabinet by seemingly leaving it to backbench MPs.

Labour got off to a good start in 1964, when it provided parliamentary time for Sidney Silverman's private member's bill to abolish hanging. This had not been in the manifesto, and it was considered a matter for a free vote, though the anti-hanging majority had risen in the previous decade. The murder bill secured its second reading by 355 to 170, being carried with the support of labour and liberal MPs in July 1965. The lords restricted abolition to five years, but both houses would vote in December 1969 to make it permanent.

The first issue Jenkins – surreptitiously – tackled was homosexuality, following the Wolfenden committee's recommendation that acts between consenting adults in private should be legalized. Humphrey Berkeley, then a conservative MP, introduced a private member's bill, which received its second reading on 11 February 1966 by 179 votes to 99. Harold Wilson was engaged that day in settling a rail strike, and Richard Crossman records that the prime minister was opposed to decriminalization. Barbara Castle supported the reform, and was subjected to 'a remarkable diatribe against homosexuality' from George Brown. 'As an Anglo-Catholic and Socialist, he thought society ought to have higher standards ... "We've gone too damned far on sex already. I don't regard any sex as pleasant. It's pretty undignified and I've always thought so."'[55] Tripping later through the lobbies, she remarked to a female colleague that they were doing a great deal 'for the boys'.[56]

Harold Wilson also seems not to have been enthusiastic about the legalization of abortion. He had many catholics in his constituency, and had no wish to antagonize them. David Steel, a son of the manse, had entered parliament in March 1965, as a liberal, in a Scottish by-election. He introduced an abortion bill in the commons after the general election, Lord Silkin having piloted it – twice – through the lords. (Steel had declined to introduce the homosexuality bill.) His abortion bill got a second reading majority of 200. The government decided to give it time in May 1967, Lord Longford alone opposing. William Ross was also against abortion, but its strong supporters included Jenkins, Crosland, Castle, Benn, Gardiner and Crossman. Crossman had responsibility for the bill's scheduling as leader of the house, and felt that, while homosexual reform damaged the party among working-class people in the north, the legalization of abortion would 'be a pretty popular measure, especially among working-class women'.[57] There were a number of all-night sittings in July, and, despite the efforts of Norman St John Stevas, the bill was carried.

It was the law commission which recommended a reform of the divorce laws, the cabinet agreeing in October to take a formally neutral position. But it also provided government time for a bill to be promoted by a back-bencher, Bill Wilson, a Coventry labour MP. The bill received its second reading by 165 votes to 64 in February 1968, and was subsequently enacted. Jenkins had already left the home office, and it was formally under Callaghan that George Strauss's theatres bill was carried in July, abolishing censorship under the lord chamberlain. The Latey commission had recommended a reduction in the age of majority to eighteen the previous summer, and, while a speaker's conference suggested voting at twenty, the government finally decided, in May 1968, to enfranchise eighteen-year-olds.

Aside from the franchise reform, which was enacted in time for the next general election, the homosexuality, abortion, divorce and theatre censorship acts were seen to be part of the spirit of cultural change in the 1960s. This wave of legislation was to have a profound impact on the private realm of male–female relations. In the context of selective upward social mobility in the 1970s and 1980s, new values and practices were to emerge. The 'coming out' of gays and lesbians was to challenge the idea of the hetero-sexual nuclear family, while abortion and divorce did much to strengthen the position of women. This sideshow of private members' bills was seen as the epitomey of English liberalism in the 1960s. During the liberal hour of Jenkins's time at the home office, legislation had been passed of great practical and symbolic value.

The six day war in the middle east against the Arab nations, in June 1967, threatened world peace. Harold Wilson had long been a supporter of the state of Israel, but he found himself conducting British diplomacy in a major international crisis, with the foreign office attentive to Soviet intentions in the region. The prime minister initially contemplated the use of force, in alliance with the United States, though he sought to deny this subsequently.

Israel's security had been guaranteed from 1956 by the united nations' emergency force (UNEF) in the Gaza Strip and Sinai Desert, and these troops even protected Eilat, the port which gave Israel access through the Gulf of Aqaba to the Indian Ocean. In early 1967 the Zionist state became locked in sporadic exchanges with Syria to the north, Palestinian guerrillas also being involved. Egypt, which had formed the United Arab Republic (UAR) with Syria, moved troops up to its border with Israel in May; the UAR had broken down, but pan-Arabism still had an appeal. Nasser suc-cessfully demanded the withdrawal of the united nations' troops in Egypt on 18 May, and announced four days later that he would close the Straits of Tiran, leaving Israel its Mediterranean ports only. The British government opposed Egypt's intention, being committed to the right of maritime passage through an international waterway.

The foreign office, for all its traditional pro-Arabism, found itself out of touch with Cairo, diplomatic relations having been broken off over Rhodesia. The day after Nasser's announcement, 23 May, when it seemed that the United States was to send ships to the straits, Wilson, Brown and Healey decided to join their ally, in order to prevent Israel going to war. Johnson had no intention of getting involved alone in another Vietnam. '"I want to play every card in the UN", [he] told [his] advisers, "but I've never relied on it to save me when I'm going down for the third time. I want to see Wilson and De Gaulle out there with their ships all lined up too.'"[58] The foreign secretary later recalled: 'I hoped that a body of Maritime Powers might make a simple declaration that they could not tolerate the closure of the Strait of Tiran because it was an international waterway ... and that if necessary an international naval force would be assembled to escort convoys through the Strait.'[59] It was only when the defence secretary changed sides, having learned that British ships could not be got easily to the area, that an emergency cabinet meeting that afternoon decided to send George Thomson, a foreign office minister, to Washington, to find out about American action.

Britain was taking the initiative, and trying to get the cooperation of the United States on sending a multinational task force through the Suez Canal. Washington was keen on the 1950 triple declaration, which it had made with France and Britain, upholding existing frontiers in the middle east. Thomson discussed joint action in the united nations with Dean Rusk, the secretary of state. According to Johnson:

> The British proposed two steps. First, there would be a public declaration, signed by as many nations as possible, reasserting the right of free passage through the Gulf of Aqaba. There was hope that the declaration might be endorsed by the United Nations. Second, a naval task force would be set up, composed of as many nations as possible, to break Nasser's blockade and open the Straits of Tiran. During the next few days we explored the British proposal fully with key Congressmen and with other interested governments.

The middle east task force – 'known informally as the Red Sea regatta' – initially comprised the United States, Britain, Holland and Australia.[60] The state department was keen on this plan, but Johnson was worried about congress. Wedgwood Benn was in north America at this time, and met Johnson on 23 May, at a conference in Washington. 'He looked absolutely drained of energy, totally exhausted ... The leaders of the US and USSR really do carry a load far beyond the capacity of a single person. What was interesting was the way the American President moved, with no protocol but absolutely maximum security.'[61]

Harold Wilson had written to the prime minister of Israel, Levi Eshkol, revealing his intentions. Britain was aligning with the United States on the 1957 proposal to make the Straits of Tiran an international waterway, and this remained the cornerstone of British policy. Wilson was keen to emphasise free passage, and not argue about land frontiers. 'If we are to give you the international support we wish, it must be based on your undoubted rights.'[62] Abba Eban, the foreign minister, was on his way to New York, via Paris and London. He saw the British prime minister in the cabinet room, on the evening of 23 May. 'His demeanor was solid and assured. Our dialogue was on a low, pragmatic key with no attempt at rhetoric or stylized discourse; I seemed to have crossed the Channel into the twentieth century. There was also a current of unembarrassed sympathy.'[63] Eban admits Wilson did not advise for or against armed action by Israel. 'I thought that Wilson was showing a distinguished statesmanship. He was prepared for the maximum degree of commitment compatible with his country's real strength and responsibility. These were not as broad as they once had been, and Wilson moved with assurance and precision within their limits.'[64]

George Brown had flown to Moscow, to ask that Nasser be restrained from going ahead with the closure, but the Russians were suspicious of western support for Israel. General de Gaulle had called for four-power talks between France, Britain, the United States and Russia, but Moscow refused to participate. Harold Wilson then took up the idea. The use of force was again discussed in cabinet on 30 May, where Wilson's idea of an Anglo-American 'joint maritime force for action'[65] was criticized by Healey. 'Though [Richard Crossman] was passionately pro-Israeli [he] agreed ... about the danger of being isolated and classed as a Western imperialist trying vainly to reassert [British] suzerainty when [they] hadn't the military force to do so.'[66]

The government agreed to continue with contingency planning 'to enforce ... an international declaration ... if all else failed'.[67] Wilson shortened an already arranged visit to Canada and the United States, flying out on 31 May and returning on 3 June. He found Johnson was only prepared to support an international declaration by maritime powers through the united nations, and he wanted Britain to take the lead in this. The United States, according to Wilson's version, was not going to come to the aid of Israel. France vetoed the proposed British declaration in the security council, backing the secretary general, U Thant, and the prime minister arrived back in London on Sunday, 4 June empty-handed. Johnson was to write of a joint United States/British plan to make an independent declaration of the right of free passage; they would have the support of Israel, Holland, Australia, Iceland, Belgium and New Zealand by 4 June. West Germany, Argentina, Portugal, Canada and Panama were close to joining a naval intervention. This attempt to do Israel's work was about to be overtaken by events. Johnson would protest to Abba Eban after the war, that he should have been given 'a little more time'. 'I did not feel', Eban was to recall, 'that there was much conviction in his voice.'[68]

A little under three years later, on 9 April 1970, the *Daily Mail* was to publish a story, 'The Day Wilson Almost Went to War', by Walter Terry, derived from Patrick Gordon Walker's recently published book, *The Cabinet*. Gordon Walker gave an account of a supposedly imaginary cabinet meeting, the book having been vetted in the cabinet office by Burke

Trend, but Terry took this to be a thinly disguised version of the story of British deployment of force in the middle east in 1967.

Number 10 issued an immediate denial. Gordon Walker had accurately suggested in his book that the task force idea came from the foreign office, that the defence secretary changed his mind, and that the prime minister, with a divided cabinet, supported the foreign secretary. 'This is a time for stout hearts'[69] he has his fictional prime minister say. He went on to present the major arguments: Russia would intervene if there was a war, Israel would back such a task force, and it would allow Britain to get on good terms with the United States. Wilson argued in cabinet later that morning, that the government should deny the whole story, in order not to damage relations with the Arabs. As ministers searched their memories, the prime minister modified the statement to be issued. Gordon Walker denied the *Daily Mail* story, but this was after he had been seen by Wilson. The prime minister also ordered Crossman to say nothing, in the Godkin Lectures he was delivering at Harvard on prime ministerial government. George Brown discussed the matter with Ray Gunter in the bar of a train to Norwich, both now being backbenchers. Wilson telephoned Brown at his hotel at 1.30 p.m., and the two discussed the statement to be released. Brown had forgotten the task force, but he remembered the following day that the British initiative had fallen, first because Washington was not interested, and secondly because the Israelis moved too quickly. 'It seems to me that it would have been bloody stupid, to put it mildly if at that stage the Foreign Office hadn't been thinking of every bloody possibility and every impossibility.'[70]

'Not one sentence, or thought, contained in the article had the remotest connection with fact',[71] Wilson was to write in 1971. He claims Lord Gardiner conducted an investigation in 1970, with access to all the cabinet records, and reported to Wilson that there was no truth in the story. This is not borne out in accounts by Brown (1971) and Gordon Walker (1972). The diaries of Crossman (1976) and Castle (1984) reveal what went on in the cabinet meetings of 23, 25 and 30 May 1967, and Crossman had written on 29 May of the two previous meetings he had missed: 'the account which ... the Cabinet Secretariat ... circulated was trimmed down to suit the conclusions the P.M. wanted to have recorded.'[72] His informants were Roy Jenkins and Barbara Castle.

It was not until 1981 that Harold Wilson acknowledged he had tried to set up 'a naval task force'. 'We were joining with the United States Government', he was to write, 'and such other maritime countries as could be enlisted in support, in announcing our intention to establish a naval force, whether under the auspices of the United Nations or not, to keep the Gulf of Aqaba open to the shipping of all nations, or to reopen it. It was in our view very desirable that such a declaration should be made at

once, although no effective force could be assembled immediately.'[73]
(Wilson's 1971 denial, which would be typical of his statements on other
embarrassing issues, was revealed, by him, to be a lie.)

Israel attacked on Monday, 5 June 1967, taking the Gaza Strip and Sinai
from Egypt, east Jerusalem and the west bank from Jordan, and the Golan
Heights from Syria, all in six days. The Arab forces were routed, and the
position of the Palestinians rendered appreciably worse. Britain immediately declared its non-involvement, George Brown calling for a ceasefire.
Contingency planning for military action was no longer necessary, and an
arms embargo was imposed only to be rescinded. (Merlyn Rees, who was
in the ministry of defence in 1967, would blurt out, six years later, in a
meeting of the shadow cabinet, that the government had supplied arms clandestinely.) Israel responded to a UN resolution of 6 June, but Egypt and
Syria continued their defensive actions. The Israeli attack was seen as
1956 all over again by the Arabs, and Nasser, who had closed the Suez Canal,
accused Britain and the United States on 6 June of militarily supporting Israel.
Embassies and consulates came under attack, and an oil embargo was
imposed by many Arab states. Arab sterling deposits held in London were
withdrawn.

There was significant enthusiasm for the Israeli victory within the
government, even though the dalliance with the use of force meant
diplomatic problems with the Arab states. Wilson held talks with General
de Gaulle in Paris in mid-June, seeing it as an opportunity to gain Arab
recognition of Israel's right to exist. But responsibility for the balance of
power in the middle east remained with the two superpowers. George
Brown now attacked Jewish determination to keep conquered territory,
in a speech at the united nations. The government was concerned about
Arab oil and the sterling balances, and envisaged a peace settlement in which
the Jewish state would retreat to a secure frontier. The foreign secretary
'told [Abba Eban] with clarity that Britain would only advocate Israeli
withdrawal in a context of permanent peace, to secure and agreed boundaries
which Israel would find satisfactory for its security'.[74] Resolution 242 was
tabled by Lord Caradon on 22 November after considerable negotiations,
and unanimously adopted by the security council. Gerald Kaufman was
strongly pro-Israel during and after the war, and besported in number 10
a commemorative ribbon sent from Israel. Wilson became impatient with
his aide occasionally. 'Looking at that ribbon, he would retort that but for
the closure of the [Suez] Canal Britain's position would have been better
and our ability to help Israel might have been correspondingly greater.'[75]

Abba Eban was to single out Wilson as Israel's closest friend in Europe:

Whenever I came through London, he not only would want to know about our international fortunes, but would also show a detailed curiosity about our domestic relationships and rivalries. To be frank, he enjoyed Israeli gossip. Yet when I came away from him, I could never recall a malicious word. He was usually regarded as a cerebral rather than an emotional man. However, he was capable of strong fidelities that sometimes got him into trouble but were, in general, an ennobling dimension of his character. He and his colleagues came to terms with Britain's dwindling power in the Middle East and gave short shrift to the 'Arabists' who still dreamed of a Pax Britannica sustained by friendly Arab clients.[76]

CHAPTER 18

Devaluation and After, 1967–8

Harold Wilson had been heckled about Vietnam by demonstrators, while reading the lesson at the pre-conference service in Brighton in 1966. Carworkers from the midlands, who were experiencing the effects of the July deflationary measures, massed angrily outside the Grand Hotel the following day, Monday, 3 October; when twelve shop stewards, instead of the agreed six, crowded into a meeting with the prime minister, Wilson made a scarcastic comment about over-manning. The cabinet met in the prime minister's room on Tuesday evening in emergency session, to allow the government to activate part four of the prices and incomes act, immediately imposing the six months' freeze. Delegates to the party conference voted to back the government's incomes policy by 3,925,000 votes to 2,471,000, but also narrowly supported Frank Cousins's call for work sharing instead of redundancies. The prospects for Wilson's government, months after the general election, did not look good.

The balance of payments remained uppermost in the prime minister's mind, following Callaghan's actions in the summer. There was a surplus in the last quarter of 1966, but the current account deficit for the year was £61 million (compared with £393 million in 1964). The July measures marked the end of any possibility of a serious challenge to capitalism, despite Crossman's attempt to argue that it was 'a stage in our socialist development'.[1] This was Balogh's view. 'He thinks', noted Wedgwood Benn, 'that the freeze may give us an opportunity to develop a real plan for our wages and incomes and prices, which will allow us to come out of this squeeze with a socialist economy and in this way we may have stumbled into socialism.'[2] Baloghism was dirigisme.

Wilson lectured the TUC in September on the need for increased productivity, tapping an old explanation for Britain's problems: 'The restrictive practices that are still too prevalent today amount simply to a means of laying claim to a full day's pay for less than a full day's work.'[3]

The government's strategy was worked out in the steering committee on economic policy (SEP), which included Wilson, Stewart, Callaghan, Crossman, Brown, Healey, Gunter and Jay. Devaluation remained a forbidden topic, and Callaghan, as a deflationist, met with only mild resistance from Stewart and Brown. Wilson backed his chancellor, lending him Chequers for a weekend for a discussion of monetary cooperation with leading finance ministers; only the prime minister knew that the treasury was conducting a review on floating the pound versus devaluation. The idea of a huge, long-term American loan, to save sterling from speculation, was mooted in February 1967. Callaghan was extremely interested, though it became linked to Britain remaining east of Suez. When the 10 per cent import surcharge had been abolished finally at the end of November 1966, it was not replaced by quotas on imports as expected.

Unemployment began to increase that autumn, reaching nearly half a million in mid-1967. It was the highest figure for July since 1940. This had been the intended consequence of the July measures, and Callaghan was aiming for something under 2.5 per cent out of work. The government's prices and incomes policy stuck, the freeze giving way to the period of severe restraint in January 1967. Union executives voted on 2 March to support a TUC-operated voluntary incomes policy, when the statutory one came to an end. Wilson immediately suggested that the government could announce, after meeting industry each year, a 'National Dividend for distribution between all forms of income ... for distribution to workers by hand and by brain'.[4] This was to be the quintessence of Wilsonian corporatism, though his speech at Greenford in Middlesex was little reported.

Callaghan had reduced bank rate to 6.5 per cent on 26 January, and it was at 5.5 per cent by May. The budget in April was unexciting, with only a slight reflation from the relaxation of hire purchase controls. 'Steady as she goes'[5] was Callaghan's order. Wilson had been banking throughout on Britain's entry into the EEC, but this was to be vetoed in mid-May and confirmed in November and December, as de Gaulle's rejection made the position of sterling insecure once again.

The war in the middle east further upset the government's economic policy. The closure of the canal in June raised the cost of British imports, and this had to be borne until it was finally cleared and reopened in 1968. British oil supplies were held up at source, and the effects of the civil war in Nigeria were to be added to the Arab ban. Alternative supplies had to be sought in north and south America at higher prices. 'The Middle East crisis', Harold Wilson would write, 'was the biggest contributing factor to the devaluation which came five months later.'[6]

Devaluation was first discussed at Chequers on Saturday, 22 July 1967, Wilson summoning Crossman, Silkin, Castle, Shore, Wedgwood Benn, Judith Hart, Tommy Balogh, Marcia Williams and Gerald Kaufman to a private meeting. The prime minister felt that it was "'too risky'",[7] after an exposition of pros and cons by Balogh, but Barbara Castle concluded that he was 'very pragmatic ... terribly tempted to find ad hoc solutions, at which he is very good'.[8] Dock strikes in September to November added to the government's problems. Following the Devlin report of 1966, which recommended the decasualization of dock labour, guaranteed minimum wages were introduced on 18 September 1967. Dockers struck unofficially for wage increases in Liverpool, while the grievance in London was new working practices. The Liverpool dockers secured increases after six weeks, due to the intervention of the prime minister. Jack Jones had been sent up from London by Cousins, now back in charge of the TGWU, and they secured the appointment of an inquiry by Sir Jack Scamp. Wilson was staying overnight at the Adelphi, and saw that the findings were accepted by local employers. 'I told him what was involved', Jones was to recall, 'so that he could be ready to put whatever pressure he could on the employers.'[9] Working arrangements in London were revised two weeks later, after Cousins intervened with Jack Dash, the dockers' unofficial leader in the port.

It was clear by mid-October that the balance of payments would not go into surplus that year, and bank rate was raised 0.5 per cent on the seventeenth. The French foreign minister, Couve de Murville, then asserted that sterling's position as a reserve currency would have to be abandoned if Britain wanted to join the EEC, endorsing the conclusion of a commission report. Devaluation was now firmly on the political agenda. Callaghan was to argue that 'the fundamental reason was that the world was not convinced that Britain could establish a long-term equilibrium in its balance of payments', and he would opine twenty years later that 'no one can say that the international observers were wrong.' 'Nevertheless', he continued, 'devaluation by itself was not even a short-term remedy unless accompanied by other measures. The Labour Government ... had set out with the right priorities – structural industrial change, redeployment of labour, training for the new technology, reduction of the burdens of overseas defence, and maintenance of wage increases in line with productivity.'[10]

The crisis began on Saturday, 4 November with intensive speculation. Callaghan and Wilson feared for the future of sterling. Sir Alec Cairncross, now head of the government economic service, had privately advised the chancellor two days earlier that devaluation was unavoidable. 'He added that he had consulted no one before writing and did not intend to canvass any other opinion.'[11] Callaghan accepted this advice, though he remained attached to the idea of a long-term, international rescue for sterling. He 'felt that the three years of struggle had been of no avail.'[12] Wilson abandoned any political objections to devaluation, but stated a preference for floating the pound, though both men then acted to prevent this. Sir Denis Rickett, a treasury knight, was sent to see Joe Fowler, the United States treasury secretary. The Americans expressed the view that the pound was not overvalued.

The issue of devaluation was first discussed in SEP on 8 November, with senior ministers, other than the chancellor, generally in favour. A rumoured revaluation of the German mark upwards forced Callaghan to opt for a change in the value of the pound, and bank rate was raised to 6.5 per cent on 9 November. Wilson was still keen to get help by appealing to the self-interest of the United States and Europe, but the central bankers were asking too high a price in economic policy.

The decision to devalue was taken by Callaghan and Wilson in the cabinet room, in the company of Trend and Armstrong, late on Monday, 13 November. The two ministers had just returned from the lord mayor's banquet, and were wearing full evening dress. Wilson had proclaimed the technological revolution in Europe at the Mansion House, the better to cover up the following day's trade figures. Callaghan privately informed Crosland of the decision the next morning. Roy Jenkins had asked in cabinet when the economy was to be discussed, and, when Barbara Castle said she hoped there would be some room for manoeuvre, 'Jim and Harold looked like a couple of schoolboys caught with their hand in the till.'[13] Devaluation was endorsed on 14 November by a group of seven senior ministers, comprising Wilson, Callaghan, Brown, Crosland, Healey, Stewart, Shore and seemingly Thomson. Wilson wanted to keep the decision from the full SEP committee, with Crossman and Wedgwood Benn excluded. The 'special committee'[14] was entrusted with drawing up the accompanying package. Callaghan maintains that Wilson preferred to leave some measures until the budget, but is complimentary in retrospect: 'He was as tired as I was and was beset by many concerns other than devaluation but he never showed impatience or irritation, and I was greatly indebted to him.'[15] The special committee met twice on 15 November, and the cabinet, less one member, agreed that Thursday that the pound should be reduced, on Saturday, 18 November, from $2.80 to $2.40. 'This is the most agonizing reappraisal I have ever had to do', Callaghan told his colleagues, 'and I will not pretend that it is anything but a failure of our policies.'[16]

The announcement of the 14.3 per cent devaluation was made at 9.30 p.m. that Saturday. The accompanying measures followed on the Monday – bank rate raised to 8 per cent; defence cuts of £100 million, and another £100 million in other public spending; a saving of £100 million on SET repayments; the ending of export rebates the following April, when corporation tax was to be raised in the budget. Credit of three billion dollars was arranged from the central banks and IMF. Devaluation by other countries, in response, was restricted to Ireland, New Zealand and Denmark, whereas floating the pound might have provoked more countries to follow suit. Wilson felt the 'serious break in confidence' in sterling had come, when 'manoeuvrings within the Common Market set off damaging rumours in Europe',[17] but he was looking forward rather than backwards when he broadcast the following night on television.

Wilson presented devaluation as an opportunity for Britain, even though it represented a defeat for the government's economic policies. His claim that 'devaluation does not mean that ... the pound in the pocket is worth 14 per cent less to us now than it was'[18] would cause him endless difficulty. He has blamed it on a treasury draft, and argued he was concerned to reassure the public remembering the great fear about savings in 1949. Wilson actually said on the air: 'From now on, the pound abroad, is worth 14 per cent or so less, in terms of other currencies. That doesn't mean, of course, that the pound here in Britain, in your pocket or purse or in your bank, has been devalued.'[19] He went on to admit that prices would rise as a result of dearer imports, but it was shortly after 6.00 p.m. on Sunday, 20 November 1967, that Harold Wilson's political reputation, in the opinion of a mass television audience, began its inexorable slide. Having just devalued the pound, he attempted to deny it by drawing a distinction between internal and external changes.

Richard Crossman was sitting on a sofa beside the queen, at Windsor Castle, watching the broadcast. 'Of course it's extraordinarily difficult to make that kind of speech',[20] she said, after a long pause. The lord president of the council maintained constitutional relations by turning the conversation to foot and mouth disease.

Ted Heath wrote his reply 'in the white heat of anger',[21] and accused the prime minister the following night of having – falsely – suggested that devaluation would not mean price increases.

'This is the unhappiest day in my life',[22] Callaghan had said at cabinet on 16 November. He knew he had to resign, having promised foreign holders he would maintain the value of sterling, and did so in a letter on 18 November, but the prime minister asked him to stay on. Wilson and Callaghan held a press conference at number 10 on Sunday, 19 November. Tony Crosland told his wife that night: 'If Jim were given some time, I think he could be persuaded to take another job in Cabinet. At the moment he is too knocked about to think straight.'[23]

Speaking from the cross benches in the house of lords on Tuesday, 21 November, Lord Cromer attacked the labour government for 'the humiliation that both the pound sterling and our country have been brought to suffer'. Wilson had inherited 'a substantial but not unmanageable financing problem', only to 'give first priority to Party political dogma'.[24] 'It was a speech', said Longford, 'to which there ha[d] been no parallel in [his] now rather overlong experience in [that] House.'[25] Peter Jay – the economics editor of *The Times* – drew on his experiences in the treasury to write about devaluation two days later, after Robert Neild had leaked to him the story about Wilson ordering the destruction of the economists' paper on devaluation. Arguing that the pound had been overvalued since 1962, Jay blamed Macmillan and then Wilson. As for Callaghan, who just happened to be his father-in-law, Jay wrote: 'No one will perhaps ever know what in his heart Mr Callaghan's real attitude was, if indeed he had one. Like King Henry VIII's Cardinal Wolsey he judged that the only viable policy was the King's policy, whatever its strengths and weaknesses.'[26] This was also the opinion of Douglas Jay, who was to report that someone characterized Callaghan as 'a "non-issue-motivated" man'. 'To him, I felt, the men and women were the realities, and the issues by comparison were the transient and embarrassed phantoms.'[27] Following Callaghan's speech on 22 November, Wilson and his kitchen cabinet believed he 'was intriguing with the Tories and the City'.[28] Susan Crosland was throwing up at the thought of moving to number 11, while, with the possibility of a reshuffle, other labour wives suffered for their husbands' careers.

The prime minister finally decided on a straight swap between the outgoing chancellor and his replacement, an idea which may have originated with Richard Crossman. Nearly two weeks after the fateful cabinet meeting, it was announced on 29 November that Callaghan was going to the home office. If he had refused, Wilson might have offered it to Crossman. Roy Jenkins became Wilson's second chancellor of the exchequer, though he had been kept off economic committees until then.

Callaghan was to recover in time from political ignominy, though the effect on Harold Wilson was the opposite. Callaghan would write years later: 'Our economic advisers and those others who had advocated devaluation for so long always underrated the political damage that such a step would cause. Not only did the Government's fortunes plunge immediately, but in my view the adverse effects were still being felt at the time of the 1970 election.'[29] Andrew Graham, one of Thomas Balogh's economists, who would attend meetings in number 10 in 1968–9, remembers that the prime minister 'was never quite the same person after devaluation':

> He had always thought of himself, perfectly appropriately, as the cleverest boy in the class, and, therefore, that everything had come very easily to him. And he couldn't quite believe it when suddenly things that he had not expected to happen did happen and he had basically been humiliated. Events that he had thought ought not to have occurred had occurred.[30]

1967 had already seen important changes in the government. Patrick Gordon Walker was brought into the cabinet on 7 January, as minister without portfolio, replacing Douglas Houghton who had looked after social services. Fred Lee became chancellor of the duchy outside the

cabinet, and helped at the DEA. There were further changes in the ranks
of junior ministers. A mini-cabinet reshuffle was announced on 29 August.
Out went Douglas Jay, who was told of the change by Wilson in the station
master's office in Plymouth. Herbert Bowden was ennobled, and made
chairman of the independent television authority (ITA). Arthur Bottomley
was replaced by Reg Prentice, outside the cabinet. Tony Crosland became
president of the board of trade, Gordon Walker took over at education and
science, and George Thomson became commonwealth secretary. Michael
Stewart remained as first secretary, but took over the coordinating role from
Gordon Walker. The DEA was given to Peter Shore, the prime minister
taking personal charge.

Wilson had believed the previous summer that there were six possible
successors to his leadership, including Jenkins and Callaghan. With his
reshuffle, he felt he now had 'seven potential Chancellors[,] and [had]
knocked out the situation where Jenkins was the only alternative to
Callaghan'.[31] He was quickly to be proved wrong. Roy Jenkins had done
well in the government, and Wilson must have believed he would make
a good post-devaluation chancellor. 'Harold', Barbara Castle noted, 'has now
finally nobbled his one serious rival: they stand or fall together.'[32]

While Callaghan fell on the battlefield of devaluation, George Brown
finally resigned from the government four months later. The occasion was
a threat to the dollar, but the reason for the foreign secretary's departure
was to be personal. The United States was committed to paying gold at the
rate of $35 to the ounce, and Washington experienced a financial crisis in
early March 1968. The Americans were thought to favour a two-tier
pricing arrangement, and this rumour had an impact on London. The bank
of England was forced to sell gold, in order to maintain the new value of
the pound. Johnson asked Wilson on Thursday, 14 March not to open the
gold and foreign exchanges the following day, but the prime minister needed
an order in council for a bank holiday. He took Roy Jenkins and Peter Shore
to the palace shortly after midnight. Wilson maintains he was unable to find
George Brown as the crisis unfolded that evening, but the foreign secretary
had reappeared in the house about 10.00 p.m. He feared another devaluation: 'There was obviously a number of us who suspected that this
decision had been dictated to the Prime Minister from across the Atlantic.'
Brown was angry at not being consulted, and was to maintain he had been
with his wife at his official residence in Carlton Gardens. Nor had he been
drinking, unlike the prime minister 'who was himself drinking quite mag-
nificently'.[33] Barbara Castle believed Brown was 'emotionally intoxicated
rather than drunk'.[34] The foreign secretary gathered ministers in his room
in the house, until Wilson agreed to an emergency meeting at Downing
Street. Wedgwood Benn tried to rustle up "'some of his [that is, Wilson's]
friends"'[35] for an expected confrontation. The Downing Street meeting

began at 1.45 a.m., and lasted an hour. Brown was peeved at the involvement of Shore, and remembers telling the prime minister: 'You and Callaghan [sic] and Peter Shore have tonight repeated what the three [MacDonald, Snowden, Thomas] did in 1931, and if you're allowed to do this you might do it again.'[36] It was not the first time Wilson had been accused of MacDonaldism, and he lost his temper in the meeting. '"George [Brown] lost control entirely and left the room shouting insults."'[37]

When Wilson and Jenkins went to the house to make a statement at 3.00 a.m., the foreign secretary pointedly sat apart from his colleagues. Nor did he attend cabinet the following morning, and a letter came finally from Brown that Friday evening. Wilson had allowed him to resign from the government, after perhaps as many as seventeen threatened departures. The reason Brown was to give for going, was Wilson's tendency towards presidential government. 'A really serious issue … has … been troubling me for some time. It is, in short, the way this Government is run, and the manner in which we reach our decisions.'[38] Brown immediately accepted £5,000 to write a two-part article for the *Sunday Times*. Crossman saw him as a Jekyll and Hyde character: 'The good part has always been extraordinarily nice and talented … But on Thursday night he suddenly blew up and Hyde appeared shouting and screaming round the lobbies like a hysterical barrow-boy.'[39] He had been under strain as foreign secretary for months.

Harold Wilson had already made 'one of the costliest mistakes of [his] near six years in office'[40] in February 1967, shortly after the visit of Kosygin to London. The issue became known as the D-notice affair, and it permanently damaged his relationship with the press. It was the practice of a Whitehall functionary to issue defence – or D – notices to print and broadcasting media editors, 'for their general guidance as to the kind of information which should not be published in the interests of national security'.[41] The civil servant in 1967 was Col. 'Sammy' Lohan, a former ministry of defence press officer. 'Lohan was anti-Labour[,] but then so were almost all the civil servants who really care about defence and the Forces.'[42] He was secretary of a committee comprising civil servants and senior journalists, under a ministry of defence mandarin. D notices were a form of voluntary censorship, designed to protect the armed services, but also MI5 and MI6. The government's ultimate sanction was the official secrets act, if a newspaper, television or radio station ignored a D notice.

Chapman Pincher, the *Daily Express*'s right-wing defence correspondent, then entered the story. Pincher prided himself on being close to the security and intelligence services. He was not unduly alarmed at the visit of Kosygin, but was visited several days later by a telegraphist who had worked for two private cable companies. Pincher revealed, in his paper, on 21 February, that the government was reading international telegrams, including those of embassies, from a government communications head-quarters (GCHQ) in Cheltenham, then a secret installation. This had been normal practice for many years, but Pincher claimed it increased in volume under the labour government.

Lohan made no serious attempt to prevent his friend publishing the cable-vetting story, as it would embarrass a labour government, and fuel the cold war. Answering a – planted? – parliamentary question the same afternoon, Wilson accused the *Daily Express* of having breached two D notices. Wilson was bent on revenge against Pincher and Lohan, having been told by Captain Kerby, a tory MP, through George Wigg, that Lohan was feeding embarrassing parliamentary questions to the opposition. Pincher considers this the prime minister's principal motive in going for Lohan, but there is probably more to Wilson's reaction.

The prime minister's parliamentary replies were immediately seen as an attempt to intimidate the press. The *Express* claimed the following morning that Lohan had told Pincher that he would not be breaching a D notice. The *Daily Mail* had also been given the story, but did not run it because it could not be verified. 'Both newspapers', argues Marcia Williams, 'were playing with something far bigger than they knew because there was much more to the story than could be revealed.'[43] Wilson was to talk later, in secretive terms, about lives being at risk. 'During the first half of 1967', writes Marcia Williams, 'when the D Notice affair hung over us, the meetings on it were so numerous[,] that ... it gradually became the case that the door ... between my room and the Cabinet Room ... remained locked.'[44] She would claim 'that fifty of our agents were lost as a result of the D-notice affair',[45] information she can only have got from the prime minister.

Wilson set up a committee of privy counsellors two days later to examine the circumstances surrounding the publication of the article. It comprised Lord Radcliffe, Selwyn Lloyd and Manny Shinwell, the terms of reference including the 'consider[ation of] what improvements, if any, [were] required in [the D notice] system in order to maintain it as a voluntary system based on mutual trust and confidence between the government and Press'.[46] Getting rid of Lohan was now the prime minister's goal. Wilson was to regret that the government chose not to be legally represented, as its witnesses endured a drubbing. Marcia Williams would be critical of the role played by Manny Shinwell. When the three wise men reported in mid-June, it was to the effect that Wilson had been wrong. Lohan had told Pincher over lunch on 20 February that there was no D notice on the cable-vetting story. 'Lohan produced two D notices, saying that they were the only two that could possibly be applicable and that in his view neither was.'[47] Wilson refused to accept the privy counsellors' report, and the government issued its own white paper repeating the foreign office and ministry of defence positions. Lohan was accused of not acting on instructions given. He was allowed to resign after an internal civil service inquiry, but claimed he had been sacked.

If this had been Wilson's sole objective, the political cost of achieving it was way over budget, not least when Radcliffe denounced the government's case in the house of lords. The prime minister now set out to revamp the D-notice system. Meeting newspaper editors, he offered to let a retired Fleet Street journalist chair the D-notice committee. Admiral Denning was appointed secretary, and the issue debated in parliament on 22 June. Williams and Kaufman strengthened the prime minister's hand in arguing that Heath should not be privately shown the documentation, and Wilson claimed the previous government had been worried about Pincher's friendship with Lohan. He revealed that the former secretary had not been positively vetted, when it was his role to maintain official secrets.

Wilson grudgingly came to accept that he had been wrong in going for Chapman Pincher and the *Daily Express*. 'Though my motives had been concerned with protecting the security and intelligence services for which I was responsible, I was wrong to make an issue of it in the first instance. It was a very long time before my relations with the press were repaired.'[48] 'The cumulative effect of the affair on the Press', writes Marcia Williams, 'sensitive as they were from the Macmillan era about the Vassall Case and Government interference in Press matters, could almost be described as disastrous. Harold bore the full brunt of this at the time and for a long period afterwards.' 'No doubt [in] thirty years', she claims, 'the full story will be given[,] and the whole thing set in its proper perspective.'[49] This is unlikely.

Shortly after devaluation, Wilson was plunged into political difficulty on the question of arms sales to South Africa in late 1967. He had promised in 1963 that labour would halt all such shipments to the apartheid regime, at a time when Britain was undertaking joint maritime exercises, as well as training pilots for the Buccaneer aircraft it sold South Africa. The government decided in November 1964 there should be no new contracts; naval vessels already agreed were sent, and the contract for sixteen Buccaneer aircraft, plus spare parts, worth £25 million, was honoured. The cabinet decided not to proceed with a further sixteen aircraft, in which the South African government was interested. 'But there were already mutterings by some Ministers', recalls Barbara Castle, 'that we could not afford such expensive principles.'[50] She was thinking of George Brown.

'More than a year [after labour came to office]', according to a defence minister, 'the joint exercises were still continuing, and Ministers were earnestly discussing the sale to South Africa of military helicopters.'[51] Brown was in frequent touch with his South Africa opposite number, Dr Muller, and he even brought Muller to see Wilson in Downing Street. 'The

Prime Minister assured Dr Muller that everything [Brown] had been saying to him was being said with his knowledge and authority.'[52] The foreign secretary had been arguing that, if South Africa did not push the question of arms supplies, they would be granted later. This he later put in a letter to Muller, informing number 10 in the usual way. The South Africans were pressing for a quick decision, and Brown also saw it as a question of some urgency for the British economy. 'The supply of arms to South Africa', he was to write in his memoirs, 'was obviously very relevant to this, both because of the amount of money involved in the order and because of the uncertainty of the effect a refusal would have on our large and growing commercial trade with that country.'[53] It is certain Wilson heard about arms sales in July from an alarmed Lord Caradon, and there is evidence he knew before that. Rhodesia had been discussed in June in the defence and overseas policy (OPD) committee; the prime minister was concerned to get a settlement, and was prepared to consider rescinding the embargo. It was necessary to befriend the South Africans, to stop them supporting Ian Smith's regime.

The issue of further arms for South Africa surfaced in OPD on 14 September – before devaluation. This was an emergency meeting, and George Brown, Denis Healey and George Thomson all spoke in favour of supplying them. The ministry of defence was concerned that the Simonstown base should remain open for British use, in view of the closure of the Suez Canal, and the Russian build-up in the Indian Ocean. It is clear there was an emergent lobby in Whitehall, mediated by Brown and Healey. Stewart and Longford wanted to maintain the government's policy, while Crosland and Crossman had open minds. Wilson remained concerned with probable resignations and a party revolt, but he expressed interest in Crossman's idea of linking South African pressure on Ian Smith with resumed sales. 'If the South Africans would help us to settle with Smith', the lord president said, 'I would consider a concession on South African arms trade tolerable.'[54] Crossman later ruminated: 'My own view is that Rhodesia and South Africa between them are costing us an enormous amount in our balance of payments. We are completely immobilized because of the moral blackmail exerted by the left-wing of the Party and Harold Wilson's personal commitments ... He was so miserable and unhappy and divided in his mind about it that my main concern was to remain close to him and to say nothing without consulting him in advance.'[55]

The issue came again to OPD on Friday, 8 December, just after Jenkins replaced Callaghan, when a shopping list from Pretoria was considered. It was decided to postpone a reply until after an economic review then in progress, a compromise suggested by Crossman. Wilson claims he argued against any sale, but if the question of exports was to be of primary concern, he insisted, then embargoes on trade with the eastern bloc should also be reconsidered. This was a point against the foreign office. Dining with labour MPs the following Monday, Callaghan, who was no longer a member of OPD, expressed himself in favour of sales. This provoked members of the parliamentary party, and labour MPs began to sign a motion on 12 December, insisting on the maintenance of government policy. When John Silkin, as chief whip, reported this to number 10, 'Harold Wilson not only agreed: he was enthusiastic.'[56] The prime minister in fact was trying to organize labour MPs against his opponents. The story began to appear of a split in the cabinet and party. Barbara Castle was prepared to resign, and Wilson speculated about moving Healey from defence. He told Crossman he might stand for reelection as party leader, and would leak this to the *Manchester Guardian*.

The prime minister took the issue to cabinet on 14 December, but, with Brown delayed in Brussels by fog, it was not discussed. Waiting for the foreign secretary, 'the atmosphere got more and more unpleasant and the air was loaded with charges and countercharges'.[57] In parliament that afternoon, Wilson promised a statement the following week. George Brown was back in London the next morning – Friday, 15 December – in time for a special cabinet. It was to endorse the OPD decision of the previous week, Healey remembering it as 'the most unpleasant meeting I have ever attended'.[58]

Brown, Healey and Crosland protested vigorously about Wilson's manipulation of the party and press, and the foreign secretary had 'a great row' with the prime minister. 'I then claimed in front of my colleagues that he had authorised every move I had made to which he made the astonishing reply that he didn't expect me to put in a letter.'[59] As well as Healey and Crosland, Brown had the support of Callaghan, Gordon Walker, Thomson and Gunter. 'Instead of isolating Brown and Healey so that he could get rid of them and keep the rest[,] the Prime Minister had consolidated the opposition.'[60]

A group of eight, including Wilson, fought against arms sales, the prime minister's supporters being Stewart, Gardiner, Castle, Greenwood, Shore, Wedgwood Benn and Hughes. In the middle were Jenkins, Crossman, Peart, Marsh and Longford. The deadlock was only broken by Crossman's mediation. George Brown began to claim victory in off-the-record press briefings, this being the point at which his relation with Wilson collapsed. 'That I think is where it all began', he was to recall, 'and that time I came firmly to the conclusion that it didn't matter what one did he was capable of the utmost duplicity and would let one down and would be coordinating two different operations (four different operations) at the same time.'[61] Brown came very close to resigning in January 1968, when the cabinet was to be discussing post-devaluation deflation, the issue being the decision to postpone raising the school-leaving age to sixteen. This saw Lord Longford quit the government. As that cabinet meeting was breaking up, Brown hinted to Longford that he might join him.

The division in the government became increasingly obvious from 15 December 1967. Despite a prime ministerial edict to maintain public silence, the right dominated the press that weekend. 'We must force these buggers to eat dirt', Wedgwood Benn told Crossman, 'make them accept unconditional surrender. The P.M. must reassert himself.'[62] The cabinet was summoned at the last moment for Monday, 18 December, and, with intense speculation in the press, the government decided to maintain the embargo. Wilson had confronted the right, in the form of Brown and Healey. As this faction moved towards the centrist position he himself had been forced to accept, the left gained the initiative. When Callaghan switched sides, the prime minister's supporters were able to push home to victory. There the issue rested. 'It was the first and last time', wrote Wilson, '... that I had to fight rough with any of my colleagues – and I had done it by forbidding a counter-attack against tendentious press briefing.'[63] A trap had been set for the foreign secretary, and George Brown walked into it.

This was not to be the end of arms for South Africa. OPD was to be asked to sell Wasp helicopters in October 1969. These were on the cancelled shopping list of 1967, but Wilson concurred, on the grounds that 'they could only at great expense be adapted to riot control'.[64] The cabinet would insist on maintaining government policy on South Africa.

Civil war was then raging in Nigeria, one of the new members of the commonwealth. This west African country had become independent in 1960, with a federal government in Lagos, only to be confronted with the problem of tribalism. The British-trained Col. Ojukwu, an Ibo, led a seizure of power in 1966, during which the prime minister was killed. Ojukwu was soon unseated, in another military coup by General Gowon, who became the new national leader. When talks on confederation broke down later in the year, Ojukwu pressed separatist claims for the eastern region, which was proclaimed the Republic of Biafra on 30 May 1967. Fighting began on 6 July, and the country was soon divided on tribal lines. While Ibos suffered in the northern and western regions, there were counter-propaganda claims that the secessionists committed atrocities, particularly in the new states of Rivers and South East. General Gowon requested arms from Britain that autumn, the Wilson government acceding to the request. Military chiefs advised against any sort of intervention, and scuppered the idea of Britain contributing to a commonwealth peace-keeping force.

The united nations was hamstrung throughout, the war being considered an internal matter for Nigeria. The labour government came out in favour of maintaining the integrity of Nigeria, as did the Organization of African Unity (OAU). Only four black African states supported secession. Biafra secured international support on humanitarian grounds, but there was also some recognition of it as the home of an Ibo nation.

Biafra became one of the causes of the 1960s, left and right supporting Ojukwu for varying reasons. It became an issue within the labour party dividing the left, young and old, from the government. Most left-wing MPs supported Biafra, Michael Foot and Jack Mendelson alone warning of the dangers of Balkanization. Wilson was conscious of the moral appeal of a struggling people, but he stuck by Gowon. The British prime minister accepted that liberal opinion in the advanced world was committed to supplying food and medicine. He resented the military exigencies of the Ibos' struggle, French arms being flown in at night under the cover of aid, while genocidal policies were attributed to Lagos and London. 'Long before the major parliamentary debates in June and August 1968', he was to write, 'Nigeria had replaced Vietnam as our major overseas preoccupation. It took up far more of my time, and that of ministerial colleagues, and far more moral wear and tear than any other issue.'[65]

London was concerned to get both sides to negotiate, and a ceasefire remained the prerequisite. Wilson sent Lord Hunt, of Mount Everest fame, to Nigeria in July, to investigate the need for relief, but Lagos insisted that relief could only go into the eastern region by road or on daylight flights. The issue was debated when parliament was recalled during the summer recess.

Wilson blamed the continuation of the war on French military aid to Biafra, and continued to send arms to the federal government. Ojukwu expressed interest in a temporary ceasefire in December for tactical reasons, but Gowon, with the military advantage, favoured a political settlement. The federal head of state did not attend the 1969 commonwealth conference, and informal pressure was exerted, unsuccessfully, on the Biafran representatives in London to talk.

The war intensified. The federal military government used Egyptian pilots on bombing missions, which proved disastrous for its cause. Wilson had failed to arrange a Christmas visit, but the prime minister, with Lord Hunt in his party, flew to Lagos on Thursday, 27 March to meet Gowon. The now-famous *Fearless* was stationed for a possible meeting with Ojukwu. Wilson persuaded the federal government to stop bombing, and also visited relief centres and hospitals in territory formerly held by Ojukwu. The secessionist leader finally declined Wilson's invitation to meet outside Nigeria, and the British party flew to Ethiopia on Monday, 31 March, for talks in Addis Ababa with the emperor, Haile Selassie, who was attempting to mediate in the civil war. Wilson left for London on 2 April, '[his] own private hesitations [having] been removed by what [he] had seen and learnt during [his] visit'.[66]

The federal military government insisted in July that planes flying into Biafra at night should land for inspection. In the first days of 1970 the federal government finally won its civil war, Ojukwu fleeing to the Ivory Coast. Relief for the defeated Ibos was stepped up, but Wilson was only prepared to increase the number of foreign observers to ensure that the victorious troops behaved themselves in reconquered territory. He had not wavered in the support he lent the federal government, and foisted responsibility on the labour party for the long, slow destruction of Biafra.

Wilson had had an overall majority of five or less in his first parliament. He had been reelected party leader unopposed on 26 October 1964 for the duration, George Brown being confirmed as deputy leader. Ted Short, the chief whip, announced that pairing would be restricted, junior and senior ministers being required to attend the house where parliamentary business wended its way late at night. Wilson asked for no special privileges. With a former Bevanite as prime minister, left-wing MPs quickly formed the Tribune group. Its relationship with the paper was to be informal, but the group had little difficulty in operating openly as a parliamentary faction.

Trouble broke out in the party in early 1965 over Vietnam. That December, sixty-eight labour MPs signed a telegram to Wilson, when he was in Washington to meet Johnson, protesting about the bombing. There was a major storm over foreign office support for the United States in a meeting of the parliamentary party, Wilson telling his own backbenchers, on 8 February, that they should also address their calls for peace to Hanoi. But it was opposition to steel nationalization in 1965 which had the greatest impact on government policy. The third major issue was immigration, the adoption of tory controls being considered anathema by many labour MPs. When the − conservative − speaker of the house died in September, Wilson had to put Dr Horace King, a labour member, into the chair. It was Herbert Bowden who pulled off the coup in getting a liberal to become deputy chairman of ways and means. Wilson chose when to end the short parliament though his majority had dropped to one, the government having avoided a major defeat in the lobbies for nearly eighteen months.

His problems really began in the 1966 parliament, when the government had a safe majority. The prime minister soon found a new chief whip in John Silkin. With Crossman as lord president, the parliamentary party came under a new style of management. The cohort of over seventy new labour MPs also altered the political character of the party. 'The majority', Wilson was to write, 'seemed to feel more strongly on racial questions and on human rights than on issues which had divided the party in the past, including Vietnam.'[67] They began inauspiciously by helping reelect Wilson and

Brown on 18 April for the duration of the parliament. But in early 1968 ninety labour MPs were to ask Wilson to break with the United States, when he was off once again to discuss Vietnam with the president. Silkin was soon faced with the problem of incomes policy, with labour abstentions during the passage of the bill after the July measures. When the government sought to renew its powers in May 1967, the parliamentary party voted 205 to 42 to back the government. But in the defence debate on 28 February 1968, despite the promise of cutbacks, some sixty-two members of the parliamentary party abstained. Wilson read the riot act at the next party meeting on Thursday, 2 March, castigating the left for abstaining in the knowledge that the government would not fall. He also criticized some on the right who were trying to provoke the leadership to tighten up discipline. Every dog was allowed one bite, said Wilson, after which the owner might not renew the licence. He had told the cabinet that morning that 'none of the[se] dissidents would be in Parliament at all ... if it wasn't for him; they had queued up to have their photos taken with him for election purposes.'[68] Crossman and Silkin had been running a liberal regime in this parliament, to the disgust of Manny Shinwell, the chairman, and his friend, George Wigg. The lord president and Shinwell had clashed at a party meeting on 26 January, and Crossman threatened to resign after the dog licence speech if Shinwell was not sacked. Crossman attacked the disciplinarians in the party in a public speech on 8 March. Wilson tried to mediate by backing Crossman and Silkin, Shinwell eventually resigning on 15 March, to be replaced by Douglas Houghton. The common market was debated at three meetings of labour MPs from November 1966, 'a very clear majority support[ing] British entry and an early application'.[69] When the post-devaluation economic package secured parliamentary approval on 18 January 1968, twenty-six labour MPs, including Michael Foot, abstained. John Silkin moved immediately to withdraw the whip, but Wilson saved the situation by bringing forward the proposed new code of conduct. It would allow members to abstain on matters of personal conviction, but not votes of confidence.

Harold Wilson was more concerned about threats to his premiership from within the cabinet. After his two leadership contests with Brown, he came to see Callaghan as his potential rival. He kept him at the treasury, disregarding Crossman's advice to make him leader of the house. When Wilson went off to Moscow during the July 1966 economic crisis, and ministers mobilized for and against devaluation, it was Brown, rather than Callaghan, who momentarily considered ousting the prime minister. Crossman thought the following month that Callaghan had ambitions to be prime minister, and Wilson continued to keep his eye on the chancellor. Roy Jenkins emerged as a new rival, Crossman describing him in November 1966 as 'the most conspiratorial member of the Cabinet'.[70] He became more powerful when moved to the treasury after devaluation. George Brown soon dropped out of the running, though he remained deputy leader. Callaghan had been elected party treasurer at the 1967 conference, and this made him a considerable threat to Wilson. He had to be kept at the home office after he resigned as chancellor, to prevent him causing mischief on the back-benches. Wilson 'talk[ed] brutally frankly about the power set-up in the Cabinet', to Crossman and Castle, plus Marcia Williams, in April 1968: 'I will break his heart', the prime minister said. 'It may be the other way round. "He will break ours first," [Castle] retorted.'[71] The main conspiratorial threat to Wilson came from the 1963 club, 'a dining club of old supporters of Hugh Gaitskell'.[72] Christopher Mayhew had been asked to '"keep an eye on Harold"'. Mayhew believed that the death of Gaitskell 'was a major turning-point for the Labour movement. From this moment, its fortunes and integrity began their long decline.'[73] Mayhew was peeved at not being made a foreign office minister in 1964, feeling that his support for the Palestinian people was inimical to Wilson's 'unqualified commitment to Israel'.[74] He became navy minister under Denis Healey, though he was excluded from OPD, and quickly found Wilson's goal of defence cuts incompatible with remaining east of Suez. Mayhew resigned from the government shortly before the 1966 election, along with the first sea lord, over the phasing out of aircraft carriers in the following decade. He would later contrast Gaitskell, the 'doer', with Wilson, the 'be-er'. 'Gaitskell was committed to social democracy and the Atlantic Alliance. Wilson – witness the famous photograph of the short-trousered schoolboy in Downing Street – was committed to taking up residence at No. 10 and staying there as long as possible.'[75] Mayhew set out to evict the prime minister shortly after devaluation, while working on a book which was to be published in 1969 as *Party Games*. He 'had decided not only to work for a reformed party but for a subsequent alliance of moderate members of all three parties'.[76] The leader was to be Roy Jenkins.

Mayhew went to see the new chancellor on 19 December 1967. 'I thought', he recorded in his diary, 'the two essential things were for the anti-Wilson, anti-left Cabinet Ministers to stick together, and for them to be supported by a very discreet group of militant back-benchers, having no overt contact with himself.' Jenkins did not think Wilson could be unseated immediately, but the prime minister was considered weak on the issues of 'party discipline', and 'the major national problem of trade unions and wage restraint'.[77]

Mayhew had twelve supporters at a meeting of the 1963 club that evening, including Jack Diamond, Dick Taverne, Neil McDermott [sic], Dennis Howell, Bill Rodgers and Dickson Mabon – all junior ministers. Taverne – still at the home office – was the only real activist. Jenkins told Mayhew on 22 January 1968 that little could be expected from within the cabinet, and 'he thought Jim (Callaghan) was a bit jealous of himself'.[78] Wilson's overthrow would have to be promoted by a backbench conspiracy.

Mayhew then brought together 'a discreet group of ten militant back-benchers' – Gordon Walker, who did not leave the cabinet until April, Bill Rodgers, a foreign office junior minister until July, Austen Albu, a former junior minister, Dick Taverne, who moved to the treasury on 6 April, Ivor Richard, David Marquand, Carol Johnson, David Ginsburg and Will Howie. They met secretly, initially at the Gayfere Street home of Roy Hattersley, a junior labour minister, and later at Richard's chambers in Middle Temple. This group canvassed secretly among over 100 labour MPs, finding 35 certainties, 39 probables, 63 possibles, and 7 unknowns. The certainties included David Owen, Bob McLennan, Brian Walden, Douglas Jay and Woodrow Wyatt. Mayhew took the list to Jenkins in late May 1968. The two wanted to ditch the left in the party, and believed a Jenkins-led party could attract the liberals, by embracing 'far-reaching constitutional reform'.[79] The chancellor did not want 'to do a Ramsay MacDonald'[80] and break as a minority, but Harold Wilson provided no precipitating issue during the summer on which he equivocated or sided with the left. When Wilson embraced the idea of trade-union reform, Jenkins had to support his leadership.

This was the issue which brought Callaghan back into the political ring. He had been approached in June by thirteen labour MPs asking him to stand against Wilson, and Mayhew talked to the home secretary on a plane from Glasgow in December. Callaghan, with his copy of *Farmers' Weekly*, ruminated about the 150 acres farm he had bought recently in the Sussex Weald, but all ambition was not spent. He suggested March 1969 had to be a deadline for a change of leader, in time for the next general election. 'He ... went on to say that the future leader must be well in with the trade unions and the party and people told him that Roy carried no weight in these circles.' Mayhew suggested that Callaghan and Jenkins should join forces, simply to bring down Wilson at a meeting of the parliamentary party. The chancellor and home secretary could then fight it out for the leadership. Callaghan promised to think about it over Christmas, but never got back to the Jenkins's camp. 'I guessed', recalls Mayhew, 'that Callaghan had decided on a different course, that he would win substantial union and party support ... and in due course go for the party leadership against both Wilson and Jenkins.'[81]

Sixteen attended a 1963 club dinner, sometime in the week beginning Monday, 28 April. The prime minister replaced John Silkin as chief whip on 29 April with Bob Mellish, a disciplinarian who had the support of Shinwell. Wilson also agreed to the idea of an inner cabinet to pull the government together. Tony Crosland was present at the club dinner. He had not been involved in previous conspiracies, but 'opened ... with a very frank statement to the effect that at the proper time Harold must be got rid of'.[82] Crosland had been a Callaghan man, and his relations with Jenkins varied. His dinner companions were keen to make a move, and Dick Taverne, still at the treasury, even suggested Friday week, 9 May. Labour was universally expected to do badly in the borough elections. Mayhew sent his colleagues off to update their lists, but was not optimistic. 'My guess was that fewer people today would be willing to strike against Harold, because of the confusion over the Industrial Relations Bill and the lack of a clear successor.'[83]

The prime minister quickly got wind of the conspiracy, noting on 30 April that 'the professional WMG [Wilson Must Go] group was also at work',[84] but he was more concerned about the left. Barbara Castle was furious about the sacking of John Silkin, and discussed with Richard Crossman unseating the prime minister. Crossman had supported the change, and Castle wrote the prime minister 'a really stinking letter'.[85]

This – temporary – political break had a profound impact on Wilson. He feared the left uniting with the right. He even took to his bed, complaining of a gastric disorder as a result of a state dinner, though others thought he had a hangover. There was talk in the lobbies of a round-robin of 100 labour MPs on Thursday, 1 May. Crossman spoke to Wilson late that night, Barbara Castle apparently not being present. He had just brought James Callaghan into his inner cabinet. 'For the first time since I have known him', recorded Crossman, 'Harold was frightened and unhappy, unsure of himself, needing his friends. The great india-rubber, unbreakable, undepressable Prime Minister was crumpled in his chair.'[86] Wilson made – what he modestly calls – 'one or two dispositions'[87] to rally the left. News of a ferment against the prime minister dominated the media on Friday and through the weekend, but a speech by Crossman at Yardley, on 2 May, defending Wilson's leadership may have raised his spirits. He would have been less pleased to know that Brian Walden, meeting Crossman on the train to Birmingham, had tried to recruit him to the anti-Wilson cause. Wilson bounced back at a May Day rally at the Royal Festival Hall on Sunday, 4 May, telling the London Labour Party: 'I know what's going on. I'm going on.'[88]

Jenkins had been in Washington that week, and was not considered to be involved in the conspiracy. Mayhew went to see him at number 11, possibly on Monday, 5 May, believing 'there was a good chance of getting Harold out over the weekend'.[89] Three backbenchers planned to publish a letter in the Sunday press, calling for a meeting of the parliamentary party to consider the leadership. Their supporters would then endorse this call. Mayhew saw Callaghan as the frontrunner, 'with the support of the left and the old-fashioned trade union types',[90] but the chancellor was not uninterested in being promoted for leader. 'Roy ... said there was no hope for the party under the kind of backward-looking traditional leadership Jim would provide. We had to break out with a fresh image or we were lost.'[91] He was very keen on Callaghan being stopped, and Mayhew felt this had to be done at cabinet level. Jenkins conspired with Wilson, Crossman, and Castle, to rein in Callaghan, before a meeting of the new inner cabinet on the afternoon of Thursday, 8 May. The canvassing returns requested by Mayhew proved disappointing: only 48 out of 138 MPs approached were prepared to come out now against Wilson. Some were still for taking an initiative to strengthen the possibility of a future social democratic breakaway, but Bill Rodgers and David Marquand were opposed.

Harold Wilson's premiership had come under threat from another bizarre quarter in May 1968, 'the *coup d'etat* that never was'[92] associated with Lord Mountbatten.

Cecil King – a nephew of the press barons Northcliffe and Harmsworth – had become chairman of IPC in 1963. IPC owned the *Daily Mirror* and other papers, and King immediately cast himself in the role of kingmaker. Wilson had lunched on the fourteenth floor at Ludgate Circus, and enjoyed being returned to Westminster in King's Rolls, although he took the precaution of wearing spectacles, and stepping out before reaching the house. King forcefully backed labour in the 1964 election, flying a party pendant on his limousine. Wilson sought repeatedly to put King in the lords, largely out of a desire to retain the support of the *Mirror*, and even wanted to bring him into the government. The chairman of IPC would settle for nothing less than an hereditary peerage, and claims he began to lose faith in the prime minister from mid-1965. His group of newspapers supported the labour party, albeit less enthusiastically, in the 1966 election, but King's deputy, Hugh Cudlipp, remained wedded to supporting the government. King referred to the possibility of 'a National Government'[93] in a letter to Wilson on 25 June, though he was still seeking to strengthen the prime minister's leadership. With his intimate political lunches for two, King soon decided that Wilson had to go, 'owing to the government of the country being in a horrible mess'.[94]

Word of this must have reached the prime minister by November. The *Mirror* became increasingly critical of the government, especially over the D-notices affair in 1967. Devaluation made things worse for Wilson, and the paper planned a 'Wilson Must Go!' campaign for the beginning of 1968, which was supplanted by a build-up of Roy Jenkins. King was a part-time director of the bank of England, and decided there would have to be an emergency government. This he discussed with Cudlipp. The prime minister considered the idea of a national government 'fatuous',[95] and criticized Lords Shawcross and Robens for endorsing it. The institute of directors' periodical flippantly suggested a government of businessmen to run Great Britain Ltd.

King expected a second devaluation by the summer, and, after labour had done badly in local government elections, he steered the *Daily Mirror* against the prime minister on Friday, 10 May. Under the title 'ENOUGH IS ENOUGH', King argued that 'a fresh start under a new leader' was necessary given the threat of 'the greatest financial crisis in our history'.[96] 'I had neither the power to suppress', claims Cudlipp, 'nor the ammunition to negotiate yet another postponement'[97] of King's hostility to Wilson. King appeared on both the BBC and ITV that evening. He had written his resignation from the bank. Roy Jenkins received it on 9 May, but did not inform Wilson in Bristol.

Crossman countered on behalf of the government, portraying King as another megalomaniacal press lord given to dictating to prime ministers. The immediate effect was to strengthen Wilson's leadership, Marcia Williams 'preserv[ing] for posterity a box file of fascinating letters from all over the country commenting on the occasion'.[98] King himself was replaced at the end of the month by Hugh Cudlipp in a palace revolution.

There was more to the incident. Cudlipp, then acting with King, had run into Lord Mountbatten in the early summer of 1967, two years after he quit Whitehall. The former chief of the defence staff had drafted a maiden speech for the lords on the eve of the 1966 election, protesting about the cuts in aircraft carriers, and Wilson was relieved when Mountbatten decided not to speak. The prime minister continued to use the queen's uncle in a number of ways. Mountbatten declined to go to Rhodesia as governor, but he accepted a request from Roy Jenkins to head an inquiry into prison security. Mountbatten confirmed to Cudlipp that someone had suggested 'our present style of government might be in for a change',[99] but it is not clear who this might have been.

Cudlipp met Mountbatten the following spring, at the latter's request, at his country home, Broadlands, in Hampshire. The two discussed the decline of the nation on the morning of Monday, 6 May. 'What he was hoping for was a massive resurgence of the British spirit',[100] Mountbatten wondering if Barbara Castle would become a national leader. He agreed to talk to King and Cudlipp the following Wednesday, in his London flat. Perhaps to cover himself, he asked Solly Zuckerman, the government's scientific adviser and a friend, also to attend at 4.30 p.m. According to three of the four principals present that afternoon, King asked Mountbatten to head a government of national unity. 'He explained that in the crisis he foresaw as being just around the corner the Government would disintegrate, there would be bloodshed in the streets, the armed forces would be involved. The people would be looking to somebody like Lord Mountbatten as the titular head of a new administration.'[101] The latter turned to

Zuckerman, who described the idea as 'rank treachery'. He advised Mount-batten to have nothing to do with it, and stormed out of the flat. King and Cudlipp left shortly afterwards, when Mountbatten, according to his official biographer, Philip Ziegler, 'courteously but firmly stat[ed] that he could not even contemplate such a proposition'.[102] King's version was to be excluded from his diary published in 1972. He maintained that Mount-batten made the running, stressing that the queen was anxious about the state of the country. Morale in the army was low, and petitions being sent to Buckingham Palace were being forwarded to the home office. There is some evidence of a cabinet office – meaning MI5 – investigation: 'No military personnel were discovered to be directly involved.'[103]

It is unlikely that the former chief of the defence staff was committed to a *coup d'état* in 1968. King noted in his diary that 'Dickie does not really have his ear to the ground or understand politics ... He has no wish to intervene anyway.'[104] Mountbatten wrote 'dangerous nonsense!'[105] in his entry for that day. He was to rebuff King again in July 1970. But Zuckerman would note in his diary in 1975, 'Dickie was really intrigued by Cecil King's suggestion that he should become the boss man of a "government".'[106] He might have become more implicated in King's fantasy without Zuckerman. 'There is an ocean of difference', argues Mountbatten's biographer, 'between playing idly with the idea of taking power if it were offered in an emergency, and plotting actively to attain it. Nobody at the meeting said anything to suggest that a *coup d'état* was necessary or even possible, still less that steps should be taken to make it more likely. A collapse of authority was the danger to be feared, not the end to be sought.'[107] Philip Ziegler is correct to pour cold water on the stories of a military conspiracy, but it remains the case that a member of the royal family discussed replacing a labour government. There is no evidence that he reported the incident to Wilson, but he told Cudlipp in early June: '"By the way, I reported all that conversation to Her Majesty."'[108]

Mountbatten was to express a very different view of Wilson in 1974. Returning together from Dublin in November, he told the prime minister of a recent discussion of national government at a dinner at the eleven club. It was the opinion that Wilson was occupied balancing left and right in the labour party, 'whereas what he ought to be doing was keeping together all the people of good faith who wanted to see the monarchy and democracy survive and to prevent the Communists getting control through the trade unions'.[109] *Private Eye* began to hint at the story of the 1968 coup that never was in 1975, and Cudlipp published his autobiography late the following year, seeking to dissociate himself from King throughout the Wilson government. Mountbatten appears to have asked him to remove any reference to 1968, and he, Cudlipp, and finally Zuckerman agreed a version of events. Cudlipp deleted any reference to the queen being informed. 'This was a remark made to you in utmost confidence',[110] Mountbatten wrote. He showed Wilson the correspondence in November 1975, and this may have been the first the prime minister heard of the meeting. Zuckerman seems to have told Wilson of Cudlipp's autobiography at the Savoy on 11 February 1976. When Wilson was made a knight of the garter, Mountbatten noted in his diary: 'To have a Labour Prime Minister ... is an excellent idea to keep a balance between parties and classes.'[111]

In opposition, Harold Wilson had handled the media well. He was on good terms with the lobby at Westminster, though he only had party news to feed his favourite print journalists. He found the British press to be predominantly pro-tory. Wilson saw television as an alternative means of communication, and one more suitable for a labour party leader. Broadcasting was less apposite at conveying political messages, but he was more concerned with appearance and style. Television showed well the contrast between the man of the people, Wilson, and the establishment, represented by Douglas-Home.

Harold Wilson preferred ITV from the first. It had sympathetic company bosses, such as Sidney Bernstein at Granada, and its content was regulated by a statutory independent television authority (the ITA). ITV was widely perceived as the popular, and therefore more working-class, station. Little did Wilson realize that, where ITV trod, the BBC, by the logic of competition, would have to follow, and that television populism could be turned against a labour government.

Wilson's entry into Downing Street signalled 'the start of a brand new era of electronic politics',[112] with the prime minister seeking to associate himself with everything dynamic and modern in Britain. Typical of his style would be his appearance in Liverpool, on Saturday, 23 July 1966, just after the government had gone for deflation, to reopen the Cavern Club. The prime minister, who was accompanied by Gerald Kaufman, 'seized the opportunity to deliver a speech'; he mentioned the Beatles and others, giving 'the impression that ... [he] was quite a friend of these luminaries'.[113] Richard Ingrams, editor of *Private Eye*, was to attend a party at number 10 as late as February 1970. '"Y'know", [Wilson] said earnestly, looking round at the extraordinary assortment of guests that included Cliff Michelmore, Iris Murdoch and Morecambe and Wise, "There are people here from all walks of life – artists, musicians, sculptors. Jack Kennedy's parties at the White House had nothing on this!"'[114] Camelot might have crossed the Atlantic in the 1960s, but this was little more than a synthetic froth on a deeply unhappy relationship between the labour prime minister and the national, particularly electronic, media.

Harold Wilson had set out to cultivate the Westminster lobby at number 10 from 1964, even taking many of the daily meetings himself. But the fact that his press secretary, Trevor Lloyd-Hughes, came from a provincial paper seems to have annoyed more senior journalists from the national press. The prime minister recruited Gerald Kaufman in 1965 from the *New Statesman*, though he was appointed technically 'parliamentary press liaison officer' with an office in 12 Downing Street. Kaufman was to be Wilson's real press secretary, and one of his most loyal courtiers. But he could do little with a tory press, and, as for other publications, getting a good story, even if it meant challenging the authority of the prime minister, became the priority. Wilson quickly developed an antipathy to Anthony Howard, appointed Whitehall correspondent by the *Sunday Times*. The prime minister ordered he be boycotted. Ministers were also instructed to only give interviews with a civil servant present. But members of Wilson's cabinet continued to talk to the press on the phone at home, or at the many social engagements where politicans and journalists rubbed shoulders. The prime minister was unable to do anything about such contacts, on the part of what were, after all, party rivals. Wilson took, in time, to lecturing his colleagues at the beginning of cabinet meetings, behaving like the civil servant manqué he was, with increasing signs of paranoia.

As for the broadcasting media, initial advantage appeared to lie with the new prime minister as the potential maker of news. While the traditional BBC might have had difficulty adjusting to a parvenu Wilson, the corporation was already being reshaped by a dynamic director general, Hugh Greene, who quickly realized that even the state television station had to get into the business of satisfying popular demand. By the time Wilson entered Downing Street, 'the BBC was ... firmly committed to the needs of the nation as an audience, not to the needs of the nation as represented by government or opposition.'[115] The growing professionalism of producers and presenters, based on the establishment of lucrative career paths, saw increasing priority given to getting the story. Initially, Greene's style of management was considered in tune with the opening up of Britain which labour promised. When this government quickly moved to assert managerial control, it lost the sympathy of increasing numbers of cultural workers.

'The Labour party's disenchantment with the BBC, quick to follow their election to office in 1964, sprang from the shock of discovering that the BBC now behaved towards them exactly as it had towards the Conservative party since the mid-1950s.'[116] Harold Wilson came to see the BBC as biased against labour, failing to perceive that prime ministers of either party were becoming fair game for ambitious broadcasters. His early programme criticisms to Broadcasting House were not widely circulated by editors and controllers. Wilson's honeymoon with print and broadcasting journalists lasted just about into 1966, though the tory press backed the untelegenic Ted Heath in the general election. Richard Crossman observed towards the end of the campaign: 'If you want to get Party policy across, you need party political broadcasts to contrast with television's own treatment of the election, which concentrates so on personalities and leadership and gimmicks that the viewer gets a picture of bickering politicians and no real understanding of the issues involved.'[117] Harold Wilson failed to appreciate that sound, but especially vision, were more than an antidote to the conservative press; they were means of communication with their own structures and values. But he was the first electronic prime minister, playing along with television as it became the centre of cultural attention.

Harold Wilson slighted the BBC on the train back from Liverpool after the 1966 election. It had a mobile studio on board, as did independent television news (ITN), whose editor, Geoffrey Cox, had been introduced to Wilson by George Wigg. The prime minister gave his interview to ITN, the commercial channel being the first to broadcast to the nation from a moving train. There followed a series of incidents in 1966–7 – the seamen's strike, the putative July plot, and especially the D-notices affair – which made Wilson increasingly angry. The BBC was to suffer prime ministerial ire. He began his speech to the 1968 party conference on an – unscripted – sarcastic note, thanking delegates 'for what the BBC, if they are true to their usual form, will tonight describe as a hostile reception'.[118] 'The BBC were terribly upset',[119] and Sir Hugh Greene came to believe Wilson 'had an almost paranoid belief in plots'.[120]

When the chairman of the BBC, Lord Normanbrook, died in mid-1967, Wilson chose a politician, Lord Hill, to succeed him. Hill, a former conservative minister, and then chairman of the ITA, was hastily summoned to Wilson's room in the commons on 26 July, to be told that 'the press had got wind of what was in [the prime minister's] mind'.[121] If just about everyone, including Hill, was surprised at this appointment, Wilson was to be disappointed at what he took to be Hill's failure to rein in the BBC. 'He ceased to be a politician', in the opinion of a Wilson aide, 'and became a television Chairman.'[122] (Hill's job at the ITA was given to Herbert Bowden, who left the cabinet to take control of the other channel.)

When Hill was summoned to Downing Street on 9 December 1969, after a *Panorama* programme on Biafra, Wilson 'recited from his extraordinary memory all the items of difference of recent years that [Hill] had heard so often before, plus a few [he] had not heard.'[123] But it was the labour prime minister who had done most of the damage to himself, not least in his devaluation speech on television. The medium which had hitherto shown the adept politician, now revealed a cornered prime minister. He might have been trying to conjure optimism out of reality, but many ordinary people considered he was simply lying. Those who live by television, it might be argued, also perish by the same means.

The Westminster lobby had been banned from Downing Street sometime after the 1966 election, the prime minister becoming increasingly annoyed at political attacks in the papers. He had first taken umbrage at some articles by Nora Beloff in the *Observer*, and tried to stop ministers talking to her. James Margach, who worked for the *Sunday Times*, suggests it was because she wrote about the kitchen cabinet, and the influence of Marcia Williams. Beloff, as she told Tony Crosland towards the end of 1968, was being exiled to Washington for a year, her editor, David Astor, declining to report the prime minister to the press council. Wilson then tried to negotiate the relationship, inviting senior executives and journalists from a particular paper to dinner at Chequers on a Sunday evening, or lunch at Downing Street. At one of these Chequers dinners, in reply to a question from Lord Thomson who was then proposing to buy *The Times*, Wilson suggested a new proprietor should get rid of four journalists, including David Wood the political correspondent (this is unlikely to have been a joke). Senior members of the lobby were eventually invited each fortnight, for a discussion with the prime minister in the white boudoir, one of the state rooms at number 10, but this only caused offence to the journalists excluded. Wilson continued to talk off the record, trying to explain the complexities of problems he handled. He could not resist showing off, and confided in the fourth estate to orchestrate popular presentation. When Alastair Hetherington was asked by the prime minister why he had not used a piece of information, the editor of the *Guardian* replied: 'But Harold, you told me it was confidential.'[124] Wilson had also used Crossman to do his leaking, until the lord president, an habitual talker, broke off relations with certain journalists in early 1968. Wilson railed against leaks in cabinet, but his ministers knew he was briefing from his own point of view, and sometimes against his colleagues. 'I brief, you leak'[125] must have been observed by wags.

The prime minister had even established a committee on leaks under the lord chancellor, Lord Gardiner reporting in September 1967 of one such incident that 'there had been no deliberate leaking of ... information'.[126] He had to run investigations repeatedly for Wilson, and a procedure involving questionnaires and interviews was established. Discussing the press in April 1968 with David Astor, editor/proprietor of the *Observer*, Wilson showed that '"[his] people"'[127] were keeping an eye on journalists contacting members of the cabinet. After listening to Wilson fulminating about his enemies in the cabinet two months later, Barbara Castle noted that 'sometimes [she thought] he [was] going mildly off his rocker'.[128]

The full lobby was invited back to number 10 on a daily basis in 1969, when Wilson once again reorganized his press office in time for the election. It was during this summer that the prime minister had extensive dental work done, press photographs showing, from September, a glistening row of crowned teeth. Joe Haines had come from the *Sun* to act as Lloyd-Hughes's deputy, and replaced the prime minister's press secretary six months later. Gerald Kaufman was to remain at Wilson's elbow until the end, though he would be a candidate in the general election. Haines believes he was selected because Wilson thought he would be sympathetic. 'I don't pretend to have been impartial', says Haines. 'Everybody who knew me, knew that I was a socialist councillor, for example, that I was an active member of the Labour Party.'[129] The new press secretary was not in agreement with the government's trade-union policy, but he proved a better manager of the lobby. Wilson began to feel happier with his press coverage, though the personalization of politics saw the prime minister of Britain portrayed as 'cunning, devious, a liar and a cheat'.[130]

The year 1968 was to acquire a meaning for extra-constitutional, and even revolutionary, politics, Harold Wilson becoming an icon of failure in this universe. The phenomenon of 1960s' revolt owed much to students, drawn from the middle and working classes. Annual cohorts of post-war baby boomers were being pushed through the expanding institutions of higher education, in order to become functionaries in an increasingly organized society. It was a highly competitive generation, waves of boys and girls having been failed by the education system, and not a few of the more successful rebelling. Some of the middle-class children of the affluent society revolted against their parents.

The political year began in Paris in May, when student demonstrations stimulated wider working-class activity. This threatened the political system, including the communist party, and nearly brought down de Gaulle. There was also a significant student movement in Germany. Cecil King wrote of the impact of the May events on Britain: 'Though widely regarded as a pessimist, I now think the tunnel we are entering longer and darker than I had supposed.'[131] Members of the labour government would have concurred, though Richard Crossman considered they were 'living through the most momentous year that [he] could remember since the war'.[132] He even invoked the spirit of 1848, and considered he might be the chronicler of the last days of the British ancien régime. As on most things, Crossman was to change his mind about the class of 1968. This was also the time Anthony Wedgwood Benn began to try to rethink British socialism in a series of lectures, beginning with a speech on popular democracy in Llandudno on 25 May. Wilson dismissed this initiative, and sought to restrain his former acolyte. Wedgwood Benn attended the 'free university' in Bristol in June, there being sessions on revolution, black power and Vietnam. 'I realised all of a sudden', the MP for Bristol South-East wrote in his diary, 'that for three and a half or four years I have done absolutely no basic thinking about politics. I have just been a departmental Minister and this is the great gap – this is how parties get ossified and out of touch … I thought they asked a lot of important questions and I enjoyed it. I wasn't recognised. I opened my shirt collar and put on my specs and took off my jacket and nobody took the slightest notice of me.'[133] He suggested to a group of Bristol students twelve days later 'a sit-in one night, starting at about 10 and going on until about 3'.[134] A now plainer Tony Benn succeeded in having his late-night meeting with activists in a student flat in March 1969, his impressions of the sit-in leaders being presented to the inner cabinet at Chequers a year later. Some – perhaps the majority – of these students had 'distrust[ed] the idea [of meeting a member of the government] on principle',[135] though a suggestion that the minister's red box should be purloined was not acted upon.

Protests about the war in Vietnam had impinged on the Wilson administration, with a major anti-war demonstration in Grosvenor Square, close to the United States embassy, on 17 March 1968. Though peace talks with North Vietnam opened in Paris in May, the broad-based Vietnam Solidarity Campaign in London called for a mammoth protest on Sunday, 27 October. A small demonstration in July alarmed the government. 'I urged the Commissioner [of the Metropolitan Police]', recalls Callaghan, 'to review police practice and training to ensure a well thought-out, disciplined approach.'[136] The shadow home secretary demanded that the autumn march should be banned, but Callaghan 'had maintained contact with one or two political friends on the fringes of the preparation, and they told [him] that the main groups organising the demonstration were anxious that it should be non-violent.'[137] The cabinet decided against having troops on standby. Some 30,000 people, according to official figures, marched to Hyde Park in October, a minority attempting to get to the embassy, which was occupied by American marines. The police commissioner had advised the home secretary not to show his face during the demonstration, but Callaghan congratulated the police after they had used force to disperse demonstrators. The home secretary addressed the police federation shortly afterwards, having for many years been its consultant: 'There is a move among a relatively small faction', he said, 'which is anxious to prove, by some inversion of argument, that our tolerance is really repressive. They are determined to show that you are the instruments of repression by provoking you to repress them when they attack you. It is a queer and twisted sense of logic.'[138] At least one civil servant, unlike the student militants, had been reading his Marcuse. This was the political baptism of the class of '68, as it came to be known. While Soviet-style communism was eclipsed abroad by Maoism, it was largely Trotskyism which grew on the far left of the spectrum in Britain. The International Marxist Group and international socialists (later, the socialist workers' party) were the main organizational beneficiaries. They numbered their members only in hundreds and thousands, though the turnover was to be great. The loser was the labour party. Its individual membership had been over a million in the early 1950s, but it dropped throughout Wilson's time in power.

The most important events of 1968 took place in Czechoslovakia, where, following the election of Alexander Dubcek as first secretary of the communist party in January, the Prague spring bloomed. Russian tanks were to reimpose Moscow hegemony on 20/21 August, this being the first crisis of international significance to unfold, blow by blow, on television.

The defence and foreign secretaries, asked in mid-July about Britain's response in the eventuality of a Russian invasion, had replied that the government would do nothing, the Soviet ambassador gathering this from Michael Stewart at the end of the month. Despite a labour party protest in Hyde Park on Sunday, 4 August, addressed by Jennie Lee, George Brown and Richard Crossman, Moscow gave London advance notice of the invasion. Number 10 refused to pass on this information to Wilson in the Scillies by – scrambler – telephone, using the secure teleprinter line to the office which had been set up in the customs house. The prime minister returned to London in the morning, by helicopter and plane, to meet the foreign secretary, who had flown from his holiday at Swanage. Activity, not action, was to be the order of the day. A statement was issued condemning the violation of the united nations' charter, and parliament recalled for the following Monday, 26 August. A special cabinet meeting was summoned, but ministers abroad were not asked to return. 'There wasn't much we could do', noted Tony Benn, 'but we felt we owed it to the Czechs to show that we did care.'[139] The Soviet Union vetoed a security council resolution in New York, but thirteen members voted for the withdrawal of foreign troops from Czechoslovakia. Wilson repaired to Chequers to read statements of condemnation, and prepare a speech 'which, while it could not disguise the impotence of the world outside the Eastern bloc, would express the feelings of members of all parties ... and, still more, the reaction of public opinion throughout the country'.[140] The prime minister came out against a cultural boycott of the Soviet Union, but a tour of Britain by the red army ensemble was cancelled. Wilson spoke of the need for détente in east–west relations. Michael Stewart continued with his plans to visit Romania, the one country in the Warsaw pact which had opposed the invasion.

Czechoslovakia did a great deal to inspire the idea of socialism with a human face. Yugoslavia was ready to condemn the Soviet Union, and many communist parties in western Europe dissociated themselves from Moscow. It was the beginning of the break-up of international communism, though pluralism was mainly a response to political embarrassment. Trotskyism was the beneficiary in Britain. Crossman found the labour party's platform at the Hyde Park platform 'surrounded by a whole mass of red banners, on one side Troskyites and Biafran supporters and on the other Vietnam demonstrators'.[141] Musing subsequently on the disenchantment of the young with social democratic rule, he noted that the labour government, among others, had 'disappointed those who wanted the application of principle to politics'. 'We have shown ourselves competent politicians, administering the country, introducing what social justice we can but not undertaking radical change.'[142] But he dismissed delegates to the party conference as 'unrealistic',[143] when they argued that Czechoslovakia should not lead to a strengthening of NATO. Dubcek was portrayed in the west as the restorer of capitalism, but was to say twenty years after his experiment in socialism that 'the West in the political sense of the word ... was in no way concerned that the Czechoslovak reform movement should succeed. In a way, August 21, 1968 suited them.'[144]

Harold Wilson began to fade on the international stage in 1968, due to the opening of peace talks on Vietnam. Johnson had offered to stop the bombing in a speech at San Antonio the previous September, in return for 'prompt and meaningful talks'[145] with Hanoi. He met Wilson three months later in Australia, at a memorial service for the prime minister Harold Holt, when Johnson, according to Wilson, asked him to sound the Russians on the new American formula, during his visit to Moscow in January 1968. This was hardly a major request on the part of the president, and Johnson does not even mention it in his memoirs. Hanoi responded by saying it would move towards talks if the bombing stopped.

Wilson flew to Moscow on Monday, 22 January, his third visit as prime minister. Kosykin sought to persuade Wilson that the North Vietnamese declaration was a breakthrough. The British prime minister maintained that Johnson was sincere, believing he would be running for office at the end of 1968. Wilson was wrong in this judgement, though he may not have appreciated that some of Johnson's aides were seriously worried about his mental state. These talks were also bedevilled by other American attempts to negotiate with Hanoi, and Wilson left Moscow after two days unaware that a Romanian deputy foreign minister was also involved. There followed the Tet offensive, and the United States embassy in Saigon came under attack. Wilson flew to Washington on Wednesday, 7 February, and argued at a White House dinner that no military solution was possible in Vietnam. Johnson hinted on 9 February that he might call off the bombing, and publicly asked Britain and the Soviet Union on 31 March to help the peace process. The American president also announced in this broadcast that he would not be running again for office. Wilson failed to secure an invitation to return to Moscow, and talks commenced several weeks later in Paris, though the fighting continued. The United States finally halted all bombing on 1 November, this being seen as an attempt by the White House to promote the candidacy of Hubert Humphrey, the vice president, in the presidential elections.

Wilson was keen to resume relations with Moscow after the Soviet invasion of Czechoslovakia in August. Trade had not been stopped, but ministerial visits were restricted. Tony Benn was eventually allowed to go in May 1969, but Michael Stewart asked him to keep off politics. On the eve of departure Benn rang Wilson, asking if he had a personal message for Kosygin. After checking that a private secretary was recording the conversation, the prime minister asked him to convey his warmest greetings to the Soviet leader. '"Although we had had a difficult year, for reasons which we all understood" (referring to the invasion of Czechoslovakia), he now wanted the best possible relations.' Wilson welcomed a Soviet initiative in the middle east, and hoped, with the resignation of de Gaulle, that the Russians would turn more to Britain. British membership of the EEC had been conceived partly in terms of containing Germany. 'I was also', Benn noted, 'to tell Kosygin how much he still regretted the fact that the work they had done together on the Vietnam peace initiative at Chequers in 1967 had not come off.'[146] Benn managed to see the Soviet prime minister, and Kosygin expressed a wish to see Wilson in Moscow in June or July. On the middle east, he 'replied that he wished that Britain was not so dependent on other parties who exercised a negative attitude, which [Benn] took to be a reference to the Americans'.[147]

The American people had – narrowly – voted in November 1968 for Richard Nixon, a man Denis Healey was to describe as 'more lacking in self-confidence than any leading politician I have known'.[148] John Freeman must also have been discomfited. He had just been appointed ambassador to the United States, Wilson having presumably expected a victory for Hubert Humphrey. The president-elect invited Wilson to Washington through an intermediary, wanting 'a really meaningful exchange of views'[149] after his inauguration in January 1969.

Nixon decided to make his first international trip an eight-day visit to the allies in Europe, de Gaulle having relations with Hanoi and Peking which would be useful to the Americans. Nixon flew to London on Monday, 24 February after visiting NATO headquarters in Brussels, and ritualistically endorsed the 'special relationship'. Wilson was meant to accompany Nixon in an American helicopter to Chequers at the insistence of the secret service, but English fog saved the prime minister this indignity. He travelled in Nixon's presidential limousine. The new president was more of an Anglophile than his Texan predecessor. Discussing the commonwealth over dinner at Chequers, Nixon clearly impressed Wilson with his reference to the speaker's whig in Ghana being a British inspiration. Vietnam had been touched on before dinner, but Nixon was concerned mainly with NATO. The highlight of the visit for the president was lunch the next day at

Buckingham Palace. The two leaders had got down to business at number 10 that morning, Nixon recalling a private conversation with Wilson in his study on the first floor: 'A warm fire cast a glow over the room and after a few minutes Wilson leaned back in his chair and put his feet upon the table. He was wearing carpet slippers.'[150] There was another dinner that night in Downing Street, Nixon alluding to the new British ambassador in his toast. He stated he had forgiven Freeman for hostile comments in the *New Statesman* when he was editor. Wilson immediately wrote a message on the back of his menu and passed it to the president: 'That was one of the kindest and most generous acts I have known in a quarter of a century in politics.'[151] 'John Freeman', according to Tony Benn, '[had] apparently made a statement to the effect that he had ceased to be a socialist and to this extent has repudiated his past, but then again Nixon is supposed to have had psychoanalysis and repudiated his, so I suppose it is evens.'[152]

The prime minister had laid on a post-prandial meeting for Nixon and the American ambassador around the cabinet table, suggesting for discussion 'issues of the future, problems of the environment, of young people, of students, of race and colour, of freedom under the law'.[153] Wilson invited the younger members of the cabinet to respond to Nixon's comments. Tony Benn noted his own intervention: '"Mr President, I spend five days a week trying to introduce technology and the other two thinking about the effect this has on society. Young people today are aware of this and they take it for granted; they have nothing to forget, as older people have, and they think we are suffering from acute institutional obsolescence – and I suspect they are right. It is all very well to mock them for not knowing what to do but I am not sure that we know what to do." … I said I had a son of seventeen and had learned more from him than he had from me.'[154] Crossman was eventually asked to wind up. He compared 1968 with 1848, 'the year of unsuccessful revolutions'. Student activists were dismissed now as 'sentimentalists with no understanding of power'. Nixon concluded this bizarre parody of a British cabinet meeting: '"I'll swap our Professor Marcuse any day if you will give me your Professor Crossman."'[155] Wilson had made 'a few rather coarse jibes at Marcuse', only to be 'put … in his place' by Judith Hart.[156] And this in front of the men from Washington. The American president flew on the next morning, continuing 'to dramatize for Americans at home that, despite opposition to the war, their President could still be received abroad with respect and even enthusiasm.'[157]

Later that year, Wilson flew by RAF helicopter to the United States air base at Mildenhall in Suffolk, to meet Nixon on Sunday, 3 August. The American president was dropping in at the end of a world tour, which had included several Asian countries plus Romania. He had been to South Vietnam, and the war was discussed in detail, though British mediation was clearly a thing of the past. The president had proclaimed the Nixon doctrine at Guam, whereby American aid would only be supplied to dependent regimes prepared to put their own forces in the field against aggression, this being a response to the Brezhnev doctrine, under which Moscow reserved its right to intervene in eastern Europe. The meeting with Wilson was a media smokescreen, because Henry Kissinger, the national security adviser, was to have his first secret meeting with the North Vietnamese in Paris the following day. Ho Chi Minh died on 3 September, and it was 4 November before Nixon revealed that Hanoi had rejected negotiations on a settlement. The United States continued to withdraw troops, 60,000 being taken out in 1969 in keeping with its policy of Viet-namization.

Wilson was due to visit the United States in early 1970, and met the president on Tuesday, 27 January, at which the Russian proposal for a conference on European security was considered. Wilson urged that the west should respond favourably, but the main point of the visit seems to have been the British application to join the common market. The United States welcomed this on balance. Wilson, Stewart and Freeman were invited to sit in on a meeting of the national security council the following day, a response to Wilson's mock cabinet meeting. Nixon later rejected a British foreign office plan for the middle east as being too anti-Israeli, but Wilson was not too upset, being equally concerned about his Jewish vote at home. The prime minister slipped on a bathroom floor in the British embassy that afternoon sustaining several minor injuries, shortly before he was due to give a farewell press conference. American and British television audiences saw him with pipe held in front of his mouth 'in order to keep blood off the television screens'![158]

CHAPTER 19

Recovery and Defeat, 1968–70

After devaluation, it was economic management which crucially underlaid the government's performance in domestic and foreign affairs. The new Britain had long been forgotten, and it was a case of trying to solve, as the government saw it, the country's principal economic problem. Wilson would only be able to boast in January 1970 – in the United States – that Britain's balance of payments was coming right. A mixture of public expenditure cuts, budgetary policy, and control of wages was deployed in 1968 to try to make devaluation work.

The public expenditure cuts of £200 million accompanying devaluation had proved insufficiently deflationary, and the new chancellor, Roy Jenkins, informed his colleagues, in early December 1967, that the pound was still under attack. He called for additional cuts of some £800 million, to switch further resources from domestic consumption to industrial exports. Wilson announced a review of 'all major areas of policy, both at home and overseas, where substantial expenditure [was] involved'[1] on 18 December, at the height of the row over arms for South Africa. This had been foreshadowed in the letter of intent to the IMF published on 30 November. Jenkins largely took over the package which had been prepared under Callaghan. Wilson claimed it was to be 'the most difficult public expenditure exercise any Government [had] attempted since the war.'[2] He and the new chancellor had already sketched out a programme after devaluation, to go to a meeting of ministers on 27 December, and the cabinet on 4 and 11 January 1968 – for announcement the following Monday. The goal of the treasury was a balance of payments surplus of £500 million in 1968–9.

Senior ministers assembled at number 10 two days after Christmas, before Wilson went to the Scillies, to discuss the chancellor's 'slaughter [of] some sacred cows in order to appease the bankers'.[3] Wilson and Jenkins had just met the defence chiefs, and cuts in this area were still being worked out. The prime minister and chancellor favoured postponing, from 1971 to 1974, the rise in the school-leaving age to sixteen, and they also wanted to reimpose prescription charges. Wilson was baulking at Jenkins's proposal to renege on the housing target of half a million homes. Crossman had been stimulated by earlier Wilsonian references, about selling Polaris back to the Americans, to suggest cutting the British independent nuclear deterrent. Denis Healey laughed at him. Ending Britain's role east of Suez by 1971, and the cancellation of the American F 111A plane, were to be on the agenda, even though Wilson, ever attentive to the Realpolitik of the special relationship, had been strongly identified with maintaining Britain's world role.

It was feared, towards the end of 1967, that Healey, Callaghan and Brown might be encouraging Cecil King in the anti-Wilson crusade expected in the new year, so Anthony Wedgwood Benn, Tommy Balogh, Peter Shore and Barbara Castle were invited to dine at Richard Crossman's on 3 January 1968. The prime minister's left-wing supporters came up with the idea of an inner cabinet of five, which would be politically balanced, in order to save Wilson from the right. 'But it is unlikely that Harold will agree to this', Wedgwood Benn noted, since the prime minister was 'full of euphoria about his success ... in preventing the South African arms deal and not feeling sufficiently threatened to call in his friends.'[4] The same dozen senior ministers met the following day, but Healey, Callaghan, Brown and Stewart were still resisting defence cuts. They only gained three or four allies in cabinet later, against Wilson and Jenkins, who wanted to pull out entirely from the far east and Persian Gulf. Thomson, Peart, Hughes and Ross were for the status quo of gradual withdrawal as envisaged in the 1967 defence white paper, which had been described as 'the death knell of the British Empire east of Suez'.[5] The prime minister used his casting vote for cancellation of the F 111A.

The cabinet turned to domestic expenditure the following day, a weak Gordon Walker recommending the postponement of schooling to sixteen for two years. 'I am suggesting this in place of the cuts in university expenditure', he said, 'because the universities represent such an influential body of opinion.'[6] Opposition came from Brown and Callaghan, neither of whom had had the benefit of higher education. Harold Wilson proposed exemptions on prescription charges, only two or three ministers voting against any cut. It was decided to keep Concorde.

The cabinet met again on the following Tuesday, Thursday and Friday (twice). George Brown, who had been to the United States, via Japan, reported to the last meeting that the Americans were most concerned about the Persian Gulf, but it was Roy Jenkins who reaffirmed the need for a major reorientation in foreign and defence policy. When the final package was considered by the cabinet on Monday, 15 January, Wilson, having met an angry Lee Kuan Yew of Singapore over the weekend, offered to delay

withdrawal there by nine months until December 1971. He had to struggle
to prevent other items being reconsidered. Thus it was the need to make
devaluation work which speeded Britain's withdrawal from east of Suez,
effectively bringing to an end an age of active imperialism.

Wilson presented the package of cuts to parliament on 16 January 1968,
amounting to over £700 million (£325 million in 1968–9, and £441
million the following year). It was widely considered to be balanced
between military and civil expenditure. The former included closure of bases
in the far east, Persian Gulf, Malaysia and Singapore, the end of aircraft
carriers, and reductions in military and civilian personnel, plus the cancellation of fifty F 111A aircraft. The plan to raise the school-leaving age to
sixteen was put back two years from 1971. Prescription charges were
reimposed at 2s 6d (12^1/2p) per item, and free milk in secondary schools
was abolished. There were also cuts in housing, roads, help for industry and
local government, and a ceiling on central government employment.

The keynote of the package was prescription charges. The chancellor had
argued that £40 million here was worth £140 anywhere else, in the eyes
of international bankers, Wilson telling his colleagues that he had not
favoured the return to free prescriptions. The only cabinet resignation was
Lord Longford, George Brown failing to join him. Michael Foot was
included among the abstainers in the vote two days later, but Jennie Lee
was persuaded to stay in a government which was fast running out of credibility. 'This is a policy which could have been sold positively and dynamically', noted Crossman. 'Cabinet worked on it for thirty hours and now
it has been largely thrown away by Harold's failure to provide the strategic
framework within which the economic cuts should be seen and partly also
by the re-emergence of an open cleavage between left and right.'[7]

The cut back on public expenditure did not impress the city, and
sterling was to suffer during the gold crisis caused by the United States. It
began on Sunday, 10 March, reaching a climax the following weekend. A
second devaluation suddenly became likely when Wilson insisted the
pound had to be maintained against the dollar. Sir Donald MacDougall
describes 1968 as 'a nightmare', given that the balance of payments
worsened after devaluation. 'I began to understand', he recalls, 'how a
country really could go bankrupt and how this could quickly necessitate
controls of all kinds reminiscent of war-time, and risk upsetting our social
fabric if imposed in peace-time.'[8] This was averted when President Johnson
asked Wilson to close the London gold market, which remained shut for
a week. Wilson favoured ending gold's role in the world financial system,
but was forced to accept the American idea of a two-tier price system, which
was agreed at a meeting of finance ministers and central bankers in
Washington. The British suspected Paris had a hand in destabilizing the
dollar, and it looked like the sterling area was breaking up.

Jenkins presented his first budget on Tuesday, 19 March, to cut back on private expenditure. He had wanted it, with the cuts, in February. The budget was a massive deflationary attempt to make devaluation work, his theme being the need for two years' hard slog. There was to be an increase in taxation of £775 million in 1968–9; the standard rate remained the same, but there was a one-year levy on unearned income. Much of the increased revenue was to come from indirect taxation. 'It was the most punishing Budget in Britain's peacetime history ... and, despite its contents, Roy Jenkins received a great ovation ... from both sides of the House.'[9] The chancellor tightened hire purchase payments on 1 November, but it did not avert another sterling crisis, occasioned by rumours of the devaluation of the French franc, and revaluation of the German mark. London urged Bonn to increase the value of its currency, Wilson even summoning the German ambassador to Downing Street. (The mark was not to be revalued until after elections there in late 1969.) The treasury also prepared an import deposit scheme, designed to deter the inflow of industrial goods. Jenkins announced on 22 November that the 10 per cent regulator, which allowed indirect taxes to be increased, was to be activated. There was also further monetary restraint, but this did not stop another round of speculation on Friday, 6 December. *The Times* called for a coalition government the following Monday.

Roy Jenkins's second budget was presented on 15 April 1969, and was designed to increase tax revenue by £270 million in 1969–70. There was no change in indirect taxation – except wine; when the chancellor quipped that this was against his personal inclination, he established an association with claret which was to dog his political career. There were increases in corporation and selective employment tax, but Jenkins improved income tax allowances and rebates. There was also to be relief on a new save as you earn (SAYE) scheme.

Jenkins's third – and last – budget was presented on 14 April 1970 with a general election in the offing. He was to describe it subsequently as 'a bad one economically but good politically'.[10] This time the aim was to reduce the yield from taxation by some £200 million, the allowances on income and surtax being increased, and stamp duty abolished. There were many minor changes, but the chancellor relied upon a too optimistic forecast for growth. 'Jenkins settled for a mildly reflationary budget whereas we should have had a more expansionary one.'[11] The chancellor's speech was a resumé of his economic management in the preceding two years: public-sector borrowing had been turned round in 1969–70; there had been an increase in the gross national product due to export-led growth; the balance of payments had come into surplus in 1969–70 with the rapid growth in world trade. 'It was clear that the balance of payments had really been solved'[12] by the summer of 1969, and there was to be a visible surplus for the year 1970. The board of trade had discovered, in May 1969, that exports had gone under-recorded for six years, and further statistical deficiencies were to be discovered in late 1970. It was 1971 before the true economic position under labour became available. The accumulated deficit had been £817 million, or £306 million on current account. 'In our five years', Wilson was to write, 'with a small total deficit, the movement was improving, reaching, in the final year, an all-time record surplus.'[13]

The government had operated its wages standstill in the wake of the July 1966 measures, followed by the period of severe restraint in 1967 with a norm of zero. Michael Stewart was responsible for implementing this tough policy, but Ray Gunter, at labour, preferred the TUC's voluntary approach to industrial relations. The statutory powers to freeze wages and prices expired in August 1967, when Peter Shore took over at the DEA.

A second act in 1967 extended the original part two, on compulsory notification of proposed increases, the government having declined to impose a norm from 1 July. A DEA scheme for controlling the outcome of plant bargaining was rejected by cabinet, on the initiative of George Brown, but Jenkins was adamant that there had to be some sort of incomes policy to appease the bankers. It was March 1968 before the government agreed a ceiling of 3.5 per cent on pay increases, the exception being an improvement in productivity. This was to run through to the end of 1969, Wilson wanting to avoid October 1970 when there might be an election. A third act in 1968 extended compulsory notification for that period.

Wilson made Barbara Castle first secretary of state in April 1968, in charge of a new department of employment and productivity. This was a revamped ministry of labour, from which Gunter was shifted. It took over responsibility for prices and incomes from the DEA, the latter being abolished eventually in October 1969. Shore had wanted more powers to control prices and incomes. 'This might have been accepted in wartime but was quite impossible in peacetime ... It was obviously impractical and, for this reason, he lost responsibility for prices and incomes policy.'[14]

The TUC had voted against such a policy in 1967, and by '1969 trade union acceptance of an incomes policy effectively dwindled to the point of no significant contribution.'[15] TUC vetting of member unions' claims had proved less than universal, not least because an early attempt to help the low paid proved divisive. The prime minister had to struggle to retain the support of the parliamentary party, a varying minority remaining totally opposed to a statutory incomes policy. The vote on 15 May 1968 was 205 to 42 in favour of the third bill, with the Tribune group organizing the opposition.

The 1967 party conference had supported the government, but when Jenkins and Castle put the case to the 1968 conference, Frank Cousins won support, by 5,098,000 votes to 1,124,000, for opposing the use of the law in collective bargaining. Castle had a socialist commitment to the planning of incomes, and waded into the process of wage determination while also fighting price rises. The secretary of state for employment and productivity also advocated productivity agreements. At the end of the year, Crossman observed: 'Barbara chases round the country with water pouring through the dam, patching it up, trying to stop this leak and that leak, dealing with the builders, busmen, agricultural workers.'[16] The government recommended increases, of between 2.5 and 4.5 per cent, at the end of 1969, for the following year, promising another phase of government by exhortation. The cabinet, especially the chancellor, sought to retain compulsory notification, Barbara Castle, with the backing of the prime minister, suggesting the prices and incomes board be merged with the monopolies commission, to make a new commission for industry and manpower. It was her view that the government should now seek to control the 400 largest firms through prices, but the general election intervened. Wilson was to lose office after five years of trying to run a largely voluntary policy of norms and ceilings, interspersed by an explicitly statutory one in 1966–7. Wages rose faster than prices during his two governments, in spite of the efforts of the national board for prices and incomes.

Barbara Castle had been promoted to first secretary of state in 1968. Her move to employment and productivity was the centrepiece of Wilson's major reshuffle, designed to get the cabinet into final shape for the next general election. Crossman wanted to remain lord president, and stay in his beautiful room in the cabinet office, but he was earmarked for a major new department. Castle had been vetoed by Jenkins for the DEA, but she inherited Roy Hattersley as under secretary in her new department. Ray Gunter was moved from the ministry of power, only to quit on 1 July when he was not offered the general secretaryship of the party. Roy Mason entered the cabinet in his place. Richard Marsh had been moved under protest to Castle's old job at transport, the prime minister considering he would be good on television. Patrick Gordon Walker was simply dropped from the government. He was replaced at education and science by Edward Short. Cledwyn Hughes took over agriculture, releasing Fred Peart to become leader of the house as lord privy seal. The Welsh Office was taken over by George Thomas.

Wilson had long been pressured to have an inner cabinet to coordinate government strategy, and he agreed to what was called a parliamentary committee of senior ministers in April 1968. It initially comprised Wilson, Stewart, Gardiner, Healey, Jenkins, Crossman, Peart and Castle, the Scottish and Welsh secretaries being added later. It gradually expanded until it became almost half the cabinet, this being the cornerstone of the Wilson mark two regime. It was summoned to meet before the usual Thursday cabinet.

The parliamentary committee was as tame as its name suggests, mainly giving rise to resentment on the part of excluded cabinet ministers such as Gunter and Wedgwood Benn. With a plethora of cabinet committees, through which the prime minister controlled government business, the inner cabinet fell far short of what Crossman, and others, had long been demanding. Wilson reverted to using informal groups of ministers on particular subjects. 'I am sure Harold has dozens of these miscellaneous committees', Crossman wrote in February 1969, 'because he is more and more inclined to solve a problem by setting up a new committee where he can select who deals with what.'[17]

The parliamentary committee lasted a year, to be replaced by a management committee at the time of John Silkin's sacking. Wilson reluctantly decided to include Callaghan, the other members being Stewart, Jenkins, Crossman, Castle and Healey. It met first on 5 May 1969, just after the threat to Wilson's leadership, it being agreed the meetings should be 'informal, frank and forward looking'.[18] Decisions would be recorded, but not circulated to cabinet ministers. Wilson had an 'inner inner cabinet'[19] secret meeting with Crossman, Castle, and Jenkins just before the next meeting on 8 May, these four deciding four days later to exclude Callaghan, given his opposition to government policy. Fred Peart then rejoined what was effectively the old parliamentary committee, and Crosland and Benn became members in the autumn. The discussions helped make the cabinet a more productive deliberative body.

The management committee was used that summer to discuss the reform of industrial relations, and a meeting called for Chequers on Friday, 5 September to discuss the general election. Bob Mellish was now a regular attender. Wilson argued that Callaghan, who was now doing well in Northern Ireland, had to be brought back into the inner cabinet, but Brown was insisting upon returning as deputy prime minister. 'If you can get down to fewer than seven important Ministers', Crossman noted later, 'something like a natural conversation takes place between fellow-politicians who are not just pontificating from briefs.'[20] The election was discussed again on 14 January 1970, the autumn still being considered the most likely time. It was clear Wilson was becoming worried by Heath. The date was discussed at Chequers on Saturday, 8 March, the prime minister now coming round to the idea of June.

The foreign and commonwealth offices had finally merged on 17 October 1968 under Michael Stewart, George Thomson becoming minister without portfolio in the cabinet. Crossman gave up the lord presidency to Peart on 1 November, becoming secretary of state for social services in Alexander Fleming House at the Elephant and Castle. The new department of health and social security (DHSS) was a merger of health, under Kenneth Robinson, who went to housing and local government, and social security, under Judith Hart. She was taken into the cabinet, and number 10, as paymaster-general. John Diamond was also brought into the cabinet that autumn, still as chief secretary to the treasury.

Wilson had another major reshuffle a year later after the 1969 party conference, consequent upon a reorganization of the machinery of government. Peter Shore became minister without portfolio with the abolition of the DEA. George Thomson resumed the chancellorship of the duchy of Lancaster, with a view to further common market negotiations. The ministry of power was abolished, and absorbed by technology. Mason moved to a downgraded board of trade, which also lost responsibilities to Tony Benn. Tony Crosland was made secretary of state for local government and regional planning, a new environment portfolio. Greenwood was dropped from the cabinet as minister of housing and local government. Richard Marsh was sacked, and Fred Mulley took over transport, outside the cabinet. Judith Hart left the cabinet, to take over overseas development. Harold Lever entered, as paymaster-general, to work with mintech. Wilson had not touched Jenkins, Stewart or Callaghan, but he had created four super-ministers in 1968–9 – Castle, Crossman, Benn and Crosland – three of whom had been his closest supporters.

Civil service reform was an important part of the Wilsonian project, Thomas Balogh having written a seminal essay, 'The Apotheosis of the Dilettante: The Establishment of Mandarins', for a volume, *The Establishment,* edited by Hugh Thomas. Central government was employing nearly a million people by the time the book was published in 1959. Over a third were industrial workers, many working outside London. The administrative class – numbering some three thousand – predominated in Whitehall as a ruling elite, its professional organization being called, for historical reasons, the first division association. This group was led by the permanent secretaries, who ran the civil service through an over-arching committee, and it has been rightly called the permanent government of Britain. Governments might come, these mandarins thought, but they also went. Continuity, and self-regulation, were important to the civil service.

Tommy Balogh and Robert Neild were included on a Fabian Society committee to consider the civil service, publishing their report in 1964. The report recommended hiving off the civil service commission from the treasury, and importing more economists. Harold Wilson had been consulted, and the document was considered a blueprint for the labour government.

The prime minister set up a royal commission on the civil service shortly before the 1966 election, to be chaired by his old friend, John, now Lord, Fulton – then vice-chancellor of the University of Sussex, and vice-chairman of the BBC. Fulton was not the first choice, and the treasury was to be very critical of the way he failed to control his committee. It included

MPs, some academics, and – surprisingly – senior civil servants. This was to be the first major inquiry into British public administration in over a century, but the civil service excluded from the terms of reference major questions, such as the adequacy of the Whitehall machine, and the relationship of civil servants to ministers (the limited terms of reference being used subsequently as an argument to query the commission's detailed recommendations). The government also changed the fifty-year rule on the release of state documents. Failing to get the twenty-five years Wilson claims he wanted, he had to settle for thirty years in negotiations with the opposition.

Wilson worked behind the scenes to influence the royal commission, inviting Fulton to dine at Chequers on Sunday, 17 March 1968 only to be called back to London. Fulton reported in late June on the structure, recruitment and management of the home civil service, calling for 'a new system of training, organisation and career management'.[21] Administrators were criticized for 'tend[ing] to think of themselves as advisers on policy to people above them, rather than as managers of the administrative machine below them'.[22] The first chapter was an indictment of the administrative class, but the recommendations, no doubt watered down by the civil servants, did not do justice to the analysis.

The report – largely the work of Norman Hunt – was 'very unpopular in Whitehall',[23] but Wilson planned to commend it to cabinet on 20 June. He sought the support of Tony Benn the evening before. There was surprising opposition from several senior ministers, but it was accepted at a special meeting five days later. Crossman commented on Hunt's work: 'He and Harold are tremendous buddies who live in the same world of uninspired commonsense. The Report is perfectly sensible but, oh dear, it lacks distinction.'[24]

Fulton made three main recommendations. First, a new civil service department, including the existing commission responsible for recruitment. Second, a civil service college. And third, the abolition of the class system – administrative, executive, clerical, with specialists – in favour of a single graded structure. Wilson was angling to prise responsibility for the civil service away from the treasury, to the annoyance of Roy Jenkins. The new department was quickly established under the prime minister, with Lord Shackleton taking day-to-day responsibility. Shackleton set out to construct the new system by 1971, with Sir William Armstrong the new head of the civil service. The prime minister had the active support of Michael Halls, in seeking to implement Fulton towards the end of his government. Wilson was to record that 'the successive reforms went through smoothly and rapidly',[25] but Armstrong felt a strong need to consult staff associations, in the knowledge that differences would greatly slow down the process. Marcia Williams believes that the labour government failed to confront the civil service. 'This was a struggle', she would write, 'which we never fought with much heart or conviction.'[26]

1968 also saw the heralding of the open university, Jennie Lee having worked on it from the formation of the government. She nearly resigned in January, but Wilson's promise not to cut the arts council or open university's budgets kept her on board. Crosland is thought to have been uninterested in the idea, so Lee must have relied upon the support of Gordon Walker, and then Edward Short. Addressing a head teachers' union conference at Plymouth on 3 June, with his sister in the audience, the prime minister announced that enrolment should begin in the following year for the first courses in 1970. Britain's newest university was to have the full panoply of chancellor, vice-chancellor, governing body, administrative and academic staff, as well as radio and television personnel. Education was to be broadcast, though there would also be correspondence and residential courses. Degrees were to be awarded. The open university, as its name suggested, was to cater for those who had failed to complete a further education course, or had been unable to continue with their education after school. A site was designated in Milton Keynes, the university being founded, at a charter ceremony at the royal society in London, on 23 July 1969. Lord Crowther presided as the first chancellor.

Harold Wilson was to confide in later years, to any who would listen, that the open university was the greatest achievement of his years in power. This assessment has been endorsed by others, though the university was the result of the work of many people. It was an aspect of the expansion of higher education which owed most to the conservative governments of the 1950s, the Robbins Report recommending in 1963 six new universities and the upgrading of existing institutions. Harold Wilson at least ensured that the open university was not cut during any of his public expenditure exercises, though it may have been delayed.

The state of industrial relations in Britain had been the subject of another royal commission, set up by Ray Gunter in April 1965, and chaired by Lord Donovan, a judge and former labour MP. Wilson was wary of employers' and workers' representatives being included on the commission, but he came to accept that Gunter had been correct to appoint George Woodcock, general secretary of the TUC, and industrialists like Sir George Pollock and Lord Robens of the national coal board. There were several other members of the house of lords, a woman head teacher, and three academics – most notably Hugh Clegg, who became professor of industrial relations at Warwick University. According to Barbara Castle, into whose lap the document fell in June 1968, Wilson and Gunter had been 'worried by the effect on public opinion of the growing number of unofficial strikes'.[27] This was the vast majority of strikes in 1964–6, though Britain was not particularly strike-prone, in spite of the media attention being paid to carworkers, miners, dockers and shipyard workers. Wilson was seeking to frustrate opposition demands for legal curbs on trade unions, as recommended in the conservatives' *Fair Deal at Work* published in 1968. There can be no doubt of his critical attitude to the trade unions, despite his leadership of a party built and maintained by them. Harold Wilson had never shared in the heroic vision of many socialist intellectuals. While he believed in working with union leaders, he had no class or professional affinity with the movement. He certainly had no empathy with their defensive role, and Balogh, as his economic guru, saw unions as a restraint on economic development. At a meeting of the kitchen cabinet at Chequers in November, he was to say that 'the unions were an irresponsible group which had to be dealt with'.[28]

While her majesty's commissioners were deliberating, Wilson became involved in a number of industrial relations problems. The national union of railwaymen decided on a national strike on 4 February 1966, after the NBPI refused to improve on the employer's offer. With a general election imminent, Ray Gunter, George Brown and Barbara Castle tried to prevent industrial action. Wilson summoned the chairman of British Rail, and the union executive, to number 10 at the eleventh hour, welcoming each trade unionist into the cabinet room, where he plied them with whiskies. The prime minister had his usual brandy. Spectators and journalists waited outside. This was the occasion – the night of Friday, 11 February – when the prime minister supplied the railwaymen's leaders with food and drink from his own flat, beginning the legend of beer and sandwiches at Downing Street.

His second intervention in an industrial dispute was the seamen's strike a few weeks later. On the Friday before the national stoppage, he had the union executive over to number 10. This time it was the state dining room. He was thinking by mid-June of an inquiry into the shipping industry, which might have led to nationalization proposals, though the prime minister rapidly changed his tune by attacking the communist party.

Wilson's third major intervention occurred in October 1967, when he was in Liverpool at a commercial dinner. Ray Gunter had sent in Jack Scamp as an industrial trouble-shooter, to try to settle the dock strike, but it was Wilson who finally brought the two sides together. George Woodcock asked Wilson to intervene towards the end of the year, when the engine drivers' union, ASLEF, threatened to strike, over guards sitting in the cab of new diesel trains. The general council of the TUC and the ASLEF executive came to Downing Street late on 5 December. Wilson was meant to read the riot act to the engine drivers, but he secured a settlement with the promise of further talks.

During the general election in June 1970, when the newspaper publishers wanted to meet the two principal unions in the industry together, in order to prevent competitive claims, Wilson called in both sides on the tenth. He feared a loss of coverage during the election, even in the predominantly tory press, and made what he maintains was a purely procedural point, using the TUC to coax the unions. Wilson requested that the negotiations should take place in number 10 and the cabinet office, the employers meeting each union in a separate room. Though the presses stopped that night, all the unions were brought into the cabinet room. Wilson had to cancel two election meetings. Both sides then repaired to Congress House, where Vic Feather, the general secretary of the TUC, continued to chair round-table talks the following day. Agreement was reached on Friday, 12 June, to include a review of collective bargaining in Fleet Street. Newspapers resumed their coverage of the election that weekend, though some in the labour party had not been sorry when they did not appear.

In the national dock strike the following month, when Wilson was once again leader of the opposition, the conservative government of Ted Heath criticized him for having institutionalized the practice of prime ministerial intervention. Wilson was clearly sensitive to the charge of having used prime ministerial power to extract further concessions from employers, and wrote shortly afterwards that he had only intervened in five major strikes. He had done this only where there was a 'procedural deadlock',[29] but conceded that there were exceptions to the rule – damage to the economy, the possibility of a change of heart, to back up ministers, and to allow for face saving. This was a case of protesting too much. Other accounts show Harold Wilson set about resolving industrial disputes with all the gusto he deployed in other affairs of state.

The Donovan report revealed that there was a 'formal system embodied in the official institutions' conceived by the Whitley reports of 1917–18, and behind this an 'informal system created by the actual behaviour ... of managers, shop stewards and workers'.[30] Donovan's two systems lacked sociological rigour, the informal system being highly institutionalized, but the notion pointed to historical change, national collective bargaining having been augmented by shop stewards. These new industrial representatives were products of shopfloor power under full employment, and with recognition by local management. The report called for the reform of collective bargaining, advocating factory and company agreements covering wages and conditions, to be registered with the department of employment and productivity. Donovan also suggested an industrial relations commission, a national bureaucracy to aid the extension of the formal system into the area of informality. Incomes would become more subject to policy considerations, though this was to remain the preserve of the NBPI. Reform was also seen as leading to a better use of manpower. On the all-important question of unofficial strikes, the report saw these as 'a symptom of a failure to devise institutions in keeping with changing needs'.[31] The problem was conjured away. The royal commission believed that agreements, given existing circumstances, should not be legally enforceable. In cases of unfair dismissal, workers could appeal to labour tribunals, which would be renamed. Donovan largely accepted the 'closed shop', whereby workers had to become union members to secure employment. The report called for a slow approach towards industrial unionism, one union for all employees in an industry. A role for the TUC was envisaged in improving inter-union cooperation. The report found little room for the law in industrial relations. In promoting voluntary solutions – thus voluntarism or voluntaryism – it showed that the members of the commission held to a pluralist notion of industrial relations. Workers and their unions were considered to have some say in the management of largely private industry, though a majority came out against workers' directors on the boards of companies.

Donovan was the work of liberal intellectuals, not unsympathetic to a labour party based on the trade-union movement. Wilson was already putting the party through a severe trial, with his prices and incomes policy. Since Balogh had long believed this policy was essential, it was the view of some of the prime minister's advisers that he could not risk draconian industrial relations legislation. The conservatives were prepared to raise a hue and cry about unofficial strikes damaging the country, and it was the legalism of Ted Heath and the shadow cabinet which most influenced the prime minister in the summer of 1968. Wilson told Denis Healey at lunch that, having failed to win the labour movement to incomes policy, he now wanted to gain public support for the government. Action was promised in the queen's speech, and the problem then handed to Barbara Castle at DEP. She believed Wilson had conceded to the tories in setting up the royal commission, and then 'pack[ed] it with pretty harmless people'. 'George Woodcock stopped anything being said at all, practically.'[32]

Castle characteristically threw herself into every responsibility she was given, and now had to do something about strikes in the run-up to a general election. Interventionism was bound to be her solution, though her department combined a commitment to legalism with a need to work with the TUC. James Callaghan welcomed the voluntarism of the Donovan report, and advised the unions to regain control of their members. He complains that Castle ignored the cabinet's industrial relations committee, of which he was a member, and 'established a small group of four to assist her in drafting her own remedies'[33] – Harold Walker, an under-secretary at DEP, Tony Benn, Peter Shore and Hugh Clegg.

Castle did arrange a weekend at the civil defence college at Sunningdale from Friday, 15 November to help develop policy. She was accompanied by two junior ministers, her parliamentary private secretary, and departmental officials. Also present was Peter Shore, but not Wedgwood Benn. Both cabinet ministers were to be at Wilson's kitchen cabinet at Chequers the following night, in the company of Judith Hart, John Silkin, Harold Davies, Gerald Kaufman, Marcia Williams and Tommy Balogh.

'We agreed', Wedgwood Benn noted of that discussion, 'we should have strike ballots and a cooling-off period, and in this way we would say we were going to control the trade unions by democratising them.'[34] Castle also invited several employers, members of the NBPI, and Hugh Clegg to Sunningdale. She had been prepared to accept many of the Donovan report's recommendations, welcoming the idea of an industrial relations commission. She was less keen on the philosophy of the report. After meeting the TUC on 2 July, Castle noted: 'I can't see any revolutionary changes being carried through unless the Government is prepared to impose them on an unwilling TUC.'[35] Whatever of voluntarism in the long term, 'the confessed failure', according to Wilson, 'of the Commission to find any short-term remedy for unofficial strikes could not be accepted.'[36]

Donovan had not 'failed'[37] to find a solution, believing such strikes were a consequence of unregulated activity which required institutionalization. As for state intervention in unofficial disputes, Donovan had simply favoured an officer of the department investigating the facts with a view to their publication. The DEP accepted the minority – Clegg – view that trade-union immunity should continue to apply in the case of unofficial strikes, and Castle was to present this as a sweetener to the unions. The gathering at Sunningdale came out against 'collective laissez-faire', and in favour of state intervention. Castle suggests this was 'to a man'.[38] She was alert to the argument about using the law against trade unions, but seems to have been convinced already of two propositions. One, that the state could force employers to make all sorts of concessions, including recognition, collective bargaining and participation, and, two, that it could be positive towards the unions, guaranteeing trade-union rights. These would have the combined effect of modifying behaviour on both sides of the industrial divide. The question of sanctions against unions was implicit in her model, but she agreed with Donovan in opposing the legal enforcement of agreements, and resisting the banning of sympathetic strikes or the closed shop. It was Peter Shore who suggested a legally enforceable cooling-off period in an unconstitutional strike, whether official or unofficial. Support also emerged for strike ballots. Donovan had rejected the idea, and Castle was later forced to accept that ballots did not automatically mean no strikes. The industrial relations commission was to have powers of enforcement, against employers or unions, in recognition disputes. Three definite sanctions against the unions emerged from Sunningdale, and were to be subsequently known as penal clauses in the draft legislation. 'Altogether a fabulously successful weekend', Barbara Castle noted on 16 November. 'We can all see our way on Donovan quite clearly now.

We agreed that we would never get anything positive out of the TUC and that the Government would have to risk giving a lead.'[39]

A draft white paper was ready by early December, the first secretary being congratulated on this by the prime minister. 'As I said to Marcia', he was reported, 'Barbara has not so much out-heathed Heath as outflanked him.'[40] Barbara Castle states that Wilson fully supported her. This is not surprising given she was developing the idea of state regulation of union behaviour, but not simply in a legalistic manner. Wilson arranged an ad hoc meeting of ministers (MISC 230) for 19 December, which included the law officers plus Gardiner, Lee and Peart. Callaghan was excluded. Castle then confided her proposals to George Woodcock, who was shortly to accept the chairmanship of the commission on industrial relations, to be known as the CIR. She addressed the inner cabinet of the TUC five days after Christmas, some members – probably Frank Cousins – breaking their pledge of confidentiality. She saw the CBI on 31 December. The leaks were to make it difficult for members of the government, the first secretary developing policy on her own at an unprecedented pace.

A special cabinet only considered Castle's white paper on 3 January 1969, and she wanted it published six days later. A majority – surprisingly – supported the strike ballot. This was not the case with the conciliation pause, where it was feared that Castle might end up intervening in every small-scale dispute. Wilson had to ask for further papers, albeit on tougher legal approaches.

There followed two meetings of the cabinet, and three of an industrial relations committee, the white paper being approved, by ten votes to six, at a final gathering on 14 January, during the commonwealth conference. The opponents in cabinet included Crosland, Greenwood, and the three trade unionists, Callaghan, Mason and Marsh. Much of the internal political resistance came from Crossman and Judith Hart, doubtful of whether an industrial relations bill could get through the party. Callaghan – whose political maxim had long been 'wait till the Trade Unions decide their line and follow them' – also voiced his doubts at this point. 'From the moment I set eyes on it I knew that such a proposal, which ran counter to the whole history of the trade union movement and to the ethos of the Donovan Report, could not succeed ... The legal sanctions would not stop unofficial strikes ... would not pass through parliament ... [and] would create tension between government and unions at a time when morale was low, to no real effective purpose.'[41]

It was Castle's husband, Ted, who came up with the title *In Place of Strife*, after Bevan's *In Place of Fear*. The white paper was published on 17 January, with three of the twenty-seven proposals involving the use of penal powers – ballots, cooling off and the attachment of wages for fines. Castle and Wilson wanted to be seen as the architects of trade-union reform, but to the unions and the labour party they were behaving almost like a tory government.

The labour cabinet had decided it could not legislate before the autumn. It was believed Wilson did not want another prices and incomes bill in the 1969-70 session, and trade-union reform would take the political stage. Some even believed he was simply trying to prove labour would tackle the unions, if returned in an imminent general election. Castle wanted time to put over her general philosophy, including the penal powers, and did not want to rush through a short anti-trade union bill. She had said in cabinet: 'The old carthouse [the TUC] is stirring in its stable. If we show doubts it will turn over and go to sleep again.'[42]

The TUC general council came out against penal powers. David Lea, the officer who drafted the TUC's evidence for Donovan, thought Wilson might have been able to live with the report. 'He did not know how big a stone he was throwing into the pond.'[43] Public opinion could have been assuaged by Donovan, and the status of the commission's members used against critics. The TUC issued a twenty-eight paragraph document, while the white paper was before the cabinet. The assistant general secretary, Vic Feather, took charge at Congress House when Woodcock left, and was probably even more attentive to members of the government, including the prime minister. Jack Jones had joined the general council in September 1968, and was to be critical of the role Feather played during *In Place of Strife*. Feather had known Castle's father, Frank Betts, a leading socialist intellectual in Bradford, in the 1920s, and was to refer throughout to the first secretary of state as Barbara Betts. Feather dined in a private room at Brown's Hotel with Castle on 22 January 1969, but all he could say was: 'Why did you do it, luv?'[44] He then offered to help with union conferences. Whatever the general secretary might say in private meetings, he was to be the agent of the TUC in carrying out a strategy of resistance.

Castle had been given a sullen hearing by members of the 137-strong trade-union group of labour MPs, at gatherings on 17 and 20 January, but she defended the penal powers, in February, at meetings of the parliamentary party. When the white paper was debated in the chamber on 3 March, it was approved by 224 votes to 62. Fifty-three of the latter were labour opponents, and another thirty-nine abstained.

Opposition was also gathering on the party executive. The mineworkers' leader, Joe Gormley, moved opposition on 26 March to '[any] legislation based on all the proposals in the White Paper'.[45] This was carried by sixteen votes to five. Callaghan had suggested dropping the word 'any', which was accepted by Gormley, and the home secretary then voted against an unsuccessful Castle amendment to remove the sentence altogether. Callaghan voted with the trade unionists on the substantive motion, Castle having the support of Brown, Greenwood, Benn and Arthur Skeffington. Jennie Lee abstained.

Callaghan's stand was all over the papers on Thursday, 27 March. Wilson was about to leave for Nigeria, but resolved to chastize Callaghan upon his return. 'Things are pretty bad, quite frankly',[46] Tony Benn noted, after spending some time talking to fellow labour MPs. The home secretary arrived late for the next cabinet, in Wilson's room in the commons, on Thursday, 3 April. 'The thunderbolt never materialized', according to Castle, 'and [she] heard [her]self listening to [her] astonishment to some very generalized and conciliatory noises indeed. It was Jim who pushed his own position firmly into the open by saying he had no reason to apologize for what he had done on the N[ational] E[xecutive] C[ommittee].'[47]

Callaghan argued that the government had only decided to consult the unions on the white paper. No decision had been taken to legislate. 'Harold then asked the Cabinet to reaffirm their belief in the White Paper. Jim objected to this and Harold said it was all subject to consultation. We left the meeting', says Benn, 'without knowing more about where we were than at the beginning. I am afraid Jim is winning.'[48]

Wilson then briefed the lobby, telling Westminster correspondents that he had been tough with Callaghan. He was subsequently to recount that he had insisted that ministers, unable to accept the doctrine of collective responsibility, must resign from the government. 'It was a perfect example of instant politics', noted Tony Benn. 'It was so disrespectful of Harold to suggest he had kicked his Ministers into line … It … does reveal what a very small man he is.'[49] Benn's disenchantment with Wilson was becoming apparent.

Castle and Jenkins had come round to the view that there should be a short industrial relations bill, and no further prices and incomes legislation. This could be announced in the budget speech on Tuesday, 15 April. Castle had changed her mind about waiting until the next session, after witnessing Callaghan's stand at the party executive. She now felt that the penal clauses had to be rushed through, before the unions mobilized. '"In Place of Strife"', writes Callaghan, 'was suddenly to be turned into instant government.'[50] The plan was stitched together in number 10 on Thursday, 10 April with Crossman present, this being the first occasion on which Wilson seemed amenable to having a seven-strong inner cabinet. Jenkins's suggestion was agreed at the pre-budget cabinet meeting four days later, the industrial relations committee immediately afterwards settling the terms of an interim bill. The strike ballot was dropped at this point on the suggestion of Tony Crosland. Tony Benn put to Paul Johnson of the *New Statesman* 'the idea that the whole debate about industrial relations ought now to be taken to the people[,] and that we ought to argue the case much more systematically at factory gates and so on.'[51]

A second cabinet on 14 April supported proceeding with legal sanctions, Callaghan stating that the package was now less draconian. Barbara Castle 'emphasized how [she] had only come to accept an interim Bill reluctantly, but it was clear that, however long [they] gave the TUC, they would not negotiate until they were under the threat of immediate legislation.'[52] 'The Government and Harold Wilson himself are in a very shaky position', wrote Tony Benn. 'The morale of the Parliamentary Labour Party is about as low as it's been for a long time.'[53] At the parliamentary party on 17 April, Wilson told labour MPs that 'the passage of [the] Bill [was] essential to [the government's] continuance in office. There [could] be no going back on that.'[54] Crossman described his performance 'as a flop',[55] and the prime minister was to be forced to eat his words. 'Member after member warned the Government that you couldn't intervene, and the meeting was almost unanimously against.'[56]

The TUC general council had been holding a series of industrial conferences involving member unions, to work out the movement's response to Donovan. Vic Feather asked to see Wilson on 10 April, and *Action on Donovan* was presented by the TUC inner cabinet the following day at a meeting in number 10 with senior ministers. The trade-union leaders wanted a 'tripartite agreement', whereby the CBI, TUC and the government would tackle unofficial strikes. Wilson insisted the cabinet must be free to decide its legislative programme, and he broke the news of the short bill to Vic Feather at a meeting in his study on 14 April. Castle, who was present, was perplexed. 'How far Vic is genuinely unalarmed at our proposals (he may even welcome the new power they give to the TUC) I cannot tell. I only know that in public he will trounce them vigorously.'[57] Castle met the TUC, with Wilson, at the house of commons two days later, having replied to the shadow chancellor in the budget debate. Feather and his colleagues agreed to consider her speech. Wilson was thinking of having a provision in the bill to delay the penal clauses, to give the unions time to come up with voluntary solutions.

The TUC general council called a special congress eight days after the announcement of the industrial relations bill, to be held in Croydon on 5 June. There followed the challenge to Wilson's leadership consequent upon the sacking of John Silkin, Wilson wanting Bob Mellish to get the industrial relations bill through. The climax of the leadership crisis was the meeting of the parliamentary party on 30 April. Bob Mellish warned labour MPs about opposing the bill, and threatened a dissolution of parliament. 'Only the Prime Minister can talk in this language',[58] Wilson was to write. Douglas Houghton, as chairman, apparently lost control. 'The whole thing ended', noted Tony Benn, 'with the same sort of awful ill will that I remember from the 1951–7 period. It made me very gloomy.'[59]

The right wing continued to conspire, but the Wilson–Castle axis was preserved. It was by no means certain that the government could introduce the bill as planned on 22 May. At cabinet, on 8 May, Callaghan suggested that it be delayed until after the Croydon congress.

Defeatism about the general election was beginning to spread. Douglas Houghton had reportedly told the parliamentary party the previous day that an industrial relations act was not worth the destruction of the labour party. Wilson raised it as a constitutional matter with his cabinet colleagues on 8 May. 'Harold is a very small-minded man', noted Benn, 'he always gets to the least important part of the issue, suggesting ways of downing the Tories or embarrassing Heath or putting Harry Nicholas [the general secretary] in his place, when events call for a higher degree of statesmanship.'[60] It was Crossman who launched into a personal attack on Callaghan, mentioning the threat to Wilson's leadership. 'We had never had such a scene in Cabinet before', wrote Crossman, '(I was told later on that it was a phenomenally dramatic moment) and there was an awkard silence. Then Jim muttered, "Of course, if my colleagues want me to resign I'm prepared to go if they insist on my going." He had been punctured. He hadn't responded, he had crawled, and it was quite a moment.'[61] '"We don't want you to go. We think you should stay and be convinced"', Wilson said, according to Castle. 'Nonetheless I could see [Harold] was secretly delighted.'[62] Castle, Jenkins and Crossman sneaked into Wilson's room in the commons that afternoon, for their 'inner inner cabinet'[63] to talk behind the home secretary's back. The first secretary explained about her concession, but was worried that Callaghan would be seen to be the victor. 'Harold assured me', she noted, 'he would steer discussion at inner Cabinet so as to indicate that he and I had already been discussing the possibility of postponing the Bill.'[64]

A joint meeting of the cabinet and party executive had been arranged for number 10 for Friday, 10 May, Callaghan using this forum to criticize his cabinet colleagues for attacking the unions. 'The Government's job', he was quoted as saying, 'is to build up the popularity of the trade union movement.'[65] It was this intervention which would lead Wilson, after consulting Jenkins, Crossman and Castle, to drop Callaghan from the inner cabinet before the meeting on Tuesday, 13 May. Castle replied in the joint meeting that the government's job was 'to build up the strength, authority and status of the trade union movement so that it could make *itself* popular'.[66] She privately considered the views of Jack Jones – now general secretary designate of the TGWU – as 'facile and one-sided',[67] but informed the party executive that its proposals on industrial democracy, which Jones had largely originated, were contained in her white paper.

Vic Feather was smuggled into number 10 on 10 May for a private dinner with Wilson and Castle, bringing a draft of the general council's position, its 'Programme for Action'. Castle recalled:

> I was rather snappy with him while Harold was at his most conspiratorial. Under pressure Vic admitted that the TUC document had 'soft edges', but maintained that if he had taken his proposals any further he wouldn't have got away with it. But he added, encouragingly, 'I don't mind how diamond-hard you go, so long as it comes from you.' ... I excused myself after dinner and left them conspiring over the brandy.[68]

When the full general council came to number 10 on Monday, 12 May, the trade-union leaders only showed a willingness to move on inter-union disputes. Wilson told them that the bill was being postponed until after 5 June, and promised to consider the TUC's programme for action.

The trade-union leaders published their programme a week later. The TUC condemned unofficial strikes, but refused to move in the direction of the government. Wilson and Castle unsuccessfully appealed on 21 May to the general council to tighten up its rules, reaffirming that the bill was still on course. Wilson had said at the inner cabinet the previous day, in response to a weakening in the government's position: '"Brinkmanship is essential; we have to push it right up to the edge."'[69] Crossman and Mellish wanted to drop the conciliation pause, while the rest favoured a legislative delay in its implementation. Some opposition was expressed two days later in cabinet to proceeding with the bill.

Feather had already asked for a very private meeting, between himself, plus Jones and Scanlon (and the chairman of the general council), and the prime minister, which was arranged for Sunday, 1 June at Chequers. Castle insisted on being flown back by military plane from the Mediterranean, where she and her husband were cruising. Wilson confided to her that it was now a confidence matter. If he lost the party leadership, he would show himself tougher than Heath in staging a comeback against Callaghan. When Jack Jones, who had also been abroad, turned up at Chequers on 1 June, he found the TUC would not be able to do a deal with Wilson behind Castle's back. The prime minister had beer with his roast duck at dinner, no doubt to impress his trade-union colleagues. The rest drank wine. Talk became more frank as the evening wore on. Wilson stated his position: '"I will never consent to preside over a Government that is not allowed to govern ... There are two types of Prime Minister I have made up my mind never to be: one is a Ramsay MacDonald and the second is a Dubcek. I'm not going to surrender to your tanks, Hughie."'[70]

Jones concluded that 'Wilson and Castle were basically academics and it was difficult to persuade them to see things from a shop-floor angle.'[71] Castle relented slightly the following morning, coming up with the idea of two bills. Wilson was to maintain his stance. The special trade-union congress voted that Thursday at Croydon, almost unanimously, to back the general council.

Its voluntary approach got a surprisingly good press, but the inner cabinet decided on Sunday, 8 June to go for penal powers, under pressure from Wilson and Castle. These would be held in cold storage for a time, while the TUC acted on unofficial strikes. The general council found Wilson willing the following day to drop the penal clauses, in return for action from Congress House. The cabinet agreed to negotiations. The general council appointed a sub-committee of six, including Jones and Scanlon, on 11 June. The TUC could not move far from its 'programme for action', in terms of changing its rule – number 11 – governing unofficial strikes. The general council came back with the idea of an interpretative declaration of intent at a third meeting the following day, and Hugh Scanlon suggested it could be drafted by the government. Wilson rejected this, and a break looked inevitable.

There had been a cabinet that morning, and Tony Benn noted that he was joining 'th[e] anxious group, fearing that an Industrial Relations Bill just can't work.'[72] At some point Wilson said to Joe Haines that he didn't mind having a green cabinet, but he was damned if he was going to have a yellow one. There the matter was to rest until a special cabinet the following Tuesday, 17 June. Barbara Castle wrote that this was 'the most traumatic day of [her] political life'.[73]

Wilson accepted a new version of the conciliation pause early on 17 June, but the inner cabinet was doubtful about legislating with the TUC opposed. Crossman and Mellish were hesitant, Jenkins and Stewart more willing to proceed. At cabinet immediately afterwards, Castle found 'the wreckers were not interested in the merits or demerits of [her] proposals. All they wanted was a settlement: peace at any price.'[74] It was Peter Shore who suggested that the first secretary was now largely concerned with securing a victory over the TUC, but Wilson maintained they had got nothing on unofficial strikes. He stated that capitulation was '"a situation in which neither this nor any other Government [could] carry on"'[75] when he closed the meeting at 12.30 p.m. The cabinet resumed later that afternoon in the house of commons, with Wilson fighting his colleagues as he had never done before. He was reinforced by three double brandies in the last half an hour.

Tony Benn had announced his support for the white paper, but felt 'statutory authoritarianism had its limits'. 'To move from absolute silence about industrial disputes', he said, 'to statutory penalties was too big a jump. We wouldn't win assent for it and it was contrary to the idea of self-regulation. It underestimated the power of public pressure and therefore we should challenge the TUC, open the industrial debate, continue the talks and get them to strengthen their Letter of Guidance on disputes.'[76] Wilson accused his cabinet colleagues of being cowardly. "'I won't negotiate on your terms. If you order me to go back to the T.U.C. and say I'm to accept a declaration of intent I refuse to do it, because a declaration would not be worth the paper it is written on. I insist on getting the change of rules or on standing for the penal clauses. You can't deny me this.'"[77]

It was finally agreed that Wilson and Castle should have a free hand, when they met the TUC the following day, but the cabinet would be at liberty to accept, or reject, any agreement. Vic Feather gave the impression that the TUC might accept a reworded rule 11, on yet another of his secret late-night visits to Downing Street. A government draft was presented to the general council the following morning, Wednesday, 18 June. The nego-tiating sub-committee accepted the wording, but not as a rule amendment, preferring something like the 1939 Bridlington regulations, which prevented inter-union poaching of members. Beer and sandwiches were served yet again.

Responding to Scanlon's prediction that he might not be able to hold his national committee, Castle suggested a binding undertaking to Wilson, to be drafted by the government. The prime minister proposed this in the afternoon, to the evident relief of the general council. The TUC quickly agreed to 'a solemn and binding undertaking' governing the operation of rule 11, with the force of Bridlington.

Congress House agreed to intervene in major unofficial strikes to help promote a settlement. Where procedure had not yet been exhausted, it would oblige the union concerned to get the strikers back to work. The sanction was being reported to congress, and even suspended from membership. Wilson and Castle then reported to the cabinet, the first secretary saying: "'In the end we have got complete acceptance of our formula and this is entirely due to the superb way in which the Prime Minister has handled the talks.'"[78] There followed a press conference, in which Wilson, flanked by Feather and Castle, announced the deal. It was welcomed by the parliamentary party, though Crossman was sceptical of the reception Wilson reportedly received: 'I think the Party was relieved and that they heard the speech with somewhat cynical disdain. They had got the climb-down they wanted but you don't greatly admire a leader who climbs down, even when it is you who have ordered him to do so.'[79]

The short industrial relations bill was scraped, and the non-punitive parts of Donovan, accepted by the government, remained to be legislated, after further consultation, in the 1969-70 parliamentary session – only to be aborted by the general election. The demise of *In Place of Strife* on 18 June 1969 was universally seen as a retreat by the labour government, due to the opposition of the parliamentary party to penal powers in the face of trade-union resistance. 'A victory had been scored in defence of the right to strike without fear of legal sanctions', recalls Jack Jones, 'but the TUC took aboard some big new responsibilities.'[80]

If *In Place of Strife* was the major issue of the Wilson government, Northern Ireland was to prove the most enduring in British politics. The self-governing British province in Ireland – also known as Ulster – politically exploded on Saturday, 5 October 1968, in front of television cameras.

The return of Ireland to the agenda of British politics was related to the constitutional settlement of 1920–2. The Irish Free State was established, but Britain partitioned Ireland, setting up Northern Ireland within the United Kingdom. One was a concession to nationalism, the other to unionism. London erred in allowing a regime to be established in Belfast, and compounded the problem by including a sizeable catholic minority within the area of what could only be a protestant state. The result was sectarian domination, with unionism a state force, and nationalism the expression of catholic grievances. Discrimination was part of the system of government, but Ulster's structural inequality was a legacy of colonialism.

The idea of a unitary state survived the early 1920s, though successive Dublin regimes never tried to unite the people of the island. British supporters of Irish nationalism, in the liberal and labour parties, invariably replied that a united Ireland, whatever the problem, must be the solution. When Eire declared itself a republic in 1949, the Attlee government guaranteed Ulster as part of the United Kingdom, enraging the friends of Ireland in the parliamentary party, led by Geoffrey Bing.

Sentimental support for Irish unification coexisted, in the labour party of the 1960s, with the duties of office. London had a desire for closer relations with Dublin, but it was also ultimately responsible for Northern Ireland. Harold Wilson represented a large number of second- and third-generation Irish catholics in Huyton, and was attentive to the issue. He had committed the labour party before the 1964 election to reform in the province, in reply to supplications from the campaign for social justice in Northern Ireland, declaring in favour of 'new and impartial procedures' in housing allocation, 'joint tribunals' to consider unfairness in public appointments, and 'any other effective means that can be agreed'.[81] He banked all such measures on the political advance of the Northern Ireland Labour Party (NILP), pro-conservative unionists being returned for all twelve Westminster seats in October.

Wilson engaged in a grand gesture as prime minister, returning to Dublin the remains of Roger Casement in February 1965. His bones were probably a consolation for the import surcharge which greatly affected the Republic of Ireland. It was also a sweetener for the free trade agreement signed at Downing Street the following December, allowing for the gradual removal of all quotas and tariffs on trade across land and sea frontiers. The 1966 election occurred shortly before the fiftieth anniversary of the Easter rising in Dublin, but politics in Ireland were dominated by the 1965 exchange of visits between Sean Lemass, the Irish taoiseach, and his opposite number at Stormont, Captain Terence O'Neill. Paul Rose had become first chairman of the Campaign for Democracy in Ulster (CDU), and was supported by Stan Orme in the Tribune group, Kevin McNamara – the victor of the Hull by-election in early 1966 – 'start[ing] a small group in Parliament to raise the issues brought up by the C.D.U.'.[82]

O'Neill met Wilson and Jenkins at Downing Street on 5 August 1966, and reassured them about continuing progress on questions of human rights. Regular meetings were also agreed, the first following on 12 January 1967. O'Neill had applied cosmetics to the face of Ulster politics since 1963, his advocacy of regional planning – the new Ulster – being a response to the loss of party support among protestant workers. Harold Wilson was prepared to back O'Neill as the only force for change in 1966, and was to later recall: 'I was satisfied then, as I am today, that we had not been taken for a ride.'[83] The British government took little active interest. Rose, Orme and Maurice Miller visited Northern Ireland on behalf of the CDU in April 1967. Backbench interest in the province had been stimulated by Gerry Fitt, a catholic who had been returned for West Belfast as a republican labour candidate. The reformers demanded a royal commission on the province, while the newly formed civil rights association (NICRA) looked to progress within the United Kingdom.

Callaghan inherited responsibility for Northern Ireland when he became home secretary, but it was Wedgwood Benn who opened a new factory in Craigavon, in the company of the local minister of commerce: '[Brian] Faulkner is a bright guy, very ambitious, they say. He's obviously done a successful job selling Northern Ireland to industrialists abroad and he is a popular figure … Listening to him talking about his world tours to get industry … gave me an idea of what a tremendous advantage it is to have a separate Government.'[84] O'Neill was coming under reactionary pressure from the likes of Ian Paisley, and the civil rights movement took to the streets in 1968, propelled by young catholic militants. It was the behaviour of the Royal Ulster Constabulary (RUC) which signalled the beginning of the end for the unionist regime.

Gerry Fitt was on the Derry march on 5 October, in the company of three labour MPs. They reported back to Callaghan, and Wilson invited O'Neill to talks. The British prime minister stressed Westminster's ultimate responsibility for the province on 4 November, Wilson having hitherto quoted the 1920 act to justify British non-interference. Wilson told O'Neill's colleagues that any palace revolution would incur British displeasure, Whitehall being responsible for the annual subvention which maintained Stormont. Callaghan claims Wilson was thinking of ending

Northern Ireland's representation at Westminster, the twelve unionists having caused him problems in the 1964 parliament, but it would have meant the loss of Gerry Fitt. There is no evidence of Wilson seriously advocating a united Ireland, whatever may have been said in the parliamentary party or the foreign office.

A joint statement issued after the meeting with O'Neill mentioned a number of reforms: there were to be changes in local government and housing, and an ombudsman appointed for the province; the special powers act was to be amended. British determination secured movement on all these issues, and O'Neill made an impressive television appeal. But the pressure of marches, particularly one from Belfast to Derry at the beginning of 1969, saw him call a general election for 24 February. He lost support within the protestant community, and resigned in late April.

'From that time forward', James Callaghan would recall, 'events moved towards the disasters of the 1970s and 1980s.'[85] The fall of O'Neill ended British hopes of reform, but London had to work with his successor, Major James Chichester-Clark. Callaghan had already announced that British troops were to guard remote public utilities, and told the cabinet on 24 April that the aim of the government was 'to influence while getting embroiled as little as possible'.[86]

The orange order celebrated William's victory over James in 1690 every 12 July, and troops were quietly moved to Derry for the 1969 march. The event passed off relatively peacefully, but this was not the case when the so-called apprentice boys celebrated the lifting of the Jacobite siege in 1689 on 12 August. Troops were deployed on the streets after several days of rioting by the catholic population of the Bogside, during which CS gas was used. Wilson and Callaghan had wanted to ban this march, but relented under pressure from the Northern Ireland government. The deployment of British police was ruled out, on the grounds that they would not operate under the special powers act, and a plan to use them the following summer collapsed with the change of government.

The British army appeared in Derry on 14 August 1969 to relieve a demoralized RUC, and went into Belfast the next day, following sectarian pogroms. 'It looks', noted Tony Benn, 'as though civil war in Ulster has almost begun.'[87] The decision had been taken by Wilson and Callaghan at a secret meeting at St Mawgan RAF station in Cornwall, the actual request from Stormont coming as the home secretary was flying back to London. It could not be refused, though the cabinet had only authorized, on 30 July, the use of CS gas to prevent the involvement of troops. 'Harold stressed', according to Barbara Castle, 'that our aim must be to keep out the troops at all costs ... He asked that the small group of Ministers should be authorized to take any urgent decisions.'[88] This was probably Wilson, Stewart, Callaghan and Healey. On 3 August Wilson and Callaghan, in a telephone conversation, took the crucial decision to accede to any request from Stormont, on or after 12 August. This was an operational and not political matter. Both men knew it would be difficult to get them out, but Roy Hattersley, in the absence of Denis Healey, was actually responsible for the deployment. The action of Wilson and Callaghan had later to be ratified by the cabinet, the implications for the relationship between London and Belfast being ignored in favour of continuing to work through the unionist government.

Wilson and Callaghan embraced their opportunity for statesmanship with gusto. Stormont had conceded it could not maintain internal security, but London had become directly involved with only two civil servants in the home office responsible for the province. The Irish government rejected an absurd invasion plan, to call unsuccessfully for a united nations' peace-keeping force, with the diplomatic connivance of Lord Caradon in New York. Callaghan had told Chichester-Clark that 'a government which could not control the streets or the population was not a government in [their] understanding of the word.'[89] The cabinet was summoned for the afternoon of Tuesday, 19 August, and Chichester-Clark invited to Downing Street for 5.00 p.m. Callaghan had seemed prepared for eventual direct rule of the province, but the government decided only to push the Northern Ireland prime minister as far as he would go.

Tony Benn records: 'Jim then considered the possibility of a broadly-based Government. Denis stressed again, "Let's keep Chichester-Clark carrying the can." Jim agreed. "Yes, I too want to avoid responsibility."' The home secretary cannot have been too intent upon taking over Northern Ireland. 'Britain cannot walk out of Ulster entirely', argued Michael Stewart, 'although we had considered it as an alternative ... He thought that awful as it would be to take over responsibility, it would be less awful than walking out.'[90] Tony Benn noted the foreign secretary's words. 'Harold [had] said', according to Barbara Castle, 'we were not going to underwrite a reactionary Government. We had agreed to put in troops to *restore* law and order but not to keep them there indefinitely to *maintain* it. We must keep firmly in the middle of the road and be "firm, cool and fair". Above all we must not take provocative decisions (such as to recall Parliament, or legislate to take over control) at the moment.'[91]

Wilson, Callaghan, Lord Stonham, a junior minister at the home office, Healey and Stewart then met the Northern Ireland delegation. The home office had a list of demands ready, but Chichester-Clark surprised everyone by conceding that the army should assume control of security, including the police and the controversial part-time B specials. The general officer commanding (GOC) would report daily to Chichester-Clark's minister of home affairs. Wilson insisted upon the rebuilding of the RUC. The B specials should be removed from near catholic areas and disarmed, and a

British chief constable take over the regulars and irregulars. There was to be an inquiry held into the role of the RUC in Northern Ireland. Whitehall saw it as a case for British policing, but it was to be perceived in Ulster as a case of taking away the B specials in the face of a catholic revolt. The Ulster delegation effectively accepted the eventual disbanding of the B specials. Lord Hunt was to recommend this in October, having been ready to scale yet another political mountain for Wilson. Hunt also recommended a new Ulster Defence Regiment (UDR), as part of the army, for part-timers.

London wanted its own officials at Stormont, and Oliver Wright, who had been in Wilson's private office before becoming an ambassador, was to occupy a room near to Chichester-Clark 'to thicken up the political relationship'. (Wilson had wanted to send a member of the cabinet, thought to be Lord Shackleton. A foreign office man hardly suggested that London saw the province as an integral part of the United Kingdom, but Wright was to be Wilson's eyes and ears, 'rather less than a governor and rather more than an ambassador'.[92] Wright was kept informed by Ken Bloomfield, of the Northern Ireland civil service, but the British communicated with Whitehall from offices in the Conway Hotel.) The idea of a non-unionist minister of community relations was rejected.

The talks lasted some six hours, Wilson and Chichester-Clark signing the so-called 'Downing Street declaration'. This stated that 'the border [was] not an issue',[93] and British standards would henceforth prevail in Northern Ireland. The unionists' willingness to listen to London on matters of civil rights 'marked the turn of the tide in the relations between Westminster and Stormont'.[94] It was agreed that Callaghan was to visit the province, and he arrived on 27 August for three days of discussion with ministers and officials, army and police officers, and members of both communities. The home secretary was well received in 'free Derry' and other areas outside the control of the unionist government, it being – in the opinion of Crossman – 'the only successful diplomatic episode in the[se] five years of a Labour Government'.[95]

Wilson was unwilling to allow Callaghan his public relations success, and sought to claim joint credit when they reported to the cabinet on 4 September. Further measures had been forced on the unionist government, mainly joint working parties on housing allocation, ending discrimination in public employment, and the prohibition of incitement to religious hatred. There was also to be an economic mission from London departments. It was announced on 8 September that the army was to construct a peaceline between catholics and protestants in Belfast, so that barrricades could be removed. The home secretary started to advise the minority to work with the unionist government, but, at the labour party conference in Brighton, he mused about 'raising the whole Irish problem to a new plane'.[96]

This was contrary to the Downing Street declaration, and the same rhetoric would be returned from Dublin a decade later. The IRA was still insignificant, splitting at the end of the year into 'official' and 'provisional' wings, and Sinn Féin following in early 1970. The latter, more traditional, group was becoming established in the catholic ghettoes by the summer, and the army had to deal increasingly with disturbances, given Hunt's plans to turn the RUC into an unarmed force.

The reform process was in motion, and Britain was being sucked in further, for what threatened to be a very a long time. A British-style police force might have contained the troubles, but with Westminster pulling the political rug from under Stormont, republicans and loyalists increasingly emerged. This required further reliance upon troops, soldiers first opening fire in October on protestants in the Shankill Road, after an RUC man had been killed. Easter 1970 saw rioting in the – catholic – Ballymurphy area of Belfast. The government was concerned about Chichester-Clark's position in early 1970, the return of Paisley and a colleague to Stormont representing a real threat from the right. The impact of the British government on the province remains debatable, but it is clear that Callaghan in the home office became a considerable force within the state towards the end of the decade.

MI5 was unravelling a Czech spying plot in London, for what it was worth. Josef Frolik, a Czech intelligence officer, had arrived in Washington on 21 July 1969, one of many to quit in the wake of the Soviet invasion. He had lived in London from 1964 to 1966, posing as labour attaché at the embassy. Frolik revealed to the CIA the names of four labour MPs – Tom Driberg, Will Owen, Sir Barnet Stross and John Stonehouse – though he had not actually run them himself. He was probably telling the CIA what it wanted to hear. This information was passed quickly to MI5, Furnival Jones exercising his right to report directly to the prime minister. Wilson authorized surveillance, and had Frolik flown to London for debriefing by his security service.

Driberg's name occasioned little worry. This was not the case with Will Owen, who had been elected MP for Morpeth in 1954. Owen had been involved with the Czechs for years, and was charged under the official secrets act. He was thought to have passed information from the house of commons' estimates committee from 1961, and all the documents for 1962-3. Frolik's evidence was ruled out as hearsay, and Owen acquitted in May 1970, though he did not stand again for parliament. Sir Barnet Stross was the son of Polish refugees who became a medical expert, and a labour MP in 1945, and his connections with Czechoslovakia may have been perfectly innocent.

John Stonehouse was the only real cause for concern. Stonehouse had become an MP in 1957, and entered the government in 1964 – holding junior posts at aviation, the colonial office, and the ministry of technology, before becoming postmaster-general in July 1968. He was never a member of the cabinet. Sometime in late 1969, Wilson arranged to have an MI5 officer, Charles Elwell, put his suspicions to Stonehouse in the study at number 10, with Michael Halls taking notes. The postmaster-general recounted his contacts with Czechs, and claims he reported one suspicious approach to the security officer at the ministry of aviation. There were several further meetings between Elwell and Stonehouse at the RAC club in Pall Mall. The matter had been allowed to rest, with Wilson forbidding his minister to take any more holidays in Czechoslovakia, and Stonehouse stayed in the government as minister of posts and telecommunications. Stonehouse stayed in the house of commons, but Wilson would not offer him a job in 1974, and he went missing off Miami Beach at the end of the year. The story of Frolik's allegations then broke, and Wilson was forced to admit to parliament, on 17 December, that MI5 had not accepted them in 1969. The prime minister was departing from normal practice, but he seems to have been greatly angered by possibility of a scandal.

The 1966 parliament had, by law, to end by the spring of 1971. Wilson had feared, before his second general election, that he might be forced to go the country in late 1969, or delay through the winter of 1970. The 1969 party conference at Brighton was considered a pre-election gathering, Wilson being at his most partisan in his attacks upon Ted Heath. While 'the politics of the sixties [had] inevitably been heavily centred on the problems of economic management',[97] he told delegates, the problems of the 1970s would have to do with the environment. This ideological embrace of ecology anticipated Crosland's new super ministry, Wilson telegraphing Crosland in Japan with the suggestion that he should be called the secretary of state for the environment. This was to be Wilson's 'rallying call for those who had been disillusioned or disaffected, either on domestic or foreign affairs, over the past years.'[98]

But 1969 was not 1963 over again, and ecology was not to have the same appeal as the scientific revolution. The conservative shadow cabinet, meeting at the Selsdon Park Hotel in Croydon, agreed its election manifesto in January 1970. 'Selsdon man', as it was later dubbed by Wilson, was a reversion to traditional right-wing themes, with an emphasis upon law and order, fewer price rises, a reduction in direct taxation and trade-union reform. Wilson had already reverted to his anti-tory style in speeches, but, as prime minister, he had to recount the achievements of his administration. The conservatives had been leading labour in the polls for nearly three years, the nadir for the government being May/June 1968, when only 21 per cent of voters stated an intention of voting for the party. The tories' lead had shortened since then, and Gallup was to predict a labour victory in May/June 1970. The party had lost seventeen seats in by-elections in the course of the parliament, these going mainly to conservatives, but also to the liberals, and Scottish and Welsh nationalists. Labour held South Ayshire on 19 March, and Wilson reckoned this was the first by-election swing from the conservatives. The party was not fully to regain its position in local elections, but the poll for the GLC on 9 April showed evidence of the working class returning to the party.

Wilson claims it was on 13 April, the evening before the budget, that he decided to go to the country in June. His worry had been the world cup, to be played that month in Mexico. 'The political effect of this', Tony Benn would note, 'can't be altogether ignored.'[99] Britain was knocked out on Sunday, 14 June. The decision to have the election was made probably after one of the frequent kitchen cabinet discussions held in his study, with Shore, Kaufman, Haines and Williams. Shore and Kaufman favoured June. Haines was hesitant, and Williams in favour only if victory was guaranteed. The prime minister felt he had good economic news to broadcast, but wanted to exploit the existing wage inflation before retrenchment became necessary. He was also worried about rumours of a conservative propaganda campaign in the summer. The inner cabinet discussed a June election on 29 April, Wilson favouring Thursday, 18 June, with four weeks' notice. Jenkins was cautious, and Castle and Crossman favoured October. 'It was obvious that the Prime Minister was wanting the election', Crossman wrote after an inner cabinet on 4 May, 'just the opposite of 1966, when he had to be dragged into it. This time he was having to be dragged back.'[100] Wilson finally got his way on 14 May, following labour local gains in England, Wales and Scotland, which helped to shift the minds of Jenkins and Crossman. 'Harold', Barbara Castle recorded, 'wasn't going to let us dodge sharing responsibility. "Everyone agreed? Right: then no one will be able to claim the virtue of hindsight."'[101]

The full cabinet was not informed of the election date, when it met after the inner cabinet on 14 May. 'They were just told that there was still no decision but that it was most important to say there had been no discussion.'[102] The prime minister announced there would be a committee on the future of broadcasting, chaired by Lord Annan, a shot across the bows of the BBC in the run-up to an election. Wilson predicted a majority of over twenty, but Ian Mikardo thought it would be another 1964. With a joint executive-cabinet meeting planned for 17 May, Wilson was concerned to keep control of the manifesto's preparation. '"We're really asking for a doctor's mandate", said Harold. "We're the best doctors the country's got."'[103] The announcement was delayed until Monday, 18 May; parliament was to be dissolved in eleven days, with the election on 18 June.

A South African cricket tour was due to begin at Lords that Thursday, though the MCC had excluded the South-African born Asian, Basil D'Oliveira, from an English side in 1968. The resultant furore led to the tour being cancelled, but the MCC invited South Africa to play twenty-eight matches in England in 1970. A Springbok rugby team had toured Britain the previous winter, only to be subjected to protests led by Peter Hain. The number of cricket matches was cut back in February to twelve, but the labour government was still faced with the prospect of anti-apartheid demonstrations. Wilson was opposed to the MCC invitation, but stated '[he] did not believe they should be disrupted by digging up pitches or violence ... and not by nasty, sneaky little things like, sort of, mirrors to deflect the sunshine into batsmen's eyes and so on.'[104] 'Harold and Jim Callaghan', Crossman noted on 30 April, 'are taking enormous time and trouble over this because, if the tour takes place, black countries of Africa may refuse to come to this summer's Commonwealth Games [in Edinburgh].'[105] The prime minister was advised that using immigration control against individual cricketers would probably require parliamentary approval. It was decided on 19 May that England would not play South Africa in future until it had teams selected on a non-racial basis, though the 1970 tour would proceed. Callaghan then told the MCC that, 'on the grounds of broad public policy the Government would prefer the MCC to withdraw the invitation'.[106] This duly occurred.

The idea of a four-week election campaign was to get the labour party into shape after the desertions of the government years. Trade unionists, like Joe Gormley, advised him to delay, because *In Place of Strife* had not been forgotten. But Wilson planned to include local committee rooms in his visits round the country, due to begin in Cardiff on 29 May. The campaign was run from Transport House, but the political office under Marcia Williams was again central.

'From the outset, the election was fought as Harold Wilson v. the Conservatives', wrote one of his staff. 'The role of the Labour Party was played down.'[107] The room of Mary Wilson's secretary, Peggy Field, sister of Marcia Williams, became the prime minister's election headquarters. Peter Shore's cabinet job as coordinator of government information allowed him to act as political adviser in these months. Gerald Kaufman was a candidate in Manchester, and Will Camp was brought in from British Steel at a late point. David Candler had taken to accompanying the prime minister on his political engagements. Joe Haines – though a civil servant – wrote Wilson's press articles, and John Allen was brought over from Transport House to help. Richard Crossman had quit the executive in 1967, and intended resigning as a minister. Though again a parliamentary candidate, he went off to Malta for ten days' holiday. Barbara Castle, now a power in her own right, was also excluded from Wilson's inner circle. Thomas Balogh had been ennobled out of number 10 but returned to help as a speech writer.

Television was again important, the advent of colour further presenting Heath and Wilson to consumers. Confrontations were ruled out, though Wilson stole a march on his opponents by having the election announcement filmed in the garden of number 10. Edward Heath was not amused: 'He sat down in a very comfortable chair with the sun shining and artificial geraniums all the way round, put there for the event, and it was the old stuff all over again.'[108]

Wilson appeared on a BBC programme on 28 May to answer viewers' questions put by Robin Day. Asked if 'in view of [his] past record of lies and broken promises, [he] really [did] expect the electorate to place any reliance on [his] word?', Wilson stated his intention of 'nail[ing] those lies'. The studio was unusually hot that evening, and, according to Joe Haines, 'how it looked on television was this man wriggling under the intensely hostile questioning'.

1970 also saw the parties embrace political advertising, unencumbered by even the modest restrictions imposed on commercial purchasers of airtime. Heath was well presented against a bright blue backdrop, making short, well-crafted speeches. Wilson started to go walkabout among party supporters, an idea of Marcia Williams's who did not otherwise admire the queen. It worked for the prime minister given pleasant weather, though his advisers then panicked. He was told by his political secretary: 'God, you can't go on doing this, we have got to get you into situations where you actually make speeches that deliver the party's policies.'[109]

Wilson kept control of the manifesto, delegating the writing to Peter Shore. The executive meeting on 20 May did not even discuss it. Crossman, just back from the Mediterranean, happened upon a drafting committee in Transport House on 26 May chaired by Tony Benn, and he was able to rework the section on social services. Wilson had been attacking the opposition for making spending promises, while intending to cut public expenditure. The inner cabinet, at the behest of the chancellor, had agreed there should be no interference with a white paper in which public finance had been allocated for, effectively, the lifetime of the next parliament. Barbara Castle's proposals for capital sharing were vetoed by a cabinet committee as insufficently detailed, but she was encouraged by the prime minister to write sections on unemployment, strikes and inflation. The executive, in a six-hour meeting, with Wilson present, tackled a third, and final, draft of the manifesto the following day. Anything of interest, except the reform of the house of lords, was removed, and the subsequent press conference was described as 'nearly a shambles'.

'I am appalled at our lack of good material with "bite" as we go into the campaign', wrote Barbara Castle. 'I've never felt less well equipped for an Election but the others (Harold apart) seem so lackadaisical.'[110]

The polls remained in labour's favour for the next three weeks. Heath was having difficulties with his credibility, while ministers were attending to government business. Wilson was to become involved in the newspaper strike, and was the consummate performer on the stump. 'Harold has got the bit between his teeth and he is fighting the election in his own individual style', wrote Crossman on 7 June. 'He has dispensed with practically all policy and there is no party manifesto because there are no serious commitments at all. In that sense we are fighting a Stanley Baldwin, "Trust my Harold", election.'[111] The Sunday before polling day, he contrasted it with 1959, less because he thought Wilson was Macmillan, more because he associated Heath with Gaitskell. The conservatives were going to lose.

Barbara Castle was uneasy, and wrote in her diary the Saturday before polling: 'I have a haunting feeling there is a silent majority sitting behind its lace curtains, waiting to come out and vote Tory.'[112]

The trade figures for May were released on Monday, 15 June, showing a freak deficit of £31 million. Richard Crossman toured polling stations in his Coventry constituency on the Thursday, observing that the turnout remained low after 6.30 p.m. 'I was sure that I had found in microcosm what we were going to discover in macrocosm.'[113]

The first returns that night from the midlands showed a swing away from labour. Turnout was a post-war low of 72 per cent. Labour lost less than a million votes, the conservatives putting on something under two million. The labour share of the vote at 43 per cent was still on a par with all elections after 1951 – except 1966. The tories had been losing relatively since 1955, but 46.4 per cent in 1970 represented a reversal in fortunes. Labour had a net loss of 60 seats with 287, the conservatives securing a net gain of 68 with 330. Heath had an overall majority of thirty, much to his own surprise. Prominent labour casualties were George Brown, still deputy leader, and Jennie Lee. The liberals lost out to other minor forces. There was a swing of 4.7 per cent to the conservatives, this being highest in England and lowest in Scotland. Huyton now had an electorate of over 100,000, and the prime minister secured his highest ever poll of 45,583 votes, on his lowest turnout of 67.6 per cent. This gave him a majority of 21,074 over his tory opponent, on a swing against of 2.4 per cent. But he knew the game was up nationally.

The Wilsons left in the early hours of Friday morning for London. Marcia Williams telephoned the political office from Huyton, ordering the staff to begin packing files. David Candler and Joe Haines had already concluded the government was defeated, and were drinking whisky. Sometime after dawn a *Sun* photographer, in a car following Wilson's on the motorway, obtained a picture of the prime minister sleeping with his head on Mary's shoulder. 'It said all that there was to say.'[114] Wilson and his assistants reached

Downing Street soon after 7.00 a.m. Waiting in one of the state rooms were the television cameras, the prime minister later conceding defeat after hearing further results. He explained the surprise outcome in economic terms. While labour was leaving a strong economy for the new prime minister, the electorate had not forgotten the price which had been paid to get it right.

A depleted final meeting of the inner cabinet was held that afternoon in Downing Street. Wilson proposed giving the tories a honeymoon period, expecting an issue to arise within two years. It was assumed there would be no leadership contest. Though Callaghan was party treasurer, Crossman thought he might fight Jenkins for the now vacant deputy leadership. It was agreed to meet again on the following Wednesday, pending elections to the shadow cabinet. Tony Benn then got out his movie camera, and filmed the end of the labour government as Wilson left the cabinet room. The film was found to be blank when processed. The prime minister then left for the palace to hand in his resignation. He had been in office for a little under six years.

CHAPTER 20

Leader of the Opposition, 1970–3

Harold Wilson resigned as prime minister at 6.30 p.m. on Friday, 16 June. The family quit Downing Street immediately, Edward Heath extending the usual courtesy of Chequers for the weekend. He also let Mary Wilson remove their belongings from the flat at number 10 at her convenience. Wilson informed Crossman that he and Mary were to become his neighbours in Westminster. A house had been secured for three months at eighty guineas (£84) a week by telephoning Harrods. Fourteen Vincent Square belonged to Jerome Epstein, an American film producer/director who had worked with Chaplin, though he was to retain the use of the basement for himself and his partner; the couple were rapidly married, seemingly to avoid causing Wilson any embarrassment. Epstein also offered the new leader of the opposition his chauffeur, though this was only a temporary arrangement. Marcia Williams was relieved that Wilson would not be getting behind the wheel of a car. He was a bad driver, and the conservative prime minister was to allow him a government car and driver – Bill Housden – as leader of the opposition.

The Wilsons, with Giles, moved to Vincent Square the following Monday, taking with them their housekeeper Mrs Pollard. Wilson's secretary acknowledged the election result was depressing. 'It is impossible', she wrote later, 'to overstate the sense of shock which was felt in those post-defeat months, and its effect on politicians and staff alike, all of which had been aggravated by the ... extra workload of the campaign itself.'[1] Epstein found the Wilsons "'very gentle, kind and polite, but you felt the strain of their election failure'". "'It's nice to know we still have friends'", Wilson said. Their landlord considered they were "'a couple coming very close together again after the ups and downs of marriage'".[2] Wilson took to using sleeping pills, and was reported to be drinking brandy heavily at a dinner given by Rupert Murdoch.

Devaluation in 1967 may be seen as the turning point in Harold Wilson's political career. He had climbed the greasy pole, and then tried to prove himself as prime minister. Despite all his efforts, success on many issues eluded him. Involvement in a second devaluation may have meant he started seeing a horizon to his political career, and he certainly began to think of life after the premiership. It was to be said that he told a group of foreign correspondents in number 10 that 'he saw himself as a *mélange* (his word) of Gladstone, Lloyd George, and Churchill!'[3] Wilson only reached his fifty-fourth birthday in 1970, but he had been in Whitehall and Westminster for three decades continuously. He was then in the sixth year of one of the most demanding jobs in the country. Wilson had considerable physical and mental stamina, and greatly needed such stimulation, but he endured considerable knocks and adversities, and his behaviour had often been characteristic of a person under stress. One labour MP has even written of Wilson being close to a mental breakdown at the time of the dog licence speech. Joe Haines believes that he went into the 1970 election thinking of his ultimate retirement. 'If Harold had won in 1970, he would have stayed a couple of years.'[4] This is credible. Wilson would then have won three elections in a row, and might not have wanted to risk a defeat. As a peacetime premier in the twentieth century, he would have soon overtaken Stanley Baldwin's record of six years and ten months. Asquith and Churchill had both occupied number 10 for eight years and eight months, partly in wartime. Wilson would have overtaken these giants in June 1973. Tony Benn talked to Wilson at a party on 5 December 1970: '[He] told me that had we won the Election he would only have continued as Prime Minister for three years. I have often suspected this but he has never said it specifically before.'[5]

The 1970 defeat was a considerable personal setback for Wilson, given his penchant for political timing, and he later tried to blame the late Richard Crossman for the election date. Wilson lost because of unexpected trade figures three days before polling, and he would have avoided this with an 11 June election, as Joe Haines may have advised. The fault was his alone. Undoing the labour defeat became his medium-term goal, even though there was always a risk he might not win again. Harold Wilson gambled on the chance of historical rehabilitation, as he settled back in opposition with the prospect of four parliamentary sessions before the labour party.

He was a shadow of his former self, as a number of witnesses testify. Richard Marsh was to say in March 1971 that Wilson '[took] little part in the business of the House ... [He] embarrass[ed] new members by recounting the brilliant speeches he made years ago.'[6] Douglas Houghton later described Wilson as having 'no inspiration or enthusiasm to impart, dwell[ing] on the glories of the recent past, and [having] no vision of the future.'[7] Ray Gunter also had a house in the Scillies, and still saw Wilson from time to time. 'He looks old and bent, a very different man from the old Wilson', Cecil King noted in his diary after dinner with Gunter in September 1971. 'According to Ray, Wilson is in two minds whether or no to retire – he certainly will if he thinks Labour will be defeated next time ... Mary will exert all the influence she has in favour of retirement.'[8] Andrew Graham was only to see Wilson once during his time in opposition, when Tommy Balogh organized a gathering of economic advisers about 1972. 'Wilson was completely and utterly uninvolved with the meeting in any way whatsoever'. Graham remembers him going on about speculators having ruined devaluation. 'I came back to Oxford and I told my wife I couldn't conceive that Wilson could ever be prime minister again. [It] ... seemed ... as if somebody had just switched off the adrenalin.'[9]

Marcia Williams hunted for a more permanent home for the Wilsons in the first months of the new parliament, often accompanying them to visit properties. Mary Wilson had stated a preference for living in the centre of town, and they moved that December to 5 Lord North Street, Wilson paying £20,000 on a twenty-year lease. Their new house was within easy walking distance of the Palace of Westminster and Transport House. Originally occupied by one of Lord North's mistresses, the front door of number five opened on to a dining hall, off which was a small room used by Mary Wilson as a study. In the basement was the kitchen, and Mrs Pollard's room. The drawing room on the first floor looked on to the street at the front, and a small paved garden at the back. Here the Wilsons kept the many presents they had received while in Downing Street. Wilson took the larger bedroom on the top floor, Mary and Giles having smaller rooms. They also acquired a third home in 1970, Grange Farm near Little Missenden in Buckinghamshire, not far from Chequers. Grange Farm was a five-bedroomed, oak-beamed farmhouse costing about £20,000. An Elizabethan barn was converted into a study, with an extension for the storage of Wilson's papers.

Wilson had discussed labour's political future with Williams, Balogh, Shore and Kaufman during his last weekend at Chequers. Peter Shore thought he recovered quickly from the defeat. Marcia Williams wanted Wilson to resign the leadership, presumably to come back stronger in the party. He had already decided only to speak in the queen's speech, and at the party conference at the end of September. Wilson returned to the leader of the opposition's room at Westminster on 22 June, but did not attend dinner the following evening at the Castles' flat in Islington. As leader, and especially a former prime minister, he would probably be above caucusing with the left. The others present at the Castles were Crossman, Balogh, Shore and Harold Lever. Crossman had taken on the editorship of the *New Statesman* though still an MP. 'Tommy Balogh explained that the economic policy hadn't succeeded because the wrong people were in the wrong place.'[10] Lever in contrast condemned the obsession with the exchange rate, and advanced a Keynesian defence of deficits. 'There is a difference between a deficit associated with real growth and a deficit associated with living beyond your means.'[11] Lever was emerging as a considerable political figure. Barbara Castle wanted to stand for the deputy leadership, but there was a feeling that *In Place of Strife* had destroyed her chances. Benn mooted the possibility of his candidature, though seemed more keen on standing for chief whip. He had thought about the general secretaryship of the party in 1968, and would only consider the leadership in December 1970: 'If I am going to make any sort of bid for the leadership at any stage, I shall have to begin preparing for it soon.'[12]

The former inner cabinet met the following afternoon, Wilson announcing the leader was to be reelected by acclaim by the parliamentary party. He suggested that the chairmanship of the parliamentary party should not revert to him, and Douglas Houghton was duly reelected to this separate post. As for the deputy leadership, he hoped any candidates would come and see him. He tried hard to dissuade Barbara Castle from standing at some point that week, on the grounds that she would split the party, and even said he would refuse to carry on in such circumstances. According to Joe Haines, 'Barbara left saying she would stand, but she never did. When she had gone from the room, the leader's defences fell away and he visibly sagged. For a time he was utterly dejected, depressed and defeated. At that moment he might have resigned.'[13]

The new parliamentary party assembled the following Monday, 29 June in Church House. Wilson was reelected unopposed to the leadership, but not before Leo Abse had insisted that it was the party which licensed the leader, and not the other way round. As the new house of commons assembled, Wilson expressed the hope that labour MPs and their 'expert groups' would work closely with the party executive. This 'was never really done successfully before'.[14] Roy Jenkins stood for the deputy leadership. Jim Callaghan chose not to oppose Jenkins, seemingly because he preferred being on the executive as treasurer. Callaghan quickly seized the chairmanship of the party's home policy committee. Jenkins's campaign was organized in Dick Taverne's flat, the others present including Bill Rodgers, George Thomson, David Owen, David Marquand and Bob Maclennan. These former Gaitskellites, called 'the Reform Club set'[15] by Wilsonites, had been the conspirators of the 1960s, though Jenkins was the success story of the second labour government. Fred Peart decided to run for the deputy leadership, as did Michael Foot with his reputation as a backbench rebel. Jenkins was elected on 8 July on the first ballot with 133 votes. The surprise of the contest was the 67 votes for Michael Foot, who had shot forward as a left-wing tribune in the wake of defeat. From about 50 members in the 1960s, the Tribune group was to grow to 93 in this smaller parliamentary party. But party unity was temporarily preserved in

1970. Roy Jenkins's election to the deputy leadership reassured an establishment concerned about labour opposition to the common market.

Left-wingers were mainly elected to the constituency section of the executive at the party conference in Blackpool; successful candidates, in descending order, were Castle, Benn, Joan Lestor MP, who had come on in 1967, Mikardo, Frank Allaun, also 1967, Driberg and Denis Healey. The latter was the sole right-winger. The five-strong women's section was to become more interesting, with Judith Hart and Renée Short on the left. It was November, with the return of parliament after the recess, before the shadow cabinet was elected. The twelve positions went, in descending order, to Callaghan, Healey, Crosland, Houghton, Benn, Foot, Shirley Williams, Harold Lever, Short, Peart, Thomson and Castle. Wilson had had the power of patronage as prime minister for six years, but was now surrounded by elected frontbench colleagues. Former Gaitskellites greatly outnumbered the left, but he followed the pattern of government office in appointing frontbench spokesmen and women. Michael Stewart had not been elected by his colleagues, and Healey was asked to shadow the foreign office. George Thomson took care of defence, Lever was given a new European watching brief, and Shirley Williams replaced Crossman in the health and social services slot. Michael Foot was given the fuel and power industries to look after, these being taken from Tony Benn's wide range of responsibilities.

The new parliamentary session had begun on 2 July. In the debate on the queen's speech, Harold Wilson stated that the new government, in contrast to 1964, was inheriting a balance of payments surplus. 'As a government', he said, 'we were ready to sacrifice a great deal in political terms to put sterling on a firm foundation, honoured and respected, and we shall show the same sense of responsibility in opposition.' He announced a strategy for labour. 'We shall wait for each new development of policy, wait watchfully and keenly, but we shall not rush into condemnation for the sake of it.'[16] Wilson expressed the hope that Selsdon Man, having been gagged during the campaign, would not be resurrected now that Heath was in Downing Street. Benn thought Wilson 'incredible, just like an India rubber man, bouncing up again after his defeat, completely unphased by the fact that he lost'.[17]

It was 29 September, at the party conference, before the public heard from Wilson. Relaxed after his usual summer holiday in the Scillies, and with the cares of office having lifted, he gave a knockabout anti-tory performance, larded with quotations – including reducing prices 'at a stroke'.[18] The former prime minister defended the record of his past six years, 'in which [the government] almost doubled the provision for social services, health, housing, education and the attack on poverty'. This was to be his defence in 1970–1 of his two administrations. Now espying 'Selsdon Minister', Wilson promised a vigorous parliamentary defence. 'I warn [ministers] that if they lay their hands on all that has been built up by the British people, by this Movement, then whatever their mask of cold indifference and doctrinaire arrogance, the fight we shall put up by day and by night against their legislation will make even the battles they had to fight to get the Rent Act through seem mild in comparison.'[19]

Harold Wilson's political office at number 10 had become his private office on 19 June, awaiting transfer to Westminster. Heath's aides were initially reluctant to vacate the leader of the opposition's office just behind the speaker's chair. Following several phone conversations between Marcia Williams and Douglas Hurd, Heath's political secretary, access was promised for the evening. Two – black – ministry of works' porters, upset at labour's defeat, began the first political strike of the Heath years, only to be sacked.

Marcia Williams had taken charge of the packing on the second floor at number 10. Harold Wilson had had a private office of three at Westminster in 1963–4, but 'as an ex-Prime Minister, his own standards were now considerably higher.'[20] Marcia Williams claims he left number 10 with an overdraft, but another source says he and Mary had about £14,000 at this time – the sum he got from the sale of his Hampstead Garden Suburb home. It seems likely that his prime ministerial salary had failed to cover all necessary expenses, the post having traditionally been occupied by men of wealth. Marcia Williams reverted to being Wilson's secretary at £30 a week, MPs having been granted an allowance of up to £500 per annum in 1969 to employ such a person. Joe Haines left the civil service, to become full-time press officer to the leader of the opposition, a post funded by a fortnight's lecture tour of the United States in the summer recesses of 1971–3. Other, clerical and research, staff were lent by Transport House, but Marcia Williams found them insufficiently devoted to her boss in working unsocial hours. Wilson and Williams had called in management consultants, but they underestimated the demands on the private office by working in the summer of 1970. Running costs of £20,000–25,000 per year were estimated, though this was to be less than adequate by 1974. Some £6,000 came from Transport House. Joe Haines had initially been suggested as office manager, but the job went to Marcia's brother, Tony Field, on a unpaid, part-time basis. He was a geologist turned businessman, and, though not a member of the labour party, he had become a friend of Wilson's, and regular golf partner at Chequers. He stayed until his marriage in June 1973, to be replaced by an organizer from Transport House, Ken Peay. Peay left that October, having failed to oust Marcia Williams, the job going to Albert Murray, a former junior minister who had lost his seat in the election.

Wilson received no state help in 1970 for his office, so some of his friends decided to establish a trust fund. The details were drawn up by Wilson's solicitor, Lord Goodman, the fund being kept secret from the labour party. It was chaired by Lord [Wilfred] Brown, former head of Glacier Metal, who had been a junior minister in the board of trade. Brown had belonged to the 1944 association, a secret group of wealthy businessmen serviced by the general secretary's office, which provided funds in Attlee and Gaitskell's time. The other members of Brown's group were Samuel Fisher, a diamond merchant, and Rudy Sternberg, an Austrian-born businessman.

'So discreet were [Brown, Fisher, and Sternberg] about the organization of the Trust Fund', claims Marcia Williams, 'that, although Harold Wilson knew of its existence, neither he nor anyone else knew the full details about it. Certainly, it was rarely discussed. It operated quite separately from the Private Office, and we did not know at any one time exactly who contributed to it.'[21] Joe Haines is adamant it continued after Wilson returned to Downing Street in 1974, when he again had a political office run by Marcia Williams. 'It's been denied, but it continued', he says. 'I've got the proof at home ... It certainly continued into his second premiership.'[22] The fund paid for 'four to five secretaries and research assistants, and an office junior'.[23]

It is thought that a dozen or so businessmen contributed up to £2,000 a year to the fund. Brown and Sternberg certainly did. A former member of Wilson's staff – who was paid out of the fund – says 'Joe Kagan was also putting money in.'[24] The name of Eric Miller, of Peachey Property, is also mentioned, as is Emmanuel Kaye, of Lansing Bagnall. Other contributors are thought to have been George Weidenfeld and Arieh Handler, a banker with Israeli connections.

A separate research fund was established in 1973. This was not secret, as Wilson shared it with other front-bench colleagues, £20,000 being contributed by Sigmund Sternberg. No relation of Rudy's, he was a Hungarian-born scrap metal dealer. Sigmund Sternberg was, at that time, vice-chairman of, what was called, the industry group, founded the previous year, also by Lord Brown, as a continuation of the 1944 association. Marcia Williams has admitted that 'a number [of members] were subsequently honoured – some by Harold Wilson during his first government, others earlier by Clement Attlee and Hugh Gaitskell – for the contribution they had made to the Party and to public life.'[25] The following honours were bestowed by Wilson, on those thought to be associated with his trust fund: knighthoods – Samuel Fisher (1967), George Weidenfeld (1969), Rudy Sternberg (1970), Joseph Kagan (1970), Emmanuel Kaye (1974), Eric Miller (1976), Sigmund Sternberg (1976); peerages – Wilfred Brown (1964), Arnold Goodman (1965), Beattie Plummer (1965), Fisher (Lord Fisher of Camden, 1976), Rudy Sternberg (Lord Plurenden, 1975), Weidenfeld (1976), and Kagan (1976).

Wilson had suggested in 1966 that there should be no further political honours, awarded at new year and on the queen's official birthday in

June. These went to party faithful and financial contributors, the recipients often being simply friends of the prime minister's. Such honours could be bought – indirectly. Anthony Wedgwood Benn had argued for reform of the system in 1963, getting a barely polite hearing in an executive sub-committee the following June. Wilson promised in 1966 that there should only be honours for public service, names being suggested by government departments. He privately suggested that labour party agents could be included under public honours, but Crossman told him this was 'merely a gimmick because you *haven't* cut out political Honours'.[26] Wilson announced at the party conference that there would be changes in the system, and this seems to have been brought about by administrative action. He did not recommend any labour MPs, party officials, or coun-cillors, though local government service, regardless of party, continued to be recognized for public honours; labour councillors received twice as many awards as conservatives. He also reduced the number of virtually automatic honours for senior civil servants, which cannot have helped him manage Whitehall. Wilson failed to do the same for defence and diplomatic personnel, because of pressure from the departments. The honours system remained an aspect of prime ministerial prerogative, and few realized that Wilson did not exclude political service, when it came to dissolution honours. The same was to apply when he resigned. Heath reverted to the old system in 1970, and members of the shadow cabinet, such as Callaghan, Peart and Mellish, wanted to support him. The labour opposition limply asked for a committee to look at the honours system. 'The discussion revealed the Party at its worst', wrote Tony Benn, 'believing that it is entitled to the prerequisites which go with being part of the ruling class.'[27]

Wilson had refused to appoint hereditary peers from the first, but hereditary honours had to be maintained for the royal family. There were only about forty labour members of the upper house in 1964, which numbered roughly 1,000 attenders. Wilson's strategy of slowing turning the house of lords into an effective second chamber, by awarding life peerages, led to proposals for its reform in 1968. Crossman agreed with the opposition parties that there should only be 230 salaried voting peers, divided between the parties. The government would always have a majority. The bill was defeated in 1969, largely due to an unholy alliance of Michael Foot, Enoch Powell and Robert Sheldon, acting partly out of fear of a prime minister having the power to appoint 105 peers after each general election. Wilson had started with the view that new life peers should work, ideally for the government, but he lost interest towards the end of his government. In his dissolution honours list in 1970, he elevated George Brown and Harold Davies – two labour MPs who had lost their seats. Leslie Lever had released a Manchester seat for Gerald Kaufman, but had to wait for his peerage until Wilson returned to power. In 1976 the *Sunday Times* was to investigate Wilson's house of lords appointments. Of the 146 peers then taking the labour whip, he had been responsible for elevating 103. Some of his nominees chose to sit on the cross benches, and a few must have been tories. The first appointments were political, designed to strengthen the party in the lords; eleven of the twenty-five new life peers in 1964–5 were given government jobs. The largest group comprised former labour MPs, numbering some forty. The other groups were: business (12), academic (10), miscellaneous (9), journalism (8), local government (8), trade unions (8), and spouses of former labour figures (4). 'Taking Wilson's Labour peers as a body, the voting and speaking record is distinctly patchy, with a noticeable deterioration towards the end.'[28]

Wilson had tried to keep a diary while in office, occasionally dictating at night to Marcia Williams. Before he even vacated Downing Street in June 1970, he was looking forward to selling his account of the labour government. The prime minister was not the only one looking to posterity, however. The *Observer* had reported in early 1967 that Richard Crossman was to publish a book based on his political diary. Barbara Castle was also said to be working on her memoirs. Wedgwood Benn admitted to being the third diarist in the cabinet. Others were thought to be Roy Jenkins and Fred Peart. Benn noted Wilson as saying he wanted to write three books: '"One, I will write immediately we leave office and that will be an absolutely factual record of the Administration. Later, when I retire, I shall publish a much fuller account in which I will give far greater detail ... Thirdly, I shall write a book about what really happened with instructions that it should not be published until after my death.'[29]

George Brown raised the matter at cabinet on 26 January, arguing that this undermined confidence between colleagues. Wilson had long known of Crossman's plan to write a volume of memoirs, and another on the British constitution, and suggested a committee under the lord chancellor to review the conventions. 'Any private and personal recording of what went on in Cabinet', he said, 'was to be deprecated and contracts which might bring a Minister under any kind of improper pressure were obviously wrong.'[30]

Lord Gardiner did not report until September, and ministers disagreed on the question of the cabinet secretary vetting their manuscripts. Wilson wanted the party leader to be the judge – even in opposition. It was George Brown who threatened to be the first minister to publish his memoirs, though he did not begin working until April 1970. On the eve of the general election, Wilson told Crossman that his first book would run to three or four volumes. 'The big job [would] be the twenty-volume memoirs [he would] leave for posterity.'[31] He seems not to have been joking.

Lord Goodman had already initiated negotiations with Lord Thomson's Times Newspapers to serialize Wilson's book in the *Sunday Times*. The editor, Harold Evans, was no admirer of the prime minister, considering him hostile to the freedom of the press, but the company had bought the private papers of the likes of Montgomery, and this was also to be the case with Wilson. The volume was to be published in hardback by Weidenfeld and Nicolson and Michael Joseph. This was the first such joint venture for a Wilson book, and the two houses seem to have put up £30,000. This was a great deal of money, but small beer for a former prime minister. Goodman was talking in the context of a labour defeat, but Wilson is understood to have been relatively sure of victory. The approach to a newspaper was necessary to raise the big money. Four days before the election was called, Heath told Cecil King that Wilson was asking for £225,000. It is thought that the figure of 'something over £215,000'[32] was eventually agreed, about July 1970. (Hugo Young, who was in the know, claimed, in 1990, that the *Sunday Times* paid Wilson the equivalent of over half a million pounds at today's prices.) During the recording of a television interview with David Dimbleby in 1971, he exploded in uncharacteristic anger when asked about his earnings: 'I would not believe any of the stories you read in the press about that. If they got the facts, they twisted them. Anything personal – if they did not get the facts, they invented them.'[33] Marcia Williams acknowledges that 'a satisfactory large sum of money was in question – enough to clear his overdraft and make some provision for his future retirement, for staff pensions and for the Private Office.'[34]

Wilson had begun to think about his book on the way back from Liverpool in the early hours of 19 June 1970. According to Joe Haines, 'the volume would ... serve as a handbook of the successes of the Government which party workers could use during the next General Election campaign.'[35] Wilson began to dictate his account into a tape recorder that summer. Haines had signed a contract to do the writing, and was paid by the *Sunday Times* for a year; Peggy Field was also employed as a typist. Wilson quickly abandoned this method on the grounds that the volume would prove too long, though he still seems to have been thinking of three volumes as late as November. Wilson sat down in Vincent Square to write the remainder of the text himself on Wednesday, 2 September, finishing the first draft in Lord North Street on Monday, 1 February 1971. He then worked on it with others for another two months or so. Joe Haines was director of research, responsible for checking official records and other sources. 'I worked bloody hard on the book.'[36] Martin Gilbert, fellow of Merton College, Oxford, was brought in as an adviser on the manuscript, at the suggestion of Marcia Williams, and was most active in the first three months of 1971. Gilbert then employed Jane Cousins (formerly Mills), a graduate of the University of Kent, as a research assistant. She was also involved in the book, and would stay and work for Wilson as a political researcher.

The result of all this effort was published a little over a year after the 1970 election. *The Labour Government, 1964–1970: A Personal Record* ran to 836 pages. The book contained twenty-six photographs, judiciously selected to show the many faces of Wilson's government – all his own. There was not one official cabinet photograph, and the former prime minister, who railed against the charge of presidential rule, also figured in all the seventeen newspaper cartoons. The book was serialized in the *Sunday Times* and other papers abroad, but would not appear in paperback until 1974. Wilson claims he asked his colleagues in government to refresh his memory on particular events, and thanked many – unnamed – friends who helped with its 'compilation'.[37] It is dedicated to the labour party's supporters, and bears a quotation from Aneurin Bevan on the difficulty of economic planning in a parliamentary democracy.

Harold Wilson had written the first draft in longhand early each morning before his normal working day, and also at weekends, using ruled A4 paper. Two sample pages show he wrote clearly, and with little correction. (Wilson's drafting ability has often been remarked upon.) Much of it came from memory, which is not surprising for Wilson. He produced something under half a million words in five months, writing twelve thousand words in one weekend alone. The final volume was a little under 400,000 words, after Joe Haines edited it down. Wilson wrenched his right shoulder in November, and the writing also led to cramp; he was using cortisone the following March. It is true that the burden of the premiership had lifted, and he was not around much in 1970–1, but it was a Herculean task for a man who was an MP and party leader, with obligations to vote, speak, attend meetings, see people, and travel on political, and private, business. Joe Haines was to write that 'the physical and mental toll was such that he did not recover fully from the effort for more than a year.'[38] Other close associates also see Wilson as having aged during this period, though Martin Gilbert was impressed by Wilson's industry. He noted of a Wilson speaking engagement in Perth on 1 April 1971: 'He works every weekend. He is harder working than anyone I know.'[39]

A photocopy of the first draft had been sent to Gilbert in Oxford, and Jane Cousins also had a copy. Gilbert was not involved in any initial discussions of the project, but he clearly agreed with Wilson on the structure of the volume. Gilbert certainly worked with him on the final preparation of the manuscript. His role was literary prompter, and he tried to keep official accounts, which resulted in Wilson's civil service prose, out of the text. The Oxford historian wanted the former prime minister's own account, albeit hopefully located in objective reality. There were discussions about passages in the draft, and topics not included. 'He was extremely open to all suggestions and ideas', Jane Cousins recalls, 'and if you could argue it through,

you won the argument.' If Marcia Williams was present, it was an interesting debate. Wilson was 'very sloppy on dates', though this was Haines's
responsibility to check.[39] Gilbert recalls maybe a dozen major meetings with
Wilson, and a similar number of shorter ones. He remembers that, when
he suggested elucidation, Wilson would actually draft in front of him; several
hundred words on the highlands and islands development board owed their
origin to such a cue. 'He was determined to finish the book and finish it
quickly.' Wilson drank whisky, well-watered, and smoked cigars between
pipes. Gilbert recalls being in the presence of a significant political figure:
'I have never known anybody to conduct such an exciting running
commentary on what he was reading, in the case of the memoirs, on who
he was seeing, in terms of the people who came into the room, and left,
on the events of the day. It was a perpetual running commentary ... It was
irreverent, but he was somehow always thinking a little ahead ... It was
as if he was sorting out his own thoughts and ideas, doing it aloud, with
great humour and irreverence.' Rhodesia and Vietnam, he remembers, as
dominating the discussion of Wilson's premiership. The book was conceived
as 'an interim statement', Wilson having his eye on the next general
election.[40] The labour leader had told Heath three times on a flight to Paris,
that he intended to tell all, but Douglas Houghton reported the labour leader
was 'warned by his colleagues that any "rough stuff" would be answered
in kind – and that there were more of them than of him'.[41]

Martin Gilbert also attended a planning meeting with the publishers, at
which production details were discussed. When the question of a title was
raised, Wilson joked about 'old men forget' having been used already by
Duff Cooper. 'This book is meant to be serious history', he said. 'On the
whole I prefer a flat title. It's how I saw it from Downing Street. I was on
top of the elephant.' Several titles were suggested, Wilson finally coming
up with 'the labour goverment, 1964–1970'. When Weidenfeld suggested,
as subtitle, 'a prime minister's record', he demurred. 'It isn't a prime
minister's record. That makes it sound like presidential government. It's a
record of what the government did.' Martin Gilbert wanted galley proofs,
and Haines was also concerned about mistakes. 'I don't care about mistakes',
Wilson insisted. 'I've been reading the *Guardian* for years.'[42] He wanted
it published before September so people could take it with them on their
holidays. Wilson agreed to do a publicity tour, but not on Fridays.

Wilson's volume weighs over three pounds, and is divided into thirty-
eight chapters. It bears the hallmarks of its author's intellectual and political
worldview, lacking a structure and having very little dramatic content. It
reads in parts like Wilson's dictated speeches, with short journalistic
paragraphs spilling out in a disjointed succession. Wilson's book shows the
perspective of a man at the centre of an administrative machine, with little
in the way of moral or cultural susceptibilities. There is a seemingly

endearing resort to self criticism, as, for example, over the D-notices affair, but the book is substantially an apologia, and embarrassingly egocentric. He portrays the world of the 1960s as revolving around the British prime minister, quoting many favourable – and a few unfavourable – comments about himself.

Few British prime ministers burst so quickly into print about their time in Downing Street, and his book was the first detailed account of his government to appear. It is an important source by virtue of its length and author, though one critic and reviewer observed at the time: 'Politicians belong to that special class of liar who seem to be genuinely unable to discriminate between special pleading, the suppression of material evidence, and outright falsification of the record.'[43] The book received unfavourable reviews. 'The general feeling', according to Cecil King, '[was] that this orgy of self-justification [had] done him a lot of harm.'[44] Roy Jenkins, surprisingly, intimated that it was 'frightfully good in a way[,] but after a while it's rather like spending a month in a brothel.'[45] The *Sunday Times* serialization had proved dull reading, and it was considered Thomson had wasted his money. Despite considerable publicity by his two publishers, the book did not sell. Only 22,000 copies had been ordered towards the end of the year, including stocking for Christmas. The joint publishers were said to be regretting their £30,000 investment.

As a work of contemporary history, Wilson's *Personal Record* is obviously written from the Downing Street record of his activities. It starts on 16 October 1964 and rushes breathlessly through to 19 June 1970. The chapters are simply blocks of events. This has the virtue of showing how government may be experienced, with meetings, agendas, minutes, papers, notes, letters, speeches in parliament and elsewhere, broadcasts, visits around Britain and trips abroad, formal and private lunches and dinners, to say nothing of the parliamentary party ever needing to be conciliated, all crowding in on a busy schedule. Wilson played along with the civil service, enjoying work for work's sake, usually in gargantuan quantities. He lacked either ruling passion or reforming zeal as a prime minister, and gives the impression that things simply happened to him. He was responsible – it would seem – for very little, except appointing ministers and picking election dates. He had access to all relevant cabinet documents, but seems to be summarizing reports of his own and perhaps even transcripts of international exchanges and national gatherings. He quotes directly occasionally, claiming the privilege of mentioning two cabinet discussions, albeit from his point of view.

These are very unreliable memoirs. Wilson often gets his facts wrong, and discretion leads him to disregard material facts. In repeatedly placing himself at the centre of events, he ignores the real structures of global power in which the British state had to manoeuvre. The conclusion one is forced to draw is that Harold Wilson, as a political leader and would-be statesman, exists only through his repeated interventions in a wide range of affairs. 'So compulsive is the philistinism of this book, its celebration of contingency, its resistance to thought, that the reader is conditioned to see all in the same diminished perspectives, and to say ... "This is what politics is about. Poor manikin, he could do nothing else."'[46]

Wilson did not have things all his own way, with former colleagues determined to put their point of view at the end of their political careers. Just before the end of the labour government, Patrick Gordon Walker, in *The Cabinet* (1970), had revealed some of its processes. This was an academic book, but he dropped important political hints. The putative middle east intervention in 1967 was elaborated upon in 1972. Lord George-Brown published his own political memoirs in March 1971, *In My Way* being anticipated by excerpts in the *Sunday Times* in late 1970. Brown at least revealed something of his political beliefs, including Harold Wilson's tendency to a presidential style of government. Lord Wigg also produced his memoirs the following year. He was discreet about matters of national security, but his book was the first to discourse on the role of Marcia Williams: 'She ... gradually came to take on responsibilities which I thought extended beyond those appropriate to a personal secretary and to behave towards myself, among others, as if she were a political force in her own right and a power to be reckoned with.'[47]

Weidenfeld and Nicolson published Marcia Williams's account of her time in Downing Street, *Inside Number 10*, in 1972. It was edited by Terence Lancaster of the *Daily Mirror*, a long-standing friend of Wilson's and Jenkins's, from tapes she dictated. This was the work of a Wilson supporter, and Williams acknowledges that she received his permission to do the book while in his employ. It is rare that a political secretary, albeit one of her ability, should have an apparently free hand to write about her majesty's leader of the opposition, shortly after the publication of a prime ministerial apologia. Wilson felt he had nothing to fear.

Marcia Williams had never been self-effacing about the role she played as political adviser, and this comes across in the book. While she is circumspect, it is clear a kitchen cabinet existed in Downing Street. The volume, embarrassingly for posterity, contains a photograph of Joe Kagan and his family, taken at Chequers. It would be dropped from the 1975 revised edition, and the foreword was also altered; Joe Haines would no longer be described as 'Mr Wilson's constant companion, helper and adviser'. There is a reference to Wilson's own opus; she may have used it, but there is little sign that she sought to write an account which corresponded with Wilson's. At the party conference that year, Tony Benn thanked her, in front of Wilson, for having sent him a copy of the book. 'I must say your references to me in it were much kinder than in Harold's book.'[48] Her reflections have a ring of self-censored accuracy, and the book is eminently superior to Wilson's. She is able to observe and describe those she encountered as his personal and political secretary, and it is clear Marcia Williams continued to see Harold Wilson as a significant political figure.

The only other publication of the 1970 parliament was James Callaghan's book on Northern Ireland. *A House Divided* (1973) was written by John Clare of *The Times*, from recorded conversations with the former home secretary. It was seen as marginal to the work of the labour government, but it is more insightful than Wilson's, and a better source on the workings of government. *A House Divided* remains an important book. 'When it came to formulating conclusions, Clare says that to his surprise Callaghan asked for his views on what they ought to be ... The rather woolly endorsement of ultimate Irish reunification stems, in Clare's view, from a temperamental attachment to and preference for the word "unity" (as against the dreaded "division").'[49]

The Heath government had moved swiftly in 1970 to reform the trade unions, the defeat of *In Place of Strife* setting the context. The TUC was still formally committed to its 'solemn and binding undertaking', and stated a willingness to be consulted by the new government. It was no longer quite as welcome in the – soon to be renamed – department of employment under Robert Carr, and he and his cabinet colleagues began to draw up plans against the background of the dock strike in the summer of 1970. The government aimed to shackle the unions in a framework of law, and an industrial relations bill was introduced in December, to muted protests from Vic Feather. While labour opposed it in parliament, the movement took to the streets. Harold Wilson kept a low profile, and James Callaghan chaired the crucial home policy committee in Transport House, which recommended to the party's executive the repeal of all tory industrial relations legislation by a future labour government. It was a significant commitment from a loyal opposition. 'Our objectives', stated the party, 'will be to secure greater industrial democracy, better working conditions, and the development of voluntary reform on the basis of the Donovan Report which emphasised the role of the C.I.R.'[50] This had not been the case with *In Place of Strife*.

The bill took up 450 hours of debate, spread over 60 days of the first session of parliament. It started with 150 clauses and 8 schedules, and went to the lords on 25 March 1971 with 160 clauses and 9 schedules. There it was strongly resisted, going back to the commons on 20 July longer still. The government imposed a guillotine after only 30 clauses, and, with pairing suspended, there were 241 divisions. On 23 March 1971, MPs spent eleven hours simply tramping through the lobbies, at the direction of party whips. 'Here was the Party purging itself of Government', Tony Benn had observed of an earlier night of voting, on 28 January. 'It was the final occasion on which we ate our words as a Government and as Ministers on industrial relations, and we went through the lobby time after time after time.'[51] The bill finally received the royal assent on 5 August, its passage having been accompanied by an unprecedented mobilization on the part of the trade-union movement.

Tony Benn had attracted the attention of the new labour MP for Bedwelty, in south Wales, Neil Kinnock, who came to Westminster with a reputation as a left-winger. He told Benn on 25 January of an organized demonstration on the floor of the house being planned against the government's guillotine. 'I argued with him for a long time', noted Benn, 'as sympathetically as I could, saying this would be a big step and it would annoy other members of the Party.' Jim Sillars was later to identify his co-organizers as Kinnock, Denis Skinner and Heffer. Benn reported to the chief whip, who called a meeting of the shadow cabinet, but 'Michael Foot very sensibly said it would be stupid to make a big thing of this.'[52] Despite attempts by the labour front bench to appeal to the militants, Kinnock and his friends succeeded in having the sitting suspended. Reg Freeson, a front bench spokesman, had joined Heffer in the protest, and Wilson later sent for both party spokesmen. No assurances about their future behaviour were sought, and Heffer and Freeson told the press they would not have given any. Harold Wilson's authority as leader seemed to be draining away.

Wilson described 1970–1 at the October conference as a parliamentary session 'such as we have not seen in this generation',[53] though he had been much preoccupied writing and promoting *The Labour Government, 1964–1970*. Despite the views of his labour colleagues, Wilson still regarded trade unionism from a prime ministerial perspective. Speaking at an international symposium on industrial relations, in New York, in early May 1971, he had looked forward to 'a voluntary compact between Government and industry – both sides of industry – in which the Government can go forward boldly with economic policies necessary to increase productivity, knowing that this need not lead to inflation so long as it could count on industrial co-operation and restraint.'[54]

Most of the opposition to the industrial bill had been conducted outside parliament, the TUC general council being initially shocked at the new style of tory government; it decided it 'had to persuade [its] members and the public in general to oppose the Government's policy',[55] despite the recognized unpopularity of trade unions. A publicity campaign was undertaken. It was more difficult to agree on a national day of protest for 12 January, with meetings in workplaces and a rally that evening in the Albert Hall addressed by Harold Wilson. '[He] was constantly heckled and interrupted by cries of "Judas" and "hypocrite": Vic Feather was not allowed to finish his speech.'[56] No politicians were to be invited to the TUC's 'great march' from Hyde Park to Trafalgar Square on Sunday, 21 February 1971. 'It was the biggest demonstration since the Chartists moved working men to demand the right to vote, 130 years earlier.'[57] Upwards of 200,000 trade unionists marched. 'There was a total absence of cranks and rowdyism, no arrests and no scuffles – although Trafalgar Square and its surrounds were not large enough to hold the crowd and many marched on to another meeting on the Embankment.'[58] One day strikes followed, on 1 and 18 March, but Jones and Scanlon failed to get majority support for industrial action at a special congress at Croydon. The TUC agreed on a policy of non-cooperation, and, against the advice of the general council, it was to vote in September to instruct member unions not to register. Tony Benn was much impressed by a trade-union dinner in Newcastle on 6 March, at which Vic Feather and Joe Gormley spoke. 'Legislation', he wrote, 'has succeeded in shutting off the idea that somehow you can escape from your class and come up in a Davis Escape Apparatus, one by one, to join the ruling class, because the ruling class has let you down and is trying to suppress you. There is a tremendous self-confidence in being yourself and what you are. It is "black is beautiful" applied to the working class, which is marvellous.'[59]

The 1971 industrial relations act was designed to reduce unofficial strikes, but it did no such thing. The number of days lost had shot to nearly eleven million in 1970, and it was over thirteen million in the year the act was passed. It was to reach almost twenty four million in 1972, falling back to seven million the following year. A major weakness in the government's policy was the employers; they allowed collective bargaining agreements to be disclaimed as legally enforceable contracts, keeping the unions out of the firing line. Some small, and several large, unions felt a particular need to be registered, the general and municipal workers (GMWU) being least opposed to the new act. If the TGWU had been forced to remain registered, in order to keep its members, the TUC front would have collapsed. The GMWU, and other large unions, were to vote to deregister in 1972, and, after that year's TUC came out in favour of expulsion, the general council suspended thirty-two smaller unions. Twenty of these would be expelled at the 1973 congress. It was one of the most successful attempts to defy an act of parliament.

Deregistration was encouraged by events in the summer of 1972, dockers up and down the country taking unofficial action to preserve jobs threatened by containerization. (This restructuring had been advocated by Patrick Blackett, and he was to be criticized for having no solution to the labour upheavals which resulted.) Injunctions had been issued to prevent picketing and blacking. Three London dockers were arrested on 16 June, for contempt of the industrial relations court, the hitherto unknown official solicitor securing their release in the appeal court the following day. Another five dockers were gaoled in Pentonville on 22 July, but, after the TUC called a national one-day stoppage for 31 July, the dockers were released, again by the official solicitor. The house of lords had ruled that the TGWU was liable to pay a fine, after members, and non members, blacked Heaton's, a haulage firm on Merseyside. This action led the TUC to ease up on non-recognition of the national industrial relations court set up under the act.

Harold Wilson could only profit from the conservatives' embarrassment. Robert Carr had been replaced, in April, by Maurice Macmillan, son of the former prime minister. The leader of the opposition did the round of union conferences that summer, and criticized the government, in a parliamentary debate on 3 July, for 'consistently regard[ing] the world of industrial relations as a battleground for ideological confrontations, as part of a wider political conflict'.[60] Wilson did not countenance industrial action, subscribing as a parliamentarian to the observation of the law; this was the case even with bad law, as the TUC considered the act. 'The whole question of one's attitude to the law', Tony Benn had noted in June, 'has become dominant this summer, indeed over the last year, with U[pper] C[lyde] S[hipbuilders], the sit-ins, the work-ins, the flying pickets, the railwaymen, and so on.'[61] He did not believe in countenancing others to break the law, but hearing on 22 July that Reg Prentice had criticized the dockers, he came out in their support. 'Tomorrow is the celebration of the Tolpuddle Martyrs' meeting down in Dorchester', he wrote that night, 'so I drafted a statement saying that millions of people would respect the dockers for sticking to their beliefs.'[62] The national executive, on a motion from Benn, called four days later for the release of the dockers, and it later supported the TUC's call for a one-day strike. Harold Wilson was 'absolutely furious' over Tony Benn's support for the Pentonville five, 'but there was nothing much he could do about it'.[63] Benn told the shadow cabinet on 31 July, that '[his] father went to the 1889 dock strike on his father's shoulders. [He] was always taught to believe that the dockers were the best workers of the lot.' Denis Healey described him as 'a middle class Robbespierre',[64] but the *Daily Mirror* allowed 'Citizen Benn' the centre pages three days later to unfold his vision of the changed political situation in the country.

Government economic policy, in particular indirect, and then direct, attempts to control wages, stimulated much of the industrial action. Heath had come to power firmly opposed to any idea of a statutory incomes policy, but the government sought to use its position in the public sector to run a secondary policy of wage restraint. This was broken in November 1970, when Sir Jack Scamp made an award for local authority manual workers which was slightly inflationary. Industrial action by electricity supply workers, and a national post office strike, followed that winter, though both disputes were settled after the establishment of official courts of inquiry. Ford ended a strike with a substantial increase, encouraging workers throughout the car industry. The miners, led by their president, Joe Gormley, came out on strike in January 1972, a state of emergency being declared after a month, as power supplies were affected. The labour party national executive held a special meeting on 14 February, support being forthcoming for the miners; party members were invited to help local authorities deal with the consequences of power cuts.

Wilson was generally subdued, but advanced the opinion that the government had miscalculated, and called upon Heath to bring about a settlement. The national union of mineworkers was having success with mass picketing; a coke depot was closed at Saltley in Birmingham, a Yorkshire official called Arthur Scargill proclaiming the victory. A court of inquiry, under Lord Wilberforce, made a generous award to the miners, and further concessions were extracted in Downing Street. When railway unions later embarked upon industrial action, Macmillan got the industrial relations court to order a cooling-off period and strike ballot. The men voted for action, and extracted further concessions. There followed struggles in the engineering and building industries, and a national dock strike in August.

Heath had expressed a wish on the day of the miners' award 'to find a more sensible way of settling our differences'.[65] Talks followed with the confederation of British industry (CBI) and TUC between August and October, Jones and Scanlon being major interlocutors. The former was not unduly critical of the conservative prime minister: 'I had known that Heath was not unsympathetic to labour ... [and] the exchange at Chequers [in the summer of 1972] strengthened my conviction that he genuinely wanted to get on with working people.'[66] The talks broke down, possibly because the cabinet reined in the prime minister. The government rushed a counter-inflation bill through parliament, with a standstill on prices and incomes imposed from 7 November. This was hailed as a policy U-turn, the government having abandoned Selsdon Man for the previous administration's statutory approach. Stage two followed in March 1973, with a compulsory ceiling of £1 plus 4 per cent. That November, a twelve-month stage three, with a ceiling of 7 per cent, commenced. The government had been running a voluntary prices policy, but the counter-inflation act imposed stringent controls in stages two and three. Macmillan even returned to Wilsonian institutions, a separate pay board and price commission being set up to administer restrictions. The number of days lost through strikes declined as the statutory policy bit, and the government was to envisage in the summer of 1973 some sort of return to free collective bargaining. The miners were again looming into view, with negotiations due on a new claim in September.

Harold Wilson was enjoying the comfort of the opposition front bench, from where he observed Heath's difficulties over prices and incomes. He had chosen as the title of his address in New York in 1971, 'collective bargaining in a free society'. Arguing that the whole question had to be considered in terms of industrial democracy, he came out in favour of a voluntary prices and incomes policy. Wilson said in New York that statutory action could only be a short-term emergency measure, because anomalies would then make it unworkable. This would 'discredit not only the policy, but even the system of society in which it operates'.[67] Certain conditions were necessary to make voluntary restraint work: 'Its greater acceptability if it is associated with national crisis; its totality and fairness; the absence of provocative incomes or gains elsewhere, the social service supplement – the social wage helping the industrial wage – and the absence of discrimination between the public and private sector.'[68] A necessary corollary was action on prices. Wilson went further. He envisaged full employment, social services, and fair taxation as guaranteed aspects of the bargain. With all this, individual unions, he inferred, might make 'a sectional sacrifice, perhaps, a short-term price, for a long-term gain for themselves and for the community.'[69] He dubbed this process a 'compact' between government and industry – shades of the 'national dividend' he had unsuccesssfully advocated in March 1967.

When in power the labour government had not given up on trying to get into Europe in the late 1960s. George Brown had been reluctant to accept de Gaulle's veto in 1967, and the British application was left lying on the table. The French president privately dangled the possibility of a looser economic association, but his resignation in April 1969 was seen as clearing the way for British entry. George Thomson was reappointed chancellor of the duchy on 6 October, within the cabinet, to prepare for talks. The six met at The Hague that December, it being agreed that talks on enlarging the EEC should begin the following summer. The new French president, Georges Pompidou, promised not to veto British membership, but insisted it had to prove its willingness to become truly European. A white paper outlining the cost of admission was published on 10 February 1970, Wilson having left this to officials with assistance from outside the civil service. He repeated that Britain could survive outside the EEC, but also argued that 'a failure of the negotiations ... would involve a cost for Britain, a cost for Europe and a diminution of Europe's influence in world affairs.'[70] The labour government's position was still that entry depended upon the right terms, but it looked like the party would take Britain into Europe.

The responsibility of office lifted on 19 June, and, with Edward Heath a convinced European, the ultimate test of Harold Wilson's leadership was to prevent the labour party coming out against the EEC in principle. Talks began shortly after the general election, with Geoffrey Rippon handling the negotiations as chancellor of the duchy. Sir Con O'Neill had been ambassador to the community in 1963–5, and was brought back into the foreign office by Michael Stewart. O'Neill now led the officials on the British delegation in Brussels. He maintains that Wilson had planned to start negotiations on 30 June, and that Heath simply took up where the labour government had left off.

The pro-marketeer Harold Lever was given responsibility for Europe on the opposition front bench. He had been appointed to the cabinet in 1969 to help Tony Benn, the latter being then broadly in favour of membership (as was Eric Heffer). Benn distinguished his position from Peter Shore's on 6 April 1970: 'I don't think economics are everything by any manner of means and if we have to have some sort of organisation to control international companies, the Common Market is probably the right one. I think that decision-making is on the move and some decisions have to be taken in Europe, some in London, and an awful lot more at the regional and local level.'[71] This substantive position was to be overwhelmed by the question of sovereignty, and opposition to the common market would become a great left-wing cause. Wilson stated he still favoured entry at the 1970 party conference: 'I have not changed my view, although I respect the view of many here who think differently, that provided we can get the right terms, entry will be advantageous for Britain.'[72] A composite resolution moved by the TGWU opposing entry was narrowly defeated – by 3,049,000 votes to 2,954,000. The writing was on the wall. This was to be the last vote from a labour party conference in favour of Europe.

Wilson's difficulty was the common market sceptics and opponents in his party, who had remained relatively silent while in government. He knew Europe could become the most divisive issue for the labour party in opposition, and intimated to Benn, as early as 7 December, that he would be coming out against entry; 'he made it absolutely clear [Benn noted of Wilson] that he was going to get off the hook by discovering the conditions for entry into Europe were not right.'[73] Benn had raised in September the question of a special conference before the parliamentary labour party met to consider the government's terms, and this was agreed by the national executive on 16 December. He had also suggested a referendum on the government's terms of entry, when still in government, believing the public should participate in such a political decision. Wilson then stopped him putting the idea to the party executive, but Benn first argued for it in an open letter to his constituents in November 1970. At a meeting of the shadow cabinet on 11 November, Callaghan said: '"Tony may be launching a little rubber life-raft which we will all be glad of in a year's time"'[74] – a prescient observation. Benn believed a referendum could be won by the pro-marketeers, but he also saw it as labour's way of handling the common market issue. Wilson took this point, but thought he was being too hasty. Callaghan outlined his political view of the issue to Benn, about the middle of January 1971: 'He says he is sitting on the fence but he sees no reason at all why we as a Party shouldn't come out against the Common Market now and if we ever won an Election, apply to join ourselves; indeed this would seem to him perfectly acceptable as a political manoeuvre.'[75] Callaghan decided in February publicly to oppose entry, in order to rehabilitate himself with the party in parliament, Transport House and the country. It was becoming clear that opposition to Europe was a vote winner. The shadow home secretary made his pitch in a speech at Southampton on 25 May: 'If we are to prove our Europeanism by accepting that French is the dominant language in the Community', said Callaghan, 'then the answer is quite clear, and I will say it in French to prevent any misunderstanding: *Non, merci beaucoup.*'[76]

Wilson anticipated his own position. He believed 'Callaghan would purport to lead the party away from Europe while actually preparing the ground for a consolidation of Britain's role (under Labour) in the "re-negotiated" EEC.'[77] The party executive decided a month later only to 'take note' of the special conference discussion when it was held. Wilson knew any labour conference would come out against the EEC, but only wanted it to discuss the terms. He was waiting for the white paper. The party leader wanted the executive then to endorse his statement, and present it to the annual conference. The parliamentary party would vote after that. He hoped to swing the party round, while minimizing division. The left believed it could strengthen its opposition at the special conference, and then present a 'definitive resolution' to the annual gathering in early October. Wilson changed his position on the common market that July, or rather he made known his intention of rejecting the government's terms. 'He privately told some of us', Barbara Castle recalls, 'that he was going to come out against the terms, even though he knew it would destroy his credibility.'[78]

The negotiations had come to an end on 23 June, and the white paper was published on 7 July. Wilson reiterated his opposition to a referendum the following day, a 'take note' debate on the white paper being arranged in the commons for 21 July – four days after labour's special conference. Roy Jenkins argued for accepting the government's terms, at a meeting of the parliamentary party on 19 July, attacking socialism in one country as a slogan not a policy. 'It took you right back to 1951 or 1961', wrote Benn, 'the Party at its worst.'[79] The special conference had met on the Saturday in Central Hall, Westminster, with 140 international observers present, including diplomats from 67 countries. The 479 trade-union delegates were outnumbered by the 539 from constituency parties, but no decision was made, Wilson having persuaded the executive to rig the conference. An early left-wing attempt to get the party to call for a general election was lost on a card vote, by 3,185,000 to 2,624,000. The chairman, Ian Mikardo, attempted to balance the debate, calling speakers, for and against, from the constituencies, trade unions and the ranks of MPs sitting apart in the balcony. George Thomson MP spoke for one camp when he stated he would have recommended the terms received, while Peter Shore MP bemoaned 'the abandonment of the 120-year-old policy of cheap food for this country, a switch of supply from traditional low cost suppliers to the high cost, inefficient farms of Western Europe'.[80] Wilson spoke last, stating he would put a motion to the next meeting of the party executive on 28 July, which '[took] full account ... of all that [had] been said [there that] day'.[81] 'I have never', an EEC representative said to a British journalist, 'seen a man pour shit all over himself.'[82] Wilson stated the party's position over the years, arguing that the terms were unacceptable, and ended by stating that it was his duty 'to recommend the course [he] believe[d] right in the interests of Britain and our people', but that he had also 'to do all in [his] power to maintain the unity of this Party'.[83] For this he was applauded. Delegates then signified their willingness to make a decision at Brighton. It was clear that labour was coming out against entry, though a significant proportion of the party favoured supporting the government.

While the Jenkinsites celebrated their brief reprieve at St Ermine's Hotel, Benn attended the left's celebration in Ian Mikardo's office. 'It's all over bar the shouting now',[84] he recorded later.

The labour party finally made a decision on the first day of the annual conference (Monday, 4 October), with Tony Benn due to take over the chair for 1971–2. He also finally decided to stand for the deputy leadership, accepting that Michael Foot had the prior claim to be the left-wing candidate. Denis Healey moved rejection of the terms on behalf of the executive, calling for a general election, and inviting labour MPs to oppose the government. Royden Harrison, a constituency delegate from Sheffield, found himself, to his surprise, seconding. He proclaimed 'the beginning of the end of ... [the] politics [of consensus] in our Party'.[85] Harold Wilson did not speak in the debate, and it was Callaghan who wound up for the platform. The resolution was carried overwhelmingly, by 5,073,000 votes to 1,032,000. A composite opposing entry on any terms was defeated, and another from the post office engineers, which called for a referendum, was lost by over two to one.

It was not until after the autumn party conferences that MPs debated entry, being asked, in October, to consider the principle 'on the basis of the arrangements which [had] been negotiated'.[86] The shadow cabinet decided on 13 October to recommend opposition to the terms. When Heath announced five days later there was to be a free vote, Wilson felt he had to allow labour MPs the same. Tony Benn argued it was the British people who should have the free vote. Labour MPs voted on 19 October to support the shadow cabinet by 159 to 89.

Wilson now tried out the idea of calling for a general election at the shadow cabinet, but got little support, though it was endorsed by the party executive on 27 October. He spoke in the sixth, and last, day of the debate, having intervened during a number of conservative contributions. Wilson resolutely denied that, before leaving office, the labour government had agreed to a negotiating position. He stated his own, and the party's, position succinctly: 'namely that we saw great advantage in getting into Europe if the terms were right, but that, if the terms were wrong, we thought that Britain was strong enough to stand outside and prosper.'[87] Obviously expecting to lose, he warned that labour, once returned to power, would seek to renegotiate the terms. Wilson insisted that better terms could be secured, and this was taken as an admission that a future labour government would accept the EEC. Taking a leaf out of the book of the late General de Gaulle, Wilson implied that a labour government would accept expulsion from the community; this, as the home secretary, Reginald Maudling, commented, was a case of the leader of the opposition 'going rather further than, on reflection, he will wish to have done'.[88] The house then voted 356 to 244 in favour of going into Europe. Sixty-nine labour MPs, led by Roy Jenkins, and including Michael Stewart, defied the three-line whip, and voted with the conservatives. Douglas Houghton, the party chairman, had announced he was voting for the government, and another twenty labour MPs abstained. Out of a party of 287 members, something under 100 refused to follow Wilson, making this a major crisis of his leadership.

It was at this point that Wilson's father died in his ninetieth year. Herbert Wilson had long been retired, and was living with his daughter. He had flown out to Western Australia, with Marjorie, to meet his late wife's family, but 'Grandpa' Wilson, as he was known to his son's staff, suffered a heart attack there in November. 'His second coronary occurred [a week later] while he was sleeping and so he died without knowing anything about it.'[89] He was buried in Australia. When news of his death reached London, 'there were no tears or weeping'[90] in the family. The father Harold Wilson had struggled to please and impress was no more.

The question of Wilson's resignation had been raised in 1971. Following Jenkins's speech to the parliamentary party on 19 July, Wilson sought to reassert his leadership at another meeting the following day. It was a disastrous performance. He made accusations of a party within the party, and wondered how right-wingers could fulfil front-bench responsibilities; he was to sack Bill Rodgers the following January. Wilson mooted the possibility of not continuing beyond October. Earlier, with Tony Benn, at Lord North Street, he had become maudlin about the cost of leadership: 'They can stuff it as far as I am concerned.'[91] Harold Wilson was only in his fifty-sixth year, and Benn tried to reassure him that he now had the support of the left, following the special conference: Callaghan and Jenkins had discredited themselves in different ways; Michael Foot was emerging as an opponent of Roy Jenkins's; Denis Healey, who was now opposed to entry, had changed his mind twice; Crosland had also come out against, determined not to support Jenkins, his ally turned rival. On 20 July, Benn first thought of his own leadership bid. He felt Foot could only be a stop-gap deputy leader, given age and lack of cabinet experience. 'I am almost ashamed to talk about this in my diary because it makes it seem that I am mainly concerned with that, which I hope I am not. But egoism eats up all politicians in time, which is probably the case for getting rid of them.'[92]

The Times stated on 20 October that Harold Wilson must never again be prime minister, just after the parliamentary party voted to oppose the goverment's terms: 'to put party before country on a matter of preeminent importance is one of the crimes for which a party leader can never be forgiven.' When nominations closed for the deputy leadership on 4 November, Jenkins was opposed by Foot and Benn. The three secured, respectively, 140, 96 and 46 votes on the first ballot. The parliamentary party was well and truly split.

Jenkins had the largest following, but barely a majority, though he had secured seven more votes than the previous year. One Jenkinsite urged a right-wing breakaway upon the deputy leader, with Owen, Marquand and Maclennan thinking he should challenge Wilson for the leadership. Foot was rising fast for a man who had only recently joined the shadow cabinet. Benn had been extremely nervous about his bid, and was relieved not to have done worse. Jenkins held on to the deputy leadership by 140 votes to 126 in the second ballot; some of Benn's supporters had not transferred their votes to Foot. According to Barbara Castle, who must have been at her politically closest at this time: 'The strain on Harold Wilson began to tell. He became dispirited and more than once hinted at resignation.'[93] Changing his position on the common market saw his credibility at its lowest, but he had to continue maintaining party unity after the parliamentary split of 28 October.

This was to lead to a second political shift. Immediately after the 1970 election, Douglas Jay had argued for a referendum on European membership. He assumed that the British people would vote against. Jay was soon joined by Tony Benn, but the option continued to be rejected through 1971. 'I found myself', Benn was to recall, 'in a minority of one both in the shadow cabinet and on the national executive.'[94] Early in 1972, two anti-market conservatives, Neil Marten and Enoch Powell, put down an amendment, asking for a consultative referendum. A treaty of accession had been signed in Brussels on 22 January, and the European communities bill was introduced in the commons shortly afterwards. Tony Benn now came out against the proposal to ally community law to Britain's, on the grounds that it raised

the question of 'the future of parliamentary democracy in this country ...
There may have to be a battle for the soul of the Labour Party and this could
be the issue.'[95] There was talk of referenda in Europe, and even Northern
Ireland. The European communities bill secured a second reading by only
eight votes on 17 February. The prime minister had opponents in his own
party, and Heath would have been defeated if it had not been for labour
abstentions. Wilson was depressed: 'The fact that he had held the Party
together ... was a great achievement and he couldn't understand why people
weren't grateful to him.'[96] Benn again suggested a referendum on 15
March, but only three or four fellow members of the shadow cabinet
supported him. Wilson spoke and voted against this unBritish constitutional
device, and Benn momentarily considered resigning. The French then
announced a referendum on whether to let Britain into the EEC. With
Wilson, Callaghan and Jenkins absent, Benn, as chairman of the party, put
the idea to the national executive a week later. It was carried by thirteen
votes to eleven, some members seeing it as more realistic than a general
election. Wilson then swung into the referendum camp, the shadow
cabinet reversing its position on 29 March by eight votes to six. Edward
Short followed Wilson in switching. Ross and Healey, who had been
opposed, were absent from the meeting. The opponents were Jenkins,
Williams, Lever, Crosland, Houghton and Thomson. Labour MPs were
to be whipped into the lobby in support of a motion whose seconder was
Enoch Powell. On 18 April 208 followed Wilson, and there were 63 abstentions. The party had divided for a second time.

There had been little chance of Heath having to hold a referendum, but
Benn's success in the executive had implications for a future labour
government. Roy Jenkins had done much to maintain party unity after the
election defeat, voting loyally with the party against the European communities bill. 'This was utterly inconsistent, and a painful humiliation ...
The effect of [the Jenkinsites'] grand gesture of self-abasement was undercut
by the strong suspicion on the left that they were in collusion with the Tory
whips to ensure that there were no embarrassing defeats.'[97] Dick Taverne
claims that the Jenkinsites voted with the party, in return for an understanding with Wilson that he would not oppose the EEC in principle.
Jenkins now decided to make the referendum an issue of principle, and
resigned from the shadow cabinet, and, effectively, the executive, on 10
April. He believed he had been in with a chance for the leadership. Benn
felt he was using the referendum as an excuse to vacate the deputy
leadership, given the anti-EEC trajectory of the party. The chairman,
who had conceived the referendum to maintain unity, was now portayed
as the splitter of the party.

The parliamentary party only voted on 12 April to support the referendum
by 129 to 96. Jenkins was joined by Lever and Thomson, leaving Shirley

Williams as the only thorough European in the shadow cabinet. Roy Hattersley declined to abandon his front-bench position. Tom McNally, then in Transport House, believes the deputy leader was badly advised, and criticized the Jenkinsites for being willing to nail their man to the cross. Jenkins stated he could not accept 'this constant shifting of the ground'[98] in his letter of resignation. Aware that labour was becoming opposed to the very idea of the common market, he warned of the divisive effect of a referendum on the party. He again openly voiced an implicit criticism of Wilson's style of leadership: 'I ... want to see that future Labour Governments have a clear sense of direction. It is not easy at the best of times to preserve this through the buffetings of the week-to-week crises which are the lot of any Government ... If a Government is born out of opportunism it becomes not merely difficult but impossible.'[99] Though Jenkins was to return to the shadow cabinet in 1973, this was probably the greatest rupture in the collective leadership of the party since the war.

Edward Short, the most popular member of the shadow cabinet, beat Foot by 145 votes to 116 in April 1972. The two places on the shadow cabinet were filled by the runners up, Reg Prentice and John Silkin. Following the 18 April 1972 parliamentary split over the referendum, the question of the party conference's position on Europe loomed. Callaghan feared complete opposition to the EEC, which would have forced a future labour government to withdraw. Benn told Wilson on 3 May he wanted the referendum in the executive's resolution, otherwise he would vote against the common market. Wilson refused to commit himself to coming out and again talked of resignation, declaring himself in favour of the referendum on 10 June.

Wilson had quickly reassigned front-bench responsibilities after Jenkins's resignation. Crosland was again overlooked for treasury affairs, Jenkins being replaced by Healey, and foreign affairs given to Callaghan. The latter was still recovering from a prostate operation, and being generally benign. Shirley Williams was asked to look after home affairs, and Merlyn Rees became responsible for Northern Ireland. Harold Lever gave way to Peter Shore, a strong anti-marketeer. Michael Foot, as shadow leader of the house, was to coordinate opposition to common market legislation.

The executive accepted 'Labour's Programme for Britain' on 5 July, including the idea of the referendum to be presented to the conference. Wilson was still worried about a leadership challenge, fearing Christopher Mayhew might launch a symbolic threat. Benn feared a split. 'If ... [Harold] felt he couldn't lead the Party any more, then it would create a frightful crisis because it would divide the Party into the Marketeers plus Wilson against the rest.'[100] As for Jenkins, 'he simply kept on playing the Labour game according to the rules, honourably but unhappily and unconvincingly'.[101] With the parliamentarians leading the retreat from Europe, the

1972 party conference at Blackpool voted, by 3,335,000 votes to 2,867,000, for renegotiation, followed by 'a general Election or a Consultative Referendum'.[102] The party had reversed its position on a referendum. A vote to oppose membership in principle was only defeated by 128,000 votes. The pro-market position still attracted a sizeable minority of votes, but Roy Jenkins, in the opinion of Barbara Castle, 'had no stomach for political in-fighting'.[103] He declined to speak during the common market debate. The success of the left, as measured by growing anti-Europeanism in 1972, owed something to the right cutting and running.

Dick Taverne, labour MP for Lincoln, resigned his seat in October 1972, deliberately choosing the last day of the party conference, and announced his intention of standing as an independent. Taverne had voted with Jenkins in October 1971, and he wanted the right to break then from the labour party. His local party called upon him to retire as its member of parliament, and his appeal to the executive was overturned in July 1972. Closing the party conference on 6 October, Benn hinted at the precedent of MacDonald. 'It is the first time', he said, 'that the mass media has actually put up a candidate in the election. I wish the workers in the media would sometimes remember that they are members of the working class and have a sense of responsibility to see that what is said about us is true.' Wilson was furious, and Benn's advisers thought he had made a mistake. He considered his colleagues on the conference platform 'gutless'.[104] Taverne was returned in a by-election five months after his resignation as a democratic labour candidate, but his parliamentary career was to come to an end in October 1974. Roy Jenkins refused to speak for the labour candidate, but Healey and Crosland went to Lincoln to try to stop this dissident right-winger.

Harold Wilson, it is asserted, preserved the unity of the labour party, this being seen often as his major claim to historical fame. The price was opposition to the common market in the Heath years, when he was to fight for a 'yes' vote for continuing membership in a referendum after returning to office. Harold Wilson mitigated all-out opposition, by taking up an anti-market stand in 1971–2, being prepared to put his leadership on the line. This did not satisfy the right, and Wilson merely postponed the exeunt of the Jenkinsites until 1981. His behaviour in opposition seriously damaged his reputation at the time, with the *New Statesman* calling for his removal from the leadership following Jenkins's resignation. 'His very presence in Labour's leadership pollutes the atmosphere of politics.'[105] Wilson's loyal henchman, Crossman, also criticized him in *Inside View* (1972), advancing the theory that he had simply lacked any strategy in office. 'Twists and turns are morally acceptable', Crosland had said of party leadership, 'if they're not motivated by purely personal ambition.'[106] Ambition may have accounted for Harold Wilson's tactical political style, but the party has to accept historical responsibility for containing a coherent right-wing faction, and parliamentarians who changed their minds when they went into opposition. In Harold Wilson the labour party retained the leader it needed in the early 1970s.

The European communities bill had a rough ride in the commons in 1972. There were ninety-six divisions, Heath's majority dropping as low as four on two occasions. Within months of the prime minister taking office, labour had gone into the lead in the polls, and the opposition hoped it might actually defeat the government in 1972 on an issue which would provoke a general election. Hostility to European membership, as some had predicted, was a vote winner, though the bill secured its third reading on 13 July by the relatively narrow margin of 301 votes to 284. It received the royal assent on 17 October. That day the commons debated the summit to be held in Paris, when the new members of the EEC were to join the six in a meeting of the council of ministers. Arguing that 77 per cent of all voters wanted a referendum, Wilson dragged up Heath's promise from the 1970 election that he would not join the market 'against the wish of the British people'. 'He has not secured that consent', Wilson argued. 'His action is against the wish of the British people. And in so far as he claims the authority of Parliament, it is a Parliament which was deliberately denied information available to him, and a Parliament whose legislative proceedings were themselves robbed of authority by the denial of free debate and the refusal to consider a single Amendment.'[107]

Britain became a full member of the European economic community on 1 January 1973, when Ireland and Denmark also joined. Norway had been involved in the negotiations, but membership was rejected in a referendum. Harold Wilson refused to participate in the 'fanfare for Europe' by which entry was celebrated in Britain, having already dubbed the EEC 'the European agriculture welfare state'.[108] A new commission was installed in Brussels by the nine member states, two of the portfolios being filled by the British government. Christopher Soames, a former tory agriculture minister, took over responsibility for external affairs, and George Thomson was plucked from the labour backbenches, to become the commissioner for regional policy. This was an issue Wilson had made much of when criticizing the terms, but the government's bipartisanship was not reciprocated by the official opposition. Labour boycotted the European parliament, where it had been allocated fifteen of the thirty-six nominated British seats, and the TUC refused to participate in the economic and social committee.

Northern Ireland was becoming a major problem. Relations between the catholic community and the British army began to break down in 1970, and Paisley was elected to Westminster. The provisional IRA took the offensive, the first British soldier being killed in February 1971. Chichester-Clark was soon replaced by Brian Faulkner, who introduced internment on 9 August against the advice of the police and army. Paratroopers fired on a demonstration in Derry on Sunday, 30 January 1972, killing thirteen civilians. The British embassy in Dublin went up in flames. London imposed direct rule on 24 March, after Heath failed to wrest security policy from the northern government. The province now became the responsibility of William Whitelaw, at the head of a new Northern Ireland Office (NIO). 1972 was to be the year of greatest violence, a loyalist backlash adding to an escalating republican campaign. The IRA declared a truce from 27 June, and the RAF flew six of its leaders to London on 7 July for a secret meeting with Whitelaw. 'The meeting was a non-event.'[109] The truce collapsed two days later, and Whitelaw furnished details of the meeting in a written parliamentary answer. There following a bombing blitz in Belfast on 21 July, which was dubbed 'Bloody Friday'. The army went into catholic 'no go' areas in Derry and Belfast on 31 July, ending any possibility of negotiations between the IRA and the British government. Whitelaw held all-party talks at Darlington in Co. Durham in September, and a green paper followed on 30 October, laying down constitutional parameters. Northern Ireland was to remain part of the United Kingdom, but the minority was to have a say in its government. Support for reform was to be sought from the Republic's government, despite its constitutional claim over the north. Both states joined the common market in 1973, and a plebiscite was held in March on the question of Ulster's status. Protestants voted overwhelmingly to remain part of the United Kingdom, and, with catholics abstaining, 57.4 per cent of the electorate of Northern Ireland endorsed the existence of the border.

A white paper followed, proposing a new assembly to be elected by proportional representation. The secretary of state would appoint an executive, but its devolved powers were not to include security. There was to be a council of Ireland, to be agreed at a conference involving the London and Dublin governments and northern parties. The seventy-eight members of the assembly were elected on 28 June. In favour of power-sharing were nineteen social democratic and labour party (SDLP) members, eight alliance, one NILP, and twenty-two followers of Brian Faulkner. Opposed was a coalition of twenty-seven unionists, led principally by William Craig and Ian Paisley. The new assembly opened inauspiciously on 31 July, and an executive was agreed on 5 October, a social and economic programme emerging by 6 November. Heath agreed a council of Ireland with the Dublin government and the executive-designate at Sunningdale in early December. Brian Faulkner returned to office at Stormont as chief executive on 1 January 1974, with SDLP leader Gerry Fitt as his deputy. The new administration comprised six unionists, four SDLP, and one alliance member, with the participation of catholics guaranteed by the British government.

Harold Wilson had not taken a great deal of interest in Ulster until internment in August 1971. He met Brian Faulkner in London a number of times on privy councillor terms, and the labour party generally supported the government. A party delegation met the NILP, SDLP and Irish labour party on 1 September, but little was to emerge from fraternal consultations. The Dublin government would be more significant. Jack Lynch, the Irish taoiseach, and Faulkner were to meet Heath at Chequers later in the month, shortly after Wilson put forward a twelve-point programme, calling for a Northern Ireland minister, proportional representation and an all-Ireland council. Wilson repeated these ideas towards the end of the month when parliament was recalled to debate Northern Ireland. He did not come out in opposition to internment, though a group of backbenchers voted against the government. The platform defended the bipartisan front in parliament at the party conference shortly afterwards. Callaghan led a party delegation to Belfast in November, for a meeting with the labour and social democratic parties of Ireland. Internment was seen as a major issue, and Tony Benn thought security should be transferred to London. 'There was a press conference at the airport', he wrote, 'and it was really awful. We were surrounded by paratroopers with Sten guns, looking in every direction and at any moment there might have been a bomb thrown. One felt as if one were in Hanoi or Saigon at the height of the war.'[110]

It was November 1971 before Harold Wilson paid his first visit to Ireland as labour leader, in preparation for another two-day parliamentary debate. Wilson 'met every conceivable interest group [in Belfast, Derry, and Dublin in three days]: politicians, of varying shades of orange and green and pale pink; trade unionists, some courageous and a few racist; leaders of every religious denomination; businessmen; surgeons; and the General Officer Commanding.'[111] Wilson had lunch with Jack Lynch in Dublin, and meetings with the two opposition parties. Haines had failed to shift Wilson from the idea that the Republic of Ireland might rejoin the British commonwealth, in return for a united Ireland to be achieved after fifteen years without violence. 'The fascinating moment at the Taoiseach's lunch came', Haines writes, 'when Harold Wilson put forward the plan for turning the dream of unity into reality. I had thought they would jump for joy. But their reaction was more akin to falling through the floor.'[112] (Conor Cruise O'Brien of the Irish labour party was soon to sketch the consequences of withdrawal: 'A British Government announces its agreement to the unity of Ireland, for which it receives many telegrams of congratulations from America, and urgent private messages of alarm from Dublin.'[113])

Harold Wilson should have learned something important about Ireland, but he was primarily concerned with Britain and its problems. He wanted to advance the profile of the labour party, by seeking talks with the government on Northern Ireland, in the hope that such an approach to politics would inspire the Irish on both sides of the border. A section of the parliamentary party had come out against government policy, and, at the shadow cabinet on Monday, 22 November, Wilson was furious to find that no debate on Maudling's failure in Northern Ireland had been arranged for that week. He would be abroad promoting his book the following week. The opposition had to offer up one of its supply days, and it was on 25 November that Wilson made public the fifteen-point programme he had trailed privately in Dublin. Britain was to remain the sovereign power in Northern Ireland for fifteen years, continuing to provide finance and troops for perhaps twenty-five years. The Republic was to achieve – bluntly – British standards of social welfare and personal freedom, and suppress the IRA. The minority was to participate in government at Stormont. Talks at Westminster were to involve the northern parties, and then the Dublin government. The goal was 'a constitutional commission of the three Governments [or all parties in the three parliaments?], to examine the implications of a united Ireland with protection for minorities, north and south'. 'Any resulting constitutional agreement ... [was] to be based on a study of such possibilities as a Federal constitution, a dual system, or on the four historic Irish provinces, or on a system of meaningful devolution.'[114]

Wilson had killed two political birds with one stone. It did not matter greatly how the speech was received in Ireland, even if it stored up trouble for a future labour government. 'The practical possibilities of the plan were nil, but the effects of putting it forward were dangerously explosive.'[115] Paul Rose moved the ending of bipartisanship at a meeting of the parliamentary party later in the day. Benn suggested to Wilson a parliamentary resolution, but the labour leader was about to do a television programme on his speech. Benn then went to Callaghan, who was angry at being upstaged. 'You'll have to do it', he told Benn. 'I'm going. I'm late for seeing my grandchild.'[116] The parliamentary party committed itself that night to opposing internment, while supporting British troops. 'This was a very important statement', asserted Benn, 'because it did break bipartisanship.'[117] The labour opposition voted against the government on 29 November, but the breach was only to be momentary. Little was heard of Harold Wilson's Irish solution after the autumn of 1971. Callaghan and Benn returned to Belfast on 20 December, for another meeting with the three fraternal parties. The shadow home secretary was against getting too close to the SDLP. Harold Wilson addressed them during a three-hour lunch, hinting at the transfer of security to London. It proved impossible to achieve any major political agreement. When the conservatives embarked on a process of internal reform in Northern Ireland the following March, the labour opposition returned to supporting the government, though it was to oppose the emergency provisions bill in 1973. The executive acknowledged Wilson's fifteen-point plan at the 1972 party conference, but the emphasis was on talks in Northern Ireland which the southern parties could join later. Wilson would later describe his constitutional edifice as 'not realistic, for it was a much milder version of the White Paper following the Sunningdale Conference'.[118] But this only envisaged a council of Ireland, and it is clear he had been playing ducks and drakes with the Ulster problem.

Wilson had told the house of commons that he 'would not meet any men who sought to change the existing order by violence'.[119] He was to change his mind after Bloody Sunday, when the IRA's seven-man army council decided in March 1972 to negotiate a truce. 'The truce was a gesture to the increasing political contacts the Provisionals were having at that time',[120] shortly before Heath suspended Stormont. The IRA approached an interested labour member of the Irish Dáil, Dr John O'Connell. The latter flew to London bearing the IRA's terms, and approached the leader of the opposition. Wilson showed the terms to the prime minister, and O'Connell believes the draft ceasefire came back with changes by Heath. Wilson then asked for a meeting with the IRA, euphemistically with 'friends' of the republican leadership. He vetoed Ruairi Ó Bradaigh, president of Sinn Féin, and Seán Mac Stiofáin, chief of staff of the IRA, the movement's two principal leaders. A suitable cover story would have to be arranged. O'Connell was actively mediating, and the army council agreed to a meeting with a man it considered virtually an envoy of Heath's. The IRA unilaterally announced a three-day truce on 10 March, and expected a British response. Harold Wilson was to arrive in Ireland on 13 March to be interviewed by Irish television (RTE); few queried why it was necessary to go to Dublin for this. He booked into the Shelbourne Hotel with Joe Haines and Tony Field, and proceeded to meetings in the nearby Leinster House. One of these was with labour leaders, including Conor Cruise O'Brien. The latter wrote shortly afterwards:

> I shall not here divulge any confidences of Mr. Wilson's; indeed I am not sure he did any confiding … .He … told me, as he usually does when he meets any elected Irish representative, that he, in Huyton, represents more Irish voters than I do, which I am sure is true. For the rest, he patiently performed a pipe-filling ritual, so exquisitely long-drawn-out and so charged with implications of wise negotiation, that I am sure, at any Red Indian pow-wow, it would bring down the wig-wam. We, having heard some disquieting rumours, said how unwise it would be to negotiate with the I.R.A., under present conditions … .Mr. Wilson did not dissent. He continued to play with, or on, his pipe.[121]

Wilson dined that evening in his hotel room with Dr O'Connell. The leader of the opposition then drove, with Haines and Field, to the RTE studios in a British embassy car. Merlyn Rees was to meet them there. O'Connell drove out and waited in the carpark, telling Irish special branch officers that he was taking Wilson to his house near Phoenix Park for a drink afterwards. O'Connell asked them to be discreet, and they left Wilson unprotected for several hours. Waiting for Wilson, Haines, Field and Rees at O'Connell's house were the friends of the republican movement: Daithi Ó Conaill, the provisionals' leading political thinker, Joe Cahill, the former commander of the Belfast IRA, and John Kelly, a co-defendant, with Charles Haughey, in the 1970 arms trial in Dublin. Watching Wilson on television, they 'judged his performance ... [to be] a typical piece of politician's opportunism, playing to his audience, and riddled with ambiguities'.[122] When Wilson and his associates arrived, there were no formal introductions. Wilson's press secretary started to take notes, but the IRA objected, though there seems to be a shorthand record of the exchanges. Wilson passed Ó'Connell a sheet of paper during the meeting, on which the latter wrote the names of the republican leaders. Ó Conaill presented the IRA's five points of the previous September, the main one being 'hold[ing] free elections to establish a regional parliament for the Province of Ulster as a first step towards a new government for the Thirty-two Counties'.[123] The British labour leader clearly wanted the violence stopped. Wilson asked if the IRA would accept the SDLP as negotiators: '"If there were talks could you promise that your friends would not intervene? Not shoot them [the SDLP] in the back?"'[124]

Ó Conaill and his associates maintained that the IRA's three-point peace proposals – withdrawal of troops, abolition of Stormont, and an amnesty – 'were the minimum that would bring about a prolonged truce'.[125] Kelly said at midnight it was then too late to talk of extending the IRA's ceasefire, and Wilson was unwilling to accept an amnesty. The end of Stormont was on the cards, but was a matter between Faulkner and Heath. As for withdrawal of troops, the IRA had failed to defeat them militarily. It could hardly hope to secure their withdrawal politically, in the context of a united Ireland they expected to be created by Britain. 'I had detected no signs', Merlyn Rees was to admit, 'that the South was preparing itself to take over Northern Ireland.'[126] Ó Conaill had particularly impressed the British party, Joe Haines later writing: 'Though he and his colleagues were to us light years away from reality, especially when discussing what was politically possible, he demonstrated an intellectual quality greater than many politicians we had met in the North ... He is not a man to be underestimated.'[127] The meeting broke up in the early hours of 14 March, the IRA having secured no political concessions. If the IRA had expected Wilson to intercede with the British government, he was unable and/or unwilling to play such a role. He had been concerned to project himself as the man who could do Heath's job better; it would have been a bonus to have persuaded the IRA to call off its military campaign, but the IRA's truce was not extended beyond the third day.

Wilson's meeting with the IRA was a precedent for Whitelaw's equally fruitless encounter several months later. The government could hardly then be criticized by the leader of the opposition. The truce which had begun on 27 June broke down on 9 July. Wilson and Rees were in Whitelaw's flat that night, and the secretary of state was to admit the following day that he had met the IRA. Whitelaw 'did not demur when Harold said that he was thinking of meeting the Provisional leaders to try to get the temporary ceasefire restored.'[128] Wilson quickly got in touch with Dr O'Connell again. The IRA's army council was divided on his request to talk again, but it was agreed to send a lesser delegation to Britain on Tuesday, 18 July. Joe Cahill was to be in charge, and he would be accompanied by a man called Ford from Belfast, and Miles Shevlin a lawyer sympathetic to the IRA.

The party was flown to Luton Airport under O'Connell's guardianship. They were met, it is thought, by Tony Field, and driven to Grange Farm. Wilson opened the meeting by saying he was not acting on behalf of the government, which wrongfooted the IRA. They could then only rehearse the reasons for the breakdown of the truce nine days earlier. Wilson tried to talk them into another ceasefire, but the discussion hit rock bottom when Shevlin reiterated the demand for a withdrawal of troops by the beginning of 1975. Merlyn Rees joined the discussion later. 'The aim of the meeting had been to try and get the Provisionals to see political reality, to get them back to a ceasefire. On any terms', Rees recalls, 'it was a failure; we were wasting our time.'[129] O'Connell and his companions were flown back to Dublin, where a number of Wilson's colleagues were attending a party at the British embassy. During the evening Stan Orme took a call from Wilson, reporting later to the gathering on the meeting at Grange Farm. 'The effect was electrifying, the conversation animated, and the comments of the British MPs about their leader made me glad it was a stag party with no ladies present. (This is no breach of confidence', writes the ambassador at the time, 'it all could not have been more public.) Anyway, it made the evening.'[130]

This was the last time Harold Wilson was to treat directly with the IRA. He may have been expecting some sort of reply, because Cahill had to report to the army council in Dublin on the visit. The reply came three days later in Belfast in the form of Bloody Friday. Twenty-seven indiscriminate IRA bombs killed eleven people.

Marcia Williams had suddenly resigned on 26 June 1970. Wilson was not perturbed, having seen it many times before. She was back the following Monday to take charge once again.

Others found her behaviour more difficult. She intimidated the private office staff, according to Joe Haines. 'The roll-call of girls and women who were reduced to tears by her sarcasm is a long one.'[131] Secretaries were terrified of her, and Jane Cousins became a particular object of criticism. Joe Haines was the principal threat to her influence over Wilson. She continued to act as Wilson's political conscience, the telephone being her means of communication. There were many shouting matches during the years of opposition, and Wilson travelled to Wyndham Mews (her London home) when he wished to discuss political matters. 'These meetings ... often degenerated into quarrels that would go on past midnight.'[132] On one occasion she insulted Mary Wilson, and was forbidden to come in to Westminster. (Haines is discreet on the reasons for Wilson's anger, but the issue must have been serious.)

Wilson was 'really quite avuncular' when he asked Jane Cousins to become his political researcher, work John Allen had been doing. She remembers the former prime minister saying on the first day, 'you work with me not for me', and 'I really hope you won't become too disillusioned'.[133] When she later got in trouble with the sergeant at arms for going barefoot at Westminster, Wilson delighted in studying Erskine May to find there was no such prohibition.

Jane Cousins was given the small room in which Wilson's papers were stored. She was to see little of Marcia Williams, and believed she was not talking to Harold Wilson. Cousins helped with speeches, and parliamentary questions, using the house of commons' library, and Transport House. She was to later answer constituents' letters and other political correspondence, working more closely with Marcia Williams. Jane Cousins endorses Joe Haines's view of Williams: 'I didn't see socialism in practice in that office.' As someone who was becoming involved in feminism, Cousins developed a strong critique of Marcia Williams. Though a lone parent, she was no feminist exemplar. Williams was seen as someone who disliked women, and 'look[ed] to men for power', which led Jane Cousins to be more critical of Wilson. 'He was personally a nice boss to work for, until I concluded that you can't be that nice if you employ people who are vindictive, irrational, sometimes off their rocker.' 'One of Harold's great misfortunes was that he didn't read people very well.'[134]

It was during the years of opposition that Harold Wilson came under most attention from within MI5, the reason being Sir Joseph Kagan.

In late 1969, Richardas Vaygauskas, a Lithuanian party official, came to London as a second secretary in the Soviet consulate. He suggested that Wilson's associate, Kagan, establish a business connection with Lithuania.

The two became friends, playing chess each week in Kagan's flat in Bayswater. Kagan denies Vaygauskas ever asked him leading questions about the prime minister: 'I knew that he was very careful of the relationship not to embarrass me, as I knew ... he was under control of KGB[.] I would not ask him something that he would have to worry about. It was a politically platonic relationship.'[135] 'It was partly because Joe knew it would not be approved of', says John Parker, who worked for him in London. 'He'd do anything to upset people for the hell of it.'[136] Wilson got Arthur Young, former head of the City of London police, who had taken over the Royal Ulster Constabulary, to advise Kagan to be discreet.

Kagan and his wife visited the Soviet Union, including Lithuania, in the summer of 1970. The following February, Oleg Lyalin, who worked at the Soviet trade delegation in Highgate, began to supply information to the British. Lyalin was a member of the KGB, involved in contingency planning for sabotage in Britain, though the ambition of his supposed instructions was matched by the insignificance of his putative agents. Lyalin, who was the responsibility of Christopher Herbert, and two agent-runners, Harry Wharton and Tony Brooks, referred to Vaygauskas's relationship with Kagan, it being suggested that he got information from number 10. MI5 now began actively to investigate Wilson and his friends. Kagan must have been under surveillance for some time, as a result of Vaygauskas being watched, and Marcia Williams was among those recorded talking to him on the telephone. Tony Brooks went to Huddersfield, to recruit agents at Kagan's factory; posing as Col. Brewster, he signed up John Parker in London. Lyalin was arrested for drunken driving in the autumn of 1971, and his defection had to be admitted to save him from the law. The Heath government then expelled 105 Soviet diplomats and trade attachés, including Richardas Vaygauskas. Peter Wright claims this was to give MI5 less to do, the treasury being reluctant to meet demands for further expansion of the security service. Kagan and Wilson sought out Young in order to clear themselves with MI5, and 'Young expressed surprise that Wilson had not spoken to Furnival Jones [when prime minister].'[137] Harry Wharton was sent to interview the leader of the opposition, and Wilson defended Kagan, though unaware of the exact suspicions. Kagan and his wife continued their relationship with Vaygauskas back in Lithuania, and John Parker even travelled to the Soviet Union. None of this, of course, made Wilson a Russian agent.

But the Kagan story confirmed, for some in MI5, an old theory. The interview with Wilson went into a file in Furnival Jones's safe, under the name Henry Worthington. It was not Harold Wilson's personal file, but one on the subject of his friends. It had been opened about 1967, after Wigg had become suspicious of Kagan and Rudy Sternberg. 'There was nothing very sinister about it', said Alec MacDonald of MI5. 'I reported it back.

We took it from there.'[138] The file grew and grew. Peter Wright saw four volumes before he retired. Following Wilson's election defeat in 1970, however, a MI5 officer, in the company of a CIA man, had shown William Massie, of the *Sunday Express*, material from Frolik's debriefing about Stonehouse. It began to circulate among journalists. References to Kagan and Williams began to appear in *Private Eye* from May 1971, and the sources are believed to have been other Wilson aides. On 24 October the *News of the World* ran the old story about Gaitskell having been murdered by the Russians, attributing it to Lyalin. Auberon Waugh, nephew of the novelist, had announced, in July, that Wilson had until October to resign, otherwise all would be revealed in *Private Eye*. His source is considered to have been his uncle, Auberon Herbert, who had worked for MI6 and MI5, and could remember Wilson's trips to Russia in the late 1940s. Another source is David Candler, who had stopped working for Wilson in 1970, and took a critical view of Marcia Williams. When asked much later why he circulated tittle tattle about Wilson, all Waugh could say was that 'it was a lovely idea to have a Prime Minister who's a major security risk, and who may be open to influence from the KGB or the Soviet Union ... We played with it, you know, like mad.'[139] For once he was telling the truth.

CHAPTER 21

Return to Office, 1973–4

The Heath government found itself wrestling, as had Wilson, with a British economy in considerable difficulty. The conservatives had the nostrums of Selsdon Man to hand, but a series of U-turns was to be the theme of economic policy. Where labour had failed in 1968–9, the conservatives followed in 1972–3.

In opposition, Wilson and the labour party engaged in the rethinking of economic, and especially industrial, policy, in a context of popular disillusion about the ability of any administration to govern. 'There will be no lurches of policy from what we did in Government', the labour leader had said in July 1970, 'but I hope there will be some healthy developments of new thinking.'[1] Wilson, as usual, was having it both ways.

The key to the party's development of policy was the parliamentary leadership's relationship with organized labour, in the form of the TUC. The labour movement took up three significant positions in the early 1970s. First, it opposed the conservatives' industrial relations legislation, having scuppered labour's earlier attempt. Secondly, it came out against the common market, union votes being crucial at the 1971 party conference. Thirdly, it opposed a statutory incomes policy from the standstill in late 1972, through stages two and three, the latter beginning in November 1973. The memory of labour in power saw the unions alienated from the party leadership in 1970. 'For Labour to regain power there had to be a new confidence between both sections of the movement.'[2] It was Jack Jones who served as the architect of labour's renewal, helped by the Tribunites in the parliamentary party, through their base in the constituencies. Michael Foot returned to the executive in 1972, and Tony Benn played an increasingly important role in Transport House. It was the alliance between the unions and the left which was to prove decisive, though the policy rethink proceeded through a network of committees and groups run by the party organization. 'Wilson was not involved in the minutiae of policy-making, with its time-demanding month-by-month discussions inside the multifarious

415

committees. Here, he had his informal contacts and sources, and was to keep his main challenge until the last minute.'[3]

Jones had argued early for a liaison body to work out a new programme, this being a case of the TUC seeking to influence the labour party. The party leadership did not respond, relations with the trade-union leaders remaining chilly for about eighteen months. The idea took root in the unlikely setting of a Fabian fringe meeting at the 1971 conference, when Roy Jenkins stated there could be no return to the recent past, when the political and industrial wings had been divided. Callaghan was still chairing the home policy committee of the party's executive, which included David Lea as a representative of the TUC. Lea suggested an opening to the parliamentary party, since trade unionists were not talking to shadow ministers. 'I think you'll be treading on a thousand principles',[4] said Callaghan. The latter recognized that the labour movement had two wings, and it was but a short mental leap to the idea of the labour party having two heads – the shadow cabinet and national executive. This was something the party's constitution had long tried to contain. A liaison committee between the TUC and labour party was set up in January 1972, comprising six members from the general council, six from the party executive, and six members of the parliamentary party, who just happened to be from the shadow cabinet. The chair rotated between the three constituents on a three-monthly cycle, starting with Harold Wilson. Callaghan was 'a liaison man to his fingertips'. He was 'much more thoughtful about these matters than Wilson'.[5] The liaison committee met first on 21 February, with Wilson conciliatory in the extreme. He claimed the TUC's review of the economy was compatible with party policy.

Wilson and a few colleagues dined that evening with leaders of the CBI. During the dinner, Wilson attacked Jones and Scanlon in front of the employers. 'The Government have big ears', he is reported to have said, 'and we know what these two men are up to.' Bragging about his knowledge of MI5's intelligence was too much for Benn. 'Since we had met with them that very morning and they were political colleagues, I thought that was a pretty scandalous thing to say to one's political opponents.'[6]

The TUC–labour party liaison committee was to be one of the most publicized policy-making bodies in the history of the labour movement. The party's national executive was dominated by trade unionists, and they were reluctant to share power with the parliamentary committee. But it was the view of the TUC leadership, that the best way to control a future labour government, was to meet with the parliamentarians when they were in opposition. Going to Westminster direct, rather than through Transport House, was the key to the strategy. 'We wanted commitments', writes Jones, 'especially on the repeal of the Industrial Relations Act, and only the leaders of the Party could deliver these.'[7] The repeal of the act occupied the first meetings, the shadow cabinet wanting something to replace it. There was still the problem of strikes, about which a future labour government would be expected to do something. There had to be another industrial relations bill. Jones advanced an idea in a *New Statesman* article in February, for a state-run conciliation service. The liaison committee announced in July that the next labour government would set up an advisory, conciliation and arbitration service, which became known as ACAS. The service was to be independent of the department of employment, seeking to help both sides of industry avoid strikes by offering a range of free services.

The next issue tackled was incomes policy, the trade unionists extracting a promise that labour would not again resort to statutory measures. When Wilson and his colleagues mentioned a voluntary policy, Jones insisted that it would be 'disastrous'[8] if such talk leaked from the meeting. There was clearly some basis for doing business, and the idea emerged that the unions might consider a policy for wages, in a political climate of opposition to inflation. This would be where a labour government was prepared to tackle not only prices, but also a range of issues which made up the totality of social policy. For the TUC to make a concession on free collective bargaining, the shadow cabinet had to offer to consult it on economic, social and industrial policy.

The liaison committee published the eight-page statement *Economic Policy and the Cost of Living* on 28 February 1973. The government was indicted for using the law against trade unions. 'The problem of inflation', the statement argued, 'can be properly considered only within the context of a coherent economic and social strategy – one designed both to overcome the nation's grave economic problems, and to provide the basis for coop-eration between the trade unions and the Government.'[9] The key to an alternative strategy was statutory action on prices. It went on to mention council housing, compulsory purchase of housing land, public transport, a redistribution of income and wealth, and social benefits. In the section on 'investment, employment and economic growth', it was argued that national growth and increased productivity were essential. The question of incomes policy was skated over. A promise of 'new public enterprise' was made, along with 'effective public supervision of the investment policy of large private corporations'.[10] Reference was made to 100 companies, known to control more than 50 per cent of manufacturing output. The final question was industrial democracy. 'The collective bargaining process', read the statement, 'is the essential means whereby the most important factors affecting the livelihood of workpeople can be subjected to joint regulation. But these areas must be extended to include joint control over investment and closure decisions.'[11] The statement appeared to offer a great deal, but there were important reservations. 'It will be the first task of [a] Labour Government on taking office', it ended, 'and having due regard to the circumstances at [the] time, to conclude with the TUC, on the basis of the understandings being reached on the Liaison Committee, a wide-ranging agreement on the policies to be pursued in all these aspects of our economic life and to discuss with them the order of priorities of their fulfilment.'[12] The statement suggested that a labour government would negotiate 'a wide-ranging agreement' with the TUC upon assuming office.

Economic Policy and the Cost of Living was subsequently referred to as the social contract, though it had no serious philosophical inspiration from Locke or Rousseau. It certainly had nothing to do with the citizen's relationship with the state, being about the internal structure of the labour movement. Wilson had first used the term 'voluntary compact' in April 1971, drawing on the corporatism of the 1960s. The critical relationship for the former prime minister was between government and industry, both management and unions. The *Guardian* characterized his suggestion as a 'social compact',[13] and Wilson used the term 'great compact'[14] at the press conference for the liaison committee's statement. He was now talking about government and the unions, and an agreement between labour in opposition and the TUC. Wilson wanted to keep the trade-union movement on board to get him back into office, after which there would be a different relationship. The unions could make the labour party in opposition, but, once in office, a Wilson government would deal with both sides of industry. The question of whether there was an agreement between the party and the TUC, or not, had to be fudged, but the social compact became the social contract at some point in 1973. It remains unattributable, and ultimately undescribable.

Wilson's 'great compact' was a bargain struck between two sets of leaders on future domestic policy, the collective bargaining analogy being uppermost. According to Jones, 'in many ways it was like negotiating a collective agreement, with the highly experienced political leaders – Denis Healey, Barbara Castle, Shirley Williams, Jim Callaghan and Harold Wilson amongst them – seeking to make sure that they did not give too much away.'[15] The policy concessions made, according to *Economic Policy*, would 'further engender the strong feeling of mutual confidence which alone [would] make it possible to reach the wide-ranging agreement which is necessary to control inflation and achieve sustained growth in the standard of living'.[16] This is the sentence Wilson subsequently chose to quote from the last paragraph, to justify his argument that a voluntary incomes policy was implicit in the social contract. This view, he claims, was confirmed by Lionel Murray, who became general secretary of the TUC in 1973. It is a difficult conclusion to draw from the document as a whole, and the liaison committee did not formally endorse a policy for even the voluntary restraint of wages. While there was a reference to further work in the coming months, no detailed social contract had been agreed within the leadership of the labour movement by the time of the general election. The social contract was nothing more than a blend of aspirations. Wilson knew that an incomes policy was absolutely essential, but he failed to impose this on the TUC. 'The politicians were still uneasy, but [the statement] was the nearest they could get to voluntary incomes policy.'[17]

Economic Policy and the Cost of Living codified a new rhetoric for the labour party, some of which would come back to the leadership in changed circumstances. Party documents and papers were being written increasingly by bureaucrats, trained only in a number of academic disciplines. There was to be much talk of strategy, especially with the left.

Wilson gave the impression of being outside the social contract process, having 'a lion tamer sort of approach to things'.[18] Policy formulation was proceeding within the party proper, and again Wilson was also aloof. Callaghan had presented an executive statement, *Building a Socialist Britain*, to the 1970 conference, which was intended as the basis of a new labour programme. 'In preparing that programme', according to Wilson, '[labour would] be the Party of protest as well as the Party of experience.'[19] This was not dialectics but more Wilsonian ambiguity, and he and Callaghan privately thought the statement too radical. The labour leader was also opposed to any inquest on the general election defeat. 'You can't have a post mortem when there isn't a body',[20] he said in a radio interview conducted when he was on the Scillies.

With the memory of a labour government fresh in delegates' minds, there began at Blackpool in 1970 an internal democratic struggle. A motion was carried narrowly, by 3,085,000 votes to 2,801,000, deploring the way conference decisions were ignored by the parliamentary party. This was to challenge the parliamentarist structure and ideology of the labour party, where the autonomy of the parliamentary party, based rhetorically on the people who elected its members, was jealously guarded. The party's constitution barely penetrated the preserve of MPs and the parliamentary leadership, the shadow cabinet and parliamentary party having their own rules. Wilson urged the motion's rejection at Blackpool on behalf of the executive. When it was passed, 'Harold didn't like that very much.'[21] It was not up to party members to instruct its parliamentary representatives. The manifesto was the responsibility of the parliamentary leadership, in accord with the doctrine of electoral mandate in Wilson's view. But the labour party saw conference decisions as sacrosanct, and entrusted to the executive. Any contradiction was to be resolved, in accord with the constitution, in a joint meeting of the shadow cabinet and national executive. Manifesto items were to be selected from the party programme, this being the responsibility of the conference and national executive. Wilson claimed he had left the manifesto to the executive in 1966 and 1970, but it is the case that he did not involve the cabinet, and had it secretly drawn up by Peter Shore. The party leader kept control of labour's commitments, variously using the cabinet, or shadow cabinet, and national executive to get what he wanted. A joint meeting of the executive and shadow cabinet discussed the first draft of *Labour's Programme for Britain* in May 1972. A policy coordinating committee, linking the two heads, had begun to meet in February, under Benn as party chairman for the year. It was not to be as important as the liaison committee. The new draft programme was accepted by the executive on 5 July, and later approved by that year's party conference. The common market was still the principal issue. Callaghan then gave up the chair of the home policy committee, which was controlling the policy review through a number of sub-committees.

One of these had been formed in April 1971 to consider industrial policy, and was to engage in the most radical policy rethink during labour's period in opposition. Old-style nationalization was effectively dead, but the idea of control was uppermost. Jones's advocacy of industrial democracy may have inspired a conference at the Bonnington Hotel in February 1971, at which Tony Benn welcomed a paper by Geoff Bish, number two in the party's research department. Industrial democracy tended to be seen at this stage only in terms of collective bargaining, and a separate working party was set up to consider the issue. There was little continuity with the mintech of the 1960s in the work of the industrial policy sub-committee. Tommy Balogh had been the father of the ill-fated national plan, and, while he was in office, Stuart Holland gave Wilson copies of French planning agreements between the government and leading companies. France – and Europe in general – was to be the inspiration for socialist thinkers in the party on the question of industrial policy, and this at a time of growing opposition to the EEC. Two ideas were developing. First, newly created public enterprise. This had been in Wilson's 1963 conference speech, but it was to be developed in the form of a state body selectively acquiring parts of industries. Second, the idea of the state regulating industrial activity. Stuart Holland, now working at the Centre for Contemporary European Studies at Sussex University, was to be influential. He published an edited collection, *The State as Entrepreneur*, in 1972, and Roy Jenkins asked him to draft a speech on regional policy which was part of his ghosted volume, *What Matters Now* (1972). On the recommendation of Geoff Bish, Judith Hart and Ian Mikardo invited him to write a paper on economic planning. Holland was keen on Italy, on the ideas of a state holding company and a regional development bank. This he presented to the industrial policy sub-committee, then being chaired by John Chalmers of the boilermakers' union. 'I was quite consciously trying', recalls Holland, 'to get as wide a consensus in the party for something which was actually progressive.'[22] There emerged the idea of a national enterprise board, to invest selectively in industry, and thereby slowly socialize it. Perhaps more important was the idea of planning agreements, to be negotiated by a future labour government. The state would only aid companies in return for promises on production. *Economic Policy and the Cost of Living* referred to 'new public enterprise' and 'effective public supervision of the investment policy of large private corporations'[23] in Febrary 1973. It was shortly before the so-called social contract was published that Wilson was informed, by Transport House, of the working of the industrial policy sub-committee. Judith Hart had tried to involve him in their thinking, only to be fobbed off by Marcia Williams, and Wilson was to find now that plans for industrial ownership and control were being developed.

Judith Hart chaired a public sector study group, associated with Chalmers's sub-committee, in which the idea of nationalizing 25 of the 100 largest companies was being considered in early 1973. *Economic Policy and the Cost of Living* referred to 100 leading companies, but the use of an actual figure in this document had more to do with the scope for planning agreements. The figure of twenty five companies went to an all-day meeting of the party executive at the Churchill Hotel on 30 May.

The meeting was to be historic. Wilson had asked Terry Pitt, head of the research department, to remove any reference to nationalizing twenty-five companies. This he could not do. 'Quite clearly [Wilson] was desperate to have it removed and yet did nothing when his best opportunity arose. As a result, his subsequent actions ensured even greater controversy within the party.'[24] Callaghan and Healey backed Wilson, and Tony Benn supported Judith Hart. When Healey pressed an amendment, he was joined by Callaghan, Williams, Foot, Walter Padley and Sid Weighell. The amendment was lost by six votes to seven, Harold Wilson not voting. The executive was now saddled with the twenty-five companies commitment with a conference due in the autumn. It was to go into the redrafted party programme to be issued the following week. The labour leader issued a statement the next morning, insisting he had a veto on the selection of election issues from the party programme. 'Wilson ... was determined to kill the specific proposal for nationalization ... [and] spent the whole summer in the attempt.'[25] Tony Benn did not want an issue made of the number of companies, but the substantive question of socialization was well and truly caught up in the procedural one of internal party democracy, with the labour leader taking a reactionary position on both counts. Wilson's putative veto after the Churchill Hotel executive led to the formation of a rank and file pressure group, the campaign for labour party democracy (CLPD), which was to become a rallying centre for the left.

Wilson prepared the ground for the party conference in Blackpool that October. He told the shadow cabinet, a week before, that he was going to propose a joint meeting between the parliamentary leaders and the national executive, to select manifesto items from the programme. This was already the constitutional position. Even if the conference went for the twenty-five companies, the shadow cabinet would be there to strengthen opposition on the executive. He even prepared his own statement on public ownership. Wilson wanted the shadow cabinet to meet jointly with the executive in Blackpool, on the Friday before the conference. This was an innovation, and the executive decided a joint meeting should only be held after the conference. It also threw out his statement, but it was accepted two days later with two amendments to the text. The shadow cabinet met in his room that Sunday before another executive meeting in the afternoon. There were three resolutions on public ownership to be debated at the conference. One called for the nationalization of 250 companies, the second backed the executive, and the third was against a specific shopping list. The first, from constituencies in Brighton and Liverpool, let Wilson off the hook, allowing the executive to unite in recommending rejection. Wilson offered to withdraw his statement, on condition he could put it in his speech, and he was assigned to introduce the public sector debate on Tuesday, 2 October, on behalf of the executive.

He began his speech on the constitutional question, distinguishing conference support for a resolution from the view of the British people. 'We are debating not what we would like to do if we had political power', he said, 'we are debating what we must do to turn our debates into the reality of political power.'[26] The labour leader then discoursed at length on social ownership. 'It is the commanding heights, not of the forties and fifties, we seek to storm, but those of the seventies and eighties.'[27] Labour's *Programme for Britain, 1973* promised 'a fundamental and irreversible shift in the balance of *power* and *wealth* in favour of working people and their families.'[28] This amounted, in the public sector debate, to the idea of a national enterprise board, and the more open-ended notion of planning agreements. When he came to the national enterprise board, Wilson referred to the twenty five companies mentioned in the programme. 'My own view on the twenty-five companies proposal has been stated', he said. 'I am against it. The Parliamentary Committee is against it. I will leave it with these words, that the Parliamentary Committee charged by the Constitution with the duty of sitting down with the Executive to select from the Programme adopted by the Conference the items for inclusion in the election manifesto, entirely reserves its full constitutional rights on this matter, and there could be nothing more comradely than that. (*Applause*)'[29] The substantive issue was lost in the procedural one, as Wilson asserted the autonomy of the parliamentary party at a delegate conference. It was clear the shadow cabinet would remain opposed even when sitting down with the executive. Tony Benn concluded the debate on behalf of the executive, acknowledging that the 250 companies resolution was in accord with clause four of the constitution. But it was 'a composite that confuse[d] strategy and tactics'.[30] It was lost by 5,600,000 votes to 291,000. The executive position was endorsed unanimously, but Benn was still trying to avoid the twenty-five companies commitment. He argued at a press conference that, since Heath had nationalized twenty-seven companies, labour should not plump for a definite figure.

Harold Wilson did his best to manage the policy rethink, to prevent labour swinging too far left. He began in 1972 to look towards the next general election, as he had done in 1963–4 as leader of the opposition. The labour leader had to find a new idea to unite the party, and give it a progressive image, without unduly hamstringing a future Wilson government. It was to be a case of history repeating itself as farce. Roy Jenkins delivered a series of speeches on economic and social issues in 1972, and Wilson can only have seen this as a threat to his ideological leadership. He began privately to consult advisers.

There had been something of a change in politics in the 1960s, Wilson's electioneering speech to the 1969 conference being an attempt to tap growing concern for the environment. Tommy Balogh was still involved as economic guru during labour's time in opposition, and Geoffrey Goodman remembers a series of ad hoc groups, which met in the leader of the opposition's office. He was a member of one on trade unions and industrial relations. Marcia Williams was not actively involved in organizing these, but other members of the kitchen cabinet were around. Gerald Kaufman was now a member of parliament. Tony Benn is unlikely to have been involved this time round. Peter Shore was probably loyal. Michael Foot was becoming increasingly preeminent. The new model Wilson appeared in 1973, in the form of the so-called Edinburgh series of policy speeches. This was for no reason other than that Wilson spoke first, in Leith, to the East of Scotland labour party, on 20 January 1973. He took 'Individual Choice in Democracy' as his theme. It could not have been further removed from the collectivism which was exciting the party, nor even Jenkins's revamped managerialism. It was a strange excursion into philosophical individualism, of the sort which would be characteristic of the right of the labour party in the 1980s. Wilson blamed the failure of his governments on international finance and multinational corporations. He drew a very different sort of lesson: 'What we failed to recognise ... was how many and how remote were so many of the decisions which were being taken, not only in this country but in the wider dimension of the world industrial complex.'[31] This was to turn questions of economic and political power into issues about the alienation of individuals. Psychology became

the chosen discourse. Wilson warned of the consequences of individual powerlessness, in an apparently authoritative historical judgement. 'The danger
that, not from desperation, not even from inflation resulting in unemployment ... but from frustration and a sense of deprivation of real power,
we could see a lurch into fascism.'[32]

Wilson spoke to the local government conference of the labour party in
Newcastle Upon Tyne three weeks later, addressing them on 'Democracy
in Local Affairs'. Never one to forget parliamentary political rivalry, he
blamed powerlessness on the conservatives. 'The whole of Conservative
thinking is directly opposed to any idea of meeting the over-riding need
to associate the individual more and more closely with the taking of
decisions affecting the environment in which he lives; in which his family
is brought up, and educated, and works and spends his leisure-time.'[33] His
practical political argument was that, while some of the new local authorities were too small for planning purposes, most of them were too remote
from the people. There was an element of self-criticism on the reform of
the national health service. 'It was only in the later months of the Labour
Government that the Secretary of State and I came to appreciate the
degree of fetishism in the Treasury and the Civil Service generally about
appointing the members of the government authorities.'[34] Wilson had
outlined the party's policy on local government reform, arguing that this
should be in accord with what he called 'the Edinburgh principle of consultation and participation'.[35]

His third lecture in the series dealt with 'Democracy in Industry', and
was given to the labour party's north west regional conference on 17
March. Picking up his general theme, he argued that the failure to increase
democratic participation would lead to 'a vain search for a solution to our
problems in the spurious doctrines peddled by the anti-democrats of the
extreme right and the extreme left, ending in the assertion of authoritarianism in Britain.'[36] He had once persuaded a train driver to go to Ruskin
College in Oxford. That individual, Wilson said, was now a personnel
director in British Steel. 'But how many did he leave behind? How many
are being left behind today?'[37] The extension of collective bargaining was
the way forward. Wilson acknowledged the efforts of the party's industrial
democracy working party, where Jack Jones's ideas had taken root. He
suggested a system of compulsory works committees, with shop-floor
elections managed by the unions. This was entirely in accord with new party
thinking, though Wilson was normally reluctant to concede the democratic
pretensions of trade unions in the wider society. He even quoted the
figure of the top 100 companies being responsible for half of manufacturing output. The European solution was some sort of codetermination
between management and workers – two-tier boards for private industry,
and worker directors in public industry. This implied reform within trade

unions. 'It means … a continuing willingness to overhaul and develop the structures and internal democracy of the unions, and to rationalise inter-union agreements, joint servicing and so on.' Wilson saw his 'new deal in industry' strengthening the rights of individuals, implying a responsibility 'to ensure that decisions are taken in the wider interest of society'.[38]

He promised to deal with the question of public ownership and state control in a further speech, but philosophical reflection soon hit the ground with a bump when the recommendations of Judith Hart's working group went to the national executive meeting at the Churchill Hotel. The Edinburgh series died a premature death, though the three lectures were published by the labour party. Harold Wilson had had nearly six years as prime minister to prove his political worth. The left might be interested in participation, but not Harold Wilson's theorization of this advanced democratic concept. The labour leader lost any initiative he had to the party in 1973, the party in turn losing it to the national union of mineworkers, which was about to return to the centre of the political stage.

The Heath government could have been expected to last until late 1974, or even the following spring, but popular industrial pressure was to determine otherwise. After the successful strike in 1972, the national union of mineworkers accepted the coal board's offer in the next annual wage round. Union delegates voted the following July, to demand increases of £8 to £13 on basic wages from March 1974. Stage three of the government's statutory incomes policy was due to begin in November 1973, with a norm of 8 to 9 per cent. Provision was made for an allowance for 'unsocial hours', in order to give the miners more, and the national coal board offered the maximum possible. This was rejected by the union, and an overtime ban began on 12 November. There was no better time to prove a number of points: Britain needed coal; the closure of pits had been short-sighted; and well-paid miners were the key to a successful energy policy.

There had been another flare up in the middle east, a concerted Arab attack being repulsed by Israel in the Yom Kippur war of 6–22 October. The Zionist state was beginning to develop a reputation for invincibility. Harold Wilson would admit later that he had been in daily touch with the Israeli ambassador; he pressed Heath and Douglas-Home, privately and then publicly, to resume arms supplies, but was unsuccessful. Wilson, and Callaghan to a lesser extent, were particularly concerned about ammunition and spares for British Centurion tanks supplied in the 1960s. Wilson had some difficulty getting his pro-Israel position through the shadow cabinet. Roy Jenkins had returned to the front bench at the beginning of the 1973–4 session, and was taking a pro-government line on not sending arms. "'Look, Roy'", Wilson was to quote himself as saying, "'I've accommo-dated your [expletive deleted] conscience for years. Now you're going to take account of mine. I feel as strongly about the Middle East as you do about the Common Market.'"[39] Somewhat preposterously, Wilson compared the middle east war with the defence of the Spanish republic in the 1930s. The Arab states set out after the war supposedly to help the Palestinians by cutting back on oil production. If this was designed to secure diplomatic support from leading states, it was counter-productive. The oil producers were strong enough greatly to affect the world economy. Britain was especially dependent upon Arab oil, its own supplies from the North Sea having not yet come on stream. Heath's stand during the war did not save Britain, and Harold Wilson, as leader of the opposition, was hardly responsible for what ensued. Amid panic buying at the pumps, there was a fourfold increase in price. A 50 mph speed limit was introduced. Ration coupons were even issued, though they were not to be necessary. The government declared a state of emergency on 13 November to conserve coal stocks, with a cut back in electricity supply. Street lighting was curtailed, and television instructed to close down at 10.30 p.m. The end of civilization beckoned.

Heath invited the miners' executive to Downing Street on 28 November, and offered the prospect of improvements in an expected report from the pay board on relativities. Douglas Hurd was subsequently critical of the briefing the prime minister had received, arguing that the civil service was found wanting (as it had been after Bloody Sunday in January 1972, and during the discussion on inflation in the summer of 1973). The 28 November meeting was the occasion when Mick McGahey, the miners' vice president, said he wanted to bring the Heath government down. The miners' leaders voted not to put the new offer to a ballot of the membership. William Whitelaw was working wonders in Northern Ireland, and Heath sent him to the department of employment on 2 December, a move which only encouraged the miners to believe that more would be on offer. It was announced nine days later that there would be a three-day week in the new year, further to conserve electricity. There were rumours of a general election, but Heath was almost certainly prepared to see the overtime ban through. With Whitelaw at employment, Joe Gormley suggested privately that the government could find a way out by paying miners for waiting and bathing time. When Gormley explained this to Wilson at Lord North Street the following morning, the labour leader said: '"Oh! Well, of course, Joe, you do realise you're pulling the Tory Government's irons out of the fire for them?"' Wilson then made the idea public, thereby preventing the government from doing a deal. 'It was bad enough', Gormley wrote later, 'to have the Tories playing politics with an industrial dispute, but to have our own Party doing the same thing to us was beyond belief.'[40] Whitelaw admits he 'was furious at the time',[41] and Joe Gormley records: 'I will never forgive Harold Wilson for it.'[42]

Parliament was being recalled early after the Christmas recess for 9 January 1974, and pressure built up within the conservative party for an election on 7 February. It was believed the government could secure a mandate to deal firmly with the national union of mineworkers. Harold Wilson did not accept an election was imminent, but he feared Heath might be encouraged by some of 'his Pearl Harbor boys'[43] to go to the country. Labour had no wish to be associated in the eyes of electors with the miners, but the national executive and shadow cabinet had met in December to draw up a campaign document. An emergency meeting of the liaison committee was held at Congress House on 4 January, but the trade unionists refused, yet again, to accept a voluntary incomes policy. Wilson, echoing Tony Benn, said: '"What we need is more the creation of a mood than a compact."'[44] A social contract hardly existed, and it was hoped the TUC would respond positively to the campaign document. This was finally agreed, after redrafting by Michael Foot, at a second joint meeting on 11 January, and was published immediately. It later became the manifesto.

Efforts were being made to get the miners to call off the overtime ban, and the TUC stated, at a meeting of NEDC on 9 January, that it would not consider any settlement, outside stage three, as a precedent for other workers. Heath met the TUC the following day, and also on 14 January, abandoning the option of a 7 February election. The prime minister and Whitelaw were inclined to be conciliatory, fearing the consequences of being returned to power after a confrontation with the unions. A fresh electoral mandate would mean little if there was an embittered, but not neutered, trade-union movement. Lord Carrington, in the new energy department, mooted the possibility of a four-day week on 17 January, thinking the coal stocks might last through to the spring.

The miners' executive decided, a week later, upon a strike ballot. The deputy chairman of the pay board, Derek Robinson, had conducted the inquiry into relativities, and was trying, through Barbara Castle and others, to press his report as the basis of a solution. It was published on 23 January, the day before labour's national executive carried a resolution from Tony Benn, supporting the TUC's initiative. Mick McGahey said on 28 January that, if troops were called in, he would appeal to them not to break a strike, only to be repudiated by Joe Gormley, and members of the parliamentary party led by Wilson and Callaghan. The latter, who was closest to the unions, sought to dissociate the party from such revolutionary talk. 'We utterly repudiate', said the shadow foreign secretary, 'any attempt by the communists or anyone else to use the miners as a battering ram to bring about a general strike or to call on troops to disobey orders.'[45]

Wilson wrote to Heath the day afterwards, suggesting the relativities report as a way of avoiding a national coal strike. The prime minister replied on 30 January that, if the miners went back to normal working, their case would be the first referred to a relativities board, providing the TUC supported the government's action. Barbara Castle had been an early advocate of using Robinson's report, but she felt Wilson had conceded too much. 'He really is the most reckless tactician', she wrote in her diary, 'always getting himself into corners.'[46] The miners voted four to one to support their executive, which decided on 5 February to call an all-out strike. Two days later, Heath called a general election for 28 February. It was not clear how this would led to a solution. The conservative government had been pledged not to have a statutory incomes policy, and the election was probably an alternative to fighting the miners. A section of the cabinet must have seen it as securing a mandate to take them on subsequently. Heath was going to the country after only three and a half years, but some of his colleagues were aware that the economy were getting worse. With the pits about to close down for an indefinite period, the prime minister now sent the miners' claim to the pay board, raising the question of whether the election was necessary at all. Joe Gormley sought, unsuccessfully, to have the strike postponed, and the 1974 general election was the first to be conducted against the background of national industrial action. Observers considered this would militate against the labour party's chances, and Wilson was to claim he tried to avert the strike. 'Throughout the three months ending with Mr Heath's decision to go to the country', he was to write, 'I did all I could to avoid it, including meetings with the NUM, and attempts to find a formula which Mr Heath could accept.'[47] He certainly did not want an election on this single issue. Labour had led the conservatives in the opinion polls for most of the parliament, but, in January, the government had the support of 33 per cent of electors to the opposition's 31.

The challenge to the conservatives' incomes policy saw Sir William Armstrong, the then head of the civil service, succumb to a mental breakdown. A civil service trade-union leader had dubbed Armstrong 'the deputy prime minister',[48] and he played a key role in trying to control inflation under Heath's administration, from the time of the statutory incomes policy in November 1972. When the miners were balloting in January 1974, Armstrong was with other civil servants, politicians and business men, at Ditchley Park, for a weekend meeting with congressmen from the United States. Douglas Hurd described him as being full of notions, ordinary and extraordinary. Campbell Adamson of the CBI remembers another occasion: 'We listened to a lecture about how Communists were infiltrating everything. They might even be infiltrating ... the room he was in. It was quite clear that the immense strain and overwork was taking its toll.'[49] When Armstrong told a meeting of permanent secretaries on 1 February that they should all go home early, to convince the public that the government was in control of events, 'Douglas Allen got up and gently led Armstrong from the room.'[50] He was spirited to Barbados to rest, and resigned shortly afterwards from the civil service.

The policy for prices and incomes was to be a major issue of the February 1974 campaign. The labour manifesto, *Let Us Work Together*, which had been agreed on 8 February, came out for strict price controls on key goods and services. The conservatives, in *Fair Action for a Fair Britain*, stated they would strengthen their price commission. It was announced on 15 February that the retail food price index had risen 20 per cent in the past year – higher than at any time since 1947. As for incomes, labour announced it would abolish the pay board. Wilson stated the need for a 'social contract' between the government and both sides of industry at Nottingham on 17 February. This was prime ministerial talk, not the labour leader dealing with the TUC. Heath poured scorn on the existence of a social contract, and admitted to now favouring a statutory policy, if a voluntary one could not be negotiated with the TUC and CBI. Labour was not advocating a statutory incomes policy, and was promising the alternative of cooperation with the unions. It had more credibility than the government in the context of the miners' strike. A week before polling day, the pay board, in the form of Derek Robinson, suddenly announced that, as a result of the coal board getting its figures wrong, the miners had underestimated their claim. Wilson was quick to claim that the election was an unnecessary farce. Heath had put Britain on a three-day week, to defend an incomes policy the miners might not be breaking. The state of industrial relations formed the background to the electoral struggle. The conservatives had promised to amend their industrial relations act, tough new policies being promised on trade-union elections, and ending the payment of social security to the families of strikers. Labour was to repeal the act, and replace the legal approach with an independent service for employers and workers. On 26 February, Campbell Adamson of the CBI, being recorded unwittingly by the BBC at a management conference, stated that he favoured the repeal of the conservatives' act. This was a bombshell. The CBI dissociated itself as an organization, and Adamson even offered his resignation. It is clear that the employers had scored an own goal, with Heath between the posts.

It had been ten years since Harold Wilson had fought an election as challenger, and he had less control of the manifesto than in 1966 and 1970. He sought to mount a characteristically presidential campaign, based on his Westminster office and home in Lord North Street. Ron Hayward, the party's general secretary, had to persuade Wilson to move his staff into a set of offices on the first floor in Transport House. Volunteers were left in the leader of the opposition's office at Westminster to deal with correspondence, its manager Albert Murray accompanying Wilson on his nightly speaking engagements. Marcia Williams still avoided the house of commons, but again considered herself one of his political advisers. Joe Haines also played an important role. He had been critical of Wilson's limp speech writing in the early days, and took over the task with others. The fourth member of Wilson's entourage was Bernard Donoughue, then a reader in politics at the London School of Economics. Also involved in the campaign were Peter Lovell-Davies and Dennis Lyons, who ran a small publicity group on behalf of the party. Tommy Balogh and Gerald Kaufman took an interest in Wilson's campaign.

Each day began with a meeting at 8.00 a.m. between Wilson and his small entourage at Lord North Street to discuss that evening's speech. The campaign committee met at 9.00 a.m. at Transport House chaired by Ron Hayward, and Wilson put in an appearance at all of these. Something of his attitude towards labour headquarters can, perhaps, be inferred from Donoughue's description of Transport House as 'a central organization of almost unbelievable inefficiency'. 'Much of the energy as existed in the upper levels', he was to write, 'was devoted to petty jealousies and internal squabbling.'[51] Wilson then went to his office or back to Lord North Street, to discuss the following night's speech, and, probably, his statement at the party press conference. Labour's was held after the conservatives' at 11.45 a.m., allowing Wilson to reply to points made by Heath. Other labour figures, also engaged in their constituencies and national speaking tours, took part in these conferences, Transport House imposing a more collegial leadership on the party. Wilson then travelled to a provincial centre to address rallies of the party faithful.

Marcia Williams, remembering the tories' performance in 1970, had discussed the labour leader's presentation on television with Stanley Baker, the actor. David Wickes, a film producer, plus Neil Vann, from Transport House, were taken on to style Wilson's image. Wickes and Vann travelled ahead of Wilson in their own vehicle to set up a backdrop, incorporating a Union Jack motif, which had been made at Pinewood Studios. There was also a prepared platform, which allowed Wickes and Vann to control the positioning of television cameras. Wilson even had his own professional make-up man, but he 'disliked this form of grooming intensely'[52] and was resistant to changing his suit. David Wickes recalls: 'we made the whole place look professional and smooth and clear and clean so that it gave this reassuring image.'[53] He arranged it so that Wilson entered from the back of the hall, with cameras and lights on him as he processed up the middle, to be greeted by party members assigned the seats on the aisle.

Wilson gave radio and television interviews during the day, when he was speaking in or near London. Williams and Haines usually accompanied him to the studio, but he had to share these spots with prominent front-bench colleagues. Williams, Haines and Donoughue discussed the following night's speech each evening in Transport House, the two latter having drafted it. The speech was then taken over to Lord North Street, for Wilson to read when he returned to London towards midnight. The party also supplied him with the results of daily private polls, which continued to show labour was behind. Donoughue describes Wilson as showing 'signs of tension and exhaustion'. 'He would slump in his chair, light a cigar and sip a brandy, his exhaustion showing as he talked over the day's events and the big evening meeting.'[54] Wilson suffered from an infected eye and strained voice during the campaign, and his usual confidence on the stump did not return. He complained of being unable to read the election, this being, paradoxically, an accurate reflection of the national mood.

Neither the leader of the party nor Transport House expected to win, since the election was billed as being about 'who governs Britain?' Roy Jenkins shared this view. Wilson had announced to his inner circle on Sunday, 10 February that he would fight like Cromwell at Marston Moor: 'During the first week the Conservative attack would be contained; and in the second week Labour would counter-attack by asserting its better economic policies, its commitment to social consensus through the social contract, and above all its plans to reduce prices. In the third week there would be skirmishes on the flanks, exploiting Enoch Powell's expected attacks on the Conservative leadership over the question of EEC membership.'[55] Labour was known to be closely associated with the unions, but it was Wilson who had posed the question of excessive and disruptive trade-union power. Memories of *In Place of Strife* still lingered within the party. Labour knew what it was against, not what it was for. Callaghan was deputed to handle the trade-union issue, his politics consisting of appeasing, first, the union movement, and, secondly, voters sympathetic to labour. Benign paternalism was deployed to handle the contradiction. The election badly backfired on Heath over the question of the miners' strike. It was feared something worse than the three-day week was in the offing. Heath must have observed Wilson's emollient promises becoming increasingly attractive to voters. The leader of the opposition concentrated on attacking the conservatives on other issues, Europe coming up trumps for him at long last in the unlikely form of Enoch Powell. Wilson had heard before the election that the latter would speak on the detested EEC, Powell having refused to stand in what he considered an unnecessary election. As a former conservative member of parliament, he suddenly announced on 26 February that he had already completed a postal vote for the labour candidate in his midlands constituency. Wilson synchronized his speeches on the market with Powell's appearances, a journalist, Andrew Alexander, acting as go between. The trade figures for January had been published the day before Powell's dramatic revelation, showing a deficit of £383 million. As with labour in 1970, so it was to be with the conservatives: the poor state of the balance of payments was blamed on the government. The liberals, and other minor parties, cast uncertainty over the prospects of the two major parties in the closing days of the campaign. Neither labour nor conservatives berated the liberals, as each feared losing support to the third party. Both hoped that the liberals would eat into the other's vote. They had won five by-elections in the 1970 parliament, breached the 20 per cent figure in the polls the previous August, and were running 517 candidates under the leadership of Jeremy Thorpe. Plaid Cymru contested all thirty-six Welsh seats. This was also the case north of the border, with the Scottish National Party (SNP). It had won one seat in 1970, and another in a by-election. There were also the Northern Ireland parties, fighting for twelve seats at Westminster.

The turnout on 28 February was 78.8 per cent, back to the level of 1959 and with three million more voting. The miners' strike was proving conducive to democratic participation. Labour found that the three-day week was helpful to the party, since their supporters cast their votes during the day, and bad weather set in during the evening. But there was no simple relationship between the strike and popular electoral support, labour losing over half a million votes. With 11,639,243 supporters, it received 37.1 per cent of the poll – the lowest percentage since 1931. The turnout was a 77.2 per cent in Huyton, Harold Wilson securing 31,767 votes to his conservative opponent's 16,462 and a liberal's 7,584. The conservatives came back with slightly more support than labour, their 11,868,906 votes representing 37.9 per cent of the poll. This was a loss of one and a quarter million votes, and their lowest percentage in over fifty years. The conservatives faired worse than labour. Though Heath had more national votes than Wilson, labour came back as the largest party. It had 301 seats, a gain of 14, to the conservatives' 297, a loss of 33. Wilson failed to reach an overall majority, 318 being the target figure: he needed at least 17 minority votes to form a government, while Heath required 21. Nothing like this had happened since the 1920s, when labour replaced the conservatives twice with the reluctant support of the liberals. The 37 minority seats, representing 7,825,517 voters, and 25 per cent of the poll, were decisive in 1974. The balance of power was well and truly held by the minority parties, though they were far from united. The largest was the liberals with 14 seats – a post-war record – and 6,063,470 votes or 19.3 per cent. But this was not enough either to keep Heath in power or put in Wilson. The other 23 seats, and 7,462,047 votes, were divided between a number of minor parties: the Ulster unionists, 11; SNP, 7; Plaid Cymru, 2; SDLP, 1; and 2 independent labour candidates. Heath could no longer be sure of the 11 unionists, and the other 12 were more likely to go to Wilson. The fourteen liberals, under Thorpe, to determine who would be the next prime minister.

CHAPTER 22

The Third Wilson Government, 1974

The resignation of Harold Wilson as labour leader had been on the cards in February 1974. Joe Haines testifies that Wilson planned to step down, on Friday, 1 March, if he did not pull it off. This is confirmed independently by Marcia Williams and Bernard Donoughue. The latter states Wilson made 'quite bizarre secret preparations to go into hiding should he be defeated',[1] but this involved nothing more than booking rooms in the Golden Cross Hotel in Kirby, a hotel he used frequently on constituency visits.

Wilson had flown to Liverpool on the eve of poll, with senior members of his entourage, establishing himself in the Adelphi. After touring Huyton on election day, he returned to his suite to watch the election coverage on television, surrounded by a circle of friends. He paced the room as was his custom, returning to his regular chair by the bedroom door when he wished to discuss some point or other. The polls had closed at 10.00 p.m. on 28 February, and the first results suggested a labour victory, but, by midnight, BBC and ITV computers were predicting a deadlock. Wilson secured a special branch bodyguard, and the party left for Huyton. Haines and Williams were admitted to the count, and, after Wilson's assured return, there was a visit to the local labour club. Wilson and his entourage retreated to the Golden Cross Hotel, in accord with the plan to disappear. Accounts are confusing but it seems the press found them, and they returned to the Adelphi. It was becoming clear that Harold Wilson was going to be in the position of Ramsay MacDonald in the 1920s, because of the liberal revival. He and his party flew back to London on Friday, 1 March, returning briefly to Lord North Street before repairing to Transport House. There was deadlock. The advance of the minority parties registered in the late results, and Heath clung to office. He was not interpreting the election result as a vote of no confidence, and, after an emergency cabinet meeting in the late afternoon, the prime minister went to see the queen, who had just returned from Australia. Heath wanted to try to form a new government.

Wilson had called the shadow cabinet together in Transport House, and the opposition announced its willingness to serve. With Heath likely to be busy through the weekend, the Wilsons drove off to Grange Farm. He telephoned Callaghan at some point, the latter advising they should stick to their agreement not to issue any statement. Jeremy Thorpe visited Downing Street on the Saturday afternoon, and again late on the Sunday, but the 14 liberal MPs unanimously rejected a coalition offer on Monday, 4 March. Thorpe had been prepared to give support to 'any minority government on an agreed but limited programme'.[2]

Wilson had refused even to consider a national government, and discussed labour's return to office with his private staff at Lord North Street on the Sunday night. Jeremy Thorpe was to find him almost pathologically opposed, fearing charges of MacDonaldite treachery. Donoughue believed that moderate policies would gain the support of the liberals, and knew that Thorpe's colleagues would not countenance a coalition with the conservatives. It was mid-afternoon the following day before Robert Armstrong, Heath's principal private secretary, finally telephoned Wilson. The prime minister was going to the palace to resign at 6.30 p.m. The leader of the opposition followed, at 7.30 p.m, accompanied by his family and senior staff. Wilson undertook to form a government. Marcia Williams, in the courtyard below, told Haines to accompany Wilson back to Downing Street, in order to discomfit Robert Armstrong, who was waiting in the prime minister's car. Wilson's party reached number 10 just before eight o'clock. 'It's Joe Gormley come to take office',[3] a wag shouted from the crowd. A second car containing Donoughue, Albert Murray, an apparently reluctant Marcia Williams, and Gerald Kaufman stopped further down the street. With his kitchen cabinet in tow, Harold Wilson was greeted by the number 10 staff, lined up on either side of the hallway leading from the front door.

Wilson believed it would be different this time. The labour leader now had experienced colleagues, and the party had divided in opposition. He told Donoughue that he would play as the 'sweeper' in defence, and not as the 'striker' in attack if returned to office. Ministers would be left to run their own departments. He took to describing himself as 'a deep-lying centre half'. 'There would this time be "no presidential nonsense", no "first hundred days", and no "beer and sandwiches at No. 10" to solve crises.'[4] This political autocritique may have been the outcome of brainstorming sessions in the leader of the opposition's room, but Wilson probably had no alternative, as the party became increasingly difficult to manage. The problems of civil society, especially the relationship between capital and labour, were proving beyond the British system of government, and this was to be reflected in his new style of premiership. The prime minister told a special meeting of the national executive on 6 March that ministers were being left to do 'the bloody work'. 'My job is to be the custodian of the

Manifesto', he said. 'I have already recruited a political team at No. 10 which will have access to all the documents. I am asking all my colleagues to appoint political advisers to their private office.'[5]

There had been changes in number 10, as Heath had imposed his own ideas on decor. One of Wilson's first instructions was that the Napoleonic war pictures should be restored to the state dining room, and a wartime Churchill portrait was put back in the lobby outside the cabinet room. Wilson was proving himself the true conservative. Marcia Williams returned to her room, the idea of a political office being less of an innovation for the civil service. Wilson had decided to retain Heath's appointee in the private office, Robert Armstrong, and he also kept the other private secretaries, contrary to the advice of his personal staff. Kenneth Stowe was later to become principal private secretary. Joe Haines returned to the civil service and the press office, dismissing four of his eleven officers; when Armstrong mummered about civil service morale, Haines sacked another one. The most important innovation was the number 10 policy unit under Bernard Donoughue. It had been the latter's idea, and was only agreed during the hiatus after the election. Balogh was to be excluded, though Andrew Graham returned from Oxford to become number two in the unit. Donoughue took two years' leave from the LSE, entering the civil service as the prime minister's senior policy adviser. The policy unit did not come under the cabinet office, now headed by Sir John Hunt, and Wilson left the central policy review staff — or think tank — in place, with Victor Rothschild in charge.

Wilson had decided to retain his home in Lord North Street, presumably to appease Mary Wilson. She had been upset at the way messengers interrupted their privacy during his first two governments. The flat in number 10 was to be used only occasionally, Wilson later telling Martin Gilbert he had been unable to sleep in that prison. The prime minister had a strong liking for Chequers, believing it was where he had his best ideas. Mary Wilson would be dropped off at Grange Farm at weekends, unless required for some official engagement. They had long lived separate lives within their marriage, and work was to take up most of Wilson's time at Chequers in the 1970s.

The first priority on the evening of Monday, 4 March 1974 was the selection of senior ministers. Wilson states the parliamentary party had elected the shadow cabinet he voted for, which is another way of saying he wanted a balanced leadership. He now had parliamentary colleagues with whom he had worked in government, and had arranged the key appointments that afternoon. Denis Healey was to go to the treasury, and Jim Callaghan have the foreign office. Roy Jenkins had to be content with a return to the home office, though his supporters wanted him to demand the treasury; 'how many votes', Bill Rodgers asked, 'are there in prison reform'?[6] Wilson was now less concerned with threats to his leadership; Healey had no base, Callaghan was becoming even more benign as a grandfather at the age of sixty-two, and Jenkins had shown political cowardice. Wilson offered Sir Elwyn Jones the lord chancellorship that evening, and Fred Peart agriculture. Tony Benn went to the department of industry, mintech having absorbed the board of trade in 1970. Shirley Williams was placed in charge of prices and consumer protection, with a seat in the cabinet. The department of energy had recently been hived off, and was given to Eric Varley, a former parliamentary private secretary of Wilson's. Peter Shore took charge of a new trade department, also with a cabinet seat. The surprise appointment was Michael Foot at employment. Jack Jones had vetoed Reg Prentice, and Bernard Donoughue stressed the importance of good relations with the unions. Foot believes he owed his job to the TGWU's general secretary. Prentice was given education and science, and defence went to the former miner, Roy Mason, whose 'biggest disappointment in life'[7] had been his failure to be accepted by the RAF. Barbara Castle, who had been on the backbenches since 1972, became secretary of state for social services. Other cabinet ministers seen by the following morning were: Edward Short, the deputy leader (lord president), Lord Shepherd (lord privy seal), Tony Crosland (environment), Harold Lever (duchy of Lancaster, to advise Wilson on economics and finance), Merlyn Rees (Northern Ireland), William Ross (Scotland), and John Morris (Wales); John Silkin, who had shadowed social services, took charge of planning and local government. He was to enter the cabinet in October. Mellish joined as chief whip in July. Thirteen of Wilson's cabinet of twenty-one had been senior ministers in the 1960s, and Foot was the only one with no experience in government. The 1974 cabinet was the first to contain two women, Castle and Williams. It was also politically balanced, the left being represented by Castle, Foot, Benn and Shore, while Jenkins, Williams and probably Lever constituted a modern right. Most of the others – including Callaghan, Healey and possibly Crosland – were more traditionally rightist. The majority remained the prime minister's men. Wilson appointed fewer senior ministers outside the cabinet – Judith Hart at overseas development, Sam Silkin as attorney-general, Peter Archer as solicitor-general, plus the two Scottish law officers.

The junior appointments took a little longer. Lord Balogh went to the energy department, to take charge of North Sea oil. Other notable junior ministers were Edmund Dell (paymaster-general), Joel Barnett (treasury), David Ennals and Roy Hattersley (foreign office), Lord [John] Harris (home office), Denis Howell (sport and recreation), Brian O'Malley (social services), Eric Heffer (industry), and Stan Orme (Northern Ireland). The likes of Callaghan and Jenkins selected their own junior ministers, but Wilson was responsible for choosing many of the others. He was assisted in this by his personal staff, seemingly at the first working lunches in the small state dining room. This was a new development, designed to allow Wilson and his kitchen cabinet to discuss business daily, often with a party official or other outsider present. Wilson wanted to direct his administration politically, but Marcia Williams was to storm out after a few weeks, and the prime minister stopped attending shortly afterwards.

The miners' strike was continuing, with Britain still on a three-day week. As soon as he had entered number 10, the prime minister asked to see the TUC at noon on Tuesday, 5 March and the CBI at 2.30 p.m. to discuss industrial normalization. The first cabinet meeting was held at 5.00 p.m. The pay board report on miners' relative pay recommended increases, with faceworkers to get more than those on the surface. Michael Foot wanted the government to allow the coal board to resume negotiations, it wishing to settle the miners' basic claim in full. Healey sanctioned a further slight increase the following day, and a settlement was announced. The state of emergency was declared at an end on 7 March, though Heath's stage three was still in force. The labour government decided to let the act run its course until July, as a result of which Wilson was to preside over highly inflationary threshold payments. The pay board remained in existence until the summer.

The government had been under pressure to prepare its first queen's speech for 12 March. Though Wilson, and just about everybody else, knew that there had to be another election in 1974, he asked ministers to come up with measures for a year's legislative programme. The cabinet office had produced a draft speech, based on labour's manifesto, for a full parliament. The queen's speech promised food subsidies and consumer legislation, council-house rent increases were to be frozen, the price commission retained, and pensions and benefits uprated. Talks about 'methods of securing the orderly growth of incomes on a voluntary basis' were to be held, the industrial relations act replaced by ACAS, and the modernization of industry promoted. The coal industry was to be reexamined, and North Sea oil used 'to confer maximum benefit on the community'.[8] Wilson had formed his government in the knowledge that it would be tested over the queen's speech. When Heath threatened to vote against, the prime minister stated he would call an immediate general election. Parliamentary brinkmanship was the order of the day. Wilson was confident that the queen would grant a dissolution, and number 10 used a couple of highly-placed lawyers to convey this news, by a round about route, to the opposition. The conservatives abstained on 18 March, the government winning the vote by 294 to 7.

In the annual budget on 26 March, Denis Healey increased pensions and benefits, plus food and housing subsidies. Nationalized industries were to raise prices. The chancellor sought to reduce the public sector borrowing requirement (PSBR) by £1,500 million, it having reached £4,250 million in 1973–4. This required a substantial increase in taxation. 'The oil situation', according to Wilson, 'had in fact created a fiscal problem not very different in character from the requirements of a war budget, and measurably similar in extent.'[9] The cost of imports had risen rapidly. Value added tax (VAT) was extended, and other indirect taxes increased. As for direct taxation, the basic rate was raised three points, to 33 per cent, and the highest rates commensurately. The idea of a wealth tax was later to be criticized by a select committee.

Healey's first budget was mildly deflationary, being introduced against the background of a resumed balance of payments crisis, which had preceded the fourfold increase in the price of oil. Under-investment in industry meant unemployment was rising, and this at a time of inflation. The quadrupling of the oil price gave rise to an inflationary recession, or – as it was to be known – 'stagflation'. Harold Lever was to argue for increased borrowing, to cover the balance of payments deficit, and defend sterling; he would be the last Keynesian defending the fort. The shortfall in demand in Britain, accentuated by deflationary measures, could only be corrected by increased demand in countries running a surplus – mainly the oil producers but also Germany, Japan and Switzerland.

Even before Healey's budget was enacted, the chancellor was forced to introduce further measures on 22 July, intended to bring about a slight reflation given the increase in unemployment. VAT was reduced from 10 to 8 per cent, and central government relief provided on excessive rate demands. Food subsidies were extended, the regional employment premium raised, and the limit on dividends increased to help investment.

The mainstay of government economic policy in 1974 was a proposed industry bill, to create the national enterprise board and allow planning agreements. This was the responsibility of Tony Benn, and his minister of state, Eric Heffer, who were not to have a good working relationship. Benn's permanent secretary, Sir Anthony Part, would play a key role. Wilson requested a white paper, with a view to the next manifesto. 'It was vital', he would write, 'that no vague statements or half-veiled threats should be left around for use as a scare by the Opposition.'[10] Stuart Holland had been lined up as a political adviser, and believes Wilson cryptically vetoed Benn's request. Holland became a member of the working party under Heffer, which was to produce the first draft of the white paper. Conscious of the right-wing orientation of the cabinet, Heffer decided 'a severely practical document was needed, in which the radicalism was presented as realism.'[11] He 'walked on eggs from time to time',[12] but the secretary of state 'redrafted it as a socialist manifesto'.[13] Michael Meacher, a junior minister in the department, described the language as having been radicalized.

This was more than Heffer could bear, and, according to John Silkin years later, 'he told us the experience had been hell.'[14] Heffer was afraid of provoking Wilson, as Sir Anthony Part, through the cabinet secretary, fed criticisms of Benn back to number 10. The white paper 'created a major crisis in Whitehall', when it emerged from the department of industry in July. Its 'very aggressive[ly] interventionist language' was dubbed Bennery by civil servants and ministers, and it 'disturbed' the prime minister.[15] The latter described it as 'a sloppy and half-baked document, polemical, indeed menacing, in tone, redolent more of an NEC Home Policy Committee document than a Command Paper.'[16] The white paper went to a cabinet committee, which decided it should be rewritten. Benn was initially in the chair. Exception seems to have been taken to compulsory disclosure of financial information, and the purchase of shares in companies by workers. Wilson attributes the redrafted white paper to Michael Foot, but Bernard Donoughue claims the work was done in the number 10 policy unit. The prime minister seems to have dictated a synopsis of the redraft himself. Wilson's senior policy adviser states the prime minister supported the 1973 programme, but 'the united hostility of industry could not be discounted'. 'A minority government', Donoughue was to argue, 'has great difficulty in imposing a non-consensus partisan policy, especially in a major policy area.'[17] Benn and his associates thought Wilson had never believed in a serious extension of public ownership, and that he only took over the chair when he thought he was losing. The secretary of state for industry recalls 'long arguments, the most exhausting and bitter disputes [he had] ever been involved in'. Benn describes them as 'a series of meetings which I hope I never have to live through again'.[18]

The rewritten white paper, *The Regeneration of British Industry*, emphasized the role of the national enterprise board. It was to invest in industry, taking a share of the equity capital in return; promote industrial reorganization; act as a holding company for existing public assets; and provide short-term assistance. 'The extension of public ownership into profitable manufacturing industry by acquisitions of individual firms'[19] was envisaged. The NEB was to be less the agent of socialist encroachment, and more a form of state aid for ailing industry. The white paper listed the industries labour wanted to take into public ownership – development land, North Sea oil, shipbuilding and aircraft manufacture, aspects of road haulage and construction, and ports and docks. It was made clear this was a finite programme. Unlike Benn, Heffer and their advisers, Wilson had little interest in planning agreements, which he saw as dangerously open ended. According to labour's 1973 programme, such agreements were to be the means to increased social ownership. The state would intervene increasingly in the control of large companies. As things turned out, planning agreements were to be voluntary. Writing four years later, Wilson was almost to take pride in the fact that only one – with the nationalized coal industry – had been established. This was a veritable disarming of the labour threat to push back the frontier of private industrial power. It is clear that number 10 successfully sabotaged one of the most radical proposals to come up through the labour party. Given Wilson did not back Benn, 'civil servants', according to Sir Anthony Part, '... had the problem of asking themselves where their principal loyalty lay', an interesting light being shed on the question of prime ministerial government.

A second problem for Sir Anthony was 'the radical and novel nature of many of Mr Benn's ideas. A good number of them connected with consultation with, or pressure from the unions, and to such initiatives as worker co-operatives.'[20] Bernard Donoughue reveals something of the atmosphere in the summer of 1974. 'To someone such as myself', he writes, 'the son of a factory worker from the poorest working class, listening to the aristocratic fantasies of Tony Benn or the middle-class fantasies of Mrs Frances Morrell or Mr Francis Cripps [Benn's advisers] was always entertaining, but it had nothing to do with the realities of industrial life.'[21] Wilson hoped to provoke Benn into resigning in 1974, and thought of moving him to a lesser job. 'It seemed transparently clear to a detached observer that there was no humiliation which Tony Benn would not swallow in order to stay in the Cabinet.'[22]

Shortly after his return to Downing Street in 1974, Harold Wilson became involved in the so-called 'land deals' affair. Its beginnings were modest enough. Tony Field, Marcia Williams's brother, had purchased some slag heaps at Ince-in-Makerfield near Wigan, plus a stone quarry, in 1967, the material being sold for use in civil engineering. Field's friendship with the prime minister was not well known, nor was the fact that Marcia Williams, her father, and her sister, Peggy, had financial stakes in his company. During the period of labour's opposition, Tony Field used Wilson's office to carry on his business, obtaining planning permission in 1971 for industrial development at Ince-in-Makerfield. It was during this time that the party came out in favour of taking development land into public ownership, in response to the property boom orchestrated by Heath's chancellor, Anthony Barber. Field's relationship with the prime minister was personal, but Harold Wilson was a politician above all. Finding himself running out of slag, Field decided to sell his thirty acres of empty land, with planning permission attached. He entered into negotiations with a number of companies, including one run by a Victor Harper of Birmingham; Harper seems to have become his agent for the land. Field agreed eventually to sell it, plus another four acres, to a Wolverhampton developer, Ronald Milhench, in early 1973, the purchaser also being committed to a larger neighbouring site, without full planning permission (which seems to have caused problems).

Towards the end of the general election in February 1974, Gareth Parry of the *Guardian* came to Joe Haines with a story about Wilson engaging in land speculation. Haines convinced Parry there was nothing to it, and Wilson also reassured the editor. The *Daily Mail* was then reported to be on the look out for Marcia Williams, and Haines suggested she stay hidden at home until after the election. 'That the *Daily Mail* intended to use the story about Mr. Wilson before Polling Day is beyond doubt.'[23] Wilson called Lord Goodman his solicitor to stop the paper. The *Mail* broke the story of the Wigan slag heaps on 18 March, claiming that Milhench had been involved in a £950,000 land deal, though only £341,000 of this was for the Field family. The story suddenly took off on 3 April, when the same paper alleged that someone had forged Harold Wilson's signature on a letter to Milhench, expressing the hope that the deal with Field would go through. Another story in the *Daily Express* of the same date by Chapman Pincher claimed that 'A.A. Field, private secretary' had written in August 1972 to Warwickshire County Council, from Wilson's office, but on behalf of Harper, asking about another possible property development. Harper's request to a political representative would not have been remarkable if it was made to Wilson, but he was taking advantage of Field's dual role of businessman and political aide at Westminster; Field mentioned in his letter that Wilson was not be be involved. The two stories then became tangled, some inferring that Field – or Marcia Williams – had used Wilson's notepaper to help Milhench carry off his deal. Nobody suggested that Wilson was directly involved, and number 10 took the view that the papers were intruding upon 'the legitimate business activities of former employees'.[24]

Wilson immediately issued writs against the *Mail* and *Express*, but he faced questions in the commons on 4 April. The prime minister insisted that Field was engaged in 'land reclamation', not 'land speculation'. This was a case of applying cosmetics to something pretty unsightly. The prime minister's attempt to protect his secretary and her brother was considered by tory MPs a piece of Wilsonian wiggling. Haines and Donoughue had advised against such sophistry in a parliamentary answer, and the two stories were recycled through April. The national press was to carry over 6,000 column inches between 3 and 11 April. Journalists doorstepped Marcia William's town house in Wyndham Mews, and reporters were sent to tease out the activities of the Field family. The existence of Marcia's two illegitimate children came close to being splashed all over the *Express*, but Walter Terry, their father, made sure it was not used. A statement from Marcia Williams appeared exclusively in the *Mirror* on 11 April, insisting that her involvement in her brother's land dealing had been simply to secure a pension for her retirement. This was becoming a preoccupation bordering on the obsessive in the Wilson camp, but Fleet Street had the bit between its teeth. There would be a further 1,100 column inches in the national press from

13 April to early May. Wilson's relations with the press sank to an all-time low, and his press secretary was unable to limit the damage. Milhench (who kept a signed photograph of Wilson on his desk) was arrested on 22 April, and charged with forgery, having allegedly stolen notepaper from Wilson's office. He admitted the offence, and was to be gaoled in November on this and other charges for three years. His arrest effectively brought the story to an end, and the writs were dropped.

The most bizarre aspect of the affair was Marcia Williams's elevation to the peerage. Wilson considered strengthening the labour contingent in the lords shortly after the stories broke on 3 April, and, returning from ten days on the Scillies at Easter, he told Haines that his political secretary was to be included on the list. 'It is hard not to see in the life peerage an act of defiance to all those who have questioned her power and position, and a reply to the publicity that surrounded Mrs Williams and her family over the land deals affair.'[25] Williams hints that she was virtually forced to accept the honour, and gives three reasons: 'to enable [her] to concentrate on something entirely different'; to 'create a pause in press attention'; 'to give public acknowledgement to the work [she] had done'.[26] None of these had to do with any possible contribution she could make in the lords, and she was not to speak or vote over the next two years. She was known as 'a highly intelligent woman ... who was inordinately shy or apprehensive of public engagements, who would be unable to make a speech'.[27] The civil service was appalled when it learned of Wilson's intentions. Donoughue, Haines and Murray sought to save the prime minister from himself, interceding with Wilson on 23 May – the day before a list of fifteen new peers was to be announced. Haines led in arguing that it would damage the government and party. He himself was to turn down the offer of a peerage two years later. Wilson countered that Williams would be easier to control, and it was probable she would go off to become an executive with Weidenfeld and Nicolson. This was not to happen, and the announcement backfired on Wilson and Williams. The latter changed her name by deed poll to Falkender, a place near Whitby with which her family had been associated. She was to become The Baroness Falkender or simply Marcia Falkender.

Installation was on 23 July, and *The Times* began a two-part profile of Williams by Caroline Moorehead that morning. Moorehead confirmed for the first time that the new peeress had two children by Walter Terry, though *Private Eye* had been first with the news on 19 April. 'So dog has at last eaten dog!',[28] Barbara Castle observed of *The Times*. Williams's private life was being used as part of a public critique of her elevation to the upper house. Membership of the lords hardly bestowed sanctity, though it may have offered security. *The Times* had made a conscious editorial decision to use a woman journalist critically to portray another, under the heading 'From a secretary's chair to a seat in the House of Lords'.[29] 'Those who do not like her', wrote Moorehead, 'say she has used her position to wield power, both real and petty, that she is a highly strung woman of prejudices, and that her presence by Mr Wilson's side has tended to isolate him from the main course of Labour Party politics.'[30] An unnamed civil servant was quoted as saying that, in only four cases over four and a half years, had Wilson accepted his advice when it conflicted with Williams's. An adviser on election campaigns said he thought 'she [was] the most powerful person in the country after Harold Wilson since he came to power'.[31] With a fanfare like that, it is not surprising that the press gallery in the lords was crammed for the introduction. The new Lady Falkender observed the prime minister sitting on the steps of the throne with other privy councillors. She had already announced she was to remain Wilson's political secretary, but Marcia Falkender was now a national figure in her own right – her temper, children, and brother being all in the public domain. She was increasingly becoming a problem for Wilson, and, when he put her in the house of lords, it was clear they were going to sink or swim together.

The land deals affair of April 1974 occurred at a difficult political time, with the government and opposition roughly equally matched. Wilson and Heath were like a pair of stand-off cats through the summer. Wilson's return to Downing Street had alarmed the conservatives, because they feared he might secure a quick dissolution to strengthen the government's position. This was unwarranted since the prime minister was concerned to accumulate political capital, but he, in turn, feared that Heath might try to get him out early, and was not going to take any risks. When the conservatives decided to allow the government to proceed with its legislative programme, it was clear Heath was backing down. The revelations about Tony Field were understood to be inspired by the conservative party, but it is possible that the tory press was simply being opportunist, taking delight in pressing the charge of land speculation against the leader of a left-wing labour party. Wilson was mainly suspicious of the timing of the 'land deals' affair; he knew it had been intended for the general election towards the end of February, and must have assumed in April there was some ulterior political purpose. Pincher, from the *Express*, claims he was in touch with a tory party official that spring, and was led to believe the leash might be slipped. 'While the leadership still disliked the whole idea of using personal denigration, these were desperate times and to use such means to prevent an election was not so reprehensible as using them to win one.'[32] The conservatives were fearful of Wilson calling a June election, and Pincher believes Heath may have authorized a press campaign. But this was to reckon without Wilson getting to Sir Max Aitken, the proprietor of the *Express*. Aitken ordered that there were to be no more personal attacks on the prime minister or Marcia Williams.

The labour government set up a royal commission on the press that May. This was in the Wilsonian tradition, the prime minister having joked about royal commissions sitting for years and taking minutes. It was to be chaired by Sir Morris Finer, and later Prof. McGregor. There had been similar inquiries into the press in 1947–9, and 1961–2. Wilson made reference, in a parliamentary debate on 14 May, to problems in the Beaverbrook group of newspapers, and also stated that labour had received little support from the press in the general election. Two of the eleven members of the royal commission, David Basnett and Geoffrey Goodman, were sympathetic to the view that the British press was biased against the left. The establishment of the royal commission, which did not sit until September, may have had a slight deterrent effect on the press, but was unlikely to be of any immediate use to Wilson. Number 10 believed – certainly in retrospect – that a generalized conservative-inspired press campaign was in progress in the summer of 1974, and this is considered to have been targeted on several members of the labour government in addition to Wilson. The prime minister had told the cabinet, at the height of the land deals affair, that two other ministers were being investigated: 'One had been tailed for five years and on the other they had got a dossier two feet thick. They both would be regarded as being in the leadership stakes if I went.'[33] There were several stories. Edward Short, the deputy leader, was reported in July to have a secret Swiss bank account, after copies of a false statement were sent anonymously to journalists. The *Express* claimed, on 1 May, that Short had received money eleven years earlier from T. Dan Smith. The latter was a former chairman of the housing committee in Newcastle, who had just been sentenced to six years' imprisonment for corruption. Short admitted receiving some money, thought to have been £250. Callaghan believed his business interests were being investigated, given his involvement with the Italian International Bank when in opposition. He had also been associated with the Commercial Bank of Wales, run by Sir Julian Hodge. John Silkin was alleged to have engaged in land speculation in south Wales, but he immediately denied it in a full statement. Tony Benn was the subject of 'even more bizarre and fanciful'[34] stories, one of which concerned cruelty to rabbits.

This was the year of the Watergate scandal in the United States; President Nixon resigned in disgrace on 9 August 1974. The burglary at the headquarters of the democratic national committee in Washington, in June 1972, had not become an issue in that year's presidential elections, but journalistic investigation saw Nixon besieged in the White House, in his second term, by an increasingly hostile legislature and judiciary. In Britain the name of the architect, John Poulson, was on many lips at the same time, following his bankruptcy in 1972. Reginald Maudling, the home secretary, was forced to resign that July, having taken money from him when in opposition. Poulson was convicted of bribery on 11 February 1974, just before Wilson returned to office. His trial in Leeds created an impression of widespread corruption, particularly in the north-east, involving labour politicians. T. Dan Smith was one of those irreparably damaged by the Poulson affair. Andy Cunningham, a trade-union member of labour's executive, was also imprisoned for corruption. Given the popular perception that there can be no smoke without fire, a climate of suspicion clearly existed. Harold Wilson set up a royal commission in December, under Lord Salmon, on standards in public life.

It was this climate of suspicion that Chapman Pincher, and other right-wing journalists, sought to exploit, in order to embarrass the labour government. Pincher and his wife attended a lunch party at a country house in Hampshire on Saturday, 25 May, the day after the announcement of Marcia William's peerage. He recalls a former senior official from the ministry of defence being present. The dozen or so guests were younger, and not Pincher's usual companions. After lunch he claimed the prime minister had lied over the land deals affair. He also insisted that Wilson had 'acted improperly'[35] over Williams's second positive vetting. He revealed a forthcoming legal action by Marjorie Halls, who worked in the lord chancellor's department, and was the widow of Michael Halls, Wilson's principal private secretary until 1970. She believed his sudden death had been brought on by the unreasonable behaviour of Marcia Williams in Downing Street. Finally, Pincher also stated that Heath had been persuaded to sanction a press campaign against the labour party; the actual words he used were 'green light',[36] this apparently having come from the leader of the opposition's private office. According to Pincher's own later published account, he stated he would not be participating given the ban on the *Express* attacking Wilson and Williams.

One of the house guests was Martin Gilbert. Pincher had been introduced to him, but forgot his name. Nor did he make the connection with Wilson. Martin Gilbert is not keen to be involved in the story, and declines to say where the lunch took place. Pincher was to complain about the breach of confidentiality on Gilbert's part. The latter may not have behaved as a gentleman in Pincher's opinion, and Gilbert admits he was upset at Pincher's journalistic braggadocio. He was opposed to smear campaigns in politics, though Pincher made the point that the smears were true. Gilbert wrote to Pincher the following Thursday, 31 May from Oxford, repeating what the latter had said, and suggesting Heath had to be given the chance to dissociate himself. Gilbert wrote, in due course, to the leader of the opposition, as he informed Pincher in a second letter. Heath denied any such campaign, but Pincher argues that it was Gilbert's letter which led the tories to call off the dogs. Gilbert had been invited with his wife to

Chequers for lunch on Thursday, 31 May. Wilson was in a mood to reminisce, and it is possible Gilbert did not say anything to the prime minister at this stage about Pincher. He may only have told Wilson after his exchange of letters with Heath, when he would be able to report that Pincher was spreading false rumours, presumably for his own gratification. Pincher states he suspected, and confirmed later, that Gilbert told Wilson about an anti-government press campaign. He also suggests Gilbert showed the prime minister Heath's letter of denial. Joe Haines certainly knew about a putative press campaign, and describes the prime minister's source as a senior academic. Wilson respected Gilbert, and would have taken anything he said, or implied, very seriously. After he resigned as prime minister, Wilson asserted, in words drafted by Haines: 'A prominent journalist, known for his virulence of opposition to the Labour Government, spoke at length – and had his words taken down by one of our most distinguished historians – at a private house party – about his determination to "expose" all manner of things. A full record of his tirade exists.'[37]

Back in April, during the land deals affair, Haines had heard from a journalist about a woman colleague, with a story on Wilson's tax affairs. This she gave to the *Express*, but the paper decided to hold it until the general election. 'It was only one of many similar messages received at that time',[38] and he promptly forgot it. Haines recalls that a number of Fleet Street contacts told him about a press campaign during the expected autumn election. A great deal lay behind Wilson's arrangement with Times Newspapers over his 1971 book, and little of it became public. Wilson's tax papers went missing at some point in 1974, between the two general elections. Joe Haines is now adamant that the labour leader simply mislaid his tax papers, being generally careless with documents. 'He'd put wanted papers on top of unwanted papers and then throw the lot away.'[39] There is some circumstantial evidence to confirm this.

Wilson was also preoccupied with a series of burglaries, some eight in all, and asked Haines to draw up a list of break-ins in the summer of 1974. Wilson was later to make the point that while papers were scrutinized or stolen, valuables were not. 'I put everyone in', says Haines of the list he compiled, 'I dredged around for everyone.'[40] The burglaries had started in 1969 with Michael Halls. Also included was Wilson's accountant, his solicitor, Bernard Donoughue and Marcia Williams. Wilson seems to have been alerted by the loss of papers from a store he used in Buckingham Palace Road. Haines now believes this crime wave was typical for the time and place, reporting he was not burgled in law-abiding Tunbridge Wells. He claims Wilson only lost old speeches from his store: 'I couldn't give them away when they were new.'[41] Haines seems not to have been so sure at the time. His list of incidents involving the prime minister's staff was handed in confidence to the chairman of the royal commission on the press.

The idea was that, if Fleet Street ran a story about Wilson's tax affairs during the second 1974 election, Sir Morris Finer would know it was based on stolen documentation. Wilson seems to have been more concerned with theft than the fact that such stories might be based on the truth. He was to insist later: 'I have never suggested that there is any evidence that any journalist prompted or inspired those burglaries, indeed, I have explicitly rejected the idea ... It would be foolish to ignore the possibility that some evil minded person might have regarded Fleet Street as a potential market for anything he might discover.'[42] This was to prove to be the case. In April 1976, after Wilson had left Downing Street, the police apprehended two men as a result of a prison tip-off, charging one with the Buckingham Palace Road job, and the other with receiving Wilson papers and tapes. They did not come to trial at the central criminal court until 1977. 'You hoped in the context of what was going on over Watergate', the judge was to say, 'that [Wilson's papers] might be valuable from the point of view of what could be extracted from certain organs of the Press.'[43]

Wilson was feeling insecure about his tax position as he prepared for the second 1974 general election. When he told the cabinet on 18 September of his chosen date, 'Harold said there was a rumour that his income tax returns had been photocopied.'[44] He was due to speak at an election meeting in Portsmouth two days later, and determined to frighten off the press. Wilson referred sarcastically to 'cohorts of distinguished journalists ... combing obscure parts of the country with a mandate to find anything, true or fabricated, to use against the Labour Party.'[45] The 'smear campaigns' of recent weeks, he said, 'did not emanate from any of the Parties. Nor has any Party Leader, nor would any Party Leader, lend any support to them.'[46] It was a serious matter for a prime minister, at the beginning of an election, to suggest that the press might report untruths. Haines had realized this, and removed the offending words from the draft speech, only to have them reinserted by Wilson as he was about to leave Downing Street. The prime minister opened the election campaign by shooting himself in the foot. His press secretary was alarmed about the possibility of a tax story. Haines's journalist contact telephoned him, in early October, to say that his woman colleague, who was now named, had passed the story to the *Daily Mail*, because her own paper would not use it. Lord Goodman was once again summoned, and was able to report to the police that Wilson's missing tax papers had been offered to the *News of the World*. 'Rumours of a last-minute sensation were widespread'[47] on the Thursday before polling (3 October). 'Much of the journalists' art is imitative', Haines would reveal: 'However well-bred the herd, they all feel the itch to run when the worst-bred of them stampedes.'[48] Lord Goodman prevented this, and the second general election passed without any scandal concerning Harold Wilson or his

friends. This was no consolation to the prime minister, who seems to have
expended a great deal of emotional energy in worrying about evidence of
tax avoidance. This was hardly on a par with number 10 sending disrep-
utable plumbers to rifle conservative central office in Smith Square at
dead of night. But many people in 1974 were hoping for a British
Watergate, and elected leaders across the world probably felt, after 9
August, that Nixon's fate could befall them.

After his 'cohorts of journalists' speech, the press council had publicly
asked Wilson to produce his evidence. This he refused to do, believing it
was politically hostile. Wilson was more interested in the royal commission
on the press, though it was not to produce an interim report until March
1976. Finer died in December 1974, and McGregor took over as chairman.
Sometime late in 1975, Wilson asked Haines to prepare evidence for him
to submit. The evidence was in two parts. Haines wrote an annex telling
the story of the land deals affair, and the missing tax papers. 'The inquiries',
he wrote, 'were never restricted by Mr. Wilson alone. His personal staff,
anyone connected with him, anyone even thought to be connected with
him, ran – and runs – a constant risk of his or her private life being raked
over.'[49] Much of the main body of the evidence from Wilson was also
drafted by Haines. 'In its editorial opinions', the prime minister argued, 'and,
often, by its treatment and presentation of the news, the Press in Britain
is, largely, hostile to the Labour Party.'[50] The earliest case cited was late
1964, when the *Daily Mail* had gone through the dustbins at number 10
after a party. But his concern was largely with 1974: 'It is my contention
that by deliberate and painstaking exploitation of the smear technique [the
Daily Express and the *Mail*] sought to influence the result of two General
Elections ... Whether they had a marginal effect, or any effect at all, it is
impossible to say. That they tried, I have no doubt.'[51] There was little in
the way of documentation which would impress a royal commission.
Wilson mentioned Ted Short, the Poulson/T. Dan Smith axis, references
to the commercial interests of labour MPs, supposed extra-marital affairs,
the threatened legal action of Mrs Halls, and the birth certificate of an illegitimate male member of his staff. There was no reference to Marcia
Falkender's children. The essence of his case was that, just as the land deals
affair had threatened to break during the February election, so the *Daily
Mail* was reported to be holding something for Monday, 7 October.
'Certainly the Chairman of the Newspaper Publishers' Association [Lord
Goodman] had reason to believe a story was in the offing, possibly based
on stolen documents, since he spent some time telling me how inaccurate
the story was when I had no precise idea what it was.'[52] Wilson was
being disingenuous. This evidence for the royal commission was shown to
Lord Goodman, perhaps in early 1976, and he advised, as Wilson's solicitor,
that it not be submitted. The most likely reason is the allegation about stolen

tax papers, since this was a crime still under investigation by the police. Wilson had to hold his peace. 'I believe', he concluded, 'that there was a sordid quality about sections of our national press during the middle six months of 1974.'[53] He had to remain silent during the rest of his second premiership, and for months after he was to retire. The royal commission continued to take evidence, and reported finally in July 1977.

The February general election had been disastrous for Northern Ireland, but only Whitelaw, and his successor as secretary of state, Francis Pym, had kept the issue before the government in the winter of 1973–4. The Faulkner unionists, SDLP and alliance felt unable to agree a pro-assembly slate of candidates, though they were partners in the new executive. The anti-assembly unionists, having formed the united Ulster unionist council (UUUC), secured control of the unionist party, Faulkner being replaced by Harry West. The UUUC won eleven seats in February, with Gerry Fitt as the sole proponent of power sharing in West Belfast. The UUUC secured 51 per cent of the vote. Wilson had supported the setting up of the power-sharing executive, but he had no deep attachment to an institution of the Heath years. 'We had feelings of parents', Whitelaw would write, 'for the new child which our Labour successors naturally did not possess ... I knew they believed that the executive was doomed sooner or later anyway.'[54] Merlyn Rees was installed as Northern Ireland secretary in Stormont Castle, promising a continuation in British policy, with Stan Orme as minister of state. The province was low on the agenda of urgent government business, Joe Haines observing that 'bipartisanship [was] often not a policy but a disguise for the lack of one.'[55] Wilson chaired the Northern Ireland cabinet sub-committee, which comprised Rees, Callaghan, Jenkins, Roy Mason and Sam Silkin. Officials from the Northern Ireland Office, plus foreign office, sometimes attended, as well as senior army officers. There was also a committee of officials, which included Bernard Donoughue. Rees, so he was to claim, did not see the executive having much of a future, and expressed this view in a confidential minute to Wilson on 8 April. 'I thought that we should prepare in the strictest confidence plans for alternative methods of government',[56] but he was not keen on Wilson's idea of an all-party conference. On 10 April the cabinet, meeting in Wilson's room in the commons, decided, after hearing from a frightened Rees, to 'begin considering the implications of a total withdrawal. Of course, if that got out', Tony Benn recorded, 'it would precipitate bloodshed but we felt we simply had to do it.'[57]

Wilson cut short his Easter holiday to fly to Northern Ireland on Thursday, 18 April, having already seen Faulkner in London on 1 April. He met the army and police, and also the provincial administration in Stormont Castle, but the prime minister's first official visit was hardly considered an enthusiastic endorsement of the Sunningdale agreement. The

SDLP was trying to woo its coalition partners into the proposed council of Ireland, but the unionists were resistant to any further concessions. 'The only approach was to take it slowly', Rees was to write. 'I was not prepared to have a shooting match with unarmed civilians and a slip would have led to bloodshed.'[58] Bernard Donoughue recalls that the prime minister gave some thought to Ireland, in conversations with him and Haines. 'Harold Wilson had radical instincts on the Irish question and nurtured the same ambition to make progress there which had tempted and misled several previous British Prime Ministers.'[59] There was some talk of an Algerian solution with Wilson playing de Gaulle, and the prime minister even drafted a doomsday scenario involving a British withdrawal, but this was hardly with the knowledge of the Northern Ireland Office. More thought was given to dominion status, leading to an independent Ulster, 'a bold and imaginative, if risky, proposal', in the opinion of Donoughue. Wilson 'seemed almost afraid of its implications', and only circulated it to 'a few very senior officials'.[60] The labour government continued to maintain Whitelaw's solution, but they lacked the will to command the British state in a confrontation with a popular movement such as loyalism. Rees had begun to see anti-government sentiment in the protestant community as a form of Ulster nationalism, a bizarre combination of the perception that Northern Ireland was not like Britain, and the hope that Ulster would disappear as a problem. As for Wilson, he was annoyed that Rees continued to use the term loyalism, without putting it in inverted commas.

The UUUC called for immediate elections in the province a week after Wilson's visit, with a view to restoring the old northern parliament. It even threatened a communal general strike, the Ulster workers' council (UWC) having been set up in late 1973. Rees had met the UWC as early as 8 April 1974 and felt then that the game was up for the executive. The assembly voted against a loyalist motion calling for the scrapping of Sunningdale on Tuesday, 14 May, and the UWC announced an immediate 'constitutional stoppage'. A most unusual political strike followed. The UWC was a right-wing, loyalist, organization, largely outside the trade-union movement. It was disapproved of by the (British) TUC and the Irish Congress of Trade Unions (ICTU); Stan Orme placed a great deal of faith in the labour movement standing up to this loyalist usurper. The strike began with unionist paramilitaries encouraging protestant workers not to go to work, the RUC and army giving little appearance of trying to keep roads open and prevent intimidation. There was some popular support for the strike, but such action was untypically legitimized by protestant leaders opposed to Sunningdale. 'Both the leaders of the farmers and the CBI nightly visited the Hawthorden Road strike headquarters to obtain passes and visas, though neither group would have responded in this way to an industrial dispute in Great Britain.'[61] There was no hint of class war, or analogy with the successful miners in 1972 and 1974. The UWC had gained control of the highly centralized system of electricity generation, and began to pull the plug on normal life in Northern Ireland. Rees was to maintain that they 'were in fact beaten technically on all aspects of the strike',[62] but only because of 'an overall lack of planning and thought about the consequences of a political stoppage in Northern Ireland in the months and years before'.[63] He accepted the advice of the manager of the electricity service, and not that of the executive: the power station near Derry could not supply the whole province; if troops were put in, the middle managers would leave. Stan Orme was to try to recruit such personnel in Britain. By the following Monday – 20 May – industry, shops and offices were effectively closed, though both communities continued to be served with existing goods on a rationed basis. The ICTU tried to organize two back-to-work marches the following day. One was led by Lionel Murray of the TUC, who naively put his authority as general secretary on the line. He came at his own initiative, having been to tell Wilson. 'I didn't believe at the time', Lord Murray now says, 'and I don't believe now that they did all that they could have done to open up the estates, and let the men come off the estates.'[64]

It was too late for trade-union resistance, without a concerted stand by the British government, which could only defeat the strike by defending the executive. The Ulster volunteer force (UVF) had been responsible for three bombs in Dublin, and one in Monaghan, the previous Friday, 17 May, twenty-eight people being killed indiscriminately. This action was an outrage even by the standards of the IRA, and it led many in the Republic to reconsider their aspiration about reunification. The perpetrators were the responsibility of Merlyn Rees, and he telephoned Wilson at Chequers on the evening of 18 May. A state of emergency was declared the following day, though the secretary of state was content simply to bring over another battalion of troops to try to keep roads open. Naval personnel were also assembled, with a view to manning the power stations. This was crisis management at best. Rees declined to ask the cabinet on 21 May for technicians to take over electricity generation, and advised that it was not possible to take out road blocks. The UWC took control of petrol supplies the following day, a coordinating committee having been set up embracing the UUUC leaders and the paramilitary organizations. Wilson wanted to distance himself from Ulster. A British reporter wrote later of the government's stance: '[the strike] was a mutation outside the realm of their political experience and ... until the strikers won, they were to react with a mixture of political stubbornness, indecision and sheer disbelief.'[65] John Hume raised the question of a fuel oil plan at a meeting of the executive on 22 May, a contingency which had been prepared for an earlier industrial dispute. It was discussed the following day with Rees, and communicated to Wilson. The prime minister invited members of the executive to meet him at Chequers on Friday, 24 May. Talk of the council of Ireland had provoked the strike, but the loyalists' objective became the power-sharing executive. The new Stormont administration was under siege in its own land, though Rees refused to negotiate with the UWC. When the Wilson government showed little inclination to take on the loyalist workers during the first weekend, some unionists in the provincial government began to weaken. Faulkner announced on Wednesday, 22 May that the executive had agreed to implement the council of Ireland in two stages. There would be assembly elections in 1977–8, before executive powers were given to any all-Ireland bodies. This was unacceptable to the Republic, and it had also come too late to appease protestant opinion in Ulster.

Faulkner, Fitt and Napier, the alliance leader, flew to London on 24 May, and were closeted with Wilson, Rees, Mason and Sam Silkin at Chequers. Haines and Donoughue, and a number of other officials, were also present, as was General Sir Peter Hunt, just back from a secret visit to the province. The local politicians wanted the strike broken, and there was reference to Hume's fuel plan, which Rees claims he supported. An offensive was being constructed, but, according to the latter, there was not going to be any large-scale incursion of troops. 'What we were seeking was some action to show moderate opinion that the government and the Executive had the will to govern and were capable of influencing events, something to retain their credibility.'[66] Wilson agreed that the roads should be kept open, and fuel provided for essential transport, but it had to go to an emergency meeting of the cabinet in London that evening. The three Northern Ireland politicians believe he was also going to seize the power stations, but Wilson was to be less than forthcoming on the all important question of electricity. 'Our search for Army specialists to man the power stations', he wrote later, 'had produced a useful number, but they could not run power stations on their own. Power engineers ... had remained at their posts, but it became clear that this would not continue ... . The professional association of power station engineers in Britain made clear that their members would not be allowed to go and help out in the North.'[67] Faulkner and his colleagues left Chequers believing they had got all they wanted, little realizing they were going to be allowed to fall. 'There seemed little hope of breaking the strike or of maintaining the Executive in being', Wilson was to argue, 'but they returned to their beleaguered Province determined to fight on to the last.'[68] Bernard Donoughue believes 'the Government's capitulation to the strike was suspiciously and unnecessarily quick'.[69] At Chequers 'we decided to stand firm against Protestant intimidation and terrorism, but once we returned to Whitehall the advice flowing in from all sides turned very pessimistic.'[70] The Northern Ireland Office and the home office were for making concessions, and the cabinet office then lost nerve. 'Wilson was not at this moment inclined to embark on a more courageous and risky course.'[71]

Ian Paisley later expressed the view that the army was to be moved in, 'to arrest [him] and his group and try them for high treason'.[72] High treason may be slightly fanciful, but something greater than actually happened seems to have been intended. Rees maintains that 'a grandiose scheme had never been on the cards',[73] and cites a Northern Ireland Office report on the strike, but this seems to have been requested to find out where policy had gone wrong. It is thought Wilson saw army leaders, and officials from the ministry of defence, that Friday evening in Downing Street. Rees insists that the army was against getting involved in emergency services where there was public opposition, and it would only move in when they had broken down. Donoughue believes that the army was prepared to act, given sufficient government will. Faulkner, Fitt and Napier had asked Wilson to broadcast to Northern Ireland, and Wilson returned to Chequers late that night to prepare such an address. It was to go out on Saturday night, the seizure of the petrol stations being put back to Sunday night. The first draft is thought to have included provision for the arrest of the UWC leaders for rebelling against the crown, and it is believed Wilson only finally abandoned the executive on the afternoon of Saturday, 25 May. All such references were removed from the speech. Wilson told British and Irish listeners that the strike was designed 'to set up ... a sectarian and undemocratic state'. The labour government, he said, would 'not negotiate on constitutional or political matters in Northern Ireland with anyone who chooses to operate outside the established constitutional framework'. Wilson formally supported the executive, but it was a very English intervention designed more for a British audience.

Wilson then departed for the Scillies, but had to be helicoptered the following morning, Sunday, 26 May, to Culdrose in Cornwall, to hear Merlyn Rees report that the executive was on its last legs. The secretary of state had learned Faulkner was going to resign, no doubt because of the content of Wilson's broadcast. The SDLP had threatened to resign by the Monday, if troops were not used. The army seized twenty-one petrol stations on the Monday, to wrest control of fuel rationing from the UWC. The unionists then called on the secretary of state to negotiate with the loyalist workers, but he refused. The British government was holding firm to something. 'There was a wider context to be considered', Rees wrote. 'Whatever we did, the Executive would certainly fall, but it must not fall because of indecision on our part.'[74] Wilson returned to London on Tuesday, 28 May, the day the Faulknerites resigned. The UWC called off the strike on 29 May, and London prorogued the assembly. The so-called power-sharing experiment had collapsed in the laboratory.

The issue was debated in the commons early the following week. Wilson returned to his point about the cost to Britain of Northern Ireland before discussing the future, but he had nothing to offer. The prime minister seemed resentful of the failure of the British government's writ to run in Ulster, this being mental – rather than political – withdrawal. The UWC had brought down the executive, but when Wilson ruled out talks with the strike leaders, he saved the British government from direct defiance by the Ulster protestant community. The key to defeating the strike all along had been troops, but Rees refused to go on the offensive, largely because he lacked confidence in the possibility of a military solution. Rees would later note:

> Although there may have been marginal mistakes in the handling of the Ulster workers' strike, I feel strongly that there was, and is, no way of putting down an industrial/political dispute supported by a majority in the community. The counter-insurgency methods used by the army for dealing with the Provisional IRA and other paramilitaries were not appropriate to a political strike ... It is one thing to fight the IRA and quite another to fight a whole community.[75]

Two months after the fall of the Northern Ireland executive in 1974, Turkey invaded the Republic of Cyprus, which had been granted independence in 1960. Britain's strategic interest was secured with two sovereign base areas, and Cyprus resembled Northern Ireland in that it had two communities. The majority Greek population had fought for independence, under the secret joint leadership of Archbishop Makarios and Colonel Grivas. The latter's guerrilla organization, EOKA, wanted union with Greece – *enosis* – and it was an achievement for Makarios to become president of an independent Cyprus. He might have been able to conciliate the Turkish minority, which was disadvantaged if not oppressed, but inter-communal rivalry persisted under the Cypriot government. Makarios lost the support of Grivas in 1964, when the latter took over the national guard, and his relations with Athens also deteriorated, following the colonels' seizure of power in Greece in 1967. Nicos Sampson, a Greek nationalist, led a coup in Cyprus on 15 July 1974, with the support of the military junta in Athens. Makarios escaped to a monastery near Paphos, where a British helicopter rescued him. Callaghan consulted Wilson, and the archbishop was brought to London and to Downing Street on 17 July. Makarios blamed the coup on American tolerance of the anti-communist Greek colonels, while Cyprus tried to maintain good relations with the Soviet Union. Wilson supplied him with a clean shirt, and ordered that a cassock be found from an orthodox priest in London. The deposed Cypriot president then left for the united nations in New York. Callaghan was concerned largely with the British bases, but, under the treaty of guarantee of Cyprus's independence, Britain had undertaken, with Greece and Turkey, to avert either *enosis* or partition.

The Turkish prime minister, Büleat Ecevit, flew to London on 17 July to ask Wilson, Callaghan and Mason to militarily convenience a Turkish invasion in order to unseat Sampson. Ankara had declared its hand in private. Britain could not risk its bases by allowing Turkish troops to land, since this would only jeopardize relations with whatever regime was in control in Nicosia. Wilson could only cite the 1960 treaty, arguing for a meeting between the three guarantor powers. Callaghan hinted that the position of the Turks could be improved in a new independent Cyprus, and the foreign office was hoping to unseat Sampson, by mobilizing international opinion against Athens. Contingency planning for the use of force was premissed on the United States cooperating with Britain. Wilson was awakened early on Saturday, 20 July with news that Turkish troops had landed in the north of Cyprus. He ordered that the bases should be secured immediately with air support, and, back in London, sent ships and planes to evacuate British residents and holiday-makers. A ceasefire was to be agreed eventually on 22 July, with Ecevit's troops in possession of the northern part of Cyprus. Greeks had fled in front of the invasion, and Turks in the south had no alternative but to quit their homes.

The Greek government came under internal challenge the day after the Turkish invasion, and the junta was replaced on 23 July by a democratic regime under Constantine Karamanlis. Sampson was replaced as acting president of Cyprus by Glafkos Clerides. The US secretary of state was busy working on a ceasefire, as Greece's threat to declare war on Turkey was also a threat to United States' strategic interests. Ecevit believed a regime sympathetic to the Soviet Union was taking over in Athens. Cyprus was now militarily divided, but a small united nations' contingent, including British troops, was unable to restore peace. Reinforcements were flown to the island to secure the international airport from encircling Turks, and, when Ankara threatened to bomb Nicosia airport on the evening of 24 July, Wilson called Ecevit's military bluff on the telephone. He had ordered the RAF to prepare to counter any such attack. It was probably the nearest Britain came to war during Wilson's premiership, and Callaghan seems not to have been involved.

With the fighting stopped, but numbers of Greek Cypriots unaccounted for, the focus shifted to Geneva, where it was hoped the Greek, Turkish and British governments would negotiate some sort of settlement. Callaghan remained in charge in London, informing Downing Street of developments, the three guarantor powers meeting on 25 July. 'Once again', according to Wilson, 'the intervention of the United States was missed.'[76] British policy was now much more pro-Athens, and Turkey refused to budge. The de facto partition of the island had become a constitutional reality. The ceasefire had been underwritten on 30 July, and it was agreed to meet again in Geneva on 9 August. Callaghan could barely keep the talks going, though he was to admit of the Cypriot leaders that 'if it had been left to them it is conceivable that they might have hammered out an understanding.'[77] Britain was now proposing a federal state, but the conference collapsed on 14 August. Turkey then broke the ceasefire, and with Gerald Ford installed in the White House, the United States turned to the strategic implications of the Cyprus problem. Wilson and Callaghan countenanced giving up the British bases later in 1974, but, during a cabinet discussion of the defence review on 20 November, it was reported that 'the Americans ... were unhappy about the idea of [Britain] withdrawing from Cyprus and could see the eastern Mediterranean becoming a Russian lake.'[78] Britain stayed. The United States Congress suspended arms to Turkey the following year, and Ford, for reasons of NATO strategic defence, asked the Europeans to make up the shortfall. Foot and Castle alone resisted in cabinet, Callaghan arguing that Britain should follow the example of France and Germany, otherwise 'it would merely make the Turks bloody-minded and less likely to make concessions over Cyprus.'[79]

Europe was a simmering foreign policy issue in 1974. Labour had been committed, in opposition, to 'a fundamental renegotiation of the terms of entry', the outcome to 'be submitted to the British people for final decisions'.[80] Callaghan attended his first council of ministers in Brussels on 1 April, and spoke obviously for a party audience at home: 'We should negotiate in good faith and if we are successful in achieving the right terms we shall put them to our people for approval. But if we fail, we shall submit to the British people the reason why we find the terms unacceptable and consult them on the advisability of negotiating ... withdrawal.'[81] The community, however, was not prepared to tolerate a renegotiation of the treaty of Rome. The view of the Brussels commission was that some changes could be made for Britain, while European business proceeded relatively normally. Callaghan's initial shot had the effect of convincing the Europeans that the British government was serious about negotiating. Wilson chaired a strategic cabinet committee (ES) which included Callaghan. 'Without actually saying so to each other', he was to write, 'the Prime Minister and I implicitly seemed to understand that we must both work in the closest unity.'[82] Jenkins, Lever and Williams represented the Europeans, and were balanced by the anti-marketeers, Foot, Shore, Varley and Silkin. Healey, Peart and Short were also members. This composition allowed the prime minister and foreign secretary to take the lead, and Wilson also got the cabinet office to coordinate policy between all interested departments. Callaghan was put in charge of a tactical committee (EQ) to look after ongoing European business, and handled negotiating positions. It included the majority of the strategic committee, plus Benn, Crosland,

Rees, Ross, and – later – Castle (and a number of junior ministers). 'My committee', claims Callaghan, 'was firmly in charge of settling our policy and tactics in each subject and took the lead in coordinating overlapping problems at regular meetings held in my room at the Foreign Office.'[83]

The government made it clear it wanted to remain in the community. Even if new terms were considered unacceptable, there was still a chance that a referendum would not lead to withdrawal. Callaghan was also saying that, as all negotiation involved compromise, Britain would shift its positions if the EEC talked. Further integration was to be halted in the interim, particularly as it affected food prices, but British ministers were to continue to play a full part in council meetings. Callaghan was most prominent on the EEC scene. 'Sometimes I grumbled to my officials', he was to write, 'that I felt not so much a Foreign Secretary as a multiple grocer.'[84] Wilson minimized the number of meetings he had at head of government level in European capitals, and it was clear, in 1974, that the Europeans were not too keen to embark upon a renegotiation, given the uncertainty in British politics. The labour cabinet became much less hostile to the EEC during the summer, as the responsibility of office revealed the difficulty of withdrawal. When Callaghan set out his demands in detail on 4 June, it looked like Britain might be accommodated. Areas of difference had been narrowed down to the budget, agricultural policy, the developing world, and regional and industrial policies.

Gradually Wilson's team came to favour staying in. Callaghan claims he began the renegotiations without having any idea of the outcome, but was in favour of staying by the late summer. The foreign office played along with his putative agnosticism, and seems to have won him over on the question of political cooperation. Peart abandoned his erstwhile opposition at agriculture, leaving Castle, Foot, Shore and Benn as the principal opponents. Shore was the only possible resignation, if Britain remained a member. On the other side, Jenkins, Williams and Lever would hardly have tolerated withdrawal. But this was still the position of the labour party, and the executive set up a committee to monitor the renegotiation. It was chaired, initially, by Tony Benn, and included Mikardo, Foot and Joan Lestor; it had only two meetings, because Wilson forbade ministers to attend. He had issued a minute on 14 May, telling all ministers that collective responsibility overrode all other obligations, and reaffirmed the rule, after an anti-Callaghan document, prepared in Transport House, was leaked on 10 July to *The Times*. The executive decided a fortnight later, on a motion from Benn, that there would be a two-day conference to examine any package brought back by Callaghan from Brussels.

The cabinet and national executive met the following day in Downing Street, to consider the draft manifesto for the autumn general election. Wilson wanted a commitment to hold a referendum within twelve months, not being keen on the idea of another general election; he argued that the queen might not grant it. The right was opposed to a referendum. Robert Mellish, the chief whip, said: "'Why are we raising all this issue again? I don't find the Market the great burning issue some of you do. Why not leave well alone?'"[85] Jenkins rushed to Wales, and issued a clarion call to the right on 26 July. The labour party was implicitly condemned as intolerant, and emphasis placed on the need to win over moderate voters. Right-wing labour MPs had been meeting for some time, and were formally to constitute the manifesto group in December, stressing the sanctity of their electoral mandate, as a counter to the Tribune group, which had secured the election of Ian Mikardo, albeit on a split vote, as chairman of the parliamentary party after the February election. In Paris on 14 September Wilson restated British objections to its budget contribution, as well as opposition to European union, but President Giscard d'Estaing proposed a second summit of government leaders in December, assuming this would be after a second British general election. The final draft of the labour party's manifesto was considered again jointly on 16 September in number 10. The EEC was the only divisive issue, the wording now being that the British people should have the final say 'through the ballot box'.[86] It was assumed this meant only a referendum, and Jenkins was worried about a low poll being binding on the government. With labour's careful compromise being unravelled, anti-marketeers rushed to reassert the need for a referendum. Barbara Castle was most aware of the electoral damage of a split, and she countered Shore's attempt to strengthen opposition to the EEC in the document. "'I think we can say there is a consensus'",[87] chipped in Wilson, bringing the discussion to an end.

The devolution issue within the United Kingdom was less traumatic for labour, even given the nationalist breakthroughs in the February election. Wilson undertook to hold discussions in Scotland and Wales, following the 1973 Kilbrandon report on devolution, but he made Lord Crowther-Hunt, who had signed a memorandum of dissent, his constitutional adviser. The Scottish secretary, and many labour MPs from north of the border, were not keen to conciliate the nationalists. But the conservatives there came out, in May 1974, in favour of an indirectly elected assembly, which led the executive of the Scottish labour party to vote, on 23 June, to oppose devolution, which had been suggested in a government discussion document. The national executive in London then committed the labour party, in July, to devolution in Scotland, at the behest of the Scottish trade unionist Alex Kitson, and this was later endorsed, despite their earlier opposition, by a Scottish party conference. Scottish and Welsh ministers took local soundings during the summer. John Morris, the Welsh secretary, was keen on devolution, which had long been party policy in the principality. Edward Short, as lord president, chaired a cabinet committee on devolution, but, with an election pending, Wilson appropriated some proposals from an executive sub-committee chaired by Shirley Williams. Another thirteen labour seats in Scotland were thought to be vulnerable, and Wilson believed it was necessary to take the wind out of the nationalists' sails. A white paper was finally issued on 17 September. It was becoming clear that labour MPs from the north-west and north-east of England were worried about being overshadowed. Scotland was to have an elected assembly with a legislative role, but the Welsh assembly was to be a lesser body. There was still a strong emphasis on the integrity of the United Kingdom, and Scottish and Welsh MPs were to remain at Westminster, with secretaries of state in the cabinet. Development agencies for Wales and Scotland were also proposed. This was policy-making on the trot, Wilson being determined to get a result out of the civil service machine.

The next day, Wilson announced a general election. His strategy had been quickly to implement some measures, such as the repeal of the industrial relations act, and the government carried thirty-eight bills, albeit at the price of eighteen defeats in the commons. Wilson concentrated upon the preparation of a series of green and white papers, promising legislation in the next parliament. This included the extension of trade-union rights: action on sex discrimination was promised on 6 September; consumer protection on 10 September; pensions 11 September; land 12 September; and devolution 17 September. When parliament had adjourned for the summer on 31 July, it was not expected to reassemble on 15 October. Previously, Michael Foot had urged the need for an early election, if the government could first alert the country to the crisis it faced. The June option came and went, but, while ministers avidly discussed the possibilities, the decision remained the prerogative of the prime minister. Wilson seems to have made up his mind in August on the Scillies; addressing the TUC at Brighton on 5 September, he hinted strongly at his intentions. The cabinet and national executive had discussed the manifesto on 25 July, and it was agreed at the second joint meeting on 16 September. He told the cabinet two days later the election would be on Thursday, 10 October, allowing a twenty-two day campaign. 'I don't think anyone was certain we would win', wrote Barbara Castle, 'but no one seemed to doubt we were right to go to the country – or that, in choosing that date, Harold had taken every conceivable consideration into account.'[88]

The labour manifesto was launched at a press conference on 16 September. It emphasized the social contract as an alternative to 'the authoritarian and bureaucratic system of wage control imposed by the Heath Government'. Labour dismissed the possibility of a coalition government, on the grounds that 'there [was] no meeting point between [the party] and those with quite different philosophies.'[89] The section on public ownership was watered down to accord with the industry white paper, and the government was acknowledged to be still working on banking and insurance. The manifesto was that of February less the achievements of the short parliament, which were listed. The labour government also declared in favour of devolution for Scotland and Wales; Northern Ireland was also mentioned. There was a promise to scrap the official secrets act.

The party had decided on the campaign slogan 'Britain *will* win with Labour' in August, to be printed on a rosette symbol. A publicity campaign began at the end of the month, mounted by Denis Lyons, Lord Lovell-Davies and Mike Oxley. Lyons and Lovell-Davies had been given an office in number 10 during the summer; Davies became a peer in July, and Lyons was to be elevated in December. Stanley Baker again advised on television presentation, and he was joined by the playwright John Mortimer. Wilson was doing better in the polls than Heath, but this political double act, which had been on the British stage for nine years, was a waning attraction. Lyons resurrected the second half of his 1970 'Yesterday's Men' campaign, the labour front bench being presented as a winning team. The novices of 1964 were, after ten years, among the most experienced ministers in parliament, and were given a more prominent role in the campaign. Ministers shared press conferences with Wilson, and were to do election political broadcasts. The second campaigning theme was that 'Labour keeps its promises'. Wilson had stated nine promises in Bolton the previous December, which he claimed a labour government would realize within three years. He was to state during the campaign that substantial progress had been made on all nine issues in six months. Thirdly, labour argued that it had the policies to solve the problems of Britain. These three themes were merged in the idea of the social contract, labour's alternative strategy for dealing with the unions.

Wilson's aides were again Marcia Falkender, Bernard Donoughue and Joe Haines. The two latter, as civil servants, could not be seen to be involved in the campaign, and Jean Denham, who worked in the number 10 press office, went on leave to work for Wilson. Haines considers that he and Donoughue were frozen out of the election planning by Falkender. There was no attempt to exploit the fact that Wilson was prime minister, and, in the main, the team of ministers eschewed major domestic and international political events.

Wilson's day began in his Westminster home in a meeting with Falkender, Donoughue and Haines. He then attended the campaign committee, chaired by the general secretary, at 9.00 a.m, accompanied by John Grant, a junior minister in the civil service department, who had been liaising with Transport House since the return to office. There was then another meeting with his aides before the 11.30 a.m. press conference, labour having again decided to follow the conservatives. Wilson attended every one of the fifteen press conferences, though he was always accompanied by other ministers. Wilson then left for his evening speaking engagement, the campaign beginning as usual in Glasgow, on Monday, 23 September. As with the first 1974 election, there was a great deal of emphasis upon television presentation. The 'Britain *will* win with Labour' rosette was added to the backdrop behind Wilson, and two sets, in separate vans, were transported up and down Britain, to allow more time for construction on alternative days.

Falkender, Donoughue and Haines worked each evening in Downing Street on the following day's speech, often dining later in the private flat. Wilson had initially assigned the task to Lovell-Davies and Lyons, but Haines took over the preparation of his speeches. Donoughue and Haines also helped write the questions for the party's private polls, run by Robert Worcester's MORI organization, and financed by a group of supporters led by Harry Kissin. The results were presented to the information committee each morning at 8.00 a.m., though Wilson reviewed them the night before on his return to London. Marcia Falkender claims Transport House expected to win with a majority between ten and thirty, but the private polls became more depressing. It was not certain that Wilson would continue as prime minister, though he later said he expected a majority of ten to twelve. Falkender claims that the 'teamwork [was] even more effective than in February',[90] but Donoughue insists that the campaign was 'blighted by administrative inefficiencies and hysterical tension within the team',[91] Wilson and his entourage flew to Liverpool on 9 October, where they were joined by friends in the Adelphi Hotel the following evening for the election results.

More rain fell during the October campaign than in any post-war general election. Wilson was on the look out for any conservative-inspired scandal in the press, but the common market was his principal political worry, given the balance in his government. Shirley Williams was asked what she would do if Britain voted in a referendum to pull out. She replied she would quit politics, and Roy Jenkins reiterated this view the following morning. Peter Shore, possibly after discussion with Wilson, said he would accept any popular verdict. Margaret Thatcher, for the conservatives, repeated her housing policy on 27 September, involving a reduction in the mortgage rate to 9.5 per cent, and the abolition of local rates. It caused Wilson less difficulty than the conservatives' idea of a government of national unity. In order to avert a loss of votes to the liberals, Heath came out in favour of coalition on the last Sunday of the campaign. The election on 10 October produced little change. The target for an overall majority was 318 seats; turnout at 72.8 per cent was down by over five points. Labour secured slightly less votes, just under eleven and a half million, but this was 39.2 per cent of the poll. Wilson romped home with 31,750 votes in Huyton, to 15,517 for the conservative and 4,956 for a liberal. The conservatives dropped nearly a million and a half votes, securing 35.8 per cent. There was a swing of 2.2 per cent from the official opposition to the government. The liberals were also slightly down. The SNP gained votes, nearly a third of those in Scotland. Labour secured 319 seats, an increase of 18, and the conservatives dropped 21, to 276. The liberals had 13. The SNP put on 4, to make 11 seats, while Plaid Cymru moved from 2 to 3. Anti-power-sharing unionists had 10 in Northern Ireland, to the minority's 2 seats. Labour had a healthy lead over the conservatives of 43, but when the minor parties' 39 are discounted, Wilson had an overall majority of only 4, allowing for the speaker. It was the smallest margin of a majority government since 1922. It was also one that 'could be transformed overnight by death, disaster or by-election'.[92]

CHAPTER 23

Economic Crisis, 1974–5

Harold Wilson had pulled it off, and was able to form a fourth government, but few realized he was thinking of going during this parliament. Joe Haines confirms this had been mentioned to 'a small group'[1] after the first election, and Donoughue recalls that Wilson intended to retire on his sixtieth birthday. Others present on this occasion – possibly Sunday, 3 March 1974 – are believed to have been Albert Murray, Terence Lancaster and Marcia Williams. The latter was to write that 'some who knew of [Wilson's] plan believed that he might be persuaded to stay on longer if he thought this was necessary for the country or Party.'[2] For Harold Wilson, each week from 11 October was to be a long time in politics.

Wilson's only change to his administration was to bring John Silkin into the cabinet on 18 October; there were some alterations at junior level. Judith Hart, as minister for overseas development had aroused the suspicions of MI5's new director, Michael Hanley, largely as a result of confusion over her name. Hart was concerned about Chile, where the socialist president Allende had been toppled by the military in September 1973. After she joined the government in 1974, she insisted – unsuccessfully – that Wilson should refuse to honour existing naval contracts. Hart telephoned communist party headquarters that September, stating she would not speak at a Chile protest meeting in Scotland alongside a prominent communist. The phone was tapped, but the transcript was to be described as 'completely innocent, benign'.[3] The transcript of her September telephone call, and a photograph of a different person attending a peace conference in Warsaw in 1950, were shown to Wilson after he returned to office in late 1974. He sent for Judith Hart on Thursday, 17 October, and told her she was being positively vetted. Potential ministers were only negatively vetted. Judith Hart later confided to Barbara Castle. 'Harold had accepted her assurances, but she was clearly shaken to the core.'[4]

The postponed 1974 party conference was held in London between 27 and 30 November. An emergency resolution on the EEC was carried, by

3,007,000 votes to 2,949,000, calling for safeguards on eight points. It also demanded a special party conference before a referendum. Callaghan, as party chairman, had secured an invitation from the executive to Helmut Schmidt, the German socialist chancellor, who appealed the following day to delegates not to leave Europe. Schmidt then repaired to Chequers for talks with Wilson, after which the prime minister came out on the issue at a London labour lord mayor's dinner on 7 December. Wilson stated that if the renegotiations were successful, he would recommend staying in the European community. Foot, Shore and Benn wrote jointly asking his permission to make similar personal statements.

Wilson and Callaghan flew to Paris on 9 December for the first two-day summit of community leaders. The prime minister was not feeling well. The conference was hosted by President Giscard d'Estaing, who felt that generalized economic difficulties in Europe warranted such summitry. It was at this first meeting that Wilson set out Britain's seven demands: first, the common agricultural policy, where arrangements were necessary for Britain to continue importing from the commonwealth; second, the community budget, which he wanted made fairer; third, opposition to economic and monetary union by 1980, since it required a fixed parity for sterling; fourth, parliamentary sovereignty, particularly in the areas of regional, industrial and fiscal policy; fifth, capital transfer provisions, to protect the balance of payments; sixth, safeguards for developing countries; and seventh, no harmonization of VAT. Wilson stated that some progress had been made on all these points, or that the recent experience of the community was not deleterious to British national interests. He reported to the commons on 16 December, saying that the community had agreed that a 'correcting mechanism' should be worked out on the all-important question of the budget.

The communiqué from the Paris summit alarmed the left-wing ministers. Michael Foot may have already suggested to Wilson an agreement to differ on Europe. Following public stands taken by Tony Benn, Roy Hattersley and Peter Shore, Wilson put a suggestion to the cabinet on 21 January 1975. Once the cabinet had made its recommendation for or against the EEC, the minority in the government should 'be free to support and speak in favour of a different conclusion in the referendum campaign'.[5] This was announced in parliament two days later. While there was widespread derision of Wilson's constitutional initiative, both sides in the cabinet were relieved that a split – involving resignations – had been avoided.

The climax of the renegotiations was reached in Ireland on 10–11 March, during the second European summit in Dublin Castle. Wilson and Callaghan agreed that the renegotiations could not run on past the Dublin summit, given the split in the cabinet, and the area of difference had been reduced to the budget, New Zealand dairy products and lamb, and, a lesser item, steel. Negotiations proceeded for two days, the Irish being keen to find a solution, as they were dependent upon Britain remaining in the EEC. Agreement was finally reached late on 11 March – Wilson's fifty-ninth birthday – the final compromise owing much to the president of the European commission, François Ortoli. Provision was made for an annual refund to Britain on the budget, if its contribution should prove excessive under new criteria. As for New Zealand, continued access to the British market was to be permitted. The problem of steel seems to have paled into insignificance.

Wilson reported immediately on the Dublin summit to parliament and the cabinet; on Monday, 17 March, ministers met to consider whether to recommend the deal to the British people. The prime minister and foreign secretary had been negotiating about Britain's differences with the EEC for a year, but the real contradiction was between Wilson, as labour leader, and the anti-Europeans in the party. This was about to be fought through the cabinet, national executive, parliamentary party, and special conference, in the run up to the June referendum. The prospects did not look good for Wilson as battle commenced in cabinet. The Dublin terms produced a pre-dictable Europe/anti-Europe split, as ministers debated papers showing how progress had been made on the seven points in the manifesto. The prime minister met the rest of his government in number 10 later that day, and he and Callaghan then faced the full parliamentary labour party. Wilson's cabinet had been evenly balanced for and against staying in the EEC in early 1974, but, on Tuesday, 18 March 1975, it split sixteen to seven in favour of recommending continued membership. Opposed were Shore, Foot, Benn, Castle, Silkin, Varley and Ross; Varley was known to be close to Wilson, and Ross did not like the left. Short, Peart, Prentice, Mellish, Elwyn-Jones, Morris and Healey backed the prime minister and foreign secretary, as did Shepherd, Rees, Mason and Crosland. The real Europeans were Jenkins, Williams and Lever, but they were not yet home and dry with their considerable victory. The previous Sunday evening, Barbara Castle and her husband, Ted, now a labour peer, had entertained over twenty people in their Islington flat. It was a 'referendum conspiracy meal'.[6] Plans were laid for mobilizing a no vote. Peter Shore led the onslaught on the foreign secretary's recommendation over the next two days, arranging a press conference for the antis at 5.30 p.m. on the Tuesday, shortly after Wilson made his lengthy statement to parliament. Word of the planned press conference came to the prime minister's attention, probably through Robert Armstrong. Wilson asked Castle and the others not to attend, but Shore, Castle, Foot, Benn and Silkin defied him. Later, at a meeting of about eighty anti-market labour MPs, called by Douglas Jay and Joe Ashton, signatures were collected for an early day motion. This was later abandoned on tactical grounds. Barbara Castle was watching *News at Ten* on Wednesday, 19 March when she received a telephone call: 'It was Harold, angrier than I have ever heard him in my whole life. He was almost beside himself. The venom poured out of him. He had generously allowed us to disagree publicly on the Common Market and what had we done? "Made a fool of me", he declared.'[7] She immediately rushed back to the commons, where Foot and Callaghan had also been summoned to the prime minister's room. Wilson immediately apologized, and Castle kissed him on the forehead. '"Don't I get a kiss?" said Jim [Callaghan] gloomily. "God knows I need it." So I kissed him too', wrote Castle, 'and sat down next to him.'[8] Wilson was upset by Mikardo's motion for the following week's national executive, which described Callaghan's terms as falling 'very far short'[9] of the manifesto requirements. The prime minister was in a resigning mood; with the party split widening, he feared being left with a 'rump Government'.[10] Castle and Foot were conciliatory, although Castle was privately to be critical of Foot's reasonableness.

Wilson criticized left and right, the following morning at cabinet, for factionalism. Clearly he was worried about the national executive coming out against the government. Ministerial freedom to dissent, he had argued, did not extend to organizing together on the executive. The prime minister's strong stand saw Foot suggest that Ron Hayward, as general secretary, should promote an agreement to differ for the party.

The five principal dissenting ministers, plus Judith Hart, nailed their colours to the mast over the weekend, issuing a statement on 23 March to the effect that British democracy was being curtailed by the EEC. It was decided at the executive on 26 March, that the right of party members to campaign individually in the referendum would preserve unity. The party was not to pitch itself against the government in a referendum campaign, which would have been the outcome of Mikardo's motion. Transport House was to hold a special conference asking delegates to oppose staying in the EEC, and then allow pro- and anti-factions to use the machinery of the party to propagandize in the referendum. Wilson recalls that 'for only the second time ... [he] laid [his] leadership ... on the line, ... a formula [being] produced with the help of the General Secretary'.[11] The government was recommending acceptance of the terms with a minority opposed, but, when that minority became the majority within the party, the executive declined to push its opposition home. Wilson had been absent in Northern Ireland the day before, when the cabinet threw out his draft guidelines on ministers' behaviour during the campaign. He considered he made 'a serious error of tactics'[12] in not attending, but the leading anti-EEC ministers were not to speak in the parliamentary debate on the government's white paper held after Easter between 7 and 9 April.

Cabinet government was largely suspended until after the referendum. Wilson reiterated his – rejected – guidelines on the first day of debate, insisting that ministers opposed could not act officially against government policy. Members of the government could not publicly debate with each other when it came to campaigning. This was to be relaxed on 23 May for the last four days of television coverage. Despite a warning from the prime minister, Eric Heffer spoke in the house on 9 April against the government's recommendation, and was immediately sacked. Wilson won the vote by 398 to 172 with 59 abstentions, making the government dependent on the support of the conservatives and liberals. 137 labour MPs supported the motion, while 145 voted against, and 33 abstained. The cabinet voted 14 to 7, but junior ranks split 31 to 31 with 9 abstentions. Backbench MPs divided 92 to 107, with 24 abstentions. The parliamentary labour party had come out against the government it was meant to keep in office, on an issue which was considered the most important of the decade.

The struggle then shifted to the details of the referendum, the date being announced as – most likely – Thursday, 5 June. The bill was given its second reading on 10 April, and received the royal assent by 8 May. A number of issues were debated by the pro- and anti-camps. First, the count, which was to be for the United Kingdom as a whole. The government later changed this to a county basis. Second, broadcasting, where the BBC and IBA decided to treat the referendum as a general election between two equal parties. Third, expenditure, which was declared unlimited, though £125,000 was granted to each of the campaigns. Fourth, the wording of the question. The antis secured the insertion, in parenthesis, of the term 'common market' after 'European community'. Fifth, information. The government agreed to send pro- and anti-appeals to each household, along with its own statement of the renegotiated terms, *Britain's New Deal in Europe*. The title may have been Wilson's.

With the authority of the government behind a yes vote, pro-marketeers anticipated victory. Their organization – Britain in Europe (BIE) – had been set up secretly by Sir Con O'Neill, at the beginning of the year, though it was not announced until 26 March. The organizers quickly realized the key to success was labour support, which had to be mobilized behind the prime minister. Roy Jenkins became president, with William Whitelaw as effectively his deputy. Wilson and Callaghan initially eschewed public association with BIE, in line with the argument that they were EEC agnostics, who had just been won over by the terms. The former addressed only eight meetings in the last fortnight, and the latter five, organized on an ad hoc basis by the prime minister's political office. There was some contact towards the end of the campaign, and Lord Harris, at the home office, was called in by number 10, 'to give advice on the Prime Minister's personal campaign presentation'.[13] Vic – now Lord – Feather provided the prime minister with a platform in the form of a pro-EEC trade-union group, 'a front organization of the European Movement'.[14] Callaghan wanted to appear on the BIE's last television broadcast, but Lord Harris, who was jointly in charge of BIE publicity, told the foreign office it would not be acceptable to the broadcasting authorities. Wilson and Callaghan were largely kept off radio and television, on the grounds that airtime had to be equally divided between the campaigns. A referendum steering group had been meeting each morning in Whitehall, chaired by the foreign secretary or Roy Hattersley, the attendance including Shirley Williams and Bernard Donoughue. Private polls were commissioned from MORI at a cost of at least £15,000, which was charged neither to public nor party funds. The pro-EEC campaign is thought to have cost something approaching two million pounds.

The national referendum campaign (NRC) spent £134,000 getting out the no vote. It had also been formed at the beginning of the year on an all-party basis, to coordinate a number of disputatious anti-EEC groups. The chairman was a conservative MP, Neil Marten, and Douglas Jay was probably its most prominent figure. Jack Jones and the TGWU were instrumental in its foundation. It attracted support mainly from the labour party, but also the Scottish and Welsh nationalists and Ulster unionists. Enoch Powell played the major public role. Jones had shared a platform in Yorkshire, the previous summer, with Lord Wigg and Enoch Powell. When he found TGWU members queueing up for the latter's autograph, he 'wondered whether [he] had done the right thing'.[15] While the labour cabinet minority, less Tony Benn, became associated with the NRC, Foot, Castle and Shore tended to continue to speak as ministers against the market. They met each Thursday in Barbara Castle's room in the commons, where statements were drafted by Jack Straw, Frances Morrell and Tony Banks, the political advisers, respectively, of Castle, Benn and Hart.

The no campaign concentrated on economic issues, such as food prices and unemployment, but also political ones, especially independence and sovereignty. It owed most of its strength to labour as a national party, despite Hayward's success on 26 March in preventing the executive pitting itself against the government. Callaghan had criticized a Transport House document on the renegotiations, but the executive agreed on 23 April, at a meeting from which Wilson absented himself, that this, plus the government's statement of its case, should be laid before the delegates to the special party conference, to be held in Islington on Saturday, 26 April. The TUC had endorsed its anti-EEC stance on 23 April, while acknowledging the right of unions to disagree; a minority of unions, especially the GMWU, favoured membership. Hayward had arranged that Wilson and Callaghan would open and close for the pro-lobby. Fred Mulley in the chair was to allow opponents equal say. Barbara Castle found Wilson 'obviously unhappy before he began and even more unhappy at the lukewarm reception he received at the end'. 'My heart went out to him', she wrote, 'because I am very fond of him.'[16] The conference voted 3,724,000 to 1,986,000 to reject the government's new terms, in accord with the executive's position. Labour pro-marketeers feared the executive would now use the party machine in the no campaign, but the anti–EEC members were more afraid of Wilson neutralizing the party by appealing to a notional right to dissent. When the executive held a special meeting the following Wednesday, 30 April, Hayward stated that the party was now opposed to the renegotiated terms. There would be no campaign. The party had no money, and some pro-EEC unions were opposed to their contributions being used. Transport House staff saw it as an open question, as did party organizers, and some constituency parties. Wilson and Callaghan had turned their special conference defeat into a victory for the government, forcing the majority to accept responsibility for party disunity. Transport House was not at the service of the cabinet minority; Foot, Castle, Benn, Shore, and Silkin, plus Judith Hart, were forced to work through the NRC or independently. They remained a collection of prominent individuals, organizationally detached from the anti-EEC sentiment in the country. Barbara Castle had privately predicted defeat at an early stage in the campaign, and feared Wilson becoming a prisoner of the right. Benn, Shore and Foot argued that the left would prevail.

According to public and private opinion polls, Britain favoured staying in Europe by about two to one. This figure had first been registered the previous October, when the question of being for or against the EEC became one about staying, if the government argued withdrawal was not in Britain's interest. This was the question from March, and two to one remained the position regardless of the efforts of BIE or NRC. Britain voted on a 64.5 per cent turnout on 5 June to stay in the community, by 17,378,581 votes to 8,470,073. Every county, bar two in Scotland, favoured remaining in the EEC. England was most keen, followed by Wales, and then Scotland. The turnout in Northern Ireland was lowest. Opposition to the EEC had haunted the labour party from 1962, but the issue was now settled. The prime minister had appealed over the head of the party, in parliament and the country, and won. It was his finest political hour, though few socialists were prepared to accept this.

The largely pro-European press acknowledged the service he had performed for British politics. It had been, according to Marcia Falkender, 'the most hectic and hard-working [sixteen months] of Harold Wilson's life'.[17] It was also an important defeat for the labour left. 'Tony Benn's army of the left', writes Bernard Donoughue, 'was diverted from the dangerous fields of British industry [onto] ... the deceptively inviting marshes of the EEC. Once committed and trapped there, Mr Benn was blown up by a referendum of the British people.'[18] Benn had come under attack for his work in the department of industry, as one of the leading anti-marketeers in the public eye. While attending the commonwealth conference in Jamaica in early May, Wilson told a *Daily Telegraph* correspondent that Benn was going to be moved. He later admitted that he planted this story, 'the only time I [had] taken such action in my whole period of office'![19] Later, on ITV's *Weekend World*, the prime minister described his secretary of state as having 'some of the qualities of an Old Testament prophet, without a beard'.[20] Wilson was to remain attached to this political metaphor.

The prime minister offered Benn the energy department on Monday, 9 June. 'He took it extremely hard, and it looked virtually certain that he would choose to retire to the back-benches, the last place where I wanted to see him.'[21] Benn accepted the following day. Foot had acted as go between, and Varley agreed to be moved to industry. Ian Mikardo spent all day working on Foot, realizing that defence of the industrial policy was crucial for the left. Tony Benn had been forced to come to the aid of ailing firms, including Ferranti and British Leyland, while preoccupied with his – emasculated – industry bill. Wilson, despite his proclamations about being a reformed character, sought to seize control of these rescue operations. It was Eric Varley who saw the industry bill enacted belatedly in November 1975, the NEB being established under Sir Don Ryder. Planning agreements were virtually still-born. Wilson also shifted Reg Prentice, an increasingly right-wing member of the government, from education to overseas devel- opment. He was forced to retain him in the cabinet, probably because of threats from Roy Jenkins. Judith Hart had to be removed from overseas development, and was offered transport outside the cabinet. Having caused Wilson concern during the referendum campaign, he does not seem to have struggled to prevent her resigning. Others feared prime ministerial retri- bution, but Foot, Castle, Shore and Silkin were left in their posts. As the prime minister was about to announce the changes to the commons, late on 10 June, the left, less Shore and Castle, prepared to protest to Wilson about Hart's sacking. Foot and Benn, plus Castle, interceded later. Hart – at the prompting of Tony Banks – told the house the following day she was being sacked. Barbara Castle noted critically of the prime minister: 'He subordinates all considerations, not only of principle but of administrative effectiveness, to his balance of power manoeuvrings.'[22]

A second general election, and then the referendum, meant the labour government did not address the economic crisis until June 1975. Economic policy in Britain was out of step with the rest of the advanced world. One senior treasury official was to say, 'when the rest of the world was deflating in 1974–5[,] we were not'.[23] 'In the absence of a clear macro-economic or counter-inflation strategy', writes Bernard Donoughue, 'our interventionist industrial proposals were then Labour's most visible economic policy.'[24] The 1975 industry act was to be an extension of Heath's 1972 act, Tony Benn ironically only ever using Heath's. The NEB 'as it developed was very different from the original conception of Labour left-wingers of an organisation which would spearhead the transformation of Britain's industrial economy from capitalism to socialism.'[25] With the sacking of Tony Benn, the labour government's industrial strategy was effectively brought to an end. It became a case of propping up lame duck industries with government money, a task to which Sir Don Ryder, a businessman, was willing to turn his hand.

Something of the government's frame of mind, at the beginning of Wilson's fourth administration, had been evident at an informal meeting of the cabinet, held at Chequers on Sunday, 17 November 1974. It was meant to consider economic strategy, and ministers had put in papers. 'As the discussion unfolded, revealing problems of almost insurmountable gloom', Barbara Castle wrote, 'I had the quiet feeling that so much expertise, sense and conviction of purpose *must* enable us somehow to win through.'[26] The CPRS, under its new head, Sir Kenneth Berrill, was responsible for the agenda. 'We have only a 50 per cent chance of avoiding world catastrophe',[27] said Harold Lever before he left complaining of gastric flu. Roy Jenkins recalled that it was ten years since the Chequers defence review: 'The world has changed out of all recognition since then.'[28] Benn was visionary: 'We cannot win consent to a technocratic solution. We must redistribute power in this country by peaceful means. Beyond the slump must be the perspective of a better society.'[29] Michael Foot, taking the lead from Lever, argued for contingency planning in case of catastrophe, but Denis Healey was less pessimistic: 'We could not sensibly plan ahead for a doomsday-type catastrophe.'[30] Callaghan then spoke with all his wealth of experience, fearing a siege economy would damage British democracy: 'When I am shaving in the morning I say to myself that if I were a young man I would emigrate. By the time I am sitting down to breakfast I ask myself, "Where would I go?" (Laughter)' He went on to argue that Britain would continue to decline. 'Nothing in these papers makes me believe anything to the contrary. I haven't got any solution. As I said, if I were a young man, I should emigrate.'[31] Wilson ended the morning's discussion by describing it as first class, 'the best I have ever heard in this type of gathering'.[32] After lunch the deputy head of CPRS announced there was 'no surefire recipe for economic growth'.[33] Berrill saw inflation as more important than the standard of living, and pointed to wage bargaining as the key to policy. Tony Crosland was unable to explain Britain's relative decline: 'All we can do is to press every button we've got. We do not know which, if any, of them will have the desired results.' He was for 'grit[ting] our teeth till the oil flows'.[34] Foot, to cheers from

Castle, insisted that a statutory incomes policy was not on. He favoured cutting ministerial salaries. Jenkins, trying to do Healey's job, insisted that 'the danger of hyperinflation [was] the greatest that [they] face[d]. I agree that we need a contingency plan, though not a siege economy. We must face the danger that the Social Contract may fail.'[35] Shirley Williams took the view that after 'the devolution of power' must come 'the devolution of responsibility'.[36] Healey was for giving the social contract until the following Easter, when the alternative of unemployment would have to be considered. He described Benn's idea of subsidies to industry to prevent redundancies as one which would 'create paralysis in our economic system, leading to rigor mortis'.[37] 'We broke up', Barbara Castle concluded, 'congratulating ourselves on a valuable day. The problem, as always, will be whether we have the time to follow our own lessons through.'[38]

It was the rise in the price of oil which fuelled the inflation of the mid-1970s, in the context of a world commodity boom. The consequence was the threat of global unemployment. Western nations, with memories of the inter-war years, turned to deflationary solutions, as the influence of new right-wing economists increased. Britain had two options as a member of the EEC. It could either seek to change international policy, which was impossible, or pursue national economic objectives, in the context set by the leading industrial states – Germany, the United States and Japan. Harold Lever was the leading advocate within the government of global reflation, but it was Tony Benn, as an opponent of the common market, who espoused an alternative strategy of economic nationalism. The prime minister was fundamentally opposed to the latter, but the promotion of global economic expansionism, which he instinctively favoured, ran up against the views of his economic ministers, particularly Denis Healey at the treasury.

'Harold Wilson sometimes gave the impression of being reluctant to face the growing economic crisis. He had also shrewdly learned from long and painful experience that if a major economic crisis is looming it is politically better to wait until the seriousness of the situation is unmistakably apparent to one's ministerial colleagues.'[39] Bernard Donoughue had briefed Wilson in May 1974, on the basis of a paper by Andrew Graham. Graham accepts Wilson may have been biding his time, but recalls it did not feel like that. 'Sitting in number 10 in 1974–5 was the most weird experience … You had the feeling that the whole world economic system was in danger of much more serious collapse.' The international economy was slowing down, producing massive liquidity problems for British companies. A major clearing bank was to find itself in considerable difficulty. Wilson must have been terrified. 'There seemed no good reason why the Arabs were keeping their money in London. It just looked as if the whole situation could run away from you.'[40] Peter Shore argued that, towards the end of 1974, virtually all the major institutions in Britain were technically bankrupt.

Graham argued in his paper that Britain faced hyperinflation and devaluation, and there would be treasury demands for cuts and a statutory
incomes policy. From a rate of 16 per cent between 1973 and 1974,
inflation was rising to over 24 per cent in 1974–5. The July 1974 budget
slowed the rate of increase for a time, with a decline in the rate of increase
of import prices, but the escalating cost of wages and salaries increasingly
drove up prices. Average earnings rose by 25 per cent between late 1973
and 1974, in an explosion determined by the end of the Heath controls.
Over 700,000 people were unemployed by the beginning of 1975.

The number 10 policy unit recommended in a 'long and gloomy'[41] paper
that the government should adopt a crisis package, comprising public
expenditure cuts, import controls or tariffs, and the dampening down of
wage inflation. Robert Armstrong arranged for Graham to see Wilson in
his study about this time. Graham recalls the prime minister had 'that sort
of glazed look'[42] about him. Benn outlined two strategies in a paper to the
economic strategy committee on 25 February. The first, A, was the conventional treasury one of increasing unemployment, to reduce the balance
of payments and get inflation down. The second, B, involved selective
assistance to industry, import controls, restrictions on capital outflows, and
the downward floating of the pound. Benn's paper was not allowed to go
to cabinet, and he claims any possibility of a radical approach had been
foreclosed at Chequers in November. 'I was forced to attend as a sort of
captive and watch the whole thing being reversed.'[43] His alternative
economic strategy (AES), as it was to be called, had been derived from
Francis Cripps of Cambridge, a colleague of Wynn Godley's, and had been
discussed beforehand with Heffer, Frances Morrell and Michael Meacher.
It was dismissed by Roy Jenkins as making for a siege economy, though
the concept of an alternative strategy was taken straight from the liaison
committee's key document of two years earlier.

The government was doing something about prices, but on wages it
merely invoked the social contract as a justification for restraint. 'The
problem, not so much for government as for their partners in the Contract,
was that of selling eminently reasonable pay restraint proposals to millions
of workers and their wives, who could see their standard of living being
reduced month by month – even before the pinch of unemployment
began to be felt.'[44] Healey introduced a 'rough and tough'[45] budget on 15
April, in an effort to achieve a deflation of £1.75 billion. Direct taxes were
raised, the standard rate becoming 35p, and indirect taxes also rose, but not
the basic rate of VAT or corporation tax. There were cuts in defence, food,
housing and nationalized industry subsidies. 'Once again', noted Barbara
Castle, 'I felt caught in that sense of inevitability when social democratic
dreams come up against the realities of the mixed economy.'[46] The
chancellor ruled out a statutory incomes policy, but he warned that 'unless

... the voluntary policy achieve[d] stricter adherence to guidelines laid down by the trade unions of their own free will, the consequence [could] only be rising unemployment'.[47] Wage negotiators, according to the TUC, should only seek increases in line with rises in the cost of living.

Labour's treasury team had come to office without any clear idea of what public expenditure was possible. 'We naturally discussed the likely immediate economic situation we would face', writes Joel Barnett, the chief secretary to the treasury, 'but medium- and long-term planning on the allocation of resources rarely, if ever, entered into our thinking and discussions.'[48] The cabinet had agreed a white paper on public expenditure in November 1974, covering the four years, 1974/75 to 1978/79, which was published in January 1975. The first cuts were agreed on 25 March, totalling over a billion pounds for 1976/77, and were announced in the budget. The treasury was now concerned about the two following years. Healey made much of the fact that public expenditure, as a proportion of gross national product, had risen from 42 to 58 per cent in twenty years, and Roy Jenkins was to be particularly appalled at this figure. 'The survival of society is threatened', he said. In a speech in January 1976, Jenkins, though he harboured leadership ambitions, was publicly to attack the idea of such a large public sector. 'I had been particularly struck by [Healey's] implication', noted Barbara Castle of the earlier meeting, 'that public expenditure was wrong in itself. What then were we in business for?'[49] For Tony Benn it was 1931 all over again, 'when the government of the day refused to accept protection and gave us a depression instead.'[50]

The pound came under attack after the referendum, dropping on Monday, 30 June 1975 to a 28.9 per cent depreciation on the 1972 figure, when it was floated. The treasury demanded a statutory incomes policy, but Wilson had his political eye on the NUM conference in Scarborough, which he was to address on 7 July. He hoped to be defending there a voluntary policy, in keeping with the social contract.

The cabinet had held another economic strategy meeting at Chequers on Thursday, 20 June, where ministers agreed to a wages norm of 10 per cent, with some form of monitoring body and a tough stance in the public sector. Foot, Healey and Williams were sent off to talk to the TUC, and the following week the number 10 policy unit came up with the idea of a £5 norm. This had been suggested by Joe Haines, and it was to be backed up by sanctions, a price code and restraint in the public sector. Healey had mentioned a £5 norm, as an alternative to 10 per cent, at the Chequers cabinet, so the idea was in play in the treasury. Wilson had asked his unit for ideas on wages restraint, but he was reluctant, despite pressure from the treasury, to abandon the idea of a voluntary policy. A cabinet committee (MISC 91) accepted the number 10 idea of 'a voluntary policy backed by sanctions' on Thursday, 26 June, but '[Wilson] did not want to commit himself to an incomes policy and then find his colleagues backing off'.[51] Michael Foot was still keen to get a voluntary agreement with the TUC, where Jack Jones was also arguing – successfully – for a flat-rate increase. He wanted a limit of perhaps as much as £10 on all salaries up to £7,000, though the rate later became £8. This proposal annoyed the left. Wilson decided the following day to tell the treasury to cease working on a statutory policy, though it is not clear whether, and how, he did this. The prime minister, with his characteristic irreverence towards establishment figures, predicted to Joe Haines that the governor of the bank of England would be round at the beginning of the following week. Sure enough, there was a financial crisis on Monday, 30 June. The treasury did not provoke the run on the pound, but it had been biding its time. The governor and chancellor came to number 10 demanding immediate action. The key meeting seems to have been between Healey and Wilson that afternoon in the prime minister's study; a note would have been taken by Robert Armstrong, and Bernard Donoughue also appears to have been present. Andrew Graham observed them coming out of the room. 'Wilson gave me a look of a kind which indicated to me that something was up, and I was not supposed to know about it.'[52] A meeting of MISC 91 was held, while Graham went off to the treasury, to be told by friends that the governor had been to number 10. Donoughue and Haines suspected a conspiracy between the treasury and bank of England, an attempt to 'bounce'[53] the government into a statutory policy. They warned the prime minister of this after the cabinet committee, but Wilson seems to have been badly shaken by the run on the pound. He feared it dropping below $2.20, when the oil producing states would start moving out of sterling. Wilson now began to weaken towards the treasury, where a statement was being prepared for an emergency cabinet the following morning. Donoughue and Haines continued to work on Wilson during a state dinner for the Belgian prime minister, Leo Tindemanns. 'He snapped at us that we were not being sufficiently realistic', recalls Donoughue. 'It was quite a gruelling evening.'[54] The draft treasury statement reached number 10 just after midnight, providing for a 10 per cent norm with criminal sanctions. It may have gone to another meeting of MISC 91. Donoughue and Haines drafted a minute stating the treasury had not attempted to defend the pound on the Monday. It was now trying to 'stampede [the government] into a statutory pay policy, against every pledge which we have given'.[55] They predicted government resignations, and a split in the party. Andrew Graham also drafted something to give to Robin Butler in the private office. Wilson read the minute from Donoughue and Haines in his study in the early hours of 1 July, and it led him apparently to change his mind. Andrew Graham acknowledges the role of Donoughue and Haines at this crucial point, but stresses that Wilson was opting for another hypothetical policy. Getting his press secretary at his home on the phone at 1.40 a.m., Wilson told Haines that Healey had now been instructed to bring a different statement to cabinet.

Ministers met at 9.30 a.m. in number 10 on 1 July. Healey was allowed to announce his 10 per cent norm, but he was now talking of £6 as an alternative. Any question of legislating to compel employers was to be postponed, pending further negotiations with the TUC. Criminal sanctions against workers had been ruled out by Wilson, after contact with Lionel Murray. The prime minister had been thinking again of 1966 until 3.00 a.m., and suggested taking general powers which would only become law by regulation if needed. 'Can social democracy ever work?', Eric Varley asked Barbara Castle in a note. 'Do you think the Government will still be in office this autumn?' was his next question.[56] Jack Jones was flown from his union's conference in Blackpool on 2 July, for a meeting with Wilson and Healey. The chancellor agreed to a flat-rate increase in a tough bargaining session, in return for Jones coming down to £6 (the limit was later set at £8,500).

After the cabinet meeting on 1 July, the number 10 policy unit and treasury vied to draft a white paper, which was formally the responsibility of Healey's officials. Graham started work with his colleague, David Piachard, on an alternative paper on Thursday, 3 July. At a meeting of the Oxford political economy club a few weeks earlier, addressed by Derek Robinson, Graham had hit upon the idea of separating the private and public sectors for the purpose of wage restraint. It was 'a conceptual breakthrough', though would it be called 'a fudge'[57] by some. A draft was ready by the Friday evening, to be developed in the unit and rewritten by Donoughue. Thus the so-called statutory voluntary policy was drawn up. 'Relations with the Treasury officials', Donoughue writes, 'henceforward improved dramatically since, as true professionals, they bore no malice but recognised that we were an important part of the Whitehall power game.'[58] Wilson flew to Scarborough the following Monday, where the miners were being urged to demand £100 a week for faceworkers. The NUM decided that £100 should be a long-term objective, and, thanks to the 'consummate skill ... [of] Joe Gormley and his colleagues',[59] the union, in a ballot, accepted the £6 limit. Meanwhile, Castle, Foot, Benn, Shore and Eric Varley had met in secret. Resignations were on the cards if Healey prevailed.

The white paper, *The Attack on Inflation,* was considered in cabinet on Thursday, 10 July. Healey still wanted reserve powers, on the grounds that the TUC vote had shown declining support for the social contract. The prime minister supported this position, and it looked like the treasury might still win. It was then suggested that the government should say it had a bill waiting if the £6 did not work, this being a compromise between the voluntary and statutory camps. Healey left the cabinet room promising that, if there was another run on the pound, he would have to legislate immediately. Proponents of the voluntary approach had agreed to support a white paper, which the chancellor was now claiming contained a statutory policy to all intents and purposes.

Wilson made a statement in the house the following day on the government's new incomes policy, which was designed to get inflation down to 10 per cent by September 1976. He agreed at the later press conference to publish the text of the bill, but then had to backtrack in order to appease the employment secretary and his supporters. Wilson acted on an earlier idea of Barbara Castle's, setting up a counter-inflation policy unit in the cabinet office to be run by Geoffrey Goodman, industrial editor of the *Daily Mirror*.

Healey had still not given up on public expenditure cuts. At what was meant to be a special cabinet on the medium-term economic assessment on 14 July, the chancellor presented a demand for £2 billion off the 1978/79 figure, in order to eliminate the balance of payments deficit by 1978. He was prevented from mentioning this figure in the debate on the government's white paper on 21–22 July. The £6 policy was accepted by 327 votes to 269, but 36 left-wingers defied the whips and voted against the government. 'The breach between Mike [Foot] and the Tribune group', Barbara Castle had noted the previous evening, '[was] now almost as great as the breach was between me and them in the previous Labour Government over *In Place of Strife*.'[60] The second reading of the counter-inflation bill was moved the next day, and it was ready for royal assent by 1 August. At the Tribune rally during the party conference, Jack Jones was to criticize Ian Mikardo for attacking the government. The unions and the left, having made common cause in the early 1970s, were splitting.

As soon as the government's incomes policy was enacted, the cabinet returned to public expenditure in a special meeting at Chequers on Monday, 4 August. This was originally intended to work out detailed cuts. Ministers again divided for and against the chancellor, treasury ministers considering the meeting 'wholly inconclusive'.[61] Priority was assigned to various commitments. Healey told the house of commons in November he was seeking a special drawing from the international monetary fund (IMF). He wanted £575 million now, and perhaps £400 million later. 'Although he was not pressed to spell out the detailed consequences of what we would need to do to meet the requirements of the IMF, informed opinion had a pretty good idea, even if it did not wholly appreciate the difficulties involved.'[62] By 13 November the chancellor was demanding a cut of £3.75 billion in 1978/79, and hinting at resignation if he did not get £3 billion. Crosland proffered a £2.5 billion alternative, and the cabinet – according to Wilson's record of the vote – marginally agreed to the higher figure. The lower figure was reached by 9 December, and the final package – less £172 million – was agreed two days later. Bilateral meetings between the treasury and spending departments were to follow for the financial years 1977/78 and 1979/80. A public expenditure white paper for 1976/77 was published on 19 February 1976, this effectively marking the end of Harold Wilson's conduct of economic management by cabinet government.

The white paper contained projections for the future, the treasury wanting a levelling off in public expenditure from April 1977, so that industry could take advantage of an expected upturn in world trade. It itemized cuts of £1.6 billion in 1977/78, and £3 billion the following year. Thirty-seven Tribunites abstained on the vote on 10 March 1976, ensuring a defeat for the government by twenty-eight votes. The following day was Wilson's sixtieth birthday, and the cabinet decided to ask for the first vote of confidence of his premiership, which was secured by 297 votes to 280. He was to resign as planned five days later.

Denis Healey now began to warn his colleagues that the treasury's assumptions, used for the public expenditure exercise the previous December, were overoptimistic. 'The most obvious change since the last medium-term appraisal' on 14 July 1975, he argued,

> is that the world recession has been deeper and more prolonged and the upturn so far more sluggish than we had reckoned on. If our anxiety should prove well-founded, we should have to pursue our national objectives on employment and the balance of payments in an international environment more difficult than at any time since World War II. The economists suggest that in this case it would be dangerous to base resource planning on the firm assumption that we can devise a combination of policies which will enable us, by 1979, to achieve the state of affairs represented by the central case in the White Paper projections.[63]

The year 1976 was an important watershed in economic thinking and management. Keynesianism had been around for nearly forty years, this guide to practice being based on the ideas of economic growth, public expenditure and full employment. In 1974, the number 10 policy unit proposed a committee on monetary questions, and, by December 1975, Donoughue was arguing for the increasing centrality of monetary policy. Inflation was the most important economic problem, and it was believed the government's incomes policy could be aided by tighter control of the money supply. 'In the modern world inflation [was] a printing press phenomenon'[64] according to Milton Friedman. This proposition was to become – under the generic term monetarism – the basis of an alternative strategy for reversing the structural decline of the United Kingdom. 'The prevailing belief among [senior civil servants] was that our poor industrial and economic performance meant we must restrain the growth of public expenditure.'[65] It was but a short step to full-blown monetarism, the practice – as often in Britain – coming before the theory. 'Mr Wilson', according to his senior policy adviser, 'seemed to have lost interest in contemporary developments in economic thinking before the debate on monetarism emerged.'[66]

It was Tony Crosland, talking of local government spending, who had first announced that 'the party [was] over, at least for the moment'[67] in the spring of 1975, in spite of the role he was to play in resisting Healey's first round of public expenditure cuts. But it was not until the 1976 party conference that the monetarist doctrine was to be proclaimed by a labour government, with a new leader in place. James Callaghan, inspired probably by Peter Jay, said: 'We used to think that you could just spend your way out of a recession and increase employment by cutting taxes and boosting government spending. I tell you, in all candour, that that option no longer exists.'[68]

Harold Wilson attended this conference as a backbench MP, but he was not to be allowed to escape historical association with the international monetary fund, when, in December, it was effectively to dictate British economic policy. An IMF loan had become an option in the summer of 1975, as an alternative to devaluation or import controls. The latter had been rejected as altogether too radical, and Harold Wilson had no desire to become involved in a third devaluation. The resort to the IMF was to fund the public sector borrowing requirement, considered by Healey to be too large. 'In his letter of application [the chancellor] ... not only reiterated his intention to continue with his present policies, but undertook not to impose new restrictions on payments or trade without prior consultation with the Fund.'[69] The letter of intent that November must have been agreed between the chancellor and prime minister.

Wilson's second premiership crossed with the final months of Nixon's presidency, but Gerald Ford was in the White House when Wilson visited north America in January 1975. The British government had already tentatively raised the question of its defence commitments, because of financial difficulties. The Americans seem to have been prepared to accept withdrawal from the Simonstown base in South Africa, but they wanted Britain to remain in Cyprus. Washington also asked for further facilities on Diego Garcia, in the Indian Ocean.

The labour party remained opposed to the further development of nuclear weapons. Polaris had been modernized in 1969 in the Antelope project, and Heath declined to purchase Poseidon from the United States as it would require the conversion of British submarines. Heath secretly authorized Polaris's improved penetration of Soviet anti-ballistic missile defences, shortly before he left office, this being known as the Chevaline project. Harold Wilson inherited this decision, and Britain carried out a nuclear warhead test between the 1974 elections. Wilson told the commons on 24 June that this had been authorized by the conservative government, but Michael Foot raised the question three days later of why it had not been brought to the cabinet. 'I could not consult Cabinet', the prime minister replied, 'because a leak of any kind would have very serious effects for reasons I can't give now.'[70] He was forced to concede there would be no more tests, until defence policy was reviewed. Wilson next argued in cabinet, on 20 November, that Britain should remain a nuclear power. This was for reasons of diplomacy, since it gave access to American thinking and reassured the Germans. The Soviet Union had never objected. The prime minister insisted that further modernization was to cost £24 million per annum for ten years, this having been unanimously accepted by the defence and overseas policy committee of the cabinet. Wilson did not refer to it as the Chevaline project, and described the work as 'a very minor addition to the present nuclear weapons system'.[71] A billion pounds would be expended without any further recourse to the cabinet.

Michael Foot raised the question of nuclear bases on 20 November, only to back off. 'Mike then said', according to Barbara Castle, 'that he remained of the view that we should rid ourselves of nuclear weapons, but recognized that he was in a minority and so would not press the matter.' 'Mike's comments were so muted', she concluded, 'as to be almost token.'[72] Tony Benn's note is not that dissimilar. Castle records Shore and Benn as not saying anything. She then made the point that it was contradictory to say nuclear weapons were important, and then not fully modernize them. The sum of £240 million could be much better spent. 'Harold summed up cheerfully, saying that Cabinet, with a few of us expressing dissent, had endorsed the policy and he added unctuously that he was extremely grateful for the constructive spirit in which those who disagreed with the policy had put their views. He then took himself off, looking pleased with himself, as well he might.'[73]

Wilson and Callaghan flew to Washington, via Canada, in early 1975. The British party was officially received at the White House the following morning. He and the foreign secretary discussed problems of the global economy with the president and Henry Kissinger, the secretary of state. They were concerned about possible producer cartels, on the model of the organization of petroleum exporting countries (OPEC). Wilson also mentioned the forthcoming commonwealth conference, and his trip to the Soviet Union. The prime minister later met members of the foreign policy community on Capitol Hill. There was an official dinner at the White House with toasts and speeches, appropriate for a NATO head of government, but hardly an important world figure.

Wilson and Callaghan left for New York the following day, meeting the secretary-general of the united nations, Kurt Waldheim, plus colleagues on 1 February. The principal items were the middle east and Cyprus. Wilson backed Kissinger's diplomatic approaches on the former, while partial Turkish military domination in Cyprus was being increasingly accepted. Britain shared with the United States alarm at the growth of third-world power in the general assembly, and Wilson undertook to raise with his commonwealth colleagues the counter-productive nature of ambitious initiatives being promoted by the oil-producing states.

The prime minister reported back to the cabinet that relations with the United States were '"as good as they have ever been"',[74] and, at the 1975 party conference, he teased the anti-marketeers on the left about their Atlanticism during the referendum. Wilson went on to tell delegates that Anglo-American relations were 'now more constructive, both in political and economic issues, than at any time in the political life of most of us'.[75]

He also quoted the Soviets as having described his visit in February as 'historic'.[76] Wilson claimed that 'the 1975 talks covered more ground than any since Winston Churchill's historic visits in the Second World War.'[77] Heath's exlusion of the 105 Russians in late 1971 had frozen relations between London and Moscow. 'It seemed to me', Callaghan was to write, 'that a change of government was a suitable occasion to mend fences, to explore prospects for increasing our stagnant trade and to get to understand current Soviet thinking and objectives.'[78] Wilson and Callaghan arrived in Moscow on 13 February, to be greeted by the Soviet prime minister, Kosygin. They met the ailing Brezhnev that evening, to agree an agenda for the talks. Britain was interested in joint cooperation in a number of economic areas, but there was also concern about the Portuguese revolution. The Russians had a political interest in European security. A preparatory conference was then meeting in Geneva, the United States and Canada, as NATO members, negotiating with thirty-three European states. Wilson reiterated the western position, and dismissed general Soviet talk of world peace. He asked that both sides might speed up the conference on security and cooperation in Europe (CSCE). At some point, Brezhnev offered to provide full information on Soviet military dispositions, if the United States removed its nuclear weapons from Germany. Callaghan was impressed by the Russian leader's horror of war, but the offer was hardly taken seriously.

Discussions resumed the following morning. At a Kremlin lunch, Wilson reiterated the British position on European security, even making reference to coexistence between east and west. At the final meeting on the Monday, 17 February, Brezhnev asked for a restricted talk with Wilson to discuss the middle east, at which Wilson reiterated support for Kissinger's diplomacy. There followed a major signing ceremony, in which Wilson and Brezhnev put their names to a joint statement. They also signed a protocol on consultations, and a declaration on the non-proliferation of nuclear weapons. Wilson and Kosygin then signed further documents. There was an agreement on medical cooperation, another on economic and industrial cooperation, and a third on scientific and technological cooperation. The statement referred to 'the opening of a new phase in Anglo-Soviet relations', and to 'improved ... prospects for deepening détente in Europe'.[79] At another official lunch at the British Embassy, Kosygin stated 'th[e] visit [would] be a major factor in the history of Anglo-Soviet relations'.[80] Wilson reported to the cabinet three days later, 'immensely proud of his achievement'.[81]

The commonwealth was now of declining significance for Britain, as the fissure which had opened up over Rhodesia was exacerbated by the growing preeminence of north-south relations on a global scale. Given his involvement in Rhodesia in the 1960s, it is interesting that Wilson was now leaving it to his foreign secretary. Wilson and Callaghan secured a modest success at the 1975 commonwealth conference in Jamaica in late April/early May. The prime minister of Guyana, Forbes Burnham, was keen that the third world should unite economically against the advanced countries. He wanted them to establish what was to be known as the new international economic order. The Guyanese leader had been much impressed by the growth of Arab oil power, but Britain had been working on a plan to head off any threat from the third world, and the commonwealth was to be approached to give its backing. Wilson called for a general agreement on commodities in line with GATT, and claims his initiative was 'well received'[82] by the commonwealth heads of government. It was backed by a government report, *World Economic Interdependence and Trade in Commodities*. Wilson argued that 'commodity prices should be equitable to consumers and remunerative to efficient producers and at a level which would encourage longer-term equilibrium between production and consumption.'[83] Wilson advocated a commodity by commodity approach, citing tea and jute as possible candidates for commonwealth agreement. He saw prices being stabilized through buffer stocks, either international or national. In the case of the poorest countries, this could be done through schemes to stabilize export earnings. All this fell within the model of capitalist cooperation, the structural inequality of the world's economy being managed by inter-state relations. The cheap food of empire days was a thing of the past, now that British was in the common market. But the cabinet antis were playing up the commonwealth in the referendum campaign, and Wilson was not inattentive to a bit of domestic politicking during his time in the Carribbean. The so-called Lomé convention had recently been agreed between the EEC and forty-six African, Carribbean and Pacific countries. This was a great deal more meaningful than sentiment for the commonwealth. The Jamaica conference included a paragraph in the final communiqué, which implied that Britain should remain a member of the community. Wilson claims he knew nothing of its preparation, but the commonwealth declaration undoubtedly helped him and Callaghan at home.

The diplomatic high point of Wilson's second tenure of number 10 was the conference on security and cooperation in Europe, which met finally in Helsinki, between 30 July and 1 August 1975, after two years of preparatory work. Heads of state and government met to sign what was called the final act. Wilson was randomly selected to speak first, and also to chair the final session on 1 August. In his speech on 30 July, he compared the Helsinki conference with the congresses of Vienna and Berlin. Wilson argued that, in the age of détente, 'the only alternative to co-existence [was] co-death',[84] a phrase which had been used first by Attlee. He saw the final act as 'the start of a new chapter in the history of Europe'. 'With the peoples of North America and the Soviet Union', he said, 'we want to maintain the diversity of European civilization, but we want to end its fratricidal divisions and give it a new and better sense of direction.'[85] A diplomatic signal was sent to the Soviet Union, to the effect that Berlin was now protected against possible aggression. No reference was made to NATO, and, in the rest of his survey of areas of possible progress in international relations, Wilson concentrated upon Europe. He was to admit later that 'it [was] disappointingly true that [the final act had] been more a statement of principle than anything approaching a reality.'[86]

Helsinki was something of a diplomatic bazaar, and Wilson and Callaghan devoted a great deal of time to Portugal. Salazar had died in 1970 and the army became discontented at the attempt to hold on to its African colonies, mainly Angola and Mozambique. There was a military coup in Portugal on 25 April 1974, led by the armed forces movement (AFM) under Spinola. One of the first acts of the revolution was the freeing of Portugal's colonies, their liberation tilting the struggle in Rhodesia in favour of the nationalist guerrillas. The Portuguese revolution was seen in terms of the cold war. It was the loss of a ruthlessly anti-communist regime, for NATO and the United States, while, for the Soviet Union, the communist party was one of the forces participating in the democratization of the metropolitan power. Having survived underground in the days of Salazar, the party was able, under Alvaro Cunhal, to play a leading role in the AFM. Its political advance alarmed Washington, which drew cold comfort from the argument that a pro-Soviet regime in Portugal would vaccinate Spain and Italy, where communism was strong. 'The Labour Government's policy', Callaghan writes, 'was to ensure that the[se] democratic groups were given a fair opportunity to appeal to the Portuguese people without being shut out or dominated by the Portuguese Communist Party.'[87] This was nothing less than interference in the internal affairs of another country. 'I made use of all the facilities at the Foreign Office', he was to admit, 'to support Portugal's struggling democracy and in conjunction with Mario Soares and a handful of others, we laid plans against the worst-case scenario of an attempted Communist coup, but it would not be appropriate to detail them here.'[88] He can only have been referring to MI6, and the information research department.

Portugal was one of the issues discussed in Moscow in February 1975, as Wilson and Callaghan saw the role of the Soviet Union as absolutely crucial. Callaghan and Soares were much struck by the analogy of Czechoslovakia in 1947, when the communists, with the backing of Moscow, seized control of the coalition government in Prague. The British foreign secretary asked Kosygin to call off the Portuguese communists, insisting that détente and CSCE were at stake. The Russians defended political pluralism in Portugal. 'We concluded', Callaghan wrote, 'that the Kremlin was not seeking a new adventure in Portugal and regarded the success of their detente policy as more important than the success of the Portuguese Communist Party.'[89] The AFM stood by its promise to hold national elections to a constituent assembly, and Callaghan visited Portugal in the spring to support Soares's party.

The socialists emerged as the largest party and the communists much smaller, but the AFM remained the dynamic of the revolution, in ultimate control of the provisional government. General Costa Gomez was president, and General Vasco das Santos Goncalves became prime minister of the new coalition, but the socialist party left the government. Soares was replaced as foreign secretary by Major Melo Antunes. The new foreign secretary visited London in June, only to be lectured by Callaghan about communist influence, but Antunes insisted that the AFM was a popular national body, and not a stooge for Moscow. The EEC then promised economic aid in July 1975, on condition that a bulwark should be constructed against communism. Portugal was represented by President Gomez at Helsinki, but Wilson was to refer later to 'as choice a bunch of thugs as I have ever met.'[90] He demanded 'pluralist democracy' in Portugal, and Gomez responded that a 'pluralist socialist system' was being created. The British prime minister showed himself to be actively hostile to the military dictatorship he perceived to be developing in Portugal, his comments on the regime matching in virulence any he had ever made about any other government.

Wilson and Callaghan again interceded with the Soviets at Helsinki, asking Brezhnev to use his influence to end political uncertainty in Portugal. The general secretary replied that it was an independent state. He promised a discussion in the politburo upon return to Moscow, and Callaghan offered to send a memorandum. 'After Helsinki', Callaghan writes, 'we observed that the political situation in Portugal began to improve slowly, although the same could not be said of its economic prospects.'[91] General Antonio Ramalho Eanes was to be elected president in a national election in June

1976, and Soares would become head of the first constitutional government without an overall majority in the national assembly. 'The Portuguese people themselves', Callaghan writes, 'had played the biggest part in ensuring the survival of their "young democracy", but I believe it can be claimed with truth that the determined attitude and help of a number of European Governments, with Britain in the lead, materially assisted.'[92] Immediately after Helsinki, the socialist leaders had travelled on to Stockholm, at the invitation of Olof Palme, the socialist prime minister, to be joined by others, including Soares. A committee of friendship and solidarity with democracy and socialism in Portugal was agreed, a continental form of political activity in which Wilson had not hitherto been particularly interested. He was made a member of the committee, and the first meeting arranged for the following month in Downing Street. It was duly held on 5 September, with Soares attending. Though this was a political, and not official, gathering, Wilson was clearly acting in accord with the policy of NATO. The Portugese socialist leader addressed the labour party conference in Blackpool, some months before he was to become prime minister.

Spain was also greatly to concern the leading western states. President Giscard d'Estaing had convened an important conference of international leaders in November 1975, at Rambouillet, south of Paris. This was the first in a series of world economic summits, where the United States, Britain, France, Germany, Italy and Japan could discuss the prospects for capitalism. Summitry was becoming infectious. The Spanish dictator Franco had just died, and Giscard sought to alert his fellow leaders to another possible Iberian revolution. But the conference was mainly concerned with the world economy, the French being worried about an export-led recovery in Europe, where national budgets were running into deficit. President Ford was much more confident about the American economy. Wilson, accompanied by Callaghan, predicted that Britain would have a balance of payments surplus by 1977. North Sea oil would then be flowing and inflation down to 10 per cent, but he accepted that an international recession was on the way. This group of six world leaders was able to condemn economic nationalism, but it was another matter to impose a strategy for international trade and development on the United States. Ford was primarily concerned with tariff barriers against American exports. Britain was suspected of protectionist tendencies, though Wilson refuted this. He complained about state-subsidized competition in textiles from some eastern bloc countries, and even animadverted to the growing interest of officials in north-south questions.

Ulster in the period after the UWC strike continued to be a major problem for Britain. 'It was an extraordinary Parliamentary defeat for the combined efforts of all the major parties at Westminster', Wilson was to admit, 'a defeat for law and order, with all this meant for Britain, not least in our overseas relationships.'[93] The view of the government in London was that it had little to contribute. Northern Ireland would have to have a go at finding a settlement, and it should also relate more closely to the Republic. Michael Cudlipp was sent to Belfast as a public relations consultant, later becoming coordinator of information policy. Rees and his ministerial team of two, augmented in June by another two, took over the portfolios held previously by members of the executive. Northern Ireland legislation was to be passed as orders at Westminster. The cabinet committee responsible for Northern Ireland began to consider a new white paper on 12 June 1974, *The Northern Ireland Constitution* being approved by the cabinet on 2 July 'without any argument'.[94] A bill was then enacted allowing for a constitutional convention in the province, the chairman to be appointed by the queen on the advice of her ministers. The job of the convention was to discover 'what provisions ... would be likely to command the most widespread acceptance throughout the community there.'[95] It was envisaged that this might take some time.

The second 1974 general election then intervened, but it saw little change in the Northern Ireland representatives in the United Kingdom parliament. Rees told the cabinet committee on 24 October that the proposed assembly for Northern Ireland was the way forward. 'Although it was idle to pretend that the Convention had a strong chance of succeeding – indeed there was a high likelihood of failure – this time the politicians could not blame the British for the outcome. The ball was now in their court.'[96] Dublin was worried about the convention, fearing it was 'a device ... to pull out leaving a Congo situation'.[97] Rees suggested holding the assembly elections in March 1975. The cabinet committee reported rarely to cabinet, but, with Wilson in the chair, it seems to have considered other options in the winter of 1974–5. These included withdrawal, repartition and a 'no-man's land'[98] along the border. All the options were rejected by the cabinet committee as unworkable. The labour government 'tried not to get too deeply involved in the Irish problem. Our policy became one of consolidation, trying to contain terrorism and just to get through from year to year.'[99] Tony Benn was later to complain that the labour cabinet 'didn't really discuss Irish policy at all, apart from the Ulster workers' strike ... and one or two individual issues',[100] and Rees would reply that 'he must have conveniently forgotten the discussions at this time [in the summer of 1974]'[101] (to say nothing of the cabinet meeting on 10 April).

The convention was only a substitute for a policy, and Benn remained in ignorance of the wide-ranging constitutional discussions in the Northern Ireland committee after the second 1974 election. Absence of discussion was not the problem; it was the lack of a solution. 'There could neither be a United Ireland on the one hand', Rees discreetly concludes of this period, 'nor a move to integration on the other. Our aim would remain to move away from direct rule.'[102] 'It was internment and special category status', the secretary of state would admit later in a moment of singular clarity, 'that came to concern [him] more than other policy matter.'[103] Doing something about internment became the ultimate end of British policy in the wake of the UWC strike. Lord Gardiner was asked to find a solution in October.

In so far as a British strategy can be detected, it was slowly to withdraw the army. There was a reduction from sixteen to thirteen battalions in 1974. Handing over to the RUC and UDR became known, on the analogy with Vietnam, as Ulsterization. Meanwhile the IRA would be considered a terrrorist organization. Its actions in Northern Ireland were one thing, quite another on the British mainland. The IRA killed five off-duty soldiers with bombs in Guildford pubs during the second 1974 election, but this had little political effect. The death of twenty-one civilians in three Birmingham pubs on 21 November shocked the British people. A measure of the hysteria was the arrest, and conviction, of the wrong men, for Guildford and Birmingham; attempts to secure their release would, much later, dramatically expose the British system of justice. The Birmingham atrocity led Roy Jenkins to rush the 'draconian' prevention of terrorism act (PTA) through parliament, allowing the police to hold suspects for up to five days. Rees, Sam Silkin the attorney general, Foot, and a number of others were alarmed at the proposal to deport suspected republicans to Ireland. Wilson only got the policy of exclusion orders through the cabinet, by promising a review in six months. On the very day of the Birmingham bombings, the cabinet committee had authorized Rees to release further internees and detainees if the IRA declared a ceasefire. Ministers agreed on 17 December 1974 to phase out detention by, at the latest, mid-1976, in accord with the Gardiner report. Rees saw some protestant churchmen in London the following day, who had talked secretly to the IRA at Feakle in Co. Clare. The IRA announced a truce two days later, as from 22 December, to run until 2 January 1975. It believed a great deal was on offer, and Rees felt Sinn Féin wanted to participate in the elections to the convention. Fifty-two detainees were to be released up until 17 January, and Rees and Orme met the four main church leaders from Northern Ireland on 30 December 1974, asking them to seize the opportunity provided by the temporary cessation of violence. The leaders saw Wilson in Downing Street on new year's eve, 'the meeting [going] on and on, with Harold being more generous on time than he ever was to the Cabinet'.[104] It was announced on 2 January 1975 that the truce was being extended by fourteen days.

Dr John O'Connell in Dublin was put into play by the IRA for the third time. He had been to the British embassy on 18 December 1974 'with new proposals'.[105] 'When I heard this', Rees recalls, 'I told Harold's office to be wary. Belfast was bad enough without Dublin joining in.'[106] O'Connell brought a document to the embassy on 2 January 1975. The IRA wanted a commission of three to study the Irish problem: this was to comprise Sean MacBride from the Republic, and Desmond Boal from Northern Ireland; the third member was to be from Britain, and five candidates were mentioned, though Joe Grimond seems to have been the favourite. Secondly, the IRA wanted a private commitment to an amnesty. Its third demand was a bilateral truce, involving the progressive withdrawal of troops to barracks. This document was relayed to Rees, and presumably Wilson and Callaghan. Jack Lynch is known to have discussed it with his party colleagues, but the official British response to O'Connell cannot have been encouraging. Publication of Lord Gardiner's report on 14 January represented the limit of British policy, and the IRA announced, two days later, it was resuming its military campaign from 17 January. Rees talked to the four church leaders that day in Belfast and again a week later, blaming the breakdown of the ceasefire on the IRA. 'Our basic problem lay with the Provisional Sinn Féin representatives in Belfast, who were inexperienced and not up to their task.'[107] Conditions for a resumption of the ceasefire were presented on 21 January, but Rees decided to end all contact with Sinn Féin while violence continued.

He was aware John O'Connell had been trying to get in touch with Tony Field, but the British ambassador in Dublin was asked to tell O'Connell that Field no longer worked for Wilson. 'I had been kept informed of these various moves', Rees recalls, 'and when Harold spoke, to me, he was firm that there was to be no freelancing. All talk would take place in Northern Ireland.'[108] O'Connell eventually contacted Field, seemingly at the point at which the ceasefire was collapsing. He telephoned Marcia Falkender, and she apparently rang the prime minister 'in a highly excitable state'.[109] Falkender wanted to go to Dublin, something the prime minister immediately vetoed. Wilson then decided to go behind Rees's back. It was decided that O'Connell should come to London, on Friday, 17 January. Albert Murray drove Joe Haines to the Old Vic Theatre where they picked up O'Connell at 6.00 p.m. and drove them to the Southwark headquarters of Murray's trade union, where the prime minister's press secretary and the IRA's emissary talked in a private room. It seems the IRA was dissatisfied with the Laneside meetings, and wanted the British government to send two envoys to Daithi Ó Conaill. Haines gave O'Connell an assurance that Rees would not be informed, but Wilson reported fully to his Northern Ireland secretary, even sending O'Connell's document by messenger to Rees's home. Haines feels he was let down. 'Obviously', Rees writes, 'Dublin was trying to bypass me because I had stopped the contacts with the Provisional Sinn Féin in Belfast.'[110] Rees insists that a civil servant wrote to O'Connell, to the effect 'that the message had been passed on to [him] and that [his] responses would be gravely damaged if there was violence.'[111] O'Connell was back in London the following Tuesday, 21 January to meet Albert Murray, but the latter handed over a handwritten letter from Wilson, saying he could not exclude the NIO. Any meeting was out of the question.

Contact was resumed between Sinn Féin and the NIO. On 9 February Sinn Féin announced there would be an indefinite ceasefire as from 10 February. Wilson held out the prospect of troops being withdrawn to barracks, and the IRA claimed the following day that British civil servants had accepted their twelve points, amounting to an undertaking to withdraw, but Rees insists there were only four meetings at Laneside over six weeks to discuss the ceasefire. 'I concluded that facts had been sacrificed in order to show lukewarm Provisional IRA supporters of the ceasefire that the British were conceding important demands.'[112] He announced the same day that incident centres would be set up to monitor the truce, and staffed by civil servants in direct contact with Sinn Féin, though the republicans were to take these over, and use them to communicate with the NIO. Rees told his ministerial colleagues a week later that he wished to preserve the ceasefire, 'short of conceding anything of substance, to the Provisionals or of producing a loyalist backlash'.[113] He hoped the IRA as a military organization would be weakened, and opt for political activities due to battle fatigue.

The lord chief justice was announced as the convention chairman on 21 February 1975, and Wilson visited the province on 25 March to announce the date – 1 May – for the elections. The term 'power sharing', though not the concept, was absent from his speech, and there was no reference to an Irish dimension. Rees confided to his diary on 20 April that he was thinking about after the convention. 'The Provisional IRA', he wrote, 'could never "push out" the British but another UWC strike or similar loyalist action supported by the majority in Northern Ireland could transform the situation.'[114]

There was a 66 per cent turnout on 1 May. The UUUC captured 47 of the 78 seats with 55 per cent of the vote, a clear majority. The figure includes two independent loyalists, only one of whom was endorsed. Ranged against this coalition for a return to the old Stormont, were 5 Faulkner unionists, 17 SDLP, and 8 alliance members of the convention. The ceasefire held until 10 May according to Wilson, in spite of a wave of loyalist killings of catholics. The IRA probably did not sanction the resumption of operations by local units, and Rees certainly considers the ceasefire continued through the summer. The incident centres remained in operation until 11 November, when the last ones were closed, though the IRA claims it remained in touch with the British government. It never announced the resumption of its military campaign, but talks with Sinn Féin ceased.

The Northern Ireland parties failed to produce a unanimous report by November. They did agree there should be an assembly with an executive, but the UUUC's concession of all-party committees resembled that which had been rejected by the minority in 1971. The failure of the convention was considered by Rees's ministerial colleagues on 11 November 1975. 'I did not have an answer to the problem', the Northern Ireland secretary admits. 'Continually to talk of solutions was, [he] asserted, an English disease.'[115] It was back to a continuation of direct rule. Rees announced that month that special category status for political prisoners was to be ended, and set a date of 1 March 1976 for the commencement of the policy of criminalization. Wilson made a surprise Christmas visit to the security forces in Northern Ireland on 18 December. Catholic gunmen stopped a minibus early in the new year in Co. Armagh, and shot dead ten protestant workers. It was a nakedly sectarian act.

Wilson argued in a series of ministerial meetings for the deployment of the special air service (SAS), though it was already involved – secretly – in Northern Ireland. He announced on 12 January that the spearhead battalion was being sent into Co. Armagh, to engage in undercover work along the border. The general officer commanding flew to London to see Rees, objecting to some of the planned measures, but there is evidence that the prime minister was concerned principally to assuage protestant feeling. The convention was reconvened on 3 February 1976, and talked unsuccessfully until 23 February. It was dissolved finally on 5 March. During the convention's second round of talks, Wilson suggested to Rees a Lancaster House conference, involving Westminster and Northern Ireland politicians. 'Its real purpose', the prime minister wrote, 'would be to impress the Westminster parties of the "insufferability" of the Northern Ireland politicians and to stop the Ulster Unionists making common cause with the Tories.'[116] Rees objected, and the prime minister then invited all the Westminster parties successively to Downing Street, supposedly for open-ended discussions on the Northern Ireland problem. He wanted to associate the other parties with the British government's failure to construct an internal solution.

Richard Crossman had been told, in September 1973, he was suffering from cancer of the liver, and given six months to live; he was to die on 5 April 1974. For two years he had been working on the three volumes of his diary of a cabinet minister, with the help of Dr Janet Morgan of Nuffield College, Oxford. It had been Crossman's intention to update Bagehot 'by disclosing the secret operations of government, which are concealed by the thick masses of foliage which we call the myth of democracy'.[117] This he intended to do in his memoirs, and also in a study of British government, but, once in office, the idea of publishing his own unexpurgated ministerial diary became attractive. He consulted Wilson and Callaghan during labour's period in opposition, and both begged him not to publish his first volume before the next general election. Hearing he had but a short time to live, he appointed literary executors – his wife, Anne, Michael Foot, and Graham C. Greene, of Jonathan Cape, co-publisher, with Hamish Hamilton. They were asked 'to make sure that the pressure, which will undoubtedly be brought from Whitehall and from Westminster to prevent publication of parts of the manuscript, is completely rejected'.[118]

The first volume was in press by the time of the February 1974 election. Crossman had substantially finished the second volume, and was commencing the third, but only volume one had been checked against the records in the cabinet office, by the time he died. He had lunched at number 10 with Wilson a few days before, accepting the offer of a peerage. The *Sunday Times* announced on 28 April it was to serialize the first volume in the autumn, prior to publication. The cabinet secretary, Sir John Hunt, immediately asked to scrutinize the manuscript, in accord with established practice. Crossman had agreed to this, but without prejudice to his freedom as an author. 'How much to publish is not a matter of Government ruling, far less of the Official Secrets Act, but a concern of personal taste and personal conscience.'[119] Hunt told Wilson on 7 June 'of the reasons why he felt unable to clear the text submitted to him', and the prime minister concurred. The cabinet secretary wanted to suppress the diaries for thirty years, believing that former ministers had a duty to preserve 'the confidentiality which is necessary to maintain collective responsibility and mutual trust'.[120] This applied even when they wished to publish their memoirs. It was known that Wilson had allowed previous books to be published and that he himself had breached convention on two important matters in his own book, though he had deferred to the authority of the then cabinet secretary, Sir Burke Trend, and removed some passages. 'Wilson did not in fact play a decisive part' in the summer of 1974, according to Hugo Young, the political editor of the *Sunday Times*. The cabinet secretary was to testify that the manuscript was laid before Wilson on 7 June. It was claimed that:

he did not read the book, though he may have had it read for him by a political aide; and ... with an autumn election imminent, he was concerned to act correctly. Above all, he wanted to take no part in any discussion of possible litigation ... What actual influence he may have had, if only by his silence and deliberate distancing, on the handling of the Crossman case by Hunt and the Attorney-General, Sam Silkin, is impossible to know.[121]

Crossman's executors sought to have the first volume of the diary edited in order to satisfy Hunt. The exercise proved unproductive. The cabinet secretary laid down four parameters of limitation: cabinet discussions; advice by civil servants; senior appointments; and other discussions of policy but not personality. The *Sunday Times* then tried to negotiate with Hunt, but its intended extracts proved equally unacceptable. The executors next decided to let the paper publish extracts of its own choosing. The cabinet secretary alluded on 23 January 1975 to legal action, and demanded seven days' notice of publication. There was now a threat of the official secrets act being used, but the *Sunday Times* ran its first extract on 26 January. Number 10 sent a despatch rider to pick up copies for Hunt, and Wilson at Chequers. Hunt sought to modify each following extract for the next eight weeks, as the paper tried to minimize the possibility of legal action. Two days after the fourth extract appeared, tragedy struck on 18 February. Crossman's seventeen-year-old son Patrick hanged himself. Barbara Castle noted that night, though she was later to change her view: 'I cannot get rid of the haunting feeling that this is some grim retribution for the publication of the [diaries], which nobody likes very much and which made Dick's insistence on publishing them seem in bad taste.'[122] Nearly 100,000 words had been published by 23 March, each extract having been tactically edited. The government's law officers refused to accept that serialization altered things, and insisted that the first volume should not be published as a book. The executors resolved to go ahead.

Wilson's own account of his first two years in government had been challenged by the serialization, as the *Sunday Times* pointed out on 22 June. 'Many episodes receive from Crossman a treatment which is not just fuller than Wilson's but raises a straightforward question of historical accuracy.' Wilson was repeatedly to attempt to discredit the Crossman diaries as factually inaccurate, and did his best to discredit the account by attacking their author. It is said that if Harold Wilson did have a view in 1975, he was opposed to taking legal action against Times Newspapers, the publishers, and executors. Moreover, Michael Foot was an important member of his government, and Anne Crossman the widow of the man who had been his most loyal supporter. The cabinet secretary was to testify that he did not consult Wilson about prosecution, but Hunt left open the possibility that the prime minister might have discussed it with the attorney general. Sam Silkin was not to rule out this possibility, admitting he was taking action 'reluctantly'.[123]

He began proceedings on Monday, 9 June, immediately after the referendum. A writ was served on Foot and his two colleagues, and the

Sunday Times injuncted from publishing any further extracts, including the recollections of other ministers. The court of appeal discharged the injunction against the paper, in return for an undertaking to publish nothing before the trial. It began on 22 July, before Lord Widgery the lord chief justice. Sam Silkin chose not to use the official secrets act, which would have meant a criminal trial. He argued instead that Crossman had breached an arcane law of confidence. Evidence was heard over six days, and Widgery stated on 29 July he would give his judgement after the long vacation, on 1 October. The lord chief justice found in favour of the defendants, though the attorney general was permitted to seek an injunction in the case of further volumes, but only if the circumstances were different. Widgery conceded that the law of confidence could be applied to public affairs. 'None the less, his judgment destroyed the principle of Cabinet secrecy and it curbed the Cabinet Secretary's power.'[124] This was a surprise decision. The *Sunday Times* was vindicated, Hunt routed, and a precedent set for the publication of ministerial diaries. It was a major victory for press freedom and contemporary political history. Where Richard Crossman had ventured, Barbara Castle and Tony Benn would follow. A unique source on Wilson's governments was to become available, long before access was allowed to public papers under the thirty-year rule.

Shortly after the last newspaper extract on 11 April, Wilson had set up a committee of privy councillors, under Lord Radcliffe, to consider the publication of ministerial memoirs. The committee sat during the Crossman trial, completing its report on 16 December. Wilson was among those who gave oral evidence. Widgery's ruling muddied the area of ministerial memoirs. Whitehall now looked to Radcliffe for its defence. The committee endorsed the conventions first announced to parliament in 1946, arguing that they should 'be regarded as concessions made to the author, rather than as restrictions imposed on him'.[125] Former ministers were free to write about their careers. In the areas of national security and international relations, the prime minister was to have the final say. On the question of collective responsibility, ex-ministers were to wait fifteen years or until civil servants had retired. The cabinet secretary was to check manuscripts against the rules, on behalf of the prime minister. The law was considered inappropriate, though the Radcliffe committee observed that the official secrets act, and civil law, were still in place. It was effectively a question of honour, and ministers, on taking and leaving office, were to have their attention drawn to their obligations. In the case of diarists, they should make provision in their wills for any publication. The first volume of *The Diaries of a Cabinet Minister* came out that month, to be followed by two more in 1976 and 1977.

The prime miniser wanted to accept the Radcliffe report when it came to cabinet on 15 January 1976, but Tony Benn was in favour of more open government. It was considered again on 21 January, with Foot, Castle and Benn putting up resistance. The Radcliffe report was published the following day, with an accompanying prime ministerial statement saying that ministers would be asked 'to sign an appropriate declaration'[126] to the effect that they had been made aware of the rules. The prime minister was slow to request affirmation, and Jenkins, Foot, Crosland, Benn, Shore and Castle declined. Wilson then told the cabinet secretary, on the eve of his retirement, that it would be unrealistic to ask his successor as prime minister to pursue the matter, but Radcliffe's guidelines were included in the Questions of Procedure for Ministers, prepared when Callaghan became prime minister. Wilson was to defend the idea of a closed period of fifteen years, and chide Harold Macmillan, in 1978, for observing a ten-year rule in his six volumes of memoirs.

The October 1974 general election had seen the return of eleven SNP and three Plaid Cymru MPs, and Northern Ireland contributed in its own complex way to the devolution debate. Scotland posed the greatest threat to labour rule, the SNP being the challenger in a further forty-two seats north of the border, thirty-five of which were held by labour. This was enough to threaten labour's position as a party of government. Wilson had brought Dr Norman Hunt, as Lord Crowther-Hunt, into the government, to help Ted Short with the legislation. Devolution was considered at a cabinet committee meeting on Friday, 17 January 1975 held at Chequers. The majority view on the cabinet committee was that devolution for Scotland and Wales was necessary to counter the nationalists, but Tony Benn saw devolution as subordinate to the question of Europe. Membership of the EEC meant the break-up of the United Kingdom; he believed that industrial democracy was a better way of sharing power. The same ministers returned to Chequers on Monday, 16 June. The doubters were still seeking to delay government action, but Tony Benn favoured publication of a white paper. A third Chequers meeting on Wednesday, 10 September rehearsed the principles yet again. Barbara Castle came up with the formula of legislative proposals, and these were promised in the 1975 queen's speech. A second white paper, *Our Changing Democracy: Devolution to Scotland and Wales*, was published on 27 November, but there was to be no enactment for national assemblies in that session. Jim Sillars, and another Scottish labour MP, defected from the party in the following months, to set up their own Scottish labour party. Nationalism was being seen as a stimulus to socialism north of the border.

The five-day debate in the commons was opened by the prime minister on 13 January 1976. Wilson explained that the directly elected assembly in Wales was only to have executive functions, while the Scottish assembly in Edinburgh would also be a legislative body. Both were to elect their own executives. This was the state of play when Wilson handed over to his successor.

The parliamentary session which began after the second 1974 election ran through to 12 November 1975, and was one of the busiest in post-war history. The government began with an effective overall majority of only three, which dropped to one after the West Woolwich by-election in June 1975, the first of seven seats labour was to lose in that parliament. 1975 was the year of the EEC referendum and important foreign trips for Wilson, and at home it saw the £6 incomes policy and important domestic legislation. The government had promised in the queen's speech the previous November to set up ACAS. Labour would tackle 'the lump' in the construction industry, and protect dockers' jobs. There was to be reform of the social security and pensions systems, as Barbara Castle integrated occupational pension schemes into the earnings-related state system. By aiding the growth of pension funds, she unwittingly brought about, what Wilson has called, 'an economic and financial revolution perhaps greater than all the post-war nationalization measures put together'.[127] There were also proposals for the community ownership of development land. In order to secure a share of North Sea oil profits, a British National Oil Corporation (BNOC) was to be established by Lord Balogh, later the deputy chairman of BNOC. Wilson had also anticipated the formation of the national enterprise board, bringing Sir Don Ryder into the cabinet office, as industrial adviser, to report directly to the prime minister. Wilson quickly became involved in rescuing British Leyland, recommending, in March 1975, its division into four units as part of a capital investment programme. When the industry bill was finally enacted in November, the company became the principal responsibility of the NEB. Wilson had already hailed the NEB as 'the biggest leap forward in economic thinking as well as in economic policy'.[128] Wilson was keen that the industry bill should not 'operate like an industrial rogue elephant'.[129] With Eric Varley as secretary of state, its guidelines were to be made public. Development agencies for Scotland and Wales were to be legislated in the following parliamentary session.

Aside from the special case of industry, the prime minister seems to have kept to his promise of not interfering in his ministers' work. He addressed labour MPs shortly before he led the party into a general election for the fifth time, espousing the idea of 'collective leadership'. 'I hold it self-evident', he said, 'that this Party cannot be led by anyone except on the basis of a collective leadership which includes every strand of thought and idealism.'[130] He proclaimed labour the 'natural party of Government'[131] at the 1974 party conference, hastily organized for the end of November in London. Callaghan was in the chair, and he was effusive in the extreme at the end of Wilson's parliamentary report. 'Your contribution, Harold, in the first 74 years of our birth will probably never be surpassed', said Callaghan, 'and I doubt very much if it will be equalled.'[132]

The 1975 conference at Blackpool was to be Wilson's last as leader. He chose to rail against factionalism in the party in his parliamentary report. 'The activities of small groups of inflexible political persuasion, extreme so-called left (Applause) and in a few cases extreme so-called moderates (Applause) having in common only their arrogant dogmatism.'[133] He appeared even-handed, in condemning both left and right, but Wilson's enemy was principally the left. It had not worried him unduly in the past, but a post-1968 left was entering the party to capture the conference, and influence the executive, under the emerging leadership of Tony Benn. Wilson's uncharacteristic outspokenness signalled an internal struggle, in which he would not have to participate. It was one of his strongest speeches to a party conference in many years. There was no similar declaration of war against the right. It was to be another six years before they broke away from the party.

Wilson claims the period from the queen's speech on 19 November, to the end of 1975, was 'the most hectic [he had] ever known either as Prime Minister or as a member of ... Attlee's ... Cabinet'.[134] This was hardly because of the legislative programme. Few major measures were proposed, and the shipbuilding and aircraft bill was reintroduced, only to fail again. The major provisions were the phasing out of private practice in the national health service (NHS), and the abolition of selection in secondary education.

This was a thin programme, occasioned by the government's tiny parliamentary majority. When the two Scottish labour MPs defected in December, the government's overall majority disappeared. Wilson's administration was again a minority one, and it became a question of constructing votes on each and every measure. The two defectors could probably be relied upon to support the government, if it came to a vote of confidence. It was fortuitous for the prime minister that his last few months were not to be dominated by a succession of major parliamentary defeats. Barbara Castle's proposal to abolish pay beds in NHS hospitals angered the doctors, and Lord Goodman was summoned yet again. The government agreed to phase out the beds, and allow its doctors to work in private hospitals. A second crisis arose that autumn. The Chrysler Corporation of Detroit decided upon the closure of its British subsidiary, which employed 27,000 people. Wilson invited John Riccardo, the company chairman, to dinner at Chequers, on 3 November. He accused Chrysler of seeking to blackmail the government, but asked for talks on possible restructuring. The department of industry was prepared to let the company pull out of Britain, given its falling share of the market and the government's commitment to British Leyland. Eric Varley leaked this to the press.

Harold Lever nevertheless believed parts of Chrysler were viable. When Scottish ministers threatened to resign, Wilson backed the retention of the company's plant at Linwood near Glasgow. He was prepared to sacrifice Coventry. This decision was taken by the cabinet on 12 December, a planning agreement being a condition for financial help – the only one in private industry. According to his senior policy adviser, Wilson had 'wished to settle at almost any price'.[135]

CHAPTER 24

Towards Resignation, 1975–6

Joe Haines claims that, by early 1975, 'the physical and mental strains of thirty years at the top were beginning to show.'[1] He dates Wilson's weariness from the writing of his book, but it was the pressures of office which produced signs of stress. 'Whenever we had a major event, like visiting overseas leaders – there was one particular one with Helmut Schmidt [in November 1974] – he would get a severe stomach upset ... He was no longer able to do the job.'[2] Wilson was also unwell during the Paris summit in December. 'Undoubtedly he was bored with government', Donoughue admits, 'having seen it all before and he was fed up with managing the squabbles within the Labour party, where many on the left wing seemed more interested in attacking the Labour leadership than in resisting the return of a Conservative Government.'[3] Robin Wilson's wife, Joy, gave birth to twins on 13 March 1975, and the prime minister was called out of the cabinet to hear he had become a grandfather. Harold Wilson began to talk of going within months.

The treasury bounce, on Monday, 30 June, was probably the decisive event. Wilson was so shaken by the financial crisis that he countenanced a statutory incomes policy. Haines had a row with the prime minister outside the cabinet room, and told him – probably in anger – he should resign. Donoughue was present. Wilson rang his press secretary, in the early hours of 1 July, to say he was going to resist the treasury, and remarked at some point: '"Joe, the trouble is that when old problems recur I reach for the old solutions."'[4] He was thinking of 1966. 'He realized that he was no longer up to the job. That was the basic thing ... And to his great credit he recognized it, which is why he got out.'[5] Bernard Donoughue quotes Wilson as saying on one occasion that '"[he had] been round this racetrack so often that [he could] not generate any more enthusiasm for jumping any more hurdles."' It was 'perhaps the single most important reason'[6] for going. Andrew Graham remembers a similar metaphorical phrase from that summer, and Marcia Falkender confirms that Wilson decided to go in July

1975. He was to tell his cabinet colleagues that he decided not to go in September 1975, because of 'the paramount importance of ensuring the national acceptance and success of the counter-inflation policy',[7] but, for much of July, he was determined to go after the summer. When he asked workers to 'give a year for Britain',[8] in a broadcast on the economic crisis, Marcia Falkender seized upon this phrase to argue that he had to see his policy through. Wilson may have discussed resignation at Chequers on Sunday 3 August, with the cabinet due to meet there the following day. Marcia Falkender was certainly present. The idea of an announcement at the party conference was abandoned: a labour prime minister springing his resignation on the delegates would lead to unedifying electioneering. Wilson had a second deadline – Christmas – but Marcia Falkender opposed this as impractical. She sensed that too many families would be disturbed by a message that would be considered dramatic rather than seasonal. The prime minister's mind may not have been made up entirely, but it was probably on the Scillies, later that month, that he abandoned the October option. He and Mary spent some time with the queen at Balmoral in September, the customary prime ministerial visit. Wilson finally acted at the party conference at the end of the month, asking Joe Haines and Ken Stowe, his new principal private secretary, to prepare a timetable for retirement. He asked that no copies be made, and Haines possesses the original. 'People don't believe the simple explanations', he says. 'There is no great revelation.'[9] Mary Wilson wrote 'D-Day in very large letters'[10] in her diary for one day the following March, but Marcia Falkender was not keen on leaving number 10, and, 'throughout the winter of 1975–6, she fought and argued with [Wilson] over his decision to resign.'[11] The end of Wilson would be the end of her.

The prime minister had never found it easy to keep a secret. He entertained George Thomas, at Chequers, immediately after the party conference, and told him about the intended resignation during that weekend. Harold Wilson first informed the queen directly of his imminent resignation at Buckingham Palace on 9 December. The prime minister dined that evening with leading press barons at the invitation of Lord Goodman, and attempted to preempt his resignation becoming a source of gossip. Wilson turned to Goodman towards the end of the dinner and said: '"Oh, Arnold, I mentioned that matter to the Queen."' Wilson recalled:

He felt I had done it a little crudely, and that my meaning would be recognized – but it was not. My reason for doing this was that when I finally resigned I knew I could safely count on at least one or two papers knowingly saying that my real reason was not the one stated: in those last months paper after paper was telephoning anxious enquiries about stories that I had this or that serious syndrome, most of them terminal.[12]

This story is believable, given Wilson's reputation for deviousness. He had always disliked public references to his state of health, and he was in fact to be unwell before Christmas. A new year's visit to Egypt had to be cancelled. Haines mentions that Wilson often had to deal with 500 submissions in his red boxes during his weekends at Chequers, and this increase in paperwork squeezed out much needed recreation. He let the machine take him over, and needed to use Chequers for longer periods, but it was doing him little good because he looked 'yellow and lined'.[13] Marcia Falkender acknowledges that, 'by the beginning of 1976, those of us close to Harold Wilson ... had begun to feel ourselves in a curious political no-man's land – a sort of twilight period before the end.'[14] There was a certain insecurity on the part of some Wilson appointees, and the future of the counter-inflation unit seemed to be in doubt. Marcia Falkender was hoping Joe Haines would take it over, but she also wanted Wilson to stay. 'He himself was quite aware that he might be forced to change his mind because of, say, a run on sterling or the need for a vote of confidence in the House.'[15]

Barbara Castle went to see Wilson in number 10 on Thursday, 4 March, to tell him of her intention of going in the autumn. 'He was relaxed and talkative, full of his ploy on privacy and the press, which he told me with great satisfaction he was going to develop in a speech that weekend.'[16] When Castle asked about his next ministerial reshuffle, Wilson swore his closest political friend to secrecy. He informed her of his own decision:

> I want to talk to you as an old friend who has always been loyal to me, [he said]. You are the only person I know who never leaks. I am getting tired of this job. I've spent thirteen years trying to keep this party together and it's been a pretty thankless task. Do you know I have only been to the theatre about twenty times in all those years? Because I have had to keep on top of everything that is happening. Every weekend I have about ten one-hundred-page documents to read – and I read them all. It's the only way. I have to think of everything ... When I became PM this time I told the Queen the date on which I would retire from this job. She's got the record of it, so no one will be able to say afterwards that I was pushed out.[17]

He declined to tell Castle the date he had given the queen, mentioning Rhodesia and Northern Ireland as possible reasons for staying on for six months or so. A sterling crisis was to break the following day, but it only delayed his resignation announcement. 'It was soon obvious', Callaghan was to write of 11 March 1976, 'that his mind was totally made up and he would not be deflected.'[18]

Much thought had been given to the politics of Wilson's resignation. Salisbury, Campbell-Bannerman, MacDonald, Churchill, Eden and Macmillan had all gone on grounds of health or age. Bonar Law died in office. 'Of all the Prime Ministers in the present century[,] Harold Wilson is the only one who came to an end of his own volition. Baldwin would come nearest to him in this respect. But Baldwin, we are told, had a nervous breakdown before his last year in office and another one at the end of it.'[19] Four – Balfour, Asquith, Lloyd George and Chamberlain – were forced to resign. Attlee, Home and Heath were defeated in elections. 'I thought the nation would be stunned and shocked', Marcia Falkender was to write, 'at the sudden disappearance of this man whom they had come to regard as a permanent fixture in their lives – right or wrong, agree or disagree, Labour or Tory, Harold Wilson was there. I felt that it was something that should happen more gradually and at a time when things were easier.'[20]

Harold Wilson also wanted 'to discourage others attributing [his] "sudden" resignation to an impending national crisis, or, as one newspaper blatantly [would seek] to suggest, some great revelation which would shortly break on the world – whether a bank robbery or genocide was not [to be] specified.'[21] He makes no mention of scandal, but it has been impossible to avoid this putative explanation since 1976. 'No scandal', Marcia Falkender was to write in 1983, '[has] surfaced either then or subsequently.'[22] Scandal – in the context of English prurience – usually means sex, money being less of a problem. Joe Haines was to write of his time with Wilson in 1977, and his book would be serialized in the *Daily Mirror* shortly before publication. Haines was to be accused of sensationalism, though he describes his account as an 'understatement'.[23] He made no reference to scandal, describing Wilson as having resigned 'for a variety of reasons'.[24] Bernard Donoughue would also publish an account of his time in Downing Street in 1987, and denies there was any 'impending scandal'.[25] Haines would have much to say about Falkender, and Donoughue a little about both of his former colleagues. They have all gone in different directions since working at number 10, but these three independent accounts published over a period of ten years correspond. Harold Wilson did not resign because of some threatening scandal.

Wilson had failed to script his last major dramatic political performance, but it is possible to analyse the personal and political forces operating upon him from 1974.

First, his wife Mary. It was no secret that she would have preferred him to pursue a career other than politics. She was quoted in the *Sunday Times Magazine* in early 1964: '"When he comes home after a bad day I say why don't you go back to Oxford? I lie awake worrying, but he can go straight to sleep.'[26] Mary Wilson, with her two sons, stuck faithfully by him when he was prime minister, but she also chose to exclude herself from some of the duties of consort. 'She tried to fix a system of priorities: "Family and friends first. Labour Party engagements next; then duties concerned with Number 10, and then engagements [she] would accept [her]self."'[27] She was to recall with affection the three commonwealth conferences her husband attended, the liveliness and lack of snobbery contrasting with the British style of political life. Mary Wilson was no doubt delighted when he decided to give up the burdens of office.

Secondly, Marcia Falkender. She had, by her own admission, tried to persuade him to stay in office. There can be no doubt that Marcia Falkender was increasingly verbally violent to the prime minister and his associates from 1974. 'It was a curious aspect of Mr Wilson's tolerant and apparently masochistic character that he always invited contradiction and harsh comments in private from those working close to him.'[28] Joe Haines would testify to Marcia Falkender's hysteria at great length, and Bernard Donoughue acknowledges the press secretary's book as an important source 'on the realities of life inside Harold Wilson's Downing Street'.[29] But he also refers to 'the bizarre fratricide within [Wilson's] own personal team',[30] which does not necessarily excuse Haines's own contribution to an unpleasant atmosphere. 'Marcia Williams', writes Donoughue, 'was often humiliatingly severe as well as perceptive in her remarks, and Joe Haines was totally incapable of being a lackey to anyone.'[31] Others tend to blame Haines as much as Falkender. Wilson and Haines were to separate, but his relationship with Marcia Falkender would continue. Haines's view of her impact on Wilson in 1976 is credible: 'She was a substantial part of the burden which made him too tired, mentally and physically, to contemplate changing his mind and carrying on.'[32]

Thirdly, the labour party. Harold Wilson had been leader for thirteen years. This was something less than Attlee's two decades at the top, but six of those years had been during the war when there was a national consensus. Wilson contrasted the two leaderships before the summer recess in 1974, when he told the parliamentary party that Attlee had had 'a pliant National Executive'.[33] Wilson lost control of his executive in the early 1970s (though claimed he had been in a minority from 1968), and only attended two of the ten meetings in 1974-5. He had also had to read the riot act to the party conference, and wrote later of his speech to delegates in 1975: 'had the different varieties [of the left] been locked in a room without food or water until they produced an agreed policy statement, the mortality rate would have been high. All they could conceivably agree on would be the destruction of our present system of society, without any named positive replacement.'[34] He was to win the vote of confidence on his sixtieth birthday, but the parliamentary party had also become unmanageable. Wilson told them on 30 July 1974: 'Just as ... I am the custodian of the Manifesto on which we were elected, so equally am I custodian of the constitutional position of the Government, and its relations with all other Bodies. As Attlee was.'[35]

Wilson was making himself increasingly vulnerable. His arrogant statements about his leadership reveal growing insecurity, an admission that time was nearly up. His challenges to the conference, national executive, and party constitution would do much to stimulate the campaign for internal reforms of the labour party. This emperor was rapidly losing his clothes, and Harold Wilson would have felt the chill. He had lost the support of the parliamentary party, in April 1975, over the EEC, and his victory in the referendum did little to strengthen his leadership of the party. Marcia Falkender has argued that, 'if [Wilson] had been staying on, I have no doubt he would have formulated an effective strategy to deal with [the left]',[36] but it is by no means certain that a labour prime minister could have done this in the mid-1970s. Splitting the labour party would have been a poor epitaph for the man who had done so much to keep it united.

Fourthly, the government. During his second premiership, Wilson succeeded in keeping the ship of state off the rocks. There had been a general progression in his first two administrations. This is certainly the case with the balance of payments, though *In Place of Strife* was an unfortunate blemish towards the end. His third and fourth administrations were relatively less successful. It is certainly true that Wilson kept Britain in the EEC, but the prime minister helped the establishment by appealing directly to the people. Wilson was left with a minority government at the end of 1975, and was to acknowledge that it began to run out of steam after the loss of the West Woolwich seat and the Scottish labour party defections. Wilson did carry the £6 incomes policy and public expenditure cuts, but it was the latter, in combination with the problem of the doctors and the threatened Chrysler pull-out, which saw him claim that 'December 1975 was by far the most hectic and harrowing month [he had] experienced in nearly eight years as Prime Minister.'[37]

Wilson was to tell the public when he announced he was going, that 'there [were] no impending problems or difficulties – economic or political – known to the Cabinet, which are not known to the country.'[38] This rebuttal of the charge that he was running away from responsibility was another Wilsonian subterfuge. Things were to get worse – much worse – after April 1976, and this was known, or could have been anticipated, at the time of his resignation. Wilson must have been sniffing the political air, and would have realized he could not improve on his reputation by staying. It did not require great foresight to see what lay up ahead.

First, labour was to lose three seats to the conservatives in by-elections within a year. Wilson's successor would agree a pact with the liberals, in which parliamentary support was offered in return for a say on policy. There was to be no devolution of power to Scotland and Wales, and the Ulster unionists became an important part of the parliamentary opposition. Michael Foot was to increase their parliamentary strength at Westminster, in a deal for support. Secondly, unemployment was still rising in early 1976. A 4.5 per cent incomes policy agreement with the TUC, later in the year, further tested the social contract. There were to be even more public expenditure cuts in July, which would not avert an autumn sterling crisis, nor a deal with the IMF at the end of the year, which involved increased taxation and further cuts. Monetarism took root in the British polity in 1976. Thirdly, the new labour prime minister was to seek to perpetuate Wilson's tough line with groups in the parliamentary party. But the left under Tony Benn, and against the background of growing union disenchantment, was to promote its alternative economic strategy. Roy Jenkins would decamp for Europe in September 1976, but the prince waited to be called back from Brussels. He would proclaim a future for the right outside the party after the winter of discontent of 1978–9, though the rest – the social democratic party – is already history. The labour government was brought down in March 1979, after five years in office; like the wounded beast it was, it took only one vote – that of Gerry Fitt – to finish it off. It was the first vote of confidence lost by a government since 1924, and the conservatives were returned to power in the subsequent general election. Between 1976 and 1979, the ground for the politics of the 1980s was to be prepared. James Callaghan could hint to Bernard Donoughue at the seachange in British politics, when the forces of Thatcherism reached the gate of Whitehall, with a trite image of a thirty-year historical cycle. It was an endearing utterance of philosophical detachment on the part of Callaghan. Harold Wilson, in contrast, could never have admitted, in 1979, the game might be up, though he would probably have gone to the country in the autumn of 1978.

A moment of counter-factual speculation is appropriate in every life, and absolutely crucial in a discussion of Harold Wilson's exeunt. If he had not resigned in 1976, when could he have gone with dignity? He would have had to have led labour into another general election, which would undoubtedly have been his second defeat. His leadership would have been worthless, and his historical reputation even further devalued. Harold Wilson would have been forced out of British politics, by resignation, with rival packs of labour wolves howling for blood.

Harold Wilson could have resigned as labour leader in 1970, but he needed an electoral victory before he departed. He had largely ceased to play the role of party unifier by 1974, the only one he was suited to perform (Edward Short was to write of this being one of the Wilsonian laws of politics.) Wilson's difficulties that year flowed from the fact that labour formed the government, as can be seen in the split on continuing EEC membership. He had long been attentive to the exercise of state power in Britain, and for him there were no other politics. Principle always implied impotence for Wilson, but it was increasingly difficult to reconcile capitalist management with working-class advance. Tony Benn was to say in 1976: 'I really think politics is about education and not management',[39] an admission that labourism had had its day. If Wilson had discovered the limits of corporatism in the 1960s, Edward Heath proved its inapplicability to British capitalism in the early 1970s. Harold Wilson must have been aware, by 1976, that his experience of politics was becoming outdated. He quit at a relatively young age, but after thirty-six years in Whitehall and Westminster. Nearly eight of those had been at the top. He had arrived in Whitehall at the dawn of a new political era, the age of consensus politics originated under Winston Churchill. Keynes and Beveridge were to be considered its prophets. The era was to be perpetuated by all post-war governments, of left and right. That it broke down is clear, though expiration is variously located in 1976 or 1979. Harold Wilson fits exactly into an historical epoch, an aesthetic delight of real biography, allowing a human form to express the times. His name will be inextricably associated in British history with the 1960s and 1970s. For Harold Wilson the show came to an end, as it always does, and he was enough of a nimble political performer not to be hit by the curtain as it closed.

Harold Wilson resigned because he came to lose faith in himself. The knocks were becoming punishing, and he was no prime minister born to rule. As labour leader he was constrained by his party, especially its stunted and hand-me-down vision. Even Harold Wilson found he had limits. His voluntary departure from Downing Street, in 1976, was a twentieth-century first, but it was also an admission that the politics of labourism were virtually played out. He would tell Roy Jenkins in Brussels, in April 1977, that he did not think there was any future for the labour government, or party, coalitionism being the only solution. Wilson had already allowed himself to be washed up on the shore of cold-war rhetoric, and this in an age of détente, from the one British politician who had frequently visited the Soviet Union. He took to describing political obligations in his last months as 'boring'.[40] This was no simple regression to the satiation of pampered youth, but how Harold Wilson came to feel about himself, his office and the country. His ennui may have been battle fatigue, but it was also lack of imagination and, ultimately, a failure of duty as a socialist leader. It is not surprising he had difficulty explaining his resignation. For a deeply conformist Englishman, born outside the structure of power, Harold Wilson wanted to go down in history as above all patriotic. Sir Harold (and later, Lord) Wilson was all that was left. How could a political leader of the party of progress say there was no promised land in 1976, only bureaucratic problems of amplifying complexity which had finally defeated the ambitious administrator, while labour was dividing between socialist fundamentalism and managerial realists with their own mythologies?

Harold Wilson was not the only British political leader to go in the mid-1970s. Both the conservative and liberal parties underwent cyclical changes, in the case of the former, with the emergence of Margaret Thatcher. The fall of Jeremy Thorpe would presage the end of a great – now minor – party. Thatcher became leader of the opposition a year before Wilson resigned, and his departure was quickly followed by that of Thorpe. All this produced some excitement at the top of British politics. Who was in, out, where, why, when and how, provided British print and broadcasting journalists with enough questions, not to need any answers. All change at the top in 1975–6 was to be a nodal point in British political history, the key to which lay in 1973–4 when the miners – assisted by OPEC – brought about the fall of a British government.

Harold Wilson was not greatly perturbed by the emergence of Margaret Thatcher, when she secured 130 votes on 4 February 1975 to Heath's 119. Barbara Castle 'felt a sneaking feminist pleasure',[41] but was unable to elicit any opinion from Wilson. On the day the final result was announced, she found the prime minister enjoying an official dinner at New Zealand House: 'Nothing like a bit of sex challenge for bringing the best out in a man.'[42] Wilson had paid a courtesy call on Thatcher earlier in her new room in the commons, but this was considered less chivalry and more a breach of parliamentary convention. The prime minister was, no doubt, pleased that Heath would not be leading the opposition's challenge to the EEC renegotiations. But he became perturbed about the former conservative leader after the referendum, having been informed that Heath had been to Jenkins's country cottage at East Hendred in Oxfordshire. Wilson began to fear his home secretary was seeking to construct a coalition government, this being an old obsession on the left of British politics. It is said that leading members of the labour cabinet were delighted at Thatcher's election, believing the tories would lose the next election. Marcia Falkender and Peter Shore were not so sure. Tony Benn looked forward to the end of centrist politics. Barbara Castle considered Thatcher a professional politician, and thought a woman leader would have a political knock-on effect on the labour party. 'To me', she wrote, 'socialism isn't just militant trade unionism. It is the gentle society, in which every producer remembers he [sic] is a consumer too.'[43]

Harold Wilson was more concerned with the liberal party, which had done badly in the second 1974 election. Jeremy Thorpe, as leader, found himself coming under challenge from his parliamentary colleagues. A department of trade report criticized him, on 29 January 1976, for his role as director of London and County Securities, a fringe bank which had collapsed. Here was the making of a real political indictment, but it was to be obscured by a sexual scandal. On the same day a man calling himself Norman Scott was charged in a Barnstaple court with a minor supplementary benefits fraud. Scott alleged – not for the first time – that he was being harassed, because of a homosexual relationship he had once had with the liberal leader.

Thorpe was quick to deny any such impropriety, but the press uncovered the fact that Peter Bessell, liberal MP for Bodmin in 1964–70, paid money to Scott, for a year or so, presumably to keep him quiet. Tony Benn had heard a rumour the previous month that Thorpe was being blackmailed, but it was Marcia Falkender who responded quickly to the reports of Scott's courtroom outburst. (Joe Haines had known all about Thorpe in February 1974, and two senior party members, afraid that the liberal leader might enter a coalition under Heath, considered broadcasting the Scott story.) Marcia Falkender pressured Wilson on 30 January 1976 to come to the liberal leader's rescue, the prime minister immediately attributing it to South Africa. Wilson had been friends with Thorpe since 1964, and used him as a secret envoy to Rhodesia. But the prime minister, to say nothing of Lady Falkender, had his own reasons for bringing South Africa into the story.

The prime minister asked Sir John Hunt for a report on Pretoria's agents in Britain, this being a request to MI5. He also seems to have done some briefing, because, the following day, the *Daily Mirror* carried a report about Gordon Winter, a Yorkshire-born, South African journalist, who had been trying to interest the British press in Thorpe. Winter had heard Norman Scott's story in 1971, but had only been able to drop hints about Thorpe in *Private Eye*. The *Mirror* alleged Winter had connections with the South African Bureau of State Security (BOSS), a charge he would subsequently exploit to great personal financial effect.

Harold Wilson came to Thorpe's room in the commons on the afternoon of 3 February, and asked to see the liberal leader at 4.00 p.m., after the election of George Thomas as speaker. The prime minister may not yet have heard from the security service. The two leaders spoke for thirty minutes in the prime minister's room on privy councillor terms, Thorpe later telling a colleague, Cyril Smith, that 'it's good. It will be pushed on to South Africa ... The P.M. believes that there are South African influences at work.'[44]

Thorpe would say on 27 October 1977, after Wilson and he had gone: 'I had no reason to disbelieve this, coming from so authoritative a source. I did not myself promote this belief, and it is fair to say that Sir Harold himself has now expressed his doubts.'[45] Thorpe clutched at the South African connection in February 1976, on the eve of meeting his parliamentary colleagues. Wilson gave every appearance of believing the story at the time, but Thorpe also fed the prime minister's suspicions. He gave Wilson a memorandum from Peter Hain, chairman of the young liberals, drawn up on 24 February, in which Hain recounted a meeting – also on 3 February – with a businessman called Kenneth Wyatt, who alleged that the Anglo-American Corporation of South Africa was out to discredit British public figures. His information was second hand, and Hain was cautious, but he passed the allegation to Thorpe. When Hain met the liberal leader at the house of commons, Thorpe said to him '"I have the three most powerful pillars of the state on my side – Harold Wilson, Lord Goodman and MI5."'[46] Goodman was now Thorpe's solicitor.

The prime minister lunched at the commons on 4 February 1976, and told some of his colleagues the South African government was behind the Norman Scott revelations. Agents of the apartheid regime were out to discredit the liberal leader, because of his party's strong opposition to its policies. 'He hinted darkly that he knew all about that sort of thing and had his spies working on it, because he had been the victim of it: the theft of his own confidential papers.' Barbara Castle wanted him to 'deal with it coolly, discreetly and silently, as a calculated expression of political principle, instead of in this erratic and dramatic Goldfinger way'.[47] Thorpe survived the weekly meeting of the parliamentary liberal party that Wednesday, refuting all allegations. He argued that his personal popularity was crucial for the party, but this was only to provoke Scott to make further charges.

Wilson discussed the matter with Castle again on 5 February. 'He believes that the Tories, or someone even more sinister, put Scott up to announcing his alleged association with Jeremy. "The Tories had this information as long ago as 1972. Why didn't they use it then? My theory is that they thought it would rebound on Heath."'[48] Wilson still seems to have believed Thorpe, but the problem was less the truth, and more the use to which information was being put. He asked Castle to find out who had decided to prosecute Scott, thereby giving him a platform in court, and she put Jack Straw, her political adviser, to work on Scott's personal file. The permanent secretary at the department was informed. Castle reported to Wilson before cabinet on Thursday, 12 February. 'Harold's face dropped a bit when I told him it seemed to show Jeremy's relationship with Scott had been longer and more domesticated than he had so far admitted. My aim is to warn Harold against going overboard for Jeremy too recklessly.'[49] Wilson had already attacked the press for hounding Thorpe, only to be criticized for this in a *Daily Mirror* editorial that day. 'He really is an incredible mixture of caution and recklessness',[50] Barbara Castle concluded.

Wilson joined Castle at lunchtime, at the communal table in the members' dining room, on Tuesday, 9 March. As labour MPs drifted away, Wilson was left with Castle. The prime minister confided that

BOSS was behind the Thorpe story. '"It's been a great detective exercise, I can tell you"', he said. '"Detective Inspector Falkender has been up to her eyes in it. I've got conclusive evidence that South African money has been involved. After all, she's been through the same thing. So have I. No Minister or political party is safe unless we expose this."'[51] He inferred that his source was MI5, by referring back to a meeting he had had with Macmillan about Profumo. Wilson was prepared to reveal the evidence to Thatcher on privy councillor terms, if she challenged him. 'Those of us who were left were completely mystified', Castle recorded, 'but Harold was like a Boy Scout playing cops and robbers. He was chuckling at the way he had arranged to make his great announcement that afternoon through the medium of a Question that was only remotely to do with it ... I almost despair of him. I can see him getting involved again in a complicated manoeuvre which will merely make him look devious rather than a Sir Galahad.'[52]

Wilson had arranged for James Wellbeloved, a right-wing labour MP, to ask a supplementary question that afternoon, which the prime minister himself had drafted. Planting questions was not unusual, but it was unparliamentary to boast about it. Wellbeloved duly asked if there was any South African involvement in the 'framing' of leading liberals. The prime minister replied that he had 'no doubt at all there [was] a strong South African participation in recent activities relating to' Thorpe. It was privately masterminded, and 'based on massive resources of business money and private agents of various kinds and various qualities'. He went on to exclude 'the South African government or its agencies ... [from] these unsavoury activities'.[53] Barbara Castle was sitting beside Callaghan, and asked the foreign secretary if he knew anything. Callaghan shook his head. '"What is it all about?" I went on. "I haven't a clue", he replied.'[54] As for Tony Benn, he thought Wilson was trying to defend the liberal party for electoral reasons, gain credit for coming to Thorpe's rescue, and, possibly, scapegoat South Africa because he feared a scandal involving himself. The *Mirror* responded positively to Wilson the next day, but the paper could not desist from pursuing the follies of Jeremy Thorpe. Cyril Smith was in hospital on 9 March: 'I was certainly baffled when I read the papers, and remain baffled to this day. Of all the enigmas attached to the Thorpe Affair, Harold Wilson's intervention is the most mystifying.'[55]

It is certainly perplexing, and the prime minister seems to have been caught up in something he was unable to control. He was fighting against an enemy, which, in his own mind, changed identity, South Africa being merely the latest in a line of bogies. The starting point was the land deals affair. He had also mentioned, on 4 February, his missing tax papers. Wilson may have been correct to infer that professional burglars were after his papers, and, in 1974 and 1975, he associated the break-ins with Fleet Street election scares. He suspected the tories might be behind it all. Wilson would persist with this theory after he left office, not submitting his evidence to the royal commission on the press until April 1977. But there was barely a suggestion then that South Africa was responsible for the burglaries, nor had there been before 3 February 1976, when he first discussed Thorpe's difficulties. BOSS may, or may not, have been involved, and the wave of Wilson burglaries, about which he was to become obsessed, may, or may not, have been part of a non-political crime wave. Peter Wright would claim his jobs for MI5 were not detected, so his friends from Pretoria were presumably just as skilled, but, according to Peter Bessell, 'it must be stressed that not a scintilla of evidence has been found to suggest that the South African Government had any connection with the scandal that engulfed Jeremy and the Liberal Party.'[56] It is not clear what the South Africans would have been trying to achieve with a labour prime minister in London. The party had long opposed apartheid, and it was now more left wing. But Wilson had dealt with the regime in the 1960s, despite an arms ban, and he renewed the ban when he returned to office in 1974. The Simonstown agreement was brought to an end, but the British navy did not immediately break off contact with the South Africans. Wilson and his colleagues allowed some existing contracts to be completed. There was room here for diplomacy on the part of Pretoria, which would only be disrupted by dirty tricks, disinformation or attempts to discredit the British prime minister. Wilson deliberately refrained in his parliamentary answer from accusing the South African government, because – as he explained to Castle beforehand – he needed Pretoria's help over Rhodesia.

The problem of Ian Smith had returned to haunt the British government on 13 February, when Lord Robens reported to Callaghan on a visit he had paid to Salisbury. The foreign office was forced to pay attention to the possibility of a settlement through March. Callaghan revealed the government's position to the house of commons six days after Wilson said he was going. It is certain the prime minister had been kept informed, and unlikely that he tried to sabotage Callaghan's initiative. A Rhodesian, not South African, agent had managed to get information from number 10 when Wilson was first prime minister. A secretary in the cabinet office, Helen Keenan, had been sentenced to six months in 1967, for stealing papers on Rhodesia, which were passed to a Norman Blackburn. Blackburn admitted to being a Rhodesian special branch officer, though there may have been some South African connection. 'It was Harold Wilson's first major encounter with espionage.'[57] If there were any African dirty tricks in the 1970s, they were more likely associated with the rebel regime in Salisbury. The Rhodesian intelligence chief, Ken Flower, was to admit before he died that 'a crude smear campaign by him against Wilson and Thorpe [was] organised in Britain and the US.'[58] It may be possible to link Flower with the Wilson burglaries, and Norman Scott's court appearance, in the absence of less fanciful explanations, but it is difficult to associate such activity with Ian Smith's political overture to the British government in early 1976.

Wilson seems to have plumped for South Africa, and then disregarded the information he got from his security service. Falkender knew about Gordon Winter on 30 January, but it is unlikely MI5 would have reported by 3 February. The prime minister heard sometime later in the month, judging by his conversation with Castle on 9 March. *Panorama* would claim in late 1988 that the cabinet office 'pointed the finger'[59] at BOSS, but this is not very precise. In 1978, Chapman Pincher correctly described Hunt's report as coming from MI5, but, citing a private conversation with Wilson, was much less definite about South African activity. He quotes Wilson as saying of the report, that '"there had been suspicions that people used by BOSS had been paying attention to certain black Commonwealth diplomats in London."'[60] This is certainly likely, but it is not evidence of a conspiracy to discredit Jeremy Thorpe because of the liberals' hostility to the South African regime. Wilson refused to accept the evidence of Norman Scott, and was to continue to do so for some time. Marcia Falkender believed implicitly in the liberal leader. 'She was personally fond of Jeremy Thorpe, enjoyed his company and felt a natural sympathy for anyone who found himself the target of attacks in the press, which she regarded as biased and right-wing.'[61] She and Wilson were to be proved bad judges of character.

When the prime minister spoke to Barbara Castle on 5 February, he suspected the tories might be paying Scott to speak out now. He also thought there might be some conspiracy involving the Barnstaple department of health and social security. When Castle found out there was some sort of private relationship between the two men, the prime minister seemed unable to let go of his hypothesis about South Africa. The cabinet office had been asked to report principally on the Thorpe affair. '"As regards Thorpe", Wilson was to tell Pincher, "MI5 could not say that the South Africans were guilty but they could not say they were innocent either. There had also been one or two suggestive articles in the South African papers, so I felt justified in going ahead."' Though Pincher is hardly the person to say it, 'it was a thin basis for the very serious parliamentary accusation'[62] of 9 March. Barbara Castle was prepared to believe 'that the South African security forces [were] active in this country and are capable of anything', but described Wilson as having 'been obsessed with this defence of Jeremy for weeks'. When the prime minister referred to South Africa, she asked him the key question: '"Are you saying that there was nothing in the Jeremy–Scott affair and they have been inventing it, or that there was something and they are exploiting it?"' '"I dare say there may have been something at some time", said Harold indifferently, "but they are out to destroy the Liberal leader and they would destroy any successor to him. There is big money involved in this."'[63] It is not known how much MI5 told Wilson about Thorpe, but the security service had suspected him of homosexuality from the time he became an MP in 1959 and it was most unlikely, in February 1976, that Sir John Hunt did not convey some of this suspicion to the prime minister.

'I doubt we will ever know the answer', Cyril Smith would write in 1977, 'unless Harold "tells all" in his memoirs. Whatever the reason, it needs to be good. The South African Connection was never taken very seriously, not even by the press, to whom it was surely a source of much sensational material.'[64] Smith can only speculate that Wilson wanted to retain Thorpe in the leadership, as the liberal party syphoned conservative votes and the labour government needed the support of the liberal party. Chapman Pincher was to advance this political explanation of Wilson's behaviour, but argue that the prime minister was trying to stop a lib-lab pact. His theory is dependent upon Jeremy Thorpe being opposed to a deal with the government. Thorpe, however, had been at one with David Steel, in June 1974, in favouring a coalition government, to the displeasure of some liberal MPs.

Wilson would continue to try to help Thorpe after he left office. Norman Scott had been trying to retrieve two letters written to him by Thorpe, which were seized by Scotland Yard in 1962. Harold Wilson seems to have known about them, and assumed the tories could have used them in the 1970s. Thorpe and Goodman decided, on Friday, 7 May 1976, to publish the two letters, having obtained copies. 'They knew that Scott would not hestitate to reveal the contents of the letters once he had the originals as documentation. Any action to suppress their publication, would look as though there was something serious to hide and they reached the view that the letters, though awkward, were perhaps not as bad as more lurid speculations surrounding them.'[65] 'Bunnies can (& will) go to France' was the postscript to one of them. Goodman approached the *Sunday Times*, but Thorpe was unable to explain the postscript to Harold Evans. He could not remember what it meant. There was also to be a six-point statement by Thorpe denying Scott's allegations. All this, with other editorial material, including a report of Wilson's speech, appeared on 9 May. The letters only fuelled the rumours. Liberals MPs had had enough, and Thorpe was finally forced to resign as party leader on Monday, 10 May. He did so referring to a 'campaign of denigration' and a 'sustained witchhunt' by the press.[66]

Thorpe might have protected what was left of his reputation, if he had settled on to the backbenches, but things were to become even more peculiar, as Harold Wilson tried to keep the South African story alive. As a result of Wilson's leaking behind the scenes, the truth about the former liberal leader began to emerge – with devastating consequences for the supposed victim of South African dirty tricks. It became clear that Thorpe and Scott had been homosexual lovers, and suspicions were aroused of a bizarre murder plot, first in 1968, and then again in 1974. The police became involved. 'One of the great ironies of the whole situation is that if it had not been for Wilson, Thorpe would never have gone to trial.'[67]

Wilson began to backtrack in October 1977. 'My intervention [in 1976]', he told Chapman Pincher, 'was purely for the purpose of coming to the aid of a parliamentary colleague.' 'He insisted that he had no knowledge then of any alleged murder attempt or plot against Scott. And he admitted that he might have been wrong about his South African connection allegations and might be prepared to withdraw them. He would not say whether he or Thorpe had first thought of the South African "scenario".'[68]

Thorpe was finally to be charged in December 1978, with others, of conspiracy, and incitement to murder Norman Scott. Only the latter's dog had ended up dead in October 1975, but Scott was thought to have been at risk from friends of the liberal leader. Thorpe was acquitted on 22 June 1979, having lost his parliamentary seat in the general election. He would not be allowed to return to public life.

It is difficult to avoid the hypothesis that Harold Wilson may have been paranoid, this being suggested by his hostility to the media from an early point in his premiership. His perception of enemies, and belief in plots, became more accentuated in the 1970s, the obsession with South Africa being the best documented. No doubt there is a multiplicity of stories here, but Wilson's inability to distinguish between all his various enemies is strongly characteristic of a paranoid personality.

Following prime minister's question time on Tuesday, 9 March 1976, Joe Haines had been surrounded by members of the lobby. They wanted to know what Wilson knew. '"Now what do I say?" he asked the prime minister, as soon as he had returned. "Tell 'em nothing", said Wilson jovially. "I can't tell them nothing", protested Haines. "If they ask, just say there's nothing to say", insisted Wilson. Glumly the Prime Minister's press secretary passed on the message, to the outrage of waiting newsmen.'[69] Joe Haines did not suggest, in 1977, that Harold Wilson was showing signs of paranoia in his second premiership, but he now does associate such a response to stress with Wilson's general weariness. 'The zip had gone by the end of 1971'. He was 'under very considerable strain' in the last months, and had been 'working hard for a great number of years'. 'He had come to believe that there was a conspiracy against him ... A series of unrelated incidents, or even coincidences, became part of the conspiracies.' Joe Haines now admits Harold Wilson was paranoid 'towards the end'.

On 17 July 1977 the *Observer* had run an article by two freelance journalists, on Wilson's relationship with MI5. (This was the first the public was to hear about a so-called Wilson plot, a story that would run and run, and bring many, including Peter Wright and Colin Wallace, into the open with more and more allegations.) Joe Haines was then working for the *Daily Mirror*, and immediately came out, on Monday, 18 July, 1977, with a story about bugging (and South African burglaries). Haines's revelation was, in turn, to inspire Chapman Pincher to an even higher flight of fancy. Haines claimed, in his *Mirror* piece, that Harold Wilson believed MI5 was spying on him in number 10. He later reported Wilson looking behind a picture of Gladstone in his study, and an independent expert being called in to examine what, the prime minister suspected, might be a bug. It proved to be a light fitting. Haines admits Wilson was suspicious of his cabinet secretary, Sir John Hunt, who was his link with MI5, but is less critical of him calling in the electronics expert. '[Wilson]'s not an electrician, he's a politician,'[70] (James Callaghan also confirms Wilson's suspicion of what was behind the Gladstone picture.)

Harold Wilson was responsible, as prime minister, for relations with the United States, which involved the CIA, and formally in charge of MI5 and MI6. In this wilderness of mirrors, his suspicions, in 1975–6, led to some rather unusual actions for a head of government. Conspiring against conspirators probably tipped him into paranoia, though Wilson would be careful not to go public with his suspicions. The prime minister did not even share them with his cabinet colleagues.

Joe Haines's bursting into print about fears of bugging in July 1977, in response to the *Observer* article, raised the question of surveillance by MI5. Chapman Pincher countered on 29 July, after a second *Observer* article, that Wilson had been subjected, on several occasions, to electronic surveillance in Downing Street. (Merlyn Rees, then home secretary, told Tony Benn that there was electronic surveillance at number 10 to keep out intruders.) The following day in the *Express*, Chapman added the house of commons, and Wilson's private homes, to the list of properties penetrated electronically by MI5. Pincher was to claim the following year that his source was an intelligence contact, and claims 'one of Wilson's closest confidants'[71] confirmed the then prime minister's fears. Marcia Falkender denied Haines's allegations in 1977, but Wilson issued a statement on 30 July to the press association: 'Since contrary to everything known to me and my Number Ten and Cabinet Office advisers, [Pincher] is confident of his facts, it is essential that the information in his possession must be made available to, and fully investigated by, the Home Secretary [Merlyn Rees].'[72] Callaghan came under conservative pressure to hold an inquiry into Pincher's allegations about MI5, and, on 23 August, Downing Street issued a statement about 'detailed inquiries' having been conducted by the prime minister. Callaghan gave MI5 a clean bill of health: 'The Prime Minister is satisfied that at no time has the Security Service or any other British intelligence or security agency, either of its own accord or at someone else's request, undertaken electronic surveillance in 10 Downing Street or in the Prime Minister's room in the House of Commons.'[73] There was no reference to Wilson's homes. Callaghan was privately to dismiss his predecessor's anxieties, though he claimed Wilson accepted his statement. The last word on the subject was to come from Chapman Pincher, after he turned against Peter Wright, and published *A Web of Deception* (1987). Pincher then admitted that his 'regular contact who had access to highly classified Intelligence'[74] was the late Bruce MacKenzie, a white Kenyan politician, who just happened to have been a neighbour of Pincher's, in the Berkshire village of Kintbury. MacKenzie had looked after MI6 interests in Africa, and his source on the bugging of Wilson, he had implied to Pincher, was Sir Maurice Oldfield, chief of MI6. Pincher went direct to the latter in 1977, only to be told that Oldfield's source was Wilson. The story about bugging, and electronic surveillance, amounts only to the fact that Wilson believed he was being bugged. Haines never suggested anything more than this, but it took Pincher ten years before he admitted the scare he had raised was incorrect.

Weeks before Norman Scott's dog was killed on Exmoor in October 1975, something important – rumours of a communist cell at number 10 – were brought to Wilson's attention. He was due to have lunch with Sir George Weidenfeld, at the house of commons, on Thursday, 7 August, an exceedingly hot day. The £6 incomes policy had become law on 1 August, and the cabinet discussed public expenditure cuts at Chequers on the Monday. That Thursday, there was another run on sterling, and Barbara Castle feared a crisis cabinet would be called. Wilson was already thinking of going. The prime minister's mind was distracted at lunch, when Weidenfeld told him of the anti-Wilson rumours being spread. 'Well they came and went', Weidenfeld told John Ware, 'but they were sort of repeated in clubs, in drawing rooms, in country houses, and retold, embroidered, second and third hand, and it did look as if there was an orchestrated effort to denigrate and smear him and cut him down to size.' Sir George was an habitué of salon life. Given his close identification with the prime minister, it is unlikely that Wilson was cut down to size in his presence. Weidenfeld may have heard something from the wife of Winston Churchill, the grandson of the wartime leader, as her husband had already warned Wilson that Kagan was associating with known KGB officers. Sir George also knew Martin Gilbert, who was now developing as a Zionist historian. 'There were people in [Wilson's] entourage who were pro-Russian', ran the rumour, '... there were people in Downing Street who were ... in contact with the Soviet Union ... they could lean on him for this or that reason.' 'It's absolutely ludicrous', claims Weidenfeld, 'indeed idiotic, anybody who really knew Wilson or read his speeches, had contact with him, knew that right from the beginning he was a very loyal, very staunch Atlanticist, staunch NATO supporter and an anti-Communist.'[75] Chapman Pincher was to claim later that he originated the communist cell at number 10 thesis, which Weidenfeld was now reporting to the prime minister. This was not the first time Wilson had been associated with the Soviet Union, but Weidenfeld's reports from polite society propelled the prime minister to act.

Wilson returned to Downing Street 'quite distressed',[76] and summoned officials. Sir Maurice Oldfield was the first to come to number 10. MI6 was not considered to be uneasy about the prime minister, or the labour government, though intelligence chiefs had been concerned in 1974 about passing papers to, possibly, three junior ministers. One was probably Judith Hart at overseas development, possibly because of her concern with Chile, but she left the government in June 1975. Another may have been Joan Lestor, an under-secretary at the foreign office, but Wilson moved her to education after the EEC referendum, at the insistence of Callaghan, and she was later to resign from the government, in February 1976, in protest at cuts in her area of responsibility. Eric Heffer may have been the third junior minister, also because of his stand on Chile, but he is unlikely to have required much foreign intelligence at the department of industry, before his resignation in April 1975. Harold Wilson had not been displeased with the secret intelligence service, and it does not seem to have caused him problems, even after he appointed Foot and Benn to the cabinet.

Oldfield is thought to have told Wilson, on 7 August 1975, that there was opposition to him within MI5. Sir Maurice was thinking of Peter Wright, whom he knew. Wright had taken early retirement, at his own request, about 1973, and was then seeing out his time in the security service, as a technical consultant to the director general. The Oldfield meeting is the first occasion on which the prime minister was told that a section of his security service was unreliable (and is the origin of the story of 'the Wilson plot', as it was dubbed belatedly in 1988). The head of MI6 later reported his conversation with the prime minister to Chapman Pincher, and Anthony Cavendish, a friend and former MI6 officer. According to Cavendish, Wilson asked Oldfield to investigate MI5, and South African activity, and then reveal the evidence. Cavendish gives a senior intelligence officer only as his source. Oldfield apparently declined the prime minister's overture, and reported to Callaghan as foreign secretary. The chief of MI6 may have understood Wilson to have said something like this, but the story is highly improbable. The prime minister would not have encouraged further inter-service rivalry, nor instructed the intelligence chief to go public. Wilson was too cunning for that. The concern with South Africa did not surface until several months later. But there is no doubt of the impact Oldfield had on the prime minister. Wilson was to tell the story of his meeting to two journalists after he retired: 'There was a man', he said, obviously referring to Peter Wright, 'who had once held high office in the Security Service …'.[77]

Sir Michael Hanley was next round to Downing Street that Thursday afternoon. The prime minister put Oldfield's claim about MI5 to him. 'The career Security Service chief … apparently also confirmed the existence within his Service of a disaffected faction with extreme right-wing views.'[78] That is what Wilson was to tell the two journalists the following year. According to Chapman Pincher, Wilson said of Hanley: '"He replied that he believed it was true [that Wilson was considered a security risk] but that only a small number of right-wing officers were concerned."'[79] Hanley acknowledged the existence of, what he may have described as, 'young Turks'[80] – a perverse term. He may have explained they were frustrated, in the context of MI5's internal inquiries to find its own Kim Philby, but probably did not reveal the identity of Sir Roger Hollis. Wilson was to tell Falkender, later that day, that a former head of MI5 was now suspected of being a Soviet agent, his source being possibly Oldfield, but would claim that Hanley sought to reassure him that MI5's internal problems had been cleared up.

The prime minister left, as planned, for the Scillies that night. His decision to resign had long been in motion, but Wilson's conversations with Weidenfeld, Oldfield and Hanley undoubtedly affected him. He almost certainly ruminated upon them during his summer holiday, but his eventual resignation cannot be attributed primarily to the events of 7 August 1975. The revelation about a small section in MI5 may have reinforced his decision, but, having been engaged in fighting a battle with the press from 1974, he was beginning to see ghosts at each and every corner.

Wilson would only go public once on the alleged plot against him. When Callaghan denied, in August 1977, that the former prime minister had been bugged, Wilson came clean on his concern about MI5. He said in a statement published in the *Observer*, on 28 August 1977: 'My impression is that what has been going on over a period of years has come from[,] or been fed by, a small mafia group of MI5 who have contacts outside in one or two sections of the Press, and a few self-appointed private enterprise Security agents.'[81] A 'small mafia group' is Peter Wright, and whatever support he had. The journalists may be Chapman Pincher and Gordon Winter. The former now admits he had no sources inside MI5, and Gordon Winter's connections were South African. The private-enterprise security agents could be those responsible for the burglaries of Wilson and his friends. Wilson was to go back on his statement, in 1978, claiming '[he] had no reason to believe that MI5 were at all involved in these questions'. This can only have been a reference to the security service as a formal organization. 'My reference to a small section of MI5', he would continue, 'who had made oral allegations to pressmen and others about myself and other

Ministers of the 1964–70 Government, was qualified by my statement that
I thought they were mostly now on the retired list.'[82] Peter Wright had
indeed retired in January 1976 to a stud farm in Tasmania. The conspiracy,
according to Wilson, amounted to a section of MI5 talking to journalists.

Someone else had done a great deal of talking to journalists, namely Colin
Wallace, who had moved to London in late 1975. Wallace went to a
solicitor, Graham Dodd, in Blackheath, in November, about his dismissal
from the civil service. Twelve years later, Dodd would recall, for *Channel
Four News*, without any apparent documentation, that Wallace talked
about being involved in dirty tricks against mainland politicians, including
Wilson. In the summer of 1976, Wallace leaked information to Airey Neave,
the conservatives' Northern Ireland spokesman, and friend of Margaret
Thatcher's. In late 1976 he moved to Arundel in Sussex, and helped
David Blundy of the *Sunday Times* with an article on psychological warfare
in Northern Ireland, which appeared on 13 March 1977. When Wilson's
views on MI5 became public that summer, Wallace wrote to the former
prime minister, saying he had helped members of the security service
discredit the then labour leader. Marcia Falkender asked for further information on 5 August, but Wallace did not secure his interview with Wilson.

The Wilson plot was to be first described in print by Chapman Pincher
in 1978. He then collaborated with Peter Wright, publishing *Their Trade
is Treachery* in 1981. Peter Wright finally came out in print with *Spycatcher*
in 1987, the collaboration of Paul Greengrass being acknowledged later.
But Pincher then attacked Wright in another book that year. 'He was totally
wrong', Pincher was to insist, 'professionally, ethically, and, I believe,
legally, in disclosing MI5 secrets to me in 1980 and in publishing *Spycatcher*
in 1987.'[83] The 1981 volume had elicited a statement from Margaret
Thatcher on 26 March: 'The book', she told parliament, 'contains no information of security significance that is new to the security authorities, and
some of the material is inaccurate or distorted.'[84] It was 6 May 1987
before the conservative prime minister responded to the Peter Wright
version, as told by Paul Greengrass. She insisted that Hanley had not told
Wilson, in 1975, of 'a disaffected faction with extreme right-wing views
… within the Security Service'. This is taken to be a simple refutation of
everything said in the previous eleven years, but it is possible to square her
account with what Wilson leaked. She went on to say that the current
director general, Sir Anthony Duff, had investigated what came to be called
the Wilson plot: 'All the Security Service officers who have been interviewed
have categorically denied that they were involved in, or were aware of, any
activities or plan to undermine or discredit [Harold] Wilson and his
Government when he was Prime Minister.' Thatcher then sought to tie
down all rumours: 'No evidence or indication has been found of any plot
or conspiracy against [Harold] Wilson by or within the Security Service;

or any misuse of information obtained in the course of their investigations ... [Harold] Wilson has never been the subject of a Security Service investigation or of any form of electronic or other surveillance by the Security Service.'[85] This was stronger than Callaghan's denial of 1977, though it implies that MI5 collected information on Harold Wilson's friends. Thatcher's statement remains the official version (and has been reaffirmed in 1990 in the Colin Wallace affair). Harold Wilson was interviewed in May 1987, and appeared on television conceding that, as the prime minister was closer to events, she must be correct. The so-called 'Wilson plot'[86] remains to be unravelled without help from government sources.

Chapman Pincher revealed, in *Inside Story* (1978), that 'certain officers inside MI5, assisted by others who had retired from the service, were actually trying to bring the Labour Government down and, in [his] opinion, they could at one point have succeeded.'[87] He refers to one – unidentified – senior MI5 officer who was Peter Wright, but Pincher did not yet know him. Wright, according to Pincher, knew about, what has now been revealed as, the MacDermot affair in the 1960s, and also had something on two ministers in the 1974 Wilson government. He was intending to disclose what he knew, at the risk of losing his job, and perhaps prosecution under the official secrets act. The MI5 officer approached 'a very senior Whitehall personality',[88] whom Pincher calls Q. This is now known to be Lord Rothschild. Wright was looking for alternative employment as a security consultant, and Q contacted 'one of the best known figures in the City'.[89] This person was unable to get Wright a job. 'On being told this by Q, the MI5 officer completely lost heart and kept both his silence and his job. Had he been sufficiently encouraged to go through with his venture, the naming of three ministers in Labour governments as serious security risks might have been enough to bring the existing government down.'[90] This is the Wilson plot in rough outline. It overlaps with a story from 1974, about a disgruntled MI6 officer, Stephen De Mowbray (who had been in Northern Ireland). Sam Silkin had told Wilson, in about June 1974, that Anthony Blunt was the fourth man, though this was not admitted, until November 1979. De Mowbray was concerned that Hollis, who had died in 1973, should be revealed as the fifth man, but got little joy from Sir Maurice Oldfield at the top of MI6. De Mowbray went to see Sir John Hunt in the summer of 1974, and demanded an interview with the prime minister, claiming to represent a group of officers in the security and intelligence services. His companions were Arthur Martin and Peter Wright from MI5, and the three are the so-called young Turks, whose existence Hanley would reveal to Wilson. Their views were conveyed to the prime minister, but 'Wilson', it is suggested, '[did] little but initial Hunt's suggestion.'[91] He asked Lord Trend, now presiding over an Oxford college, to conduct an investigation, the former cabinet secretary being given a fifth floor office in Leconfield House, to work part-time, for a year, on a review of the Hollis case. Trend had all ten volumes of the so-called 'fluency' working party report, over which Peter Wright had presided, he and his five colleagues having concluded Hollis was a Soviet agent. Hunt informed De Mowbray, in late 1975, that the former head of MI5 was not under – posthumous – suspicion, though the conclusion of the Trend inquiry was not to be made public until 1981. De Mowbray quit the intelligence service, and subsequently championed Golitsin's view of the world along with Arthur Martin.

Peter Wright, in turn, quietly quit the country in 1976, Rothschild lending him £5,000 to get established in Tasmania. The security commission, in the wake of Hanley's meeting with Wilson, on 7 August 1975, was soon to report on its investigation of MI5. It recommended a reform of the security service's recruitment, officers to be drawn from a wider social background. It advised that Hollis's reputation should be defended, in official statements by way of reply to public charges, but suggested preparations be made in case Blunt was exposed. 'The firm', Hanley wrote cryptically to Wright in Tasmania, 'has passed its recent examinations, and is doing rather well.'[92] The director general was to be replaced, in 1978, by Sir Howard Smith, a safe foreign office man, and it looked like the ructions within MI5 would pass unnoticed into history. Peter Wright returned to England on a visit in 1980, when he was trying to write a book provisionally entitled 'The Cancer in Our Midst'. 'The present state of Britain is part due', he would assert later, 'to the penetration of the establishment by the Russians, and the subsequent cover-up.'[93] The decline of Britain, a weak establishment, Soviet penetration, and cover-ups were all related in Wright's febrile imagination. Anthony Blunt had been exposed publicly the previous year, and Rothschild, who had associated with him in the 1930s and 1940s, feared he would be accused of being the fifth man. He needed Peter Wright's support, and sent him an airline ticket. Wright was introduced to Pincher at Rothschild's country house in Cambridgeshire, and a lengthy collaboration followed. Hollis was the target, and *Their Trade is Treachery* was published in 1981, without any acknowledgement to Peter Wright. It saved Rothschild's reputation, made Pincher money, but only left Wright more frustrated. Following the arrest of Michael Bettaney, Paul Greengrass and John Ware, working for Granada Television, flew out to Tasmania in 1984, and gave Peter Wright free rein in a *World in Action* programme. MI5 refused to let Alec MacDonald put the official security service line, though he believed that 'Wright should never have switched from scientist to molehunter – a job for which he had no training'.[94] Wright was still after Hollis, but he had no papers or other documents, save a few letters. Paul Greengrass then set out to ghost Wright's memoirs, using taped interviews and conversations. When he discovered the Hanley letter the following summer, 'suddenly Wright dissolved in tears. He was ashamed and embarrassed. Just ten (sic) words had implicated him in treasonable acts and destroyed his self-image as a patriot and defender of the realm.'[95] The publishers, Heinemann, were keen to rush *Spycatcher: The Candid Autobiography of a Senior Intelligence Officer* out in 1987, though title and subtitle, it could be argued, breach the trades descriptions act. Due largely to Margaret Thatcher, and the then cabinet secretary, Sir Robert Armstrong, the book attracted unprecedented international attention, Whitehall seeking to apply the general rule of not commenting on MI5 in this particular case. Much of the public attention in Britain focused on Harold Wilson, though Greengrass, responding to Hanley's cryptic letter, only addressed the question at a late stage. 'I don't believe the *Spycatcher* account of the Wilson plot is very accurate', he now says. 'It is a very interim first draft.'[96] But Peter Wright had achieved his revenge, and Wilson's resignation – in the minds of very many people – was associated either with MI5 skulduggery, or a scandal Wright threatened to expose. Lord Rothschild had been forced to write to the *Daily Telegraph*, on 3 December 1986, asking MI5 to confirm publicly he had not been a Soviet agent, something the prime minister did most laconically in the house of commons. When the house of lords finally permitted, in October 1988, the publication of Wright's book in Britain, *Panorama* broadcast a special programme, 'Spycatcher', the reporter being John Ware. It, plus David Leigh's book, *The Wilson Plot* (1988), also published by Heinemann, critically examined Wright's allegations, the media taking little interest in their conclusions. Good investigative journalists analyzing facts, which point to a much more complicated, and less sensational, world, is of little commercial interest.

After Hanley took over MI5 in 1972, Wright was appointed to his personal staff as a consultant in the area of counter-espionage. Wright is believed to have been considered unreliable by the management of MI5, this sideways move being an attempt to constrain him pending his departure, at the age of sixty, in August 1976. His grudge against MI5 was his pension, Wright believing the management had gone back on the promise it made in 1955. Something of his worldview can be detected in what he later said to a journalist. '"Have you ever asked yourself why Britain is in the mess it is in? Why fifty years ago it was a great country?"'[97] He was to have plenty of evidence in the miners' strike of 1973–4 that Britain had gone to the dogs, and confirmation in the return of Harold Wilson to office. Relative decline did not mean subversion by a foreign power, or treachery by a political administration motivated with destructive intent, but a post-imperial nationalism, comprising a mixture of nostalgia and paranoia, flourished among the most devoted servants of the empire. In an office next to the director general's suite in Leconfield House, and then Gower Street, Peter Wright had access to Sir Michael Hanley's safe, where resided the four-volume Henry Worthington file on the friends of the labour prime minister. Wright recounts in his book approaching Rothschild for a job, seemingly towards the end of 1973, after Hanley vetoed his going to the firm of N.M. Rothschild. He was invited to meet a prospective employer at Rothschild's flat in St James's Place, who is described simply as 'a businessman ... a wealthy industrialist'.[98] This individual invited Wright to lunch at a London hotel with others. 'They were retired people from various branches of intelligence and security organizations whose best years were well behind them. There were others, too, mainly businessmen who seemed thrilled to be in the same room as spies, and did not seem to care how out of date they were.'[99] This group was out to prevent labour returning to power, and was prepared to buy damaging information from Wright. Harold Wilson was explicitly named. Wright reported to Hanley, who advised keeping well away, but the director general was persuaded to look at the Henry Worthington file. Hanley concluded: '"There's lots of smoke, but not a lot of fire."'[100] In the spring of 1974, Wright continues, 'MI5 was sitting on information which, if leaked, would undoubtedly have caused a political scandal of incalculable consequences. The news that the Prime Minister himself was being investigated would at the least have led to [Wilson's] resignation. The point was not lost on some MI5 officers.'[101] Wright was approached by two colleagues about this time, who were in the company of three or four other officers. This group was keen to use any information against Wilson in the election expected later in 1974. About thirty members of MI5, Wright claimed in *Spycatcher*, were prepared to try and swing the election, by leaking information to sympathetic pressmen, and even trade-union leaders. This was very much in the manner of the 'Zinoviev letter', used in 1924 against Ramsay MacDonald. Wright admits to having thought about joining the conspiracy, by copying the files on the labour party in Hanley's safe. 'I felt an irresistible urge to lash out. The country seemed on the brink of catastrophe. Why not give it a little push? In any case, I carried the burden of so many secrets that lightening the load a little could only make things easier for me.'[102] He claims he was talked out of it by Rothschild, and was out of the country for the rest of 1974, and an early part of 1975. 'It was obvious to [him]', during this time, 'that the boys had been actively pushing their plan as much as they could.'[103] Wright dined with Sir Maurice Oldfield at Locketts that summer, the day after the MI6 chief had been called in by Wilson. Oldfield told Wright of the allegations about the communist cell at number 10, involving Marcia Falkender. Hearing of the plot of the previous year, Oldfield insisted that Wright should tell Hanley. This he did the next morning: 'He might have suspected that feelings against Wilson ran high in the office, but now he was learning that half of his staff were up to their necks in a plot to get rid of the Prime Minister.'[104] Hanley asked for the names of the officers involved, and they were handed over.

Wright's account of the Wilson plot, which is historically unreliable, had to be extracted from him. He felt bad about betraying his colleagues, and being a moral coward. The structure of the narrative is suspect, putting Wright outside the events he narrates, but a number of facts may be discussed. One, Peter Wright's personal, professional and political disenchantment was the starting point, about mid-1974. Two, Rothschild is the key patron. Wright admits he discussed reopening the Hollis case with Rothschild in 1974, and, when it was believed Blunt was dying in 1975, there was great fear that he might leave an incriminating last will and testament. Wright claims he gave Robert Armstrong forty names associated with the ring of five, spreading suspicion widely in other directions. Three, the unidentified businessman. Victor Rothschild knew James Goldsmith, who had a business and personal relationship with Jacob Rothschild. Goldsmith was 'an excitable man of radical right-wing opinions'.[105] 'In one generation', he was to say, 'we have been transformed from a rich country into a poor country'.[106] David Leigh denies, in parenthesis, 'that Goldsmith was involved in any misconduct'.[107] Four, the lunch sounds like something on the extreme right, possibly Unison. This committee for action had been set up in 1973, by George Kennedy Young, former deputy chief of MI6, to counter trade-union militancy. (His name was removed from the published version of *Spycatcher*.) Young had argued publicly, in the 1960s, for the compulsory repatriation of non-white immigrants, and he stood unsuccessfully, in February 1974, as the conservative candidate in Brent East. Anthony Cavendish was also involved in Unison. Peter Wright is known to have taken an interest in the private armies phenomenon, which saw retired military and naval officers try to come to the aid of the civil power, by organizing against the unions, though it is unclear whether he, as an MI5 officer, was working for or against them. The essence of the Wilson plot concerns MI5. Paul Greengrass admits that the reference to 'the boys'[108] leaking to the press was a throwaway phrase, and Peter Wright, under questioning from John Ware, also plays it down in the case of the Henry Worthington file. 'I am shattered about the leaking thing. I have no recollection of that, except as a complete last resort.'[109] The number of thirty conspirators initially led some to suspect K5 in MI5, the counterespionage section which had been merged with MI6 counter intelligence. Harry Wharton was the MI5 head of K5, and it was housed away from headquarters. Hanley had demoted K branch, at about the time he took Wright into his office, and Russian spies went out of fashion, being eclipsed by domestic subversion, which was the responsibility of F branch. Hostility to Wilson was greatest in K5, given the Kagan connection, and

Wharton, after all, was the man who had personally interviewed the then leader of the opposition in 1971. Peter Wright now admits to being at the centre of the conspiracy within MI5, he being the one with access to Hanley's safe. He also says there were only about eight or nine meeting, after hours, in his room over a period of a few weeks, but often there were only three. Members of K5 came to hear about Wright, but only one, considered to be Harry Wharton, was prepared to go along with him. 'It is commonly known as cold feet', Wright said later of his reluctant co-conspirators. 'I don't blame them because they were all younger than I. They had careers still in front of them. I was very nearly at the end of the road.'

Wright's plan was similar to De Mowbray's. He proposed that he, and his colleagues, should march into number 10. 'What I wanted to do was to show Wilson that we'd got it and that we wanted him to resign, that there would be no publicity if he just quiety went ... I honestly think that Wilson would have folded up. He wasn't a very gutsy man, you know.'[110] This is the Wilson plot Peter Wright was reluctant to explain in *Spycatcher*. He now states Greengrass must have misunderstood him, but he also admits he did not bother to correct the typescript sent to him for approval. 'I think basically ... I never thought there would be a fuss about it. I didn't see why there would be ... because it had been stopped.'[111] This casts considerable light on Wright's attitude to history, and probably to his profession as a security officer. Facts are subordinate to their intended effect. Wright still insists he told Oldfield, and then went to Hanley. The director general was silent. 'Then I said don't worry too much about it, or words to that effect because I am not going to do it. I have come to tell you about it.'[112]

The Wilson plot begins and ends with Peter Wright: 'There was a faction unjustifiably suspicious of [Harold Wilson] and occasionally they leaked. MI5's internal inquiry doesn't seem to have uncovered all the facts. As for a conspiracy to bring down Harold Wilson, we still only have Peter Wright's word for that. But if there was one, it didn't get very far.'[113] Peter Wright is known to enjoy spy thrillers, and this literary genre may have stimulated his imagination as a security officer. Four years after Wright and Wilson retired, a left-wing journalist, Chris Mullin, published a – not very good – political thriller called *A Very British Coup*. Tony Benn was fighting Denis Healey for the deputy leadership of the party, and Mullin was to become a labour MP in 1987. The book tells the story of a future labour government, under a left-wing leader, Harry Perkins, who is brought down by a conspiracy, involving the United States government and the British security service. The television adaptation, by Alan Plater, made the ending more ambiguous, when it was shown as a mini-series on Channel 4, in the summer of 1988. Lady Falkender attended the preview, and it is reported she enjoyed this fictional account of life at the top. It is gripping as a thriller with a fine performance from Ray McAnally in the lead, but other characterization is weak. The film's politics are simplistic, not least in the view that an uncorruptible salt of the earth could be elected leader of the labour party. He or she would never get that far, and the complexity of societal power cannot be reduced to a conspiracy against an encumbent prime minister in a stable democracy. The mini-series won three BAFTA awards in 1989, from an industry reacting to government heavy handedness in television, but mainly because it articulates the political worldview of the class of 1968. This is so on the nature of state power, and particularly on the idea that the labour left of the 1980s was a profound threat to western capitalism. The class of 1968 has heard stories about the destabilization of Wilson's government from 1976, and *Spycatcher* became compulsory reading in 1987. Chris Mullin makes no claims to have written a fictionalized account of what might have happened, but Peter Wright's 1988 version of the Wilson plot comes straight from *A Very British Coup*.

Back in the world of prime ministerial politics, a certain tactical disengagement was evident in Harold Wilson's final months. At the Rome EEC summit in early December 1975, Wilson supported Callaghan's protest about Britain's exclusion from the French global initiative, a Paris conference on north–south development. 'I backed him mainly out of loyalty', he was to write later, 'for it soon proved he was out on an uncomfortable limb. In truth, I considered the Conference would prove such a dreary failure that it hardly mattered ... whether Britain was represented.'[114] This was hardly the Harold Wilson of nearly thirty years before, when international conferences had been about the enthusiastic defence of national interests. Harold Wilson worked for a Euro-compromise at Rome, while Callaghan was invited to speak on oil supplies for a few minutes at Giscard's conference.

Wilson and Callaghan were at a meeting of socialist leaders at Elsinore in Denmark, in January 1976, when François Mitterrand, of the French socialist party, spoke on the Mediterranean countries. He argued for an electoral alliance between social democrats and communists, where national parties had broken from Moscow – the phenomenon known as Eurocommunism. If such alliances were electorally successful, they would lead to coalition governments of the left. This Gallic proposal greatly annoyed Wilson and Callaghan, attentive as they were to the anti-communism of the United States. The British prime minister 'was given the task of the hatchet job' on the French socialist leader, coming up with the concept of 'Mitterrandisme', and quoting 'There was a young lady of Riga/ Who went for a ride on a tiger/ ...'. 'There is little that established traditional parties can do about [Eurocommunism's] arrival in each country', Wilson said, 'except either ignore it or fight it.'[115] He was later to argue that there could be no rapprochement between parliamentary socialism and Eurocommunism. 'The arrival on the scene of Eurocommunism demands that, in meeting this latest of threats, this generation suffers a weakening neither of ... vigilance nor of ... resolution', he wrote subsequently. The French socialists complained to the labour party, and the national executive rebuked Wilson. 'This I noted', he was to write, 'but have not troubled to acknowledge.'[116]

It was also at Elsinore, at the beginning of 1976, that Harold Wilson hit upon the idea of Roy Jenkins as the next president of the European commission. 'I liked to say', Jenkins was to recall, 'only half as a joke, that I kept my European faith burning bright by never visiting Brussels.'[117] Harold Wilson was thinking less of what Roy Jenkins could do for Europe, and more that the presidency would get him out of British politics. The prime minister was looking no further than his successor as labour leader. Wilson hinted to his home secretary about the possibility of the Brussels job, on 22 January, saying the Europeans wanted Heath or Jenkins. The latter had learned just after Christmas that Wilson was going, but was prepared for a prime ministerial change of mind. Jenkins describes his informant as an impeccable source, and declined the offer of Europe for a chance at the labour leadership, only to have second thoughts within days. 'It would be an opportunity', he wrote later, 'to do something quite new for me and in which I believed much more strongly than in the economic policy of Mr Healey, the trade union policy of Mr Foot, or even the foreign policy of Mr Callaghan.'[118] He withdrew his rejection on 26 January, but still wanted to keep open the chance of the leadership, if Wilson should suddenly go. Callaghan, who favoured George Thomson for the presidency, had also heard, just after Christmas, about Wilson's intentions, from Harold Lever (as did Denis Healey). Callaghan warmed to the idea of Jenkins's departure, but both were to throw their hats in the ring when Wilson announced he was going. Jenkins was unsuccessful in the leadership contest, and, when Callaghan became prime minister, he lost the much-desired foreign office to Tony Crosland (Jenkins believes Wilson would have offered him this, if they had won in 1970). He then asked the new prime minister to send him to Europe, and was not prepared to stay with a promise of the treasury in six months. 'Once the decision to go to Brussels had been finally made', Jenkins writes, 'I felt both liberated and excited. I realised how ill the shoe of British politics had been fitting me for some years past.'[119]

The £6 pay policy was working in late 1975, and public spending was being reorientated towards industrial investment. The pound had settled at just over two dollars by early 1976, the bank of England managing the exchange rate by occasionally buying sterling. Given the uncompetitive character of British industry, a strong pound did not help exports, and it was government policy to prevent it rising too high. The market became unsettled in early March 1976, due to an international surge in demand for sterling, and the treasury instructed the bank to begin selling. As the result of 'an amateurish technical mishandling',[120] the pound dropped, on Friday,

5 March, below the psychologically critical level of two dollars. This alarmed the international money markets, and it continued to drop the following week, despite bank support. The treasury was thought to favour the rate of $1.88. The condition of sterling worried the prime minister, in the days leading up to his planned resignation, and he asked to be wakened at 6.00 a.m. on Tuesday, 16 March, to hear the latest report from Singapore. This was also the day he had picked to tell the cabinet he was going. Barbara Castle had been told in confidence on 4 March, though she was to be surprised when Wilson finally told his colleagues. Marcia Falkender was given the date at Chequers on Sunday, 14 March. Tony Benn had heard a rumour at Michael Foot's on 7 March, which may have started with Castle, and suspected a scandal. Wilson personally informed the foreign secretary, late on 11 March, when they were driving to Westminster from a dinner party at Sir George Weidenfeld's home in Cheyne Walk, on the occasion of Wilson's sixtieth birthday. Callaghan believed the mantle of office was being passed to him, though there is just a suggestion that Wilson may have thought Healey a suitable successor. But the chancellor was about to lose the crucial vote on public expenditure cuts, and slog it out with the left-wing abstainers while the vote proceeded.

The prime minister saw the queen on Tuesday, 16 March, unusually at 9.30 a.m. Princess Margaret's separation from her husband was to be announced that day, but it is unlikely Wilson delayed his resignation to convenience the royal family. Returning to Downing Street, he called Ted Short and James Callaghan into his study, just before the cabinet meeting. Wilson told Denis Healey in the lavatory near the cabinet room. Jenkins was being excluded. Marcia Falkender passed the news to Peter Shore, still her favourite. Once the cabinet began at 11.00 a.m., Wilson said he had a statement to make, and autographed copies were then distributed to members. 'He certainly has developed a flare for drama',[121] Barbara Castle noted. This statement was also being released to the press. It remains the one and only official explanation of his action, in which Wilson gives four reasons for his resignation. First, his length of service: thirty-one years in parliament, almost all of it on the front bench; over eleven years in cabinet, thirteen as leader of the party, and nearly eight as prime minister. This was 'longer than that of any of [his] peacetime predecessors in this century'.[122] Second, the need to let another, who might be over sixty, have a chance as party leader. Callaghan was grateful for this Wilsonian dispensation. Third, to give his successor a chance to prepare effectively for the next general election. The fourth reason was the problem of repeating decisions made in different circumstances. Wilson obviously had to give an explanation as to why he was going. Reasons one and four ring true as personal, while two and three are the diplomatic utterances of a prime minister who now had to wait for the labour party to elect a new leader.

Wilson went on to thank the cabinet, mentioning he had presided over 472 meetings, and answered more than 12,000 parliamentary questions. It is not known who did the counting. The prime minister presented a hopeful picture of the British economy, expressing confidence in his successor continuing the counter-inflation policy, and maintaining '*in full measure our commitment to our allies and partners overseas*'.[123] Wilson insisted that he would go to the backbenches. He was not going into industry or accepting consultancies, nor would he accept the headship of a university college. He ended by telling his successor that the job was stimulating. A prime minister had to know all that was going on, while thinking of the government's strategy. It was important to get out into the country. Having finished reading, he tried to explain his timing (a two-page addendum being added to the original statement when it was released). He had decided to stay only two years. His birthday had been ruled out because of two by-elections. The summer was too late for his successor to prepare for the party conference. The next pay round was also approaching. Timing was still everything.

There followed a silence which was broken by Ted Short. A tribute then followed from Callaghan, 'Jim conclud[ing] haltingly, "Thank you, Harold, for all you have done for us.'[124] Wilson then left the cabinet room to discuss his successor's election with the chairman of the parliamentary party, Cledwyn Hughes, Short taking over the meeting. Hughes found "'the Prime Minister alone [in the study at 11.35 a.m.] with his pipe and half a pint of beer"'.[125] Shirley Williams and Barbara Castle left to draft a statement, which was accepted by the cabinet. 'John Hunt add[ed] the discreet prefix that the statement had been agreed "in the Prime Minister's temporary absence". These civil servants think of everything.' Barbara Castle began to muse, 'and some irreverent questions about Harold's whole manoeuvre began to creep into [her] mind':

> Okay, so a man has the right to decide he will give up office, and whatever date he chooses will have its snags, but for Harold to do this so gratu-itously and so apparently senselessly, in the middle of a perfectly reasonably successful term of office, almost looks like frivolity. Has one the *right* to throw one's party into turmoil for no apparent cause, to face them with a *fait accompli* because one knows they would plead with one to stay if they knew in time? What exactly was Harold up to? More than had met the eye, I had no doubt.[126]

And this in spite of the conversation they had had twelve days earlier. If Barbara Castle was suspicious, it is not surprising that the man and woman in the street was to be perplexed. Harold Wilson was no doubt amused to learn, after all that he had been through, certainly since 1970, that some members of the labour party wanted him to stay. He had speculated about his successor with Castle on 4 March 1976, and still saw himself as on the left. There was a 'soft' left, to which he, Castle and Foot belonged, separate from a middle group, and 'the really vicious group'. This distinction between a hard and soft left was to take root in time. Wilson's ideal choices were Varley, though not this time, and Shore, who had 'really become very impressive'.[127] Both had served him as parliamentary private secretaries. Wilson had ruled out Healey on the grounds that the left hated him, and, when Castle then discounted Callaghan and Jenkins, the prime minister implicitly endorsed the former, by rejecting the latter as too much of a bon viveur.

Castle and Shore pressed Foot, immediately after the cabinet meeting, to become the candidate of the left. Benn also stood on 17 March. The main concern was to stop Callaghan, some of the left even preferring Denis Healey. Barbara Castle sought to persuade the chancellor to run, telling him he could pick up votes on the second ballot. The first ballot was arranged for Thursday, 25 March, with six candidates. Callaghan and Healey looked the best leadership prospects. Jenkins and Tony Crosland came from the right, Foot and Benn from the left.

Wilson was due to take prime minister's questions on the afternoon of 16 March, after his dramatic announcement to the cabinet. Barbara Castle found everyone 'shell-shocked'[128] at lunch in the house, and a crowded front bench. Senior ministers decided not to stand for the prime minister, unless backbenchers took the initiative. They only cheered, and some waved their order papers. Tributes were paid to Wilson from opposition parties. Heath was particularly generous, as the only former prime minister in the house: 'May I thank the Right Hon. Gentleman for the courtesies that he always extended to me when I was Leader of the Opposition and for the way that he responded to my invitations during the time I was Prime Minister.'[129] Wilson then attended a press conference in the ministry of defence.

The Wilsons dined that evening with Sir George Weidenfeld, Marcia Falkender being the only other guest. She had appeared earlier on television, commenting upon the resignation. The papers that evening, and the following morning, were taken by surprise, much of their coverage perforce being drawn from filed obituaries. Columnists and commentators were surprisingly kind. Attention focused on Callaghan as the likely successor, the foreign secretary having discussed it, after Christmas, with his closest friend, Merlyn Rees. Callaghan claims he was confident of victory. Rees was joined by Gregor MacKenzie, John Cunningham and Tom McNally, to run a campaign for a leader who would be entitled to become prime minister, but Callaghan came to fear Healey and Crosland's candidatures. Michael Foot's campaign was managed by Stan Orme, ironically Rees's deputy at the Northern Ireland Office. Roy Jenkins had the support of the principled right, and Tony Benn would thank Joe Ashton, Frances Morrell, Francis Cripps, Ken Coates and Audrey Wise.

Wilson invited the cabinet to a farewell dinner, in the state dining room at number 10, on Monday, 22 March, though the wear was to be informal. A valedictory photograph was taken in the main reception room, in the presence of other photographers and television crews. Wilson had arranged the seating as at cabinet, and added Marcia Falkender and some officials. The six contenders for the leadership all attended, though some were keen to get back to lobbying in the house of commons. Barbara Castle, who kept quizzing Falkender about the resignation, noted later: 'as the evening went on I thought there was something artificial about it. It did not come alight. This was a real event, Harold's abrupt and unnecessary departure, and I felt that this ought to be expressed spontaneously in some way.'[130] Wilson made a short speech. He said it was best to go in advance of expectation, and cited the open university as his major achievement. Others paid tribute. Tony Benn had been busy with his camera, and 'got very political, which did not fit in with the mood of the evening',[131] though a recording of his speech shows there was gentlemanly table thumping. He had the transcript of an obituary of Wilson he had recorded in 1965, and joked about Joe Haines trying to control ministers' broadcasting. There was some banter about Wilson having given government cars to former prime ministers the previous year, in order to assure one for himself.

The queen had let it be known she would be prepared to attend a farewell dinner for Wilson in Downing Street, as she had done for Churchill twenty-one years earlier. The historical analogy was not lost on the prime minister, and the occasion was arranged for Tuesday, 23 March. Wilson invited some senior ministers, former prime ministers, senior officials and some of his personal staff. Michael Foot turned up in a dinner jacket with an NUM badge on the lapel. Marcia Falkender made a 'superbly executed'[132] curtsey, according to Haines, her republican hostility muted for the evening. The dinner was more relaxed than that for the cabinet. The queen joked that she had seen five prime ministers out of number 10, and expected to see a few more (Callaghan was to be the only one for a considerable time). The guests then repaired to the state drawing room, and were joined by more number 10 staff. The fact that the queen and the duke of Edinburgh stayed until near midnight was judged a success.

The result of the first leadership ballot was announced two days later. Foot had come top with 90 votes, and Benn had 37. Callaghan received 84 votes, to Jenkins's 56, Healey's 30 and Crosland's 17. The right had 187 votes to the left's 127, so there was no fear of a Foot premiership. Crosland had to drop out and switched to Callaghan, as did Jenkins, at the insistence of his followers. Healey stayed in the race for the second ballot, but Tony Benn switched, as expected, to Foot. It was now a contest between Foot and

Callaghan, with a third candidate hoping to run a 'stop Jim' campaign. Healey only picked up an additional 8 votes on 30 March, Callaghan securing 141 to Foot's 133. But for Healey, Wilson would have been out of Downing Street by the end of the month. A third ballot was fixed for 5 April, and the prime minister was forced to attend a final European summit on 1 April in Luxembourg. A special cabinet had gone cold on the question of direct elections to the European parliament, and Luxembourg was mainly an occasion for farewells. The other European leaders were more concerned to do business with Callaghan, though still foreign secretary. Wilson was also in an end of term mood at this gathering, suggesting a music channel on the translation facilities for European conferences.

During his last weekend at Chequers, Wilson left foreign telegrams and cabinet committee papers to one side. But he had to preside over a budget cabinet on Monday, 5 April, when Healey revealed his assumption of a 3 per cent increase in wages. Wilson was being implicated in continuing government policy. There followed a private lunch, when the Wilsons were joined by senior number 10 staff. Wilson saw Cledwyn Hughes, the chairman of the parliamentary party, at 3.15 that afternoon in the commons. Callaghan had won the third ballot, with 176 votes to Foot's 137. Only four of Healey's had gone to Foot, the parliamentary party having split between left and right. Wilson telephoned the palace, while labour MPs assembled to hear the result at 4.00 p.m. Callaghan read his prepared speech, stating he would make changes in the government. Foot received a warmer reception for his contribution, and the future of party unity rested largely with him. He was to veto Roy Jenkins as foreign secretary, but could not save Barbara Castle. 'Harold got the biggest reception of all, with a standing ovation. I think everyone in the room realized that in his own funny way he had been a big man.'[133] He then returned to Downing Street, and left for the palace at 5.15 p.m. to tender his resignation. Callaghan later offered to form a government. The Wilsons drove to Chequers for the night, though he would be back in the commons, as a backbencher, the following day. 'It's not just goodbye', a labour party official had said a few days before. 'It's the end of an era.'[134]

CHAPTER 25

The Years of Decline, 1976–91

It is the prerogative of every outgoing prime minister, at dissolution or resignation, to make personal recommendations for honours to the sovereign.
Wilson was looking forward to having his resignation honours announced
on the day he left. Marcia Falkender produced the first set of names and
Wilson then made some changes in his own hand. 'The names added by
[Wilson] improved the quality of the list, but the substantial majority of the
knights and peers who were in the published list were those originally
proposed by Lady Falkender.'[1] The recommendations went then to Ken
Stowe, who had responsibility for the honours section in number 10,
neither Haines nor Donoughue being asked to comment.

The civil service set about vetting the candidates for honours, and
inquiring into their willingness to accept. There were a few refusals. Two
on the list approached a very important lawyer, and, according to *The Times*,
he recommended they decline. They accepted. The list was not ready to
be announced on 5 April, possibly because the palace asked number 10 to
have second thoughts, the limit of the sovereign's power in such matters.
It was also considered on the day Wilson left office, by the political
honours scrutiny committee, an all-party committee of three peers,
supposed to prevent any prime minister doing a Lloyd George. Selling
honours was forbidden; bestowing them on political friends and contributors to party funds was not. The committee was chaired by Lord Crathorne.
According to Lady Summerskill, the labour member, the committee was
not in favour of at least half of the names. It refrained from immediately
resorting to the queen, but the story broke in the *Sunday Times* of 2 May.
Three names had gone to the committee, 'people either not known to have
rendered personal or political service to [Wilson] or the Labour Party, or
people not regarded as leading public figures'. The implication was that the
former prime minister might have been selling political honours, but
Wilson denied any of his putative peers was the difficulty. Some of the names

began to appear in the press. David Frost, whom Joe Haines had advised should not get an honour, presumably because Wilson would be working with him, was ruled out, on 2 May, as a likely recipient. James Goldsmith, Sir Joseph Kagan and Jarvis Astaire were first mentioned on 23 May, as were Sir Lew Grade, Sir Bernard Delfont and Sigmund Sternberg, plus Sir George Weidenfeld.

Wilson complained privately to Callaghan about these leaks, and Sir Philip Allen was asked to find the culprit. When Joe Haines was interviewed by Allen, he 'expressed the hope that if [Allen] discovered the leaker he or she would qualify for inclusion in a future list'.[2] The Crathorne committee succeeded in stopping only one knighthood, for Jarvis Astaire the impresario.

The list was eventually published on Thursday, 27 May, to be greeted with widespread disapproval. The establishment was almost as offended as the left. 'There was an immediate furore, because those named were either tycoons of the entertainment business or financiers, whose contributions to national glory, public welfare or party interest had, in most cases, escaped notice.'[3] 'The former prime minister', according to the *Economist*, 'chose to extend his customarily generous patronage once again to a clutch of businessmen and showbiz men some of whose services to politics, public life, even to [Wilson] himself, remain obscure.'[4] 'A pity about Harold', a member of the cabinet said. 'Such a graceful exit – and then he does this on the doorstep.'[5] Tony Benn described the recipients as 'inadequate, buccaneering, sharp shysters'.[6] Over 100 labour MPs sought to dissociate the parliamentary party from the action of its former leader, hostility being expressed to 'the inclusion of those we regard as symbolic of the less acceptable face of capitalism'.[7] 'In the [following] weeks ... the coolness amongst his colleagues was discernible. On at least one occasion they refused to move up to make space for him on the "Churchill seat" on the front row just below the gangway. As more and more revelations emerged, more and more Labour MPs were heard to say, "That's finished Harold for me!"'[8]

Wilson's list contained forty-two names, including nine new peers. Resignation honours traditionally go to those who have been of personal service to the prime minister, but members of the Chequers and number 10 staff were 'accommodated in the steerage section of the list'.[9] His doctor, Sir Joseph Stone, was given a peerage, as were two former labour MPs, Terry Boston and Albert Murray. Joe Haines was opposed to being offered a peerage, and most attention focused on the famous names honoured. Peerages went to Weidenfeld and Kagan, already Wilsonian knights. The brothers Sir Lew Grade and Sir Bernard Delfont, leading impresarios, were also sent to the upper house, as were Sir Max Rayne, a property millionaire, and Prof. John Vaizey. Most attention was paid to the knighthood awarded to James Goldsmith. The knighthood was awarded

'for services to export and to ecology', suggesting Wilson had to find a justification for Goldsmith's honour. Sigmund Sternberg, who also got a
knighthood, was to be acknowledged by Transport House as the only con-
tributor to labour party funds.

There were two further Wilsonian knights. James Hanson, whose
interests included television, was known to be a conservative supporter, and
Eric Miller, considered especially close to Marcia Falkender, was specifically cited as 'recently treasurer of the Socialist International'. This may have
been another attempted justification. 'The list remains a bizarre one for a
socialist ex-Prime Minister', argued *The Times* leader that day:

> If one takes the baronies and knighthoods, a majority go to people who
> are very clearly capitalists, and capitalists of the tough risk-taking type.
> These are not, by and large, the men who run the great industrial
> companies, but men who have carved out their own fortunes with
> their own sharp swords ... The impression [the list] creates with
> cumulative and striking force is one of unrepentent Darwinism, of the
> business survival of the fittest and of nature red in tooth and claw ...
> Whether these untamed capitalists hold theoretically socialist views or
> not, it is they – the tigers and wild dogs free-ranging on the veldt – rather
> than the captive pseudo-capitalists on display in the safari park of the CBI,
> who are capable of destroying socialism ... These are the very people
> whose lives are the contradiction of everything for which the Labour Party
> stands.[10]

The *Sunday Times* of 30 May had an article by its Insight team on 'The
Wilson Connection'. 'The most striking feature of the latest list', it argued,
'is that it points to a degree of personal croneyism, reaching back to the
beginning of Wilson's political career, which has encouraged the honouring
of men who often (but, of course, not always) have no convincing record
of public or political service. On this process ... Lady Falkender[,] has set
her own mark for many years ... Some of the friends and associates
recognised have belonged as much in her circle as in Wilson's'.

George Hutchinson had denounced the resignation honours in *The
Times* the previous day. He accused Wilson of having demeaned the office
of prime minister, embarrassed the queen, injured the labour party, and discredited the honours system. Hutchinson detected the cloven hoof of his
political secretary: 'It might be as well if Lady Falkender were to lie low
for a while, perhaps a long while, avoiding the House of Lords. After all,
there is a limit to what even the most patient, indulgent and generous of
the two Houses can stand.' The latter immediately drafted a 2,000 word
reply that bank holiday weekend, which was published by the paper on
Monday, 31 May. She was still angry about the revelation two years earlier
that she had two children born out of wedlock. Falkender maintained that

the list was Wilson's, and queried its leaking to the *Sunday Times*. She described the hue and cry as a 'sanctimonious protest by the unimaginative half of the Establishment', and accused the critics of snobbery and of 'covert anti-semitism'. 'Perhaps behind this whole affair', she wrote, 'lies some other story, some other motive for it, where frustration, malice and envy are being expressed in a final attack upon a man who has contributed so much to our national life, to the lives of ordinary people, though not necessarily to the lives of those living within certain select circles in Metropolitan London.' She denied that the political office had handled honours lists, but the prime minister would consult her, Haines and Donoughue on the arts and sports section. 'Harold Wilson, in [her] view, [had] done more than most previous Prime Ministers to uphold our institutions, to protect the Crown, to give devoted and loyal service to his party and to uphold the office of Prime Minister through difficult times, and pass that office to his successor in a manner unparalleled in British history.'[11]

Wilson refused, in a statement issued on 2 June, to concede that he had done anything wrong. 'I still have the original names, substantially as published, written down by myself after consultation with no one else.' He accused his critics, especially the *Sunday Times* of 30 May, of 'anti-semitic overtones', and defended his political office, denying that Falkender had ever seen any classified documents, or participated in the formulation of government policy. 'Now that I have stated the facts', he concluded, 'I hope that those concerned will now cease this orchestrated vendetta against what I repeat is a personal resignation list.'[12] Harold Wilson played the populist in the face of upper-class criticism, but perhaps the best comment on the whole affair came from the one man who was to be most closely identified with the list. 'Those who mind don't matter', said Sir Joseph Kagan on 27 May, 'and those who matter don't mind!'[13]

Wilson's cronies no doubt assumed their patron would also be honoured by the queen, retiring prime ministers being entitled to an earldom. Ramsay MacDonald had repeatedly refused all honours, but Clement Attlee took his earldom in 1955. Wilson had told the cabinet he was staying in the commons, but Barbara Castle knew he intended to fight only one more general election. It was announced, on 22 April 1976, that he was to become a knight of the garter. This was the most ancient order of chivalry, founded in 1348, and had been awarded to Churchill. The knight of the garter was altogether more important than the knighthoods dished out to MPs after some years of service. The sovereign of the order was the monarch, and the number of knights companions limited to twenty-four. Sir Harold paid out something like £650 for the cap and cloak of the order, and another £590 to the college of arms. His coat of arms was designed by Sir Anthony Wagner, the clarenceux king of arms. It incorporated the labour party's symbol of pen and spade, the white rose of

Yorkshire (the place of his birth), the red rose for Lancashire (the county of his parliamentary seat), the Trinity House ship (since he had become an elder brother in 1968), the arms of the Abbot of Rievaulx, and the Bishop Rock lighthouse to show his attachment to the Scillies. Wilson's motto was *Tempus Rerum Imperator* – timing is everything.

He attended his first annual garter ceremony in cap and cloak at Windsor Castle on 14 June, and was invested, with the Duke of Grafton, in the throne room in the morning. The jewelled order of the garter was buckled round the slenderest part of his calf. The queen and her knights then proceeded to the traditional banquet off gold plate. After lunch, the former prime minister and his new peers processed, two by two, down the hill to St George's Chapel. Wilson and Grafton led, the former 'grinn[ing] impishly at the crowds, and look[ing] Churchillian'.[14]

The question of post-prime ministerial office accommodation had been discussed with the chief whip, Robert Mellish, two large rooms being found for Wilson and Falkender at 2 Abbey Gardens in Westminster. Wilson was also given a small room in the commons. The removal from Downing Street was supervised by Marcia Falkender, Wilson's papers being shifted in their cabinets. The Wilsons were still running homes in Lord North Street, Buckinghamshire and the Scillies. 5 Lord North Street was sold at the end of 1976 and the Wilsons moved – for the twenty-third time – into a flat in Victoria in March 1977. Grange Farm was also sold, apparently that summer. The Wilsons would quietly move to north Oxford in the early 1980s, retaining their London base.

Harold Wilson had begun work on a book ten days after leaving Downing Street, *The Governance of Britain* being published later in 1976, by Weidenfeld and Nicolson in conjunction with Michael Joseph. A paperback followed in 1977. This was not a second attempt at prime ministerial apologia, Wilson presumably having promised Callaghan he would desist from writing about his second premiership before the next general election. Wilson had been riled by Crossman's diaries, but his *Governance* was to be promoted as 'a unique insight into how Britain is run from the top'.[15] It was evidently intended to preempt what he considered to be a distorted presentation of British politics. He defined the scope of the book in the preface: 'The office, function and powers of the prime minister as an essential part of Cabinet government within our parliamentary democracy. Certain essential elements in the governance of Britain, notably departmental administration, the role of the Civil Service and the vast and growing area of local government, are not covered.'[16] It was the work of a former prime minister on 10 Downing Street, a sort of memoir elevated to an institutional study. The state, in all its complexity, was reduced to the office of chief executive of Great Britain Ltd. Wilson was concerned to 'reject the philosophies of those who write of prime ministerial dictatorship', stressing countervailing power: 'the system of democratic checks and balances, in Parliament, in the Cabinet, and not least in the party machine and the party in the country'.[17] He ended by quoting Richard Neustadt's opinion that, while the British prime minister was not yet a president, the American head of state and government was 'a sort of super Prime Minister'.[18] This was a suitably complacent conclusion for a former British prime minister, who believed that 'a sense of history'[19] was a necessary condition for success. He compared his two stints at number 10, and situated them in the line of British prime ministers, through anecdotes and institutional description. Little was revealed, and no serious contribution was made to the intellectual study of British government. 'The checks and balances', he wrote, 'operate not only as long-term safeguards, but also ... almost every day. Historians and academic onlookers not only have the inestimable advantage of hindsight, they span long periods at a time. History is not really like that, still less are the warp and woof of governmental decisions that operate under varying but ever-present parliamentary vigilance and pressure.'[20] He had stated an intention to 'set out, with full discretion about what should not be set out, how Britain is governed',[21] and turned over familiar political nostrums of little offence to the establishment.

A second book, *A Prime Minister on Prime Ministers*, followed in 1977, in time for Christmas, again jointly published by Weidenfeld and Nicolson and Michael Joseph. Wilson placed himself forty-ninth in the line from Sir Robert Walpole in 1721, though Disraeli was the first to use the term officially in 1878.

The copyright belongs to David Paradine Histories, the book accompanying a television series of the same name – broadcast between November 1977 and February 1978 – and coproduced by Yorkshire Television and David Frost. He must have begun writing it in late 1976, Barbara Twigg, the television researcher, recalling he tried to do a prime minister a week. There were to be twelve in all, and he would be delighted with his daily output of words. Twigg remembers him telling stories he had already told, and she later did some – unpaid – research for Wilson. Marcia Falkender would acknowledge her assistance in 1983. *A Prime Minister on Prime Ministers* was broadcast as thirteen thirty-minute programmes, some six and a half hours of Harold Wilson talking. David Frost and Michael Deakin were the executive producers, Peter Morley produced and directed, and Antony Jay was the series editor. Robert Blake was recruited as historical adviser, though there was no script. Each programme was structured as Sir Harold Wilson in conversation with David Frost, an historic location being chosen for its close identity with the prime minister in question: the chancellor's room in the house of commons for Macmillan; Broadlands for Palmerston; Transport House – a nice irony – for MacDonald. Access was granted to film at Chequers for the programme on Baldwin. Wilson was required for most of the filming, turning up at each location in his government car over a number of months in 1977.

A Prime Minister on Prime Ministers was a work of historical tourism, by the third labour prime minister, rather than a description, if not an analysis, of British political power. It was an attempt to situate Wilson among former prime ministers, the book being a competent summary of selected lives, interspersed with Wilsonian anecdotes already well told. His work on British government was still in mind, and he formulated a pithy critique of the argument about prime ministerial power. 'The modern working of the British constitution', Wilson writes, 'depends on the doctrine that while the Prime Minister is more important than any member of the Cabinet, he is not more powerful than his Cabinet as a whole.'[22] He engages in a dialogue with a succession of prime ministers, allowing his personal sympathy, and in some cases admiration, to come to the fore. The most startling aspect of *A Prime Minister on Prime Ministers* is the absence of politics, particularly a socialist view of the world. Harold Wilson never had a strong inclination for ideology, except a sort of nonconformist, little England reformism, but seven years and nine months in Downing Street saw him bestowing benignity on a very mixed bag of political leaders. There is a subtext to the book, Wilson alluding repeatedly to the growing importance of party, and the development of skills of political leadership. He dismisses Baldwin's traditional critique of Lloyd George's lack of principles, finally voiced in 1922: 'Lloyd George and his colleagues had long been committed to [progressive] objectives, and did not feel it necessary to repeat them as a preamble to every tactical discussion.'[23] Lloyd George appealed deeply to Wilson in his day-to-day life as a politician, but he describes Baldwin in all-round sympathetic terms:

> A healer ... does not usually get a good press. Fleet Street thrives on confrontation. The same applies to a Prime Minister's control of his Cabinet. If he uses his political skills to keep the Cabinet together in pursuit of a common aim and common policies, he is condemned as devious; if he forces splits and public recriminations then, as long as he takes the right side in the division, he is a hero. But his cabinet disintegrates. A formula worked out and painstakingly negotiated with those in industry, or in a divided party, is attacked as a 'gimmick', or even a 'sellout'. A statement which exacerbates the situation, in industry or a party setting, is acclaimed as statesmanlike, though there is some difference between the treatment of a Conservative leader and that of a leader of a Labour Government.[24]

Wilson was to write his own political epitaph in 1979, in very similar terms:

I was regarded as one who tried always to work for a formula which would unite the party ... – and if it was one which had not been aired in the press there was disappointment and a feeling of deprivation. Many of the comments on my resignation referred to my constant desire, others even said ability, to unite the party – a latter-day Baldwin in fact. I do not regard this as a condemnation ... But a good old-fashioned confrontation generates more news and livelier comment. To the extent that ... I had kept the party united through such crises as the Common Market, the adoption of the anti-inflation policy in July 1975 – not to mention speedily ending the nuclear row after becoming leader of the party in 1963 – I was something of a disappointment ... To bridge a deep political chasm without splitting a party or provoking dramatic minis-terial resignations is sometimes regarded as something approaching political chicanery. This is to subordinate the realities of two hundred years of democratic politics to the demands of sensationalism. The highest aim of leadership is to secure policies adequate to deal with any situation, including the production of acceptable new solutions and policies, without major confrontations, splits and resignations.[25]

Wilson's politics were those of 'a latter-day Baldwin', but some considered it immodest of him to seek an historical analogy.

There was a secret side to Harold Wilson's cultural endeavours after he left office, concerning the conspiracies to which he believed he had been subjected. His mind returned to 1974, to the land deals affair and the question of his missing tax papers. The royal commission on the press was still sitting in April 1976, and it was another year before he could submit his evidence because of 'legal difficulties'.[26] It was a sloppy package. He forwarded the two papers Haines had written, the evidence proper and the annex on the land deals affair. Sir Harold corrected the typescript in his own hand, references to 'last year' being changed to 'in 1974'. There was also a 'postscript' by himself, and the text of a speech he had made at the Liverpool press club on 5 March 1976

Wilson made four substantive points in April 1977. First, there had been seven further burglaries of homes of staff members in his last three months at number 10, only two of which may have been 'common crime'. Secondly, when a series of television interviews with David Frost was announced, the contracts section of Yorkshire Television was burgled. Thirdly, there had been two burglaries at Lady Falkender's house. A television set had been stolen each time, and 'papers were rifled through'. Fourthly, his study at Grange Farm had been broken into at Easter 1977. Personal letters had been taken as well as bank statements, and the typescript of a book by a former colonial judge 'about his dealings with agencies of the South African Government'. Wilson implied that all this was opportunist crime, politicians' papers after Watergate being of interest to the press. A journalist had gained access to his new flat in Ashley Gardens, when it was being decorated, and a ground plan was published in a national newspaper. 'In the 250-odd years of British premiers', Wilson wrote, 'I am sure that this has not happened in the case of a former Conservative Prime Minister ... a year after his retirement from Downing Street.' He had taken legal advice though it was a 'small matter', but would be unsuccessful most likely given no physical damage had been done.[27]

It is not clear what McGregor and his colleagues on the royal commission made of this. Wilson's evidence found its way into *The Times* on 14 May, and the phenomenon of the burglaries into political folklore. When the final report of the McGregor commission was published in July, it was stated that Wilson's evidence had been received too late for consideration. The final report was near completion, and, in an addendum to the chapter on 'performance of the press', crowned with the name of the *Daily Mail*, the commissioners stated: 'We could not have referred to Sir Harold Wilson's extensive evidence without detailed investigation which must have included giving an opportunity to comment to newspapers and journalists mentioned in it. This would have taken a great deal of time and delayed considerably the publication of our Report.'[28] The McGregor report was complacent on the question of bias against the left: 'Within the terms of the agenda actually drawn up, however, the evidence we have had does not suggest that in either the national or the regional press at present the balance against Labour is a a strong one.'[29] Fleet Street had not been roughed up by Wilson's last royal commission, though Basnett and Goodman signed a minority report suggesting their colleagues had underestimated the crisis in the newspaper industry. Basnett also appended a note of dissent on the closed shop. But there was no attempt to fight the Wilson case, in the main report, or the six accompanying research studies.

He had refused to substantiate his 'cohorts of journalists' charge of September 1974, but seems to have gone now to the press council, belatedly in 1977. The press council rejected, in October 1978, the charge of a smear campaign in connection with the two general elections, and urged Wilson to withdraw his allegations. He wrote instead to *The Times*, his letter being published on 19 October. It had been a strange four years, starting with Wilson's initial refusal to see anything wrong in the land deals affair. He also failed to appreciate the context of increasing newspaper competition, at a time of growing political polarization in Britain. This led him to see the tory press as engaged simply in a conspiracy to unseat a labour prime minister. A younger Wilson might have handled the issue better, and, once he had resigned the premiership, he was in no position to fight a one-person battle against the might of Fleet Street.

He had returned to the issue of South Africa in May 1976. Two days after Jeremy Thorpe's resignation on the tenth, Albert Murray rang Barrie Penrose at his home. The latter was a freelance journalist working for BBC television news, and was invited for drinks that evening at Lord North Street. Another version has Penrose approaching Wilson for a comment on the alleged blackmail of Sir Harry Oppenheimer, the BBC having asked him to get reactions from British politicians. It is also believed Wilson 'had already tried to interest several newspapers in stories of "massive reserves of business money and private agents of various qualities engaged in a smear campaign"',[30] and only responded to Penrose when he got nowhere with the press.

Barrie Penrose turned up on the evening of 12 May, in the company of Roger Courtiour, another freelance journalist working for the *Tonight* programme, who had been investigating South African involvement in British politics. Falkender and Murray were also present. The two broadcasting journalists were secretly to tape Falkender later, but do not seem to have done the same to the former prime minister, despite the extensive quotations they would later put into circulation. Wilson had addressed the parliamentary press gallery that day, on the threat to democratic societies, and he revealed to two young and relatively unknown journalists, in the next ninety minutes, as much as he would have told Marcia Falkender in the previous year. She had done much of the research, and held a copy of Norman Scott's DHSS file. Gordon Winter was uppermost in Wilson's mind, though he had now returned to South Africa. 'I am not certain', Wilson told the two BBC journalists, 'that for the last eight months when I was Prime Minister I knew what was happening, fully, in Security [MI5].'[31] He told Penrose and Courtiour about, *inter alia*, the burglaries, the belief that he had been bugged, his meetings with Oldfield and Hanley the previous summer, a right-wing faction within MI5, Weidenfeld's mission about the CIA, South African involvement in the political destruction of Jeremy Thorpe, and, later, West German 'slush funds'[32] for the discrediting of the British government.

Most of the stories about Wilson's last months stem from this off-the-record briefing on 12 May 1976, but none of what Wilson said was very precise. The popular press had been interested in Thorpe only as a sex scandal, but Wilson claimed 'others occupying high office in Whitehall had also been involved in the affair'.[33] This may have been a reference to a senior civil servant in social services, or the cabinet office, but the British Watergate was already showing signs of becoming a case of history repeating itself as farce.

Penrose and Courtiour must have had difficulty believing their good fortune, given their deep throat had just resigned as prime minister. Wilson wanted them to work up the story, particularly by investigating the South

African connection. He visualized a major television documentary, which would be made with his cooperation, at which point he would go public. All this was by way of provoking his former cabinet colleagues into setting up a royal commission on, presumably, the attempted destabilization of his last government. He may even have wanted to chair a select committee of the house of commons, though Britain was very far from being the United States. Penrose and Courtiour may have already begun to see themselves as the British Woodward and Bernstein, and 'Woodstein' was spawning 'Pencourt'. Wilson offered to supply them with information. 'I see myself', he said, 'as the big fat spider in the corner of the room. Sometimes I speak when I'm asleep. You should both listen. Occasionally, when we meet I might tell you to go to Charing Cross Road and kick a blind man standing on the corner. That blind man may tell you something, leading you somewhere.'[34] It is not clear what Wilson's spiders and blind men had to do with a putative crisis of the state, in which a left-wing government may have experienced interference from MI5, assisted possibly by the CIA, or a more tangential threat from BOSS. Wilson saw his two guests to the door, showing them the seven-foot high Chubb safe, newly installed in the hall for his private papers. He gave them direct access to himself, a privilege probably only enjoyed by his secretary from 1963. 'Suggesting he might be under electronic surveillance',[35] he told them the phone was unsafe.

Penrose and Courtiour latched upon the reference to South Africa. 'Though the ex-Prime Minister ... had given them relatively few direct clues',[36] he did refer to Norman Scott's file in a Chelsea DHSS office. Barbara Castle, as the former minister, was reluctant to cooperate, and Jack Straw felt vulnerable as a temporary civil servant. Straw got on to Castle, who succeeded in getting Wilson to call off his dogs. They then discovered the Chelsea file had been destroyed in March 1975. Wilson clearly persisted in the belief that Scott was a puppet of the South Africans, and that the basis of the relationship was money. Penrose and Courtiour had returned to Lord North Street the following day, and they saw Wilson four times within a week. This was almost the end of their active relationship, though they were to give the impression that it lasted about eighteen months. Their fifth meeting was to be on 16 November. Penrose and Courtiour had not been believed by their editors at the BBC, but their first meeting was reported to Sir Charles Curran, the director general. He too was initially suspicious of Wilson's motives, but, after the latter summoned Penrose, Courtiour and Curran to Lord North Street, it was agreed that he would work exclusively with the two freelancers on the South African connection. MI5 was not the issue of public concern, and the BBC had simply been worried about harrassing Thorpe, now that he had resigned as liberal leader. Curran reported the project to the BBC's board of governors, who were extremely alarmed, but Penrose and Courtiour were contracted for a six-month period. A 'special unit' was set up at Lime Grove, coordinated by Gordon Carr, a producer from the newsroom, and there began 'the most expensive investigation the BBC ever undertook'.[37] The BBC quickly had its corporate fingers burnt by the South African story, when it broadcast a Penrose interview with a 'Colonel' Cheeseman on 18 May, the latter claiming he had seen dossiers on leading liberals at BOSS headquarters in Pretoria. Cheeseman was a former sergeant in the United States airforce, who was living on the dole in England and had been convicted of fraud. He boasted, the following day, that he had perpetrated a hoax.

The British Woodward and Bernstein reported frequently to Wilson through an intermediary, who seems to have been Albert Murray. But they did not seek to follow up his allegations about burglaries, bugging, MI5, and MI6, the right-wing faction within the former, including a hint about Peter Wright, the CIA, or the West German slush funds. They pursued Norman Scott, and trawled behind the leadership of the liberal party. This reservoir of supposed political principle was proving mirky, but it was hardly 'one of the most cancerous political scandals of our time'.[38] The liberals were a declining third force in British politics, and Jeremy Thorpe a discredited MP on the backbenches. Penrose and Courtiour were to be struck by the fact that Wilson's resignation announcement, the opening of Andrew Newton's trial (on a charge of killing Norman Scott's dog), and Princess Margaret's separation had all happened on 16 March 1976. They claimed the story of the dead canine 'involved three of the world's most powerful Secret Services ... it had undermined democracy and altered the course of British politics over most of the last two decades.'[39]

The BBC became uneasy about the Penrose/Courtiour investigation, and the head of the news and current affairs departments insisted that Carr should attend the meetings with Wilson. He chose not to, in order to protect the relationship already established. Carr prepared several treatments 'to justify the whole exercise ... all involv[ing] sadly some very lurid conspiracy-type scenario'.[40] Broadcasting House sought, that July, to impose stricter contractual terms, the BBC claiming ownership of all material uncovered, and Penrose and Courtiour finally broke with the corporation in September, claiming an establishment cover-up was taking place. '"That is bunk and they were told so"', said Curran, '"The story seemed to be turning into a kind of semi-criminal investigation and I thought that for the BBC to be financing air trips for two people to California [where Peter Bessell lived] and South Africa on what was going to be a police investigation anyway seemed to me to be an unjustified use of public money. I was not interested in pushing Jeremy Thorpe further down the hole".'[41] Penrose and Courtiour were to work closely with the police on the criminal investigation, a fact which would emerge at Thorpe's trial. Wilson told them that an independent company would be interested in a documentary, but, when Curran offered Wilson two other journalists, he declined. The Carr unit continued working after September 1976, but was closed down the following February. '"It is not unusual in journalism"', the director general wrote, '" ... to pursue a line of inquiry and then, after a lot of work, be forced to abandon it ... It is no discredit if our investigations have not produced the result we were led to expect ... There is no programme at the end of the day — at least not yet."'[42]

As the story of the Thorpe-Scott relationship was pieced together in the autumn of 1976, Wilson elaborated upon the burglaries and buggings. There had been too many break-ins, he argued, for this to be a coincidence. Roy Ranson of Scotland Yard had mentioned a South African connection. He felt the purpose may have been to plant bugs, and Sir James Goldsmith was going to have Grange Farm electronically swept.

Penrose and Courtiour had now signed a contract with Secker and Warburg, the publisher, Tom Rosenthal, being prepared to fund their independent investigation. They still failed to find a South African connection, but had come across the plot to murder Norman Scott, and amassed considerable documentation. The two journalists had their first meeting with Marcia Falkender on 22 March 1977, unfolding their evidence so she might brief Wilson. Falkender predicted his reaction: '"If he heard what you are saying he would stand with his back to the wall like a wounded stag."'[43] She was afraid Wilson might do something in the house of commons, and reported, at a third meeting on 5 May, that 'Harold [found] it difficult to accept'.[44] Talk of a murder plot had frightened Wilson, and he dropped Penrose and Courtiour, on the advice of the ubiquitous Lord Goodman. Goodman raised the possibility that the South Africans could be funding the two journalists. Rosenthal was taken to see Falkender on 10 May, and there followed a meeting, a week later, between Rosenthal and Wilson at Ashley Gardens. The latter agreed they could keep in touch with him through Falkender, though it would be deniable on his part. Penrose and Courtiour only saw Wilson once again, running into him as he left Wyndham Mews on 1 July.

They went public about Wilson just over two weeks later, the *Observer* agreeing to publish some articles starting on 17 July. The first article, by Colin Smith and Andrew Wilson, was entitled 'Wilson: Why I lost my faith in MI5'. It was based on Penrose and Courtiour's work, and checked with Falkender, but the paper was not so sure: 'While we cannot be certain whether Sir Harold was justified in his suspicions about MI5 or was merely over-reacting to a series of unconnected incidents, we are satisfied that the material does faithfully reflect the considered views of the former Prime Minister.' The *Observer* article claimed that Wilson believed there had been 'a constant whispering campaign against himself, his personal entourage and Labour Ministers', and that 'the head of MI5 ... confirmed the existence of an anti-Labour element within the service'. These words, in an article which the *Observer* virtually conceded was not based on fact, were the beginning of the MI5 destabilization story, which would run, and run and run. For over three years, Wilson had suspected the press and the tories, and then South Africa, but MI5 became, from 17 July 1977, the explanation for everything that had happened. Whether Harold Wilson continued to believe this or not, it became an article of faith for a great many other people.

The *Observer* was evidently not interested in the Jeremy Thorpe story, and Penrose and Courtiour quickly returned to the alleged plot to murder Norman Scott. Wilson had first learned of their findings in March 1977, but he issued a statement, that October, saying he had only been told about Scott 'some weeks ago'.[45] Andrew Newton was released from prison in April, and on 19 October the *London Evening News* carried the story that he had been hired to kill Scott. Wilson had wanted the two journalists to pursue the South African connection only, but on 27 October Thorpe admitted finally that he knew Scott. He also acknowledged that Bessell had helped Scott financially.

Wilson now tried to extricate himself entirely, by rewriting history, in a letter to Peter Blaker MP. But Wilson's account of the investigation was 'at variance with the relationship as [Penrose and Courtiour] had experienced it'.[46] He claimed the BBC had approached him, and while he saw the two journalists, he refused to give them further information. Penrose and Courtiour finished their book on 21 December 1977, and it was published early in February 1978 as the *The Pencourt File*. 'When [it] was published it seemed a mixture of naivety and surrealism; it was thick with verbatim quotes but appeared to be peopled by fantasists and madmen.'[47] *The Pencourt File* was a missed opportunity. It could have made a judgement about whether Wilson was being paranoid, and preempted much of the discussion about Peter Wright, and then Colin Wallace, in the late 1980s. The spook hunters, if not spooks, were to be laughing all the way to the bank, however, as some British investigative journalists sought to satisfy a public appetite for revelations about the power of the state.

The Pencourt File was quickly overtaken by Joe Haines's *Politics of Power,* published on Monday, 14 February 1977. Though in the genre of 'kiss and tell' revelations, this St Valentine's Day offering from Jonathan Cape was to become the most famous book on the Wilson years. It had been serialized the previous week by the *Daily Mirror,* starting with the resignation honours list. Day two was Captain Kerby. Marcia's Williams's peerage was the third front-page story. On Thursday, 10 February, Haines's revelations went to the centre pages. Day five was Wilson meeting the IRA. Saturday was a report on Marcia Falkender's response. Print journalists had a field-day, and the *Mirror* sold an extra half million copies during the five days.

'The impact of the serialisation', says Haines, 'was much greater than I personally expected.'[48] He explained on the day of publication why he had done it: 'I wrote *The Politics of Power* because the alternative was not to write it. To keep quiet. To say nothing. That was impossible.'[49]

Haines's explanation was no explanation. Keith Waterhouse, a columnist on the *Mirror*, referred to 'political correspondents [vying] with one another to out-tittle Mr. Haines' tattle',[50] only to be accused, in a leader, of having 'a rather bogus, even pompous attitude'. Wilson lamely protested about the 'dedicated hatchet job' from his former press secretary.

Haines's motives, other than financial, are not easily discernible, and it is therefore difficult to assess his judgements. Haines sought to answer his critics in the postscript to the 1977 paperback edition. He suggests the attempt to censor the Crossman diaries, and then discredit them, was his 'Damascus road',[51] but he also makes reference to the 'cohorts of journalists' speech. Haines had privately discussed resigning from the middle of 1974. He states that Wilson placed a high premium on loyalty, and this was something he himself valued. The book reveals a high regard for many of Wilson's qualities, and Haines quotes sympathetically a friend of the prime minister's – possibly Lord Goodman – saying in December 1975: 'Mr Haines, he will not go down in history as one of the great Prime Ministers, but if it had not been for that woman [Marcia Falkender], he would have gone down as the greatest.'[52] Haines writes in the preface that '[the] book is a very personal look at power and pressures in politics ... It is not so much about the theory and structure of power as about the way it operates in practice, which is a very different thing.'[53]

Haines and Wilson had only met once after Downing Street, for lunch at the Athenaeum in May 1976, the former prime minister having recently become a member. 'Neither of us, I fear', Haines was to write, 'is an uncritical admirer of the other's work.'[54]

The major event of Harold Wilson's final years was his chairing of what became known as the city inquiry. He had stalled in the early 1970s, on the question of nationalizing financial institutions, the first 1974 manifesto noting that the party's 'decision in the field of banking, insurance and building societies [was] still under consideration'.[55] It was not until the 1976 conference that the document, 'Banking and Finance', was approved, providing for the public ownership of 'important sectors of the banking and insurance industries'.[56] This was only the first part of a four-pronged attack. Labour also looked to the development of the existing national giro and savings banks. It wanted an investment reserve fund established, as in Sweden, and the transformation of the bank of England. The TUC was also concerned about the city, the lack of finance for industry being a principal worry. The labour party was less of a worry to the new prime minister in 1976, but it was the conference decision which propelled him to act. Callaghan may have wanted to find something for Wilson to do, and his credibility was sufficiently intact for the committee to assuage the labour party and even the TUC. Thus it was by a treasury minute of 5 January 1977, that Harold Wilson was given a chance to update Macmillan and Radcliffe, and leave his name in British financial history. It was really a case of kicking the issue of nationalization into touch for the duration: 'The name of the game was keeping it off the labour party agenda for as long as possible.'[57]

The committee to review the functioning of financial institutions, as it was called, was to be chaired by Harold Wilson. He was denied a royal commission, presumably to downgrade the final report. Some members were informally approached quite early on, and the committee was to turn out to be an unwieldy eighteen strong. 'That was the time', a Congress House official recalls, 'when we could determine membership of royal commissions.'[58] The trade unions had four members, led by Lionel Murray (whom Wilson had made a privy councillor in his resignations honours, to allow him to discuss the social contract), accompanied by Lord [Alf] Allen, chairman of the TUC economics committee, and Leif Mills and Clive Jenkins from the general council. Two trade unionists had been envisaged initially, but Jenkins insisted upon inclusion because he organized in financial institutions, and Mills had to follow on behalf of bank employees. Jenkins was to do much to oppose labour party ideas of public ownership, the trade unionists being joined by the heads of the cooperative wholesale society (CWS) and the CWS Bank. The academics were Dr Ralf Dahrendorf, director of the London School of Economics, who became deputy chairman, Professor Andrew Bain, Andrew Graham and Professor Joan Mitchell of Nottingham University. Dahrendorf was absent for part of the time, and, 'though enormously rational and persuasive', did not write the report. Bain had a technical expertise, and Graham was a politically alert economist. Joan Mitchell had worked with Wilson during the war, and he was to be 'incredibly rude about her'.[59] She declines to talk about him. Hugh Stephenson, *The Times*'s business editor and a labour councillor at the time, was there from the fourth estate. The remaining six members were drawn from the city and industry, perhaps the most important being Sir Kenneth Cork, who was to become lord mayor of the corporation of London while on the committee. Others were Sir John Prideaux of the national provident assurance, and two from clearing banks, including Richard Lloyd. From industry there was the deputy chairman of GEC, and the chairman of Unilever. There was also a representative of small businesses.

The committee's terms of reference were broad, 'to enquire into the role and functioning, at home and abroad, of financial institutions in the United Kingdom and their value to the economy'. The TUC was pacified in the instruction 'to review in particular the provision of funds for industry and trade'. The injunction 'to consider what changes are required in the existing arrangements for the supervision of these institutions, including the possible extension of the public sector, and to make recommendations'[60] was a gesture in the direction of the labour party. 'Th[e] last reference', Wilson was to state while the committee was sitting, '[was] rather low down on [their] practical agenda.'[61] Wilson, according to an observer, 'had always seemed intrigued by[,] but innocent of[,] the operations within the City'.[62] He had only just stopped railing against 'the speculators'. The members of the committee were selected largely by Callaghan, but he allowed Wilson to suggest Cork, and one or two others. There was no one from the stock exchange, but David Bruce, of Cazenoves, was taken on in a full-time research capacity. Wilson had wanted Donoughue to become committee secretary, but Callaghan refused to release him, and the senior policy adviser at number 10 cannot have been too distressed. Brian Hudson was succeeded, as committee secretary, by Christopher Kelly, who was to write the report, and it was serviced by the treasury, with an address at 54 Whitehall.

The Wilson committee held its first meeting on 18 January 1977, two and a half hours being devoted to discussing the subsequent press conference and fixing the next meeting. There were to be fifty-five meetings of the full committee, spread over the next three years, usually fortnightly on Tuesdays. It met first in Whitehall, opposite the cenotaph, but this was too noisy, and, at the suggestion of Cork, it moved to the Guildhall. This was symbolic, and Wilson was to say of Sir Kenneth Cork in 1979: 'as Lord Mayor he has not missed a meeting – he sometimes comes in half an hour late and goes half an hour early, but he usually attends the luncheon.'[63] Wilson's relationship with Cork was to be crucial. As a receiver, he knew something about underinvestment in industry. Eighteen of the fifty-five meetings were devoted to taking oral evidence, invariably after the submission of written material. 'I make no secret of the fact', Wilson was to say, 'that the City did not want us to be set up, but the City takes everything in its stride and it has got over its original doubts ... In the first year the evidence poured in and from the ground the pile measure[d] about 6 ft 6 ins – 2 metres, and the second year it was rather more than that. I do not have time to read it during the week, but I spend a lot of the weekend reading it, and I have got into the habit, once I have read it, of putting it on the household scales, and it averages something between 7 and 8 lbs a week. It is very readable but difficult and weighty stuff in its content.'[64]

Harold Wilson could still joke in public, but he was much less impressive to members of the committee. He would turn up with a briefcase, empty except for his cigars, and is described by one member as 'the least serious man in public affairs that I have ever met'.[65] He had no serious views on anything, certainly not the city. Wilson was simply a procedural chairman:

'He got through the day's business.' The committee could have done with some leadership, but Harold Wilson was determined only to stop it being a forum for debate. He was seen to be past it: 'He could just about cope with the mornings, and during the afternoons he could not remember what anybody had said.'[66] He only had a little to drink at lunchtime, but one member describes him as suffering from 'pre-senile dementia'.[67] No one of any influence was likely to complain. The government and city were pleased. The labour movement was divided between its political and industrial wings, and, within the TUC, Jenkins rivalled Mills. Harold Wilson gave the impression of wanting the committee to go on for some time, his priority remaining the achievement of a consensual view, however insignificant. The Bullock report on industrial democracy, inspired by Jack Jones, served throughout as a warning. When its conclusions were presented, in January 1977, three members, all industrialists, had signed a minority report. This Harold Wilson would do anything to avoid. As the inquiry was coming to the end of its work, the chairman was primarily interested in having a standing committee on the city established, over which he would preside. Wilson encouraged witnesses to publish their own evidence simultaneously, though it is not clear who suggested the idea, and selected oral and written evidence was published by the committee as it sat. The attendant public discussion became the *raison d'être* for the Wilson committee. It divided into two panels to hear some of the oral testimony, set up a panel on research and another on statistics. Fourteen of the eighteen members made it to Edinburgh, just before Christmas 1977, to take evidence from the Scottish banks and others. Five working parties were set up in April 1978, covering the topics of small firms, bank lending, overseas direct investment and exchange control, relations between institutional investors, and company management. Their reports were discussed that October, and some of them continued with their work. The committee also went to the United States in 1978, half to study the small business administration, and the other half the exchange commission. Various studies were also commissioned.

The committee had decided, early in 1977, to look first at the provision of funds for industry and trade, this being 'agreed [as] the subject of highest priority within [its] terms of reference'.[68] The trade unionists pressed for this approach, which became known as the first stage. The TUC members were caucusing at Congress House, their strategy being to try to neutralize the industrialists and bankers by winning over the academics. Bain and Graham, plus Stephenson, would all be cultivated. Questions of functioning, supervision, and public ownership were to be considered in a second stage of evidence, but, by 1979, Wilson was talking of stage two being 'the working o[f] the institutions',[69] public ownership being relegated to a third stage – which would never come. A progress report on finance for industry was issued in December 1977, this being largely a summary of first stage evidence to be published in eight volumes. The Wilson committee fudged on the all important question of whether industry was not seeking finance, or the institutions were declining to provide it. The TUC had called, in May, for an interim report, given that 'the major strategic problem ... [was] how to prevent and reverse in the 1980s the de-industrialisation of the United Kingdom'.[70]

Oral evidence was provided, in October, by David Basnett and Harry Urwin of the general council, but principally by two officials of Congress House, David Lea and Bill Callaghan. Basnett was looking forward to 5 per cent growth in the 1980s, North Sea oil being used to fuel an industrial strategy. The *Investors Chronicle* had expressed alarm at the TUC view of under-investment as being due to the city's refusal to fund industry, and the oral evidence was taken at 'a fairly rough meeting'.[71] In the end, Wilson extracted from David Lea the admission that the funds probably existed in the city. The labour party's first stage evidence had been submitted in August, and 'aroused a great deal of hostility among the institutions of the City'.[72] The party was criticized in detail in other evidence, and it was the TUC's idea of the need for a huge injection of cash which dominated the progress report. This document apologized for the city, arguing that, if it was not investing, this was for good reasons, namely better returns were available elsewhere. 'In general', Wilson was to say, 'the lack of new investment was affected by what the economists in my day would have called exogenous factors, including the policies of successive governments.'[73]

The small firm had figured prominently in the 1931 Macmillan report. The Wilson committee produced its own interim report, in March 1979, identifying small firms as still an important part of the British economy. The conclusions of the small firms report were to be incorporated, as an appendix, in the final report, but the committee was not able to agree on the idea of a small business agency, modelled on the American institution. It decided to consider it no further, on the grounds that it was at the margins of the terms of reference. Margaret Thatcher had come to power by this time, and the Wilson committee could only bemoan the government's failure to implement the earlier recommendations. The tories' budget of early 1980, 'with credit tight and interest rates high', saw 'the difficulties for small firms ... now more intense'.[74]

The Wilson committee moved on to its second stage in 1978, taking evidence on the functioning of financial institutions. All the principal city institutions provided accounts of their operation. The labour party, mindful of the reference to 'the possible extension of the public sector', submitted a document, in January 1979, specifically on the question of public ownership. 'Our aim is to defend the concept of public ownership as an instrument for achieving greater control of the flow of funds in the economy, and for making accountable the vast concentration of private power represented by the banks and insurance companies.'[75] It advanced a general critique of British capitalism: 'There is a conservative and exaggerated caution in both financial and industrial spheres in the UK which [has] held back industrial investment and hence the embodiment of technical advances in new capitalist equipment.'[76] The TUC's second stage evidence had been agreed the previous November, and it remarked, of the reports already published by financial institutions, that it was 'concerned that much of the evidence from the institutions [had] been unduly defensive and uncritical'.[77]

The final report appeared as two volumes in June 1980, the decision to publish being influenced by the conservative government's public expenditure plans. The committee had survived a first round of cuts, but the chancellor of the exchequer, Sir Geoffrey Howe, was known to be gunning for the Wilson inquiry. The city was quite happy to have Wilson report. The first volume was the report proper, the second a set of ten appendices. The report ran to twenty-seven chapters, many of them updating public knowledge and understanding of the operations of the city. The first chapter admitted fundamental differences on the committee, in spite of Wilson's claim during its sitting that it was 'well knit, united and very happy'.[78] 'It became obvious from an early stage that widely different views were held about how the economic system functioned and that this tended to be linked to differing judgements about how well the financial institutions operated at present and about how they ought to operate in the future.'[79]

The committee was politically hamstrung, as was evident in the conclusions, these being a statement 'of what [the members of the committee them]selves regard[ed] as the most important points'. There were nine in all. One, financial institutions, particularly pension funds and insurance companies, were of growing importance in the capital market. Two, it was not generally the case that there was a shortage of external finance, 'expected profitability ... [being] the major financial constraint on real investment'.[80] This clearly was a major point of contention on the committee. Three, it was inflation which dried up the issue of long-term industrial bonds, and this required an experiment in index-linking. Four, measures were needed to help small firms, including an English development agency. Five, it was against biases in the tax system, and controls for prudential or monetary reasons. 'Unintended or unnecessary divergencies from neutrality should obviously be avoided because of their effects on competition, and because they distort the allocation of savings between competing investment uses.'[81] The committee was in favour of competition between building societies. Six, there was no recommendation for an exchange commission in the securities market, but self-regulation required more supervision. Seven, the existing review body for this market 'should be replaced by a wide-ranging body composed of outside members as well as civil servants and reporting to Parliament'.[82] Eight, while the bank of England was now subject to a parliamentary select committee, non-executive directors 'from a wider range of backgrounds'[83] were recommended. Nine, public ownership was ruled out. 'Had we been designing a completely new system', read the report, 'some of us would have believed that there would be a role for publicly-owned insurance companies and a greater role for publicly-owned banks. But we have recommended against any extension of the public sector in these areas by the nationalisation of existing institutions.'[84] The city was safe from the designs of the labour party.

A contrary recommendation would have meant little, with labour out of office, but the Wilson report remains valuable for the social democratic solution it advances to the problem of under-investment in Britain. Chapter twenty, on stimulating industrial investment, was followed by the note of dissent, 'The Need for a New Investment Facility'. The dissenters argued that there was little chance of the 'conventional mechanisms'[85] supplying essential funds for industry. 'We are conscious that the nature of the crisis facing the British industrial and financial systems is not fully appreciated.'[86] They called for 'a new investment facility', to be 'jointly funded by the public sector and the long-term investing institutions'.[87] The need for investment, it was argued, could be met, partly because of the growth of pension funds, and partly because of North Sea oil and gas. (The pension funds had been attracting attention for some time; Clive Jenkins had noticed their growth, and had alerted the TUC and labour party.) 'To safeguard the interests of policy holders and ... pensioners the return of the institutions would be guaranteed by the government at a level equal to that for gilt-edged stock, but open-ended at the top.'[88] With a government guarantee, the facility would be offering an attractive form of investment. The minority recommended that the institutions should give one billion pounds, and the government the same, from North Sea revenues. Here Wilson dissented from the dissenters, arguing that the government's billion 'should be adequate, but that as industry drew that figure down, it should be topped up by the institutions to maintain it at a steady level of £1 billion'.[89] The TUC nominees wanted to start with £2 billion, take 10 per cent of the institutions' annual outflow each year, and match it from the public sector. The goal was to have £2 billion to invest each year. The facility was to have a tripartite steering committee, of employers and employee representatives, plus civil servants.

The idea implied an element of state coercion. 'We consider that a general power of direction over the institutions would be needed, partly if a significant minority, especially of the most sizeable institutions, were unwilling to participate on a voluntary basis.'[90] This was the rub. Wilson's idea did not formally imply coercion of private capital, but the TUC's was quite frankly confiscatory, albeit with the promise of a profit at the end. It was not, the note protested, a statist approach: 'We accept the importance of developing public sector agencies but this alone will not be enough. The need to develop links between the private and public sectors, and the importance of the tripartite approach in a mixed economy such as ours as a way of ensuring public confidence and accountability are crucial.'[91] 'Tripartism', they wrote, '[was] based on a recognition of the fact that the government, employers, and trade unions are permanent and respective centres of power in the economy.'[92]

As this was being written, tripartism was being buried. The unions were being excluded from the corridors of power, and certainly from the formulation of policy. The conservative government was committed to a free market, in which the city would be allowed to continue doing what it wanted. The Wilson committee resulted in a mountain of a report, with thirteen volumes of evidence and three research reports. It was one of the taller peaks in the range of British government blue books, Harold Wilson, as chairman, securing his place in administrative history.

He had told the cabinet, in March 1976, that he would remain in the commons for as long as his constituency was prepared to put up with him. 'I hope to see more of [my constituents] and put in more time on their behalf. I am above all a Parliamentarian. I love Parliament and want to go on serving it and serving in it.'[93] For the remainder of the parliament, and the following one, he was to do very little. Wilson would ask a few – mainly written – questions, and make a handful of interventions in debates. There was not much to show for the last seven of his thirty-eight years as a member of parliament. His last speech as prime minister had been on the vote of confidence on 11 March, when he attacked the left of his party for 'luxuriat[ing] in an odour of sanctification'. Margaret Thatcher accused him of being angry 'because it [was] his own failure that [was] on trial'.[94] He continued to answer questions until Callaghan took over. It was 13 December before plain Sir Harold next spoke in the house on the devolution bill, pronouncing himself in favour of the transfer of power from Whitehall to the regions of England as well. He attacked the *Daily Mail,* in the spring adjournment debate in May 1977, shortly after he had presented his evidence to the royal commission on the press. Starting with the Zinoviev letter, he rehearsed that paper's involvement in the land deals affair and the fake Short bank account. He argued that, if the paper published a document believing it genuine, it must also realize it was stolen. Wilson accused the *Mail* of operating on the principle that 'mud always sticks'.[95] It was December before he spoke again, in a debate on the crown agents. Malpractice during his time was being alleged, and the former prime minister pointed 'to the remarkable fact of the Parliament which did not bark in the night in those years'.[96] His few questions were probably inspired by friends or constituents. He had asked Shirley Williams about the teaching of Russian in Britain in October 1977, and the following June he asked Eric Varley about financial assistance to Lucas Aerospace. He was told by Gerald Kaufman, now a junior industry minister, that the government was providing a new factory in Huyton. The past again caught up with Wilson during the debate on the queen's speech, at the beginning of the 1978–9 session. He spoke on the recently published Bingham report, about the breaking of Rhodesian sanctions, insisting he had known nothing of the activities of British oil companies at the time.

There followed the general election in May 1979, in which labour lost office. Harold Wilson was returned for Huyton for the tenth and last time. He had a comfortable majority as usual, but the conservatives improved their position. As an opposition backbencher, with Margaret Thatcher in power, he had cause to mention his work with the British film industry. He was less successful following the publication of his report on the city in June 1980. Wilson asked the leader of the house, Norman St John Stevas, for a debate that December, but nothing was arranged. When a tory MP and banker was successful in a backbenchers' ballot, he arranged for the Wilson report to be debated on the morning of Friday, 23 January 1981. It was commended as 'a non-partisan, clear and lucid report'.[97] Wilson mentioned that the committee had been unanimously against nationalization, and had raised public perception of the building societies and pension funds. 'With hardly a question to Ministers or a clear debate there has been a massive takeover – a community takeover, not nationalisation, with scarcely a debate or any knowledge of what was happening.'[98] The financial secretary, Nigel Lawson, responded for the government, describing 'the report [as] a classic text book which will be read for generations to come'.[99] It took Jack Straw, speaking for the first time from the opposition front bench, to point out that Stuart Holland, now a member of parliament, and Tony Benn, had first raised the question of finance for industry in the early 1970s. Holland spoke towards the end, dissenting from the praise being heaped on the report. He believed 'the Government must take responsibility for overall savings and investment relationships with the system',[100] and pointed out that the NEB had been prevented from becoming 'a key agency for translating savings into investment'.[101]

Wilson was keen to be seen as a responsible leader in March, when Margaret Thatcher made her statement on Chapman Pincher's *Their Trade is Treachery*. She was asking the security commission to review procedures, though the government had been forced to defend Roger Hollis's reputation. 'Will the right hon. Lady', Sir Harold asked, 'confirm that although Sir

Roger Hollis operated during seven premierships – including my own – I was the first to set up an independent inquiry?'[102] He was determined that this should be placed on the record.

Wilson came back on the question of small businesses, during the budget debate in April, and his last speech in the commons was that July, when he spoke on behalf of Bradford University, during a debate on higher education cuts. His last parliamentary question, answered orally on 4 March 1982, was on satellite broadcasting.

Wilson had been ill during part of this time. Cancer of the bowel was diagnosed in 1980. Wilson's cancer was malignant, but his operation, at St Mark's Hospital in City Road, was successful. Wilson's cancer is thought to have delayed his report on the city, and it was from his hospital bed, on 25 June 1980, that he issued his press release as chairman. Barry Cockcroft, a television producer at YTV, turned up unexpectedly at the Wilsons' bungalow in the Scillies that summer, and found Sir Harold recuperating. Wilson was welcomed back to the commons on 11 December, having recovered from the cancer, with a long rest.

During the remainder of the October 1974 parliament, Sir Harold Wilson wrote a book on his second premiership. *Final Term: The Labour Government, 1974–1976* appeared in 1979, after the fall of the Callaghan government. It was clearly intended to be son of *The Labour Government, 1964–1970,* but was mercifully shorter, with 242 pages of text and 62 of appendices. Wilson had been in no hurry to write it after he stepped down, and he probably started the book in 1978, as the manuscript was with the publishers – again Weidenfeld and Nicolson and Michael Joseph – by early 1979. He added an epilogue after the general election defeat. No help was acknowledged in its writing, and there was no major serialization, or commensurate publishers' advance.

Harold Wilson published *The Chariot of Israel* in the spring of 1981, having visited the country the previous April, to speak at a memorial evening for Yigal Allon. A postscript was added in June 1980, presumably before he went into hospital. No help was acknowledged, though Martin Gilbert was thanked for permitting the reproduction of several maps. With the subtitle, *Britain, America and the State of Israel,* it was Wilson's first attempt at a scholarly history. He had long been a supporter of the state of Israel, and involved with prominent British Jews. An account of the reality of Zionism was a legitimate intellectual project, but the book is interesting only because Wilson was prime minister during the 1967 war. Wilson protests it was not a history of the middle east, but it is not even a good monographic account of British and American policy, being written largely from secondary sources. More might have been expected from a book about state formation, in an area like the middle east, especially when the author was a member of one of the declining imperial powers at the time. Wilson lacks any appreciation, as a historical narrator, of the complexity of forces, and economic and social development is largely ignored. There is little of the drama of historical action, or the personality of key actors. It is only in the singular eleventh chapter that the multilateral character of British diplomacy in 1967 is conveyed, his skill for concise summation being to the fore.

Sir Harold Wilson retired from the house of commons in 1983, Huyton, as Knowsley South, being inherited by a local history teacher, Sean Hughes. Callaghan had resigned as labour leader in 1980, Wilson voting for Healey in the first ballot, but then switching to Michael Foot. He had gone by the time Kinnock took over after the 1983 election defeat. Wilson was in due course awarded a life peerage, taking the title Baron Wilson of Rievaulx. There was no general opposition in Huyton, even among the local labour party, to him accepting a peerage. Wilson was introduced to the house, 'in his robes', on Tuesday, 15 November, between Lords Longford and Shackleton. This was on the same day as the conservative, Lord Bruce-Gardyne, who was to later describe the place as a 'day-care centre for retired gentlefolk'.[103] Lord Kagan hosted a lunch for Wilson. There was also a tea, but this was more a family occasion, and included Sean Hughes.

It was several months before Lord Wilson of Rievaulx made his maiden speech, on 14 March 1984, in a debate on higher education. Wilson reminded the noble lords that he had first spoken there in 1945, when the commons was temporarily housed in their chamber, and, as a junior minister, he 'was assigned to the task of directing the progress of the other building'.[104] His few contributions to their lordships' debates were to be in a similar anecdotal vein, Wilson usually rising on behalf of some institution with which he was connected. On this occasion it was the open university, where his elder son was a lecturer in mathematics; his younger son was a graduate of the open university. Wilson claimed parentage of the institution, revealing he 'had partly in mind the fighting men of World War II',[105] despite the fact that this was not the generation to benefit from the open university. Lord Wilson attacked the treasury for opposing the idea. He reminisced about working for Churchill and Attlee, and uttered a heartfelt plea for the unemployed who numbered – he claimed – four and a third million. 'I am certain', he said, 'that [Churchill and Attlee's] message would have been "Action now" to stir our people and, above all, the younger generation to genuinely satisfying work and to training facilities that anticipate economic needs and opportunities.'[106] Wilson must have appreciated it was the end of an era, for all his efforts at historical recall. He addressed a question to Lord Whitelaw the following week, giving full support to the prime minister, after a meeting of the European Council at Brussels. When Wilson referred to 'the grasping habits of the French

Government, whose agriculture is almost the worst organised in Europe', the leader of the house thought 'it would perhaps be politic ... to allow his comments ... to rest in his mouth and not in mine'.[107] Wilson spoke from the front bench on 9 May, opening and closing a debate on unemployment. It was the last time he was to do so. He mentioned leading firms in his former constituency, and also described himself as 'a former head of the government manpower statistics branch under the Churchill Administration in wartime'.[108] He made the point about the pension funds having socialized British industry, and stated 'he never had such a pasting from the press'[109] as over devaluation in 1967. It was another two years before Wilson made a further intervention in the house of lords, in a debate on marine pilotage. Declaring that he had been an elder brother for eighteen years, he rose at 10.26 p.m. to speak up for Trinity House. He felt it was being slighted by the government. 'When I was a Minister', he recalled, 'officials used to take pride in presenting unbiased facts on which proper judgments could be made.'[110]

Harold Wilson was then seventy, not old for a man who had generally enjoyed good health in the hot house atmosphere of Whitehall and Westminster for forty-six years. But in 1986 he began to withdraw from public life. He had given up the chair of the British screen advisory council the previous year, and became president, because it was felt he was unable to carry out the duties. He was working on his autobiography, and may have started in the early 1980s, but his memoirs were to be written from memory, not private and cabinet papers. Wilson's recollections had long been shaped into a series of stories, which were improved in the telling, and he was planning two volumes as late as September that year. The first appeared the following month, entitled *Memoirs: The Making of a Prime Minister 1916–64*. The book is a personal account of his life until he entered Downing Street, but this relatively short work – of 214 pages – was not written by Wilson. It was ghosted by Brian Connell, probably on the basis of tape-recorded interviews, and, though widely reviewed, was not a success. For a man who had once had a prodigious memory, it contains many inaccuracies.

Lord Wilson gave a series of interviews to promote his memoirs, and John Torode did a piece for radio at Ashley Gardens. He observed later that Wilson looked 'more than his three score years and ten', and, more importantly, that 'his short-term memory [was] a little suspect'. He also described the role of Mary Wilson: 'she plants herself firmly at Lord Wilson's feet. She is ready to help him over any lapses of memory and to stop things dead if the going gets rough.'[111]

This suggests a degree of senile dementia, the most common form of this cruel ailment now being known as Alzheimer's disease. The family of Lord Wilson has not acknowledged he suffers from Alzheimer's disease, or anything similar, but it is an open secret in the palace of Westminster, to say nothing of the drawing rooms and pine kitchens of the political classes in London. Alzheimer's disease certainly accords with Wilson's behaviour since at least 1986. The delay in his second volume of memoirs is attributed, by Michael Joseph, to an unspecified illness. The transcript of a long interview with Phillip Whitehead, for *The Writing on the Wall*, shown on Channel 4 in 1985, shows Wilson hiding behind anecdotes, and occasionally making honest admissions of having no memory. His last appearance, as an interviewee, in a television documentary, was in November 1986, and it was obvious, even from the little used, that there was not much of the old Wilson left. He gradually gave up responsibilities in the late 1980s, though Lord and Lady Wilson remain socially active. He attends rounds of lunches, dinners and parties with his wife, that many old aged pensioners would find exhausting. At such social gatherings, the former prime minister launches into tales of his past, guarded by Lady Wilson, and occasionally Lady Falkender. Asked recently by a friend his opinion of *The Pencourt File,* Lord Wilson is reputed to have replied: "'Ah, Penrose, now which cabinet of mine was he in?'"[112] Those who meet him are invariably kind, and many refer to his much publicized cancer operation in 1980. The Wilsons travel frequently between Oxford and London, and to the Scillies. His photograph appears occasionally in the newspapers, and he unveiled a statue of Clement Attlee outside the library in Limehouse in late 1988. The house of lords is protective, looking after one of its own. But it remains a tragedy that a man, once noted for his formidable memory, should be so struck in his final years.

Notes and References

PREFACE

1. Cameron Hazelhurst & Christine Woodland, *A Guide to the Papers of British Cabinet Ministers, 1900–51*, London, Royal Historical Society, 1974, p. 152.

2. The first, *Harold Wilson: The Authentic Portrait*, was by Leslie Smith, a BBC producer, who had first met Wilson in 1951, and lived near him in Hampstead Garden Suburb. The book was published in June 1964, and issued as a Fontana paperback in November, with the front cover claim 'The first authentic biography of the man chosen to shape the new Britain'. Smith was sympathetic to Wilson, but not a member of the labour party, and the biography, based on taped interviews, was very much Wilson's view of himself. It had to compete with two entirely unofficial efforts in 1964: *Harold Wilson: A Critical Biography* by Dudley Smith, a journalist and conservative MP, who had observed Wilson for five years, but was obviously ignorant of the workings of the labour party; and *Harold Wilson and the 'New Britain'*, a sympathetic book by Gerard Noel, an aristocratic catholic publisher, who was much taken by Wilson's vision of the new Britain. It was republished in 1966 as *The New Britain and Harold Wilson: Interim Report, 1966 General Election*. Mention should also be made of a pictorial biography from Pergamon Press, edited by Michael Foot, but actually compiled by John Parker MP and Eugene Prager, which came out in time for the 1964 general election. The last in this line, *Pragmatic Premier: An Intimate Portrait of Harold Wilson*, came in 1967 from Ernest Kay, a former journalist and Hampstead Garden Suburb neighbour. It deals largely with Wilson's association with the Scilly Islands. The most serious book on Harold Wilson is by Paul Foot, the journalist and member of the – then – international socialists. Published as a Penguin Special in 1968, *The Politics of Harold Wilson* sold twenty-five thousand copies in six months. It did much to fuel a left-wing critique of the labour prime minister. Though written in the Hampstead home of his MP uncle, Michael Foot, the author argued that 'what [was] required [was] not a new leadership but a new socialist politics, with roots deep down in the Labour rank and file' (p. 21). It is surely a measure of socialist, and wider, disenchantment with Wilson, that only one biography

has appeared in the last two decades. This is Andrew Roth's *Sir Harold Wilson: Yorkshire's Walter Mitty* (1977). Roth, a parliamentary journalist, had intended to write a three-volume work, but came out with a critical volume the year after Wilson's resignation. The former labour leader secured an injunction on the grounds of libel. Roth claims he disproved all but one of many alleged libels, and the case was eventually settled out of court. It cost his publishers £10,000, and a paperback edition was cancelled.

3. Letter to the author, 11 September 1986.

CHAPTER 2

1. Letter from John McDonnell, 24 October 1986, editor *The Ryedale Historian*, periodical publication of the The Helmsley and District Group of the Yorkshire Archaeological Society.
2. *Journal of the Association of Teachers in Technical Institutions*, vol. 2, no. 3, April 1909, p. 38.
3. Ibid., vol. 2, no. 3, July, p. 10.
4. David Howell and John Saville, in *Dictionary of Labour Biography, Volume 3*, eds J. Bellamy and J. Saville, London 1976, p. 115.
5. Noel, *Wilson*, p. 17.
6. Harold Wilson and others, *The Party Leaders Speak on Education*, London 1963, p. 22.
7. Interview, Harold Ainley, 7 October 1986.
8. Wilson, *Memoirs: The Making of a Prime Minister, 1916–64*, London 1986, p. 10.
9. *A Brief Description of L.B. Holliday & Co. Ltd.*, booklet later issued by the company in Huddersfield, n.d.
10. Quoted in letter from M.J. Peagram, Managing Director, Holliday Dyes and Chemicals Ltd., Huddersfield, 14 November 1986.
11. Wilson, *Memoirs, 1916–64*, p. 13.
12. *Wilson*, p. 16.
13. Harold Ainley.
14. *Observer*, 9 June 1963.
15. Harold Ainley.
16. *Memoirs, 1916–64*, p. 13.
17. Quoted in Godfrey Smith, 'Notes for a Profile of a Politician', in the *Sunday Times Colour Magazine*, 9 February 1964 and Ivor Smullen, 'Could Do Better', in *Weekend*, 20–26 July 1966.
18. Harold Ainley.
19. *Memoirs, 1916–64*, p. 24.
20. Leslie Smith, *Wilson*, p. 24.
21. *Memoirs, 1916–64*, p. 23.
22. Kay, *Wilson*, p. 17.
23. *Roydsian*, no. 18, July 1928, p. 227.

CHAPTER 3

1. *Prime Minister*, p. 132.
2. Ibid.
3. Harold Ainley.
4. Quoted in Leslie Smith, *Wilson*, p. 33.
5. *Memoirs, 1916–64*, p. 17.
6. *Roydsian*, no. 28, March 1932, p. 42.
7. Letter, Irene M. Smith, 14 October 1986.
8. Ibid.
9. Letter, Winifred Large (later, Gurney), n.d., but October 1986.
10. Letters from E.H. Diggle, son of H.F. Diggle, 23 October 1986, Betty Clark, 19 October 1986, and Winifred Gurney (née Large), n.d., but October 1986.
11. Leslie Smith, *Wilson*, p. 48.
12. Letter, 19 October 1986.
13. *Roydsian*, no. 24, December 1930, p. 157.
14. F.S. Wilmut to Harold Wilson, 29 July 1945, quoted in Leslie Smith, *Wilson*, p. 54.
15. *Roydsian*, no. 20, May 1929, p 63.
16. Ibid., no. 28, March 1932, p. 41.
17. Ibid, no. 27, December 1931, p. 6.
18. Ibid., no. 30, December 1932, p. 82.
19. Interview, Douglas Richmond, 7 February 1987.
20. Ibid.
21. Wilson, *Memoirs, 1916–64*, p. 26.
22. Ibid., p. 27.
23. Douglas Richmond.
24. Leslie Smith, *Wilson*, p. 62.
25. *Huddersfield Examiner*, 2 March 1968.
26. Interview, Doreen Pitts (née Richmond), 24 July 1987.
27. Letter, Harold Wilson to Doreen Richmond, 29 October 1933.
28. Ibid., 11 March 1934.
29. *Memoirs, 1916–64*, p. 31.

CHAPTER 4

1. Interview, Prof. Albert Goodwin, 6 December 1986.
2. *Ruling Passions*, London 1978, p. 55.
3. Interview, Rev. Eric Sharpe, 7 December 1986.
4. *Jesus College Magazine*, March 1937, p. 469.
5. Interview, John Branagan, 23 October 1986.
6. *Jesus College Magazine*, June 1937, p. 491.
7. *Memoirs, 1916–64*, p. 32.
8. Ibid., pp. 34–5.

9. Interview, 30 April 1990.
10. Prof. Albert Goodwin.
11. *Memoirs, 1916–64*, p. 38.
12. R.B. McCallum to Paul Foot, 19 April 1967, quoted in Foot, *Wilson*, p. 31.
13. Letter, Margaret McCallum, 29 September 1986.
14. *The Times*, 26 January 1959.
15. Quoted in Leslie Smith, *Wilson*, p. 75.
16. *Jesus College Magazine*, June 1936, p. 435.
17. *Memoirs, 1916–64*, p. 38.
18. *Jesus College Magazine*, June 1936, p. 429.
19. Ibid. December 1936, p. 454.
20. Ibid. December 1936, p. 452.
21. Letter from Mr Justice [Raymond] Walton, n.d., but c. March 1987.
22. M.P. Ashley and C.T. Saunders, *Red Oxford: A History of the Growth of Socialism in the University of Oxford*, 2nd ed., Oxford 1933.
23. Ibid., p. 41.
24. *Oxford Guardian*, 19 October 1936.
25. Ibid., 9 November 1936.
26. Ibid., 2 February 1937.
27. *Listener*, 29 October 1964.
28. *Memoirs, 1916–64*, p. 34.
29. Ibid., p. 35.
30. Foot, *Wilson*, p. 23.
31. Ibid., p. 24.
32. Ibid., p. 25.
33. Mr Justice Walton.
34. Interview.
35. Letter.
36. *Oxford Guardian*, 2 February 1937.
37. Letter.
38. Godfrey Smith, 'Notes for a Profile', p. 9.
39. *Memoirs, 1916–64*, pp. 35–6.
40. Foot, *Wilson*, p. 29.
41. Letter to Paul Foot, 19 April 1967, quoted in *Wilson*, p. 31.
42. Letter to Paul Foot, 21 December 1967, quoted in *Wilson*, p. 30.
43. Private communication.
44. *Oxford Guardian*, 23 February 1937.
45. *Jesus College Magazine*, June 1937, p. 490.
46. Letter to Paul Foot, date unknown, quoted in *Wilson*, p. 32.
47. *Memoirs, 1916–64*, p. 41.
48. Letter from Sir William Beveridge's secretary to M.R. Lakin, 26 October 1938, Beveridge Papers, IXa 100, British Library of Political and Economic Science (BLPES).
49. Leslie Smith, *Wilson*, p. 77.
50. December, p. 502.

CHAPTER 5

1. *Jesus College Magazine*, p. 491.
2. 'Economic Research in Progress', undated 4 pp. typescript, Beveridge Papers, V 52, British Library of Political and Economic Science (BLPES).
3. Memorandum, 'Harold Wilson', 8 June 1987.
4. Letter to R. Fosdick, Beveridge Papers, V 50.
5. William Beveridge, *Power and Influence*, London 1953, p. 253.
6. Ibid.
7. *Politica*, September 1937, vol. II, no. 9, pp. 466–7.
8. *Politica*, p. 475.
9. *Power*, p. 254.
10. Beatrice Webb, *The Diary of Beatrice Webb: Volume Four, 1924–1943: 'The Wheel of Life'*, eds Norman and Jean MacKenzie, London, 1985, p. 393.
11. London, pp. x, xii–xiii.
12. Letter, 28 July 1936, in Beveridge Papers, IX a 100.
13. 'An Analysis of Unemployment III', *Economica*, vol. IV (new series), no. 14, May 1937, p. 180.
14. Beveridge, *Power*, p. 261.
15. Jose Harris, *William Beveridge: A Biography*, Oxford 1977, p. 362.
16. Harold Wilson, *The Beveridge Memorial Lecture*, 18 November 1966, London n.d., but 1966, p. 7.
17. 'Note on Needs of the Institute for Further Clerical Assistance, Computers and Research Assistants', November 1937, Beveridge Papers, V 52.
18. 'Statistics and Decision-making in Government – Bradshaw Revisited', Presidential Address to Royal Statistical Society, 15 November 1972, in *Journal of the Royal Statistical Society*, A, 1973, no. 136, p. 4.
19. Webb, *Diary ... Volume Four*, p. 418.
20. Quoted in Paul Addison, *The Road to 1945: British Politics and the Second World War*, London 1977, p. 213.
21. 2nd ed., London 1960, p. 89.
22. *Beveridge ... Lecture*, p. 3.
23. *Oxford Guardian*, 15 June 1937.
24. Beveridge Papers, V 52.
25. *Minutes of Meetings of the Warden and Tutors, 1922 -*, Bound Volume, Library of New College, Oxford.
26. *New College Record, 1937–1938*, Oxford 1938, p. 3.
27. *Memoirs, 1916–64*, p. 47.
28. Beveridge to Fisher, 25 November 1937, Beveridge Papers, V 52.
29. Beveridge, *Power*, p. 260.
30. Miss Zvegintzov (?) to M.R. Lakin, 26 October 1938, Beveridge Papers, IX a 100.
31. William Beveridge, 'A Programme of Research', June 1939, Beveridge Papers, V 50.
32. *Growing Up into Revolution*, London 1949, p. 113.
33. Ibid.

34. 'Cole and Oxford, 1938–1958', in Asa Briggs and John Saville, eds, *Essays in Labour History*, London, 1967, p. 27.
35. Lord Pakenham, *Born to Believe: An Autobiography*, London 1953, p. 87.
36. Interview, Lord Longford, 24 November 1986.
37. Ibid.
38. *Revolution*, p. 113.
39. Letter, 20 April, quoted in Foot, *Wilson*, p. 38.
40. Letter to Paul Foot, 16 January 1968, quoted in *Wilson*, p. 40.
41. *A Vote for Hitler*, Channel 4, 2 October 1988.
42. Beveridge, *Power*, p. 260.
43. P. 62.
44. Beveridge Papers, V 52.
45. William Beveridge, 'A Programme of Research', June 1939, Beveridge Papers, V 50.
46. Beveridge to Kenneth Potter, Longmans, Green & Co., 6 March 1939, Beveridge Papers, V 52.
47. Beveridge to Potter, 21 June 1939, Beveridge Papers, V 52.
48. Beveridge, *Power*, pp. 260–1.
49. Ibid., p. 260.
50. Janet Beveridge, *Beveridge and his Plan*, London 1954, p. 99.
51. Beveridge, *Power*, p. 260.
52. P. 75.
53. Wilson to Beveridge, 31 December 1939, in Beveridge Papers, V 52.
54. *Ormskirk Advertiser*, 5 October 1944.
55. Interview.
56. University of Oxford, *Report for the Year 1938–9*, Oxford, 1939, p. 6.
57. Henry Pelling, *Britain and the Second World War*, London 1970, p. 57.
58. Beveridge Papers, VIII 14.
59. Ibid.

CHAPTER 6

1. Beveridge Papers, VIII 10 14.
2. *Power*, p. 270.
3. Beveridge Papers, V 52; also copy article in XII 19.
4. Letter, 21 March 1987.
5. Ibid.
6. Ibid.
7. *Memoirs*, London 1978, p. 18.
8. S. Dennison, 'Note on Statistical Assistants for the Anglo–French Co-ordinating Committee', sent by W.L. Gorell Barnes to Sir Edward Bridges, 19 February 1940, CAB 85/32, PRO.
9. Interview, 15 April 1987.
10. Quoted in S.S. Wilson, *The Cabinet Office to 1945*, London 1975, p. 110.
11. *Autobiography of an Economist*, London 1971, p. 170.

12. Interview.
13. Letter, 3 April 1987.
14. Interview, Sir Alec Cairncross, 1 June 1988.
15. D.E. Moggridge, *Keynes*, 2nd edn., London 1980, p. 120.
16. R.F. Harrod, *The Life of John Maynard Keynes*, Harmondsworth 1972, p. 577.
17. Draft of letter to *The Times*, 9 May 1940, Beveridge Papers, VIII 14.
18. *Listener*, 13 June 1940.
19. Quoted in Beveridge, *Power*, p. 273.
20. Copy of Presidental Address, *Some Thoughts on the Organisation of Man Power*, Beveridge Papers, IXb 27.
21. Webb, *Diary ... Volume Four*, p. 458.
22. Beveridge, *Power*, p. 274.
23. Worswick, 'Cole and Oxford', p. 29.
24. *Report by the Commissioner for Man-Power Survey*, London, 5 October 1940, p. 3, Beveridge Papers, VIII 15..
25. Ibid., pp. 23–4, Beveridge Papers, VIII 15.
26. *Power*, p. 274.
27. Letter to William Beveridge, 10 June 1952, Beveridge Papers, 2b 51.
28. *Power*, p. 276.
29. *Change and Fortune: A Political Record*, London 1980, p. 86.
30. Harold Wilson to William Beveridge, 19 June 1952, Beveridge Papers, 2b 51.
31. 'Northern Ireland's Manpower Resources', 17 December 1940, COM 61/440, Public Record Office of Northern Ireland, quoted in Robert Fisk, *In Time of War: Ireland, Ulster and the Price of Neutrality, 1939–45*, London 1985, p. 453. There is also a copy, dated 1 January 1941, and numbered M.P.R. (41) 2, in Beveridge Papers, VIII 15, BLPES, and another in CAB 92/102.
32. D. Lindsay Keir, 7 March 1941, in COM 61/440, Public Record Office of Northern Ireland.
33. Beveridge, *Power*, p. 278.
34. H.M.D. Parker, *Manpower: A Study of War-time Policy and Administration*, London 1957, p. 105.
35. W.K. Hancock and M.M. Gowing, *British War Economy*, London 1949, p. 295.
36. Parker, *Manpower*, p. 105.
37. Beveridge, *Power*, p. 278.
38. Ibid., pp. 278–9.
39. In Beveridge Papers, VIII 15.
40. Dated 13 January 1941, Beveridge Papers, VIII 15.
41. Letter to Beveridge, 18 June 1952, Beveridge Papers, VIII 15.
42. *Power*, p. 279.
43. *The Second World War: A Guide to Documents in the Public Record Office*, London 1972.
44. *Power*, p. 280.

45. 'Schedule of Reserved Occupations', revised 10 April 1941, London, Ministry of Labour and National Service, p. 21.
46. 'Change of Occupation on the Military Register', LAB 6/642, PRO; also copy in Beveridge Papers, VIII 16.
47. 'The Problem of the Service Tradesmen', LAB 6/642, PRO; also copy in Beveridge Papers, VIII 16.
48. *Power*, p. 282.
49. Addison, *1945*, p. 211.
50. Minutes, first meeting, LAB 8/846, PRO.
51. *Power*, p. 284.
52. *Committee on Skilled Men in the Services*, Second Report, London, Ministry of Labour and National Service, February 1942, Cmd. 6339, p. 24.
53. Letter, 31 October 1941, LAB 25/147, PRO.

CHAPTER 7

1. Memo, S. Wright to, possibly, Sir Alfred Hurst, n.d., POWE 10/216.
2. Letter to Arton Wilson, n.d., POWE 10/216.
3. Memo, S. Wright to, possibly, Sir Alfred Hurst, n.d., POWE 10/216.
4. 18 July 1941, POWE 10/216.
5. Wilson, 'Bradshaw Revisited', p. 1.
6. Ibid., pp. 1–2.
7. Philip M. Williams, *Hugh Gaitskell*, abidged ed. with new material, Oxford 1982, p. 97.
8. Diary entry for 3 March 1942, in *The Second World War Diary of Hugh Dalton, 1940–45*, ed. Ben Pimlott, London 1986, p. 387.
9. Hugh Dalton, *The Fateful Years: Memoirs, 1931–1945*, London 1957, p. 389.
10. *The Second World War Diary of Hugh Dalton*, p. 407.
11. Memo, Harold Wilson to W.G. Nott-Bower, 7 August 1942, POWE 10/252, PRO.
12. Courtesy of Muriel Nissel.
13. Interview, 19 August 1987.
14. Robin Page Arnot, *The Miners in Crisis and War: A History of the Miners' Federation of Great Britain (from 1930 onwards)*, London 1961, p. 345.
15. Letter, 26 August 1987.
16. *New Deal for Coal*, London 1945, p. 67.
17. Memo, Harold Wilson to David Serpell, POWE 20/67, PRO.
18. Memo, Harold Wilson to Gwilym Lloyd George, 20 April 1943, POWE 20/74.
19. Memo, Harold Wilson to Gwilym Lloyd George, 21 May 1943, POWE 20/74.
20. Memo, Harold Wilson to Sir Frank Tribe, 22 December 1943, POWE 10/252.
21. Ibid.

22. *New Deal*, p. 73.
23. Harold Wilson to Eric Sharpe, 26 March 1944.
24. Harold Wilson, 'Report to Lord Hyndley on L.C.P.R.B. Mission to Washington', POWE 10/252.
25. Quoted in Wilson, *Memoirs, 1916–64*, p. 74.
26. 'Report to Lord Hyndley', POWE 10/252.
27. Memo, Harold Wilson to S. Wright, 2 November 1943, POWE 10/252.
28. Harold Wilson to Tribe, 14 January 1944, POWE 10/252.
29. Memo, POWE 10/252.
30. Muriel Nissel.
31. Letter, 11 January 1944, Beveridge Papers, 2b 43.
32. Memo, 2 November 1943, POWE 10/252, PRO.
33. Letter, Harold Wilson to Bussey, POWE 10/252.
34. Memo, POWE 10/252.
35. Personal letter, Harold Wilson to Bussey, 27 September 1944, POWE 10/252.

CHAPTER 8

1. 4 December 1942, Beveridge Papers, 1a 50.
2. Letter, Beveridge Papers, 2b 44.
3. *Memoirs, 1916–64*, pp. 177–8.
4. POWE 20/62.
5. Ibid.
6. Quoted in Roth, *Wilson*, p. 72.
7. Quoted in Foot, *Wilson*, p. 41.
8. Interview, 7 December 1986.
9. *Ormskirk Advertiser*, 5 October 1944.
10. Ibid., 19 October.
11. Interview, 1 June 1988.
12. Interview, Stanley Dennison, 15 April 1987.
13. Interview.
14. Philip Mair Beveridge, *Shared Enthusiasm*, p. 102.
15. Beveridge Papers, 2b 43.
16. Letter, 30 April 1990.
17. *Ormskirk Advertiser*, 23 November 1944.
18. Ibid., 1 February 1945.
19. Ibid., 3 May.
20. London, pp. 172-3.
21. Alan Sked and Chris Cook, *Post-War Britain: A Political History*, 2nd edn., Harmondsworth 1984, p. 14.
22. *Ormskirk Advertiser*, 31 May 1945.
23. Ibid., 21 June.
24. *Memoirs, 1916–64*, p. 79.
25. *Ormskirk Advertiser*, 2 August 1945.
26. Ibid.

CHAPTER 9

1. 14 October 1944.
2. 27 July 1945.
3. 27 July 1945.
4. *Diaries and Letters, 1945–1962*, ed. Nigel Nicolson, London 1971, p. 27.
5. 27 July 1945.
6. *The Annual Register: A Review of Public Events at Home and Abroad for the Year 1945*, ed. M. Epstein, London 1946, p. 55.
7. Diary, 30 July 1945, quoted in *Time to Explain*, London 1987, p. 86.
8. Smith, 'Notes', p. 6.
9. Fred Blackburn, *George Tomlinson*, London 1954, p. 158.
10. *Fateful Years*, p. 478.
11. Blackburn, *Tomlinson*, p. 150.
12. C.P. (45) 118, 16 August 1945, CAB 129/1, PRO.
13. Blackburn, *Tomlinson*, p. 154.
14. *Wilson*, p. 103.
15. Blackburn, *Tomlinson*, p. 153.
16. *Hansard*, 1945–46, vol. 418, col. 268.
17. H. (45) 32, in CAB 21/1745, PRO.
18. *Memoirs, 1916–1964*, p. 83.
19. Cabinet Housing Committee, Minutes, 11 December 1945, CAB 134/120, PRO.
20. Ibid., Minutes, 13 January 1947.
21. Copy of text in WORK 11/487, PRO.
22. 6 December 1945.
23. *Hansard*, 1945–46, vol. 418, col. 274.
24. Ibid, vol. 421, cols. 143–4, 25 March.
25. Ibid, 1946–47, vol. 433, col. 2423, 27 February.
26. Circular, 'National and Regional Machinery for Consultation with the Industrial Organisations in the Building and Civil Engineering Industries', 29 October 1945, in WORK 45/27, PRO.
27. *Memoirs, 1916–1964*, p. 88.
28. 20 November 1946, from Washington, courtesy of Harold Ainley.
29. Letter, 11 February 1946, in PREM 8/229, PRO.
30. James Hinton, 'Self-help and Socialism: The Squatters' Movement of 1946', *History Workshop Journal*, 25, spring 1988, p. 104.
31. Cabinet Conclusions, 78 (46) 8, CAB 128/6, PRO.
32. Committee on Squatters in Military Camps, 20 August 1946, CAB 130/13, PRO.
33. Letter to T.L. Rowan, 12 September 1946, in PREM 8/227, PRO.
34. Second Note by Attorney General, 16 September 1946, C.P. (46) 364, CAB 129/12, PRO.
35. Typescript statement in HLG 7/1024, PRO.
36. Hinton, 'Self-help', pp. 101–2.
37. Interview, Lord Jay, 13 January 1988.

38. Report on FAO Conference, Washington, 20–27 May 1946, on Urgent Food Problems, FO 371/58307, PRO.
39. Memorandum, 14 October 1946, covering C.P. (47) 374, in PREM 8/501, PRO.
40. P.P., 1945–46, XX, *The World Food Shortage* (presented to Parliament, April 1946), pp. 224–5.
41. Telegram, Lord Inverchapel to Foreign Office, 25 July 1946, FO 371/58307, PRO.
42. P.P., 1946–47, XXV, *Report of the Preparatory Commission on World Food Proposals* (presented to Parliament, January 1947), p. 269.
43. John Boyd Orr, *As I Recall*, London 1966, p. 192.
44. Harold Wilson's Report on Preparatory Commission, 28 October to 18 December 1946, in FO 371/66871, PRO.
45. Telegram, Lord Inverchapel to Ernest Bevin, 4 March 1947, in FO 371/62863, PRO.
46. 16 December 1946, in PREM 8/501, PRO.
47. Wilson's Report, FO 371/66871, PRO.
48. L. Broadley to James Helmore, 2 January 1947, FO 371/66871, PRO.
49. Letter to Gorell Barnes, in PREM 8/501, PRO.
50. To L. Broadley, 31 December 1946, in PREM 8/501, PRO.
51. In PREM 8/501, PRO.
52. Wilson's Report, FO 371/66871, PRO.
53. Telegram, Lord Inverchapel to Ernest Bevin, 4 March 1947, FO 371/62863, PRO.
54. Draft Telegram, in PREM 8/501, PRO.
55. Douglas Jay, *Change and Fortune: A Political Record*, London 1980, p. 159.
56. Rev. John Wild to Sir William Beveridge, Beveridge Papers, 2b45.
57. Diana Farr, *Five at 10: Prime Ministers' Consorts since 1957*, London 1985, p. 97.
58. Ibid.
59. Roth, *Wilson*, p. 102.
60. *Pragmatic Premier*, p. 15.
61. *Ormskirk Advertiser*, 2 October 1947.
62. Ibid. 27 September 1945.
63. Ibid., 17 January 1946.
64. Ibid., 9 May 1946.
65. Ibid., 8 December 1945.
66. Ibid., 10 October 1946.

CHAPTER 10

1. Interview.
2. From Hector McNeil, 25 April 1947, in PREM 8/668, PRO.
3. O.E.P. (47) 18, in FO 371/66325, PRO.
4. Letter to Hugh Dalton, 7 June 1947, in FO 371/66325, PRO.

5. Wilson's Report, 11 August 1947, O.E.P. (47) 32, in FO 371/66333, PRO.
6. Ibid.
7. Wilson to Board of Trade, in FO 371/66328, PRO.
8. Kenneth MacGregor, 14 July 1947, in FO 371/62362, PRO.
9. O.E.P. (47) 32, 11 August 1947, in FO 371/66333, PRO.
10. In FO 371/66334, PRO.
11. Cable to Foreign Office, 2 August 1947, FO 371/66331, PRO.
12. 2 August 1947.
13. Cable, Foreign Office to Moscow Embassy, 11 August 1947, FO 371/66331, PRO.
14. FO 371/66341, PRO.
15. Sir Maurice Peterson to Christopher Warner, 12 December 1947, FO 371/66342, PRO.
16. Ben Pimlott, *Hugh Dalton*, p. 506.
17. *The Diary of Hugh Gaitskell, 1945–1956*, ed. Philip M. Williams, London, 1983, p. 35.
18. *Wilson*, p. 124.
19. *With Malice Towards None: a War Diary*, ed. William Armstrong, London 1970, pp. 301–2.
20. Gaitskell, *Diary*, p. 36.
21. *Memoirs, 1916–1964*, p. 98.
22. Gaitskell, *Diary*, p. 47.
23. *Nothing So Strange: an Autobiography*, London 1970, p. 112.
24. Ian Angus and Sonia Orwell, eds., *The Collected Essays, Journalism and Letters of George Orwell*, Volume II, Harmondsworth 1970, pp. 485–6.
25. *Change*, pp. 179–80.
26. Gaitskell, *Diary*, p. 49.
27. Leslie Smith, *Wilson*, pp. 125, 127.
28. 10 May 1948, Attlee Papers, 70 fol. 118, Bodleian Library, Oxford.
29. Gaitskell, *Diary*, p. 162.
30. Earl of Longford [Frank Pakenham], *Five Lives*, London 1964, pp. 253–4.
31. 2 October 1947.
32. Interview, 14 July 1988.
33. Leslie Smith, *Wilson*, p. 130.
34. Ibid., p. 146.
35. 'Britain's Overseas Trade', in Frank Illingworth, ed., *British Parliament*, London n.d., but 1948, p. 15.
36. Harold Wilson, 'International Trade Agreements', in *The Pattern and Finance of Foreign Trade: With Special Reference to the City of London*, London 1949, the proceedings of an Institute of Bankers international summer school at Oxford in September 1949.
37. Interview, 4 April 1990.
38. Draft Memorandum, sent to Prime Minister, 7 May 1949, in PREM 8/1416, PRO.
39. Minutes, 3 April 1951, in CAB 134/228, PRO.
40. Interview, 27 October 1987.

41. Quoted in Morgan, *Labour in Power*, p. 368.

42. *Memoirs of a City Radical*, London 1974, p. 166.

43. Economic Policy Committee, 7 November 1947, CAB 134/215, PRO.

44. Economic Policy Committee, Memorandum, 19 February 1949, CAB 134/221, PRO.

45. Interview, 15 November 1988.

46. Harold Wilson to Sir Stafford Cripps, 10 January 1949, CAB 127/153, PRO.

47. Leslie Smith, *Wilson*, pp. 144–5.

48. *Report of the Tribunal appointed to enquire into Allegations reflecting on the Official Conduct of Ministers of the Crown and other Public Servants*, P.P., 1948–49, XVIII, p. 506.

49. Harold Wilson to Clement Attlee, 15 February 1949, Attlee Papers, 78 fols. 260–2, Bodleian Library, Oxford.

50. E.P.C. (49) 65, in T269/2, PRO.

51. *Diary*, p. 117.

52. Note, 'The Need for Disinflation', Sir Edward Bridges to Cripps, T269/4, PRO.

53. *Diary*, pp. 127, 130.

54. Ibid., p. 131.

55. Ibid., p. 132.

56. Jay, *Change*, p. 187.

57. 12 September 1949, Hugh Dalton Papers, BLPES.

58. Gaitskell, *Diary*, p. 134.

59. Michael Foot, *Aneurin Bevan, 1945–1960*, London 1975, p. 267.

60. A. Bevan to C.R. Attlee, 21 October 1949, in T269/5, PRO.

61. E.P.C. (50) 4, dated 30 December 1949, in CAB 134/225, PRO.

CHAPTER 11

1. *Diary*, pp. 163–4.

2. Labour Party, *1948 Report*, p. 121.

3. Hugh Dalton Diary, 12 & 13 October 1949, BLPES.

4. H.G. Nicolas, *The British General Election of 1950*, London 1951, p. 204.

5. Dalton Diary, 26 February 1950.

6. *Prescot and District Reporter*, 17 February 1950.

7. *The Labour Government, 1945–51*, London 1963, p. 154.

8. Harold Wilson to Harold and Dorothy Ainley, 28 February 1950.

9. *Prescot and District Reporter*, 2 June 1950.

10. Ibid.

11. *Five Lives*, London 1964, p. 202.

12. *Diary*, p. 166.

13. Letter to Harold and Dorothy Ainley, 28 February 1950.

14. *Diary*, p. 164.

15. Minutes, Economic Policy Committee, 19 January 1950, CAB 134/224, PRO.
16. Quoted in Foot, *Bevan*, p. 286.
17. Letter, in PREM 8/1183, PRO.
18. Wilson's summary, in PREM 8/1183, PRO.
19. PREM 8/1183, PRO.
20. Ibid.
21. C.M. (50) 17, 3 April 1950, CAB 128/17, PRO.
22. *Diary*, p. 72.
23. Ibid., p. 77.
24. Ibid., p. 114.
25. Quoted in Williams, *Gaitskell*, pp. 149–50.
26. Gaitskell, *Diary*, p. 193.
27. Quoted in Williams, *Gaitskell*, p. 157.
28. *Change and Fortune*, p. 201.
29. Gaitskell, *Diary*, p. 216.
30. Ibid., p. 221.
31. CAB 128/19, PRO.
32. Alec Cairncross, *Years of Recovery: British Economic Policy 1945–51*, London and New York 1985, p. 232.
33. Quoted in ibid., p. 214.
34. Bevan to C.R. Attlee, c. 21 October 1951, quoted in Foot, *Bevan*, p. 297.
35. *Memoirs, 1916–64*, p. 114.
36. *Diary*, p. 229.
37. *Wilson*, p. 152.
38. *Diary*, p. 233.
39. Ibid., p. 242.
40. CAB 128/19, PRO.
41. Gaitskell, *Diary*, p. 242.
42. Hugh Dalton Diary, 5 April 1951.
43. Quoted in Foot, *Bevan*, p. 319.
44. *Diary*, p. 244.
45. CAB 128/19, PRO.
46. Letter, 10 April 1951, quoted in Foot, *Bevan*, p. 324.
47. CAB 128/21 N.C.R., PRO.
48. Quoted in Pimlott, *Dalton*, p. 599.
49. *Memoirs, 1916–64*, p. 118.
50. *A Prime Minister on Prime Ministers*, London 1977, p. 298.
51. Smith, 'Notes', p. 6.
52. Quoted in Williams, *Gaitskell*, p. 177.
53. Smith, *Wilson*, p. 155.
54. Interview, 4 April 1990.
55. Quoted in Foot, *Bevan*, p. 329.
56. Smith, *Wilson*, p. 157.
57. Foot, *Bevan*, p. 337.
58. Smith, *Wilson*, p. 159.

59. *High Tide and After: Memoirs 1945–1960*, London, p. 369.
60. Pimlott, *Dalton*, p. 599 and Dalton, *High Tide*, p. 369.
61. *Hansard*, 1950–51, vol. 487, col. 42.
62. *Prescot and Huyton Reporter*, 1 June 1951.
63. *Hansard*, 1950–51, vol. 487, cols. 228–9.
64. Quoted in Smith, *Wilson*, p. 161.
65. *Crisis in Britain, 1951*, London 1963, p. 283.
66. Gaitskell, *Diary*, p. 257.
67. Ibid., p. 238.
68. Ibid., p. 256.
69. Interview, 22 March 1990.
70. *Memoirs, 1916–64*, p. 119.

CHAPTER 12

1. Smith, *Wilson*, p. 166.
2. *Diary*, pp. 309–10.
3. Quoted in Williams, *Gaitskell*, p. 181.
4. Quoted in Morgan, *Labour*, p. 454.
5. *Bevan*, p. 336.
6. Ibid., pp. 339–40.
7. Interview, 4 April 1990.
8. *Wilson*, p. 157.
9. *Memoirs, 1916–64*, p. 113.
10. *Hansard*, vol. 430, col. 526, 18 November 1946.
11. Smith, *Wilson*, p. 168.
12. Interview, 27 October 1987.
13. Interview, 6 December 1986.
14. Quoted in Morgan, *Labour*, p. 412.
15. *Bevan*, p. 338.
16. *Prescot and District Reporter*, 18 May 1951.
17. Ibid., 1 June 1951.
18. *The Backbench Diaries of Richard Crossman*, ed. Janet Morgan, London 1981, pp. 47–8.
19. Interview.
20. Interview, 1 December 1987.
21. *Backbench Diaries*, pp. 53–4.
22. *Time and Chance*, London 1988, p. 71.
23. A term used subsequently.
24. Foot, *Bevan*, p. 370.
25. 5 August 1952.
26. Leslie Smith, *Wilson*, p. 169.
27. Labour Party, *1952 Report*.
28. Quoted in Philip M. Williams, *Hugh Gaitskell*, Oxford 1982, p. 207.
29. *Diary*, p. 272.

30. Ibid., p. 307.
31. Crossman, *Backbench Diaries*, p. 160.
32. Ibid., p. 162.
33. Ibid., p. 183.
34. Jenkins, *Bevanism*, p. 168.
35. Interview, Ian Mikardo.
36. Jenkins, *Bevanism*, pp. 170–1.
37. Peggy Duff, *Left, Left, Left*, London 1971, p. 46.
38. Jenkins, *Bevanism*, p. 171.
39. Crossman, *Backbench Diaries*, p. 206.
40. Harold Wilson to Unknown, undated latter, c. May 1951, quoted in Smith, *Wilson*, p. 166.
41. Smith, 'Notes', p. 13. See also, Marcia Williams, *Inside Number 10*, New York 1972, p. 104.
42. *Wilson, Memoirs, 1916–64*, p. 143.
43. Interview, 30 July 1987.
44. *Memoirs, 1916–64*, p. 144.
45. 'My Visit to Moscow, May, 1953', N.E.C./24.6.1953, Minutes of National Executive Committee of Labour Party, Microforms Fiche B7, BLPES.
46. *Backbench Diaries*, p. 250.
47. *Five Lives*, p. 38.
48. Williams, *Number 10*, p. 105.
49. Roth, *Wilson*, p. 37.
50. Labour Party, *1953 Report*, p. 187.
51. Crossman, *Backbench Diaries*, p. 272.
52. *Backbench Diaries*, p. 291.
53. Foot, *Bevan 1945–1960*, p. 427.
54. Minutes, Parliamentary Committee of Labour Party, 14 April 1954, available film 199, BLPES.
55. Crossman, *Backbench Diaries*, p. 313.
56. Ibid., p. 314.
57. Ibid., pp. 315–16.
58. Ibid., p. 317.
59. Ibid., p. 318.
60. Ibid., p. 321.
61. Quoted in Smith, *Wilson*, p. 171; see also, *Daily Mirror*, 29 April 1954.
62. *Memoirs, 1916–64*, p. 146.
63. Interview, 6 December 1986.
64. Ibid.
65. *Two out of Three*, London, p. 7.
66. Interview.
67. Ibid.
68. Crossman, *Backbench Diaries*, p. 323.
69. Ibid., p. 351.
70. Foot, *Bevan*, p. 448.
71. Ibid., p. 352.

72. Ibid., p. 435.
73. John Campbell, *Nye Bevan and the Mirage of British Socialism*, London 1987, p. xiii.
74. George Brown, *Spectator*, 24 January 1964.
75. *Diary*, p. 57.
76. Crossman, *Backbench Diaries*, p. 355.
77. Ibid., p. 361.
78. Ibid., p. 395.
79. Smith, *Wilson*, p. 172.
80. *Diary*, pp. 369, 373.
81. Smith, *Wilson*, p. 173.
82. *Prescot and District Reporter*, 20 May 1955.
83. *Liverpool Daily Post*, 21 May 1955.
84. *Backbench Diaries*, p. 423.
85. Labour Party, *1955 Report*, p. 64.
86. Ibid., p. 66.
87. Ibid., p. 65.
88. Ibid., p. 70.
89. Ibid., p. 65.
90. Ibid., p. 68.
91. *Memoirs, 1916–64*, p. 151.
92. Labour Party, *1955 Report*, p. 152.
93. Foot, *Bevan*, p. 489.
94. Crossman, *Backbench Diaries*, p. 409.
95. Ibid., p. 449.
96. Ibid., p. 423.
97. Foot, *Bevan*, p. 489.
98. Ibid., p. 491.
99. Crossman, *Backbench Diaries*, p. 451.

CHAPTER 13

1. Wilson, *Memoirs, 1916–64*, p. 152.
2. Crossman, *Backbench Diaries*, p. 453.
3. Smith, *Wilson*, p. 174.
4. Ibid., p. 176.
5. Interview, 2 May 1990.
6. *Pages from Memory*, London 1970, p. 133.
7. Quoted in Foot, *Bevan*, p. 498.
8. Gaitskell, *Diary*, pp. 409–10.
9. *Change and Fortune*, p. 250.
10. Interview, 13 January 1988.
11. Crossman, *Backbench Diaries*, pp. 470–1.
12. Nikita Khrushchev, *Khrushchev Remembers*, London 1971, p. 412.

13. George Brown, *In My Way: The Political Memoirs of Lord George-Brown*, London 1971, p. 73.
14. *Pages*, p. 150.
15. *Prime Minister*, p. 310.
16. Harold Wilson, *The Chariot of Israel: Britain, America and the State of Israel*, London 1981, p. 380.
17. Interview, 27 October 1987.
18. Crossman, *Backbench Diaries*, p. 471.
19. *Diary*, p. 440.
20. Ibid., p. 459.
21. Ibid., p. 494.
22. Minutes, Parliamentary Committee of Labour Party, 23 October 1956.
23. Ibid., 7 November 1956.
24. Diary, quoted in Harold Macmillan, *Riding the Storm, 1956–1959*, London 1971, p. 17.
25. *Memoirs, 1916–64*, p. 156.
26. Alastair Horne, *Macmillan, 1894–1956: Volume I of the Official Biography*, London 1988, p. 157.
27. Labour Party, *1956 Report*, p. 117.
28. *Backbench Diaries*, p. 521.
29. *Diary*, p. 617.
30. Naim Attallah, *Women*, London 1987, p. 109.
31. Ibid.
32. Ibid., p. 823.
33. Ibid., p. 242.
34. *Inside Number 10*, New York 1972, p. 101.
35. Ibid., p. 103.
36. Williams (as Marcia Falkender), *Downing Street in Perspective*, London 1983, p. 202.
37. *Inside Number 10*, p. 104.
38. *Downing Street*, p. 201.
39. Ibid., p. 97.
40. *Backbench Diaries*, p. 581.
41. Diana Farr, *Five at 10: Prime Ministers' Consorts since 1957*, London 1985, p. 100.
42. Haines, *Politics*, pp. 159–60
43. Falkender, *Downing Street*, p. 192.
44. Daniel Kagan, quoted in *Joe Kagan: Just Another Bump in the Road*, produced and directed by Barry Cockcroft, Yorkshire Television, shown on ITV network on 12 December 1980.
45. Crossman, *Backbench Diaries*, p. 566.
46. Ibid., p. 614.
47. Labour Party, *1957 Report*, pp. 181–2.
48. *Daily Herald*, 5 October 1957.
49. London, p. 57.
50. *Socialist Commentary*, October 1957.

51. Labour Party, *1957 Report*, pp. 128–31.
52. *Remedies for Inflation: A Series of Manchester Guardian Articles*, London, p. 14.
53. Private information.
54. *Remedies*, p. 15.
55. *Backbench Diaries*, p. 624.
56. Labour Party, *1957 Report*, p. 76.
57. Macmillan, *Riding the Storm*, p. 415.
58. Ibid., p. 418.
59. Ibid., p. 415.
60. Ibid., p. 426.
61. Anthony Howard, *RAB*: The Life of *R.A. Butler*, London 1987, p. 258.
62. *Backbench Diaries*, p. 662.
63. Ibid., pp. 685–6.
64. Ibid., p. 686.
65. Ibid., p. 768.
66. Ibid., p. 769.
67. *Memoirs, 1916–64*, p. 172.
68. Wyatt, *Confessions*, p. 271.
69. *Prescot and Huyton Reporter*, 25 September 1959.
70. Labour Party, *1959 Report*, p. 83.
71. *Backbench Diaries*, p. 788.

CHAPTER 14

1. *The Awkward Warrior: Frank Cousins: His Life and Times*, London 1979, p. 241.
2. Quoted in Williams, *Gaitskell*, p. 319.
3. 'Leader of the Opposition', in W.T. Rodgers, ed., *Hugh Gaitskell, 1906–1963*, London 1964, pp. 126–7.
4. Crossman, *Backbench Diaries*, p. 790.
5. Lady Gaitskell, quoted in Williams, *Gaitskell*, p. 316.
6. *Change and Fortune*, p. 278.
7. Crossman, *Backbench Diaries*, p. 791.
8. Letter to Alastair Hetherington, 10 December 1959, quoted in Williams, *Gaitskell*, pp. 316–17.
9. *Memoirs, 1916–64*, p. 173.
10. *Number 10*, p. 109.
11. Ibid., p. 110.
12. Interview, 25 April 1990.
13. Labour Party, *1959 Report*, pp. 107–9.
14. 25 October 1960, quoted in John Campbell, *Roy Jenkins: A Biography*, London 1983, p. 67.
15. Quoted in Goodman, *Awkward Warrior*, p. 248.
16. Foot, Bevan, p. 640. The phrase had been quoted by Castle and Gaitskell.
17. Quoted in Harold Wilson, *Purpose in Politics*, London 1964, p. 264.

18. Labour Party, *1960 Report*, pp. 218–21.
19. *Purpose*, pp. 171, 178.
20. Quoted in Williams, *Gaitskell*, p. 358.
21. Ibid., pp. 358–9.
22. *Backbench Diaries*, p. 881.
23. Ibid., p. 891.
24. Ibid., p. 884.
25. *Purpose*, pp. 72–3.
26. Ibid., p. 80.
27. Ibid., p. 46.
28. Ibid., p. 51.
29. *Backbench Diaries*, p. 942.
30. Ibid., p. 959.
31. Ibid., p. 960.
32. Ibid., p. 951.
33. *Purpose*, pp. 95, 97.
34. Quoted in Williams, *Gaitskell*, p. 404.
35. Ibid., p. 407.
36. *Purpose*, p. 116.
37. Ibid., p. 117.
38. Ibid., pp. 140–1.
39. Ibid., p. 142.
40. Ibid., p. 151.
41. Alistair Horne, *Macmillan, 1957–1986: Volume II of the Official Biography*, London 1989, p. 367.
42. *For Lust of Knowing: Memoirs of an Intelligence Officer*, London 1988, p. 469.
43. Introduction to Rodgers, *Gaitskell*, p. 7.
44. Dr Walter Somerville, quoted in David Leigh, *The Wilson Plot: The Intelligence Services and the Discrediting of a Prime Minister*, London 1988, p. 82.
45. Phillip Knightley, *The Second Oldest Profession: The Spy as Bureaucrat, Patriot, Fantasist and Whore*, London 1986, p. 342.
46. Interview, 27 October 1987.
47. Walter Eden, quoted in Leigh, *Wilson*, p. 86.
48. *Spycatcher: The Candid Autobiography of a Senior Intelligence Officer*, New York 1987, p. 54.
49. Leigh, *Wilson*, p. 84.
50. 24 October.
51. Paul Foot, *Who Killed Colin Wallace?*, London 1990, p. 58.
52. Interview, 20 June 1988.
53. Wright, *Spycatcher*, p. 363.
54. *Number 10*, p. 117.
55. *My Way*, p. 83.
56. *Backbench Diaries*, p. 969.
57. Ibid.
58. Ibid., p. 971.

59. Anthony Howard and Richard West, *The Making of the Prime Minister*, London 1965, pp. 32–3.
60. *Backbench Diaries*, p. 981.
61. *Number 10*, p. 119.
62. *Gaitskell*, p. 13.
63. Ibid., p. 103.
64. Smith, 'Notes', p. 12.
65. Blackett, *New Statesman*, 11 September 1964.
66. *Volume 1*, Harmondsworth, p. 8.
67. *Backbench Diaries*, p. 972.
68. *Purpose*, p. 28.

CHAPTER 15

1. Crossman, *Backbench Diaries*, p. 987.
2. Ibid., p. 983.
3. Ibid., p. 1001.
4. Harold Macmillan, *At the End of the Day, 1961–63*, London 1973, p. 434.
5. Ibid.
6. *Purpose*, pp. 208–9, 213.
7. Tony Benn, *Out of the Wilderness: Diaries, 1963–67*, London 1987, p. 40.
8. *Purpose*, p. 217.
9. Ibid., pp. 7–8.
10. *Sunday Times*, 6 October 1963.
11. Ibid.
12. *Purpose*, pp. 15–16, 23, 27.
13. John Cole, *Guardian*, 2 October 1963.
14. *Annual Register, 1963*, London 1964, p. 39.
15. *Backbench Diaries*, p. 1026.
16. Quoted in *Memoirs, 1916–64*, p. 199.
17. 2 October 1963.
18. Ibid.
19. Ibid.
20. 4 October 1963.
21. 4 October 1963.
22. 4 October 1963.
23. 5 October 1963.
24. 6 October 1963.
25. 6 October 1963.
26. Ken Coates, *The Crisis of British Socialism: Essays on the Rise of Harold Wilson and the Fall of the Labour Party*, Nottingham 1971, p. 17.
27. *Backbench Diaries*, p. 1021.
28. *Purpose*, pp. 215–16.
29. Labour Party, *1963 Report*, pp. 150–2.

30. Harold Evans, *Downing Street Diary: The Macmillan Years, 1957–1963*, London 1981, p. 301.
31. *Wilderness*, p. 81.
32. *Memoirs, 1916–64*, p. 196.
33. *The New Britain: Labour's Plan Outlined by Harold Wilson*, Harmondsworth 1964, p. 14.
34. Ibid., pp. 28, 32.
35. Benn, *Wilderness*, pp. 92–3.
36. *New Britain*, p. 91.
37. Ibid., p. 42.
38. Ibid., p. 134.
39. *Purpose*, p. 264.
40. Ibid., p. 270.
41. Michael Cockerell, *Television and Number Ten: Programme 1: 'Into the Torture Chamber'*, BBC 2, 12 November 1986.
42. Cockerell, *Television*, 12 November 1986.
43. 'Notes', 9 February.
44. Benn, *Wilderness*, pp. 104–5.
45. Ibid., p. 107.
46. Ibid., p. 135.
47. Ibid., p. 140.
48. Thomas Balogh, quoted in Benn, *Wilderness*, p. 148.
49. *Prescot and Huyton Reporter*, 18 September 1964.
50. Ibid.

CHAPTER 16

1. Harold Wilson, *The Labour Government, 1964–1970: A Personal Record*, London 1971, p. 2.
2. Ibid., p. 5.
3. Private information.
4. Sampson, *Anatomy*, p. 115.
5. Solly Zuckerman, *Monkeys, Men and Missiles: An Autobiography, 1946–88*, London 1988, p. 369.
6. Harold Wilson (plus Joe Grimond and Enoch Powell), *Whitehall and Beyond*, London 1964, p. 13.
7. Ibid., p. 16.
8. Ibid., p. 14.
9. Ibid., pp. 16–17.
10. Ibid., p. 18.
11. Ibid., p. 23.
12. Ibid., p. 20.
13. Ibid., p. 27.
14. Ibid., pp. 70–1.
15. *Change and Fortune*, p. 295.

16. Williams, *Number 10*, p. 14.
17. Benn, *Wilderness*, p. 160.
18. Howard and West, *Prime Minister*, p. 145.
19. *The Diaries of a Cabinet Minister: Volume One: Minister of Housing, 1964–66*, London 1975, p. 230.
20. *Time and Chance*, p. 162.
21. *Purpose in Power*, London 1966, pp. 3–4.
22. *Record*, p. xvii.
23. *Memoirs*, London 1978, p. 133.
24. *Time and Chance*, p. 160.
25. Sir Donald MacDougall, *Don and Mandarin: Memoirs of an Economist*, London 1987, p. 153.
26. Ibid., p. 152.
27. Kellner and Hitchens, *Callaghan*, p. 47.
28. MacDougall, *Don*, p. 153.
29. *Time and Chance*, p. 162.
30. Kellner and Hitchens, *Callaghan*, p. 50.
31. *Diaries ... Volume One*, p. 26.
32. Wilson, *Purpose in Power*, p. 9.
33. *Time and Chance*, p. 164.
34. *Change and Fortune*, p. 298.
35. Andrew Graham and Wilfred Beckerman, 'Introduction: Economic performance and the foreign balance', in Wilfred Beckerman, ed., *The Labour Government's Economic Record, 1964–1970*, London 1972, p. 24.
36. Susan Crosland, *Tony Crosland*, London 1983, p. 136.
37. *In My Way: The Political Memoirs of Lord George-Brown*, London 1971, p. 100.
38. Graham and Beckerman, 'Introduction', p. 25.
39. *Time and Chance*, p. 167.
40. Ibid., p. 168.
41. Ibid., p. 173.
42. Ibid., p. 174.
43. *Record*, p. 37.
44. *Time and Chance*, pp. 174–5.
45. Wilson, *Record*, p. 33.
46. *Purpose in Power*, p. 35.
47. Ibid., p. 14.
48. *The Castle Diaries, 1964–70*, London 1984, p. 107.
49. *Record*, p. 61.
50. *The Time of My Life*, London 1989, p. 273.
51. Anthony Verrier, *Through the Looking Glass: British Foreign Policy in an Age of Illusions*, London 1983, p. 258.
52. *Record*, p. 51.
53. Crossman, *Diaries ... Volume One*, p. 95.
54. Williams, *Number 10*, p. 42.
55. *Sunday Times*, 22 June 1975.

56. *Purpose in Power*, p. 25.
57. *Record*, p. 53.
58. *Diaries ... Volume One*, p. 96.
59. *Monkeys*, p. 369.
60. *Purpose in Power*, pp. 39, 41–2.
61. Ibid., p. 45.
62. Martin Gilbert, interview 13 July 1988.
63. *Diaries ... Volume One*, p. 145.
64. *Record*, p. 74.
65. Ibid., p. 143.
66. *Purpose in Power*, p. 167.
67. *Diary*, p. 62.
68. *Crossman, Diaries ... Volume One*, p. 368.
69. Private information.
70. Michael *Stewart, Life of Labour: an Autobiography*, London 1980, p. 170.
71. Wilson, *Record*, pp. 195–6.
72. Interview, 1 May 1990.
73. Quoted in Wilson, *Record*, p. 80.
74. *Time and Chance*, p. 188.
75. Private information.
76. *Diaries ... Volume One*, p. 253.
77. *Number 10*, p. 66.
78. Private information.
79. *Purpose in Power*, p. 55.
80. Ibid, pp. 56, 72.
81. Ibid., p. 59.
82. *Confessions*, p. 297.
83. Ibid., p. 300.
84. Ibid., p. 301.
85. Robert Rhodes James, *Ambitions and Realities: British Politics, 1964–70*, London 1972, pp. 25–6.
86. *Change and Fortune*, p. 323.
87. Wilson, *Record*, p. 129.
88. *Diaries, 1964–70*, p. 57.
89. *Time and Chance*, p. 190.
90. Labour Party, *1965 Report*.
91. Crossman, *Diaries ... Volume One*, p. 686.
92. James Margach, *The Abuse of Power: The War Between Downing Street and the Media, from Lloyd George to James Callaghan*, London 1979, p. 147.
93. Benn, *Wilderness*, p. 399.

CHAPTER 17

1. Benn, *Wilderness*, p. 400.
2. Ibid., pp. 223, 340.

3. Charles Bates, quoted in Leigh, *Wilson*, p. 89.
4. *Wilderness*, p. 131.
5. *Time*, p. 303.
6. Interview, Andrew Graham, 2 June 1988.
7. Quoted in Peter Hennessy, *Whitehall*, London 1990, p. 189.
8. *Record*, p. 230.
9. *Diaries ... Volume One*, p. 524.
10. *Record*, p. 236.
11. *George Wigg*, London 1972, pp. 332-3.
12. Benn, *Wilderness*, p. 436.
13. *Record*, p. 239.
14. *Diaries ... Volume One*, p. 554.
15. *Record*, p. 238.
16. Ibid., p. 251.
17. Graham and Beckerman, 'Introduction', p. 22.
18. Lyndon Baines Johnson, *The Vantage Point: Perspectives of the Presidency, 1963–1969*, London 1972, p. 308.
19. Barbara Castle, *The Castle Diaries, 1964–70*, London 1984, p. 151.
20. *Record*, p. 265.
21. *Number 10*, p. 149.
22. *The Lost Crusade: The Full Story of US Involvement in Vietnam from Roosevelt to Nixon*, London 1971, p. 355.
23. *Record*, p. 348.
24. *Crusade*, p. 356.
25. Ibid., p. 361.
26. *The Vantage Point*, p. 253.
27. *Crusade*, p. 362.
28. Ibid., p. 363.
29. Ibid., pp. 367-8.
30. Richard Crossman, *The Diaries of a Cabinet Minister: Volume Two: Lord President of the Council and Leader of the House of Commons, 1966–68*, London 1976, p. 83.
31. *Record*, p. 300.
32. *Change and Fortune*, p. 349.
33. *Record*, p. 390.
34. Ibid., p. 282.
35. Ibid., p. 311.
36. Ibid., p. 320.
37. *Diaries, 1964–70*, p. 526.
38. *Number 10*, p. 272.
39. *Record*, p. 570.
40. Ibid., p. 577.
41. George Thomas, *Mr Speaker: The Memoirs of Viscount Tonypandy*, London 1985, p. 91.
42. Sir Charles Cunningham, interviewed by Anthony Seldon, 29 May 1980, BOAPAH, BLPES.

43. Philip Ziegler, *Mountbatten: The Official Biography*, London 1985, p. 635.
44. Thomas, *Mr Speaker*, p. 91.
45. *Diaries ... Volume One*, p. 299.
46. Quoted in Brian Lapping, *The Labour Government 1964–70*, Harmondsworth 1970, p. 118.
47. *Diaries, 1964–70*, p. 373.
48. *Time and Chance*, p. 265.
49. *Diaries ... Volume Two*, p. 688.
50. Ibid., p. 734.
51. Quoted in Alan Sked and Chris Cook, *Post-war Britain: A Political History*, 2nd edn., Harmondsworth 1984, p. 232.
52. *Record*, p. 526.
53. *Number 10*, p. 368.
54. Transcript of interview for *The Writing on the Wall*, made by Brook Productions for Channel 4.
55. *Diaries, 1964-70*, p. 103.
56. Ibid., p. 273.
57. *Diaries ... Volume Two*, p. 407.
58. *Vantage Point*, p. 292.
59. Brown, *My Way*, p. 137.
60. *Vantage Point*, pp. 292, 295.
61. *Wilderness*, pp. 500–1.
62. Quoted in Abba Eban, *An Autobiography*, London 1978, p. 328.
63. Ibid., p. 346.
64. Ibid., p. 347.
65. Crossman, *Diaries ... Volume Two*, p. 357.
66. Ibid., p. 358.
67. Harold Wilson, *The Chariot of Israel: Britain, America and the State of Israel*, London 1981, p. 342.
68. *Autobiography*, p. 449.
69. *The Cabinet*, London 1970, p. 145.
70. Session 2, 10 April 1970, transcript of tape recording of George Brown, for *In My Way*, Anderson Papers, Bodleian Library, Oxford.
71. *Record*, p. 401.
72. *Diaries ... Volume Two*, p. 356.
73. *Chariot of Israel*, pp. 333, 335.
74. *Autobiography*, p. 449.
75. Williams, *Number 10*, pp. 193–4.
76. *Autobiography*, pp. 600–1.

CHAPTER 18

1. *Diaries ... Volume Two*, p. 21.
2. *Wilderness*, p. 470.
3. *Record*, p. 275.

4. Ibid., p. 419.
5. Quoted in *Time and Chance*, p. 214.
6. *Record*, p. 400.
7. Crossman, *Diaries ... Volume Two*, p. 437.
8. *Diaries, 1964–70*, p. 283.
9. *Union Man: The Autobiography of Jack Jones*, London 1986, p. 188.
10. *Time and Chance*, p. 217.
11. Ibid., p. 218.
12. Ibid., p. 219.
13. *Diaries, 1964–70*, p. 323.
14. Crosland, *Crosland*, p. 186.
15. *Time and Chance*, p. 222.
16. Castle, *Diaries, 1964–70*, p. 325.
17. *Record*, p. 460.
18. Ibid., p. 464.
19. Michael Cockerell, *"Full Circle"*.
20. *Diaries ... Volume Two*, p. 581.
21. Ibid., p. 583.
22. Castle, *Diaries, 1964–70*, p. 325.
23. *Crosland*, p. 187.
24. House of Lords, *Hansard*, vol. 286, cols. 926–7.
25. Ibid., col. 1025.
26. *The Times*, 23 November 1967.
27. *Change and Fortune*, p. 439.
28. Crossman, *Diaries ... Volume Two*, p. 588.
29. *Time and Chance*, p. 223.
30. Interview.
31. Crossman, *Diaries ... Volume Two*, p. 462.
32. *Diaries, 1964–70*, p. 333.
33. Session 1, April 1970, Brown transcript.
34. *Diaries, 1964–70*, p. 398.
35. Ibid.
36. Session 1, April 1970, Brown transcript.
37. Anthony Wedgwood Benn to Barbara Castle, 15 March 1967, quoted in Castle, *Diaries, 1964–70*, p. 401.
38. Brown, *In My Way*, p. 169.
39. *Diaries ... Volume Two*, p. 714.
40. *Record*, p. 373.
41. Ibid.
42. Chapman Pincher, *Inside Story: A Documentary of the Pursuit of Power*, London 1978, p. 244.
43. *Number 10*, pp. 184–5.
44. Ibid., p. 185.
45. Quoted in Leigh, *Wilson*, p. 108.
46. Quoted in Pincher, *Inside Story*, p. 237.
47. Ibid., p. 233.

48. *Record*, p. 418.
49. *Number 10*, pp. 196, 185.
50. Castle, *Diaries, 1964–70*, p. xv.
51. Mayhew, *Time to Explain*, p. 168.
52. Ibid.
53. Brown, *In My Way*, p. 171.
54. *Diaries ... Volume Two*, p. 477.
55. Ibid.
56. *Changing Battlefields: The Challenge to the Labour Party*, London 1987, p. 78.
57. *Diaries ... Volume Two*, p. 602.
58. *Time*, p. 335.
59. Session 1, April 1970, Brown transcript.
60. Crossman, *Diaries ... Volume Two*, p. 604.
61. Session 1, April 1970, Brown transcript.
62. Crossman, *Diaries ... Volume Two*, p. 606.
63. *Record*, p. 476.
64. Castle, *Diaries, 1964–70*, p. 719.
65. *Record*, p. 558.
66. Ibid., p. 639.
67. Ibid., p. 224.
68. Castle, *Diaries, 1964–70*, p. 231.
69. Wilson, *Record*, p. 388.
70. *Diaries ... Volume Two*, p. 111.
71. *Diaries, 1964–70*, p. 422.
72. Mayhew, *Time to Explain*, p. 182.
73. Ibid., pp. 177–8.
74. Ibid., p. 199.
75. Ibid., p. 178.
76. Ibid., p. 181.
77. Ibid.
78. Ibid., p. 182.
79. Ibid., p. 183.
80. Ibid., p. 184.
81. Ibid., p. 185.
82. Ibid., p. 186.
83. Ibid.
84. Wilson, *Record*, p. 646.
85. Crossman, *The Diaries of a Cabinet Minister: Volume Three: Secretary of State for Social Services, 1968–70*, London 1977, p. 465.
86. Ibid., p. 470.
87. Wilson, *Record*, p. 647.
88. Ibid.
89. *Time to Explain*, p. 187.
90. Ibid.
91. Ibid.
92. Philip Ziegler, *Mountbatten: The Official Biography*, London 1985, p. 659.

93. *The Cecil King Diary, 1965–1970*, London 1972, p. 72.
94. Ibid., p. 84.
95. King, *Diary, 1965–70*, p. 171.
96. Ibid., p. 192.
97. Hugh Cudlipp, *Walking on the Water*, London 1976, p. 330.
98. King, *Diary, 1965–1970*, p. 198.
99. Ziegler, *Mountbatten*, p. 138.
100. Cudlipp, *Water*, p. 326.
101. Hugh Cudlipp, 'The So-Called "Military Coup of 1968"', *Encounter*, September 1981, p. 11.
102. Ziegler, *Mountbatten*, p. 659.
103. Nigel West, *A Matter of Trust: MI5, 1945–72*, London 1982, p. 170.
104. Cudlipp, '"Military Coup"', p. 16.
105. Ziegler, *Mountbatten*, p. 660.
106. Quoted in ibid., p. 660.
107. Ibid.
108. '"Military Coup"', p. 20.
109. Ziegler, *Mountbatten*, p. 662.
110. Cudlipp, '"Military Coup"', p. 11.
111. Ziegler, *Mountbatten*, p. 662.
112. Michael Cockerell, *Television and Number 10: 'Into the Torture Chamber'*, BBC2, 12 November 1986.
113. Letter from Bob Wooler, disc jockey/compere, 1961–7, 25 November 1986.
114. Ed., *The Life and Times of Private Eye, 1961–1971*, Harmondsworth 1971, p. 18.
115. Alasdair Milne, *Director General: The Memoirs of a British Broadcaster*, London 1988.
116. Ibid.
117. *Diaries ... Volume One*, p. 486.
118. Labour Party, *1968 Report*, p. 164.
119. Tony Benn, *Office Without Power: Diaries 1968–72*, London 1988, p. 105.
120. Quoted in Michael Cockerell, *Television and Number 10: 'Full Circle'*, BBC 2, 13 November 1986.
121. Lord Hill of Luton, *Behind the Screen: The Broadcasting Memoirs of Lord Hill of Luton*, London 1974, p. 70.
122. Joe Haines, quoted in Cockerell, *'Full Circle'*.
123. Hill, *Screen*, p. 148.
124. *Guardian*, 31 October 1989.
125. See, for example, Crossman, *Diaries ... Volume Two*, pp. 120, 203 and Callaghan, quoted in Hennessy, *Whitehall*, p. 337.
126. Crossman, quoting cabinet minutes, *Diaries ... Volume Two*, p. 485.
127. Margach, *Abuse of Power*, p. 148.
128. *Diaries, 1964–70*, p. 468.
129. Interview, 12 May 1988.
130. Williams, *Number 10*, p. 229.

131. *Diary, 1965–1970*, p. 196.
132. *The Diary of a Cabinet Minister: Volume Three: Secretary of State for Social Services, 1968–70*, London 1987, p. 76.
133. *Office*, p. 82.
134. Ibid., p. 87.
135. Letter from Martin Roiser to Anthony Wedgwood Benn, 9 February 1969.
136. *Time and Chance*, p. 258.
137. Ibid.
138. Ibid., p. 261.
139. Benn, *Office*, p. 87.
140. Wilson, *Record*, p. 553.
141. *Diaries ... Volume Three*, p. 170.
142. Ibid., p. 179.
143. Ibid., p. 210.
144. 'The Wound Can Be Healed', interview with Alexander Dubcek, *L'Unità*, 10 January 1988, republished, *Guardian*, 11 January 1988.
145. Quoted in Wilson, *Record*, p. 478.
146. Benn, *Office*, p. 169.
147. Ibid., p. 172.
148. *Time*, p. 318.
149. Wilson, *Record*, p. 579.
150. Richard Nixon, *RN: The Memoirs of Richard Nixon*, London 1978, p. 370.
151. Ibid.
152. *Office*, p. 150.
153. *Record*, p. 621.
154. *Office*, p. 151.
155. Crossman, *Diaries ... Volume Three*, p. 385.
156. Castle, *Diaries, 1964–70*, pp. 607–8.
157. Nixon, *RN*, p. 370.
158. Wilson, *Record*, p. 756.

CHAPTER 19

1. Wilson, *Record*, p. 475.
2. Ibid., p. 468.
3. Crossman, *Diaries ... Volume Two*, p. 619.
4. *Office*, p. 2.
5. By A. Wedgwood Benn, in Crossman, *Diaries ... Volume Two*, p. 412.
6. Benn, *Office*, p. 6.
7. Crossman, *Diaries ... Volume Two*, p. 657.
8. *Don and Mandarin*, p. 173.
9. Wilson, *Record*, p. 513.
10. *Don and Mandarin*, p. 178.
11. Ibid.
12. Ibid, p. 176.

13. *Record*, p. 777.
14. Benn, *Office*, p. 117.
15. Derek Robinson, 'Labour Market Policies', in Beckerman, *Economic Record*, p. 314.
16. *Diaries ... Volume Three*, p. 298.
17. *Diaries ... Volume Three*, p. 358.
18. Castle, *Diaries 1964–70*, p. 645.
19. Crossman, *Diaries ... Volume Three*, p. 481.
20. Ibid., p. 670.
21. Wilson, *Record*, p. 539.
22. Quoted in Clive Ponting, *Whitehall: Tragedy and Farce*, London 1987, p. 190.
23. Crossman, *Diaries ... Volume Three*, p. 102.
24. Crossman, *Diaries ... Volume Three*, p. 107.
25. Wilson, *Record*, p. 540.
26. *Number 10*, p. 344.
27. *Diaries 1964–70*, p. 459.
28. Benn, *Office*, p. 122.
29. *Record*, p. 209.
30. *Report of the Royal Commission on Trade Unions and Employers' Associations, 1965–68*, London 1968, p. 12.
31. Ibid., p. 267.
32. Interview.
33. *Time and Chance*, p. 273.
34. *Office*, pp. 122–3.
35. *Diaries 1964–70*, p. 477.
36. Wilson, *Record*, p. 591.
37. Ibid., p. 539.
38. *Diaries 1964–70*, pp. 549–50.
39. Ibid., p. 551.
40. Ibid., p. 566.
41. *Time and Chance*, p. 274.
42. Castle, *Diaries 1964–70*, p. 589.
43. Interview, 21 July 1988.
44. Castle, *Diaries 1964–70*, p. 595.
45. Quoted in Wilson, *Record*, p. 627.
46. *Office*, p. 158.
47. *Diaries 1964–70*, p. 631.
48. *Office*, p. 158.
49. Ibid.
50. *Time and Chance*, p. 274.
51. *Office*, p. 159.
52. Castle, *Diaries 1964–70*, p. 635.
53. *Office*, p. 160.
54. *Record*, p. 643.
55. Benn, *Office*, p. 161.
56. *Diaries ... Volume Three*, p. 445.

57. *Diaries 1964–70*, p. 636.
58. *Record*, p. 646.
59. *Office*, p. 164.
60. *Office*, p. 166.
61. *Diaries ... Volume Three*, p. 480.
62. *Diaries 1964–70*, p. 647.
63. Crossman, *Diaries ... Volume Three*, p. 481.
64. *Diaries 1964–70*, p. 648.
65. Ibid., p. 649.
66. Ibid., p. 649.
67. Ibid., p. 646.
68. Ibid., pp. 649–50.
69. Crossman, *Diaries ... Volume Three*, p. 497.
70. Castle, *Diaries 1964–70*, p. 662.
71. *Autobiography*, p. 204.
72. *Office*, p. 186.
73. *Diaries 1964–70*, p. 672.
74. Ibid., p. 673.
75. Ibid., p. 674.
76. *Office*, p. 187.
77. Crossman, *Diaries ... Volume Three*, p. 523.
78. *Diaries 1964–70*, p. 678.
79. *Diaries ... Volume Three*, p. 529.
80. *Autobiography*, p. 206.
81. Letter to Patricia Cluskey, July 1964, quoted in Campaign for Social Justice in Northern Ireland, *The Plain Truth*, 2nd edn, Dungannon 1969.
82. Interview with Ken Pringle, January 1984.
83. *Record*, pp. 270–1.
84. *Office*, pp. 67–8.
85. Ibid., p. 271.
86. Castle, *Diaries 1964–70*, p. 640.
87. *Office*, p.. 195.
88. *Diaries 1964–70*, p. 696.
89. *A House Divided: The Dilemma of Northern Ireland*, London 1973, p. 27.
90. *Office*, p. 198.
91. Castle, *Diaries 1964–70*, p. 700.
92. Interview, Sir Oliver Wright, 1 May 1990.
93. Wilson, *Record*, p. 696.
94. Callaghan, *Northern Ireland*, pp. 62–3.
95. Crossman, *Diaries ... Volume Three*, p. 620.
96. *Northern Ireland*, p. 107.
97. Wilson, *Record*, p. 706.
98. Williams, *Number 10*, p. 288.
99. *Office*, p. 289.
100. *Diaries ... Volume Three*, p. 910.
101. *Diaries 1964–70*, p. 799.
102. Crossman, *Diaries ... Volume Three*, p. 921.

103. Castle, *Diaries, 1964–70*, p. 800.
104. *Record*, p. 783.
105. *Diaries ... Volume Three*, p. 908.
106. *Time and Chance*, p. 263.
107. Haines, *Power*, pp. 170–1.
108. Cockerell, *Full Circle*.
109. Ibid.
110. Castle, *Diaries 1964–70*, p. 804.
111. Crossman, *Diaries ... Volume Three*, p. 939.
112. Castle, *Diaries 1964–70*, p. 805.
113. *Diaries ... Volume Three*, p. 948.
114. Haines, *Power*, p. 172.

CHAPTER 20

1. Marcia Falkender (formerly Williams), *Downing Street in Perspective*, London 1983, p. 30.
2. Farr, *Five at 10*, p. 118.
3. *The Cecil King Diary, 1970–1974*, London 1975, p. 65.
4. Interview, 6 June 1988.
5. *Office*, p. 318.
6. King, *Diary, 1970–1974*, p. 88.
7. Ibid., p. 103.
8. Ibid., p. 139.
9. Interview.
10. Benn, *Office*, p. 297.
11. Ibid., p. 298.
12. Ibid., p. 318.
13. Haines, *Power*, p. 174.
14. Labour Party, *1970 Report*, p. 70.
15. Private information.
16. Labour Party, *1970 Report*, p. 71.
17. *Office*, p. 299–300.
18. Labour Party, *1970 Report*, pp. 136–7.
19. Ibid., p. 139.
20. Falkender, *Downing Street*, p. 20.
21. Ibid., p. 25.
22. Interview, 6 June 1988.
23. Falkender, *Downing Street*, p. 26.
24. Interview, Jane Mills, formerly Cousins, 10 May 1988.
25. *Downing Street*, p. 26.
26. *Diaries ... Volume Two*, pp. 47–8.
27. *Office*, p. 309.
28. 30 May.
29. *Wilderness*, p. 487; cf. also Castle, *Diaries, 1964–70*, p. 297, entry for 21 September 1967.

30. *Diaries, 1964–70*, pp. 212–13.
31. *Diaries ... Volume Three*, p. 899.
32. Roth, *Wilson*, p. 35.
33. Quoted in Lord Hill, *Behind the Screen: Broadcasting Memoirs of Lord Hill of Luton*, London, 1974, p. 179.
34. *Downing Street*, p. 32.
35. *Power*, p. 173.
36. Interview, 6 June 1988.
37. *Record*, p. vi.
38. *Power*, p. 176.
39. Interviews.
40. Interview.
41. King, *Diary, 1970–1974*, p. 62.
42. Martin Gilbert, interview.
43. E.P. Thompson, *New Society*, 29 July 1971, in *Writing by Candlelight*, London 1980, p. 55.
44. *The Cecil King Diary, 1970–1974*, London 1975, p. 125.
45. Anthony Seldon interview with Lord Shackleton, 1980, BOAPAH, BLPES.
46. Thompson, *Writing*, p. 58.
47. Lord Wigg, *George Wigg*, London 1972, p. 312.
48. *Office*, p. 451.
49. Peter Kellner and Christopher Hitchens, *Callaghan: The Road to Number Ten*, London 1976, p. 110.
50. Labour Party, *1971 Report*, p. 46.
51. *Office*, p. 328.
52. Ibid., p. 327.
53. Labour Party, *1971 Report*, p. 158.
54. Ibid., p. 165.
55. Jones, *Union Man*, p. 228.
56. King, *Diary, 1970–1974*, p. 79.
57. TUC, quoted in Jones, *Union Man*, p. 230.
58. Ibid.
59. *Office*, p. 337.
60. Labour Party, *1972 Report*, p. 76.
61. Benn, *Office*, p. 434.
62. Ibid., p. 438.
63. Tony Benn, *Parliament, People and Power: Agenda for a Free Society*, London 1982, p. 21.
64. *Office*, p. 442.
65. David Butler and Dennis Kavanagh, *The British General Election of February 1974*, London 1974, p. 22.
66. *Union Man*, p. 255.
67. Harold Wilson, *Final Term: The Labour Government, 1974–1976*, London 1979, p. 253.
68. Ibid.

69. Ibid., p. 254.
70. *Record*, p. 763.
71. *Office*, p. 258.
72. Labour Party, *1970 Report*, p. 141.
73. *Office*, p. 318.
74. *Office*, p. 316.
75. Ibid., p. 324.
76. Kellner and Hitchens, *Callaghan*, p. 116.
77. Ibid., p. 117.
78. *The Castle Diaries, 1974–76*, London 1980, p. 12.
79. *Office*, p. 358.
80. Labour Party, *1971 Report*, p. 329.
81. Ibid., p. 353.
82. Private information.
83. Labour Party, *1971 Report*, p. 359.
84. *Office*, p. 356.
85. Labour Party, *1971 Report*, p. 116.
86. *Hansard*, vol. 823, 21 October 1971.
87. Ibid., col. 2096.
88. Ibid., col. 2111.
89. Letter, Harold Wilson to Harold Ainley, 27 November 1971.
90. Falkender, *Downing Street*, p. 192.
91. *Office*, p. 359.
92. Ibid.
93. Castle, *Diaries, 1974–76*, pp. 12–13.
94. Benn, *Parliament*, p. 22.
95. *Office*, p. 400.
96. Ibid., p. 406.
97. John Campbell, *Roy Jenkins: A Biography*, London 1983, p. 143.
98. Quoted in David Butler and Ume Kitzinger, *The 1975 Referendum*, London 1976, p. 19.
99. Campbell, *Jenkins*, p. 144.
100. *Office*, p. 445.
101. Campbell, *Jenkins*, p. 146.
102. Butler and Kitzinger, *Referendum*, p. 20.
103. *Diaries, 1974–76*, p. 13.
104. *Office*, pp. 457–8.
105. Quoted in Butler and Kavanagh, *General Election of February 1974*, p. 19.
106. Crosland, *Crosland*, p. 244.
107. *Hansard*, vol. 843, col. 59, 17 October 1972.
108. Ibid., col. 795, 23 October.
109. William Whitelaw, *The Whitelaw Memoirs*, London 1989, p. 99.
110. *Office*, p. 385.
111. Haines, *Power*, p. 122.
112. Ibid., p. 124.
113. *States of Ireland*, London 1972, p. 300.
114. *Final Term*, p. 68.

115. Brian Faulkner, *Memoirs of a Statesman*, ed. John Houston, London 1978, p. 133.
116. *Office*, p. 387.
117. Ibid.
118. *Final Term*, p. 70.
119. *Hansard*, vol. 826, col. 1572, 25 November 1971.
120. Maria McGuire, *To Take Arms: A Year in the Provisional IRA*, London 1973, p. 95.
121. *States of Ireland*, London 1972, p. 286.
122. McGuire, *Arms*, p. 96.
123. Ibid, pp. 26–7.
124. Haines, *Power*, p. 128.
125. Seán Mac Stiofáin, *Memoirs of a Revolutionary*, London 1975, p. 239.
126. *Northern Ireland: A Personal Perspective*, London 1985, p. 28.
127. *Arms*, p. 97.
128. Rees, *Northern Ireland*, p. 27.
129. Ibid., pp. 27–8.
130. Peck, *Dublin*, p. 149.
131. Haines, *Power*, p. 163.
132. Ibid., p. 185.
133. Interview.
134. Ibid.
135. 'Spycatcher'.
136. Leigh, *Wilson*, p. 185.
137. Peter Wright, quoted in ibid., p. 189.
138. Leigh, *Wilson*, p. 110.
139. 'Spycatcher'.

CHAPTER 21

1. Michael Hatfield, *The House the Left Built: Inside Labour Policy-Making, 1970–75*, London 1978, p. 38.
2. Jones, *Union Man*, p. 236.
3. Hatfield, *House*, p. 154.
4. David Lea, interview, 21 July 1988.
5. Ibid.
6. *Office*, p. 409.
7. Ibid., p. 237.
8. Castle, *Diaries, 1974–76*, p. 10.
9. TUC-Labour Party Liaison Committee, *Economic Policy and the Cost of Living*, London 1973, pp. 3–4.
10. Ibid., p. 6.
11. Ibid., pp. 7–8.
12. Ibid., p. 8.
13. 5 May.
14. Hatfield, *House*, p. 137.

15. *Union Man*, p. 280.
16. Liaison Committee, *Economic Policy*, p. 8; also Wilson, *Final Term*, p. 43.
17. Castle, *Diaries, 1974–76*, p. 10.
18. David Lea, interview.
19. Labour Party, *1970 Report*, p. 185.
20. 27 August 1970; see also, Hatfield, *House*, p. 37.
21. Benn, *Office*, p. 307.
22. Interview, 3 May 1988.
23. P. 6.
24. Hatfield, *House*, p. 196.
25. Benn, *Parliament*, p. 26.
26. Labour Party, *1973 Report*, p. 161.
27. Ibid., p. 162.
28. Quoted in Butler and Kavanagh, *General Election of February 1974*, p. 50.
29. Labour Party, *1973 Conference*, p. 167.
30. Ibid., p. 186.
31. *Individual Choice in Democracy*, London 1973, p. 6.
32. Ibid., p. 7.
33. *Democracy in Local Affairs*, London 1973, pp. 4–5.
34. Ibid., p. 16.
35. Ibid., p. 8.
36. *Democracy in Industry*, London 1973, p. 4.
37. Ibid., p. 11.
38. Ibid., pp. 14–15.
39. *Israel*, p. 367.
40. *Battled Cherub*, London 1982, pp. 133–4.
41. *Memoirs*, p. 129.
42. *Cherub*, p. 135.
43. Castle, *Diaries, 1974–76*, p. 21.
44. Ibid., p. 20.
45. Quoted in Butler and Kavanagh, *General Election of February 1974*, p. 42.
46. *Diaries 1974–76*, p. 27.
47. *Final Term*, p. 5.
48. Hennessy, *Whitehall*, p. 238.
49. Quoted in Whitehead, *Writing*, p. 110.
50. Hennessy, *Whitehall*, p. 240.
51. *Prime Minister: The Conduct of Policy under Harold Wilson and James Callaghan*, London 1987, pp. 43–4.
52. Falkender, *Downing Street*, p. 55.
53. Cockerell, *Full Circle*.
54. *Prime Minister*, p. 46.
55. Ibid., pp. 40–1.

CHAPTER 22

1. *Prime Minister*, p. 47.
2. Butler and Kavanagh, *General Election of February 1974*, pp. 256–7.

3. *The Writing on the Wall*, Channel 4, 1985.
4. *Prime Minister*. p. 47; cf. also Wilson, *Final Term*, p. 17, Castle, *Diaries, 1974–76*, p. 37, and Labour Party, *1974 Report*, p. 141.
5. Castle, *Diaries, 1974–76*, p. 37.
6. Interview, Brook Productions, for *The Writing on the Wall* (provisionally titled, *The Seventies*), BLPES.
7. Interview, 25 April 1990.
8. Wilson, *Final Term*, p. 15.
9. Ibid., p. 26.
10. *Final Term*, p. 33.
11. Ian Aitken, 'Big Eric should know better ...', *Guardian*, 28 March 1988.
12. Stuart Holland, interview.
13. Aitken, *Guardian*, 28 March 1988.
14. John Silkin, *Changing Battlefields: The Challenge to the Labour Party*, London 1987, p. 45.
15. Donoughue, *Prime Minister*, p. 52.
16. *Final Term*, p. 33.
17. *Prime Minister*, pp. 54–5.
18. Benn, *Parliament*, p. 28.
19. Quoted in Wilson, *Final Term*, p. 34.
20. Interview with Anthony Seldon, 1980, BOAPAH, BLPES.
21. *Prime Minister*, pp. 54–5.
22. Ibid., p. 54.
23. Evidence of Sir Harold Wilson, submitted to the Royal Commission on the Press, April 1977, 242 E1, 'Annex A', p. 2. Copy in British Library. Also published, *The Times*, 14 May 1977.
24. Ibid., p. 9.
25. *The Times*, 23 July 1974.
26. *Downing Street*, p. 150.
27. Interview, Joe Haines, 12 May 1988.
28. *Diaries, 1974–76*, p. 153.
29. *The Times*, 23 July 1974.
30. Ibid.
31. Ibid.
32. *Inside Story*, p. 42.
33. Benn, *Against the Tide*, p. 137.
34. Marcia Falkender, *Downing Street*, p. 141.
35. Martin Gilbert to Chapman Pincher, 31 May 1974. Letter quoted to author, 13 July 1988.
36. Ibid.
37. Wilson, Royal Commission, Evidence, p. 8.
38. Ibid., 'Annex A', p. 8.
39. Interview, 6 June 1988.
40. Ibid.
41. Ibid.
42. Wilson, Royal Commission, Evidence, p. 8.

43. Quoted in ibid., postscript drafted by Harold Wilson, April 1977.
44. Benn, *Against the Tide*, p. 226.
45. David Butler and Dennis Kavanagh, *The British General Election of October 1974*, London 1975, p. 171.
46. Wilson, Royal Commission, Evidence, p. 1.
47. 'Annex A', p. 8.
48. *Power*.
49. Ibid.
50. Wilson, Royal Commission, Evidence, p. 2.
51. Ibid., p. 4.
52. Ibid., p. 10.
53. Ibid.
54. *Memoirs*, p. 122.
55. *Power*, p. 132.
56. *Northern Ireland*, p. 60.
57. *Against the Tide*, pp. 137–8.
58. *Northern Ireland*, p. 68.
59. Donoughue, *Prime Minister*, p. 128.
60. Ibid., p. 129.
61. Rees, *Northern Ireland*, p. 71.
62. Ibid., p. 69.
63. Ibid., p. 75.
64. Interview, 17 May 1990.
65. Robert Fisk, *The Point of No Return: The Strike Which Broke the British in Ulster*, London 1975, p. 66.
66. Rees, *Northern Ireland*, p. 77.
67. *Final Term*, p. 76.
68. Ibid.
69. *Prime Minister*, p. 130.
70. Ibid.
71. Ibid.
72. Cecil King, *Diaries, 1970–1974*, p. 365.
73. *Northern Ireland*, p. 80.
74. Ibid., p. 82.
75. Ibid., p. 90.
76. *Final Term*, p. 64.
77. *Time and Chance*, pp. 353–4.
78. Castle, *Diaries, 1974–76*, p. 227.
79. Ibid., p. 390.
80. Butler and Kavanagh, *General Election of October 1974*, pp. 28, 30.
81. Wilson, *Final Term*, p. 55.
82. *Time and Chance*, pp. 299–300.
83. Ibid., p. 303.
84. Ibid., p. 304.
85. Castle, *Diaries, 1974–76*, p. 155.
86. Ibid., p. 182.

87. Ibid., p. 183.
88. *Diaries, 1974–76*, p. 186.
89. Butler and Kavanagh, *General Election of October 1974*, p. 60.
90. Falkender, *Downing Street*, p. 167.
91. *Prime Minister*, p. 45.
92. Falkender, *Downing Street*, p. 167.

CHAPTER 23

1. *Power*, p. 162.
2. *Downing Street*, p. 3.
3. Lord Donoughue, quoted in 'Spycatcher'.
4. *Diaries, 1974–76*, p. 198.
5. *Final Term*, p. 99.
6. *Diaries, 1974–76*, p. 339.
7. Ibid., p. 345.
8. Ibid.
9. Ibid., p. 750.
10. Ibid., p. 346.
11. *Final Term*, p. 106.
12. Ibid, p. 103.
13. Falkender, *Downing Street*, p. 182.
14. Private information.
15. *Union Man*, p. 289.
16. *Diaries, 1974–76*, p. 379.
17. *Downing Street*, p. 180.
18. *Prime Minister*, p. 55.
19. *Final Term*, p. 143.
20. David Butler and Uwe Kitzinger, *The 1975 Referendum*, London 1976, p. 177.
21. *Final Term*, pp. 143–4.
22. *Diaries, 1974–76*, p. 416.
23. Quoted in Mark Holmes, *The Labour Government, 1974–79: Political Aims and Economic Reality*, London 1985, p. 8.
24. *Prime Minister*, p. 53.
25. Wyn Grant, *The Political Economy of Industrial Policy*, London 1982, p. 105.
26. *Diaries, 1974–76*, p. 220.
27. Ibid.
28. Ibid.
29. Ibid., p. 221.
30. Ibid., p. 222.
31. Ibid.; also Callaghan, *Time and Chance*, p. 326.
32. Ibid., p. 222.
33. Ibid., p. 223.
34. Ibid.

35. Ibid., pp. 223-4.
36. Ibid., p. 224.
37. Ibid.
38. Ibid.
39. Donoughue, *Prime Minister*, p. 60.
40. Interview.
41. Donoughue, *Prime Minister*, p. 60.
42. Interview.
43. Benn, *Parliament*, pp. 35–6.
44. *Final Term*, p. 111.
45. Sked and Cook, *Post-war Britain*, p. 301.
46. *Diaries, 1974–76*, p. 361.
47. *Hansard*, vol. 890, col. 282.
48. *Inside the Treasury*, London 1982, p. 15.
49. *Diaries, 1974–76*, pp. 399–400.
50. Castle, *Diaries, 1974–76*, p. 400.
51. Donoughue, *Prime Minister*, p. 65.
52. Interview.
53. Donoughue, *Prime Minister*, p. 67.
54. Ibid., p. 68.
55. *Power*, p. 59.
56. *Diaries, 1974–76*, p. 442.
57. Interview.
58. *Prime Minister*, p. 70.
59. *Final Term*.
60. *Diaries, 1974–76*, p. 471.
61. Barnett, *Treasury*, p. 78.
62. Ibid., p. 79.
63. Quoted in Castle, *Diaries, 1974–76*, p. 681.
64. Milton and Rose Friedman, *Free to Choose: A Personal Statement*, Harmondsworth 1980, p. 299.
65. Barnett, *Treasury*, p. 21.
66. *Prime Minister*, p. 81.
67. Crosland, *Crosland*, p. 295.
68. Quoted in Friedman, *Free to Choose*, pp. 311–12.
69. Castle, *Diaries, 1974–76*, p. 679.
70. Ibid., p. 123.
71. Benn, *Against the Tide*, p. 267.
72. *Diaries, 1974–76*, pp. 227–8.
73. Ibid., p. 228.
74. Castle, *Diaries, 1974–76*, p. 305.
75. Quoted in Wilson, *Final Term*, p. 176.
76. Ibid.
77. Ibid., p. 154.
78. *Time and Chance*, p. 364.
79. Wilson, *Final Term*, p. 281.

80. Ibid., p. 160.
81. Castle, *Diaries, 1974–76*, p. 313.
82. Wilson, *Final Term*, p. 164.
83. Ibid., p. 162.
84. Ibid., p. 291.
85. Ibid.
86. Ibid., p. 175.
87. *Time and Chance*, p. 360.
88. Ibid., p. 362.
89. Ibid., pp. 362–3.
90. Wilson, *Final Term*, p. 168.
91. *Time and Chance*, p. 364.
92. Ibid.
93. Wilson, *Final Term*, p. 78.
94. Castle, *Diaries, 1974–76*, p. 125.
95. Wilson, *Final Term*, p. 79.
96. Rees, *Northern Ireland*, p. 135.
97. Ibid.
98. Paul Bew and Henry Patterson, *The British State and the Ulster Crisis: From Wilson to Thatcher*, London 1985, p. 77, quoting *Guardian*, 19 July 1983.
99. Donoughue, *Prime Minister*, p. 132.
100. *Parliament*, p. 72.
101. *Northern Ireland*, p. 102.
102. Ibid., p. 136.
103. Ibid., p. 25.
104. Ibid., p. 159.
105. Ibid., p. 153.
106. Ibid.
107. Ibid., p. 169.
108. Ibid., p. 170.
109. Haines, *Power*, p. 134.
110. *Northern Ireland*, p. 172.
111. Ibid.
112. Ibid., p. 177.
113. Ibid., p. 180.
114. Ibid., p. 197.
115. Ibid, p. 209.
116. Ibid., p. 272.
117. Introduction to *Diaries ... 1964–66*, p. 11.
118. Richard Crossman to Graham C. Greene, 11 October 1973, quoted in Hugo Young, *The Crossman Affair*, London 1976, p. 12.
119. Introduction, p. 13.
120. Reply to parliamentary question, 15 November 1974, quoted in Young, *Crossman*, p. 15.
121. Ibid., p. 17.
122. *Diaries, 1974–76*, p. 312.

123. Young, *Crossman*, p. 56.
124. Harold Evans, *Good Times, Bad Times*, London 1984, p. 46.
125. Young, *Crossman*, p. 221.
126. Ibid.
127. *Final Term*, p. 128.
128. Labour Party, *1974 Report*, p. 207.
129. Ibid., p. 142.
130. Ibid., p. 141.
131. Ibid., p. 200.
132. Ibid., p. 208.
133. Labour Party, *1975 Report*, pp. 186–7.
134. *Final Term*, p. 181.
135. *Prime Minister*, p. 53.

CHAPTER 24

1. *Power*, p. 220.
2. Interview, Joe Haines, 6 June 1988.
3. *Prime Minister*, p. 11.
4. Interview, 6 June 1988.
5. Ibid.
6. *Prime Minister*, p. 11.
7. *Final Term*, pp. 301–2.
8. Falkender, *Downing Street*, p. 3.
9. Interview, 6 June 1988.
10. Falkender, *Downing Street*, p. 4.
11. Haines, *Power*, p. 221.
12. Wilson, *Final Term*, p. 229.
13. Castle, *Diaries, 1974–76*, p. 672.
14. *Downing Street*, p. 187.
15. Ibid., p. 4.
16. *Diaries, 1974–76*, p. 671.
17. Ibid., pp. 671–2.
18. *Time and Chance*, p. 391.
19. Frank Longford, *Eleven at 10: A Personal View of Prime Ministers, 1931–1984*, London 1984, p. 117.
20. *Downing Street*, p. 4.
21. *Final Term*, p. 229.
22. *Downing Street*, p. 2.
23. *Power*, p. 228.
24. Ibid., p. 8.
25. *Prime Minister*, p. 86.
26. Smith 'Notes', p. 6.
27. Farr, *Five at 10*, p. 105.
28. Donoughue, *Prime Minister*, p. 39.

29. Ibid., p. x.
30. Ibid., p. 34.
31. Ibid., p. 40.
32. Haines, *Power*, p. 162.
33. Labour Party, *1974 Report*, p. 141.
34. *Final Term*, p. 297.
35. Labour Party, *1974 Report*, p. 141.
36. *Downing Street*, p. 170.
37. *Final Term*, p. 200.
38. Ibid., p. 302.
39. *A New Course for Labour*, Nottingham 1976, p. 13.
40. *Final Term*, pp. 215, 203.
41. Castle, *Diaries, 1974–76*, p. 303.
42. Ibid., p. 309.
43. Ibid.
44. Cyril Smith, *Big Cyril*, London 1977, pp. 194–5.
45. Lewis Chester, Magnus Linklater and David May, *Jeremy Thorpe: a Secret Life*, London 1979, p. 285.
46. Ibid., p. 252; cf. also Smith, *Cyril*, p. 205 and Pincher, *Inside Story*, p. 278.
47. *Diaries, 1974–76*, p. 640.
48. Ibid., p. 642.
49. Ibid., p. 648.
50. Ibid., p. 648.
51. Ibid., p. 677.
52. Ibid.
53. Chester, *Thorpe*, p. 257.
54. *Diaries, 1974–76*, p. 678.
55. *Cyril*, p. 204.
56. *Cover-Up: The Jeremy Thorpe Affair*, Wilmington, Delaware 1980, p. 323.
57. Nigel West, *A Matter of Trust: MI5, 1945–72*, London 1982, p. 159.
58. Leigh, *Wilson*, p. 252.
59. 'Spycatcher'.
60. Pincher, *Inside Story*, pp. 370–1.
61. Chester, *Thorpe*, p. 244.
62. *Inside Story*, p. 371.
63. *Diaries, 1974–76*, pp. 677–8.
64. *Cyril*, p. 204.
65. Chester, *Thorpe*, p. 267.
66. Ibid., pp. 269–70.
67. Interview, Gordon Carr, 29 March 1990.
68. *Inside Story*, p. 371.
69. Chester, *Thorpe*, p. 257.
70. Interview, 6 June 1988.
71. Pincher, *Inside Story*, p. 34.
72. Quoted in West, *Trust*, p. 400.
73. Quoted in Pincher, *Inside Story*, p. 37.

74. Ibid., p. 32.
75. 'Spycatcher'.
76. Ibid.
77. Barry Penrose and Roger Courtiour, *The Pencourt File*, London 1978, p. 10.
78. Ibid.
79. Pincher, *Inside Story*, p. 19.
80. Leigh, *Wilson*, p. 250.
81. Penrose, *File*, p. 402.
82. Ibid., p. 411.
83. Letter to *Guardian*, 14 January 1988.
84. Chapman Pincher, *Too Secret Too Long: The Great Betrayal of Britain's Crucial Secrets and the Cover-up*, London 1984, p. 628.
85. *The Times*, 7 May 1987.
86. *Wilson*, p. 250.
87. *Inside Story*, p. 17.
88. Ibid., p. 18.
89. Ibid.
90. Ibid.
91. Chapman Pincher, *Too Secret*, p. 542.
92. Peter Wright, *Spy Catcher*, p. 372.
93. *Guardian*, 9 December 1986.
94. John Ware, 'The Spycatcher Affair: A Wilderness of Mirrors', *Listener*, 6 August 1987.
95. Ibid.
96. Interview, 20 June 1988.
97. Peter Wright to Barrie Penrose, July 1983, quoted in Barrie Penrose and Simon Freeman, *Conspiracy of Silence: The Secret Life of Anthony Blunt*, updated edition, London 1987, p. 482.
98. *Spycatcher*, p. 367.
99. Ibid.
100. Ibid., p. 368.
101. Ibid., p. 368.
102. Ibid., p. 370.
103. Ibid.
104. Ibid., p. 371.
105. Evans, *Good Times*, p. 133.
106. *Sunday Times*, 12 March 1989.
107. *Wilson*, p. 225.
108. *Spy Catcher*, p. 370.
109. 'Spycatcher'.
110. Ibid.
111. Ibid.
112. Ibid.
113. Ibid.
114. *Final Term*, pp. 201–2.

115. Ibid., p. 214.
116. Ibid.
117. *European Diary, 1977–1981*, London 1989, quoted in *Sunday Times*, 12 February 1989.
118. Ibid.
119. Ibid.
120. Donoughue, *Prime Ministero*, p. 86.
121. *Diaries, 1974–76*, p. 689.
122. *Final Term*, p. 301.
123. Ibid.
124. Barbara Castle, *Diaries, 1974–76*, p. 690.
125. Diary, 17 March 1976, courtesy Lord Cledwyn of Penhros.
126. *Diaries, 1974–76*, p. 690.
127. Ibid., p. 672.
128. Ibid., p. 691.
129. Quoted in Wilson, *Term*, p. 235.
130. *Diaries, 1974–76*, p. 699.
131. Marcia Falkender, *Downing Street*, p. 9; but see also, ibid., p. 699.
132. *Power*, p. 186.
133. Castle, *Diaries, 1974–76*, p. 718.
134. Marcia Falkender, *Downing Street*, p. 270.

CHAPTER 25

1. Haines, *Politics*, p. 154.
2. *Politics*, p. 156.
3. *Annual Register 1976*, London 1977, p. 10.
4. 29 May 1976.
5. *Sunday Times*, 30 May 1976.
6. *Against the Tide*, p. 571.
7. *The Times*, 28 May 1976.
8. Roth, *Wilson*, p. 20.
9. Haines, *Politics*, pp. 149–50.
10. 27 May 1976.
11. *The Times*, 31 May 1976.
12. Ibid., 3 June 1976.
13. *Evening Standard*.
14. *The Times*, 15 June 1976.
15. Blurb on jacket of paperback, London 1977.
16. *The Governance of Britain*, p. 9.
17. Ibid., pp. 10, 20.
18. Ibid., p. 231, quoting 'White House and Whitehall', in Anthony King, ed., *The British Prime Minister*, London 1969, pp. 144–5.
19. Ibid., p. 133.
20. Ibid., pp. 20–1.

21. Ibid., p. 9.
22. *A Prime Minister on Prime Ministers*, London 1977, p. 224.
23. Ibid., p. 160.
24. Ibid., p. 168.
25. *Final Term*, pp. 234, 121.
26. Royal Commission on the Press, *Final Report*, Cmnd. 6810, p. 105.
27. *Evidence*, 'Postscript'.
28. *Final Report*, p. 105.
29. Ibid., p. 99.
30. Gordon Carr, 'Why is Wilson now silent?', *Listener*, 14 May 1987, p. 5; see also, Chester, *Thorpe*, p. 272.
31. Barrie Penrose and Roger Courtiour, *The Pencourt File*, London 1978, p. 9.
32. Ibid., p. 40.
33. Ibid., p. 14.
34. Ibid., p. 13.
35. Ibid., p. 17.
36. Ibid., p. 98.
37. Interview, Gordon Carr, 29 March 1990.
38. *Pencourt*, p. 3.
39. Ibid.
40. Interview.
41. Chester, *Thorpe*, pp. 276–7.
42. Carr, 'Wilson', p. 7.
43. *Pencourt*, p. 328.
44. Ibid., p. 333.
45. Ibid., p. 404.
46. Ibid., p. 411.
47. Simon Freeman, 'How Wilson was proved Wright', *Sunday Times*, 28 December 1986.
48. *Power*, p. 223.
49. *Daily Mirror*, 14 February 1977.
50. Ibid., 10 February 1977.
51. Haines, *Power*, p. 229.
52. Ibid., p. 158.
53. Ibid., p. ix.
54. Ibid., p. 224.
55. Wilson, *Term*, p. 31.
56. Labour Party NEC, *Second Statement of Evidence Submitted by the Labour Party to the Committee to Review the Functioning of Financial Institutions, The Wilson Committee*, London 1979.
57. Private information.
58. Bill Callaghan, interview, 12 July 1988.
59. Private information.
60. Committee to Review the Functioning of Financial Institutions, *Report*, Cmnd. 7937, London 1980.

61. 'The City Enquiry – Its Progress to Date', The City-Association Accounting Lectures, London 1979, p. 1.
62. Donoughue, *Prime Minister*, p. 118.
63. 'City Enquiry', p. 4.
64. Ibid., pp. 8–9.
65. Private information
66. Ibid.
67. Ibid.
68. Report, p. xvi.
69. 'City Enquiry', p. 12.
70. TUC, *The Role of Financial Institutions*, London n.d., but 1979, p. 27.
71. 'City Enquiry', p. 7.
72. *Second Statement.*
73. 'City Enquiry', p. 7.
74. *Report*, p. xviii.
75. Labour Party, *Second Statement.*
76. Ibid., p. 3.
77. *Financial Institutions*, p. 47.
78. 'City Enquiry', p. 6.
79. *Report*, p. 1.
80. Ibid., p. 371.
81. Ibid., p. 372.
82. Ibid., p. 373.
83. Ibid.
84. Ibid., pp. 373–4.
85. Ibid., p. 274.
86. Ibid.
87. Ibid., p. 276.
88. Ibid., p. 282.
89. Ibid., p. 283.
90. Ibid.
91. Ibid., p. 284.
92. Ibid.
93. Wilson, *Final Term*, p. 303.
94. *Hansard*, vol. 907, cols. 639, 642, 11 March 1976.
95. Ibid., vol. 932, col. 1585, 26 May 1977.
96. Ibid., vol. 940, col. 1055, 5 December 1977.
97. Ibid., vol. 997, col. 548, 23 January 1981.
98. Ibid., vol. 997, col. 562, 23 January 1981.
99. Ibid., vol. 997. col. 595. 23 January 1981.
100. Ibid., vol. 997, col. 608, 23 January 1981.
101. Ibid., vol. 997, col. 609, 23 January 1981.
102. Ibid., vol. 1 [sixth series], col. 1083, 26 March 1981.
103. *Any Questions*, BBC Radio 4, 22 July 1988.
104. *Hansard* [House of Lords], vol. 449, col. 762.
105. Ibid.

106. Ibid., col. 765.
107. Ibid., col. 1244, 21 March 1984.
108. Ibid., vol. 451, col. 923.
109. Ibid., col. 925.
110. Ibid., vol. 477, col. 389, 25 June 1986.
111. *Independent*, 30 October 1986.
112. *Guardian*, 28 July 1988.

Index